In these volumes the second decade of the sixty-year diary of Charles Francis Adams, the third of the family's statesmen, is begun. As was true of the two earlier volumes of the *Diary*, the section appearing here has not before reached print.

Covering the period from Adams' marriage in September 1829 to the end of 1832, these volumes record the early years of his maturity during which he was seeking to find his vocation. Engaged in the day-to-day management of John Quincy Adams' business interests in Boston and Quincy, he nevertheless had no inclination toward commerce or the active practice of law. Son and grandson of Presidents, proud heir to a name already great and controversial in American politics, he also at this time considered himself "not fitted for the noise of public life." Dependent for support on his father and father-in-law but determined to maintain his independence, he devoted his available time to a program of studies and writing that would prepare him for a career he hesitated to name but in which he wished distinction. His own public career still years away, he was drawn at this period to the study of American history and his famous grandparents' papers, an effort that would continue and that would make him the family's archivist and editor.

These volumes offer manifold opportunities for an enlarged understanding of a complex and able man who was later to assume positions of high responsibility. In addition to furnishing innumerable personal and familial insights, this portion of the diary is of capital importance for the historian of society and culture. Probably no more detailed and faithful record exists of Boston life in the period.

The Adams Papers are edited at the Massachusetts Historical Society. Mr. Friedlaender is Associate Editor of the Papers, and Mr. Butterfield is Editor in Chief.

The Adams Papers

L. H. BUTTERFIELD, EDITOR IN CHIEF

SERIES I

DIARIES

Diary of Charles Francis Adams

Diary of
Charles Francis Adams

MARC FRIEDLAENDER and L. H. BUTTERFIELD

EDITORS

———————☆———————

Volume 4 · *March 1831–December 1832*
Index

THE BELKNAP PRESS
OF HARVARD UNIVERSITY PRESS
CAMBRIDGE, MASSACHUSETTS

1968

308.1
Ad 18 A1
serio I
v.4

Funds for editing *The Adams Papers* were originally furnished by Time, Inc., on behalf of *Life*, to the Massachusetts Historical Society, under whose supervision the editorial work is being done. Further funds have been provided by a grant from the Ford Foundation to the National Archives Trust Fund Board in support of this and four other major documentary publications. In common with these and many other enterprises like them, *The Adams Papers* benefits from the continuing and indispensable cooperation and aid of the National Historical Publications Commission, whose chairman is the Archivist of the United States.

Library of Congress Catalog Card Number 64–20588 · Printed in the United States of America

Contents

Descriptive List of Illustrations   *vii*

Diary of Charles Francis Adams, March 1831–
December 1832   *1*

Appendix: Books Borrowed by Charles Francis Adams
from the Boston Athenæum, 1830–1832   *437*

Chronology   *447*

Index   *453*

Descriptive List of Illustrations

FACING OR
FOLLOWING PAGE

1. JOHN QUINCY ADAMS' SIX BRONZE BUSTS OR "HOUSEHOLD
GODS" ON THE MANTELPIECE OF HIS "WRITING CHAMBER"
AT QUINCY   124

The desk and its chair, the globes, fireplace, and mantel in the east
room on the second floor of the Old House in Quincy as shown in
the photograph are essentially as they were in the years following
John Adams' death and John Quincy Adams' term as President,
when John Quincy Adams concluded to make the Old House his
residence and began to send to it his belongings that had been stored
in various places and for varying lengths of time as he moved from
one public post to another. Only in the absence of the books that
lined every wall does the room as illustrated here differ from the
memory of it, and of John Quincy Adams in it, that one of his grandsons carried from his childhood: "[My grandfather] seemed to be
always writing, . . . seated at his table in the middle of the large east
room, which he used as a library, . . . walled in with over-loaded
bookshelves" (*Charles Francis Adams* [2d] *1835–1915; An Autobiography*, Boston and New York, 1916, p. 9). The books began to
arrive in 1829 to be unpacked, placed on the shelves, and cata-
logued (see volume 3:32, 55, and *passim*). By 1832, prints, paintings, cups and saucers, &c., were being sent from storage to Quincy
to be restored to their owner's enjoyment of them. Chief among the
artifacts were the six small bronze busts which John Quincy Adams
had apparently had on the mantelpiece of his study in the White
House. They were to be placed on the mantelpiece at the Old House
upon his next arrival at Quincy, and to remain there (see below,
p. 399). The busts subsequently passed to the ownership of Charles
Francis Adams and afterward to Henry Adams. So far as is known,
they were never again removed from the precincts. After Charles
Francis Adams built the Stone Library on the grounds of the Old
House, the busts were transferred to the mantelpiece of the new writing room, and stand on it now. They were returned to the mantelpiece in John Quincy Adams' "writing chamber" only to be photo-
graphed there. (Photograph by George M. Cushing Jr.) Their
subjects in the order shown, from left to right, are Cicero, Homer,
Plato, Virgil, Socrates, and Demosthenes. The French ormolu
clock in the center is of Empire design with its porcelain dial framed
by an arch and supported by caryatids. It was acquired by John
Quincy Adams during his years of foreign residence.
*Courtesy of the National Park Service, Adams National Historic
Site.*

2–7. SOME DRAMATIC PERFORMERS IN THEIR ROLES AS SEEN BY
CHARLES FRANCIS ADAMS AT THE TREMONT THEATRE,
1830–1832   124

Charles Francis Adams' first attendance at the theater after his
marriage, indeed his first in more than a year, was on 3 February
1830 to see Shakespeare's *King John* with Junius Brutus Booth in the
title role and Edwin Forrest as Falconbridge (No. 2; and see volume
3:153). Forrest, in the few years since his New York debut in 1826
as Othello, had won his place as perhaps the finest American in-
terpreter of the heroic roles of Shakespeare. By 1828 he had added
to his repertoire, Brutus, Shylock, Richard III, Lear, and Macbeth,
as well as Falconbridge with which he was to be long identified
(George C. D. Odell, *Annals of the New York Stage*, New York,
1927–1949, 3:334–337, 384, 404).

The principal event of the 1831 season at the Tremont Theatre
was the twenty-five-night engagement of the phenomenal child,
Master Burke (Nos. 3 and 4), beginning on 31 January, during
which "an unparallelled excitement prevailed" as he repeated the
triumphs he had enjoyed in New York from his debut there in November 1830 until the beginning of his tour in the following January.
The twelve-year-old, who also conducted the orchestra and played
the violin, brought to Boston an astonishing repertoire of roles that
already included Romeo, Shylock, Richard III, and Hamlet, as well
as Napoleon and young Norval (in Home's *Douglas*) and a host of
Irish comic characters, of whom the most popular was Looney
McTwolter (Odell, *Annals of the New York Stage*, 3:490–495).
Charles Francis Adams, who went twice to see him and tried un-
successfully another time (volume 3:420, 423, 425), like the
critics and the established actors and actresses who played with
Master Burke, took his interpretations with the utmost seriousness.
"During his engagement, tickets were sold at auction, at advanced
prices; which, not infrequently, fell into the hands of speculators,
who found purchasers at enormous profits." (*Bowen's Picture of
Boston*, 2d edn., Boston, 1833, p. 208.)

The next theatrical season offered a number of *divertissements* of
varying degrees of importance. The American comedian and mimic,
James Henry Hackett, gave his imitations of other actors and of
American folk types and appeared in the native American plays
which he also produced, such as *Rip Van Winkle* and James K.
Paulding's *The Lion of the West*. In the latter he took the role of
Colonel Nimrod Wildfire, "an uncouth Kentuckian just elected to
Congress" (No. 5; and see below, p. 190; Odell, *Annals of the New
York Stage*, 3:419, 459, 501). Suggestive of the range of theatrical
taste was the presence on the same bill of M. Gouffe, the man-
monkey (No. 6; below, p. 190; Odell, *Annals of the New York
Stage*, 3:569).

However, the principal feature of the season at the Tremont
Theatre was the introduction of operatic performances "in a style of
excellence hitherto unattempted" of such character as to "form an
era in the annals of our stage." The stage arrangements for the
operas were under the direction of "Mr. Barrymore," and the lead-

ing vocalists of the time were employed (*Bowen's Picture of Boston*, 2d edn., p. 209). Outstanding among these was the lovely and beautiful Mrs. Elizabeth Austin, "the acknowledged queen of song," who in early 1832 brought to Boston the greatest operatic success of the previous year (and of many years) in New York, *Cinderella*, an English adaptation by Rophino Lacy of Rossini's *Cenerentola* (No. 7; and see below, p. 263–264). The critic William Cox of the New York *Mirror* had written of the production: "the most incredible transformations take place with a beautiful and dream-like facility, living fairies float on the bosom of the air, above the branches of the forest.... Cinderella offers an attraction superior to anything of the kind ever produced in the United States." Of Mrs. Austin's voice he wrote, "its liquid tones come as softly upon the sense of hearing as snow upon the water, or dew upon the flower.... We do not believe more delicate sounds can be borne upon the air, than are breathed forth in some of her cadences." But it was Mrs. Austin in *Cinderella* that brought his superlatives: "The unrivalled excellence of Mrs. Austin consists in the possession of a voice, which for bird-like softness, sweetness, and wonderful flexibility, has never been excelled in American theaters, ... a clearness like that which delights the eye upon a sleeping stream in summer, when there is not a ripple to break its motionless beauty.... Mrs. Austin discovers a curious facility of execution, as if music escaped from her involuntarily as fragrance from a flower.... She floats through the whole part with no apparent effort." (Odell, *Annals of the New York Stage*, 3:309, 461, 486, 496–498, 546.)

Forrest as Falconbridge is reproduced from a colored etching in *Elton's New Theatrical Costumes*; Master Burke as Looney McTwolter from a lithograph of Ingrey & Madeley, London, after a drawing by Allison; Burke in six favorite characters from an engraving published by R. Lloyd, London, 1830; Hackett as Nimrod Wildfire from an engraving after a painting by A. Andrews; M. Gouffe from a West London Theatre playbill, September 1829, printed by Redeord & Robins, London. All are in the Harvard Theatre Collection. Mrs. Austin in *Cinderella* is reproduced from an illustration of an unlocated original in Odell, *Annals of the New York Stage*, volume 3, facing p. 498.

Nos. 2–6 courtesy of the Harvard Theatre Collection; no. 7 courtesy of Columbia University Press.

8. THE FIRST MEETING OF THE SUPERVISORS OF THE ADAMS TEMPLE AND SCHOOL FUND RECORDED BY CHARLES FRANCIS ADAMS AS CLERK   125

The Adams Temple and School Fund was created by John Adams' gift to the town of Quincy, dated 25 June 1822, of lands the future income from which were to be used first toward the building of a stone temple in Quincy (see volume 3:xi–xii), and after its completion to the support of a classical school or academy there. By a further deed, on 10 August in the same year, Adams gave to the town with certain stipulations "the fragments of my library which still remain in my possession." The administration of both the fund and the library was placed in a board of five supervisors. After the gifts were accepted by the Town of Quincy, the supervisors and selectmen exercised joint oversight for a time. However, by act of the Massachusetts legislature, 3 February 1827, the Adams Temple and School Fund was incorporated and thereafter the Supervisors assumed full control, elected officers, &c. At about the time that the Supervisors became a corporate entity a record book was begun. The Records of the Supervisors from the beginning to 1942 are encompassed in a single volume of ledger size, bound in full leather. The stamping on front and back includes the rubric "Presented by John Quincy Adams." Into the volume was first copied in one hand the documents relating to the Fund's establishment and its administration up to incorporation. The minute book proper begins with the meeting of 18 April 1827, at which time Thomas Boylston Adams was elected Clerk. He served until his death in 1832. The Supervisors, meeting in early October to name his successor on the board, chose John Quincy Adams, and to the clerkship elected Charles Francis Adams, who recorded the first meeting he attended on 27 October 1832. He wrote up the minutes just over a week later (see below, p. 385–386 and 391–392). Charles Francis Adams continued to serve as Clerk of the Supervisors through the meeting of 3 September 1857. For the first ten years of his tenure as Clerk, however, he was not a Supervisor. Initially he could not qualify because he was not a resident of Quincy; after he became a resident, there was no vacancy to be filled until 1842.

On another of the actions taken at the first meeting recorded by Charles Francis Adams as Clerk, namely the appointment of a committee to examine the state of the library remaining in John Adams' "Office," see below, p. 139, 389–391. The charge to the same committee to move toward the realization of the donor's provisions for a school and library building came to nothing for many years, the Adams Academy building not being put into construction until 1870.

The volume of Records is kept in the Treasurer's vault in the City Hall, Quincy.

Courtesy of City of Quincy, Board of Supervisors The Adams Temple and School Fund, William Churchill Edwards, Clerk.

9. THE ANTIMASONIC CONVENTION IN BALTIMORE CARICATURED
   IN AN ENGRAVING BY DAVID CLAYPOOLE JOHNSTON   380
   A new and exhaustive study of political Antimasonry in the United States remains to be written (Charles McCarthy's "The Antimasonic Party: A Study of Political Antimasonry in the United States, 1827–1840" in the American Historical Association, *Annual Report for 1902*, 1:365–574, and George H. Blakeslee's Harvard doctoral dissertation, The History of the Antimasonic Party, Cambridge, 1903, are still the best monographs available on the subject.) Charles Francis Adams' participation in the movement began in the last months of the years covered by the present volumes when he emerged as a polemicist in a series of newspaper articles (see below, p. 349–350, 413–431 *passim*; Martin B. Duberman, *Charles Francis Adams, 1807–1886*, Boston, 1961, p. 43–55). He had resisted for

more than a year following his father's lead in assuming a public role in the struggle. John Quincy Adams' own identification with the Antimasons in May 1831 was somewhat tardy, but he was soon thought to be a prime possibility as the party's Presidential nominee. He seems to have done nothing to discourage those who were promoting his candidacy, but at the convention of the party in September 1831 in Baltimore the choice fell on William Wirt, the Attorney General in Adams' administration and a Freemason. (See below, p. 120, 149–150; Samuel Flagg Bemis, *John Quincy Adams and the Union*, New York, 1956, p. 276–304.)

Political Antimasonry and the opposition which developed to the party generated an outpouring of pamphlet and journalistic literature (see the bibliographies in the monographs cited above). Despite the opportunities offered, the political caricaturists of the day seem seldom to have been stimulated by the conflict (Frank Weitenkampf, *Political Caricature in the United States*, New York, 1953, p. 21, 27). One of those who did treat it pictorially, and on both sides of the question, was David Claypoole Johnston (1797–1865) of Philadelphia and Boston, engraver and cartoonist chiefly on political and theatrical subjects (see volume 1:xiii–xiv; Clarence S. Brigham, "David Claypoole Johnston: The American Cruikshank," American Antiquarian Society, *Proceedings*, 50 [1940], 98–110; George C. D. Odell, *Annals of the New York Stage*, New York, 1927–1949, volume 3, facing p. 150, 300).

Johnston's unsigned lampoon, here reproduced, of the Antimasonic convention in Baltimore was used on the cover of a piece of sheet music, "Corner-Stone March, as performed by the Boston Brigade Band, At the Ceremony of laying the Corner Stone of the Masonic Temple, Boston. Dedicated to the Fraternity by Ch[arles] Zeuner." Although the ceremony for which the piece was composed was held on 14 October 1830, the composition was not published until 1832. Perhaps the cartoon was employed somewhat unjustifiably to give a political relevance in a Presidential election year to a composition done for a nonpolitical occasion a year and a half before. The Freemasons themselves did not approve: "The mechanical execution of the work is creditable to the publisher. We regret being obliged to add, that good taste did not require the embellishment of a carricature. — There should have been nothing ludicrous connected with a piece of music dedicated 'to the fraternity' " (*Boston Masonic Mirror*, New Series, 3:259 [11 February 1832]; see also the same, 2:133 [23 October 1830]). Significantly, however, in the same issue in which the "good taste" of the caricature was questioned, an article on John Quincy Adams was reprinted in which he is spoken of as "a political rat catcher," and "an unprincipled political game cock" (the same, 3:257).

The employment in Johnston's lithograph of donkeys, goats, geese, dogs, pigs, mules, and other animals assembled in convention to satirize Antimasonry would seem to derive naturally from the language of political controversy at the time. In its design and lettering, in its frequent use of puns in the legends and in the words assigned to the various speakers, and in its skill in draftsmanship, the cartoon is like Johnston's other known work. There is a distinct possibility that the punning words ascribed to the mule, the pig, and the dog are clues to individual leaders of the Antimasonic party. Thus, for example, the dog puns not only on his canine nature but also nautically. (Could Seward be meant?) The sentiment expressed by the mule, who incongruously insists that the Antimasonic candidate be "full blooded," is, of course, directed against Wirt; however, the intent of the mule in damaging Wirt's eligibility in order finally to win the nomination for himself is exactly the tactic that was being charged to John Quincy Adams at the very time the cartoon was published on the sheet-music cover and may point to the identification of the mule as the stubbornly ambitious ex-President (see the article on John Quincy Adams cited above in the *Boston Masonic Mirror* for 11 February 1832).

Courtesy of the American Antiquarian Society.

10. JARED SPARKS IN 1828, BY GILBERT STUART   380
One of the last paintings done by Gilbert Stuart (1755–1828) before his death and unfinished in the sense that background and dress have been barely suggested, this portrait of Jared Sparks belongs with other such "unfinished" but superb late Stuart works as the portraits of Thomas Motley, Nathaniel Bowditch, and Washington Allston. They may well owe their character as much to a loss of interest on the artist's part in the rendering of the appurtenances to a likeness and to his preoccupation with the face and what he saw in it as to a lack of opportunity to bring the paintings to completion. The portrait of Sparks, oil on canvas, measures 25″ x 20″ and is owned by The New Britain Museum of American Art (Lawrence and Smith Funds), having earlier been in the possession of Sparks' grandson, Professor Jared Sparks Moore of Cleveland. The portrait was begun in 1827, the sittings apparently continuing until March 1828, when Sparks left Boston for several months in Europe. (Lawrence Park, *Gilbert Stuart, an Illustrated Descriptive List of his Works*, New York, 1926, 2:706–707; *Gilbert Stuart, Portraitist of the Young Republic*, Washington and Providence, 1967, p. 106, 111–113.)

Jared Sparks (1789–1866) in the years close to the time he was sitting to Stuart was still unmarried; was just beginning to accomplish his pioneering efforts to edit and publish American historical documents; was the owner and editor of the *North American Review*, 1824–1830; and was engrossed in his labors of locating and copying documents relating to the diplomacy of the Revolution. He was to publish his monumental *Diplomatic Correspondence of the American Revolution* in twelve volumes in 1829–1830. Despite its marked editorial deficiencies, it established his reputation and defined a point of view about the Revolutionary period that so insisted upon the rightness of all that Washington and Franklin believed and did that it minimized the contributions and impugned the judgment, if not the integrity, of those like John Adams, John Jay, Arthur Lee, and Henry Laurens who often differed with one or the other of them (see below, p. 214–215). It was Sparks' representation of events perhaps more than any other single thing which forced the descendants of John Adams into a defensive posture and made three generations of them into perceptive students and interpreters of the early years of the Nation.

During the years covered by these volumes of the *Diary,* Charles Francis Adams and Jared Sparks remained on fairly familiar terms. Sparks and his copyist had the daily use of Adams' study in his house on Hancock Avenue from November 1829 to March 1830 as Sparks searched the twenty-one volumes of John Adams' letterbooks which John Quincy Adams had made available there for that purpose. Despite worsening relations between Sparks and the elder Adams as Sparks' opinions of Jay and Lee appeared, Charles Francis Adams continued to observe the amenities. (See volume 3:88, 92, 160–161, 202–203; below, p. 214–215, 395.)

Sparks' literary and archival labors were carried forward assiduously in the United States and abroad. During the next decade he completed *The Life of Gouverneur Morris,* 3 volumes, Boston, 1832; *The Writings of George Washington,* 12 volumes, Boston, 1834–1837; *The Works of Benjamin Franklin,* 10 volumes, Boston, 1836–1840. Rewards came in his appointment as McLean Professor of Ancient and Modern History at Harvard in 1839 and his election as President of the University ten years later. (*Dictionary of American Biography,* New York, 1928–1936; L. H. Butterfield, "Archival and Editorial Enterprise in 1850 and in 1950: Some Comparisons and Contrasts," American Philosophical Society, *Proceedings,* 98 [1954]:159–170.)
Courtesy of The New Britain Museum of American Art, New Britain, Connecticut.

11. THE REVEREND NATHANIEL LANGDON FROTHINGHAM IN
    1842, BY THOMAS BALL   380

Nathaniel Frothingham (1793–1870) was the husband of Abigail (Brooks) Adams' oldest sister Ann. After the death in 1830 of their mother, Mrs. Peter Chardon Brooks, the two sisters became increasingly close to one another and remained so. Their husbands, drawn together by this circumstance, seemed to find common ground on which to build a long relationship that was cordial if not intimate. During the years covered by these volumes Charles Francis Adams was in the Frothingham manse many more times than he was in any other house in Boston save his own. Frequently the Adamses were guests for meals, and Charles Francis Adams seems generally to have eaten at the Frothinghams' when for one reason or another it was convenient for him to eat *out.* The two men seem not to have been naturally congenial, although Adams found Frothingham "an exceedingly amiable man" and "a man of talents." Frothingham was the older by almost fifteen years; they differed sharply in their theological and political views and in their interpretations of American history (see volume 3:289); and although Adams was not moved by Frothingham as a pulpit orator, he listened with respect to his sermons at the First Church once or twice each Sunday that

Adams was in Boston (see volume 3:42; below, p. 405–406, 426 and *passim*). They did share an absorbing interest in the classics; Frothingham's learning was solid, and his concern for music and poetry and literature in the modern foreign languages made his conversation sufficiently cultivated to meet Adams' exacting standards.

Frothingham succeeded William Emerson in the First Church pulpit in 1815 and remained the Church's minister until ill health forced his resignation in 1849. A preceptor in rhetoric and oratory at Harvard before he began his First Church ministry, he retained his identification with Harvard, serving as an Overseer from 1819 to 1850. In his retirement, until he was prevented by blindness, he pursued his literary activities, publishing *Sermons* in 1852 and *Metrical Pieces* in 1855. Charles Francis Adams wrote in his diary (6 April 1870) that the estimate of Frothingham's life and character given at his funeral in the oration by the Reverend Frederic H. Hedge "was just, discriminating and forcible": "As a preacher, he could hardly be said to be popular. . . . The circle of his admirers was small; but those who composed it listened to him with enthusiastic delight. . . . The poetic beauty of his thought, the pointed aptness of his illustrations, the truth and sweetness of the sentiment, the singular and sometimes quaint selectness . . . of the language, won my heart, and made him my favorite among the preachers of that day. . . . As a scholar, he had in his profession no superior,— scarcely a rival. . . . [I]n richness and extent of intellectual culture he stood pre-eminent among his brethren. . . . In familiar discourse, when most at his ease, the unstudied and innate grace of his mind gave a peculiar and emphatic zest to his conversation. . . . His words expressed with unerring fitness the thing most fit to be expressed." (Massachusetts Historical Society, *Proceedings*, 1st series, 11 [1869–1870]:378–380; see also, *Dictionary of American Biography*, New York, 1928–1936; Arthur B. Ellis, *History of the First Church in Boston, 1630–1880*, Boston, 1880, p. 252–284.)

Charles Francis Adams, returning from the funeral services and mindful of their long association, wrote: "I walked home meditating on the time when I first knew him in connection with the sunniest hours of my life, on the steady good will that prevailed between us all through middle life, and lastly on the fading of the scene" (Diary, 6 April 1870).

The portrait of Frothingham here reproduced hangs in the office wing of the First Church in Boston. (Photograph by George M. Cushing Jr.) It was painted in 1842 by Thomas Ball (1819–1911), who is better known as a sculptor than as a painter. He maintained a studio in Boston from 1837 to 1853 and exhibited at the Boston Athenæum almost every year from 1840 to 1867. (George C. Groce and David H. Wallace, *The New-York Historical Society's Dictionary of American Artists, 1564–1860*, New Haven and London, 1957; *Dictionary of American Biography*, New York, 1928–1936; Mabel M. Swan, *The Athenæum Gallery, 1827–1873*, Boston, 1940, p. 179–180, 199.)

Courtesy of the Trustees of the First Church, Boston.

12–13. CHARLES FRANCIS ADAMS' MARGINAL COMMENTS EN-
TERED IN HIS COPIES OF VILLEMAIN'S "HISTOIRE DE CROM-
WELL" AND ABBÉ DE MABLY'S "DE LA LÉGISLATION, OU
PRINCIPES DES LOIX"   380

Charles Francis Adams was generally not given to entering marginal
comments in the books in his library. The keeping of a diary in which
he so often recorded his opinions of what he was reading provided
ample opportunity ordinarily for the expression of his reaction.
Furthermore, beginning in 1822 and continuing during the period
covered by these volumes, he kept a commonplace book into which
he copied passages that he found particularly memorable or with
which he was in hearty agreement (Adams Papers, Microfilms,
Reel No. 312). A few books remained with which he so profoundly
disagreed that he succumbed to the urge to enter his dissent in the
form of marginalia. Two of the subjects in which he maintained an
avid and abiding interest and on which he felt impelled to write
essays and articles as well as marginalia were the Puritan contribution to the founding of New England and the Nation, and the
wisdom of deriving principles of government from experience, as
represented by history, rather than from abstract theories (see volume
3:213; below, p. 428). These interests expressed themselves in
vigorous defense of the Puritans in 17th-century England and in
vigorous opposition to the abstract theorists who preceded and gave
doctrinal justification to the French Revolution. The two works in
which his marginal comments illustrated here were entered fall within
these two subject fields.

Abel François Villemain was one of the leading literary critics and
teachers of the early 19th century in France, politically liberal, distinguished and sometimes criticized for his advanced technique of
combining in his lectures and books on literary criticism, biographical and historical material. His *Histoire de Cromwell*, first published in two volumes at Paris in 1819, was of this mixed genre, in
which through analogies drawn between Cromwell and Napoleon
he expressed highly critical views of each. The copy which Charles
Francis Adams owned, and in which he entered his numerous animadversions upon Villemain's derogations of Cromwell and other
Puritan leaders, was of an edition published at Brussels in 1829
(see below, p. 423, 429). Beyond calling the author, "humbug,"
"goose," "brazen dog," &c., and characterizing his opinions as "stuff,"
"slander," and "flat Popery," Adams expresses at times in his comments the real grounds of his disagreement with Villemain's views
and his own bias: "This Man does not understand the principles involved in this struggle. . . . He does not seem to understand how much
of public spirit and of genuine patriotism there was in the combat.
In fine, he is a Frenchman." "To stand in the fear of God, and to be
conscientious is according to this man, 'fanaticism.' " "Say what you
will, Cromwell was never absolute. It was because his Government
was in the main a very good one, that he retained his power." "[I]t
must always be remembered that all the testimony that comes from
republicans or the royalists of the court of Charles 2d is not perfectly
impartial. The first hated Cromwell's memory because they attri-

buted to him the failure of their schemes and the return of the Royalists. The second abused him to pay their Court to the new Monarch."

In criticizing the political theorists who provided the philosophical justification for the French Revolution, Charles Francis Adams followed a pattern set by John Adams. Nowhere does the grandson better reveal his distrust of theory when applied to human behavior and when used as a foundation for political systems than in the marginal comments he made in his copy of *Bibliothèque de l'homme public, ou analyse raisonée des principaux ouvrages françois et étrangers, sur la politique . . . et sur le droit naturel et public.* This work, made up of condensations and summaries of political treatises, was compiled by the Marquis de Condorcet and others. Published in 1790–1792 at Paris, its relevance to the Revolution manifest, it reached 28 volumes. Charles Francis Adams' copy (12 volumes in 6, Paris, 1790) was acquired at the sale of Edward Jackson Lowell's library in October 1830 for three dollars. He read in it with some regularity from March to June 1831 (see below, p. 9–61 *passim*). The marginalia acquire substance and pith especially in the comments on the essays of Bodin, Machiavelli, Guicciardini, Plato, Montesquieu, Holbach, Languet, Mirabeau, and Mably. Reproduced here is the concluding page of the abstract of Abbé de Mably's "De la législation, ou principes des loix" (first published in 2 volumes in 1776). This sharp dissent from Mably's praise of the system devised by Lycurgus at Sparta on the ground that it ignores what history teaches about human nature, Adams develops at greater length in the journal entry reporting his reading of Mably (see below, p. 63).

A month later, having finished his reading in the *philosophes*, he took up another work on government which he found much more to his taste, John Adams' *Defence of the Constitutions of Governments of the United States of America* (3 volumes, London, 1787–1788), constructed upon the historical and experiential method, and there found to his delight that his grandfather had reached identical conclusions about Lycurgus' Sparta and in language often startlingly similar. Thus confirmed, he noted the lesson that "merely by looking at things in a plain practical light one may succeed at arriving at wise conclusions" (below, p. 100; John Adams' strictures on Sparta are in the *Defence*, 1:256–260; *The Works of John Adams*, ed. Charles Francis Adams, Boston, 1850–1856, 4:553–556).

Courtesy of the National Park Service, Adams National Historical Site.

14. "EVENING, MADE A LITTLE FURTHER PROGRESS IN MY TRANSLATION. I HAVE COPIED IT, INTO THE MARGIN OF THE QUARTO COPY OF CICERO WHICH I HAVE"   381

Nothing occupied Charles Francis Adams so continuously or so absorbingly during the years covered by these volumes as the study of oratory or eloquence. He read and reread the orations of Demosthenes and Æschines in the original Greek and in translations, he read the orations of Cicero in their entirety; and, among the moderns, he read the orations of Burke, Pitt, and Sheridan. To familiarize himself with the art as practiced in his own country, he read through the five volumes of E. B. Williston's compilation, *Eloquence of the United States*; the reports of the debates in Congress that were available in Thomas Carpenter's *The American Senator*; and Jonathan Elliot's four volumes of debates on the ratification of the Federal Constitution in the several states. He devoted himself as well to a close study of pulpit oratory, both as it was observable in Boston and available in the published volumes of the reputed masters: Massillon and those gathered together in the nine volumes of *The English Preacher*. On the advice of his father he directed his attention to the theorists of eloquence also: to John Quincy Adams' own *Lectures on Rhetoric and Oratory*; to all of Cicero's treatises on the subject; to Quintilian "On Oratory"; to Vossius; to Fénelon's "Dialogue on Eloquence," Hume's "Essay on Eloquence," and to works on the subject by Lord Kames, Hugh Blair, and a number of others. He balanced this by making a determined effort to acquire experience in the construction and delivery of oratorical pieces in the weekly meetings of the Private Debating Society. And finally he sought to develop his literary skill and to bring his reading into focus and use by writing translations from the Greek and Latin texts and by attempting articles and essays on the principles of eloquence or on the great orators. One number of his essay "Eloquence" was published (see volume 3:168); an additional piece on the same subject, a fragment of another, and an essay-review of Williston's compilation—all by him—survive in manuscript form in the Adams Papers (Microfilms, Reel Nos. 294, 317); also the beginning of a dissertation on Cicero (Reel No. 294). The diary reveals that there were other such efforts which have not survived. Of his translations, fragments of his version of Æschines' and of Demosthenes' orations "On the Crown" remain (Adams Papers, Microfilms, Reel Nos. 312, 317); and the translation of Cicero's "De optimo genere oratorum," which he made on 6–13 September 1831, he entered in the margins of his large-paper edition of Cicero (Oxford, 1783, 1:540–544), which is in the Stone Library and one page of which is reproduced here. The quotation above recording this action occurs at p. 135, below.

Courtesy of the National Park Service, Adams National Historic Site.

VOLUME 4

Diary 1831–1832

Diary of Charles Francis Adams

TUESDAY. MARCH 1ST.

The soft weather still continues. I went to the Office as usual and passed my time rather more profitably than heretofore. For having accomplished the usual duties I sat down and read with some attention the rest of Enfield's History of Philosophy. This is on the whole a valuable book, valuable for reference after it has been read. It has succeeded in giving me what I have long felt the need of, a general view of the subject. I shall now feel better prepared to progress with the philosophical works of Cicero.

Took a walk, but I felt the enervating effect of the air, and a little of that bilious disposition which the Spring Season always produces in me. After dinner, Miss Adams paid me a visit in my study and conversed with me upon the subject of her affairs. I obtained from her what I concluded to be her desire, in order to send it to Washington, and was engaged for the rest of the day in finishing and copying my letter to this effect.[1] My father has not written to me lately. I hope nothing has offended him.

Evening passed with the ladies. I tried a little of Buffon but did not make much progress. Port Royal Greek Grammar and the Tatler.

[1] Abigail S. Adams had fixed upon May for her marriage. In conformity with "the general practice here for the Lady to furnish her House," she planned expenditures for furniture for two or three rooms in Mr. Angier's house in Medford. Her requirements therefore on 1 April would be for $625 from the legacy to her from JA being administered by JQA until she reached her majority or married. The $2,500 then remaining in her account, she wished to be put in trust for her (CFA to JQA, 28 Feb., LbC, Adams Papers).

WEDNESDAY. 2D.

Morning mild again. The continuance of this weather shows a final stop to the Winter. And the immense masses of snow that have been gathering in our Streets for months now vanish like mist before the warm rays of the Sun. I confess this is cheering, to me for it seems like the reanimation of the world, as if the heavy weight which was pressing upon Nature was to give way to life and joy.

I went to the Office and from there to the Supreme Court for the purpose of being admitted to the bar of that Court, which in due time was done. This constitutes me an Attorney to all intents and purposes.[1]

I

Returned to my Office but finding little to do, I went to the Athenæum and passed an hour in considering the subject of my Article and the correction of it.[2] Also looked into the third volume of Bradford's History of Massachusetts,[3] which I found pretty much what I supposed.

Took a walk with Edmund Quincy and returned home to dine. Found the family in trouble from the domestics, which I settled by dismissing another of the Household. Afternoon, Conversation with my Wife upon it. She is not exactly in condition now to be troubled. Read a portion of the Oration for Cæcina which is a question of pure law and therefore difficult. Read also some of the Institutes of Justinian. Evening, quietly at home, Greek Grammar and the Tatler.

[1] The Boston bar was divided into three classes: attorneys at the Common Pleas, attorneys at the Supreme Judicial Court, and counselors at law (*Mass. Register*). Advancement from one class to the next was largely, though not wholly, determined by length of experience in practice.

[2] See above, vol. 3, entry for 23 February.

[3] Alden Bradford's *History of Massachusetts* for the period from 1764 to 1789 had been published in 2 vols. at Boston in 1822; a third volume, 1790–1820, was published in 1829.

THURSDAY. 3D.

Morning mild and cloudy but it did not rain. I found myself oppressed with a severe cold which the change has given me. Went to the Office as usual and was occupied partly in the common matters, partly in reading the Institutes of Justinian, which give me now and then a little light upon the passages of Cicero read heretofore. But my attention was not perfect, as I had in the first place received a letter from my father which kept me thinking,[1] and in the second received another summons to attend the referees in the case of Farmer and Storer.

I took a walk and returned to dinner after which I went to Concert Hall where the Reference was sitting.[2] The case took a different turn from what was anticipated so that the larger portion of the witnesses were not examined. But the whole melancholy story came out by way of statement from the Counsel. It was bad enough in all conscience. I ought however to be thankful that the evidence to prove all this was not gone into.

Evening at home, excessively fatigued. I could not read dry Grammar with any attention. H. Brooks staid here from the Theatre. Finished the Tatler.

[1] 28 Feb. (Adams Papers). On the letter, see above, vol. 3:411.

[2] Concert Hall was located at the corner of Hanover and Court streets (C. H. Snow, *A Geography of Boston . . . and the Adjacent Towns*, Boston, 1830, p. 52).

FRIDAY. 4TH.

The Celebration of this day by the firing of Cannon strikes me as a new practice.[1] It is probably one of General Jackson's Reforms. But one would think it was rather the celebration of a legal day for introduction to Office than for homage to any particular event.

I went to the Office. The weather still mild. Occupied in my usual way, and made considerable progress in reading the Institutes of Justinian in the parts that relate to Testaments and Trusts, which we appear to have borrowed very much. I cannot help admiring the wisdom of the general provisions of these laws. They seem to have reached the point intended, Equity, and are not founded like some portions of our Common Law upon partial views.

Took my usual walk, but found myself quite oppressed by a cold. Went to dine with Mr. Chardon Brooks. Nobody there but my Wife and myself. Returned home at four and pursued the Oration for Cæcina in which I made considerable progress. I think it a very remarkable production, exhibiting an infinite deal of Lawyer's power. I am glad to have an opportunity to read such an effort.

Evening, Conversation with my Wife. Miss Adams spent the day out, returned in the evening with Mr. Angier. This latter gentleman is rather a dull man. Greek Grammar, and commenced the Spectator. I had intended giving an opinion here of the Tatler but find I write too much. The book has on the whole given me pleasure. I recollect few of the numbers as remarkable, and none as very striking. The character of the publication is a medium between high and low.

[1] The Boston newspapers carried no account of a celebration or public observance of this day, 1831 not being a year for the inauguration of a new national administration.

SATURDAY. 5TH.

Morning mild. Went to the Office as usual. Engaged during much of the time in reading the Institutes of Justinian which I admire exceedingly. They strike me very favourably especially as the compilation of an arbitrary prince. Nothing of particular importance took place during the period. I went down to a sale of Stocks and visited Mr. Brooks. Took a long walk returning with Quincy.

Afternoon short as Mr. Angier dined here and Miss Adams remains some days longer. I finished the Oration for Cæcina and began a review of it. The substance is difficult and it turns upon the meaning of words. But the ability it displays is not less than usual. Mr. Angier came in the evening again and sat here. He is on the whole a pretty

3

stupid man. I do not find any thing to seize upon in order to draw him out. After he went, I read Greek Grammar and finished the Tatler.

SUNDAY. 6TH.

Morning cloudy and chill. It hailed a little and then rained. Nobody went to Meeting but I during the day. Mr. Frothingham preached a Communion Sermon, and one other. Strange how I forget what it was about. The attendance was thin.

I read today Drake's fifth volume upon the Essayists,[1] and almost finished it. This is the most peculiar writer I ever read. His style is clear and easy, yet there is a something, an affectation of the suaviter loquens that is not pleasant. His criticism is not bad and yet it is superficial. His puffing is absurd. It is bookmaking if there ever was such a thing, and yet there is much curious information and amusing biography in it. On the whole I do not know whether to say that I am pleased or displeased. Tried to read Buffon but failed and determined to postpone him to a more connected moment. Evening at home. Greek Grammar *finished*, and the Spectator.

[1] That is, the second volume of the continuation of his *Essays, Biographical, Critical, and Historical* . . . ; see above, vol. 3:362, 403.

MONDAY. 7TH.

Morning mild and pleasant. I went to the Office as usual and was busy in reading and finishing the Institutes of Justinian which have on the whole paid me pretty well for my study of them. But one interruption of any consequence, that of my Tenant Mr. Gulliver boring me for further repairs. I was rather provoked and we had a pretty smart dialogue. This repairing consumes nearly all the funds, and in these times when income fails so frequently this is something of an object. Indeed of all kind[s] of Estate which I know, real Estate is the most provoking. I wish I had nothing at all to do with it.

Went to the Athenæum but did not succeed in getting any new book. After dinner, Attended the Meeting of the Directors of the Boylston Market Association, for the transaction of business. After disposing of the various subjects I took a long walk to Roxbury[1] and could not help reflecting still more in the course of it, upon this subject of property. The discussion of the Dividend of this Company is another evidence of my assertions.

Returned home fatigued, and in the evening finished Mr. Drake's book. After which I looked over Dr. Valpy's Greek Grammar[2] and read the usual Numbers of the Spectator.

¹ Roxbury would have been reached by continuing southward from the Boylston Market on Washington Street, which after entering Roxbury became its main artery. The area is included in the "map of Boston and the adjacent towns" which is reproduced in vol. 3.

² Richard Valpy, *The Elements of Greek Grammar . . .*, first issued at London in 1805, was published in several editions in England and the United States before 1831.

TUESDAY. 8TH.

The day was pleasant though much colder than it has been heretofore. I went to the Office so early that I had a good long morning and after disposing of common matters, I sat down to read the speeches of Mr. Sheridan upon the Impeachment of Warren Hastings. These are very celebrated and may have been entitled to the praise they received when delivered, but I am at a loss to see where it is merited in the abstract I read. I mean as a whole—For parts are undoubtedly splendid. But the Speech as a charge is not clear, it gives no vivid idea of the circumstances, the narration is too much clouded by assertion and invective. It fails before the distinct painting of the Orations against Verres. It requires a knowledge of facts before we enter upon it, which is a defect in a substantial part of Orations. Notwithstanding all this, it must have been a great effort and I am much more disposed to lay the faults I find to the imperfection of the Report of it, than to the original Speech.[1]

I went to the Boylston Market and drew up the Record of the Directors Meeting of yesterday. After which I took a long walk. Afternoon, reviewed the Oration for Cæcina which I admire more and more. It contains the substance of a most important Question, agitated ever since but never better settled. Evening, at home. Edward Brooks called and passed an hour. After which Dr. Valpy and the Spectator.

¹ There were numerous accounts of the trial of Warren Hastings in which the speeches of Richard Brinsley Sheridan were summarized or abstracted, all of the accounts apparently relying upon the *Parliamentary Reports*. One such, which would have been available at the Boston Athenæum, was *The Trial of Warren Hastings, Esq.* [London, 1788], where Sheridan's speeches of 3, 6, 10 June 1788, are reported in some detail.

WEDNESDAY. 9TH.

Morning at the Office. Weather fine. Before I had completed my daily Diary, I was interrupted, and the visits of different persons continued throughout the day. Mr. Noah Curtis, the Parish Treasurer of Quincy called to pay the Note which my father held against them, from my Grandfather's Estate.[1] I was obliged to return home to obtain it, and was then paid in full. This with the sum from the Fire and

Marine will make almost enough to pay Miss A. S. Adams.[2] The Fire and Marine however *again* pay no Dividend. A wretched concern. My other visitors were my Carpenter Mr. Ayer, about some little repairs to be done on Mr. Gulliver's house. Mr. Hurlbert, the Tenant of the Store about Mr. Welsh's Room which he made an offer for, that I could not accept. Then Mr. Peabody with whom I took a walk to the sale of the Furniture under the care of the New England Society.[3] It was poor. Returned home.

Afternoon employed in finishing the Oration for Cæcina and read a large part of that for the Manilian Law. This is a famous Panegyric. But perhaps Hortensius was right and Cicero wrong. In the evening, visits from Mr. Jo. Angier and Edmd. Quincy. A pleasant Supper enough but I did nothing after it excepting to read the Spectator.

[1] The sum received was $1,436.38. CFA to JQA, 9 March (LbC, Adams Papers).

[2] The legacy to Abigail S. Adams from her grandfather payable at her marriage amounted to $3,125. CFA to JQA, 28 Feb. (LbC, Adams Papers).

[3] The sale took place at 9 o'clock at Market Hall (*Boston Daily Advertiser*, 9 March, p. 3, col. 4).

THURSDAY. 10TH.

Morning fine. Our Weather is uncommonly pleasant for this month. I suffered a little from head ach during the day owing to my Supper of last night. At the Office I found a package from Mr. Everett containing his Speech on the Indian Question, with which he had at last favoured me.[1] Mr. E. thought I could buy his Speeches if I wanted them. And he had many people of more public influence than I might ever be to conciliate by these small marks of attention. Now however that he has a cheap edition to circulate, he can be gratious with one. I feel obliged to him for it, though after I had read it, I could not attach great intrinsic value to the present. He had better have been silent for he has done nothing by it.

I read a little of Lord Chatham's Speech about the Falkland Islands,[2] but was interrupted by the hour for my walk, which I took as usual. Afternoon, I finished the Oration for the Manilian Law; and began that in defence of Cluentius. The first is a little polished gem of much lustre, but not so solid as some of the law Orations. These show the greatest talent. The Oration for Cluentius is again in another style.

Miss Adams left us today. Evening alone with my Wife. I read to her a part of the Account of Captn. Parry's first Voyage to the North Seas.[3] After which Dr. Valpy and the Spectator. Horatio Brooks lodged here this night.

¹ The more recent of Edward Everett's speeches on the Indians was delivered in the House on 14 and 21 Feb. and published as *On the Execution of the Laws and Treaties in Favor of the Indian Tribes*, Washington, 1831. Earlier, he had spoken on 19 May 1830, *On the Bill for Removing the Indians from the East to the West Side of the Mississippi*, Boston, 1830. Everett's views as revealed in the speeches are closer to JQA's than to CFA's; see vol. 3: 139.

² The "Speech on the Seizure of Falkland's Islands" is in vol. 2 of the edition of *Anecdotes of William Pitt, Earl of Chatham, With his Speeches in Parliament, 1736–1778*, published at London in 1792, owned by CFA, and now at MQA.

³ Sir William Edward Parry, *Journal of a Voyage for the Discovery of a North-West Passage from the Atlantic to the Pacific . . . 1819–1820*, London, 1821.

FRIDAY. 11TH.

Morning fine. I went to the Office as usual. Received from my Father a bundle of Papers, being Powers of Attorney for himself and T. B. Adams Jr. to receive Money in the different Offices here.¹ Also a letter from John with the welcome news of some Stores for us.² After my common pursuits, I sat down and read the first part of Mr. Brougham's Abstract of the Novum Organon of Bacon,³ and was much instructed by it. My capacity has improved, for this is clearly ascertained by the fact that three years ago I made an effort to read this and failed.

Went with Mr. Peabody to see the sales of Butter and other things under the Patronage of the N. E. Society but I made no purchases.⁴ Sent for to go out with some others of the family to Medford, so we went and reached there in time for dinner. Found Mr. Brooks at home a little unwell. Quite an uncommon thing for him. Spent the Afternoon as usual and returned home before dark. Evening, a visit from Edward Brooks and a short reading of Parry. Afterwards finished Dr. Valpy and read the Spectator.

¹ Accompanying the papers was a letter, JQA to CFA, 6 March (Adams Papers).

² Letter missing.

³ Lord Brougham's *Account of Lord Bacon's Novum Organon Scientiarum* was one of the publications of the *Library of Useful Knowledge*.

⁴ "Family butter" was sold at 12 o'clock at Quincy Hall along with machinery and household goods (*Boston Daily Advertiser*, 11 March, p. 3, col. 4).

SATURDAY. 12TH.

Morning clear and pleasant. I went to the Office as usual. Nothing material took place. I went through my usual occupations and then read the second part of Bacon's Novum Organon as drawn up by Mr. Brougham. I have been enlightened by this reading. It has explained to me clearly what I only knew generally before, the merits of the inductive System of reasoning. The difficulties existing in the mind against a true examination of effects to find causes, and the proper course to remove them. I am fully convinced of the value of this short work which I am not always in what I read.

Took a walk and in the Afternoon continued the Oration for Cluentius. It is a peculiar production, rather laboured and showing marks of Orationizing if I can use such a word. The *thing* among persons at the bar now, is often felt. Perhaps the nature of the case required it. Of this we are at this day unable to Judge not being acquainted with the feelings of those who were to decide the cause.

Evening sitting quietly with my Wife. Read a part of Captain Parry's Journal. What a course amidst all the horrors of an Arctic Winter. Desolation around them, and danger in every motion. A person cannot think of this without some wonder that any thing can induce poor weak man to endure such privations. Yet such is his spirit of curiosity and enterprize. I afterwards read Buffon's Theory of the Earth. But I am now so intolerably drowsy late at night that I can do nothing with effect. I must change my plan to earlier rising. The Spectator as usual.

SUNDAY. 13TH.

A lovely Morning. My Wife went out with me to Meeting this morning and we heard Mr. Walker preach the usual Arguments in favour of Theological discussions. I was not convinced by them. That subject is not one for the rough Jarring of inflamed Passions. If there is any on the face of the Earth where humility and meekness are enjoined as a matter of daily practice it is this. Controversy carried to any height is therefore subversive of two of the clearest precepts of the whole System of pure Religion. In the afternoon I went alone and heard a Sermon upon the nature of regenerations. The character of this gentleman's mind is controversial.

Took a walk. It rained during the latter part of the day and I was caught in it. Wrote letters to my Father and to John,[1] which occupied some time. Evening, quiet at home. I continued reading Mr. Buffon's Proofs of an Air built Fabric and after it, the Spectator.

[1] The letter to JQA (LbC, Adams Papers) was in answer to his letters of 26, 28 Feb. and 6 March; that to JA2 (Adams Papers) acknowledged with thanks the receipt of the pamphlet containing the documents in the Calhoun affair and of the gift of flour and hams.

MONDAY. 14TH.

Morning at the Office after an hours reading of Buffon at home which paid me in some measure for my drowsy night. The weather has now so much changed that this will be very expedient in future. I can gain an hour of work in the morning which now I lose half of at night.

After clearing my regular duties, I began to read a Work purchased at the sale of E. J. Lowell's Library called, "Le Bibliotheque de l'homme public." It is an Analysis by Condorcet and others of the principal Works upon Government, originally published in numbers all of which I do not own.[1] The first Work is an abstract of the Politics of Aristotle. And this I read. Took a walk and returned home.

Evening after *almost* finishing the Oration for Cluentius in the general opinion already expressed of which I persevere with some modification, I despatched my letters to my Father and received one from him, the tone and spirit of which I regret. For it shows me a very stormy future.[2] Continued the Journal of Captain Parry, and was much interested with the Account of his Wintering in the Arctic Regions. A tremendous Undertaking. Read Buffon and finished his Theory of the Earth. Also two numbers of the Spectator.

[1] Although the condensations or abstracts of classic works in political theory published as *Bibliothèque de l'homme public, ou analyse raisonée des principaux ouvrages François et étrangers, sur la politique* ... reached at least 28 volumes, the edition published at Paris in 1790 which CFA purchased on 21 Oct. 1830 for $3 consisted of 12 vols. in 6. In addition to the notation relating to their acquisition, the volumes at MQA contain extensive marginalia and summary comments in CFA's hand.

[2] JQA to CFA, 8 March (Adams Papers). The letter, an answer to CFA's of 28 Feb. (LbC, Adams Papers) in which CFA had expressed his view that the controversies appearing in the public prints relating to the break between the President and the Vice-President were degrading to all those who were drawn into them, was for the most part an unflattering and detailed characterization of Hamlet as "invariably governed by an over exquisite sense of moral sensibility," a characterization which JQA wrote was but "pre- liminary to the observation which has often occurred to me, and which your letter in pale ink ... has freshened in my mind that there is something of the character of Hamlet in your composition. Your standard of morals is more elevated than belongs to the world in which we live and to the clay of which we are formed. ... Apply if you please your inflexible measure of right and wrong to your own conduct towards others, but in estimating their motives, and judging of their actions let down a little your scale of Virtue till its last step at least shall touch the earth." Spiritedly defending his own choice in the past and for the future of a public career in which inevitably "you will see Slander and vilification enough of me," he warns that if CFA should ever attempt to render important service to his country or to benefit mankind he must expect "bitter revilings and the foulest Slanders." Then pointedly, "You must take care not on this account to lose your desire to serve your Country or to do good to your fellow Men."

TUESDAY. 15TH.

Morning cloudy but the weather gradually improved to a bright beautiful day. I read a part of Buffon's Natural History before going out. At the Office as usual. Called to obtain the Report of the Commissioners upon R. New's Estate, and found to my surprise that the larger claims against the Estate had not been brought in. Occupied in looking into a Law question upon that matter. Mr. Peabody called and sat an hour or two. Conversation upon various subjects, quite agreeably. I had not much spare time but as much as there was, I devoted to a review of the Abstract of Aristotle, which contains many good thoughts. Took a walk and returned home.

After dinner, I finished the Oration for Cluentius and made a deliberate and thorough Review of the Oration for the Manilian Law. It is certainly a beautiful Specimen in its way. A brilliant Panegyric, and it *may* have been deserved, though that is doubtful. The tone adopted by the Orator is that of independence and the concluding declaration is a noble one. If he was wrong, it was a defect of Judgment, not of principle.

Evening reading Captn. Parry's Journal which continued to be very interesting. It is described with great simplicity and apparent truth. Read a little of Buffon and the Spectator, retired early.

WEDNESDAY. 16TH.

Morning cloudy, with a mild south Wind so as not to be unpleasant. I went to the Office as usual and after the regular duties, finished the reading of Aristotles Politics analyzed. A work which contains many good single ideas but which shows no practical system, nor any clear notions of the end of human existence, at least as we understand it now. The tendency to theory is also strongly visible. I began the Republic of Jean Bodin abridged.[1] I know little at present either of the name or the Author, and did not make any very great progress today. Deacon Spear called about the Houses at Quincy, with a request that I would write to Washington for instructions for him, which I accordingly did.[2]

Took my usual walk which was pleasant enough today, and after dinner continued the Oration for Cluentius, half of which I accomplished in review. It appears more striking on this perusal. And from the Author's account of himself in one of his rhetorical Works, it seems pretty clear, that he thought it one of his best. Evening a Letter from my Mother.[3] Captain Parry and his excursion over Melville Island. Still very interesting. After this I read Buffon and the Spectator. Two good Numbers.

[1] In *Bibliothèque de l'homme public*, vol. 1, with comments in CFA's hand.
[2] CFA to JQA (LbC, Adams Papers).   [3] Letter missing.

THURSDAY. 17TH.

The day cloudy with a cold Easterly Wind and a flurry of Snow, occasionally. After reading Buffon after breakfast, I went to the Office, and continued my reading of Mons. J. Bodin. No interruptions of any consequence. These two Tenements still bring two persons on an average daily but with no serious views. My progress was tolerable. Took a walk in company with Edward Brooks, and as my Wife had gone out of town to see Mrs. Gorham Brooks, I dined with Mr. Frothingham, and had a pleasant time.

Returned to my Study and sat down to the Oration for Cluentius, which I completed. On reconsideration, I must modify my Opinion in this instance. If Cicero's opinion of some points in the case were really as strong as he asserts them to be, then the Rest was superfluous and Oration making. If as is more probable the Defendant was not so clearly innocent, he was authorized in his elaborate and long argument. At any rate, this is a great model of an Advocate's effort. He says every thing that can be said. The Opinions expressed in regard to the future state, are remarkable, and conflict with the known opinions of the Author as elsewhere expressed.

My Wife returned in time for me to read some of Parry. After which I continued Buffon and the Spectator.

FRIDAY. 18TH.

Morning quite clear. I went to the Office after passing an hour in reading Buffon's Natural History of Man. Occupations as usual. I finished Jean Bodin. This Author is rather injudiciously praised. He has a good many things that are valuable but I cannot see that his System such as it is, has any merit. He talks about absolute Sovereignty as being necessary to a Prince, and although he qualifies this remark by confining him to the performance of just things, yet he seems to leave the Judgment of what is just and unjust entirely to him. We know from history that even with good dispositions power produces rather strange effects. I also read the Account of the resources of France in the Sixteenth Century. A valuable paper though showing the deficiency which existed at the time in the knowledge of Political Economy. Also the Essays and the Prince of Machiavel—These forming the first volume of the Bibliotheque.[1]

Took a long walk as far as Dorchester Heights and South Boston. What a change since the time of my boyhood. All this was Common and quite desolate.[2] Returned home and passed the Afternoon, in reading the Orations against Rullus upon the Agrarian Law. I did not complete the Second. Evening, Captain Parry until interrupted by Edmd. Quincy who spent the Evening. After which, very Drowsy. Read the Spectator.

[1] CFA's annotations accompany the "Etat du commerce en France," "Discours de Machiavel sur la Ie décade de Tite-Live," and "Le prince de Machiavel."

[2] South Boston was reached by the older South Bridge and the Free Bridge, opened in 1828. Formerly a part of Dorchester, the area was annexed to the city of Boston in 1804 at which time ten families were resident on it. By 1830 the population had grown to 2,865; numerous factories and commercial establishments had been built and several public institutions constructed. See C. H. Snow, *A Geography of Boston . . . and the Adjacent Towns*, Boston, 1830, p. 117–123, 126–127.

SATURDAY. 19TH.

Morning cloudy and dark. I read Buffon as usual for an hour and then went to the Office in snow. This continued pretty smartly until noon when it turned to rain for the remainder of the day. After my common occupations I sat down and reviewed the two pieces of Machiavel which I read yesterday. There is a great deal of knowledge of Government contained in them, and though some of the maxims they contain are horrible enough, yet there are others which deserve deep consideration from Rulers. I was also busy some time in Accounts. Returned home directly being unable to take my usual exercise.

Afternoon instead of reading Cicero as usual, I thought I would finish pasting the Crests in my Fathers books, a business which has been hanging on from day to day for more than a year. I also did a few of my own. This was not entirely finished though I worked steadily the whole time. Evening, Continued reading Captn. Parry, which is still interesting, and after it, continued Buffon and the Spectator.

SUNDAY. 20TH.

Morning clear and cold again with a high wind. This felt more sharp from the mildness of what had preceded it. I am altogether inclined to the belief that the effect of weather upon the human frame is not in proportion to the degree of its severity, but its variation. A cold day coming after a warm one is more trying than a uniform decrease of temperature to a much lower degree. This is strengthened by reading Parry.

My Wife attended at Meeting with me and we heard a learned Sermon from Mr. Frothingham upon the doctrine of the final destruction of the Earth by fire. Afternoon I heard Mr. Ripley, alone. He is very prosy. Continued reading Buffon who is both instructive and amusing. Evening, finished Parry's first voyage. An amusing work on the whole, being a history of a portion of the earth probably never before inhabited during its winter season by civilized man. He failed in his undertaking but on the whole the Voyage has not been without some profit to the knowledge of mankind. Continued Buffon and read the Spectator as usual.

MONDAY. 21ST.

Morning clear and still pretty cold. I went to the Office as usual after reading my regular portion of Buffon in the morning. Engaged pretty fully after my common matters, in reading an Abstract of the Political Essays of Hume.[1] They are well written, having the peculiar style of the Author with his philosophical manner of thinking. But the tendency of his opinions is to the establishment of absolute power, and his feelings lead him to look with more composure upon oppression by a few, than by the many. He was too cold blooded for his authority to be valuable. There are some things upon which every man should feel and speak strongly. He does not upon any thing. I then went to the Athenæum where I spent an hour instead of walking.

In the Afternoon, I accomplished though superficially the three Orations against Rullus upon the Agrarian Law. These have not much interest. They are Addresses calculated to excite the People and of course evidently upon reading, overcharged. The idea that Capua was likely to be a Rival of Rome was clearly to catch. So is much of what is said against Rullus who was probably a Popularity seeker like the Gracchi.

Evening I began the account of the second Expedition of Parry which went through Hudson's Bay.[2] Also, Buffon and the Spectator.

[1] In *Bibliothèque de l'homme public*, vol. 2, along with CFA's marginal comments.
[2] *Journal of a Second Voyage for the Discovery of a North-West Passage . . . 1821–1823*, London [also N.Y.], 1824.

TUESDAY. 22D.

Morning pleasant but still cool. Read Buffon for an hour as usual, and then went to the Office. Nothing material took place; I received a letter from my Father, and a Copy of Verses addressed to me.[1] He frequently poetizes, and what he writes is in the usual strain of lofty morals. The remainder of the morning was taken up in my common duties, and in reading over the Essays of Hume which affected me

13

much in the same manner as heretofore. They made me doubt not principles but his system of explaining them. My Uncle Judge Adams from Quincy paid me a long visit and gave me some Account of the proceedings at that place in relation to the House &ca. He seems puzzled in regard to the Posts.

Returned home, having lost my walk and after dinner was busy in reading over the Orations against Rullus. They do not strike me as very much deserving further Comment. But as a peculiar kind of Oratory, they deserve some attention. Speaking *against* the Popular Current.

Evening, Parry's second Voyage, which appears to have been unsuccessful enough. He was entangled in Bays all the time. It is on the whole somewhat doubtful whether there is any passage through Hudson's Bay. But we shall see more. Buffon afterwards and the Spectator.

[1] 15 March (Adams Papers), with an attachment, "To my Son, Charles Francis Adams," entitled *Wisdom*, being a paraphrase of Proverbs, 3:13–35, in eight of JQA's favorite eight-line stanzas. The purport would seem to be related to JQA's reflections on CFA expressed a week earlier (above, entry for 14 March, note). The apposite lines read:

My Son! thy Soul let Wisdom keep:
So shall thy heart to God be true.

Then walk thou safely in thy way:
Path's steep and rugged thou shalt meet:

But fearless march—thou shalt not stray,
Nor stone of stumbling strike thy feet.
Thy heart, no terror shall affright. . . .

In vain the malice of thy foes
Shall spread to catch thy feet the snare,
Thy God shall shelter thy repose
And guard thee with unsleeping care.
On him with stedfast soul rely;
Like him with Goodness, others bind;
The stream of Bounty still supply
And prove a blessing to mankind.

WEDNESDAY. 23D.

Morning delightfully mild and pleasant. I went to the Office as usual after finishing the fifth volume of Buffon's Natural History, and thus concluding all that I propose to do in this way just now. I have been interested by much that he says, although in a great many things he seems to me to be wrong. Particularly in the closing Dissertation upon Men and Animals. In which he does not maintain fully the ground he starts upon. After reading several Letters from Washington,[1] and T. B. Adams Jr.—The latter enclosing a power of Attorney for his stock in the Fire and Marine[2]—I sat down and considered the Analysis of Locke's Essay upon Government.[3] A very remarkable production. Took my usual walk.

Mr. Brooks and Miss Julia Gorham dined with us. The former seemed a little depressed. The latter passed the Evening. I felt languid and unable to study but I continued the reading over the Second

Oration against Rullus and nearly accomplished it. Evening, I thought I would look into Kotzebue's Voyage [4] and I became interested enough in it to accomplish one half of the first Volume. After which I read the Spectator. Two of Addison's Papers upon Tragedy.

[1] JQA to CFA, 17 March, and probably LCA to ABA, 16 March (both in Adams Papers).

[2] Thomas B. Adams Jr.'s letter and enclosure are missing.

[3] In *Bibliothèque de l'homme public*, vol. 2; CFA has annotated the text.

[4] Otto von Kotzebue, *A Voyage of Discovery, into the South Sea and Beering's Straits, for the Purpose of Exploring a North-East Passage ... in ... 1815–1818.* Translated from the Russian by H. E. Lloyd, 3 vols., London, 1821.

THURSDAY. 24TH.

Morning cloudy with a warm Southerly Wind and threatening rain. I continued reading the Voyage of Kotzebue. How different from the coolness and perseverance of Parry. The former though on the whole not an unskilful Navigator, yet possessing little of the dignity and scientific ability of the latter. His expedition to the North West commencing very favourably seems to have been left off for no reason at the very time when it is best to try it. And his voyage was conducted rather at haphazard to discover a few little contemptible Coral Rocks in the Pacific than any settlement of interesting philosophical questions.

At the Office where I finished the review of Mr. Lockes Treatise. This contains much deep reflection, it developes many truths which I believe to be sound, but it mixes with them much that seems theoretical and several things positively false. I also resumed my old task of writing out the sayings of the Wise Men.[1] Took a walk to the Athenæum.

Afternoon, finished the Orations against Rullus, of which I have already said enough and began that for Rabirius. My spirits were depressed, and I did not study with my usual zeal. Evening, Captain Parry, Kotzebue, and the Spectator.

[1] See vol. 3, entry for 25 Dec. 1830.

FRIDAY 25TH.

Morning pleasant with a warm Wind. After reading Kotzebue for a sufficient time, I went to the Office as usual and was busy as usual with my regular work after which I read a portion of the "Bibliotheque de L'Homme Public" containing Maxims of Guicciardini which on the whole did not strike me, and a part of An Analysis of the State of

France by Seigneur du Haillan.[1] I was interrupted however by An Applicant for the Transfer of a Share in the Boylston Market, and by some other little bits of business of a trifling character yet seizing time. Took a walk.

After dinner I read the rest of the Oration for Rabirius which is but a fragment, and the first Oration against Catiline. It is a little remarkable that in the first of these two, Cicero contradicts the whole of his doctrine about a future state which he adopts in that for Cluentius. This would make it appear as if he suited his Opinions to the cases he argued, a principle which I cannot quite see the correctness of.

In the evening as Mrs. Dexter had sent in to ask us to spend the evening, My Wife and I feeling refusal to be impossible, paid her a visit. Judge Ward was there.[2] She is a singular Woman, but not an unpleasant or an unkind one. Returned home to read Kotzebue and the Spectator.

[1] Both the "Plusieurs advis et conseils" and "De l'état et succès des affaires de France" are in vol. 3. CFA's comments accompany the text from Guicciardini.

[2] Artemas Ward, chief judge of the Court of Common Pleas, was married to Samuel Dexter's sister (Winsor, *Memorial History of Boston*, 2:555; *Boston Directory*, 1831–1832).

SATURDAY. 26TH.

Morning delightful—The air being soft as Midsummer. After reading an hour in Kotzebue and finishing the Voyage which ended in nothing, compared to the preparation that had been made for it, I went to the Office and found there a letter from my Father covering the Certificates of the Mass. Fire and Marine Ins. Shares. I therefore went directly and obtained the repayment of one fourth part of the Capital upon my Fathers and T. B. Adams Jrs. Shares which I deposited. This business being over I went back to my Office and sat down to answer my Father's letter which did not appear to me to be exactly the thing I wanted. He never should have meddled with that Mill. I am afraid before he has done with it, the thing will ruin him.[1] In this manner I was so much occupied that I was unable to do any thing else.

Returned home, and after dinner, Started for Quincy, with my Man Benjamin. Found the House in great disorder, as they were painting it, and in setting the new Posts they had unfixed every thing about the Fence very much. I went to find Mr. Veazie and talked with him in regard to the Work to be done.[2] It seems Mr. Beale has been very labouriously expressing his Opinion about these matters. I think the interference of Neighbours very gratuitous. Went up to see the

Judge and his lady and took Tea with them. After which I returned home. The former was sick.

Stopped at Mrs. Frothingham's where my Wife and Miss Julia Gorham were spending the Evening. After sitting a little while, returned home. Read the Spectator and retired early.

[1] JQA's instructions were to deposit to his account in the U.S. Branch Bank both the money repaid to Thomas B. Adams Jr. from his investment in the Massachusetts Fire and Marine Insurance Co. and that portion of Abigail S. Adams' legacy which she wished to have invested. JQA proposed to pay interest to each until the principal was called for or was otherwise invested. CFA's assumption, probably the correct one, was that JQA intended to utilize the funds to reduce the heavy indebtedness incurred earlier in the year in unproductive speculation in flour. CFA countered therefore with arguments to support his proposal that JQA should advise Abigail S. Adams to place her funds in an annuity at the Massachusetts Life Office in trust. Further, that Thomas B. Adams Jr.'s funds should be used to meet the outstanding obligations incurred in the maintenance and repair of the Old House until the income from rentals, &c., could be built up to a sum sufficient to equal those demands, and that interest be paid to Thomas B. Adams Jr. from 1 April. JQA to CFA, 21 March; CFA to JQA, 26 March, LbC (both in Adams Papers).

[2] On George Veazie, of Quincy, carpenter, see vol. 3, entry for 29 Dec. 1830, and below, that for 8 April.

SUNDAY. 27TH.

Morning cold, with an Easterly Wind and Rain. I attended divine Service all day and heard Mr. Frothingham in the Morning and Mr. Emerson in the afternoon. The latter delivered rather a remarkable Sermon about the spirit and its nature. It seemed to me from what I heard that he had not very permanently fixed what his idea was of the thing and therefore he talked about what he did not himself perfectly comprehend.

I looked through the life of Josiah Quincy Junr. by his Son,[1] in the course of the day. And in the Evening after reading Captain Parry to my Wife, I amused myself with Boswell's Tour to the Hebrides,[2] which was a kind of feeler put out previous to publishing the Life. After this, read the Spectator as usual.

[1] Josiah Quincy (1772–1864), *Memoir of the Life of Josiah Quincy, Jun.* [1744–1775], Boston, 1825. The copy at MQA was presented to JA by the author, 28 May 1825.

[2] *Journal of a Tour to the Hebrides with Dr. Johnson*, like the other books of voyages and travels which CFA was reading at this time, was borrowed from the Boston Athenæum. The edition was that published at N.Y. in 1810.

MONDAY. 28TH.

Morning cloudy, with a drizzly rain from the Eastward. After reading Boswell's Tour to the Hebrides for an hour, I went to the

Office and was very busy first in my regular duties, next in writing a short letter to Mr. Stetson upon the following subject. Not knowing when I was married, that it was the custom for the Husband to make compensation to the Clergyman, I did not do it until accidentally some two months after my Wedding, my Wife asked me about it. Immediately upon being informed of it, I sat down and wrote to Mr. Stetson, and inclosed a sum of Money. This letter was sent by Mr. Stone, at that time Tenant of Mr. Brooks, and I thought the whole matter settled. Lately however, the Report has got about that I never paid my Minister for marrying me, and it then occurred to me, that Mr. Stone had turned out good for nothing, and might have retained the letter. I therefore sat down and made the inquiry of Mr. Stetson today.[1]

Busy afterwards in drawing up my third Account of the Estate of Robert New, and presented it at the Probate Office. This and my accounts at the close of the Quarter took up the rest of the morning. Took a long walk with Edmd. Quincy.

Afternoon, a Meeting of the Directors of the Boylston Market. Decided upon the Dividend, and performed the usual business which kept us until nearly six. Returned home quite fatigued. Read Boswell. Evening, Parry to my Wife. Boswell and the Spectator.

[1] CFA to Rev. Caleb Stetson (LbC, Adams Papers); see also vol. 3, entry for 23 Nov. 1829.

TUESDAY. 29TH.

Morning cloudy with a cold wind and altogether uncomfortable. I read Boswell as usual and went to the Office where my time was taken up in my regular duties of drawing up Accounts and writing my Diary. As this is nearly the close of the Quarter, it made me a little more busy than usual. I therefore accomplished the work of du Haillan but rather superficially.

Went to the Boylston Market and drew up the Record of the Director's Meeting of yesterday. Then a short walk and I stopped in to see the furniture of Wm. H. Eliot's House which is about to be sold.[1] It is very genteel, and just what I should have thought expedient for a gentleman of fortune. His moving from it a little surprises me. Probably he was governed by circumstances different from his immediate wishes.

Afternoon, copied my last Letter to my Father and that to Mr. Stetson and read the second Oration against Catiline which did not appear to me particularly remarkable. Evening, Parry, Boswell and the Spectator.

WEDNESDAY. 30TH.

The weather was cloudy this morning with a warm Southerly Wind and very heavy showers at Intervals. I finished Boswell's Tour to the Hebrides this morning. This work is amusing, but it ought to have been read before the Life of Johnson to give it a proper effect, as the latter work contains much the best Picture of the Dr's mind. None has ever been so fully laid bare to the public, and none could exemplify more strongly in itself the singular medley of weaknesses and power of which the human mind generally is composed. I do not know that such books are a blessing, for they tend to destroy all the Romance about perfection of character which though occasionally it may do harm, yet will more generally produce good in leading us to think favourably of our powers of virtuous action.

At the Office, where I passed my time in reading the Analysis of the Republic of Plato.¹ Went afterwards to the Athenæum, thence home, and in the afternoon read the Third and fourth Orations against Catiline. They are able, and breath[e] a spirit of Patriotism which though it sometimes goes a little on Stilts, is on the whole very admirable. The composition of all but the fourth is simple. The arrangement of that is tolerably artful.

Evening, continued Parry, to my Wife; after which the third Volume of Kotzebue containing the Science of the Expedition. After which the Spectator.

¹ In *Bibliothèque de l'homme public*, vol. 4, with CFA's marginalia.

THURSDAY. 31ST.

Morning clear and warm but very windy. I continued reading Kotzebue's third Volume this morning and was interested in his Account of the South Seas, and the habits of the Islanders although I do not think that he makes out much with a great parade of learning. He refers to former Navigators to show he has read them and to give information which he ought to have given, or else not have pretended to say any thing about it.

Went to the Office where it being the last day of the Quarter I was very busy in making up my Account, copying it out and writing a Letter explanatory as usual.¹ This was however stopped by one Mr.

Loker from Weston who bored me two hours about a County Road which I did not care about hearing. What annoyances these men must be to a Country Lawyer.

Took a short walk and dined at Mrs. Frothingham's with my Wife and Horatio Brooks. Returned home. Copied my Letter, and read one half of the Oration for Murena—In which one sees more of Cicero's Speaking for the occasion. Read Parry in the Evening. More of Kotzebue and the Spectator. Horatio Brooks lodged here.

¹ CFA to JQA (LbC, Adams Papers).

APRIL. 1831.

FRIDAY. 1ST.

Morning clear but with a high Wind. I read Kotzebue a short time, but began today my review of the Orations on the Crown. I hope this will be of some service to me for certainly I devote time enough to it. By it I hope to keep up my knowledge of Greek. As it is now probable that I shall have the Summer entirely to myself in town, I think I shall have a fine opportunity to pursue my studies upon a more extensive scale than ever. I have almost innumerable plans. Besides my pursuit of Latin and Greek, and the reading at my Office, I have become interested in the knowledge of facts relating to the examination of a North West Passage, and I have not abandoned the project of recovering German. This may seem a little too much at once but I know no rule more decisive for a man's conduct in life than not to be discouraged by small things.

Took a walk with my Wife and made some purchases for the Quincy House. At the Office, Engaged in Accounts. Quarter day and I drew up my bills as usual and balanced my Cash Books. Then a walk for exercise, having finished the Republic of Plato and the Utopia of T. More.¹ They are the schemes of visionaries. After dinner, I finished the Oration for Muræna. A laboured and a great effort. The explanation of legal quibbles and the doctrine of the Stoics is ably and curiously managed. Evening, Parry. Finished the third Volume of Kotzebue and read the Spectator.

¹ In *Bibliothèque de l'homme public*, vol. 4, with CFA's comments.

SATURDAY. 2D.

Morning clear and weather fine. I began my morning's studies, by seriously reviewing the Oration for the Crown by Æschines upon which I propose now to study one hour every morning. Then to the Office where I was engaged in my Accounts, until eleven, when I went to call for my Wife and Mrs. Frothingham to go and see Audubon's Engravings of American Birds.[1] They are of the natural size and certainly splendid as well from the Ornithology as the Botany they display. We remained an hour.

I returned to the Office and was worried afterwards by Tenants coming which now annoys me exceedingly. I wish I could afford to throw up the thing. A short walk. Afternoon, pursuing the study of Cicero, but owing to low spirits and listlessness I did not progress very far, with the Oration for Flaccus. Evening, reading Parry to my Wife, and began Weddel's Voyage to the South Pole.[2] He went farther than any body and says he saw a clear Sea, which is extraordinary enough. Read the Spectator upon Wit—Some valuable papers.

[1] Perhaps Audubon's engravings were included under the rubric "Domestic Birds and Animals, colored" in the collection of "Beautiful Engravings & Lithographies" to be sold at auction at the Julien Auction Rooms, Milk and Congress streets, and on display there (*Boston Daily Advertiser*, 2 April, p. 3, col. 6).

[2] James Weddell, *A Voyage towards the South Pole . . . in . . . 1822–1824*, London, 1825.

SUNDAY. 3D.

Morning clear, but a cold Easterly Wind rather produced chill in the Air and hurt its pleasantness. My Wife and I attended Divine Service at Mr. Frothingham's, where we heard him deliver a Sermon upon the Communion, it being the regular day for that service. After which I took a long walk.

Finished Weddell's Voyage. It is the Account of a Man not much versed in Science who made a daring Voyage in pursuit of Commercial Speculation. He gives An Account of the South Seas somewhat varying from that of his predecessor Cook. And he says he penetrated to 74 degrees South with a clear Sea. I see no reason to disbelieve him. If so however, the question of land might easily be settled.

Attended Service in the Afternoon alone and heard a Sermon upon the invisible nature of God as a reason for scepticism. It appeared well handled as far as I listened, but I felt tired with my Walk. Commenced reading Hearne's Journey to the Mouth of the Copper Mine River and accomplished a large portion of it.[1] Evening, Parry, and the Spectator upon Wit.

[1] Probably CFA is referring to Samuel Hearne, *A Journey from Prince of Wales's Fort in Hudson's Bay to the Northern Ocean, Undertaken . . . for the Discovery of Copper Mines, a North West Passage . . . 1769–1772*, London, 1795.

MONDAY. 4TH.

Morning cloudy with a chilly East Wind and occasional Showers. I pursued the study of Æschines for an hour, and found that I had read it pretty thoroughly before. This is some satisfaction in studies of this kind as it shows that the time has not been wasted.

Went to the Office where I was occupied during the day in my Accounts and with two or three persons who came to me as usual about Houses. I went also to vote for State Officers and gave the regular ticket.[1] No excitement about this election. Read an Account of France during the period of Louis the 14th. of no interest. The time that I pass at the Office is on the whole that attended with the least satisfaction to me. My Agency Affairs annoy me, and the waste of time discourages me. Took a short walk and returned home.

Afternoon, continued the Oration for Flaccus but found I had read it so badly that I began it over again. It is a desultory examination of Witnesses conducted ably enough. But it has less interest to me than any I have yet read. Evening, continued reading Parry to my Wife, whose Account of the Esquimaux while it is interesting is melancholy. But it is well to see human nature in all its stages. After this, continued Hearne and the Spectator. The numbers on Wit are worth deeper attention.

[1] The offices of governor and lieutenant governor were to be filled and members of the state senate elected (*Boston Patriot*, 2 April, p. 2, col. 2).

TUESDAY. 5TH.

Morning dark and cloudy with very heavy rain which continued until noon when it cleared up. I continued my review of Æschines for one hour after which I went down to the Office. Little or nothing material took place, and I pursued my studies with considerable alacrity. Read this morning a portion of An Analysis of Montesquieu's great Work upon the Spirit of the Laws.[1] I have read this pretty thoroughly in extenso, but have no objection to refresh my memory with a short review of the same. Mr. Champney my former Client called and I discussed with him the propriety of his paying me my Fees, he left me as People usually do making fair promises.

Returned home and in the Afternoon sat down to the Oration for Flaccus which I finished and began that for Sylla. The first of these is in some parts dry, in others very imperfect and therefore difficult to trace the meaning, but on the whole it is worth attention as a defence against a mass of witnesses testifying very strongly to a given point.

Evening, Parry, after which I read Hearne and my usual Numbers in the Spectator.

[1] In *Bibliothèque de l'homme public*, vol. 5, with CFA's marginalia.

WEDNESDAY. 6TH.

Morning clear but cool. I passed an hour as usual in reading Æschines. As I have already said so much about these, perhaps it will be as well in future to omit any particular mention of it. I then walked down to the South part of the City and obtained the Dividends due upon the various Stocks belonging to my Father &ca. This I continued in State Street and gleaned all that was receivable. It is a little remarkable that for the first time my expectations are pretty thoroughly fulfilled. I have no reason to complain of my own Investments. I was busy nearly all the rest of the morning drawing up my Accounts and so had very little leisure to do any thing else.

Miss Abby S. Adams sent for me about her Accounts and I went home where I paid her, the usual Interest and rather more than a third of her Principal.[1] Then a short walk. Afternoon passed in continuing the Oration for P. Sylla. Each of his Orations after the Conspiracy, is full of his wonderful works, and was no doubt in some degree the cause of his subsequent difficulties as it disgusted many with his egotism. Yet he introduces the subject very naturally, especially in this Oration.

In the Evening I finished Parry's second Voyage, and Hearne's Journey. They make both of them links and important ones in the chain of testimony respecting the Northern Ocean. Two numbers as usual of the Spectator.

[1] Abigail S. Adams' receipt for $1,125 dated this day is in the Adams Papers.

THURSDAY. 7TH.

This was the day assigned according to custom, to the observance of a day of fasting.[1] A practice which has gone out of vogue with the occasions that called it forth. Perhaps in producing humility it may produce benefit, but the doctrine that the mere act of self mortification is meritorious in the sight of God, is somewhat exploded. Surely he is not disposed to look harshly upon the moderate use of human enjoyments.

I attended Divine Service in the Morning and heard Mr. Frothingham deliver a Sermon upon the comparative merits of the past and the present. It was written with unusual clearness even for him, and though I believed the doctrine to be totally erroneous, yet I was rather more interested by the errors than usual.

After service, I took an agreeable stroll. The weather was warm and the grass was green, this being the day usually devoted by the boys to their games, the Common was filled with them and presented a gay and beautiful scene.

Afternoon, read Cicero and reviewed the Oration for Sylla. One thing is remarkable in all his works, that a second reading is better than the first. My Wife was not well and our reading progressed very little in the evening. I read the Spectator, and finished the Appendix of Parry.

[1] *Boston Daily Advertiser*, 3 March, p. 1, col. 1; 7 April, p. 2, col. 2. See also vol. 3:209.

FRIDAY. 8TH.

Morning cloudy, with a cold Northerly Wind. I read Æschines for an hour and then went to the Office. My father having drawn upon me for a sum of Money according to his statement, I was obliged to go and make the necessary arrangements.[1] This with my Accounts and superintending the repairs making to Mr. Welsh's Office took up a great deal of my time. Mr. G. Veazie, the Carpenter came from Quincy and presented his Accounts for repairs made upon the House, which after consideration and discussion I paid.[2] These repairs have been made in the most expensive way owing to my Father's trusting it entirely to the Workmen and they are satisfying me every day that he would have done better to have built a house there at once.

Returned home with the intention of going to Quincy this afternoon but it began to rain and gradually increased until in the Night it became a tremendous Storm. I read the remainder of the Oration for Sylla and that for Archias. This has been too celebrated to need much remark. It is a beautiful little Ornament, sparkling like a Diamond, and with as little substance to recommend it. Perhaps this is severe. Evening, I read the Correspondence which Mr. Sparks drew up. After which the Spectator.

[1] In his reply to CFA's remonstrance of 26 March, JQA, in a letter to CFA written on 2 April (Adams Papers), persisted in his instruction to CFA to have the remaining $2,000 of Abigail S. Adams' legacy deposited in JQA's account at the U.S. Branch Bank and to have the cashier honor his draft for that amount. JQA expressed his intent, however, to confer with CFA and Abigail S. Adams upon his arrival in Quincy about a permanent investment of the funds. JQA acquiesced to CFA's proposal for the utilization of the uninvested funds of Thomas B. Adams Jr.

[2] The payment to George Veazie amounted to $348 (M/CFA/3). A large part of this would seem to have been for

repairs to the Old House contracted for by JQA, but a part may have been for the new stone gateposts. See above, vol. 3, entry for 29 Dec. 1830; also JQA, Diary, 25 Oct. 1830; 28 June 1831.

SATURDAY. 9TH.

Morning clear though with a very violent Wind remaining as witness of the Storm. I read Æschines and went to the Office, where I was occupied some time in my accounts after which I read several Articles in the North American Review, for this month. But it was quite surprising how little I thought of them. Somehow or other this publication has not any tone. Mr. Everett began well, but he suddenly became a Politician and that tied up his Fingers.

I had intended to have gone to Quincy but as the Wind was so high and Deacon Spear informed me it was very bad riding I did not think proper to go. Little or nothing else material took place.

Afternoon at home reading the two Orations addressed to the Senate and People upon his return from exile. They are full of compliments and amount to very little. Began that in defence of his House the land of which had been consecrated[1] by Clodius, which is a much more important production.

Evening at home. Began reading Parry's *third* Voyage to the North West which is comparatively uninteresting.[2] After it, I began Franklin's land Journey to the Polar Sea in 1819–20 and was much interested in the account of it.[3] After which the Spectator.

[1] Word thus in MS; it does not convey fully the situation which was the occasion of the oration: the confiscation of Cicero's house by Clodius under the excuse that the land on which it stood would be used as the site of a temple, and thus consecrated.

[2] *Journal of a Third Voyage for the Discovery of a North-West Passage . . . 1824, 1825*, London [also Phila.], 1826.

[3] Sir John Franklin, *Narrative of a Journey to the Shores of the Polar Sea . . . 1819–1822*, London, 1823.

SUNDAY. 10TH.

Morning clear but cold and still windy though not so much as yesterday. I continued reading the Account of Franklin's Journey which is much more agreeable than Mr. Hearne's book. He proceeded much in the same track, but having more authority and stronger influence to aid him, he was not subjected to similar inconveniencies.

Attended divine Service and heard Dr. Lowell preach in the morning upon the prevailing rage for public Prayer and zealous Religion. He condemns it, perhaps justly but I have had my doubts whether for the less instructed classes it is not beneficial. I do not approve of it myself from any belief in extraordinary influences claimed for it, but

I do not disapprove of it while it may be supposed to keep men out of mischief. Afternoon, Mr. Newell of Cambridge, a Common place Sermon upon the abuse of Riches, and their general ill effect.

Returned home, and wrote a letter to my Father, with one to T. B. Adams Jr. inclosing an Account of his Affairs for the last six Months.[1] I was obliged to consume a part of the Evening before I could complete the copying and therefore did not read Parry. Continued Franklin and was unwilling to leave off, to read my usual Numbers of the Spectator.

[1] LbC's of both are in Adams Papers.

MONDAY. 11TH.

Morning cloudy with a warm South Wind. I read Æschines, making quite good progress, and went to the Office. My time was much wasted, by attention to the repair of Mr. Welsh's Office, by attending at the Probate Office to pass my Account which was postponed on account of the re-opening of the Commissions. All these things are perhaps necessary occupations but they involve a monstrous consumption in proportion. I had intended going to Quincy but the rain began about noon and continued all the rest of the day. Mr. Farrar came from Quincy and left me an Account to collect.[1] A trifle of law business.

Afternoon spent in reading the Oration pro domo sua, in which I progressed but my way of reading was superficial with a translation. The Spring brings with it to me a strong disinclination to hard study. And perhaps immediately after dinner is the most indifferent time for it. I always feel disposed to write in the Spring, and am now in some degree meditating what I can do in that way.

Evening, reading Captain Parry and the unfortunate result of the third voyage. It seems almost a pity for he had some prospect of discovery if not of finally attaining his purpose. Finished the first Volume of Franklin and read two Numbers of the Spectator.

[1] Probably Isaac Farrar, who rented land from JQA in Quincy; see entry for 5 July, below.

TUESDAY. 12TH.

We were exceedingly surprised this morning upon awaking to find the ground covered with snow, and a pretty thick drifting storm. After having had so much mild and agreeable weather, this was a very disagreeable return of Winter. The sky cleared however at Noon and the melting process began quickly.

I went to the Office. Not interrupted materially so that in the course of the morning, I accomplished all the principal Articles in the North American Review, which appears to me but a poor number. None of the vigour of good writing. Not much else accomplished. As the snow was still partially to be seen, I concluded it would not be worthwhile to go to Quincy today as I should be unable to accomplish any thing for which I should go.

Remained in my study and pursued the study of the Oratio pro domo sua, which I concluded, but as I propose to review it with more care I shall postpone remark upon it. Pursued Parry in the evening and finished the Account of the third Voyage. He certainly has earned the reputation of a bold and indefatigable Navigator. Read afterward, a part of Captn. Ross's Voyage in 1819[1] and the usual Numbers, finishing the first Volume of the Spectator.

[1] Sir John Ross, *A Voyage of Discovery . . . for the Purpose of Exploring Baffin's Bay, and Enquiring into the Possibility of a North-West Passage*, London, 1819.

WEDNESDAY. 13TH.

Morning fine at last, though uncommonly cool for the season. After an hour's progress in Æschines, I went to the Office and having no particular occupation to distract me, I did pretty well in my study of Montesquieu. I find many more questionable propositions than I thought. But the fund of actual thought contained in this Author is prodigious. He is one of the few writers who does understand the relative value of thoughts and words, therefore he uses none of the latter which do not correspond to something he has of the former.

I went home early today as this was an opportunity, the first good one I have had for some time, of going to Quincy. After an early dinner, I started with my Man, Benjamin, and we were very busy all day in working upon different parts of the Garden. I first cleared away the rose bushes in front of the House and then commenced the very necessary work of transplanting some of the English Oaks and the Elms which had been suffered to grow in the Nursery ever since I set them there. My only difficulty was to find place to put them, our limits being rather scanty. I again tried the drying ground being the third effort. We accomplished a good deal though not all I wished. We were busy until dark, when I got in my Gig and drove to the Judge's to accomplish my business there. Sorry to find Miss Abby quite ill and discouraged. But I could not stay to console her, so drove home to Boston, which I barely reached by nine o'clock. Fatigued, so that I accomplished little in Ross, and began the second Volume of the Spectator.

THURSDAY. 14TH.

The morning was fine and the air mild, so that we seemed about to be paid for the tempestuous weather of the preceding week. I pursued Æschines as usual and then went to the Office where I was busy in reading Montesquieu Analysed. My attention was however not so fixed as I wished. This Author requires constant reflection. I resumed my Elements of Knowledge also.[1] Went to the Athenæum and from thence to Mr. Frothingham's where I dined in company with Mr. Baury, a Clergyman of Mr. F's acquaintance in Europe,[2] where they were together.

Returned home and though feeling drowsy and stupid from the influence of the Spring, I accomplished some sections. Evening, began reading Parry's Attempt to reach the North Pole, being the last of the series.[3] It was a singular idea and deserved by its boldness to be successful. Finished Captain Ross's Voyage, the results of which were unimportant and the authority has been destroyed. Spectator as usual.

[1] That is, "Sayings of the Wise Men"; see vol. 3, entry for 25 Dec. 1830, and above, entry for 24 March.
[2] Perhaps A. L. Baury, Episcopal min- ister of Newton (*Mass. Register*, 1831).
[3] *Narrative of an Attempt to Reach the North Pole in Boats ... in 1827*, London, 1828.

FRIDAY 15TH.

Morning cloudy with light rain, but it afterwards cleared away and became sultry. After an hour at home I went to the Office where I was busy as usual. Some time taken up in superintending some little repairs wanted to the different rooms in this building. This Property has been suffered to depreciate constantly while the rage for making handsome Offices has counteracted the necessity which could only keep them in demand. I am doing perhaps too much, though I am not sensible of being very extravagant. Little attentions given in time will do more and be less expensive in the end, besides giving an air of neatness which makes the place attractive. I feel as if I wish I had not nothing[1] to do with this business however for it involves a responsibility I do not at all admire.

Read and finished the Analysis of Montesquieu, and also the Laws of Plato.[2] This is a more sensible work than the Republic, although it still betrays the visionary and the Poet, rather than the practical clear minded Philosopher. After calling at the Athenæum, I went home.

Read some sections of the Oration pro domo sua, and was very much provoked at my laziness in not going faster. John Gorham took tea here.

Attended in the evening, a Meeting of the Republican Institution. Of this I am not a Member, but was invited to attend as representing my brother's Estate which owns one Share.[3] The question was upon a return of the Money. This was settled in the affirmative and a Collation for the Members provided to finish the Evening. I remained for a short time. The People were all unknown to me and I had a stupid time. Returned home and read a Review of Ross's Voyage in an old Quarterly[4] after which the Spectator.

[1] Thus in MS.
[2] In *Bibliothèque de l'homme public,* vol. 5, with CFA's annotations.
[3] On the Republican Institution of Boston and GWA's investment in it, see vol. 2:411–412; vol. 3:159.
[4] *Quarterly Review,* 21:213–262 (Jan. 1819).

SATURDAY. 16TH.

The day was dark and rainy. I read Æschines as usual and went to the office where my time was passed with little interruption in reading and my usual occupations. Completed a Dissertation by Condorcet upon the question whether Errors are at any time useful in government.[1] It is not very valuable, as the tendency of it is to weaken the belief in *true* Institutions the practical benefit of which no reasonable man can doubt. My own notion is that Religion is necessary to the human mind, and, even if I suppose it an error which *I* never could, that the error is practically productive of much of the whole amount of human happiness. This is an argument about which I should never reason, nor think of weighing the logical sentences of Condorcet or even much better writers. In truth if there is any thing which leads me more particularly to doubt the great benefits of the spirit of Revolution which is overrunning the Continent of Europe, it is the connection which seems evident between it and Scepticism. This leads to the unsettlement of all Society and brings us to a State of utter confusion.

Walked down to the Athenæum where I looked over the European Papers. Full of moment. Afternoon, continued the Oration pro domo sua. It displays a good deal of vanity, let him say what he will, yet these little things are not to be weighed in the great scale of merit.

Evening, Mr. N. Hall, a Cousin of my Wife took Tea and passed the Evening. After which, I began reading Mackenzie's Track to the Arctic Ocean,[2] and my usual numbers of the Spectator.

[1] "Dissertation philosophique et politique" in *Bibliothèque de l'homme public*, vol. 6.

[2] Sir Alexander Mackenzie, *Voyages from Montreal, on the River St. Laurence, through the Continent of North America, to the Frozen and Pacific Oceans, ... 1789 and 1793. With a preliminary account of the ... fur trade of that country*, London, 1801.

SUNDAY. 17TH.

Nothing but rain, which today afforded us only the variety of heavy and light drops. I passed the morning in reading some Articles in the Quarterly Review upon the nature of the North West passage. They were written previous to the Northern discoveries lately made by Parry, and show on the whole much correctness, although clearly and rather arrogantly wrong in some particulars—The whole doctrine of the Polar basin being very probably incorrect in all its parts. The subject however has not lost its interest.[1]

I attended Divine Service all day and heard Mr. Frothingham upon the subject of fear as making a part of Religion. He was not interesting. Afternoon, Mackenzie whose first Voyage I finished. It is an important link in the Chain of evidence relating to the Artic Sea, and seems to deserve more attention than it at first obtained. Men are *incredulous* animals sometimes. The fact is there is no fixing a true limit for believing and disbelieving.

Mr. N. Hall dined here. He is studying Theology after having been Secretary of an Insurance Office. Could not resist his feelings. Poor fellow, I pity him. He forgets the fact that Wealth gives Power, learning only indigence and contempt.

Read Parry and finished this last Work. Every thing that Man could do he did, and his labours had little success only because he tried things next to impossible. The Spectator.

[1] During the period of greatest interest and before the account of Parry's fourth voyage appeared, the Northwest Passage was the subject of repeated treatment in the *Quarterly Review*: 18:431–458 (Jan. 1818); 25:175–216 (April 1821); 30:231–272 (Oct. 1823); 34:378–399 (Sept. 1826); 38:335–358 (Oct. 1828).

MONDAY. 18TH.

Morning clear and pleasant weather. After an hour devoted to Æschines, I went to the Office. My quiet pursuits interrupted somewhat this morning by business, for Mr. Conant, the Tenant of the Weston Farm came in and proceeded to settlement for the Wood sold last November as also for the Rent of said Farm for the past Year. This was very far from unwelcome as I had paid out so much for my father as not to leave sufficient to pay me my regular compensation, due the first of the Month. The counting, assorting, changing, and depositing the Money, with the Receipts and charges took up so much time that I had no opportunity to resume my reading. Walked to the Athenæum and obtained a book. I find this place more attractive and my Office less so every day. But I must not neglect what I receive a consideration for.

Afternoon finished the Oration pro domo sua. Cicero thought this one of his best. It certainly has great power but it does not please me so much as many others. I like the earlier Orations best. There is not so much egotism which will be disgusting let apologists say what they may. The invective is powerful however, and Clodius if he had any feeling must have quivered under it.

Evening, began Dr. Walsh's Journey from Constantinople[1] aloud to my Wife. After which Mackenzie's Journey to the Pacific, and the Spectator.

[1] Robert Walsh, *Narrative of a Journey from Constantinople to England*, London [and Phila.], 1828.

TUESDAY. 19TH.

The morning was foggy with occasional rain but the weather cleared away in the course of the day. After reading Æschines I went to the Office and was busy there with my Accounts after which I began reading an Analysis of a Work called La Politique naturelle[1] which seemed to contain much that was good. I could not give it my undivided attention from the nature of my morning work and interruptions which have the effect of preventing any continued action of the mind upon one subject. I lose though not without perpetual regret much of my most valuable time.

Afternoon. I completed a large part of the Oration de Haruspicum Responsis. It seems to have been a burst of Anger against Clodius in the usual manner of this Orator, attacking him at all points. As specimens of Invective these are wonderful but it is to be doubted whether on the whole this species of Oratory helps a man. It was the source of most of Cicero's sufferings and it will always make abundance of enemies so watchful that your fortune must be surprising to escape their shafts at every point. I think this remark applicable to my father who has drawn much of his manner from these sources.

Evening, we continued Dr. Walsh but Edmund Quincy came and spent two hours. After which I continued Mackenzie and read the Spectator. My Wife received a letter from my Mother,[2] containing nothing new.

31

[1] By Paul Henri Thiry, Baron d'Holbach, in *Bibliothèque de l'homme public*, vol. 6.
[2] 15 April (Adams Papers).

WEDNESDAY. 20TH.

Morning at the Office after the usual portion of time passed in reading Æschines. Engaged in reading La Politique Naturelle, which turns out to be a high toned paper of the Revolutionary period of France, written before it and probably contributing in some degree to the catastrophe. There is much in it of valuable [1] and then again there is a little that looks more like the ranting of Demagogues than sober sense. I was interrupted by superintending the repairs of Mr. Welsh's which have nearly reached a close. The cost will probably be greater than it ought but the room is now put into complete repair, and will I hope give me no trouble for some time. I wish I could throw up this business for it is a terrible thing to have a doubt about the propriety of what one does.

Returned home, and in the Afternoon was occupied in finishing and carefully reviewing the Oration upon the Answers of the Haruspices. Every time I do this satisfies me that the Author is not felt comparatively upon the first reading.

Evening. Received letters from my father and John which announce the probability, of my father and Mother's coming on soon.[2] Mr. and Mrs. Frothingham came in and passed an hour pleasantly enough. After which I read Mackenzie and two numbers of the Spectator.

[1] Thus in MS.
[2] The letter from JA2 is missing. It was probably an acknowledgment of a box of salt fish which CFA had sent as a gift. JQA's letter (15 April, Adams Papers) announced his intent to arrive at Quincy before the end of the month.

THURSDAY. 21ST.

Morning clear and pleasant. After my attention to Æschines, I went to the Office and was first saluted by my Tenant Mrs. Proctor who came with excuses and part payment of her rent. I received both though not with a feeling of much comfort. My time was considerably interrupted. Mr. Peabody paid me a visit, having returned from Exeter and about some business which I was glad to see as he may be encouraged to continue his Office. Mr. Hewit called upon me. This was a visit upon that old business of Farmer's. I could hardly have supposed that a man could have so many ways of teazing. He now proposes to publish, and this was one of Dr. Storer's friends who was desirous of suppressing the publication by a bribe. I told him precisely my Opinion upon the folly of any attempt of the kind but at the same time as he seemed so anxious I told him I would do my share.[1] I read but little in consequence of all this.

Dined with my Wife at P. Chardon Brooks'. He gave me some good Hock Wine. Returned home and read the remainder of the Oration de Resp. Harusp. together with a part of that for Plancius. Evening at home. Continued reading Walsh, and after it finished Mackenzie, and read the Spectator as usual.

[1] The effort to restrain Miles Farmer from the publication of his version of the affair involving GWA, Eliza Dolph, and Dr. D. Humphreys Storer was unsuccessful; see below, entries for 3 and 4 August; also vol. 2:403–404.

FRIDAY. 22D.

Morning cloudy but it cleared away with a chilly East Wind of this Season of the Year. After reading Æschines as usual I went to the Office where I occupied myself in my common way. Mr. Peabody came in and we had a pleasant conversation for some time. It is a very agreeable thing to talk with a well informed man of talent. How few in our Society are entitled to the character. I read in review of La Politique Naturelle but from some unaccountable reason or other I do not get along much in it. Yet I like it better than at first. Took a walk and returned home.

After dinner, employed with one interruption in reading the Oration for Plancius which appears to be one of the highest of the efforts of Cicero. I shall reserve what I think upon it until the time when I have finished and reviewed it.

Evening. My Wife wanted me to leave Walsh, and begin reading the second Volume of Moore's Life of Byron which I did. The impression produced by any thing relating to that individual is melancholy. Having finished Mackenzie whose book I have been much interested in, I spent an hour in reading d'Israeli's Second Series of Curiosities of Literature.[1] A book of chips. I think these are rarely useful. After this, the usual numbers of the Spectator.

[1] An edition published at London in 1823 in 3 vols. is at MQA and has CFA's bookplate.

SATURDAY. 23D.

Morning cloudy with a disagreeable cold Easterly Wind and appearance of Rain, but it cleared away leaving nothing but the chill in the Air. Finished my Review of the Oration of Æschines on the Crown and found it pretty much the same in my Opinion, perhaps not quite so good. There is more diffuseness, perhaps tautology in it than I had thought, but this may be owing to my not sufficiently comprehending the force of words, in the original language.

Went to the Office where I was busy in reading but not to much purpose. My power of attention is almost gone, in the morning at least. Had a conversation with Mr. Peabody and took a short walk. Mr. T. Davis also paid me a long and pleasant visit.

In the afternoon, I thought I would go out to Quincy and see how things looked before my father came on. My Servant went with me to set some Fir Trees I had purchased. On the whole, I was pretty well pleased and thought that my few directions had done a good deal to make the place look on the whole better than it had done for years. Remained busy until late, and returned home calling at the Judge's on the way to inquire for Miss Adams whom I found better. A Short Evening at home, and the Spectator.

SUNDAY. 24TH.

Morning cloudy but it cleared away in the course of the day. I attended divine Service during the day and heard Mr. Frothingham preach. In the morning a caustic Sermon upon the Religious excitement prevailing to some extent of late in our Community.[1] It was not in his common tone, but pungent and bitter. Perhaps well calculated. Though for my own part, I care little if the delusion is innocent in regard to others. Afternoon not remarkable.

I was informed today of the important political News from Washington of the resignation of the whole Cabinet.[2] It produced a great deal of excitement and conversation as the effects will probably be felt far and wide. What the result will be it seems vain to attempt to guess. But I confess I felt a little elation in thinking that this was the party that claimed such a triumph over my father. That these were the Men who claimed to know how to administer this government, and to bring it back to its original purity. The cunning man is sometimes caught in his own trap, and may often be a useful lesson to his successors tempted by similar circumstances. After all, honesty is the best policy. Finished the first volume of d'Israeli, I shall not take up the second. Mr. Blake came and passed two hours, talking politics. Evening, the Spectator.

[1] The most recent outbreak of bitterness in the long-standing conflict between the orthodox and conservative wings of Congregationalism related to the adoption of statutes governing the Theological School by the Harvard Board of Overseers.

[2] Washington newspapers of 20 April had carried accounts of the resignations and printed such letters as were avail-

able. The papers apparently arrived in Boston on the 24th; the news became public in Boston on the 25th. The resignations seem to have begun on the 7th with the letter of John H. Eaton, secretary of war. Van Buren's resignation as secretary of state followed on the 11th. Samuel D. Ingham, secretary of the treasury, and John Branch, secretary of the navy, submitted their resignations at the request of the President on the 19th. JQA, Diary, 20, 25 April; *Boston Daily Advertiser*, 25 April, p. 2, cols. 1–2. On the issues underlying the resignations, see below, entries for 2, 11, 14 May, and 27 June, notes.

MONDAY. 25TH.

Morning cloudy but it cleared away. This is the case now every day. A cold East Wind rises and prevails during the course of the Sun over us. After beginning Demosthenes upon the Crown I went to the Office but the News from Washington prevented my sitting down to any thing. I had quite a conversation about it with Mr. Peabody and the rest of my time excepting what was necessarily spent in my regular avocations, was wasted. This is too bad, for all the Administrations that ever were made can have no interest to me compared to my time. Took a walk and returned home.

After dinner, continued and finished the Oration for Plancius but determined to give it a faithful Review. It strikes me as one of his best. His observations upon Popular humor are excellent and for every age. These are the only ones worth writing. What is the fame based upon trifles of the day? It is not worth the labour it requires to obtain it.

Evening at home with my Wife, read to her a part of Moore's Life of Byron. Interesting but very immoral. I was struck with Moore's own immoral tone. Afterwards, I began Captain Franklin's Second Journey to the Polar Sea.[1] And the Spectator as usual.

[1] Sir John Franklin, *Narrative of a Second Expedition to the Shores of the Polar Sea ... 1825–1827. ... Including an Account of the Progress of a Detachment to the Eastward, by J. Richardson* [and with an appendix by Richardson], London [also Phila.], 1828.

TUESDAY. 26TH.

Morning fine with a clear cold air from the Eastward. This weather for such a succession of days has put the Country and the season back to its common place. I read a portion of the Oration for Ctesiphon with more ease than I had anticipated. Then to the Office where much time was wasted as usual in talking, and I accomplished only a little of my review of La Politique Naturelle. Nothing else material took place. Took a short walk and returned home to dine.

After dinner, as my Study was in a state of confusion from cleaning which it very much needed, I went to the Athenæum, and sat down to a very deliberate examination of Mr. Gallatin's Article upon the subject of the Bank.[1] It is a very elaborate performance and so long that nearly three hours of reading did not complete it. I was therefore obliged to reserve the balance for another opportunity.

Returned home calling by the way at the Post Office, where I received a letter from my Father dated Baltimore, and informing me of his progress.[2] He says he shall reach Quincy tomorrow but I doubt it. Evening. Read to my Wife a part of Moore's Byron, and afterwards continued Captn. Franklin—and the Spectator.

[1] "Banks and Currency," *American Quarterly Review*, 8:441–528 (Dec. 1830).

[2] 22 April (Adams Papers). LCA, accompanied by her granddaughter Mary Louisa, Mrs. Nowlan, and Mrs. Pitts, and driven by John Kirk, had departed from Washington on the 20th. JQA had followed by stage on the 21st. The journey to Philadelphia was to be resumed on the 23d. Their plan was to reach New York on the 25th.

WEDNESDAY. 27TH.

Morning fine with the usually cold Wind from the North and East. As my room was in a State of such confusion, I was obliged instead of continuing my pursuit of my study of Demosthenes, to read Franklins Journal downstairs. This is a very interesting work, and contains much information upon the point of the Sea existing North of the Continent of America.

At the Office, conversation with Mr. Peabody as usual in which we discussed the letter of Mr. Ingham and its bearing upon the present State of Affairs.[1] This is a most unaccountable business. We shall see what comes. I finished La Politique Naturelle. A piece that contains a good deal of truth put up in a frothy, declamatory way. The matter of Government is not Child's play, although the experience of the last fifty years would lead us to suppose that some people thought so.

Returned home and in the afternoon, went to the Athenæum where I finished Mr. Gallatin's Article and one in the next Number of the same Review.[2] Both good, but a man could hardly write otherwise than well, knowing the facts on that subject.

Took tea at Mrs. Frothingham's, and went to receive the payment of my brother's share at the Republican Institution which was however postponed. Returned home and read Franklin, with the Spectator.

[1] Secretary Ingham's letter to the President, along with attendant facts and speculation, appeared in the *Columbian Centinel*, 27 April, p. 1–2.

[2] "Bank of the United States," *American Quarterly Review*, 9:246–282 (March 1831). The two articles were afterwards expanded and published as *Considerations on the Currency and Banking System of the United States*, Phila., 1831; in this form it appears in Gallatin, *Writings*, 3:231–364.

THURSDAY. 28TH.

Very heavy rain this morning with a high Easterly Wind which continued throughout the day. I continued Franklin being unable to prosecute my regular studies on account of my disordered room. Then to the Office where much time was wasted in a long conversation with Mr. Peabody, and a little in writing a political Article upon the late Affair at Washington. But what is the use of this. I will say in excuse for myself that I forgot to bring down my book of regular reading and was thus without employ.

Home, after dinner my study having become fit to enter upon again, I continued the Oration for Plancius which I do extremely admire. The tone is so admirable and the principles it displays are highly valuable. The Story of his return from his Quæstorship is good, and fairly told. Many a man has felt equal mortification and said nothing about it. I did not quite finish it.

Evening, reading Moore's Life of Byron. Walsh calls it "the Life of a Profligate written by an Accomplice." Interrupted by Edmund Quincy who staid so late, that I had only a few Minutes, in which however, I finished Franklin's Journal and my usual numbers of the Spectator.

FRIDAY. 29TH.

The heavy rain continues though with little Wind. I am anxious for my father's family who must be somewhere upon the Road. Resumed the reading of Demosthenes and made rapid progress in it. The Text is easier than that of Æschines which I mastered more slowly but more thoroughly. At the Office where after my usual occupations, I continued my Article which I am trying to make able. Col. J. B. Davis called upon me and I agreed to send it to him. Attended a Meeting of the Bar of Suffolk for the first time.[1] It was upon the application of a person for admission and of another for dismission.

Returned home and in the Afternoon, read the remainder of the Oration for Plancius. On the whole, this pleases me particularly. The tone of it is a relief from the general invective, the management of the feelings both of opponent, Judges and Client is wonderful, and the beauty of the principles laid down as well as the language, in his defence of himself, all these make this Oration in my opinion among his very best. I began the Oration for Sextius.

The day was dark and cheerless, and my Wife's spirits seemed to flag. Continued reading to her from Moore's Life of Byron after which

I read some of Dr. Richardson's Appendix to Franklin's Journal,[2] and the Spectator.

[1] Full membership in the Bar apparently followed upon admission as attorney at the Supreme Judicial Court; see vol. 3:422; and above, entry for 2 March.

[2] See above, entry for 25 April, note.

SATURDAY. 30TH.

The Weather would not clear away although it made repeated efforts so to do. The consequence was a mist and drizzle altogether comfortless. My Wife was so unwell that I concluded to send for Dr. Stevenson. Nothing alarming however. After reading Demosthenes as usual I went to the Office, and with the usual avocations was entirely occupied in finishing my Article upon the troubles of the Cabinet. I think I write well, but my constant tendency is to be dissatisfied. This business appears to be an opening but on the whole it may be deceptive. In these days of diffused instruction, it is difficult to obtain reputation on mere writing.

After dinner, as the weather was too bad to allow Abby to go with me, I rode out alone to Quincy. Found my Father only, the rest of the family not having yet reached the place. They came however late in the Afternoon.[1] My Mother looks better than he does. I hope she will remain so. I had a great deal of conversation with them and regretted the necessity which made me return to town, but I was obliged to go.

The ride was dark and I did not get home until nearly Nine. Found Mr. and Mrs. Frothingham at my House, and my Wife already better. So tired that I could do little or nothing.

[1] The family and attendants had left New York on the 27th for Providence by the steamboat *President*, Capt. Bunker. A stormy passage delayed their arrival at Providence until the 29th. All except JQA remained there overnight. He continued as far as Dedham, reaching Quincy on the morning of the 30th (JQA, Diary).

SUNDAY. MAY 1ST.

Our morning was clear but as if we were not to see too much of the Sun, it clouded up shortly afterwards, and remained so the rest of the day. I went to the Meeting and heard Mr. Frothingham all day, but his Sermons did not interest me. My Wife was better, but did not go out. Little took place of consequence. I finished Walsh's Journey from Constantinople. A good deal of this is valuable information and not very common as the parts of Country to which it relates are little known. But the Dr. is credulous and tells tough [1] stories sometimes.

Experience has taught me however that the toughest are sometimes fact.

Afternoon, having no book, I took up a volume of scattered thoughts of Montesquieu many of which are exceedingly good. His was a highly cultivated and deeply reflecting mind and his temperament that which gave more profoundness than Hume's with equal coolness. I think these however are better than any thing even of his. The familiar letters however have very little interest to me. They are few in number, and very little varied.[2] Read Moore to my Wife and some of the Bible after which the Spectator.

[1] Hard to believe or understand (*OED, tough,* adj., 6b).

[2] In the edition at MQA of the *Œuvres* of Montesquieu, 10 vols. in 6, Paris, 1815–1816, the "Pensées diverses" and the "Lettres familières" are in vol. 10. The set has JQA's bookplate; GWA's signature is in the last volume; a quotation from Voltaire on Montesquieu in CFA's hand is in the first.

MONDAY. 2D.

Morning cloudy but warmer than it has been. After making some progress in reading Demosthenes which is uncommonly easy, I went to the Office and spent the morning in making up my Accounts for the Month and in balancing my Books. My time was so much occupied in this business that I did not know very well how I could pursue my Articles the first of which signed Cimon appeared in the Paper this Morning.[1] Having in some degree engaged to furnish more I am somewhat puzzled about time. Conversation with Mr. Peabody. My Tenant Mr. Tenney called here and paid his rent regularly. I afterwards went to obtain the payment from the Republican Institution and was stopped by the requiring a Certificate of Administration.

Returned to my Office, but learning from Mr. I. P. Davis that one of the English Reviews had a notice of my Article in the N.A. I went to the Athenæum to read it and for the purpose of getting some books. The Notice is not disagreeable.[2]

Afternoon, reading, Cicero's Oration for Sextius which I did not complete. These latter Orations shine out in some parts. Evening at home, read Moore's Life of Byron's and after it, Grimm's Literary Correspondence of which I have heard much.[3] Closed with the Spectator.

[1] Under the heading "The Resignation of the Cabinet," CFA's article in the *Boston Patriot,* signed "Cimon," was placed in a featured position in the issue (2 May, p. 2, col. 1). By a minute analysis of the published correspondence and statements issued by the Administration, he undertook to demonstrate that what has been made available is "untenable as an explanation of the events . . . , but that it is evidently made up for the purpose of concealing from the

public the actual truth," which is that it is a "fraud upon the Nation." In consequence, he asked, "Has the ship an incompetent Commander? a faithless Pilot? or dishonest Officers?"

[2] In *The Athenæum, Journal of . . . Literature, Science and the Fine Arts,* for 12 March 1831 (p. 174), the brief report on the January issue of the *North American Review* notes, among the contributions selected for mention, "an interesting article on Graham's *History of the United States.*"

[3] F. M. de Grimm [and D. Diderot], *Correspondance littéraire, philosophique et critique, 1753–1790.* At this time CFA was using a copy borrowed from the Athenæum (see below, entry for 10 May). However, there is an edition (16 vols., Paris, 1829–1831), with CFA's bookplate, at MQA.

TUESDAY. 3D.

The Morning was lovely and seemed to pay us for all the troublesome weather we had experienced. After reading a due portion of Demosthenes which I find easy, I went to the Office for a couple of hours. The time flew with the utmost rapidity so that I had hardly accomplished any thing by the time that it was necessary for me to go home for the purpose of starting for Quincy. Abby went with me and we had a delightful ride. We had the first true Spring day for enjoying the Country.

Found both my father and Mother pretty well though I think the latter[1] in rather low Spirits considering the little one would think could trouble him. I talked with him and after dinner we walked out in the Garden and from thence to the Mount Wollaston Farm to look at the Orchard planted there.[2] Found it in pretty good condition considering every thing.

Returned to Tea, and found Mr. Degrand there making his usual first visit. Returned to town so as to reach it by Evening. My Wife pretty well tired by her first excursion. Found Horatio Brooks just arrived from New York. Read Grimm and the Spectator as usual.

[1] Thus in MS; "former" is clearly meant.

[2] JQA's journal entries for the period following his arrival at Quincy are almost wholly devoted to activities in his garden, orchards, &c., confirming his comment, "I return to my plantations with intense interest, and can take scarce any pleasure in any thing else." Contributing to his absorption in outdoor pursuits, and undoubtedly to his low spirits, was the condition of his eyes which had prevented all reading for some days. Whether influenced or not by the melancholy state of things at Quincy, CFA and ABA during the course of the day revised their earlier decision to remain in Boston throughout the final months of ABA's pregnancy and "promised to come and spend part of the Summer with us." (JQA, Diary, 3 May).

WEDNESDAY. 4TH.

Morning at the Office after paying my usual due to the Oration on the Crown. I admire that of Demosthenes more on reading it over while the other lost a little of its relish. Perhaps this is as good a test of value as any. My time was very much taken up by a great variety of little occupations being out upon Commissions for the good people at Quincy. I was at my Office engaged in writing my Journal and then went down and received at last the payment on the Shares of the Republican Institution. I went to see Mr. Bowditch as to the investment of Abby Adams' money but did not succeed. Returned and was busy until dinner.

In the afternoon, Attended a Meeting of the Directors of the Middlesex Canal for the purpose of considering the expediency of selling the Maine lands. After considerable discussion, it was decided to sell them to the persons making their offer. This and other business took up the whole afternoon, so that I returned home and spent my time in reading the Preface to Voltaire's Catiline,[1] where he gives a character of Cicero, and the Discourse upon style by Buffon, both of these having been suggested by Grimm's Correspondence.

Evening, according to invitation, Abby and I went to Mrs. Cruft's. A party to the young lady selected by Mr. T. Smith her brother.[2] It was small and consisted of the old *Set*.[3] I talked with Mr. Tarbell. Returned home at ten. Read a little of Grimm and the Spectator.

[1] *Rome sauvée, ou Catilina* is in vol. 4 of the Deux-Ponts, 1791–1792, edition of Voltaire at MQA.

[2] The marriage of Thomas Carter Smith and Frances Barnard, daughter of Capt. Moses Barnard, took place five months later (*Columbian Centinel*, 8 Oct., p. 2, col. 7).

[3] See vol. 3, entry for 9 July 1830.

THURSDAY. 5TH.

Morning clear with a very cold Wind for the Season from the North West. After reading a due portion of Demosthenes, I was busy in performing Commissions for a couple of hours, and thus my time went until I had little left even to begin my next number of Cimon. This was bad as the subject is difficult enough to require all my time. Little material took place and as my Wife had agreed to go to Medford this morning, I took a seat with Mr. Brooks. He talked a good deal about the railroad which is to go through his grounds.[1]

The table was large, Mr. and Mrs. Everett, Miss Phillips, Horatio, Mrs. Frothingham, Abby and myself. Little or nothing material took place. Mr. E[verett], Mr. Brooks and I walked to the track of the Rail Road that is to be as he wished to see its probable course. On our return we found Mrs. Gray and her daughter. I was prodigiously sleepy after my walk and was therefore glad when the time came to return home. We reached Boston in time for Tea, and I read Grimm during a part of the Evening though excessively drowsy. Two Numbers of the Spectator.

[1] That is, the Boston and Lowell, whose proposed route across Peter C. Brooks' lands was north and west of Mystic Grove on the opposite side of Grove Street almost to the six-mile mark, at which point the tracks were to cross Grove Street and then continue closely parallel to the canal from the Partings. See a map of the proposed railroad in *Medford Historical Register*, 31:60 (Sept. 1928); also vol. 3, entries for 29 May, 12 Aug. 1830, and p. xviii there.

FRIDAY. 6TH.

Morning clear and cold. The report from the Country was that there was a severe frost but of course we saw nothing of it. After reading my usual portion of Demosthenes, I went down to perform the rest of my Commissions. Called upon Mr. Bowditch at the Life Insurance Office to converse upon the subject of Abby Adams' Money.[1] I obtained from him the necessary information and then went to the Office. Employed there in writing Cimon No. 2 which I made satisfactory progress in. I hope I shall do something with this. But writing in Newspapers is pretty unsatisfactory work. Mr. Conant, from Weston came in and paid me a small additional sum for the Wood sold there. Nothing else material took place.

Walked home by the way of one of the Tenants who plagues me in Tremont Street. Found my Mother spending the day with Abby and was glad to see her. I sat the afternoon with her, she returning home at six. Evening at home not very profitably employed in Grimm. This book disappoints my expectations. I have nearly wasted a week. Finished with the Spectator.

[1] See below, entry for 12 May, note.

SATURDAY. 7TH.

Morning clear and pleasant. I read a large extract of Demosthenes and am surprised at its facility. This expression is pedantic. Went to the Office and was busy in my usual avocations after which I copied out my Article signed Cimon for the press. It took up nearly all the time I had remaining. On looking back this week, I find very little reason to be contented. Much of my time has been wasted, the remainder not properly improved. Writing for the Newspapers is not a very satisfactory Account to give of one's self. I wonder that I am tempted to do it. What good can it produce to me in any event? If reputation is to be sought, my way should lead to paths far higher than ephemeral politics.

Returned home and spent the afternoon in reading the Oration for

Sextius. I have lost the track being so long since I broke off, and therefore after a most superficial examination of it, I commenced a thorough review. This is the only way of resuming when one has a backward lurching.

Evening, I read Grimm. There is acuteness of criticism in this book though excessive partiality. Diderot and philosophy are his two great hobbies, and as he lived just at the era of the French revolution, much of the slang[1] which was then used is in his mouth. Even now the Age is infected with it. As if we possessed all that is excellent and our fathers nothing. Perhaps the old adage may turn out true, Ignorance is bliss. It certainly was so, as to the rights of Man in France at that period. Spectator as usual.

[1] That is, "cant."

SUNDAY. 8TH.

The day was Cloudy with an East Wind and heavy rain. I attended divine Service at Mr. Frothingham's in the morning, and heard Mr. Stetson of Medford preach a Sermon which struck me like an old acquaintance. It was upon the indulgence of particular sins as affecting an otherwise good character. A habit not infrequent among men, and attempted to be reconciled.[1] His manner is yet so bad that I cannot keep up my attention. I did not attend in the Afternoon.

Finished the first volume of Grimm, which has not on the whole come up to my expectation, though rather amusing than otherwise, particularly, the story of the Curè and of his two Tragedies, Baltasar and another.[2] I passed the afternoon in again reading my father's MS Reply to the Confederates, for the purpose of making the suggestions he wished from me. It is one of his ablest papers, and more conclusive than I could have supposed possible, for the case is in its nature thorny. I wrote a Letter to my father upon it, containing little more than what I suggested to him on the first perusal.[3] The copying of which Letter was my Evening's work. Two numbers of the Spectator.

[1] Sentence thus in MS.
[2] The two tragedies by "l'abbé Petit, curé du Mont-Chauvet," were *David et Bethsabée* and *Balthazard*.

[3] Letter in Adams Papers. For the opinions CFA had earlier expressed and here reiterated, see above, vol. 3, entry for 10 February.

MONDAY. 9TH.

Morning clear with a cool air. After reading a due portion of Demosthenes as usual, I went to the Office and was busy in my usual occupations. In addition to these it was the day for passing the Account upon the Estate of Robert New, and as I hoped, for making a final settlement and distribution. But the Commissioners not yet having made their return I was disappointed in the latter object. I should think that some very material amendments might be made in the system of Probate Law—In diminishing the amount of charges that eat up the Estate and in accelerating the final settlement. Two or three interruptions on various accounts. Met T. B. Adams Jr. who has just arrived from the South. He has altered a little both in appearance and manners, and not for the better in either.[1] I was glad to see him however. He left me to go and see my Wife.

In the afternoon, I continued my Review of the Oration for Sextius. All these which relate to the expulsion from Rome of himself have much the same tang. One by itself is eloquence. When they are read together there is too little variety. And the Vanity is *not* agreeable. Men never like to be reminded of a benefit by the person conferring it. In private life it is called ungenerous, why should it be a merit any where? Read Grimm. Horatio Brooks spent the night. The Spectator.

[1] LCA expressed her reactions more sharply and indicated that the unfavorable view was widely shared: "The Lieutenant is pleasant but a great Fop" (LCA to Mrs. JA2, 22 May); "Tom is an exquisite of the highest order and perfectly horrifies the rustics. He is horrified with every thing here and talks as if he had never known Quincy" (same to same, 12 June; both letters in Adams Papers).

TUESDAY. 10TH.

The day cold with clouds. A Frost is supposed to have taken place, rather injurious to the present state of the Fruit Trees. I made great progress in Demosthenes, and then went to the Office. My time pretty much occupied in making a draught of my third and last Number of Cimon. Some doubts occur to me how I can tell the truth here. Newspapers are squeamish. The story is certainly not very creditable to any one. One or two interruptions. A Mr. Libby called to hire one of the Tenements.[1] These are destined, I believe to give me trouble constantly.

Took a walk to the Athenæum and tried to find the Telegraph of the 16th of April but without success. Returned home and passed the afternoon in continuing the Oration for Sextius, which I nearly finished. It is not so perfectly handed down to us as that for Plancius nor is it to my notion so fine in itself, though the passage upon the *Optimates* in a State is very good.

Evening, read Grimm. He was beginning to be more interesting and just at that moment I am obliged to give him up for a fortnight, the

Athenæum calling for an examination of their Library. He is perfectly absurd about Diderot. Read two Numbers of the Spectator.

[1] Joseph Libby occupied tenement No. 3 at 101 Tremont Street from 17 May to 31 Aug. (M/CFA/3).

WEDNESDAY. 11TH.

Morning clear and mild. After reading a part of Demosthenes as usual, I went to the Office and spent my time in writing out the last Number of Cimon. The idea strikes me to be good but I feel out of spirits about Newspaper writing. The second Number appeared to-day. On reading it over, it seemed to me well written.[1] One or two interruptions. One for the purpose of voting for the lower House which took place today. I went for the regular ticket as far as I could, but I could not swallow Mr. Buckingham.[2] Found at the Probate Office the return of the Commissioners upon Mr. New's Estate, reducing the Dividend to 25 cents on the dollar, and payment not to be made until the ninth of June. Walked down to see Mr. Forbes and contract with him for a horse and gig. Then to the Tenements to see them and make inquiries concerning Mr. Libby.

Afternoon finished the Oration for Sextius and read that against Vatinius. A continual invective in the shape of a series of questions. This method has much power in itself but it tires by its weight very soon. Man requires variety in every thing.

Evening took a short walk with my Wife to Mr. Frothingham's, so that we had little time at home. After my Wife retired, I read with great pleasure, one half of Horace's Art of Poetry,[3] and after it, Two Spectators.

[1] CFA's second letter on "The Resignation of the Cabinet" addressed itself to an inquiry into the true, as distinct from the announced, causes. Primarily, the letter is an historical exposition of the competing forces arrayed one against the other during the second administration of President Monroe, of the ambitions thwarted by the compromise choice of JQA for the Presidency in 1824–1825, and of the uneasy alliances created in 1828 to elect a President whom none respected. "The hidden animosities now erupt." *Boston Patriot*, 11 May, p. 2, col. 4.

[2] Sixty seats in the state House of Representatives were at stake. The National Republicans offered a full slate; also on the ballot were candidates from the Working-Men's Party, and others running on Antimasonic, Jackson, and Independent tickets. In the voting 53 candidates, all National Republicans, received a majority of the votes cast and were elected. Joseph T. Buckingham, publisher of the *Boston Courier*, was among the seven National Republicans who failed to receive a majority. A second election was called for 14 May to complete the representation. *Boston Patriot*, 11 May, p. 2, col. 2; 13 May, p. 2, col. 1; *Columbian Centinel*, 14 May, p. 1, col. 3.

[3] Apparently, CFA was reading Horace's poem in the Abbé Batteux's collection, *Les quatres poëtiques d'Aristote, d'Horace, de Vida, de Despréaux*; see below, entry for 11 August.

THURSDAY. 12TH.

Morning delightfully warm, and announcing the approach of the Summer. After making my usual progress in the Oration on the Crown, I went to the Office and was occupied there in divers matters for some time, until my father very unexpectedly made his appearance, and therefore prevented any further occupation of myself upon my own affairs. He was in good spirits, and came for the purpose of making the final arrangement in regard to Abby S. Adams' affairs previous to her marriage. He gave me a draught to get accepted at Mr. Cazenove's, for the amount, which cost me two walks, but which I finally accomplished and he accommodated me by paying the Money.[1] My father went himself and completed the transaction and thus gave up this charge, much to my satisfaction.[2] This makes more than six thousand dollars he has got rid of in two years and that without much feeling it.[3] If he can do the rest with equal ease to himself, in the course of the three or four succeeding years, it will establish him very independently for the balance of his life.

He dined with me, and in the afternoon I only finished a little of the Oration against Vatinius. The rest was distracted. We went to see Greenough's group of Statuary which is very good.[4] Evening, a walk with my Wife. After which the rest of the art of Poetry and two Spectators.

[1] Charles J. Cazenove & Co., 23 Long Wharf, had taken on consignment a shipment of flour from JA2 and agreed to advance $2,500 against its sale. JA2 to Charles J. Cazenove & Co., 14 April (Adams Papers); *Boston Directory*, 1831–1832.

[2] Abigail S. Adams had accepted the recommendation that $2,000 of the legacy payable to her upon her marriage be invested in the Massachusetts Hospital Life Insurance Co. JQA had agreed to act as her trustee. The arrangement was made final at the office of Nathaniel Bowditch, actuary of the company, and a deed in trust was issued to JQA by the terms of which interest would be paid annually for the use of Abigail A. Angier independent of the control of her husband (JQA, Diary, 12 May).

[3] That is, by the payment of this legacy and that of Thomas B. Adams Jr., for which payments JQA was obligated under the terms of JA's will.

[4] Sculpture by Horatio Greenough was shown from 8 April to 1 June at No. 4 Summer Street. Included in the collection were small copies of his large busts of JA and JQA. Isaac Hull Adams, JQA's current amanuensis, accompanied JQA, ABA, and CFA. *Boston Patriot*, 3 May, p. 3, col. 3; JQA, Diary, 12 May.

FRIDAY. 13TH.

Another very delightful day. I made good progress in Demosthenes, and then went to the Office. My occupations were somewhat interrupted by the applicant for the Tenement in Tremont Street who promises to be somewhat of a bore. Having also engaged with Mr. Peabody to go and see the Marine Railway at the North end of the

Town, we started at eleven for the purpose. A vessel was upon it, being coppered. The machinery appears simple, being a groove, upon which is drawn a Frame to support the Ship. This frame is drawn by means of Machinery worked by a single horse turning as in a Mill. I should think it a very useful thing and likely to prevent a great deal of strain to the ships in the common mode of repairing their bottoms.[1] The weather was warm so that we had a pretty fatiguing walk and I did not finish Cimon though I worked at it.

Afternoon, the Oration for Cælius after finishing that against Vatinius. But study becomes now a little fatiguing. Read a Scene or two of Voltaire's Orphelin de la Chine.[2] Evening, Boswell to my Wife after which finished the Ars Poetica, reviewed. A most admirable little Poem. Two Spectators.

[1] The Marine Railway, built in 1826, was located just to the south of North Battery Wharf. The newly developed apparatus greatly expedited the repairing of hulls. C. H. Snow, *A Geography of* *Boston* . . . , Boston, 1830, p. 31–32.

[2] *L'orphelin de la Chine* is immediately preceded by *Rome sauvée, ou Catilina* in vol. 4 of the Deux-Ponts edition.

SATURDAY. 14TH.

The day tolerably pleasant, though the Wind began to show symptoms of change. I this morning made a finish of the Oration in defence of Ctesiphon. This review has not been without its utility. It has shown me more strongly the power of the Orator, and has developed beauties of thought which before escaped me. The defence is in itself peculiar in its generality. He declines embarrassing himself with the technical details of the accusation of Æschines, and yet impresses you with the idea of its weakness much more fully than if he did so. I think this is the principal alteration I trace in my mind upon this review. The charges of Æschines seem to have less weight in them, they do not bear examination. It is a very unanswerable position assumed by Demosthenes. "You knew of all you now charge me with, many years ago. You have suffered these laws to be violated time after time without remonstrance, (which you now affect to consider so binding). Why did not you speak before? Moreover why did not you accuse me at once, instead of transferring your attack to another? Or why have you not attacked others for doing the same things heretofore, which you now bring against Ctesiphon?" Inasmuch as Æschines depends in that part of his Attack upon the *justice* of his position, and goes into a panegyric upon law, this exposition of his motives in this instance seems to undo all the foundation of his best arguments. And on this account it is, I think that the defence must be taken to be complete, though the late critics in England incline to the other side. It is plain Æschines himself does not rely upon his two first points as he passes over them soon, and urges more strongly the last which engrosses much the larger share of the Oration. Yet the critics think it is only on the former that he makes out his case. Taking into consideration the result, it seems on the whole probable that at Athens the matter was very well understood, and that the first portion of the Speech must be considered rather specious than actually strong. But stop.

Office all the morning, finishing Cimon with much joy, for I had become tired of a thing that paid me nothing.[1] It is not my destiny to make my fortune by writing for Newspapers. So that the more time I spend in doing it, the more I must charge as uselessly employed. Went to vote,[2] paid Miss Adams a visit, and passed her Settlements, then went down and scolded the Tenant.

Afternoon passed in reading over the Oration for Cælius after finishing it first. I do not like such abuse. It is too bad even for a dog. Evening, Boswell, after which Boileau's Art Poetique[3]—and Two Spectators.

[1] In the third number of CFA's series on "The Resignation of the Cabinet" he concluded his analysis of a situation he maintained was replete with selfishness and intrigue: "This is the fulfilment of the glorious promises made to us at the outset; this is the new era of retrenchment and reform. An increased public expenditure, a degraded representation abroad, and a vacillating policy at home; a timid attack upon the Judiciary of the Union, . . . and a bolder attempt to substitute for the present simple institutions, a great corrupting Government Bank, under the control of the President. These are the *improvements* we have endured" (*Boston Patriot*, 17 May, p. 2, col. 2).

[2] All seven of the National Republican candidates were elected. Joseph T. Buckingham, lowest of the seven in votes, achieved a bare majority. *Boston Patriot*, 16 May, p. 2, col. 1.

[3] As with Horace (above, entry for 11 May), CFA seems to have been reading Boileau-Despréaux's "L'art poëtique" in *Les quatres poëtiques*; see entries for 11, 19 Aug., below. However, "L'art poëtique" is contained in three editions at MQA of the writings of Boileau-Despréaux, including one published at Lyons in 1816 which is inscribed "To Charles Francis Adams from his affectionate brother George."

SUNDAY. 15TH.

Foggy with a cold Easterly wind this morning. I went to Meeting at Mr. Frothingham's and heard Mr. Lunt of New York all day. I knew him at College.[1] His writing is good though it did not interest me. This is a difficulty I am totally unable to get over. Not one preacher seems to be able to fix attention. Is it in my dullness or theirs? Perhaps a little of both. A Clergyman has a hard task. It is cruel to judge him who appears weekly before us—And when Christianity has been inculcated till all its leading doctrines have become too common to be fit for use in the Pulpit. A man who should tell us that Charity, Piety, Faith, Benevolence, Meekness, and the rest of the virtues are good things to practise, would probably be laughed at for his pains. Yet these are the great topics of our Religion, and the cultivation of them the great purposes of preaching. The difficulty is not to be common place.

I read today, Racine's Esther and Athalie[2] with the Commentaries and Laharpe's Opinion. I think they justify their character. French Tragedy has not been my favourite in general, but these are master pieces in a style not known in any other author of that line. They are upon the Greek model and in management much superior. After all, the amount of genius requisite to overcome the infinite difficulties placed in its way by the French taste, must be very great. The production of passages is comparatively easy. A man may write one character in a play well and yet the Play itself be miserable. The combination is the difficulty. Edmund Quincy passed an hour. After him, Two Spectators.

[1] Rev. William Parsons Lunt, Harvard 1823, is identified at vol. 2:280. Lunt was to become co-minister of the First Church in Quincy in 1835, and a close association developed between him and the Adamses, particularly JQA. See JQA, *Memoirs, passim*, and Pattee, *Old Braintree and Quincy, passim*.

[2] Of the six editions at MQA of the *Œuvres* of Racine, that in 3 vols. published at Paris in 1750 has CFA's bookplate and also the signature of his daughter Mary, 1866. *Esther* and *Athalie* are in vol. 3.

MONDAY. 16TH.

The fog still continues thick and heavy, without rain. I passed an hour in reading the criticism of La Harpe upon Esther and Athalie, together with occasional dipping into the Volumes of Voltaire whose inexhaustible variety supplies the place of depth and judgment. By this last word I mean that *consistency* of a mind which forms opinions upon thorough reflection and adheres to them stubbornly. At the Office—My time *not* spent very profitably. Two or three interruptions. My new Tenant among others who adheres tenaciously. A true bore, I fear. Nothing of consequence took place. I went home after calling upon a Tenant.

My Wife went out of town to see Mrs. Gorham Brooks who is confined. I finished the Oration for Cælius. It is as Middleton calls it, amusing, but its general character does not recommend itself to my judgment—Abuse of vice and justification of it in the same breath. Evening, read Athalie over again to remember it. It seems the perfection of melodious versification. Read the Life of Racine in the Dictionnaire Historique, and Two Spectators.

TUESDAY. 17TH.

Morning foggy with a cold easterly Wind, but it afterwards became clear and pleasant. I went to the Office after reading a little of Voltaire's Orphelin de la Chine. This suggested itself to me by the reading of Grimm, whose criticism on its first appearance reminded me how very defectively I had read it. My morning was spent quietly in continuing the "Bibliotheque de l'homme publique" with a consideration of the influence of Montesquieu upon the Revolution. These papers all have the particular spirit which brought on that catastrophe, and a person looking back at this moment feels a singular sentiment in reflecting upon the result as compared with the earnest prophecy.[1] Took a walk after attending to two or three applicants for Houses.

Afternoon, feeling as if I had better wind up some things that had been troubling my patience for some time past, I devoted to pasting my father's papers and preparing books for the binder—Pamphlets and old things that have been in my way for some time.

Evening, took a walk with my Wife, and called to see Miss A. S. Adams who was not well enough to come down, and Mr. and Mrs. Edward Brooks, paying them the long promised visit. Read La harpe's Criticism of Voltaire's Orphelin de la Chine, and Two Spectators.

[1] CFA's marginal animadversions accompany "De l'autorité de Montesquieu dans la révolution présente" in vol. 7 of *Bibliothèque de l'homme public*.

Quincy
WEDNESDAY. 18TH.

The day was very beautiful being clear and warm. I was occupied in making the final arrangements for leaving the City on our short summer residence in the Country. At the Office where I read over the Paper on the influence of Montesquieu. It seemed to me not to destroy one of the positions attacked, for in not a single instance did it meet them fairly. The attempt to destroy the Aristocracy of France, of which this was a part, succeeded, but it brought no such advantages with it as were anticipated.

At one o'clock I started with a horse and gig to Quincy leaving my Wife to go in the Carriage. Reached there some time before her, and found the family much as usual. My Mother seemed to be in very good health and spirits, but my Father from some reason or other seems dull.[1] I am a little apprehensive about him. Quiet is not his sphere. And when a legitimate scene of action does not present itself, it is much to be feared that he will embrace an illegitimate one.

My time was not occupied very usefully. Mr. and Mrs. Cruft and Mr. F. C. Gray called in the afternoon.[2] I read two or three Sections only of Cicero, and felt on the whole dissatisfied and unsettled. Took a walk in the Garden which looks very well. Evening, Conversation with my Father about the Judge's Affairs. The Spectator as usual.

[1] Although he had been able to resume his daily reading on the 13th, JQA continued to be troubled by various physical ailments; on the 14th he began regular horseback-riding for his health (JQA, Diary).

[2] Francis Calley Gray, counselor, who is identified at vol. 2:158, had his office in Barristers' Hall and lived at 18 Summer Street. He had failed of reelection to the state Senate and was currently devoting considerable time to the affairs of Harvard College and to his horticultural interests (*Boston Directory*, 1831–1832; JQA, Diary, 18, 24, 27 May).

THURSDAY. 19TH.

A very heavy fog was hanging over us when I arose this morning but as I fancied it would not remain at all, I went to Boston notwithstanding. The rain followed it however upon my arrival and poured heavily all the time I remained. I sat in my Office, transacted a little business and read a part of another Analysis in the French work. Condorcet was one of the movers of the Revolution, and suffered for his abandonment of practical views to theoretical perfection. His labours are not without value for they have much that was useful amidst much that is extravagant. Our age has derived little or nothing from his, for the principles then opened are now established.

Returned to Quincy in the Afternoon, and read the balance of the Oration de Provinciis Consularibus. This discloses one of the most questionable portions of Cicero's policy. He continued to Cæsar the power that eventually became great enough to overturn the republic. If by a bold and decisive stroke it could have by any possibility been broken, he was wrong, but if it had already become too strong for the Senate, he has some justification. The rain continued. Evening quiet at home. Conversation and two Spectators.

FRIDAY. 20TH.

The morning opened with a heavy thunder shower which prevented my being able to go to town immediately, but at ten o'clock it seemed to hold up and my father being desirous to go, I decided upon starting. The intermediate time I employed in beginning the operation of assorting the Papers of my Grandfather for which purpose I came out more especially to Quincy.[1]

Arrived in town we were here for so short a time that I was unable to do any thing very particular. Mr. Hayford called upon me to be paid for his work as a Mason on my Father's Estate.[2] He satisfies me better than any of my Men. His work is good and his prices are reasonable.

After waiting some time I at last found my Father and we proceeded together home. The weather cleared and it became a very fine afternoon. I read a part of the Oration for Balbus which is not so interesting, the point turning upon the construction of law. There is a high encomium upon Pompey in it, which I think he did not deserve.

This business of my grandfather's papers I foresee will prove a laborious business and I do not wonder that my father has avoided it. Evening T. B. Adams Jr. down here and spent the Evening. Afterwards, I read two Spectators.

[1] Although CFA had from time to time dipped into JA's papers (see vol. 3: 103), this marked the effective beginning of the editorial labors that were to occupy him for so many years. It is clear that initially his purpose was to stimulate his father to prosecute the work.

[2] William Hayford, mason, of 11 Bridge Street (*Boston Directory*, 1831–1832).

SATURDAY 21ST.

Morning mild and pleasant. I went to Boston and was much occupied in various ways—Going to my house, thence to Mrs. Frothingham's and afterwards to execute a variety of Commissions for my Wife. Returned to the Office, I had two or three visits. One from Mr. Geitner, my German friend who at last consents to take the House.[1] Thus I hope I am released from this trouble of letting houses for a considerable period. And now there is not an inch of my father's Property in Boston unoccupied—A thing that has not happened before for a long time. And I hope that I shall begin to reap the Fruit of my new system of management, which hitherto has been sadly out of pocket. Another visit was from Mr. Hobby, a man upon an affair of my father's, and a complete bore.[2] I had no leisure for reading and soon returned to Quincy.

Afternoon, took a long walk to Mt. Wollaston with my father, to see the Orchard and look after his Plantations. We were all the Afternoon upon it. I came back fatigued, spent the Evening with the family, and read the Spectator.

[1] C. Geitner began his long occupancy of tenement No. 1 at 101 Tremont Street on 1 June (M/CFA/3).

[2] For the preceding six months JQA had been receiving numerous letters of complaint from William Hobby who in JQA's administration had raised a charge of fraud against an army paymaster and who maintained that he had not then or since had proper consideration given to

his charges. JQA had asked Nathaniel Frye Jr. to investigate the case and on receipt of his report had three days earlier written Hobby "a short final answer" (JQA, Diary, 27 Feb. – 18 May *passim*).

SUNDAY. 22D.

Morning clear and pleasant. I went to Meeting all day and heard Mr. Whitney preach a Sermon or two, upon the employment of the powers of man &ca. He is the most placidly insignificant character I know. Perhaps such men are the happiest. He at least has all the appearance of being self satisfied to a high degree.

T. B. Adams Jr. came down to dine with us. Nothing material took place. I occupied my leisure moments in my present steady employment, the methodical arrangement of the papers relating to my Grandfather, which I already see is an immense work. My father has the most unaccountable indifference on this subject that I ever knew him to have; he moves neither hand nor foot in an undertaking which might be a very honourable one. I think a great deal more to the purpose than participating in an excitement like this of Masonry.[1] But that is only *my* opinion.

In the evening, the Judge, my Uncle came down and paid us a visit. He seemed in pretty bad humour at first, but afterwards improved very much and we had quite an amusing discussion of the merits of the Masonic Question. Upon which, it is clear, my Father and I disagree.[2] After he went away, I as usual, read my Numbers of the Spectator.

[1] For a considerable period JQA had given thought to and entered into correspondence about Antimasonry. He had not, however, given any public indication of his position on the movement until two days before when he had, on invitation, attended the state Antimasonic convention in Faneuil Hall (JQA, Diary, 20 May).

[2] CFA seems to have been, currently, not so much a defender of Freemasonry as opposed to any involvement of his father or himself in the Antimasonic movement:

"Charles is afraid of the consequences of my expressing any opinion upon the Masonic [controversy], supposing it will be imputed to selfish motives. . . . I have for nearly five years abstained from taking part . . . as much as possible; but upon such questions there is a time when it becomes the duty of a good citizen to take his side. In the conflict . . . I apprehend the Time is approaching when my duty to my Country will require a free and open avowal of my opinions and whatever may be the consequences I shall not flinch from it. The danger is not imaginary" (same, 31 May).

MONDAY. 23D.

I thought that as no especial business called me to town this morning, I would not go, and employ the time instead in the work I have undertaken, to methodize the Papers of my Grandfather. This is a prodigious work, it is one that I foresee must be performed by me, or it will never be done. There is so much that is useless and cumbersome mixed among many very valuable historical materials, that my Father shrinks at the task of assorting. I looked over a vast multitude of Papers relating to the affairs of the Revolution. Also some of the correspondence relating to the Army of 1799. An eventful period in the life of my Grandfather.[1] I made some progress though not a great deal.

Afternoon, occupied in reading Cicero, but I find that out of my own house and comfortable accommodations it is not quite so easy to make progress. I was obliged to review what I had already done of the Oration for Balbus. T. B. Adams Jr. spent the day here. Evening, quietly at home with the family, reading to them a part of Moore's Life of Byron. After it, the Spectator.

[1] The reference seems clearly to point to JA's controversy with the Hamiltonians on the Provisional Army; see Stephen G. Kurtz, *The Presidency of John Adams*, Phila., 1957, p. 366–373.

TUESDAY. 24TH.

A thick mist hung over the Country followed by heavy rain. As I had made engagements that could not easily be broken, and my Father wished also to go to town, we started together and reached Boston as usual. I went to the Office where I transacted some business, received the amount of the Note taken in payment for rent, from one of my Tenants, and gave directions for the few additional necessary ones to be made upon the Tenement not yet occupied. I then went to the House and from thence to the performance of a variety of Commissions with which I had been charged. In this way my time all went, and my Father having done all he had to do, we started upon our return at one. The weather had been terrible all the time.

Afternoon, Engaged in the Oration for Balbus in which I made much progress. It is one of the series for which Cicero is responsible to his Country. His weight having by then[1] been thrown into the scale of Cæsar and Pompey, and against the Senate. In itself I see little of peculiar interest—The question being upon a point of law. My task progressed a little besides, but it is surprising how much time I am always managing to waste. Evening with the family. Nothing material. Read a little of the Spectator.

[1] MS: "them."

WEDNESDAY. 25TH.

It being Election day in town,[1] and the weather appearing very unpropitious, I thought I should do better by remaining out here, than by going. I sat down and devoted a considerable time to my task. Read many of the letters of my father to my Grandfather at the time of his first mission to Holland and was a good deal struck by them.[2] They display a power which puts *me* to shame. I am nothing, and shall be nothing, but a daudle[r?] over trifles. At my age, how infinitely superior he was to me! I feel discouraged. Read some of Mr. Jay's, and Mr. Gerry's Letters and attempted to gain some insight into the state of things in the Commission in France,[3] but my time is limited and I must avoid reading voluminous Papers as much as possible. My progress was tolerable.

Afternoon, T. B. Adams Junr. was here, and I was so much interrupted I could not progress much in Cicero. I finished however the Oration for Balbus and began that against Piso, which is invective indeed. The fury with which he attacks is remarkable. Evening, with the family as usual except that I conversed a little while with my father for the first time upon literary topics. And afterwards, I read the Spectator.

[1] This was the last "Election Day" observance. By an amendment to the state constitution approved by the voters on 11 May, a change in the commencement of the political year was effected. Instead of the election and installation of its officers by the General Court at the beginning of its session each May, the new amendment provided for only one session each year, that one to be held in January (*Boston Patriot*, 11 May, p. 2, col. 3; 14 May, p. 2, col. 5; 25 May, p. 2, col. 2). The passing of one of the most widely observed events on the civil calendar was more regretted than CFA's words suggest. JQA wrote, "It has been a day of solemn festivity, from the first settlement of the Colony, but will be so no more" (Diary, 25 May). On the traditional observance, see vol. 3:245).

[2] JQA was twenty-seven when he became minister to The Hague; the numerous letters that he wrote to JA during his service there in 1794 and 1795 are in the Adams Papers. On his diplomatic activities during the period, see Bemis, *JQA*, 1:50–65.

[3] Presumably this refers to the tangled and protracted Franco-American diplomacy during the period of the quasi-war with France while JA was President. On Gerry's and Jay's parts in these events, see Kurtz, *The Presidency of John Adams*, p. 235–401 *passim*. A number of letters from Jay and from Gerry to JA during these years are in the Adams Papers. The letters from Jay have been published in Jay, *Correspondence and Public Papers*; letterbook versions of the Gerry letters to which CFA was probably alluding have recently been published in *Elbridge Gerry's Letterbook, Paris 1797–1798*, edited by Russell W. Knight, Salem, 1966.

THURSDAY. 26TH.

Morning cloudy but it became beautifully clear by Noon. I went to Boston as usual. Busy in Commissions for the family, and in making up my Journal which by absence from town becomes burdensome, as I have two or three days to make up at a time. Went also to the Athenæum, and was so generally engaged that I could not read at all. Such is the daily course of living out of town and such are the reasons that cause me to object to it. Wrote several dunning Notes which is my amusement. Returned to Quincy, having John Kirk with me who brought in a horse my father has been trying.

After dinner, I passed an hour in reading the Oration against Gabinius, and another in assorting Dr. Franklin's Letters to my Grandfather. He had considerable difficulty with my Grandfather whose very uncompromising character did not suit him. And much of this History is a secret. And much of it is so debateable as to be dangerous matter to bring up.[1]

In the evening, I read a portion of Walter Scott's book upon demonology,[2] after which my old acquaintance, Baron Grimm and the Spectator.

[1] JA and Franklin served together, not always harmoniously, as Commissioners on all three joint American missions from 1778 to 1786. See JA, *Diary and Autobiography*, *passim*. Franklin's letters to JA in the Adams Papers were written largely during those years.

[2] Sir Walter Scott, *Letters on Demonology and Witchcraft*. The edition at MQA was published at New York in 1830, the year of its original publication in London.

FRIDAY. 27TH.

Morning for the first time for a considerable period clear. I started to go to town, as usual excepting that I got away unusually early. Arrived, I was busy for an hour or two in obtaining wood for my house, and also two or three articles wanted. This cramps my time at the Office considerably. Executed some business there also. Mr. Jackson the Painter called to see me, he has been quite sick. I asked him to come to a settlement, and present his bill, not having as I hope any further occasion for his services for a considerable time. My fathers Property is now in pretty good order, and I hope to keep it so. It has cost a large sum of money to put in repair but this has been owing to the inattention of a preceding period. The whole is now let, as I hope profitably.

Returned to Quincy and passed the Afternoon in reading Cicero against Piso, and in assorting Papers. I have nearly completed two cases. The evening was quite cold. We were quietly at home as usual. I read the Baron de Grimm and began the third volume of the Spectator.

SATURDAY. 28TH.

The day was fine, but I concluded that I would not go to Boston today as I have this Job before me. I sat down accordingly and worked from eight o'clock until two very steadily at the Papers, though I did not appear to make any progress. The Papers are very much mixed, and as I am occasionally very much inclined to read over several interesting ones my course is stopped. An acquaintance with the incidents of his life embraces a knowledge of the history of the whole period. And I feel as if I ought to seize every opportunity of knowing facts relating to the times. The hours flew rapidly.

After dinner, I accompanied my father to Mt. Wollaston to look at the Orchard, and at his Plantations of Trees. He is making experiments upon the cultivation of Forest and Fruit Trees from the Seed. I have little faith in the possibility of *his* doing it, as his absence and other occupations prevent the necessary continuity of care. But it is with caution that I express such a sentiment. Found things looking pretty well in general. Returned home quite fatigued. Found there T. B. Adams Jr. who passed part of the evening. Little or nothing of interest. I read a portion of Grimm and my usual Numbers of the Spectator.

SUNDAY. 29TH.

Our Weather hitherto since our stay at Quincy has been exceedingly cool, and often unpleasant. Today it was clear and very warm— The Thermometer rising to over 80° of Fahrenheit. I attended divine Service with my Father all day. We heard Mr. Flint of Cohasset, the very dullest Preacher that ever existed. It passes my comprehension to understand how a man could so totally deprave[1] what might be supposed implanted by nature, the power of delivering a man's own words and ideas to advantage.[2] This gentleman dined with us. He seems to be a Man of naturally good strong sense but rough as a block of granite unhewn.

I took the leisure time to finish the Oration against Piso. It is worth studying for those who feel disposed to deal in invective, but for my own part, I prefer the more moderate, and argumentative discussions. And I cannot get over the strong inconsistency of his subsequent conduct. For Piso and Gabinius both afterwards were defended by him. I also read Grimm. Mr. Degrand and Mr. Dodge, a reformed Consul at Marseilles, paid a visit here and took tea,[3] otherwise evening quiet and warm. Read the Spectator as usual.

[1] *Deprave* as a verb with the meaning to corrupt or degrade seems to have been already by this date an archaism (*OED*).

[2] JQA pronounced the sermon delivered by Rev. Jacob Flynt a good one but "much injured by a sluggish and ungraceful delivery" (Diary, 29 May).

[3] Joshua Dodge, who had served during JQA's administration and had been removed from his post at the beginning of the Jackson administration, was now seeking reappointment. It seems unlikely that an ironic note was intended in the use of *reformed*. CFA seems to have been using the word here and in the entry for 8 Sept., below, with the meaning, already archaic or obsolete, ordinarily restricted to the military: an officer deprived of or left without a command (*OED*: *reformed*, 4).

MONDAY. 30TH.

Morning in continuation of the preceding day. The weather somewhat warmer. I felt however obliged to go to Boston. Perhaps the heat is least perceptible in riding. For a Gig is sure to create a draught. Arrived uncommonly early and went to the House to perform some Commissions for my Wife and myself. Thence returned to my Office, and passed a large portion of time in writing my Journal which these absences make somewhat laborious. Little or nothing else was done except one or two extravagances such as buying a Cask of Claret Wine, a temptation the weather made it impossible to resist. Returned to dinner. The afternoon was so warm and my father's room so heated by his neglecting every precaution, that I did nothing in assorting, and only read very superficially some sections of the Oration against Milo.

This was early interrupted by preparation necessary to attend the Wedding of Miss A. S. Adams to Mr. Angier, which took place this evening. She has been quite sick for some time and it has been doubtful whether she would be able to be married at all at present. But the matter was now set at rest. I think this will be better for the whole family. The number present at the ceremony was large, being nearly all the Quincy acquaintance, the Boston relations, and Mr. Angier's family. Mr. Whitney and Mr. Stetson both officiated. We remained until nine o'clock, when having wished the Bride all happiness in her new State we returned home, for myself I can say pretty tired.[1] Read two Spectators.

[1] The wedding is described in greater detail by LCA in a letter to Mrs. JA2, 2 June (Adams Papers); also in JQA, Diary, 30 May.

TUESDAY. 31ST.

Another extremely warm morning. The Summer commences with some fury. I felt myself obliged however to go to town, and accordingly started at my usual hour. Went to the Office and was busy there for some time, after which I did some Commissions. I sold a part of my Cask of Claret, as I found myself unable to persuade my father to take it, and I bought bottles as well as some strawberry Plants for my Father. The Sun was so scorching as to make moving about very disagreeable.

Returned to Quincy to dine, and as it was scorching in my fathers room, I read Cicero downstairs. My progress was not remarkable. I accomplished one half of the Oration for Milo, the whole being carefully reviewed. I have never experienced so much inconvenience from heat as now. Probably, my system has got braced to the prevailing cold which makes me feel this so much more. Nothing of any consequence took place.

In the evening there was a fine breeze which cooled us very much. I conversed with my father, principally upon the subject of the present excited state of things, as they regard Masonry. He has partaken of late, rather largely of this heated feeling, and I tried as mildly as possible to put a rein over indiscretions, which it must be confessed he will commit at times. I found it dangerous to press the subject, and as I was not disposed to fret myself any more than I could help, I broke off and read two Spectators.

WEDNESDAY. JUNE 1ST.

A very considerable breeze from the North West produced very little effect in diminishing the heat of the Sun. As I had accomplished all that I had to do in town, the weather deterred me from going to town.[1] But my father keeps his room so hot, that I cannot sit in it to work. I also found a large Chest of new Papers which satisfied me of the impossibility of my accomplishing them during my stay here. I worked therefore very languidly and in a discouraged manner. My father shows so little interest in it, and affords me neither assistance nor advice. I think it highly likely that I shall be obliged to look them over hereafter, for the sake of doing what my father ought to do inasmuch as he alone has the ability, and knowledge, adequate to the task. But that is future. And I see no reason for wasting my time *now* in delving for nothing.

Afternoon, Took a bath in the Creek at Mr. Greenleaf's Wharf. The water was warm, but I felt nearly as much exhausted upon my return as I did when I went. Read a considerable portion of the Oration for Milo. But the study compared to what I do at home is nothing. I begin to feel a little restless again. There is to a man like me, "no place like home." Went to ride with my Mother and Wife. This weather affects the latter.

Evening, Mr. T. and Mr. D. Greenleaf to see my Father, and Mr. Gourgas and Miss Adams to see my Mother. It was much more still, and therefore warm. I read two Numbers of the Spectator.

¹ Sentence thus in MS.

THURSDAY 2D.

The morning promised a continuation of the excessive heat, but the change of Wind to the Eastward immediately relieved us from the severity of it. The City remained very sultry however from the heated state of the Bricks. My father went in with me. The heat has produced a great effect upon his Nerves, so that I found it advisable not to talk earnestly upon any subject. Our family is constitutionally irritable, and the fact that I am not so now, only betokens an unusually high degree of health.

I read a little this morning. Mr. Fiske called upon me about a Note given by one Derby for Wood sold at Weston. He was a Classmate of mine and was always holding ill will against me among many of that period. He was now civil enough.¹ My father made it late as the Overseers of the College were delaying their adjournment.

Afternoon, short. I read a little of the Oration for Milo, but a visit from Mr. and Mrs. E. Everett cut me short considerably. I *do* very little. I went to ride with my Mother but the rapid accumulation of Clouds threatened us with rain and we hurried home.

Evening, some Gentlemen with my Father consulting as I suppose about his delivering a fourth of July Oration here.² They seem disposed to put him in harness in every way possible. I have had a thought come across me that if he declined, it might be offered to me. But this is probably vanity. I do not really wish it, as I know that is not my forte. But as there are but three or four educated men in the town, it does not seem unnatural or extraordinary for me to suppose the thing possible. I hope my father will accept it and allow me to go on in my happy, quiet way. The air was chilly though it cleared off. I read a little of Grimm and two Numbers of the Spectator.

¹ Augustus Henry Fiske, Harvard 1825, whose law office was at 5 Court Street, agreed to pay Edward Derby's note for $21.54 when the note was presented. *Boston Directory*, 1831–1832; see also entry for 1 July, below.

² George W. Beale, Edward Miller, and Thomas and Daniel Greenleaf were, along with JQA, members of the committee appointed to arrange for Quincy's observance of the 4th of July. At their meeting the other members were unanimous in urging JQA's acceptance as the orator. JQA consented only on the condition that the committee ascertain that this was the wish also of those who appointed the committee (JQA, Diary, 31 May – 2 June).

FRIDAY. 3D.

Morning cloudy, with a thick sea fog but no rain. I went to town and was busy much as usual. I had more leisure time and was therefore enabled to read rather more than common. Finished the review of Languet,[1] who is an able writer and for his age a genius, though now the same things told in so formal and reasoned a way would make one smile. I began Mably upon Legislation and found him very absurd.[2] I begin to think the fault must be in myself who cannot relish these fancies of enthusiastic men. But every system avowedly departing from the leading principles of man's nature strikes me as Nonsense. The Republic of Lycurgus is always cited as authority for the most hypothetical projects, and moreover as an example. Now to me nothing appears more unnatural, and more undesirable than those very Institutions. Was Man made to fight his Neighbours, or to employ Slaves to keep him in suitable idleness for the purpose? Where is the so much vaunted equality of man? Where is the Law of the Creator that he shall live by the sweat of his brow? Where are all the Qualities that adorn and sweeten life? The gentle affections, the social bonds formed by nature, and only severed by the caprice and art of Man? Let us hear no more then of the Republic of Lycurgus, as an example. An abominable perversion of all natural principles.

Returned home to dine, and passed the afternoon in reading the Oration for Milo, which I finished and began to review. Took a ride with my Mother and Wife. The gentlemen came again and persuaded my father to take the Oration. I am very glad of it. For I like to be saved any trial, about which I have any doubt. And my father is not a preference of which I have any reason to complain as to vanity.

After passing the Evening with the family, I finished it by reading a little of Grimm in which I make slow progress and two Numbers of the Spectator.

[1] "De la puissance légitime du prince sur la peuple, & du peuple sur le prince" by Hubert Languet in *Bibliothèque de l'homme public*, vol. 7.
[2] Abbé Gabriel Bonnot de Mably's "De la législation, ou principes des loix," is in the same volume; both abridgments in vol. 7 have CFA's marginal notations.

SATURDAY. 4TH.

Morning warm although the wind had a great effect in cooling the air so as to be tolerable. I concluded not to go to town today, and sat down to my task. But this new Chest has somewhat discouraged me, and my Father's Apathy adds so much that I decided upon *not* working all the time as I designed, and instead of it sat down to

Rousseau's Emile.[1] This is a work on Education which I have been for some time wishing to read. The first book, all I accomplished today, appears to me admirable. It is more practical than he commonly is. Read also a part of the Oration for Milo in review. Half an hour passed in the Articles Rousseau and Voltaire in the Dictionnaire Historique.

Afternoon, my father asked me to accompany him in a visit to Genl. Dearborn at Roxbury. We accordingly rode there through Milton, very pleasantly. Found him and his daughter. Sat two hours a larger part of which I was tete a tete with the latter. And yet she was agreeable enough to get through it—A thing all young ladies could not have done. Returned late. Evening as usual. Grimm and the Spectator.

[1] The edition of *Emile et Sophie*, published at Paris in 1795, at MQA has CFA's signature and bookplate. Although CFA had heard Professor Ticknor lecture on *Emile* at Harvard (see vol. 1:414), this was apparently a first reading.

SUNDAY. 5TH.

The dry weather perseveres. Vegetation begins to suffer by it. The wind was however very high from the South West, so that it was not oppressive while quiet. I attended Meeting all day, and heard Mr. Whitney preach Sermons as uninteresting as usual. There is a placidity however and above all a shortness which is pleasing. I rank both these qualities high in the character of a country Minister. Miss Smith dined with us.

I spent much of the day in the review of the Oration for Milo which I finished. This is considered as one of the masterpieces of its author, and it deserves its reputation. For whether we consider the artful arrangement of the evidence, the selection of the defence, or the management of the Judges and of Pompey, it is a model, or whether we look into the richness and melody of the language, and the pathos of expression.[1] Perhaps this last may be considered as the most general characteristic of his eloquence. It pervades every defence, and generally the allusions to himself. Evening. Took a salt water bath, read a little of Emile, finished the second volume of Grimm and two Spectators.

[1] Sentence thus in MS. CFA's words on the Oration for Milo have much in common with those which JA wrote when he was undertaking the study of oratory. See JA, *Earliest Diary*, p. 74–76.

MONDAY. 6TH.

Morning tolerably pleasant, with a cool East Wind. I went to town as usual, though I felt a little affected by a bad Night's rest. Occupied much in my common way, in the performance of sundry Commissions, and then in reading Mr. de Mably. A book I do not admire. The principle of its foundation being wrong, it destroys the whole superstructure. I went to the Athenæum to get some books and spent a short time reading the newspapers from England which exhibit a very peculiar state of things. But the Reform seems determined. The violence with which it is conducted betokens more alarming measures to come.

Dined at Mr. Frothingham's with only the family and Horatio Brooks.[1] From thence I went to the regular Meeting of the Directors of the Boylston Market, where having transacted all the usual business which was not much, I got away to return to Quincy at about five o'clock. But from my imprudence in eating Nuts at dinner, I found myself suffering from a violent headach with some fever, which I tried to walk off by going to Mt. Wollaston, without effect. Read the Spectator and passed a restless Night.

[1] Horatio Brooks was about to sail for Calcutta to be absent for a year. Peter C. Brooks to ABA, 8 June (Adams Papers).

TUESDAY. 7TH.

A strong fog from the Eastward. I felt so much indisposed that I thought it not advisable to go to town. So that I busied myself as well as I could in arranging my Grandfather's Papers. I find the correspondence immensely large and some of it not of great value. But there is some which is valuable to preserve, as a memorial to our family of what others thought. The attempt to methodize must be well studied before it can succeed. I read a part of the second book of Rousseau's Emile that falls off from the practical character of the first though equal in the beauty of its style. It was cold though it cleared away.

In the Afternoon, I began Cicero's Oration for Rabirius Postumus, and read a large part of it. The reflection in it is fine, though perhaps he could have been better occupied. Probably his Client was no better than he should be. I cannot however study with one half the relish here that I do at home, for I am not in the way to be so thorough. T. B. Adams Jr. was here from Medford,[1] and passed the afternoon. Evening, read a little of Grimm, felt a good deal better, and finished with two Numbers of the Spectator.

[1] The Lieutenant, with his mother, had gone to Medford several days earlier for the party on the evening before at which the Angiers in their newly furnished home received their friends (JQA, Diary, 3 and 6 June).

WEDNESDAY. 8TH.

Morning foggy, but it cleared away and left us a fine day though with a cold East Wind. I felt better, though not yet entirely free from pain. My system is in a pretty healthy general condition, but it is subject to attacks from small things, and requires care. I went to Boston and was occupied some time in making some purchases for my Mother of various articles needed for her House. I had also some Commissions for my father upon Money affairs. I had in this way all my time taken up and it became necessary for me to return to Quincy. My Mother and Wife came in this morning and did not return to dinner, so that My father, I. Hull and I dined together.

Afternoon, I read the rest of Cicero for Rabirius Postumus and reviewed the first half. I also looked over a considerable number of Letters, among the rest some of Mr. Jefferson's and compared them with the printed Collection.[1] Found some curious ones omitted. But I do not know that it is not for the better. These old gentlemen were neither of them distinguished for judgment though greatly so for ability. Evening, the Judge came down from his house to pay us a visit. Afterwards I read Grimm and the Spectator.

[1] Apart from a few earlier letters of 1777–1779, the long correspondence of Jefferson and JA began in 1785 after Jefferson's appointment as JA's colleague in a commission to negotiate treaties of amity and commence with European powers. The printed letters must be those published in T. J. Randolph's edition of Jefferson's *Memoir, Correspondence and Miscellanies*; on which, see vol. 3: 74. CFA's words suggest that at least some of the letters he was reading belong to the period following the renewal of the correspondence in 1812.

THURSDAY. 9TH.

The morning was clear and warm, and a tolerable specimen of fine weather at this season of the year. I went to town as usual, though I felt still a little unwell. It is a little singular that the indiscretion in eating of Sunday and Monday should have so affected my system but so it is. My time was taken up in going to my House, obtaining some books for my Father, and in doing some business for him, which engrossed a great deal. Mr. Degrand called upon me and spent some time on the subject of the business. A very thankless task. And all these commissions make me feel sick of my residence at Quincy. Returned to dine.

Afternoon passed in reading Cicero's Oration for Rabirius which I finished, and on the whole I think it not equal to the expectations raised at the commencement of it. But the great imperfection seems to be in the defective state of the Manuscripts which stops the pleasure of reading. I also spent a short time in reading Mr. Jefferson's Letters and arranging them as usual. Afterwards Grimm, whose criticism upon Emile is to my mind exceedingly judicious. Evening Judge and Mrs. Adams called. I read Grimm and the Spectator.

FRIDAY. 10TH.

Morning warm and dry. I was a little delayed by my fathers wishing to go with me, and he is rarely ready at his time. We started at last and reached town rather after my usual hour. Found on my table the decree of distribution upon the Estate of R. New and sat about a pretty heavy work of arranging the particular Dividends of the Creditors. As the rate is 27 Cents and 318/1000, this is not an easy process. As my father wanted to converse with Mr. T. Fuller[1] I went to the Boylston Market to write out the record of that Meeting last Monday. I could not find the Clerk so that my Walk was useless. Obliged to return and hear a discussion of Freemasonry which I did not relish, and therefore sat about writing my Journal. Perhaps the record of yesterday can speak for itself, as to the confusion necessarily resulting. We returned at the usual time.

Afternoon, read the Oration for Ligarius. These are beautiful pieces of composition. They seem to flow from the power of Oratory in its highest perfection. No labour but the fruit of a habit. Although not equal to the early works as specimens of *art*, yet they will always be the most agreeable to read.

Assorted papers also. But this evening was selected for the purpose of giving a little party to the Bride, Mrs. Angier. The Quincy people generally were here and the two Mrs. Everetts from Boston. It went off well,[2] and I went to bed fatigued after reading the Spectator as usual.

[1] Timothy Fuller, counselor and figure in Massachusetts politics, is identified at vol. 2:152. Currently he was a leader in the Antimasonic party and had presided over the recent state convention in Faneuil Hall. Fuller's purpose in arranging the meeting with JQA was to secure JQA's permission for him to publish JQA's letter to him attacking Freemasonry; to secure JQA's support for the movement to block the nomination of Henry Clay for the Presidency; and to engage JQA actively in antimasonic affairs at the national level. JQA withheld his consent to all (JQA, Diary, 10 June).

[2] The party which JQA and LCA gave was held in the Old House. The guest list and some description of the event are in JQA, Diary, 10 June; LCA to Mrs. JA2, 12 June (Adams Papers).

SATURDAY. 11TH.

The morning promised to be so warm that I thought it inexpedient to go through the process of travelling to Boston. Remained busy at home in arranging Papers to which however I do not devote my whole attention. I am sick of the business at present. The Letters are however many of them very curious, especially those from Mr. Jefferson most of which have been published. I also read more of Rousseau's Emile which I like less as I progress. The man shines out at every page. A maker of paradoxes. A fashioner of gaudy instruments, bright to the eye, but utterly unsafe to use. The beauty of his style makes the wildest things easily swallowed, and the occasional clearness with which he lays down truth, in order to apply it wrong.[1]

My father, Isaac Hull and I went to bathe at Noon. The water was cold owing to an Easterly wind and Spring tide. Afternoon, read the Oration for Ligarius which may be included and make part of the subject commented upon yesterday. The flattery is rather gross, for Cæsar after all was guilty of a high crime, yet one feels half inclined to give up the principle or at least to wink it out of sight. Evening, Grimm, and the Spectator.

[1] Sentence thus in MS.

SUNDAY. 12TH.

Although the wind was high, the power of the Sun this morning was very great. I attended divine service as usual, and heard Mr. Parkman of Boston preach from the second Commandment. I was much pleased with his Sermon and thought it better than any thing I had before heard of his. He dined with us and was quite pleasant. His afternoon Sermon was upon preparation[1] and I did not think so much of it. With such weather as this, sitting in Church is irksome.

I amused myself the rest of the day reading Grimm and Rousseau. The first seems to me to be remarkable for two qualities. Considerable critical judgment in literature, and fine taste in the arts. But his mind is constantly biassed by the tone of philosophy which he wants to support, against religion and its supporters. Upon the character of Diderot's writings he is no authority. The world has long ago pronounced its decision and it is not Baron de Grimm's. Of Rousseau I have spoken so much already as to need no repetition. Evening quietly at home. After the ladies retired I continued Grimm and the Spectator.

[1] Doubtless in an ecclesiastical sense: the actions of an individual that should precede and anticipate his participation in Communion.

MONDAY. 13TH.

Morning clear and warm. I went to Boston as usual arriving quite in good season. At the Office after going to the House for the purpose of obtaining two or three articles for myself. Engaged in making out the Dividend for the Creditors of R. New's Estate which I accomplished and paid one of them upon the Spot. Mr. Degrand called but entirely without success in his purpose of investment. On the whole, so far as my purpose is concerned it is as well. Found that the New England Office disappointed me in its Dividend this six Months, which satisfies me more than ever of the expediency of my advice as to paying off all engagements here. I feel the relief sensibly now of the payment of six thousand dollars in the last year.[1]

Returned to Quincy to dinner. Afternoon, read the Oration for Deiotarus, a thing apparently thrown off without any effort. An ingenious defence though rather an unsound one. This is the last of his Orations in defence. The Philippics only remain as a close of his brilliant though agitated career. Continued filing Letters.

Evening, T. B. Adams Jr. paid a visit here. I had a business conversation with him, and took the occasion to advise him to the best of my ability as to his course. The Ladies returned from riding, my Wife not very well. I afterwards read Grimm finishing the 3d volume and the Spectator.

[1] See above, entry for 12 May.

TUESDAY. 14TH.

Morning cloudy at last. It is now three weeks that we have had constantly fine weather, so that the slight shower that fell in the morning was grateful, and the heavy rain in the afternoon and evening very refreshing. I went to Boston as usual and my time was taken up in much the same fashion as common. I had some conversation with Mr. Degrand but came to no conclusion as to investment. The difference in the New England Ins. Dividend alters my views seriously.

I went to the Boylston Market today and draughted the Record of the Directors Meeting into the Book. From thence I went to the Athenæum and obtained J. Otis's Rights of the Colonies for my Father.[1] The remainder of the morning was passed in reading it. But it was too short to progress far.

I returned to Quincy, and passed the Afternoon in reading the first Oration against Antony, which is much to my taste. The tone of it is subdued, but yet firm, willing to take things fairly, but prepared for the worst. Cicero was an extraordinary compound of timidity and courage, of sublimity in sentiment and timidity of action. His character is in itself a study. I filed Letters afterwards. A Quiet Evening at home after which I pursued Rousseau's Emile in the third Stage of his Education, and the Spectator.

[1] James Otis, *Rights of the British Colonies Asserted and Proved*, Boston, 1764.

WEDNESDAY. 15TH.

The Morning looked very cloudy and dark. I went to town never-theless and the consequence was that I was in the rain. At the Office however very quietly all the time, not having many errands to run. I was engaged in writing and in arranging my own and New's Affairs which I am rapidly bringing to a close—Having paid off the larger half of what remained in my hands. This has been a very good business to me, for the money has yielded me four per Cent besides my Compensation as Administrator.[1] I had some leisure time, during which I was occupied in finishing the Analysis of Mr. de Mably. His close upon the influence of infidelity in a State is curious and sensible. The work generally does not however recommend itself in any manner to me. It is highflying Nonsense. This world was not created for purposes of War and discord. Nor is the natural condition of man military, let Hobbes say what he pleases. I never read him therefore can only judge his doctrine at second hand.

Returned to Quincy to dinner. My father had gone as one of the delegates from the Church at Quincy to the ordination of Mr. George Whitney at Roxbury.[2] I read the first half of the second Antonine of Cicero. This is the famous one, which though not delivered, cost its Author, his life. The invective is in the usual style of bitterness, with an occasional coarse personality not to my taste. Yet if it can be excused, perhaps there is as much here to be said in its defence as any where. Evening after the ladies retired, I read Emile and the Spectator.

[1] See above, vol. 3, entries for 5 and 6 January.

[2] George Whitney, Harvard 1824, a son of Rev. Peter Whitney of Quincy, was ordained and installed at the Second Church in Roxbury. I. Hull Adams ac-companied JQA. The occasion seems to have been observed as an event of more than ordinary importance. For an account, see JQA, Diary, 15 June. On George Whitney, see also vol. 1:155–156.

THURSDAY. 16TH.

The weather was bad and I had been to town so much this week that I resolved to stay at home and busy myself in the old Papers. This morning I came across a very interesting parcel of Lovel's com-munications to my Grandfather.[1] They explain much of the private history of the Revolution. How little does a man gather of the true causes of public events from the pages of common history. How different is human nature when seen in the gross, and in separate parts. There is enough to make a man humble when he looks at the fallibility of his fellows, even when they are acting for the best general purposes. My progress was necessarily slow.

Read a part of Emile containing the famous Creed of the Savoyard, which seems to me as much levelled at the Philosophy of the period as at the Christian faith. They both took it up, the former with words, because they could use nothing else, the latter with the temporal arm. Indifference would perhaps have better served the turn of both.

Afternoon the balance of the 2d Antonine. A powerful exposition of the condition of the Republic and the worthlessness of it's Rulers. The Conspiracy of Catiline was only the first signal of universal corruption in the State. Cicero merely cut off one of the heads of the Hydra, and exhausted his powers in the process. Clodius, and Antony finished the work not by superior skill, for they were probably both inferior to Catiline, but by that steady perseverance before which every thing gives. Cæsar perhaps pulled the wires in each instance, and perished after all, because there was still a greater remnant of the ancient patriotism left than he calculated. Evening, Emile and the Spectator.

[1] James Lovell (1737–1814) was a long-time friend and correspondent of JA and AA. His letters to JA in the Adams Papers extend over a period from 1777 to 1809 and are of special interest on public matters during his service in Congress from 1777 to 1782. Many of his letters to and from AA are being printed in *Adams Family Correspondence*, vol. 2 *et seq.* See also JA, *Diary and Autobiography*, 1:288, and *DAB*.

FRIDAY. 17TH.

The weather was still foggy and damp, threatening rain. I therefore thought I would remain at home today instead of tomorrow as I had intended. Engaged in arranging a full file of Mr. Jefferson's Letters. On the whole, Washington, Jefferson and my Grandfather were the three most remarkable men of our Revolution. And the two latter had more distinguishing peculiarities. Jefferson's mind was of a very capacious character, his temper philosophical, and his personal feelings kind. But he was ambitious, hypocritical and occasionally ungenerous, besides a narrowness of mind and inveteracy of prejudice peculiar to himself. He was more than a match for my impetuous, irascible but open hearted ancestor. I read the Correspondence between my Grandmother and him and could not help admiring her letters as much the best.[1] I did little more than arrange this single file today.

Read more of Emile in the last book upon the passions. Rousseau was a sensualist, a most abandoned sensualist, and every line is tinged with that spirit. One may judge how fit he is to write upon Education. So long as he confined himself to early infancy when nothing could be introduced upon the subject, he mixed more truth than falsehood, but in rising to the age of the Passions he gradually abandons himself to imagination and to his own voluptuous fancies. I doubt if this work ever guided a single man right beyond the first book. Read the third and fourth Antonines raising up Octavius Cæsar, as a counterpoise to Antony. They display the Policy but are otherwise of no great interest. Evening, rode with my Mother and Wife, we called at Judge Adams' and paid a visit. Afterwards, Emile and the Spectator.

[1] CFA had already recognized and responded to AA's extraordinary capacity as a letter-writer (vol. 2:337). His appreciation of these gifts was long maintained and reached a culmination in his preparation of *The Letters of Mrs. Adams*, Boston, 1840, which, in that and subsequently expanded form, became the most popular of the books CFA edited from the family's papers and established his grandmother's epistolary reputation. AA's correspondence with Jefferson extends, with conspicuous intervals, from 1785 to 1817, but is most voluminous for the period 1785–1787.

SATURDAY. 18TH.

The weather was again quite warm and the air though abundant was sultry. I went to town and was busy much of my time in making up the deficiency in my Journal, occasioned by my absence. Then arranging all my Accounts. I called at Meriam and Brigham's for the purpose of paying for my Wine bought lately,[1] and attended a Sale of Stocks without succeeding in a purchase. It went however pretty low. Several at my Office. Mr. Jackson the Painter for his Money which I paid him, and hope this is the last heavy amount for which I shall be called upon, in his line. Mr. J. E. Smith came as representative of a Creditor of New's Estate,[2] and I paid out that portion leaving in my hands a mere trifle. I was delayed in this way for some time, and reached Quincy a little late.

Afternoon, occupied reading Cicero's fifth Philippic which dissuades the sending a mission to Anthony and recommends the course he thinks suitable. He was right. The Counsels of the Conspirators were feeble, they had imagined nothing beyond the mere death of the Tyrant, expecting that when he was once out of the way, the Republic would come back of itself. But Cicero acted by raising opposing forces, not calculating upon a Union of these against himself. Took a bath with my father and I. Hull. Evening quietly at home. Read more of Emile and the Spectator.

70

[1] Meriam & Brigham, wine merchants, were at 20 Congress Street (*Boston Directory, 1831–1832*).

[2] Perhaps Joseph E. Smith, attorney, whose office was in Barristers' Hall (same).

SUNDAY. 19TH.

Morning cloudy, but the day extremely sultry, clearing away in the evening with a thunder shower. I attended Meeting all day, and heard Mr. Alger of Chelsea. He was my Classmate and for four years sat next to me. The idea of his character created at College would not leave, and I lost a moment in musing upon the changes of a few years. His Sermons were well enough though I was surprised to find how little his style had formed.[1] The weather was so hot that I felt very uncomfortable in Church.

Filed a few Papers and read Emile, which I finished. Perhaps I may enlarge upon it tomorrow. Took a bath with my Father, and on our return found J. Quincy Jr. who spent half an hour, but was frightened away by the Shower. Read the Spectator.

[1] Horatio Alger, Harvard 1825, delivered his well-written sermons, according to JQA, "with propriety; but in the cold or at least temperate manner of the Cambridge School" (Diary, 19 June).

MONDAY. 20TH.

The Morning was very warm and clear, so that the riding was pleasant enough after the shower. I went to town as usual and was busy for an hour in performing my Commissions for various Members of the Family. Returned to the Office and passed some time in reading the Discourse of Agrippa to Augustus translated from Dion Cassius, and a part of that of Mæcenas.[1] The idea is that they gave the Emperor advice of an opposite character. One that he ought to resign, another that he ought not. They neither of them seem to me to touch the point in dispute—The particular character of the Roman People at the moment.

Returned to dinner, and after it, I read the sixth and seventh Philippics of Cicero, continuing his advice as to the course to be pursued with Anthony. They are all noble Monuments of his Patriotism, in the last hours of his life. He was one who battled with the times, and if he had not the Sternness of ancient Roman virtue, it was because the age did not admit of it. Cato was not so useful a Citizen, though of a more unbending disposition. Rome was degenerate.

Evening very warm and without air. The Mosquitoes were very troublesome. I read Dummer's Defence of the New England Charters[2] and the Spectator.

[1] The two orations on monarchy were taken from the 52d book of Dion Cassius' *Roman History*; they appear in vol. 8 of *Bibliothèque de l'homme public* as "Discours d'Agrippa et de Mécène à Auguste."

[2] *Defence of the New England Charters* by Jeremiah Dummer was first published in London in 1721.

TUESDAY. 21ST.

Morning warm but cloudy. The Air having the sultry character of August. I went to town as usual and have rarely experienced more of heat. My time was taken up in Commissions for my Father. First to my House, next to State Street for the purpose of finishing the business of his Loan, which I did.[1] I then answered a letter from my Brother received this morning, about a proposed loan of Mr. Frye's, which is curious from the apparent confidence of the proposition.[2] The hours passed in this way with great rapidity and I returned to Quincy.

The heat ended today in occasional showers during the afternoon. I read the Eighth and Ninth Philippics of Cicero upon the course to be pursued after the return of the Embassy to Antony and upon the Honors due to Servilis Sulpicius. This business of honors was one of the greatest signs of the decay of the Republic. For the rest, these are like all his latter Orations, fluent and honest. Took a Bath with I. Hull in the Evening, and read J. Otis' Rights of the Colonies asserted and the Spectator.

[1] JQA had given CFA a power of attorney to transfer 50 shares of New England Insurance Co. stock as collateral for a loan ($5,000 for 6 months at 4½ per cent) which P. P. F. Degrand had negotiated at the American Insurance Co. CFA received the money and deposited it in JQA's account at the U.S. Branch Bank for withdrawal by JA2 to meet his and JQA's joint note at the Union Bank of Georgetown due on 26 June (JQA, Diary, 10 and 21 June; JQA to JA2, 14 and 26 June, Adams Papers).

[2] JA2's letter is missing. In it he wrote that their uncle, Nathaniel Frye Jr., had requested him to inquire of CFA at what interest Frye could borrow in Boston with a mortgage on his house in Washington as collateral. CFA's reply was a discouraging one; he doubted that any loan would be made on property outside the state, certainly at no less than a 6 per cent rate. CFA to JA2, 21 June (Adams Papers). On Frye, see vol. 1:4 and Adams Genealogy.

WEDNESDAY. 22D.

The Morning was bright and cool. I had intended remaining quietly at home but made accidentally an engagement which I felt obliged to fulfil, so I went to town and called at nine o'clock to see Dr. Stevenson, and consult him about my Wife. Found him and was satisfied with his replies. Time taken up at the Office as usual. One or two calls. One from a Creditor of New's whom I paid. Finished the imagined address of Mæcenas to Augustus and not much edified. Began the Analysis of Mirabeau's Ami des Hommes, apparently a work upon Population and

Political Economy,[1] but I could accomplish very little of it before it was time to return to Quincy.

Mr. J. Coolidge called upon me to assist the Fayetteville sufferers which I declined doing. It is a difficult thing to resist public charities. The man who can say No in this Community must have firmness as well as judgment. I reflected upon my opinion in this instance and hope that it was just. My share of assistance from peculiar circumstances in my situation must be necessarily small, and I am therefore driven to choose what I shall patronize. The town of Fayetteville has so much excited the public sympathy that I doubt not it will have more ready Cash in it than it has had for many years, if ever. I therefore think they are not so pitiable as many objects we have nearer home.[2]

Afternoon passed in reading Cicero's Tenth Philippic upon the course to be pursued after the receipt of the Letters from Brutus. It is animated and worthy of a better age and a bolder audience. But Antony had friends in the City, who though they could not entirely destroy the ancient spirit had a considerable influence in damping it. Mr. and Mrs. Farrar from Cambridge called and took up half an hour so that I did not accomplish as much as usual.[3]

Evening quiet at home. I finished J. Otis's Rights of the Colonies asserted—A Work more applauded than it really deserves. It wants method and clearness. The ideas are just but not developed with grace. It was lucky in its time, for *now* much more would be required. Indeed the difference in the *demands* of the public is very striking— Though the masculine character of works has been injured. The Night was beautifully clear. Miss Adams and Mr. Gourgas were here. Read the Spectator.

[1] "L'ami des hommes, ou traité de la population" is in vol. 8 of *Bibliothèque de l'homme public.*

[2] Fayetteville, N.C., had several weeks earlier been ravaged by a fire that left the larger part of its population homeless. Collections for the sufferers had been begun almost immediately and a city-wide committee on relief appointed. (*Boston Daily Advertiser*, 6–14 June passim.)

[3] On Professor John Farrar, see vol. 1:100–104, 239. Farrar and his wife had been acquainted with the Adamses in England and at Washington. Now in poor health, Farrar was preparing to go abroad and wished a letter of introduction from JQA to the president of the Royal Society, the Duke of Sussex (JQA, Diary, 22 June).

THURSDAY. 23D.

Morning cloudy with an Easterly Wind which became a rain Storm for the day. I concluded to remain housed today and pursue the train of my Quincy pursuits. A great part of the morning taken up in assorting Papers of no interest. I will therefore take occasion to finish my reflections upon Emile, though I have already given so much in detached passages as to leave little to be said. Rousseau's peculiar character violently influenced all his Works. He had made the Reputation he prized, by a bold and Paradoxical Essay, and being thus made aware that his natural bias was precisely that with which the world was disposed to be pleased, he gave it scope and spread it more or less through all the rest of his Writings. The great principle he seems to have adopted was, that All civilized systems and habits in Life were corruptions from the natural happy condition of man. This foundation being good for nothing, of course all his building upon it is useless. His education he boasts is a natural one. He says what he will *do*, shall be what the Child shall take, and not what he will say. He will lead by acting upon his senses and not upon his mind. But he forgets that the foundation of man is principle engrafted upon habit, and that few opportunities can be found of acting directly upon the interests of children compared to the number requisite to fix an impression permanently in the mind. Withal, there are a multitude of maxims interwoven with the system which are undoubtedly excellent. A child cannot be governed merely by reasoning, it's principal guide must be *example*, and steadiness.

I read a part of Horace's Art of Poetry with Hurd's Commentary wherein he endeavours to prove it a connected piece of instruction upon the Roman Drama.[1] It has generally been thought an easy way of throwing out loose maxims. Whatever it is, It is a gem.

Afternoon, read the Eleventh and Twelfth Philippics of Cicero, upon the course of Dolabella and the appointment of Cassius to command against him; and the new Legation to Antony. He excuses himself because he is afraid. I do not doubt he was. But there is a principle in the human character which will never admire though it may not disapprove such a reason. Quiet evening at home. Read two or three Pamphlets on the Question of Taxation, without profit, and the Spectator.

[1] An edition of the *Epistolæ* of Horace with an English commentary and notes by Bishop Richard Hurd, published at London in 3 vols., 1776, is at MQA.

FRIDAY. 24TH.

The day was bright and absolutely cold making a singular change from the past. I rode to town as usual and spent my morning pretty quietly at my Office. Nothing of any consequence happened. I had several calls. One from a man presenting a Draught upon T. B. Adams, for his Son J.Q.A. Jr. which I paid. One from Mr. Ayer the

Carpenter about Repairs. Having finished these, I read a part of the Ami des Hommes, which appears to contain some good things.

Returned to Quincy with another Horse. My luck this Season has not been good with them. Afternoon, read the thirteenth Philippic of Cicero, upon the letter of Antony to Hirtius and Cæsar, and upon the course of Lepidus. This is peculiar as being Criticism, Paragraph by paragraph, sharpened by the venom of political and personal hatred. Cicero affords examples of the varieties of invective and perhaps it is well for a man to have them as studies. But I do not fancy the strain. It is degrading to the character of human nature. Evening at home. I resumed Baron Grimm and read the Spectator.

SATURDAY. 25TH.

Morning clear and cool with an Easterly Wind throughout the day. I went to town for the purpose of avoiding my Father's invitation to go and see Mr. Bailey which I knew would come and place me in all the heat of an Antimasonic Conversation.[1] I was engaged much as usual, though I had more time on my hands to read Mirabeau's Ami des Hommes. I finished it once and began a review. The first book is upon Agriculture and Population, tolerably good. Returned to Quincy as usual.

Afternoon finished the fourteenth and last Philippic upon the Victory gained by the Consuls and Cæsar over Antony, persuading further measures. Shortly after this, the triumvirate was formed, and Cicero fell an early victim to political expediency. This Oration is a graceful close to the series of his Oratorical labours. A series not equalled in the two thousand years which have passed since his death. I had a little time left to assort papers, which I do now at every leisure moment as my period for staying here is rapidly closing.

Evening, the ladies remained out until quite late. It was cool and I took a solitary walk. After which I continued Grimm and read the Spectator as usual.

[1] John Bailey, currently active in Antimasonry, is identified at vol. 1:444. JQA's intended visit to him was apparently postponed. Two days later he visited JQA at Quincy in order to request a letter to Albert Gallatin supporting Bailey's candidacy for a professorship of Moral Philosophy at the new University of the City of New York, of which Gallatin was president of the Council. JQA, Diary, 27 June; John Bailey to JQA, 28 June; JQA to Gallatin, 11 July, LbC (both letters in Adams Papers); *DAB*, under Gallatin.

SUNDAY. 26TH.

The Weather was cool and pleasant all day. I attended Divine Service and heard Mr. Whitney preach. His afternoon Sermon was an attack upon Miss Wright for her doctrines with a general defence of the immortality of the Soul as established by revelation.[1] Nothing material took place.

My Mother with her usual benevolence of intention, thinking to assist I. Hull has interested herself with the higher powers to get him a place in the Navy. She has obtained it and it seems he is averse to the proposition. The Warrant has been offered to his youngest brother who springs at it.[2] This family is a thorn in our side. It is craving and ungrateful. I am willing to give my best advice to the children who help themselves, but I would not raise a finger for father or mother or *gentlemen youths.* My father's life has been one constant series of benefits forgot. But I must say, the course he pursues is a premium to misconduct.

I filed Papers a considerable part of the day. In the evening had a conversation with my Father upon the character of Milton's Poetry. The first since I have been out here embracing any thing like general literature. Such are the expectations of life. Read Grimm and the Spectator.

[1] Frances Wright (1795–1852), later married to Phiquepal D'Arusmont but always better known as Fanny Wright, English agitator against slavery, against established religion, and for the emancipation of women, had earlier been to the United States in 1818–1820 and in 1824, when she settled Negro slaves on land she purchased on the Nashoba River in Tennessee. Returning in 1828, she settled at New Harmony, Ind., and from there traveled widely, exciting strong opposition by her public lectures, particularly because of her religious views, to the point that she became identified in the public mind with almost any cause that was unpopular (*DAB, DNB*). Rev. Peter Whitney, frightened by the spread of Universalism, identified her with that sect in the hope of blackening it. JQA's misinformed account of her may reflect his own views or may be wholly or in large part simply a report of Whitney's characterization:

"Fanny Wright an English female Atheist who has been delivering Lectures in the principal cities of the United States, against Slavery, Marriage, and Christianity. She has every where gained numerous Proselytes, and there is a party scattered all over the Country, who call themselves the working men's Party, but who are generally called by others Fanny Wright's Party. Fanny makes no pretension to believe in a future State; nor even in the existence of a God; but she has an inveterate aversion to Slavery of all kinds—To African Slavery—Matrimonial Slavery—Religious Slavery. She declaims against them all, and never wants an Auditory. There is a Religious Sect rapidly growing in this part of the Country denominated Universalists who approach very nearly to the doctrines of Fanny but they profess to be Christians. They suppose the Soul and body to perish together ... and particularly that there will be no future State of punishment. This is a compound of Atheism and Superstition well suited to the inconsistencies and absurdities incident to the reasoning faculties of men; and the Sect is spreading marvellously. They have had preachers here for these two years, and have taken from Mr. Whitney about one third of his Parishioners." (JQA, Diary, 22 May, 26 June.)

[2] The warrant for Joseph Harrod Adams was secured through the good offices of Commodore Isaac Hull, after whom the reluctant Hull Adams had been named. LCA to JA2, 26 June (Adams Papers).

MONDAY. 27TH.

The morning was cloudy and threatened rain, notwithstanding which my Wife and I went to town together as by agreement in the Carriage. After calling at the House, I went to the Office and occupied myself in Accounts and in reading. The Newspapers contain a Correspondence between Messrs. Ingham and Eaton, of a nature so disgraceful as to set every thing else that has happened in the back ground.[1]

I had a Call from a Son of R. New's making inquiry about the final distribution. He gave me more information respecting his father's character than I had yet received. His was a case fit for a moralizing romance. One of the humble instances of suffering from the affections of the heart, which may be found in common life, and passed over without a comment. The world heals over without difficulty, and yet the pang is as acute, the sorrow as powerful as if a King experienced it, and a Court mourned in sympathy. R. New had a daughter and four Sons. He was a Barber in a good run of business and had acquired some Property besides. This daughter was educated by him with more than usual care, he had strained his means to give her extraordinary advantages, and he looked to her more than to all his other children united, for the comfort and happiness of his old age. She had been addressed by a respectable young man, a Silversmith by trade and in all respects a suitable match for her, and had become engaged to him with the approbation of her Father. Here he seemed to look for his future hours of peace, and Providence hitherto had smiled upon him with unusual favour. The Silversmith unfortunately went to Philadelphia for a little while, during which time, she happened one evening to go to the Theatre. The whole case immediately changed its aspect. She fell desperately in love at first sight with one of the Actors, procured an introduction to him, and soon forgot her vows upon gaining his Attentions. The remainder is the pathetic portion of the Story. Her father refusing his consent, she was married without it, and from that moment, he lost all his motives to live. Unwilling to commit suicide, and yet not desirous to live, he took to using the slow but sure poison which our numerous shops afford. His affairs went to ruin and he found a happy relief to save him from the extremities of earthly misery. But on his death bed, when his unrepenting daughter, forced by her husband on pain of his displeasure, went to him at the Hospital and offered her hand, the last moments of his existence were used in a violent effort to disengage himself from her. He had been too severely wounded to remember the injunctions of Christianity. The Son told me this much more forcibly than I describe it.

I dined at Mr. Frothingham's who regaled us sumptuously, and in the Afternoon attended the Meeting of the Directors of the Boylston Market as by adjournment. Little or nothing done or to do. I came back to Mr. Frothingham's early from whence I started with Abby home and reached it before tea. Quiet evening. I afterwards read Grimm and the Spectator.

[1] The principal items in the correspondence, originally carried on in the columns of the *United States Telegraph*, were reprinted in the *Boston Patriot* and the *Boston Daily Advertiser* on this day. The controversy between the two members of the Cabinet, now resigned, began with John H. Eaton's allegations of slurs upon Mrs. Eaton (the former Peggy O'Neale) by Samuel D. Ingham and concluded with a slur upon Mrs. Ingham by Eaton and Ingham's avowal that he had been waylaid and threatened with assassination. See also entry for 7 Aug., below.

TUESDAY. 28TH.

Morning cloudy, but as I thought it probable that it would not rain, I went to town. Passed my time in bringing up my Accounts for the past Quarter and in reading Monsieur Mirabeau, who discusses the rate of Interest and the importance of Commerce. This has become a part of a leading Science of the present day[1] which has had many Writers and acquired through their means a kind of cant language rather ridiculous than otherwise to those who require that words should distinctly represent ideas. With many authors, this jargon appears fascinating. Certain positions were established by Adam Smith, and those may be considered as solid. All the building upon them that I have seen proceeds from theoretical views and not such as are reduced to the scale of the world's actual condition.

I returned to Quincy to dine. Afternoon, read some spurious Orations, attributed to Sallust and Cicero, which seemed to have been written as studied imitations of the Style of the two Authors, but they are too much alike, and the roundness of Cicero's periods is not preserved. I believe I shall stop for the present, as I do not read with the same accuracy at Quincy as in Boston and as the period for my return is approaching. I continued to file Papers with some success.

The Evening was rainy. I read a part of Timothy Pickering's famous Review of the Cunningham Correspondence. It is the essence of Wormwood. But it failed of it's effect. My Grandfather was honoured as few men have been at their death, and Col. Pickering lived to see it, in the Presidency of my Father.[2] Afterwards I read Grimm and the Spectator.

[1] A reference to "political economy." JQA comments in a similar vein in his Diary (1 July).

[2] On *A Review of the Correspondence between the Hon. John Adams and the Late William Cunningham, Esq.*, a pam-

phlet by Timothy Pickering published at Salem in 1824, see vol. 1:146. The publication, both of the *Correspondence* in 1823 and of the *Review*, was in part the expression of old animosities and in part intended to damage JQA in the Presidential election. A copy of the *Review* is in MQA.

WEDNESDAY. 29TH.

Morning sultry with heavy clouds, which fell in rain before I reached town. At the Office as usual occupied in closing my Quarterly Accounts. Paid some debts on my own and on account of the Estate of R. New, and passed the balance of the time, in finishing l'Ami des Hommes, and a short Essay to improve the Common lands in France. I have not felt much interested in these. Nothing occurred and I returned as usual.

Afternoon passed in assorting Papers. My spirits have of late experienced a slight depression from a view of my present situation. Circumstances connected with my father's affairs render it desirable for me to become as soon as possible independent of him,[1] and in looking round to consider where my means are, I can see none. The circumstances of the last year in which I have made a trial for distinction, discourage my efforts. There appears no opportunity to gain any standing and if there did, I have great doubts whether I could make any thing of it. The confidence which I had for no imaginable reason I now lose for the same. Yet in considering my present situation, how thankful ought I to be for the innumerable blessings that have been showered upon me. And I am thankful to God every day of my life. My anxiety arises only from a knowledge of my *duties*, of my situation, and of the heavy responsibilities I am under to my race[2] and to my Country. Read Pickering's review and in the evening, Grimm. His infidelity becomes more and more disgusting. The Spectator afterwards. Mrs. and Miss Adams spent the evening here.

[1] Whether aware or not that the proceeds of the loan JQA recently made were to be used to retire an earlier loan and did not increase his liabilities, CFA was made apprehensive by JQA's pledging of insurance shares from his investment reserves as collateral. See the next entry.

[2] That is, *family*.

THURSDAY. 30TH.

Morning cloudy but it afterwards cleared away very sultry, notwithstanding a change of wind. I had doubts about going to town but finally concluded upon it and reached it unusually early. Occupied an hour in performing commissions, and then busy in drawing up my Accounts to settlement for the Quarter. They present an unusual amount, but a poorer view of present prospects than any I have ever drawn up. I am endeavouring to familiarize my mind to the probable loss of all of my father's Property. I see no reason why this should not take place, so long as my brother is engaged in a floating business, of which he is not entirely capable. This opinion I am aware is peculiar to me in our family but I have formed it from the experience of years. He has all his life made a great deal of noise about his success, and I never yet knew one of his transactions, which would bear a probe. Notions pervade the whole.[1]

Returned home to dinner and passed the Afternoon in assorting Papers as usual, excepting half an hour devoted to Horace's Art of Poetry. Evening. Finished Pickering's Review. A compound of evil passions, gathering force in the bitterness of years. It was expected to have demolished my Grandfather. And it's author saw him exalted. Read over the Cunningham Letters. Grimm and the Spectator.

[1] CFA maintained an at least partially erroneous view that the family's current business difficulties in Washington were chargeable to JA2's mismanagement and speculative bent. The heavy indebtedness, amounting at this time to $15,000, and the recent losses sustained were incurred as a result of JQA's purchases of flour in the winter and early spring of 1831 partly to provide supplies for sale in the cold months during which the mill could not operate and partly as a speculation against the rising prices which JQA foresaw as an accompaniment to the European war he felt impended. When the war crisis passed, flour prices in Liverpool and London dropped sharply. JQA, Diary, 27 Jan.–21 June *passim*; JQA to JA2, 14, 26 June, 16 July (Adams Papers).

FRIDAY. JULY 1ST.

Here we are in the month of July. A considerable portion of the Summer gone and I have done nothing worthy to be recorded. The days are passing over me without my heeding, and not a mark in their course to look back upon with pleasure or exultation.

The Clouds were low and threatened rain. I went to town notwithstanding as it was Quarter day. At the Office, Mr. Conant from Weston came here and gave me Edward Derby's Note which I got cashed by Mr. Fiske almost immediately.[1] I paid several demands, and copied my Account for my Father. Some Commissions were also to be performed for the family at Quincy so that on the whole I had no spare time. Returned to Quincy.

After dinner my Uncle the Judge came in to do business with me. He seemed depressed and sick. One of his Actions was unaccountable. After explaining to me the nature of a transfer of two shares of Atlas Stock to his Son Thomas, all of which I knew before, just as he was going away, he put into my hand a seal and a gold medal with a request that I would take care of them, while I was here, for he did not know what might happen to him. After reflecting upon matters, I conclude that he means to intimate his fears of an attachment of his Property.

The Afternoon was wasted. I filed very few Papers. My Mother and Wife being invited to take tea at Mrs. Adams' to see her daughter Mrs. Angier, I walked up also, and spent a stupid evening. Mr. Marston and Miss Smith there besides the family.[2] My father appeared extremely depressed also.[3] Evening, Grimm and the Spectator.

[1] See above, entry for 2 June.

[2] The names of Louisa C. Smith and John Marston are coupled in this way on other occasions; the significance is not clear. She never married; he was the father of a family.

[3] Dissatisfaction with his forthcoming 4th of July oration, a facial swelling which threatened to make his appearance on that occasion impossible, and a discontent with his current inactivity were the immediate causes of JQA's depressed spirits (JQA, Diary, 1 July and the "day" entry at the end of his entries for June).

SATURDAY. 2D.

Morning clear. I went to Boston as usual and was occupied the greater part of the time in Accounts. Not having any book to read at the Office I must also accuse myself of negligence and Idleness. A thing I am compelled to do much more often than I could wish. Nothing of any consequence took place.

Returned to Quincy to dinner, and in the afternoon I was taken up in reading and assorting more of my Grandfather's Papers. I now confine myself to the expectation of completing the Papers previous to 1790—A Task in itself not trifling.

I went to the Bath in the afternoon with I. Hull and Joseph Adams, which took up an hour. There had been little or no rain here when I had been caught on the road in a most violent shower. These rains have all been very partial in their character, but quite heavy where they have fallen.

A quiet evening at home. I read a good deal of the Cunningham Correspondence, and of the causes of Pickering's anger, which go to show me very strongly how malignant and how unjust he was. My father seemed a little depressed by a swelling of his face. I finished Grimm's fourth volume and two numbers of the Spectator.

SUNDAY. 3D.

The Weather is becoming as warm again as it was a fortnight ago. I attended divine service all day and heard Mr. Whitney preach two Sermons neither of which made me particularly attentive. This I con-

sider such a misfortune that on my return to Boston I propose to correct it, and the only way I can think will be to carry a Bible with me,
and consult the passage cited comparing it with the Commentary.

I read a few of my Grandfathers Papers and the play of the Siege of
Calais by de Belloi,[1] in consequence of Grimm's criticism. I find it in
some respects just but very harsh—The play having more merit in it
than I expected, and many of the lines being particularly striking. But
such are the merits of Critics. Afternoon I took a Bath with my father,
and found it extremely refreshing. Mr. and Mrs. Angier called. She is
silly from affectation. Quiet evening. The Cunningham Correspondence and the Spectator.

[1] P. L. B. de Belloy, *Le siège de Calais*, Paris, 1765; a tragedy.

MONDAY 4TH.

This is the National Anniversary. And preparations had been made
to celebrate it with effect. As my father was to deliver the Oration, I
thought I would hear him for the purpose of forming a Judgment
upon the character of his Oratory. To do this, I felt as if I should make
sure of a good seat only by going through all the Ceremonies. Isaac
Hull and I therefore went up a little before nine and endured all the
excruciating heat of the sun, effect of the dust, procession &ca. for
three hours, until we reached the Meeting house, thus paying pretty
dearly for our privilege. The Oration was an hour and twenty five
minutes.[1] The manner was as I expected, perhaps a little better though
with a little of the defect I anticipated. His manner is adherence to
nature which in my estimation is superior to E. Everetts studied Style.
It is difficult to fancy to one's self how far the power of words may be
carried. Perhaps no more striking contrast would readily present itself
than that of the reading of the Declaration of Independence by Mr.
Potter, commonly called a good reader,[2] and that of passages of the
same by My father in the course of the Address. The *matter* was very
good but I fear for him lest in his age it should bring upon him the
War of words to which through all his life he has been accustomed.[3]
It is the character of my Father vehemently to attack. He does it
through all his writings more or less, and attack in every community
creates defence; Controversy rises, from which issue anger, and ill
blood. All this is not to my taste and therefore I presume I must be set
down as preferring insignificance and inglorious ease.

I attended the Dinner[4] and suffered three hours of excessive heat
without any thing to pay me for it, excepting a beautiful tribute to the

memory of my Grandfather here in his native town, which affected me even to tears.[5] *That* is worth having. Removed from all the stormy passions he sleeps in his last mansion, yet the spontaneous effusion of grateful hearts rises up to cheer and invigorate his drooping descendants. Left the Table at five entirely exhausted, and sought relief in a Salt water Bath.

Occasional visits during the whole evening. We all went to a little party at Mr. Quincy's which was pleasant enough. There was an uncommon display of Aurora Borealis this evening extending from the North West to the East over full one third of the Horizon. The rays of light shot up to the zenith changing their position and intenseness perpetually. I was so fatigued I could not look at it as much as I wished. Read the Spectator as usual.

[1] JQA began to work upon the oration, the third he had delivered on the nation's anniversary, while he was yet in doubt that, because of the current bitter division over Freemasonry, the invitation for him to speak in the Adams Temple would be ratified (JQA, Diary, 7 and 9 June). Having finished and discarded a first draft, he completed the draft of a wholly new speech on the 24th and thereafter attempted to reduce the text to no more than an hour in the delivery. He made further revision until the day before, and in the end omitted a third of what he had written (same, 29 June – 4 July). The MS of the oration, which was later published, is in the Adams Papers.

[2] William T. Potter, minister of the Episcopal church in Quincy (JQA, Diary, 4 July; *Mass. Register*, 1831).

[3] In the main, the theme of the address was an attack upon the South Carolina doctrine of nullification.

[4] At the town hall (JQA, Diary).

[5] The authorship of this tribute and its content are not known.

TUESDAY 5TH.

Morning bright with the Sun in great force relieved however in the Country by a free circulation of Air. I went to town and to the Office. Thence to the House and afterwards performing Commissions, for my Wife and others of the family. I was also occupied in my Accounts which at this period always take up some of my time. Mr. Clough called and settled with me for an execution in favour of I. Farrar,[1] and I drew afterwards my Atlas Ins. Dividend together with that belonging to the Adamses. In these various ways my time was taken up until the moment for my return.

Found my Wife not very well today, owing to the fatigue and overexcitement of yesterday and I experienced myself a languid feeling not altogether agreeable. Afternoon passed in carelessly arranging Papers. This work has been so little seconded by my Father that it is likely to turn out a grand failure. I shall leave most of the Papers in greater confusion than when I began.

Took a Bath at the Wharf with my Father and I. Hull, and from thence went to the Judge's to pay Miss Eliz. her Quarter's Interest. I was not however lucky enough to find her at home. Returned finding my Walk almost fruitless. The rest of the evening was passed quietly at home. Finished the Cunningham Correspondence and the Biography of my father [2] together with two numbers of the Spectator.

[1] See above, entry for 11 April.

[2] Despite the ambiguity of its wording, this is probably a reference to the fragmentary life of JA which JQA had begun in 1829 (see vol. 3:257) and to which he returned on 26 May with the hope that he would "no more neglect it," only to record on 7 June, "I make no progress in my father's biography" (JQA, Diary).

WEDNESDAY. 6TH.

The morning was cloudy with a warm wind from the South west which terminated in a steady rain for the day. I went to town and was occupied in making up my deficient Diary and in visiting my House for the purpose of seeing the state of my Fire place. Found it bad enough—The House being hardly a fair risk for Insurance. It seems that they cut the Fire place for my Study after building the Chimney and to give it breadth, took off a portion of the Kitchen flue without filling in with Mortar. The consequence was great danger of fire in case the Kitchen Chimney had caught. I am glad I have remedied this. Made a visit to Mrs. Sidney Brooks at her Mother's. Found her well and quite lively. Mr. R. D. Shepherd was there. Returned only in time to start as usual.

Afternoon passed in my usual way, of filing old Letters. We had expected Mr. and Mrs. Frothingham today, but the weather prevented. Evening, the Spectator.

THURSDAY. 7TH.

My father accompanied me to town this morning and consequently made me somewhat later than usual. I went to the Office and passed the time much in my usual way. Writing up my Journal and Accounts. News arrived this morning of the death of Mr. Monroe. Another coincidence as it happened on the fourth of July. He was a worthy man, and his career on the whole a creditable one, but he was not perhaps entitled by nature or education to the distinction which his fortune gave him of being elected to the Presidency by a nearly unanimous vote. A thing that will not soon occur again. His later hours have been extremely painful to himself. Poverty and debt hung like a weight about his neck and these finally put an end to his course. He was not old comparatively speaking. For my Grandfather was ninety one, and Mr. Jefferson eighty four. He was seventy two. The Country has finally faced his debts, so that perhaps he does not die insolvent.[1]

My father returned from the Meeting of the Overseers of the College earlier than I had anticipated so that we were enabled to leave town at my usual time. The afternoon was spent as usual by me in assorting my Grandfather's Papers and in replacing those which I find no time to arrange. I have done little in the time passed here, but that little is more than was called for. I read in the afternoon and evening a portion of the North American Review for July. The Number is generally good although I am a dissenter in many instances from the opinions expressed in it. Not having been able to obtain a new volume of the Spectator today, I read but one Number this evening.

[1] The death of ex-President James Monroe was the occasion of widespread retrospective comment not unlike that by CFA. JQA, invited by the City of Boston to deliver a memorial address, was so absorbed by a consideration of the life of one of the last figures of importance whose public career had spanned the whole of the nation's history that the task of condensation became impossible. See entries for 16 and 25 Aug., below.

FRIDAY. 8TH.

Morning cloudy and unpleasant. I concluded not to go to Boston this morning. My time was taken up in arranging the few Papers left belonging to the period previous to 1790 and returning the balance. Very few interesting ones in comparison with the great mass. I also read a large portion of Hurd's Commentary upon Horace's Art of Poetry. It exemplifies the art of book-making. For Horace needs nothing but a reflecting mind to relish all his beauties. It matters little to that whether it is a regular Essay, or a disconnected series of maxims.

Judge Adams and his daughter Elizabeth dined here today. The latter seemed well, and I took the opportunity to pay her, her money. The former is irretrievably dull. I walked to Mount Wollaston to look at the condition of the Orchard down there. Found it doing nicely. The trees generally look healthy though the cold weather of last Winter killed the extremities of many of them. I took off from two of them a collection of Eggs from some Insect which I did not know. It had been formed round the small limbs of the Trees, and strongly protected by a thick, black gummy substance, so as to resist considerable pressure. If I had intended to remain out here I should have pursued the investigation, but as it is, they were better away from all harm to the Trees.

Evening quiet at home. I read Mr. Everett's Article upon the State of Europe. Tolerably bold, and containing many radical principles which I cannot swallow.[1] I did not read the Spectator tonight.

[1] Edward Everett's article, "The Prospect of Reform in Europe" (*North Amer. Rev.*, 33:154–190 [July 1831]), was openly sympathetic to the democratic as opposed to the aristocratic forces in their current confrontation.

SATURDAY. 9TH.

Morning cloudy, I went to town as usual, and was engaged in performing Commissions a considerable part of the day. Also in conversation with Mr. Peabody upon matters and things in general. I went to see the exhibition of the Horticultural Society with him. Found some fine specimens of Flowers, and some very large gooseberries which are a great rarity here.[1] I then drew some Dividends and attended a Stock sale without being able to purchase any thing.

Returned to Quincy with the wind blowing a gale to the imminent danger of my hat and as I sometimes thought of my Gig. Miss E. C. Adams and Miss Harrod[2] dined with us. The afternoon passed in my regular occupations. But from some reason or other my health cannot be so good as it was, for I cannot bear for any length of time, arranging Papers. Continued Mr. Hurd's Commentary, the North American Review, and read two or three remarkable trials in the Newgate Calendar.[3] Evening, Grimm and made up my deficiency in the Spectator.

[1] In the absence of any notice of the exhibition in the newspapers, the probability is that it was a show for members. The Society's rooms were in Joy's Building, Cornhill (formerly Market Street). *Boston Patriot*, 13 May, p. 2, col. 4.

[2] Susan D. Harrod, ECA's cousin; see vol. 1:162, 2:166.

[3] Andrew Knapp and William Baldwin, *The Newgate Calendar*. . . . In the edition (4 vols., London, 1825–1826) at MQA with JQA's bookplate, vol. 1 is lacking.

SUNDAY. 10TH.

It rained very heavily during the Night, clearing off this morning with a North West Wind and absolutely cool. I attended divine Service all day and heard Mr. Whitney preach. His morning Sermon upon the necessity of redeeming time. A valuable text, and full of moral to all.[1] I feel the weight of it every day I live. The afternoon I do not particularly recollect. Feeling myself in many respects deficient in a due knowledge of the Scriptures and in attention at Church I propose to set upon a course after my return to town which shall fix me in a useful habit on Sunday. At present my Church going is rather useless. I read in the afternoon a good deal of Grimm and see more and more of his infamous infidelity. This was the cry of Reform in those days. Seeing so much of Diderot in these Memoirs I felt curious to know something of him and accordingly read the Article with that Title in the Dictionnaire Historique. I do not consider him entitled to one half the merits he seems to have thought his. Yet he did much in building up the useful heads of the Encyclopedie, though he is also responsible for it's great crimes. Evening, continued Grimm and the Spectator.

¹ Thus in MS.

MONDAY. 11TH.

The Wind was in the North and East all day, and made it so cold, I was absolutely shivering all the time my ride into town lasted. Arrived unusually early and went to the Office. Occupied by Commissions. Mr. Ayer called by appointment and I went with him to my House for the purpose of directing him about some draws, my Wife wants put in. Returned and engaged in Accounts. Time slips away without my knowing how to account for it. I made up some Arrears in my Diary which takes up a great deal of space now. It is a great question with me whether my time is suitably paid.

Went out of town, and found at dinner Mr. and Mrs. T. B. Adams, Miss E. C. Adams, Miss Harrod and Miss Smith—It being the anniversary of my fathers birth. He is now Sixty four and enjoying his powers with as much vigour as ever. Nothing material took place. He went in the afternoon to town to hear Mr. Fuller's Antimasonic Oration.¹ Mr. James H. Foster and his family came out and passed part of the Afternoon after whom came several other visitors. I did little or nothing. Read an article or two in the North American Review, and in the evening, read Grimm and the Spectator.

¹ JQA took yet another step towards public identification with Antimasonry in allowing himself to be seated on the dais in Faneuil Hall at the right hand of the orator, Timothy Fuller (JQA, Diary, 11 July).

TUESDAY. 12TH.

The morning was clear and cool, though warmer than yesterday. I went to town as usual. On looking over the Newspaper I noticed the death of Mr. T. Welsh. I do not know when I have been more shocked. The notice came so suddenly and I had seen him within a few days in the enjoyment of such full health, that I could hardly believe it real. I sent to ascertain the nature of the case and found it was something like Apoplexy, which on the whole nobody could be surprised at. Yet such things come like a thunder clap from a clear sky, as if to warn us of another world. I decided to remain in town and attend the

Funeral.[1] My time was occupied in writing my Diary. Mr. S. Brown called about some Mercantile Marine Insurance Shares which I purchased at 24 per Cent advance. They are for my Father and T. B. Adams Jr.[2] The advance looks large, but they have in addition to the ordinary profits of their business added fifty thousand dollars to their Capital, and they make regular semi-annual Dividends of five per Cent, which I think makes the Stock worth it. At any rate, it is a present investment and if my father should say a word in disapprobation of the price, I have had the shares put in my name so that I will advance their price and take them myself. I read today in the Bibliotheque d'un Homme public, a fancy called, La République des Philosophes ou Histoire des Ajaoiens, attributed to Fontenelle.[3] An amusing chateau en Espagne.

Dined at Mrs. Frothingham's quietly and comfortably, and sent a message out by them as they were about visiting the family at Quincy, not to be alarmed. At four I attended the Funeral. Found there a considerable number of persons, members of his immediate Circle and of the Bar, though but two blood relations. But a few months since I followed to the same spot his father. Thus it is that families vanish from the face of the earth. There are few men in Boston I shall miss more than this. Almost daily I saw him in his Office or in the Street and he had been more friendly to me than was customary with him to any body. I could not help feeling melancholy upon it. Returned to Quincy immediately and passed the remainder of the day and evening quietly. Mrs. and Miss Whitney called to see the Ladies. Read Grimm and the Spectator.

[1] Thomas Welsh Jr. had died on the day before (*Boston Daily Advertiser*, 12 July, p. 2, col. 3). On hearing of his death at CFA's return, JQA recounted for himself the events of Welsh's life in some detail (Diary, 12 July).

[2] CFA purchased three shares for JQA's account and two for Thomas B. Adams Jr.'s at a price of $124 per share (M/CFA/3).

[3] The work appears in vol. 9.

WEDNESDAY. 13TH.

Morning clear and pleasant. I went to the Office after riding into town as customary. My time was taken up in the ordinary way, writing my Diary, and in reading a portion of Puffendorf as abridged in the Bibliotheque d' un Homme Public.[1] But I felt disposed to conversation so I went to make a visit to my old acquaintance T. Davis. Found him alone and had quite a pleasant discourse of an hour and a half. So that I left myself little time remaining. Called to see Mr. Brooks but found him engaged so that I returned directly from town.

Afternoon quietly at home although I must plead guilty to doing very little. My present unsettled state here is the cause of this, and as usual I am forming great plans of study for my return which may or may not be accomplished as it pleases God. One thing however is certain, that only at home can I pursue any thing with that thoroughness which alone gives me any kind of satisfaction. My Wife was not very well all day. I returned to their places my Grandfathers papers, and read in a very desultory manner from several books. Evening, the family went up to the Judge's to take Tea and I to pass an hour. Returned with my father but he was very silent. Read Grimm and the Spectator.

[1] The abridgement of "Le droit de la nature et des gens" appears in vol. 10.

THURSDAY. 14TH.

The morning opened heavily, and it soon began to rain, which lasted all day. I remained at home very quietly and passed the greater part of my before dinner hours in a continuation of my yesterday's occupation. In returning home, I wish to enrich my library in Boston with as many of the Works of which there are duplicates here, as I am able. They are convenient for reference and occasional reading when I know not what to do with myself. There are hours when a man requires a power of extensive selection, when he is tired with steady reading and looks for his pleasure to short and easy Essays or broken pieces of literature. O, the desire of knowledge, the power of enriching the mind with all that others in times gone by have thought, what a fund of rich enjoyment they present to Man. What a source of innocent and profitable delight. Afternoon, read Phedre of Racine, Act 1st and admired it, though to be sure a double Love plot seems foolish. Read Grimm finishing the 5th. volume, and the Spectator.

FRIDAY. 15TH.

Fine morning. I rode to town as usual and passed my morning partly at the House making a new arrangement of my Library, partly at trying to obtain some new Furniture for our return, and the rest at my Office reading Mr. W. F. Otis Oration, which has just come out. The spirit of its principles is rather wild for a very wild age. What he can think will be the use of his advice passes my utmost comprehension.[1] I could not finish it today. Returned home to dine.

Afternoon, I was tempted by the heat to go and take a bath with I. Hull, which lasted longer and tired me more than usual so that I took a Nap after it. The consequence was that I did very little during the afternoon. Finished Racine's Phedre the poetry of which strikes me much. I had formed much too low an idea of the character of the French drama, from reading only some of the most indifferent of their best authors, always excepting Voltaire who made some alterations and is hardly classed with the old School. Evening with the Family. I afterwards read Grimm and the Spectator.

[1] As a part of the Independence Day celebration in Boston William Foster Otis, Harvard 1821, delivered an oration in the First Church, Chauncy Place (*Boston Daily Advertiser*, 6 July, p. 2, col. 1). It was published in pamphlet form as *An Oration ... before the Young Men of Boston, on the Fourth of July 1831*, Boston, 1831. In substance it was an appeal that precedents and subservience to old institutions not be allowed to deter the country from experimentation and the development of new forms.

SATURDAY. 16TH.

Went to Boston as usual this morning, excepting that I was accompanied by I. Hull. The weather was pleasant but cloudy, which afterwards came in very refreshing showers. My morning was occupied much in my common way. Giving orders for Furniture, and afterwards in reading Mr. W. F. Otis's Address which I have some idea of criticizing. I wrote a little in the way of commencement. Mr. Dunlap called upon me about the Office downstairs, and finally decided to take it at a Rent rather higher than Mr. Welsh had it for the last Quarter.[1] The truth is, it is worth more. Miss Oliver called to pay her Rent for the last Quarter. She was detained in a shower and detained me. I returned however with Hull shortly after one, and after taking one or two heavy rains without inconvenience, we arrived. Found Dr. Waterhouse here spending the day. He looks to me older, more infirm and more dull than I have seen him. He had not so much sprightliness as common.[2] I spent the afternoon doing little or nothing. This waste of time galls me. Evening at home, read Grimm and the Spectator.

[1] *Lower* was apparently intended. In the Agency's books the rental of the office for the two quarters following Welsh's death was $22.50 each quarter, replacing the $31.25 quarterly rental that Welsh had long paid (M/CFA/3).

[2] Dr. Benjamin Waterhouse (1754–1846) is identified at vol. 2:165. The subjects of the conversation of the two old friends included Dr. Waterhouse's book on the identity of Junius; a biography of Gilbert Stuart and a descriptive book on Rhode Island, both of which he intended to write; and JQA's proposal, strongly advanced, that Waterhouse write a book on the controversy relating to his professorship at Harvard College (JQA, Diary, 16 July).

SUNDAY. 17TH.

Fine morning, with occasional clouds, which only served to keep off the great heat of the Sun. I attended divine Service all day, and heard

Mr. Whitney of Hingham preach. His morning Sermon was upon Content with small gains, preferably to wealth unfairly acquired. It was very far above the general tone of his Sermons and really exceedingly sensible. His manner of delivery is very bad and his appearance far from favorable, but he is more of a Preacher than I took him to be. He dined with us, and did not support in the tenor of his conversation any opinion which his morning's Sermon might create. The afternoon's discourse was not so interesting. I finished Hurd's Commentary upon the Art of Poetry and Francis' Translation today.[1] The first is good but I am afraid a little fanciful. The latter seems very spirited.

In the evening, my father and I went down to pay a visit to the Quincys. Found them at home and enjoyed the visit. There is something pleasant after all in going to see educated people. The style of conversation is better, and the sense that your mind is not wholly unemployed makes the time appear spent not altogether without profit. Returned to read Grimm and the Spectator.

[1] There are two editions at MQA, both owned by JQA, of *A Poetical Translation of the Works of Horace . . . by Rev. Philip Francis* in 4 vols. published at London: one of 1747, the other of 1778. The "Art of Poetry" is in the 4th volume.

MONDAY. 18TH.

The day was rather cloudy, occasionally threatening rain. I went to town as usual, overtaking Mr. G. Dawes. I invited him to accompany me. I was once very well acquainted with one of his brothers, and now look back upon the time with wonder at the changes which the world has produced.[1] He seems to be one of the do nothings of this world, of which there are so many. Without industry and without resources, and his mind is limited almost to the circle of the senses. I went to the Office and was busy in my worldly affairs. Mr. Geitner called and paid me rent. I wrote Journal, went to the Athenæum to get a book for my father, and passed the remaining time in writing my criticism of Mr. Otis. I shall not find time to publish it as soon as I ought. Left town at the regular hour.

Miss Elizabeth Adams dined with us. I wasted the Afternoon in putting back Papers, and in reading the North American Review. Mr. Ballister called upon me. He is one of the Consignees of John's Flour in Boston. His request was for Instructions, as much of it was spoiling upon his hands.[2] I told him I would report to my Father. In doing so, I took occasion to express my own opinions upon the expediency of his continuing the business. I did it in a firm but temperate way expressing as far as possible my own want of individual interest in the course I was pursuing. He seemed indisposed to listen much less to follow,[3] but I have done my duty and wash my hands of the consequences. That the result would be ruin to my Father I have foreseen all along and have been trying to shelter myself as much as possible from the Storm but it comes more rapidly than I had anticipated.[4]

This is the last day of our visit to Quincy. In the evening I accompanied my Father in a visit to Mr. T. Greenleaf's which I felt that I owed. Nothing new. Returned home. Read Grimm and the Spectator.

[1] On CFA's early friendship with Horace Dawes, a brother of George Dawes, see vol. 1:1, 395; 2:301.

[2] To McLellan, Ballister & Co. and Rice & Thaxter, both of Boston, along with Charles J. Cazenove & Co. (above, entry for 12 May), JA2 had sent shipments of flour and had drawn on each against sales from the consignment. Apparently a minimum price had been fixed at which the flour could be sold. The intent had been to hold until winter when it was hoped the price would rise. The consignees, because of actual and anticipated spoilage during the hot weather, and in the face of continually declining prices, pressed for sale. JQA, convinced finally that there was small likelihood of a substantial rise in the market in the immediate months ahead, authorized each of the consignees, over the next several weeks, to sell at the best price obtainable. (JQA to McLellan, Ballister & Co., 28 July, 16 Aug.; to Charles J. Cazenove & Co. and to Rice & Thaxter, 15 Aug. [LbC's]; also JQA to JA2, 13 Aug. [all in Adams Papers].)

[3] JQA would seem to have been more impressed by CFA's words than was apparent: "Charles brought me also a message from Mr. Ballister, which gave me cause enough for Meditation, and he gave me advice, which ought by me to be pondered still more" (JQA, Diary, 18 July).

[4] JQA proposed to provide himself with a substantial sum in cash by September and had apparently made this known to CFA. Perhaps not explained to CFA was JQA's intent to use these funds to retire the remaining notes which he and JA2 had signed jointly in Washington, thereby relieving JA2 of any liability for debts which JQA felt had been contracted at his own instance. To raise the sum needed, JQA saw two possibilities, both ominous: the pledging of additional securities as collateral for a new loan he would make in Boston, or the sale of real estate he owned in Washington. (JQA to JA2, 26 June, 16 July, 13 Aug., Adams Papers; and see also entries for 29 and 30 June, above.)

Boston

TUESDAY. 19TH.

I left Quincy this morning, for the Season. The period passed here is exactly two Months, and on the whole more pleasantly spent than I had anticipated. The house has been more quiet, my Mother has enjoyed uninterrupted health and we have been extraordinarily free from trouble. My father has appeared to droop however, to feel oppressed by a kind of languor which for him is remarkable, and to take little interest in pursuits which one would have supposed, he might have enjoyed. I have been so unfortunate as to differ from him in several matters, and the consequence has been rather to increase than allay the evils of his condition. Under these circumstances perhaps it is as well that I do not remain. I regret exceedingly the dejection which he feels, and I experience the same myself, from other causes however. My reason is this, that I foresee ruin to the pecuniary affairs of the whole family and great consequent misery to his old age.

My time was occupied at my Office as usual. I wrote the first Number of a Criticism upon Otis's Oration and attended to my Accounts. Dined at an Eating house as my Wife did not come until Evening. Afternoon passed at my study, arranging my Books, and commencing upon my task of reading the Epistles of Cicero. Began the first Book ad Familiares and read several of the Letters to Lentulus. Being in the broken style, leaving much to be supplied, I found it hard. My Wife came home to tea, and my Mother accompanied her returning in the evening. The former was so much depressed that it also affected me. Read Grimm and the Spectator.

WEDNESDAY. 20TH.

My night was not a quiet one. Morning clear, I arose at my usual City hour. After breakfast began a new branch of Study, Aristotle upon Poetical Composition.[1] One would suppose I was a Poet from my studies but Nature gave me no flights. It endowed me with a tolerably strait forward sense and middling Judgment which is perhaps more than a counterbalance so far as regards the practical affairs of life. I read Aristotle and Horace to form a *critical* Judgment, and to apply much of their rules to prose composition, for which they answer equally well. Felt languid and unwell so that my exertions during a considerable part of the morning were lame. I finished a re-composition of my first number against Otis and wrote my Father a letter.[2] Mr. Ballister called upon me with a short statement of his Account with my brother, which I inclosed to my Father with an explanation. Mr. Curtis came to ask me to mention an intended visit from himself and Mrs. Boylston on Friday morning. Judge Hall called for general conversation. Nothing was therefore lost of the time, that I could save. But these interruptions from people about my *father's* concerns is something of a tax.

Returned to dinner. Afternoon, continued the Letters to Lentulus. There are some pleasures in living in town, but the situation of my Wife at present renders me anxious, and I take less interest in my books. Evening, Mrs. Frothingham called. Read Grimm and the Spectator.

[1] Although there are three editions at MQA of Aristotle's *Poetics* published as a separate work, including one in Greek and Latin (Leipzig, 1780) with CFA's

bookplate, apparently CFA was reading
the text in Batteaux's *Les quatres poë-*

THURSDAY. 21ST.

Fine morning but warm. Read for an hour Aristotle's Poetics, which
is a kind of original fountain supplying the ideas of the whole world
upon a certain subject. To be such an Author is worth while. But the
days are gone. Men spread their ideas more widely and less to the
purpose. At the Office. Engaged nearly all my time in writing a second
Number of my remarks upon Otis's Oration. My father's man Kirk
called to let me know my father was in town, but owing to the length
of his engagement and my going to the Athenæum as well as for a few
other things I did not see him.

Returned home and in the Afternoon read as usual a portion of the
Letters to Lentulus. Among others a famous long one in which he endeavours to justify his reconciliation with the Triumvirate, and his
defence of Vatinius. I detest the moral of this Letter. I believe it is all
sophistry from beginning to end, and though done with great ability
and ingenuity, it deserves no Quarter from a moral man.

Evening at home with my Wife. We had a slight shower. Sidney
Brooks and his Wife came in late and passed an hour. They had just
come from Nahant and are going back tomorrow. I read some of
Grimm whose constant snarling I am tired of, and the Spectator.

FRIDAY. 22D.

Morning fine and clear. I pursued my study of Aristotle's Poetics
for an hour, and find it on the whole more simple than I expected.
The Essay however seems to be guided not so much by any principle
founded in nature as by experience of what has been successful with
Men. Thus the Works of Homer and of the early Grecian Tragic
Poets are the sum of his lessons. Perhaps this is looking at the subject
in rather a contracted light. Yet he really deserves the name of a great
genius who can succeed in a new line.

Went to the Office and was occupied during the morning in writing.
Mr. J. T. Adams called upon me about my Article. I found myself
anticipated by a severe Pamphlet so that I shall discontinue my intended criticism.[1] Read a little of Puffendorf as abridged in the
Bibliotheque de l'homme public.

At one o'clock I returned home for the purpose of going with my
Wife to Medford. We reached there quite late to dinner. Found Mr.

Brooks, P. C. Jr. and his Wife and Miss Phillips. Passed the Afternoon doing nothing. Mr. G. W. Pratt and his Lady paid a visit. On the whole the day went pleasantly, and we returned safe and sound calling on our way upon Mrs. Angier. I read Grimm to the end of the first part of the Work, (I believe I shall not take up the second) and the Spectator. Read this evening another Letter about that business of Farmer's.[2]

[1] When CFA completed his first letter in answer to W. F. Otis' position, seemingly he sent it for publication to Joseph T. Adams, editor of the *Columbian Centinel*, and intended following it with a second. Apparently neither number saw publication although it is possible that the *Centinel's* own mildly critical review of the *Oration* (23 July, p. 1, cols. 1–2) reflected something of CFA's stance. Immediately following the *Cen-tinel's* review was a notice of the anonymous attack upon the oration, published as *A Review of an Oration.* ... This pamphlet elicited a defence signed "Chesterfield" in the *Centinel*, 27 July, p. 2, cols. 2–3, as well as another pamphlet by Otis, *The Reviewer Reviewed, A Defence of an Oration* ... , Boston, 1831.

[2] The letter has not been identified.

SATURDAY. 23D.

Morning fine but very warm. I passed an hour or more in examining the Poetic of Aristotle and comparing it with Pye's Commentary which I have obtained from the Library of the Athenæum.[1] Then to the Office where I was busy in finishing the Analysis of Puffendorf. I cannot say that I have read this with the attention it deserves.

At my Office with frequent interruptions and without the habits of thinking which seem to me to belong only to a Library, I can do infinitely less than I ought. I had no interruptions of any consequence however, and on the whole executed more than for some time past. Finished and copied a Letter to John in answer to his inquiry about the Oregon Settlement.[2] I seized the opportunity to express to him my deliberate opinion upon the matter of the Flour business and to shake off all responsibility from myself as to the probable consequences arising from the pursuit. I am sorry for John but I am satisfied that neither he nor my father are equal to the task. Returned home, a little shower fell and it was windy.

Afternoon, read over the long Letter to Lentulus, of the character of which I am more and more satisfied, and several to Curio which are very good. This Curio was a good for nothing fellow, and the immediate cause of the civil War. Yet Cicero threw away upon him abundance of the best advice. Evening, my Wife went to see her Sister. I walked until nine. Read a part of Pye's Commentary on Aristotle and the Spectator.

[1] Henry James Pye, *A Commentary Illustrating the Poetic of Aristotle; with a New Translation*, London, 1792.

[2] JA2's letter is missing. CFA's response to the request for information about a scheme, apparently centering in Boston, for encouraging settlement in Oregon noted that the manager of the scheme, Hall Jackson Kelley, was of doubtful reputation and that the essence of the scheme seemed to be to form a company of poor persons who would contribute according to their means toward the costs of a trip to New Orleans, then up the Mississippi and Missouri rivers, and thence by land to the point of settlement. CFA to JA2, 22 July (Adams Papers). Although Kelley's American Society for Encouraging the Settlement of the Oregon Territory was soon disbanded and Kelley's own journey to Oregon was a disaster, his efforts to forward migration to Oregon were not without influence in the later successful movement. See the notice of Kelley in *DAB*.

SUNDAY. 24TH.

The morning was very clear with a hot day following it. I passed an hour after breakfast in continuing Aristotle, and a little while reading Viger on the Greek Idioms,[1] a very excellent Book if I may judge of the whole from a part.

Attended divine service all day, and heard in the morning Mr. Emerson, in the afternoon, Mr. Frothingham. I began today my intended practice of examining the Bible from the Texts of the Preachers. Mr. Emerson's Sermon was from 1. Corinthians, Chapt. 2. Verse 14. "But the natural man receiveth not the things of the Spirit of God: for they are foolishness unto him: neither can he know them, because they are spiritually discerned." He drew from this the distinction existing between soul and body. He objected to the prevailing habit of forming opinions from effects produced on the senses, exhorting to a greater cultivation of mind and leading to an increase of faith and hope and trust. He spoke of the custom of judging of all things by the method in which they sensibly affected us, instancing the ideas commonly formed of Heaven. What he said was true, but if man cannot be allowed to reflect upon the future in the way that comes most naturally and indeed in the only way he can realize any idea of advantage, is not there danger that he will cease to think at all, and then be without a stimulus to good conduct? Mr. Emerson should look at the thing practically. The spirit of the Chapter from which his text was taken is the humiliation of man's powers when compared to those coming from the Spirit of God. Inspiration is to be sure the most unfailing guide. But our degeneracy has deprived us of it. And if human wisdom is liable to error, (as it most certainly is), yet it is the most desirable thing we can attain. A distinction however can be drawn between human wisdom, and worldly wisdom. Mr. Frothingham's Sermon was from Matthew 18 Chap. 10 verse: "Take heed that ye despise not one of these little ones; for I say unto you, That in heaven their Angels do always behold the Face of my Father which is in Heaven." This is a lesson of humility to Man. The Saviour frequently inculcates innocence through the medium of these living examples. Their helplessness, their freedom from the passions and consequent sins of manhood and their increased natural good feelings, afford to us, the strongest possible illustration to affect us. The moral is beautiful. Mr. Frothingham however drew only that arising from God's care of Children. I therefore thought the Sermon a failure. Returned home and consumed the afternoon in reading one of Massillon's Sermons which I intend in this way to go through.[2] I began with the Petit Careme. Luke C.2. v:34. This child is set for the fall and rising again of many in Israel. The course were addressed to Louis 15th during his minority, and were designed to give him some advice upon the conduct he should pursue when King. This first is upon the influence of example either as holding out encouragement to virtue, or taking off restraint from vice. As a lesson to a King, it was bold. And the strong dissuasion from War which forms its most eloquent Passage is in singular contrast with the praises bestowed in the close, upon the character of his Grandfather. How little did the whole avail. Louis the 15th was the age of most unbounded private licentiousness instigated by the practice of the Monarch himself.

The day was very warm. In the evening, Dr. and Mrs. Stevenson called to pass half an hour. I was pleased with him as an intelligent and well informed man. They left us and I consumed the remainder of the Evening in reading Mr. Pye's Commentary on Aristotle, many opinions in which do not strike my fancy, and the Spectator.

[1] François Viger, *Greek Idioms ... translated by Rev. J. Seager*, London [1828].
[2] At MQA are two editions owned by JQA of the *Sermons* of Jean Baptiste Massillon: one in 5 vols., Paris, 1748; the other in 13 vols., Paris, 1763–1769.

MONDAY. 25TH.

Morning clear and exceedingly warm. After an hour devoted as usual to the reading of Aristotle, I walked down for the purpose of doing some little Commissions for my Wife and myself. This took up so much time that upon arriving at my Office, I found my Father doing business there with several of his friends. They left soon and so did he to attend a Meeting of the ΦBK Society about their secrets.[1] I was engaged much of my morning in preparing Copies of his Oration to be sent away by the Mail.[2] I also began my Grandfather's principal work, the Defence of the American Constitutions, for the purpose of forming an Independent opinion.[3] Mr. Ballister called upon me about seeing my Father but he did not succeed in finding him.

Returned home and found my Mother with little Louisa come in to spend the day. This young Lady is a great trouble as I cannot treat her with the little ceremony I could with one of my own children. My nerves are not made for these trifling trials. I did not enjoy the visit.[4] In the afternoon, I continued reading Cicero's Letters, to Curio and Cælius. They are good models to learn the science by. My father and Mother went away at about Sunset and after a conversation with Judge Hall and going to the Post Office, I took a little walk with my Wife. Thus passed the time until nine, when I read Aristotle commented upon and the Spectator.

[1] At a meeting of the Harvard Chapter of the Phi Beta Kappa Society on 21 July a committee of nine, JQA being one, was appointed to propose a revision of the charter and laws of the society. Reflecting the desire of a number of members to take a stand consistent with their antimasonic leanings, the Society was bent upon the elimination of secrets. At the first meeting of the committee, JQA moved to repeal all parts of the charter and laws which required the administration of an oath and any promise of secrecy. This motion encountered little opposition, but was not adopted because of the intrusion of an attempt to amend the law governing election by eliminating the requirement of unanimity. The issues were fiercely argued through several sessions. (JQA, Diary, 21, 25 July; 8, 11 Aug. See also *Catalogue of the Harvard Chapter of Phi Beta Kappa*, Cambridge, 1933, p. 152-154.)

[2] JQA received printed copies of his oration on 22 July (JQA, Diary). Extracts began to appear in newspapers in Boston and elsewhere almost at once. See, for example, *Boston Patriot*, 25 July, p. 2, cols. 1-3. The copy at MQA of the pamphlet, *An Oration . . . on the Fourth of July 1831*, Boston, 1831, has in JQA's hand: "Mary Louisa Adams."

[3] A *Defence of the Constitutions of Government of the United States of America*, 3 vols., London, 1787-1788, was the most ambitious literary composition that JA undertook, contained his most comprehensive speculations in political theory, and was among the most controversial of his published works. See vol. 1:314; JA, *Diary and Autobiography*, 3:202. Among the copies in MQA is one of the first edition, presented and inscribed to CFA by JA, 25 Jan. 1819.

[4] Despite his disclaimers, CFA seems to have been much drawn to the two-year-old, Mary Louisa. LCA thought her "a great favorite" of both ABA and CFA and quoted him as saying "she is irresistible in her little ways." Certainly his manner with her provoked enthusiastic response from the child. LCA's frequent reports to Mary Louisa's mother throughout the summer on the child's activities and predilections leave no doubt that she had "a most extraordinary affection for her Uncle Charles"; she mimicked him delightfully and "dearly loves a romp with Charles as she familiarly calls him." LCA to Mrs. JA2, 2 and 21 May, 7 and 27 July, 11 Aug. (all in Adams Papers).

TUESDAY. 26TH.

Morning dark and rainy. I have rarely seen Water fall much faster. My man servant asked leave to go away for some days, much to my surprise and the dis-organization of my family. He has acted singularly since my return. In this Country, one of our greatest troubles is the difficulty about domestics.[1] The Country is too independent to make them very subservient. I have had infinite difficulty with them since my marriage. After reading Aristotle, I went to the Office, and passed a very quiet morning, reading the Defence. There is more merit in it than it has gained credit for. The insight into human nature is very great, and the political views are to me perfectly clear.

Returned home and passed the Afternoon in reading the Epistles to Cælius and various others. The arrangement of these Letters is very poor, and the Chronology is consequently difficult to be preserved. They are written however with great nature and have the merit of showing the behind the Scenes.[2] To be sure Cicero does not show much for the better in his public course by it, but he is only one. The weakness of human nature is the general rule by which he like others must be leniently tried. Evening at home. Mr. and Mrs. E. Everett spent the Evening with us. They seemed both rather dull. I read Aristotle and after it, the Spectator.

[1] ABA and CFA "returned to House-keeping under inauspicious circumstances as it regards their Servants. Benjamin is married to Elizabeth who is dismissed and he remains with them with an old woman from the Country. Bridget turn'd out a Sot and we had the credit of having spoilt them" (LCA to Mrs. JA2, 20 July, Adams Papers).

[2] Thus in MS.

WEDNESDAY. 27TH.

Morning clear but quite cool after the rain of yesterday. I made considerable progress in the Poetic of Aristotle. The Commentators upon all the works of the ancients make a large class by themselves. Many of them have done little but to heap up useless masses of quotation to show their learning. Perhaps of all the follies to which the human mind is subject, none is greater, than the folly of disquisition upon trifling points. To see the fury with which men take sides upon the true reading of a passage supposed to be corrupted, one would suppose that the world was to feel the consequences of a mistake.

Went to the Office and read the Defence of the American Constitutions. I was very quiet and without any interruption. Read Mr. Berrien's exposition of the causes that led to the difficulty in the Cabinet. It is very dignified, and calculated to bring men back to their senses if any thing can. But the view it gives of Genl. Jackson is disgraceful enough to the Nation.[1] Talked with Mr. Brooks and went to the Athenæum. Home to dine, found Miss E. C. Adams from Quincy who told us the family were well.

Afternoon, reading Cicero as usual. Letters to Appius. They are beautifully written but Melmoth is a painful expositor of their want of sincerity.[2] Evening, Judge Hall, and Mr. and Mrs. Frothingham, so that I had only time to read the Spectator.

[1] The account addressed "To the Public" by John Macpherson Berrien, the former attorney general, is dated 22 July and appeared in the *National Intelligencer* for 23 July (p. 1–3) along with supporting documents: letters to and from J. H. Eaton, Col. R. M. Johnson, S. D. Ingham, and Francis P. Blair.

[2] Evidently CFA was reading in Cicero's *Letters to His Friends: with Remarks by William Melmoth*, 3 vols., London. Editions published in 1753 and 1803 are at MQA.

THURSDAY 28TH.

Morning very close and sultry, the sun coming out, but being soon after enveloped in clouds, we found a little relief from rain. After reading a portion of Aristotle over again, having finished the first examination of it, I went to my Office and sat down very quietly to the reading of the Defence. I must say that of all the books upon Government that I have read, none accords with my fancy so much as this. It has fewer fancies and proceeds only upon the footing of experience. The Comments upon the Government of Lacædemon are very much the same with mine made in the margin of Mably's book.[1] They are true, and show that it is merely by looking at things in a plain practical light one may succeed at arriving at wise conclusions.

I returned home early feeling fearful of being without my Umbrella. Afternoon, concluded the third book and began the fourth of Cicero's Epistles. Read the Letters to Servius Sulpicius, and the famous one of the latter, condoling with Cicero for the loss of his daughter. It is certainly very beautifully done. This man seems to have been a very honorable character. I do not think Cicero rises in one's estimation quite so much. Short evening. Took a little walk with my Wife, and read Pye and the Spectator.

[1] See above, entry for 3 June. CFA's marginal comment is reproduced in this volume; see p. xvi.

FRIDAY. 29TH.

Morning clear with a fine wind and pleasant. My Wife did not seem quite so well as usual, but I conclude that this must be as she approaches her term. I have felt more anxiety today however, and wish that some person was with her to relieve me in case of responsibility.

After reading Aristotle as usual, I went to the Office and had a very quiet and uninterrupted morning. I spent it for the most part in reading my Grand Father's Defence, the first Volume of which I finished. When we consider that it was written previous to the formation of our Federal Government, when an experiment on a grand scale was not at all so certain of success as we are apt to think now, the earnestness with which certain principles are pushed was not superfluous, nor was confidence in the theory ill founded. As my Man Servant is absent, I was obliged to go and deliver my Notes myself, for a Meeting of the Directors of the Boylston Market.

Returned home, and after dinner read Cicero's Epistles which continue to interest me. I read today the complaint of Metellus Celer, and Cicero's reply which is pretty tart. It is a little remarkable that so powerful a mind should have so much weakness. He was timid, and though he knew the right, he did not always strive to convince himself that it ought to be pursued. Evening at home. Took a short walk with my Wife, read more of Pye's Commentary and closed with the Spectator.

SATURDAY. 30TH.

Morning clear. I read a portion of Aristotle and went to the Office as usual. First, however, executing a parcel of Commissions which I am now charged with owing to the absence of my Man. Having forgotten the second Volume of my Grandfather's Defence, I thought it a good opportunity to finish getting rid of the Papers belonging to my late brother and to R. New. To read the first always makes me melancholy. In looking over the Letters congratulating him upon his successful Oration delivered when only twenty three years of age,[1] I was struck with the difference between his actual fate and that which was predicted of him. He might have accomplished all and more. For in some respects he had great advantages. His personal character was more amiable, and formed connections easily which are of great service to a man's success in life. I have often thought that had we been able to form one character out of the advantageous portions of our two, Success would have been certain. But this would have been asking too much. We must submit to the will of the Deity who probably knows best what is for our good.

Afternoon at home, reading Cicero. Came across the famous Letter to Lucæius about History. Which is amusing enough to be sure. My Mother came to town with Mrs. Nowlan in consequence of my Note of this morning.[2] I am glad of it as Company for my Wife. Evening, quiet. Read Aristotle by Pye and the Spectator.

[1] The 4th of July oration at Quincy delivered by GWA in 1824 was attended by JA (see vol. 1:222–224, 267). Of the letters of congratulation to him, only that of LCA has been located (22 July 1824, Adams Papers).

[2] The note is missing.

SUNDAY. 31ST.

Morning clear and warm though with a fine Air. I did not rise very early and had therefore less time than usual to devote to my studies. I read a little of Aristotle during the morning and attended Divine Service. Mr. Frothingham preached all day, from 1. Corinthians. Chapt. 12. verses 4. 5 and 6. "Now there are diversities of gifts, but the same spirit, and there are differences of Administrations but the same Lord, and there are diversities of Operations, but it is the same God which worketh all in all." He drew from this text an illustration of our dependence upon the Deity, who communicates to us all our blessings through means as various as can be imagined. All of which means work to the same general end, the happiness of man. And from 1 John. C4. v. 16. "God is love." Again urging the beneficent character of the Deity, and exhorting to the cultivation of the kind affections— Which perhaps I hardly do enough. I cannot help objecting to Mr. Frothingham the very indefinite tendency of his Sermons. There is rarely a leading idea to grasp by which you can continue your attention. The reflections are distinct, and finished in themselves but not so closely connected with a leading thread as to keep the mind from wandering into fields of its own. The afternoon service was performed in a violent Thunder Storm. The first severe one we have had this Season.

Returning home, I read a Sermon of Massillon. The second in the set of the Petit Careme. The Text from Matthew 4. 1. "Then was Jesus led up of the spirit into the Wilderness to be tempted of the Devil." The subject, the temptations of the great. He makes three leading divisions. The attractions of pleasure, the exposure to adulation, and the influence of ambition. The first leads astray, the second precludes a return to right, and the third is the consequence of the error. Some passages are very fine. Now here are distinct ideas, a child can manage them, and these are after all the great means to produce effect. Evening quiet at home. I conversed with my Mother about John, and the Mills. After which read Mr. Pye and the Spectator.

MONDAY. AUGUST 1ST.

Morning cloudy which ended in a thunder Storm. I pursued the study of Aristotle as usual and formed clearer ideas of his doctrines and illustrations. A critic should not exercise his Art, until he has read him thoroughly. Went to the Office and was busy in reading over and destroying the remainder of the Papers belonging to my Brother.

Among others a great many of my letters.[1] Some of which I read and could not help thinking of the alteration in myself. I have lost ground since then, at least in genius if not in morals. I could not write so sprightly a letter now if I was to try ever so hard. Returned home.

Afternoon, Attended a Meeting of the Directors of the Boylston Market. No business of importance so that we adjourned soon. I drew up the record for both Meetings and returned home in time to avoid a Thunder Storm. Read the Fifth book of Cicero's Familiar Letters, one or two of which at the close are very obscure.

Evening quiet. My Wife continues quite tolerably. I conversed a short time with my Mother, after which I read Mr. Pye and the Spectator.

[1] Only one letter from CFA to GWA is now known, that of 16 July 1814 from St. Petersburg (Adams Papers).

TUESDAY. 2D.

The weather very sultry, though cloudy. After reading my usual portion of Aristotle, I went to the Office. Time passed quietly and with only one or two interruptions. I. Hull Adams came from Quincy and called in to say a word, and my father's man John Kirke. I read a little of the second Volume of the Defence, looked over my Accounts and went to a sale of Wine to see how it was, but did not feel like paying a high price for it. Called in at Mr. Brooks, and upon my return at the Office I sat down to copying my Father's Bible Letters, the originals of which I found in a much damaged state, in the Papers of George.[1]

Returned home and spent the Afternoon in reading Cicero's Letters. They are very interesting. The Author throws himself out of his Robe. These however still have an under dress. The letters to Atticus are said to display the man naked. My Mother and Wife went to Charlestown to pay a visit or two, so that we took Tea late. T. B. Adams Jr. called and passed the Evening. He has just returned from a Journey of considerable length.[2] After a little talk with my Mother, I read Aristotle and the Spectator.

[1] From 1–8 Sept. 1811 to 4 April 1813 JQA in St. Petersburg addressed eleven letters on the study of the Bible to GWA in Quincy. All the letters are in the Adams Papers. Copies early circulated in MS form and CFA later published the letters in an appendix to the enlarged 4th edition of his *Letters of Mrs. Adams, the Wife of John Adams,* Boston, 1848, p. 427–472.

[2] At about this time he visited his cousin, Mrs. John Peter de Windt, at Fishkill Landing, N.Y. (JQA, Diary, 20 Aug.).

WEDNESDAY. 3D.

Morning dark, with very heavy rain, but it cleared away before night. After reading Aristotle, I went to the Office. Mr. Tenney called to pay me his rent. I went afterwards to do some little Commissions. Found at the Post Office a Packet for me containing the long threatened publication about my poor brother.[1] It is bad enough to be sure, but I felt on the whole as if it was better out than kept as it has been two years hanging over us. Farmer has not spared falsehood, to increase the effect of his tale.

I walked down to the Athenæum and from thence to obtain some Wood for my family. The walk drenched me so that I went directly home and changed my dress. This made it too late to return to the Office.

Afternoon, engaged in reading the Letters of Cicero. Perhaps there is a little too much sameness in his expressions of kindness and offer of service. But his advice to Trebatius is excellent. It is this kind of encouragement that great men have it in their power to do good by. For their opinion gives force to truth. My Mother and Wife went to Cambridge to see Mr. and Mrs. E. Brooks, and did not return until late. I finished Mr. Pye's Commentary, and read two numbers of the Spectator.

[1] *Report of a Trial: Miles Farmer versus Dr. David Humphreys Storer, . . . Relative to the Transactions between Miss Eliza Dolph and George Washington Adams, Esq., Son of the Late President of the United States. Reported by the Plaintiff*, Boston, 1831.

THURSDAY. 4TH.

Morning clear but rather cool. I read my portion in review of Aristotle and went to the Office. Time occupied there mostly in copying the first of my father's series of Bible letters. Had but one or two visitors and those unwelcome ones. One man on this miserable business of the Pamphlet—Another application for money. The man did not come from Farmer, but he might destroy *this* edition. Of what avail this? Since the Pamphlet itself shows that three editions have been made one after another without any cessation of purpose.[1] This has been a regularly arranged scheme from the first to draw Money by operating upon Family pride. I gave him the same answer that I give universally—That we must not flinch. Returned home as usual.

Afternoon read more of Cicero's Letters. Those to Trebatius are very amusing, having all the Salt which belongs to the Style. The familiar style of letter writing is perhaps as rare to excel in as any, it requires wit and playfulness, which is a combination not very frequent. My Mother and Wife went to take a ride. I read this Evening the first Act of Racine's Iphigenie, and the Spectator.

[1] The relevant passage in the *Farmer-Storer Trial* pamphlet relating Farmer's earlier attempts to publish an account of the proceedings begins with his introduction of a reporter into the room in which the Reference was being held:

"It was then distinctly stated that *this reference was to be strictly private! ! ! ! !* ... Of course the Reporter was obliged to withdraw, and the task of telling the public my simple story devolved on me. "I then wrote out the facts, con-

tracted with a printer to execute the work, over my own signature, which having been completed, judge what was my surprise when I called to obtain the copies, to find that the whole edition printed, *had been destroyed between two days! ! ... Who caused this to be done?* The task, however, is again accomplished" (p. 38).

On another effort to suppress, see above, entry for 21 April.

FRIDAY. 5TH.

Morning clear, I read Aristotle as usual for an hour and then went to the Office. My time very little interrupted, and I devoted it to copying the Bible letters, two of which and part of a third I finished. The last not being taken from the original, there appear some awkward readings. The letter was probably worn out by handling upon which George made a Copy, and this bears the mark of having subsequently been corrected by my Father. But it is copied by a boy without regard to sense or periods.[1] Returned home.

Afternoon, read an act of Iphigenie and then went with My mother and Wife to Medford to see Mr. Brooks, at whose house we took Tea. They were very pleasant and very kind. Chardon Brooks and his Wife and Miss [Elizabeth] Phillips were the only persons present. We returned home calling on the way upon Mrs. Angier. She appeared well and quite contented. She did commit the folly against which I warned her, in the expense she laid out upon her rooms, but having got over that, it is to be hoped that the future will teach her a lesson, gradually. We returned late, and I continued Iphigenie in the Evening, and the Spectator.

[1] CFA accurately describes the MS of the third of JQA's Bible letters, 22 Sept. 1811 (Adams Papers).

SATURDAY. 6TH.

Morning pleasant. I finished this morning the review of Aristotle's Poetic. The reading has not been without it's use to me as I have obtained some idea of what may be called the origin of criticism. Aristotle confines himself to the successful efforts of genius for his Models of writing, and argues from them to Nature. Perhaps this is the safest though it is certainly not the most philosophical method. A thing pleases for some reason or other springing from the peculiar constitution of man. That reason should be traced to explain the subject. Aristotle merely says that it does please, therefore let it be done. Notwithstanding all this, he has given valuable advice to a Poet.

Went to the Office where I was busy in copying the Bible Letters. Thence to the Athenæum where I got hold of the History of the Western World and was amused with it.[1] If I could get, I would review it.

Home to dinner. Afternoon, read the Letters of Cicero with some of Cælius to him. The eighth book is made up entirely of these. Their style is colloquial and so concise as to be very obscure. I was amused with their liveliness. It is one of the great branches of Epistolary Composition, to touch familiar subjects just enough to excite pleasant ideas and leave off to take new ones. Evening, Mr. Degrand sat an hour. He is just from Washington. Writing afterwards, and the Spectator.

[1] This work has not been further identified.

SUNDAY. 7TH.

Morning pleasant and cool. Read some portions of Hazard's State Papers[1] and a little of Chalmers. The more I read, the more I am satisfied of the correctness of my views in the North American. Attended divine Service all day. Heard Mr. Frothingham, but I am mortified in having so continually to record that I cannot follow him. His morning Text was from Philippians 2. 12. "Work out your own Salvation." He said that the Doctrine commonly adopted was that man being under the original curse pronounced upon the fall of the first of the species was therefore to redeem himself from his original sin. He expressed his dissent from the doctrine. This is one great obstacle in my way. How the words of the Bible can be evaded.

Afternoon, Psalms 19. 11. "In keeping of them there is great reward." The merit of virtue is in itself and not in any direct advantage to be realized from it. Reward commonly means some personal advantage accruing from the performance or omission of some Act. But the Preacher meant to inculcate the use of virtue in itself as administering to the happiness of the mortal, without reference to any future state of Happiness or Immortality. This is all very well, but I do not think refinement of this kind will often reclaim from vice.

I walked home with Mr. Chadwick and he gave me Mr. Ingham's Letter to read—A violent attack upon the President.[2] What a state of things in our Country! I afterwards read a Sermon from Massillon— Text, Matthew 17. 3. "Behold there appeared unto them Moses and Elias talking with him." The subject was the respect due to religion from the great. By religion he means that of faith and practice combined. The views are two, first as it respects themselves. The exalted station given to them on earth makes it more of a duty that they should demean themselves virtuously, second as it respects their inferiors, and the public generally, by spreading a spirit of piety. He goes on to advise the support of religion as an aid to Government, and says that it is a fact, that heresy in the Church has always been connected with rebellion in the State. This is a Jesuitical doctrine. It rests upon the expediency of sustaining a particular Sect without examination of its principles, and is not worthy of the rest of the Sermon. Evening at home. I read as usual the Spectator.

¹ Ebenezer Hazard, *Historical Collections; Consisting of State Papers and Other Authentic Documents; Intended as Materials for an History of the United States*, 2 vols., Phila., 1792–1794, concerning which, see JA, *Diary and Autobiography*, 2:109.

² The editors have found no further information about S. D. Ingham's letter,

apparently published as a pamphlet, of near this date and of this character. Perhaps it was a version of his address to his constituents in Bucks County, Penna., after his return from Washington in late June, which was printed in the county newspaper. William A. Ingham, *Samuel Delucenna Ingham*, privately printed, 1910, p. 13.

MONDAY. 8TH.

Morning pleasant though Easterly Winds have prevailed all along for some time. I went to the Office and was busy as usual in writing. Copied a large portion of the Bible letters. They certainly lean to the doctrines of the stricter sects and I do not wonder at their consequent desire to have them published. My father came into town and called at my Office for a few moments. He is one upon a Committee of the ΦBK Society about their secrets. He showed me an Anonymous letter about this business of the Pamphlet which is curious enough to be sure.¹ Returned home to dinner.

My father and Mr. Brooks dined with us, and we had quite a pleasant time. They left us and my Mother who has been spending a week quite pleasantly here. I had little of the afternoon left and devoted it to making out a Catalogue of my Pamphlets, of which I can make very little use without one.² And on the whole, I have a pretty valuable collection.

In the Evening Mrs. Saml. Dexter called to see my Mother. She sat half an hour and immediately upon her leaving, Judge Hall came in. He is a little prosaic but very well meaning. Continued my Pamphlet Catalogue in the Evening and read the Spectator.

¹ JQA notes that the letter was signed James Shadel and that in it the writer

said he "would call in the course of the day." The letter's purport was "an argument threatening and persuading me to pay for suppressing the pamphlet." On his return to Quincy he was visited by one Joshua Colburn who informed him that the Jackson and Masonic forces planned to distribute thousands of copies over the country to injure JQA's chances for the Antimasonic nomination for the Presidency. Colburn also divulged particulars about the publication of the pamphlet. JQA records his refusal to pay anything to suppress and his conviction that the Jackson-men, David Henshaw,

collector of customs, and Nathaniel Greene, postmaster, "are at the bottom of this as they were of the Cunningham Correspondence. Their sting is now invenomed by the fear of losing their places. There is also Masonic Charity in the Cup" (JQA, Diary, 8 Aug.).

[2] A catalogue of CFA's pamphlet collection in his handwriting, containing publications dated as late as 1833, perhaps a continuation or revision of the catalogue here mentioned, is in Adams Papers (Microfilms, Reel No. 326).

TUESDAY. 9TH.

Morning cloudy with rain in showers and the air very sultry. I passed an hour in pursuing my Catalogue of Pamphlets and went to the Office. I was there occupied in my usual business of the Bible letters. Finished the fifth. Judge Hall called in. He mentioned to me the Pamphlet which had been published by Farmer and asked if my Mother had seen it. I said, no. He thought it advisable that if possible it should be kept from her. I have my doubts. For should a sudden unexpected disclosure take place, it would affect more than if we prepared her.

I went to the Athenæum where I sat down and read the History of the United States in the Cabinet Cyclopedia,[1] a most impudent book which I feel vehemently anxious to criticize. Returned home. Expected Mr. Frothingham to dine but he disappointed us.

Afternoon writing a little upon the History of the United States, but could not please myself. Turned to one or two of the Letters of Cælius, almost discouraging by their obscurity. Evening at home excepting a short walk. Mr. Frothingham spent half an hour with us.[2] Writing and the Spectator.

[1] Henry Fergus, *History of the United States* is contained in vols. 103–104 (1830–1832) of Rev. Dionysius Lardner's *Cabinet Cyclopædia*, 133 vols.,

London, 1830–1849.

[2] Mrs. Frothingham had borne a daughter, their first, on 29 July (LCA to Mrs. JA2, 11 Aug., Adams Papers).

WEDNESDAY. 10TH.

The day was clear, but with the atmosphere so exceedingly close and sultry that it was prostrating. I felt so languid that I was unable to accomplish as much as I generally do. Morning, one hour in writing rather in a rambling way. Then to the Office where I wrote my regular Diary and copied one Bible Letter. A single visit from T. B. Adams Jr. who had very little to say. Returned home, feeling as if I had been walking ten miles. Tried to get the History of the U. States but could not.

Afternoon, came to a stop. Cannot do anything without the book. Shall I try to do any thing at all? Almost discouraged. Took up the Letters of Cælius and finished the rest of them. He seems to have [been] a pretty well disposed man, without much principle and with strong passions. His friendship for Cicero kept him generally inclined to the right, though his sudden influences frequently drove him wrong. His letters are mutilated and obscure in their nature.

Evening quietly at home, excepting a short walk with my Wife. Read La Harpe's Criticism upon Iphigenie. He thinks the Play nearly perfect. Strange that it should not interest me. I prefer Phedre and Athalie. The Spectator as usual.

THURSDAY. 11TH.

Morning clear and warm. Having finished Aristotle's Poetic, I now took up Horace's Art of Poetry again being about to read through the Quatres Poetiques of Batteux.[1] This pleases me more every time I take it up. Every thing satisfies me that one reading of a Classic is nothing for the purpose of understanding him. Went to the Office. Wrote my regular Journal and copied No. 7 of the Bible letters. My father came in, but remained a very short time, being engaged in this business of the ΦBK again. Mr. Curtis called with a little Law matter. I went to the Athenæum where I wasted an hour in fingering books. My father dined with me.

Afternoon, read a part of the Ninth Book of Cicero ad Diversos. Letters to Varro and Dolabella. He wrote to the latter after the divorce of his daughter. This shows that little shame attended these divorces. But I cannot get over the evident political arrangement which gave cause to the marriage.

Evening quietly at home excepting a short walk. Mr. Degrand spent part of the evening here. I read more of Horace and began the fifth volume of the Spectator.

[1] *Les quatres poëtiques d'Aristote, d'Horace, de Vida, de Despréaux* with translations and comment by Abbé Charles Batteux. CFA's bookplate is in the edition at MQA, 2 vols., Paris, 1771. The text of Aristotle is in Greek and French, that of Horace and Vida in Latin and French, that of Boileau-Despréaux in French.

FRIDAY. 12TH.

Morning clear and warm. Finished Horace's Art of Poetry with great pleasure to myself. On the whole, I know nothing in its way superior to it. The beautiful passages of the different ages of Man might be compared with Shakspeare's to some advantage. And the very judicious advice seems to have exhausted the most of what Aristotle left undone. At the Office, occupied in copying my Fathers Bible Letter No. 8. One of these takes me two hours and a half steady writing. So that while they last I shall not do much else. Went to the Athenæum, but the Book I want has been spirited away. So that I wasted the time.

Afternoon at home. Continued the Letters of Cicero and closed the Ninth Book. Among them a remarkable one upon the doctrine of the Stoics as to obscene words. A discussion rather curious than useful. But it is very curious as a matter of language. There is a great deal of lively wit in these letters. Perhaps they are the best models extant. I passed the Evening with my Wife and walked with her. Afterwards, read the first book of Milton's Paradise Regained.[1] It wants interest. Why? Afterwards the Spectator.

[1] In addition to the two editions of Milton's *Works* at MQA (see above, vol. 3:350), an edition of *Paradise Regained* published separately, Birmingham, 1760, with JQA's bookplate, is also there.

SATURDAY. 13TH.

Morning pleasant. I was roused in the night by my Wife who felt herself sick, but I went to sleep again and did not get up again until ½ past six. Read part of Vida's Art of Poetry which I had commenced yesterday, and went to the Office where I was again occupied in writing a Bible letter all day. They are worth the trouble I take with them, but they allow me time for little else.

I returned home and found that my Wife was in labour. This terminated at a little after three o'clock in the birth of a daughter, and the Mother and Child both tolerably well. Thus am I at last a Parent. A new relation in life is fixed upon me of which I hope I understand the importance. When I look back upon past time, my Engagement, my marriage and the fears and hopes which possessed me, and which were spread throughout my writing whether in this Journal or in my letters, I cannot restrain a loud cry of gratitude to God for the very merciful manner in which he has heard my Prayers. In my record of the 10th of September of last year I expressed my doubts of ever being blessed with Children. This is now removed, and my feelings are now perfectly at ease. But it is now that I have still greater need of divine protection, as the responsibilities which I assumed begin to make themselves felt. May the Deity look with favour upon my virtuous efforts, and support me through all days of suffering and trial. My heart was relieved upon being told my Wife was safely through, most incredibly. My Mother did not arrive until six o'clock.

Evening quiet though I could do little or nothing.[1] Read the Spectator and took possession of my lonely bed.

[1] CFA wrote letters to JQA and to JA2 announcing the birth of a daughter (JQA, Diary, 14 Aug.). The letter to JQA is missing, but that to JA2, forwarded by JQA at CFA's request, is in the Adams Papers. A few weeks later the parents chose for the infant the name Louisa Catherine; in *The Adams Papers* she is designated as LCA2. In 1854 she was to marry Charles Kuhn, and her death in Italy, at the Bagni di Lucca, in 1870 is related in a moving passage in *The Education of Henry Adams*, p. 287–288. See also HA, *Letters*, ed. Ford, vol. 1 *passim* and Adams Genealogy.

SUNDAY. 14TH.

Morning pleasant. Arose a little after my usual hour, probably from the fatigue occasioned by excitement yesterday. Found my Wife had rested well and was as quiet as could be expected. The Infant is small but quite healthy to all appearance. I was relieved to find she was in little or no trouble.

Attended divine Service all day and heard Dr. Harris preach,[1] in the morning from Luke. 17. 20, 21. "And when he was demanded of the Pharisees, when the kingdom of God should come, he answered them and said, The kingdom of God cometh not with observation: Neither shall they say, Lo, here! or Lo, there! for behold the kingdom of God is within you." This text has abundant meaning. It conveys the great lesson of moderation to human desires. Men are always looking to some sensual enjoyment as the great end of virtuous conduct. They form ideas of reward, from the things that are prized in this life, which they are continually grasping for. Here they are taught that virtue is its own reward. That the kingdom of heaven is in a happy breast. Perhaps the Dr. did not say this, but something like it, the rest I supply from my reflections.

His afternoon text was from Hosea 6.3. "Then shall we know, if we follow on to know the Lord." This Text may be considered as an encouragement to exertion in the improvement of the spirit. It holds out the prospect of advancement in knowledge, of advantage to be gained from perseverance. Hence naturally follows exhortation to that effect. Dr. Harris is an old Clergyman of respectable character and extensive acquirement. But he does not appear to me to possess much natural power, and his Sermons are drily delivered. I called to see Mrs. Frothingham, who is yet in her room but pretty well. Her infant is large and healthy.

On my return home, I read Massillon's fourth Sermon in the Petit Careme. Luke 11. 24. "When the unclean spirit is gone out of a man, he walketh through dry places, seeking rest; and finding none, he saith, I will return unto my house whence I came out." The subject, was the increase of misery attending high rank unless supported by piety and virtue. He illustrates this in three ways, 1. by the power acquired by the Passions, when there is no inducement to control them, which operates as a constant goad. 2. by the Ennui occasioned by Satiety. 3. by the inevitable eccentricity of conduct occasioned by the total absence of method in life. The Sermon is a Corollary from the first half of the preceding one.

Evening. Conversation with my Mother. My man-servant B. P. Sawtell having for the last four days been the cause of great anxiety finally left me tonight. He selected an unfortunate moment, but I was on the whole relieved at being rid of him. Read a little of Vida and the Spectator.

¹ T. M. Harris, D.D., was the Congregational minister at Dorchester (*Mass. Register*, 1831).

MONDAY 15TH.

Morning very warm, and so it continued until I thought it might be classed among the warmest days we have had this Summer. I read some of Vida. But the sudden disappearance of my Man Servant besides worrying me, has thrown all the labour upon my shoulders, and I consequently was obliged to walk first to Mrs. Frothingham's, then to market, so that it was late before I reached my Office. I accomplished my usual Diary, which has grown so much as to make it no trifle, and wrote a large portion of the tenth of the Bible letters so that I was not altogether without producing something. Returned home and found my Wife and Child still holding on pretty well. This is my present care and if it go on favourably I shall hold it as one among my many blessings.

Returned home and in the Afternoon read the Correspondence between Plancus and Cicero. It shows good intention on his part, but the Republic was not to be saved. How could it be when Cicero advises a military man friendly to the authority of the Senate to pay no attention to it's orders, but go on doing and let them approve afterwards. How is Cicero justified in giving this advice? If it was not right, then is he to blame. If it was right, the government was not worth the blood it cost to support it.

Evening quiet at home. Mr. W. Lee called not knowing that my

Wife was confined. Read Vida, and the Spectator, besides finishing Paradise Regained. I believe the reason it interests so little is, that the hero is perfect and known to be so which takes from the interest of a story by disclosing the invariable result. The little action there is, is uniform, with a uniform termination. So that the occasional snatches of bright Poetry are not enough to keep the reader alive. I would say more but I dilate too much. How do my thoughts agree with the Critics?

TUESDAY. 16TH.

Morning cloudy with an Easterly Wind, but it afterwards cleared away. My Wife seemed pretty well but there was a difficulty about nursing. The Child is hardly strong enough to draw milk enough for its own nourishment, or it's mother's relief.[1] This is a matter for anxiety. I was obliged to do all the work in the absence of any assistance so that it kept me walking a large part of the morning.

At the Office, engaged [in] writing my Journal and also in copying the tenth Bible letter which I finished but did no more. Several interruptions this morning. Mr. Curtis, a man to pay rent, and my father. The latter came in for the purpose of satisfying his anxiety.[2] He dined at my House and in the afternoon I went down with him to try the Church in which he is to deliver the Eulogy upon Mr. Monroe. It was exceedingly hot in the place which was the Old South, and in the position in the extreme corner of the upper end of the Church, it almost suffocated me. My father felt himself much exhausted in delivering only what he designed as the Exordium of the Address. He must abridge.

Returned home and had an hour's very pleasant conversation with him upon historical subjects, and he left us to return home. My Evening was a little distracted, by conversation, by sitting with my Wife and by a visit of congratulation from Mr. Everett. I read a part however of DuBos reflections upon Poetry and Painting.[3] Executed part of my Pamphlet Catalogue and read the Spectator as usual.

[1] "She is under the necessity of resorting to a puppy for comfort which I trust will relieve her" (LCA to Mrs. JA2, 17 Aug., Adams Papers).

[2] JQA's anxiety was aroused apparently by a letter from CFA (JQA, Diary, 16 Aug.); the letter is missing.

[3] Jean Baptiste Dubos, *Réflexions critiques, sur la poësie et sur la peinture.* JQA's signature and bookplate are in the edition at MQA, 3 vols., Paris, 1719–1740.

WEDNESDAY. 17TH.

Morning rather cooler than it has been, with an Easterly Wind and cloudy but without rain. I passed an hour reading Vida's Art of Poetry of which I can say, that it contains much valuable matter for a poet. But though it may make a *good* one, he will not be *great*. A great Poet must be an original. It will not do for every man of genius to be tied down to the track of Virgil and Homer. Had Virgil struck out a new path, with the same general melody of versification, would he not have held higher rank as a Poet. I do not mean to depreciate what he did, but I mean to apply to the genius the rule that all Critics apply to the species, there must be variety. What would have been Milton's merit had he imitated Virgil as closely as this person did Homer? I do not think any great genius ought to imitate unless he is willing to admit his predecessor's superiority.

Went to the Office. My Wife not quite so well today as the child will not take. I yet feel great anxiety about both. Occupied in writing my Journal and in copying a part of the eleventh and last Bible letter. Mr. Brooks called to let me know of some grapes which I was obliged to go myself to get. So I returned home and having been sent for to see Miss Oliver continued my walk to Hancock Street. She wants to keep the House, for two years more. Talked about repairs.

After dinner I read the Eleventh Book of Cicero's Letters. The Correspondence of Decimus Brutus. The Letters of Brutus and Cassius to Antony are very dignified, and worthy of the men. The letter of Cicero to Matius and his reply are very good. Perhaps the reasoning in it is not entirely without basis. The question of the propriety of Cæsar's murder is a hard one to settle. But as a general rule one may be pretty sure that when a person is successful enough to become a tyrant, he is assisted to it full as much by the corruption of the People as by his own ability. It certainly was so here. Read Bacon's Essay upon Truth which is good. Evening with my Wife, afterwards, Du Bos and the Spectator.

THURSDAY. 18TH.

I am twenty four years old this day. And what have I done to make the reflection of this age agreeable to me? Little or nothing. Time is flying and I am almost stationary. The past year has brought with it new cares and new relations. I am now a father as well as a husband and son. I believe I am duly grateful for the many blessings which I enjoy, and if I am anxious, it is only because I cannot altogether fulfill the measure which is set for me. My labours are not small and yet my progress is mortifying. On the whole this Anniversary was one of melancholy reflection upon myself, though not with any mixture of shame. I believe I may congratulate myself that I am innocent of any criminal neglect or violation of duty, and relying upon divine assistance to guide me in my further progress, I may hope that if I do not sustain the reputation transmitted to me, I shall at least place no spot upon it.

Morning finished Vida, who to my taste is very inferior to Horace. He is diffuse and weak though smooth. There is good sense, and judgment in his Verses and perhaps in point of method he is superior to his predecessor.

My Wife was quite weak this morning, and seemed to suffer a good deal. I went to the Office and finished copying the last of the Bible Letters; the thing now is to compare them, and the case is done. T. B. Adams Jr. called to see me and, I followed him down soon to see the Gallery of Paintings for exhibition. It is good but contains a very small proportion of pictures not before exhibited.[1] Returned home and in the Afternoon read Cicero's Letters to Cassius, Trebonius, and others in the 12th book, at the time of the final struggle for liberty. Read Bacon's Essay on Death.

Evening with my Wife after which I read over the first Chapter of Grahame for further study. I want to fix firmly the early History. Read the Spectator as usual—Sir Roger at the Theatre.

[1] The annual exhibition at the Athenæum Gallery had opened on the preceding Monday and had already had a newspaper review (*Boston Patriot*, 15 Aug., p. 2, col. 2; 17 Aug., p. 2, cols. 3–4).

FRIDAY. 19TH.

Morning warm and clear. The rain appears to have ceased for some time. I went to the Office after passing an hour in reading Boileau's Art Poetique. One of the most finished specimens of versification extant. If any thing the artificial construction so apparent is the thing least calculated to please. Poetry certainly is pleasing in a negligé dress though not slovenly. Yet I admire the vigour of the style, the point of the verses and the finish of the measure. Nothing in French exceeds it in its way. But I do not think that he equals Horace in the passage imitated from him, which I have already noticed.

Went to the Office where I met again Mr. Peabody who has just lost his Father [1] and has been absent from Boston a good while in consequence. Corrected several of my fathers Bible Letters. Richardson called to pay me a visit and to inform me of his engagement to be married, upon which I congratulated him.[2]

Afternoon, reading Cicero's Thirteenth Book, many letters of which are merely recommendations. A few more interesting. Read Bacon's Essay upon Unity in Religion. Great as his mind was, he could not take in the possibility of general toleration of religious differences. And yet the Puritans have been condemned for not knowing the thing to be practicable.

Evening. Walked with my Mother to Mrs. Frothingham's. Saw her husband and passed half an hour with him. Returned, read more of Grahame, and two numbers of the Spectator. My Wife has been tolerably but is still very weak, the child seems comfortable.

[1] An obituary notice of Oliver Peabody of Exeter, N.H., appeared in the *Boston Patriot*, 24 Aug., p. 2, col. 6.

[2] John Hancock Richardson was married to Lydia Anne Thaxter, daughter of Levi Thaxter, in Watertown (*Columbian Centinel*, 7 Jan. 1832).

SATURDAY. 20TH.

Morning clear, but very warm. This weather has continued an unusual length of time, and it is the most prostrating that I have felt. I finished Boileau and read Pope's Essay on Criticism.[1] Certainly a very astonishing production for twenty years of age. I do not know that any thing of his is more quoted and though it may be defective as a whole when compared with his subsequent productions, yet some particular passages have never been excelled.

Went to the Office, read a part of Mr. Calhoun's doctrine of Nullification as by him lately declared,[2] and corrected one or two of the Bible Letters. This though meagre enough was all I can give any account of.

Returned home and passed the afternoon finishing the Thirteenth Book containing Letters of Recommendation. They are all cast in the same general mould, and have on the whole very little interest.

Evening, after passing an hour or two with my Wife who is getting along quite slowly but as I hope pretty regularly I continued Grahame's United States which I find I read thoroughly before. My present design is to supply myself with materials for the future. Continued with the Spectator.

[1] "An Essay on Criticism" is in vol. 1 of *The Works of Alexander Pope in Verse and Prose*, with notes and a life by Samuel Johnson. The edition at MQA (8 vols., London, 1812) has CFA's bookplate. Numerous passages are underlined or marked in the margins.

[2] *Mr. Calhoun's Sentiments upon the Subject of State Rights, and the Tariff*, published as a pamphlet at Boston in 1831, seems to have been a version of his "Fort Hill Letter" of 26 July 1831, "On the relation which the States and General Government bear to each other," which appears in Calhoun, *Works*, ed. Crallé, 6:59–94.

SUNDAY. 21ST.

This day was a continuation of the hot weather we have already experienced for such a length of time. My Wife and Child seem to be doing prodigiously well considering the exhausting character of the Air. In looking over some old matter I found a part of an examination of Demosthenes' Oration, which I had done some time ago. Upon reading it over, I found that it was too good to throw away and therefore began to reflect upon the possibility of working it over into something. The undertaking is not trifling, but should I be discouraged from things merely because they are great, it is clear I shall always be dabbling in small.

Attended divine Service all day and heard Mr. Frothingham. The heat was so great however that I could do little in the way of attention, particularly in the Afternoon. The Text in the morning was from 2d Samuel 24th Chapter, 14 verse. "And David said unto God, I am in a great strait: let us fall now into the hand of the Lord, (for his mercies are great) and let me not fall into the hand of man." The Chapter is a singular one. David decides upon taking an account of the People of Israel against the advice of his Officers. He repents of the Action immediately after it is committed, and deprecated the punishment which God was to inflict upon him. He has a choice of three evils, Famine, War, or Pestilence. He selects the latter. Mr. F. thought the whole allegorical, excepting the Census, David's repentance and the Plague. He conjectured that the Sin probably consisted in some scheme of aggrandisement which David meditated. And the conclusion which he draws from the whole subject was the blessing that we were not allowed to chuse our future fate, and the advantage of confiding in God in preference to Man. On the first branch he introduced a very pretty illustration from Southey's Thalaba. I called for a minute to see Mrs. Frothingham, met Sidney Brooks who has just returned from New York.

The afternoon's Sermon was from the 119th Psalm 105 verse. "Thy word is a lamp unto my feet, and a light unto my path." An examination of the practical benefits of the Christian religion as a guide to human conduct. The heat was excessively oppressive in the Meeting House. Returned home and cooled myself reading Massillon. His next Sermon in order was upon the duty of Humanity in the great. Text. 6. John 5. "When Jesus then lifted up his eyes and saw a great Company come unto him." One would think he might have found a more pertinent extract and more directly to his point. The Chapter would have done better,[1] for it is the Story of the Loaves and Fishes.

He inculcates Humanity first as a *duty*. By Humanity he means the three virtues of affability, protection and charity to the poor. In the second place he considers it as a pleasure and an advantage to the giver. The whole concludes with an application to the King, and an exhortation. Evening with my Wife. Afterwards, Grahame and the Spectator.

¹ That is, would have provided a more suitable one.

MONDAY. 22D.

The weather continued as oppressively warm as heretofore. I occupied myself in an examination of the matter of the Essay I propose to write. It must take much time and after all may be beyond my ability. Went to the Office, and finished the correction of the Bible Letters. Some of them have evident errors in the Text, there are also injuries done to the Manuscript, both of which render a revision by the Author desirable.

I went down to the Athenæum to look at the Pictures, but it was so very warm I felt as if I could not stay. Returning home I found my Mother preparing to go home to Quincy as the Carriage had come, bringing in Mrs. Nowlan and the Child.¹ My father though he had intended it,² was dissuaded by the severity of the day. I thought I had repaired the breach in my Household but found I had not as the Man I had engaged disappointed me. This is troublesome. Afternoon, accomplished a very large portion of the Fourteenth and Fifteenth Books of the Letters, being those to his Wife Terentia and to Cassius and others. The single letter of Cato is a Jewel.

Mrs. Nowlan remained in town today. My Wife and Child are doing as well as the heat of the Weather will permit. In some things this is advantageous, for it prevents taking cold.³ Evening, continued Grahame, whose book I admire more and more. It is worth putting forward as a Text book of our early History.

¹ Mary Louisa Adams. LCA relates with some amusement Louisa's account to her grandfather of the visit. See LCA to Mrs. JA2, 23 Aug. (Adams Papers).
² That is, to come in to Boston in the carriage.
³ "Charles is a delighted but very nervous father and his face changes to every colour when his child cries." LCA to Mrs. JA2, 27 Aug. (Adams Papers).

TUESDAY. 23D.

The morning oppressively warm, but friendly Clouds were gathering rapidly all day, and finally cooled the heated earth with heavy and refreshing showers. For the past week, my system has been entirely open, and I have thrown out a most extraordinary abundance of perspiration. So exhausting was it, that had the weather continued the same for a much longer period, I believe I could have done nothing at all.

Read a part of the Defence, lounged with Mr. Peabody, carried up some fruit to Abby sent by her father, and did nothing. The last more than all the rest. Dined at the Tremont House to spare trouble at home. The dinner was good but I was more solitary in the midst of the crowd than if I had been sitting at home. Returned home and got into the Sixteenth and last book of letters to Tiro. I had unaccountably deceived myself as to the length of the Books and was surprised to find myself so near the close.

Evening, with my Wife. She now encourages me. I also read Grahame and finished the first Volume. An excellent work. Read an Essay of Bacon of great profoundness on simulation and dissimulation. Spectator as usual.

WEDNESDAY. 24TH.

Morning quite cool with an Easterly Wind. After examining Mitford and several other books for the purpose of writing an article on the subject of Demosthenes, I went to the Office. After sitting there and accomplishing my Diary and several other duties, I thought it a favourable day to go and look at the Athenæum Gallery as well as to see the London Papers. I was pleased in looking at the Pictures, but more particularly with four pieces of Vernet, and one by Cole. They are in their respective styles extremely beautiful.[1] But I did not like Allston's style so well.[2]

Returned home after dining at the Tremont House. Read and finished the letters of Cicero ad Diversos. On the whole I have not often read a more interesting collection. I propose now to give up my regular studies for the purpose of finishing this undertaking of mine.

My Wife and Child both doing well. I sat with her until eight when I went upstairs and read Mitford and the Edinburgh Review, which has some Masterly Articles upon the subject.[3] Read an Essay of Bacon on Parents and Children and the Spectator as usual.

[1] The paintings by Claude Joseph Vernet (1714–1789) were seascapes, that by Thomas Cole (1801–1848) a landscape. (JQA, Diary, 2 Sept.; Mabel M. Swan, *The Athenæum Gallery*, Boston, 1940, p. 214, 282.)

[2] Washington Allston (1779–1843) had two paintings in the exhibition: "Miriam" and "Saul and the Witch of Endor" (JQA, Diary, 2 Sept.). In an article reviewing *Remarks upon the Athenæum Gallery of Paintings for 1831* (Boston, 1831), Franklin Dexter singled out the two Allston paintings as outstanding among all those exhibited (*North Amer. Rev.*, 33:506–515 [Oct. 1831]).

[3] The ambiguity of the reference does

not permit absolute identification of the articles meant. However, on the assumption that "the subject" is that on which CFA was writing, Demosthenes and the rhetoric and oratory of Greece, the likelihood is that the essay with the running-head title "Greek Philosophy of Taste" is one of those meant. *Edinburgh Review,* 54:39–69 (Aug. 1831). See also above, vol. 3:147.

THURSDAY. 25TH.

Morning cloudy with an Easterly Wind, which terminated in very heavy rain in the Afternoon and Evening. After reading over part of Æschines I went to the Office and was first taken up by a visitor. Dr. A. Phelps is the chief of the Antimasonic Party in this State. He came to shew me a Letter and to request to know when he could see my Father. His purpose was to know whether my Father would be a Candidate for the Presidency on the Antimasonic ground.[1] He shewed me a letter from Pittsburg urging the nomination of him at Baltimore very much. On this subject I told him that I could say nothing. Whatever he might reply, would of course be to me very right. But that his family felt and I felt as if it was hard that the last days of his Life should be molested by attacks more bitter even than any he had yet experienced. That this would be a war of great violence and it's result would undoubtedly be defeat. I therefore dissuaded him from making a nomination. He took the opportunity to indoctrinate me on Antimasonic subjects which I bore with great good-nature. My father came in presently and sat an hour.

Returned home early in order to dine and get the family ready to move off. This was the afternoon for the Eulogy upon James Monroe and it rained heavily. After some waiting I got my Father and Mother off in a Carriage, and we reached the Church in safety. The Crowd was great. The Eulogy was successful but not so much so as the Oration. The matter was harder to manage.[2] It was late before we reached home. But my Father and Mother decided upon returning to Quincy. She was really quite sick. My head ached badly and I was glad to go to bed after a fatiguing day. Read the Spectator and Bacon's Essay on Marriage and Single Life.

[1] Dr. Abner Phelps, a Boston physician (*Boston Directory,* 1831–1832), a few days later visited JQA at Quincy to put the same question to him. In reply, JQA stated that he would not seek the nomination in any way but if offered it with a show of unanimity would not decline it (JQA, Diary, 27 Aug.).

[2] The composition of the eulogy had given JQA unusual trouble. He was never able to compress the matter he wished to include to a length suitable for delivery. In the end he spoke for an hour and a half, using less than half of what he had written. When published (9 Sept.), the pamphlet was a hundred pages in length. The delivery of the speech was attended by numerous other vicissitudes, some allegedly imposed by design. See JQA, Diary, 25 Aug.; JQA

to JA2, 28 Aug.; LCA to JA2, 30 Aug. (both in Adams Papers). The MS of the eulogy is also in the Adams Papers.

Some hint of the reception of the speech may be had from the *Boston Daily Advertiser's* comment, "[T]he Orator has formed a much higher estimate of Mr. Monroe's talents and services,

than, we believe, will meet the sanction of most men, who have been acquainted with his public life, and has consequently celebrated them in terms of eulogy which appear a little extravagent" (26 Aug., p. 2, col. 2). For CFA's opinion, see entry of 10 Sept., below.

FRIDAY. 26TH.

Morning clear and warm again. I arose refreshed and delighted that the whole of yesterday's affair was over. This bustle is a terrible thing. I know that I am not fitted for the noise of public life. The moment it surrounds me, I feel a most unconquerable disgust. I began my first draught of an Article upon the Oration on the Crown and accomplished a little. Then to the Office where I wasted the morning doing little or nothing. Talked with Mr. Peabody. Had two or three visitors: Mr. Degrand upon my Atlas Shares, Mr. Curtis about Mr. Boylston's matters, and one or two others of less consequence. Called to see Mr. Brooks, and tried to read the Defence but could not make it out. My mind is losing its tenacity at least in the morning.

Dined at the Tremont House and after a walk went home where I spent my time in writing on my Work. This I continued in the Evening. My Wife though not quite so well in consequence of yesterday, was nevertheless getting along very tolerably. I read Bacon's Essay on Envy and my usual numbers of the Spectator.

SATURDAY. 27TH.

Morning cloudy with occasional rain. I went to the Office after writing a little upon my task with which I am already disgusted. I am sorry to say I am not equal to it. Abominable that I should fold up my hands and declare it.

Went to the Office where I passed the morning in reading my Grandfather's Defence and occasional visitors. T. B. Adams Jr. in from Quincy. Announced that my Mother was much better than I could expect, at which news I was much rejoiced.[1] Went to the Athenæum for a few moments to obtain one or two books and thus the morning went.

Dined at the Tremont House, in company with T. B. Adams Jr. and Edward Miller of Quincy. Returned home and spent the Afternoon in reading and writing on my Dissertation of which I feel more sick as I advance. How hard it is to write. Yet one would not suppose so from the mass of stuff one daily sees. Read an Essay of Bacon's upon Love, the opinions of which I do not assent to entirely. There seems to be an absence of clearness in distinguishing the excess of the Passion from the thing itself. The same error would condemn all things merely capable of abuse. The Spectator as usual.

¹ LCA had fallen on getting out of the hack which had taken the family group to Old South Church for the Monroe ceremonies. (JQA, Diary, 25 Aug.; JQA to JA2, 28 Aug., Adams Papers.)

SUNDAY. 28TH.

Morning clear with a decided change in the Weather to cool. So that attendance at Church was much more agreeable. Read and composed in the Morning but never in writing have I met with so much difficulty as in this instance. Have not I studied the subject enough? If so let me set about a re-perusal of the Orations and all the Commentary. Perhaps the real secret remains behind.

Attended divine service and heard Mr. Ripley preach. Text Revelation. 11. 15. "The kingdoms of this world are become the kingdoms of our Lord and of his Christ; and he shall reign for ever and ever." He entered into an explanation of the purpose of Christianity, the tendency of its doctrines to establish social equality, its inconsistency with the monarchical system with which it was so long connected and its increasing power with the increase of civil liberty in the world. Thus it is that the kingdoms of this world are becoming the kingdoms of our Lord. The whole made however so faint an impression that I may give a wrong idea. The Book of Revelation is a mystery. The Chapter from which the text was taken is to me incomprehensible and I can not see the application either for illustration or practice to be made by the text. He might as well have taken the first verse in Genesis, or any other. Mr. W. P. Lunt preached in the afternoon, from 1. Corinthians 7. 31. "And they that use this world, as not abusing it." The subject is old but of a plain practical nature. The Speaker entered into an examination of the true use of the world, of the folly of abandoning it entirely, and of the moderation necessary in its enjoyment. After all the Greek Sage gave the substance of all this reasoning in two words, μηδὲν ἄγαν.¹ Excess as much to be avoided in the privation as in the enjoyment of human blessings. A volume would not teach a clearer lesson. Mr. Lunt has cultivated manner with some success.

Afternoon read a Sermon of Massillon. Text from Luke 1. 32. "He shall be great." The subject, the character of Christ's greatness as explained in the Bible. Of this he made three divisions—first, because he is the Son of God, second, because he is the Saviour of the world, third, because his kingdom endureth forever. He made the application practical as far as it was possible from a spiritual to an earthly kingdom. Certainly the eloquence of this Writer is great. But his manner is too full of point. The mind gets tired and requires relaxation by variety. Evening passed altogether with my Wife. Read the Spectator as usual.

¹ Nothing in excess. The words are Solon's.

MONDAY. 29TH.

Morning fine but cool. The change in the weather for the last two or three days has been very decided. I spent the hour of my morning in a quiet way upon my Work which is in its first sketch drawing towards a close. I am resolved to persevere in my labour, and if I do not make it worth offering for publication at least I shall make something that may be profitable to me as an exercise.

Went to the Office and was occupied there as usual, in writing my Journal and Accounts. I read a part of Fenelon's Dialogue on Eloquence,¹ many of the remarks in which bring up ideas frequently expressed by me in the course of my Sunday comments upon our Clergy. I talked with Mr. Peabody and on the whole was not satisfied with my occupation of time. Dined as usual at the Tremont House.

Afternoon, I accomplished the Draught and read it over. Many of the ideas are good but not quite developed enough. Evening, passed very quietly with my Wife. Read an Essay of Bacon upon great place, the doctrine of which may be practically sound, but it is worldly. The Spectator as usual.

¹ In *Nouveaux dialogues des morts* . . . by F. S. de la Motte Fénelon, dialogue 29 is "Démosthène & Ciceron. Parallèle de ces deux orateurs, ou l'on donne le caractère de la véritable éloquence." The edition at MQA, 3 vols. in 1, was published at Amsterdam in 1727.

TUESDAY. 30TH.

Morning cool and pleasant. I wasted my hour this day in lounging and Conversation with my Wife. Then to the Office where I did not stay long. Having seen Col. White at the Tremont House and he having invited me to call on him there, I felt it incumbent upon me to go and pay my Devoirs. He not being at home, I thought I would leave Cards both for him and his Wife.¹ Thence I went to the Athenæum and lounged an Hour in the Gallery with some acquaintances I had picked up. The time went beyond calculation, so that I found it the proper Hour for Tremont House.

Returned home as usual and sat down to a review of the Orations to see if I have omitted any thing. I find I have studied them so thoroughly as to go on quite fast, reading thirty pages today. But my time is on the whole not so thoroughly employed. Evening with my Wife very quiet. Read an Essay of Bacon's on Boldness and the Spectator.

[1] Joseph M. White, delegate from Florida Territory, with his wife was staying at the Tremont House and attended the Harvard commencement (JQA, Diary, 31 Aug., 2 Sept.).

WEDNESDAY. 31ST.

Morning cool and pleasant. It was Commencement day and of course there was some little bustle in the Streets. My father came in with I. Hull for the purpose of going to Cambridge. Disliking the bustle myself, I declined accompanying him. My time however was much wasted. Went to the Office and having performed my usual duties, I thought I would go to the South end and put up an Advertisement of my Father's Tenement No. 3 to be let (the Tenant[1] having vacated this morning), and afterwards to get some Wine at Mr. J. D. Williams'. This took up so much of my time that on my return to my Office I had only leisure to read Boileau's Preface to his translation of Longinus,[2] before dinner.

Went to the Tremont House as usual but found no acquaintance. At home afterwards when I continued though languidly the Oration of Æschines. My mind is considerably distracted by the multitude of interruptions my life experiences. My Father did not return until evening, and then went off directly to see Dr. Parkman.[3] I read Bacon's Essay on Goodness of Nature and the Spectator. Made an attempt to translate Æschines.

[1] Joseph Libby. See entry for 10 May, above.

[2] Both the preface and "Les réflexions critiques sur ... Longin" by Nicolas Boileau-Despréaux are in vol. 3 of his *Œuvres* in the edition published at Paris in 1768. This volume alone of the set is at MQA.

[3] JQA went to attend a party at Dr. George Parkman's, returning to CFA's house at eleven. His day had been a full one. He had arisen at four; attended a meeting of the Board of Overseers when he reached Cambridge, then all the events of the commencement; afterward, he visited Dr. Waterhouse and was present at the reception at President Quincy's; returning to Boston, he presided at a meeting of those members of Phi Beta Kappa bent upon pressing a further constitutional reform (JQA, Diary, 31 Aug.).

1. JOHN QUINCY ADAMS' SIX BRONZE BUSTS OR "HOUSEHOLD GODS"
ON THE MANTELPIECE OF HIS "WRITING CHAMBER" AT QUINCY

See page vii

EILTON'S NEW THEATRICAL COSTUMES.

Mr E. FORREST as FALCONBRIDGE.

MASTER BURKE
in the Character of
LOONEY MACTWOLTER in the "REVIEW."

Published by M.Burke,108,Ot Surrey-St.Blackfriars Rd.

No. 2. MASTER BURKE IN SIX FAVORITE CHARACTERS. 1.d Plain.

ROMEO.   RICHARD III.d   SHYLOCK.

NORVAL.   NAPOLEON.   HAMLET.

London,Pub. May, 11th 1830,by R.LLOYD.Dramatic Repository,40,Gibson St. near the Coburg Theatre.

"Come back, stranger! or I'll plug you like a watermillion!"

Mr. Hackett as "Nimrod Wildfire."

MONSIEUR
GOUFFE

EVERY EVENING,
AT THE ROYAL
WEST LONDON
Charlotte Street,] THEATRE. [Near Fitzroy Square.
BEDFORD & ROBINS, PRINTERS. PRINTERS, 26, LONDON ROAD.

2–7. SOME DRAMATIC PERFORMERS IN THEIR ROLES AS SEEN BY
CHARLES FRANCIS ADAMS AT THE TREMONT THEATRE, 1830–1832

See page viii

Mrs. Elizabeth Austin, &c. in *Cinderella*

At a Meeting of the Supervisors of the Adams Temple and School Fund at the dwelling house of J. Q. Adams Esqr in Quincy on the 27th day of October 1832.

Present, the whole Board.

The Hon. J. Q. Adams signified his acceptance of the Trust and took his place accordingly.

Chas. F. Adams also appeared and the rate of Office was thereupon administered to him as Clerk by the Hon. T. Greenleaf President of the Board and Jus. of Peace.

Voted, That Mr. Jewett be appointed Superintendent of the Land as agreeably to the provisions contained in the Deed of gift to the town of Quincy.

Voted, That a committee be appointed to ascertain what property belonging to the Supervisors may be in the hands of the Treasurer of the town of Quincy.

Voted, That the same committee be authorized to examine the accounts of the said Town Treasurer so far as they relate to such funds belonging to this Board as may have been or may now be in his hands, since the last settlement.

Voted, That the same Committee be requested to examine the state of the Library, ascertain what number of the books in the catalogue may be missing and report thereon

Voted, That the same committee be authorized to procure a plan and an estimate of the probable expense of a building suitable for a school house and Library agreeably to the provisions contained in the Deed of gift to the Town.

8. THE FIRST MEETING OF THE SUPERVISORS OF THE ADAMS TEMPLE AND
SCHOOL FUND RECORDED BY CHARLES FRANCIS ADAMS AS CLERK

See page ix

THURSDAY. SEPTEMBER 1ST.

Morning fine. I could do little or nothing however. My father and Mother carry with them wherever they go such an Atmosphere of Agitation that one gets almost entirely discomposed from pursuing active work. He went out to Cambridge early and I went to the office. Nothing of material consequence. Some sensation was excited by an article in the Courier against my father's late Letter about Antimasonry.[1] I read it and felt so much irritated at it that I wrote an Answer from the impulse of the moment. Took it down myself to the Patriot Office after dinner and it was accepted.[2] This may be injudicious, but I feel as if it was worth-while to make some attempt to resist the scandalous conduct of this infamous scribbler. My mind was so much agitated about it, that I was not able to study to any purpose. Read Bacon's Essay upon Kings and that was all I did.

Evening, quiet until eight when my Father and I went to Govr. Winthrop's party. It was very brilliant, there being every body there of the body of Strangers with whom the City is filled. I saw many old faces of the Washington Society. Returned home before eleven and read the Spectator.

[1] On 22 Aug. JQA, in addressing a letter to the *Free Press* denying that JA had been identified with Freemasonry, had used the occasion to disclose publicly his support of Antimasonry. The *Boston Courier* (as well as the *Boston Patriot*) on this day reprinted the letter, the *Courier* subjoining it to an editorial headnote, as follows:

"We perceive that some anonymous maker of Presidents at Philadelphia, has nominated John Quincy Adams for that office. Our antimasonic friends will not be under the necessity of seeking any further; if they nominate him . . . , our word for it, he will show himself too pure a patriot to decline the trouble of the election, or the honors of the office. . . . If Mr. Rush has a prior claim . . . Mr. Adams will take the Vice Presidency, or the Speaker's chair, and in the mean time,—we speak not by his authority, but prompted by his example, —he will be happy to make speeches, write letters, or psalms, or do any other odd, antimasonic or other jobs, which may promote the honor and prosperity of the country, by—exalting such an humble servant of the people.

"But it was not our purpose to advertise Mr. Adams as a political doctor ready to physic the body politic (until it throws him up again into the presidency). . . . It seems that some person has claimed the elder Adams, as a Freemason, and the late President has taken up the cudgels to defend his father from so foul an aspersion. Ye gods, masonic and antimasonic! John Quincy Adams defending the fame and memory of John Adams! Such a work of supererogation was never before undertaken by such a laborer! We advise Mr. Adams to take care of his own reputation while living, for it may be that no one can volunteer, with so much hope of success, to make out a clean case for him, when he shall cease to be a candidate for public office—for we apprehend, that is the latest period of which he will have any earthly recollection, so never-ceasing is his love for his poor country" (p. 2, col. 3).

[2] "A Looker On" in a letter in the *Boston Patriot* (2 Sept., p. 2, col. 2) charged Joseph T. Buckingham, the editor of the *Courier*, with "impudence," "effrontery," and "gall" for his calumnies within the month on Messrs. Ingham, Branch, Berrien, Rush, and Adams. He

continued: "Mr. Buckingham is not a fortune to the party he wishes to assist. Mr. Clay may well say 'preserve me from my friends' if he has many of this character—and Mr. Adams, whom he particularly abuses, has already felt the benefit of it. A suggestion made in the *Courier* last year with a sneer, placed him in Congress, and if the same proscriptive course is adopted by him as the friend of Mr. Clay against all antimasons ... it will not only ruin Mr. Clay, but may go hard to bring about the very catastrophe which he would most of all avoid."

JQA in a letter to JA2 (13 Sept., Adams Papers) expressed his own reaction to the continuing attacks upon him: "Masonry, and Jacksonism, and federalism, and Nullification, with all their united forces cannot kill me, and if they could, they would slander my ghost for haunting them after death."

On JQA's earlier relations with Buckingham, see above, vol. 3, entries for 16 Sept. and 18 Oct. 1830.

FRIDAY. 2D.

Morning fine, but did not continue warm, the Wind coming round to the Eastward. I wasted my time as usual. My mind and body are both unwell from the distracted life I am leading, and yet I have kept as much as possible *out* of the places of excitement. My father spoke to me at breakfast of the libels published about him and of my notice of them. He begged me not to mind them and by no means to answer them. I told him exactly how I felt on the subject. That I had no disposition to notice these things in general but that I thought this particular individual rioted in indulgence. That he never treated persons so here who were able to defend themselves, and that the mere absence of this was the cause of his perpetual violence against him. If a notice now and then of him could be serviceable, I was perfectly willing to undertake it.

My time was occupied all day in running about town. Called to see Dr. John Hopkinson who is in town,[1] and invited him to dine with me. I then went to see Mr. Blunt[2] and invite him and then to T. Davis. This with Marketing and sending Notices and fifty other things again distracted my whole time. I talked a little with Mr. Peabody and wrote my Diary. Returned home early. Our dinner was a little parti quarré[3] and was pleasant enough.

Afternoon, my father went to Cambridge and I did absolutely nothing. "Waste of *hours* unemployed."[4] I retired having read Bacon's Essay upon Nobility and The Spectator.

[1] On Dr. John P. Hopkinson of Philadelphia, see vol. 2:44. His father, Judge Joseph Hopkinson, had received an honorary degree at the Harvard commencement the day before (*Harvard Quinquennial Cat.*).

[2] Joseph Blunt of New York City, a political supporter of JQA and publisher of the *American Annual Register* (see above, vols. 1 and 2 *passim*), who currently entertained the idea of writing a life of JA for *Harper's Family Library*. When Blunt inquired whether this would interfere with JQA's announced plan to write the life of his father, JQA replied that he would offer no objection to Blunt's undertaking but renewed the pledge he had made to himself to devote

his energies to the completion of his own biography. JQA, Diary, 19 Oct.; JQA to Blunt, 19 Oct. (LbC, Adams Papers).

[3] That is, *partie carée*, imprecisely or ironically applied to a party of four gentlemen. ABA still kept to her room.

Those at dinner were Dr. Hopkinson, Thomas K. Davis, JQA, and CFA (JQA, Diary, 2 Sept.).

[4] CFA evidently was here adapting from Byron's *The Giaour*: "The waste of feelings unemployed."

SATURDAY. 3D.

Morning Cloudy but it did not rain until Night, and then a mere Shower. I did very little. Went to the Office after leaving my Father to go and complete his arrangements at Cambridge in relation to the admission of Ward N. Boylston.[1] My time was not well employed. I did however succeed in reading some of Longinus. I found many views of the sublime which pleased me though I cannot say I was equally gratified by the lengthy remarks of the Commentators.[2] What a disposition there is in the human mind to be prolix; to run out ideas as far as you can drive them.

Returned home and after dressing started for Medford where my father and I found Messrs. A. H. and E. Everett, Capt. Morris, Mr. Bigelow, Mr. Gorham, Sidney Brooks and his Wife, Chardon and Edward and the usual family. The dinner was pleasant enough though I am tired of precisely the Company. Mr. E. Everett is a man of rather pleasing general manners at table, but his talk is all for effect. He aspires to shine by brilliancy till he satiates. So it is at least with me.

We returned home in the shower, and my father proceeded directly to Quincy. I am glad the week is over, a week of excitement as unusual as it was unwelcome to me. Read Bacon's fine Essay on Sedition and the Spectator.

[1] As one of the executors of the estate of Ward N. Boylston, JQA had assumed the task of arranging for the admission of Ward N. Boylston 2d to Harvard. Having been notified on the day before that the entrance examinations which had begun at 6 A.M. had been satisfactorily met and having taken Ward to the president's house to meet Mrs. Quincy and the young ladies, JQA this day completed the procedure for admission by executing a bond with John

Lane Boylston, Ward's father, in the president's office (JQA, Diary, 1–3 Sept.).

[2] Of the numerous English translations of Longinus, *On the Sublime*, with notes and commentary, the most recent was that published at London in 1830. However, the likelihood is that CFA was referring to the translation from Boileau's French version and commentary which was published in vol. 2 of the English edition of Boileau's *Works*, London, 1711; see entry for 6 Sept., below.

SUNDAY. 4TH.

Yesterday closed another Year since the day of my Marriage. And I have the pleasure of looking back upon it with unmingled satisfaction.

I have never had occasion to regret the occasion of which it was the Anniversary, though not a few had doubts about my judgment in precipitating it.[1] My affairs so far turn out as favourably as I could expect, and I have during the last revolution been blessed with a Child to make my happiness complete. May my humility keep up with the degree of my prosperity, and may I never be led to forget, that all things that I enjoy are the gifts of a beneficent Deity.

My day was a quiet and a pleasant one today. I attended Divine Service all day. Heard Mr. Frothingham in the Morning from Ezekiel 37. 3. "And he said unto me, Son of man, can these bones live? and I answered, O, Lord God, thou knowest." But what the purpose or what the connection of the discourse with the Text I must candidly confess I do not know. I heard an Allusion to the present Polish struggle and to Lord Byron's effort for the Greeks but nothing farther. Mr. Palfrey of Washington[2] preached in the Afternoon from 1 Corinthians 15. 53. "And this mortal must put on immortality." Of course the discourse was upon the immortality of the Soul, with the usual arguments upon it. The Chapter from which it is taken is a very remarkable one being a reason throughout for well doing on account of the promised future life.

Returned home and read Massillon's Sermon upon worldly glory. Text from John 8. 54. "If I honour myself, my honour is nothing." In my humble opinion the best of all I have read. The position assumed is that no glory is true unless combined with the fear of God. The division of worldly glory is into three points—the first, Worldly honour, which he asserted had no foundation to rest upon in matters pertaining to our present condition, whether wealth, rank or the rest of the factitious advantages, the second, brilliant talents which are often but a false light to their possessor, the third, distinguished successes, the offspring of fortune and without security. All this will never support a man. It is the fear of God which will carry him through the trials of life with confidence and with honour. The close is brilliant.

Evening. Tired of writing. Can do nothing with my review and begin to give up. The Spectator as usual.

[1] See vol. 1:xxxii–xxxiii; also vol. 2:363, and above, vol. 3:167.
[2] Cazneau Palfrey, Harvard 1826, was the minister of the Unitarian church in Washington; see *Harvard Quinquennial Cat.*; *General Catalogue of Bowdoin College, 1794–1950*, Brunswick, Maine, 1950.

MONDAY. 5TH.

Morning clear and extremely pleasant. My Wife having been strong enough to dine downstairs yesterday, this morning took a short ride with me, so that it was late before I reached the Office. My time was taken up pretty much in the usual way. Writing, reading a little of Boileau, Accounts and talking with Mr. Peabody. Made a purchase or two for the House, and called at Mr. Brooks room. He surprised us agreeably today, by making us a present of six Shares of the Cocheco Manufacturing Stock with a kind Note expressing his pleasure in adding to our revenue.[1] The thing was done with great delicacy and goodness, and I felt as if my blessings overpowered me. Mr. Brooks is generous with Judgment. And the consequence is that though this in fact increases the benefit, it takes away from the appearance and the credit he deserves. It will probably make a material difference in my Income and relieve me from the Apprehension I have been under respecting my Father's Affairs. Should the worst come to the worst, I can now reasonably hope to be no great charge to him. Until then however it is but fair that I should derive a little benefit to my children from my father's property and not let it *all* sink in the gulf which he and John are forming for it.

Returned home and in the afternoon, read and translated Demosthenes on the Crown. How much I try and how little I do. My attempt looked mean. Forgot in doing it, that this was the regular day for a Directors Meeting of the Boylston Market. A bad omission.

Evening, reading Fenelon's Dialogues on Eloquence which has many sensible things, Bacon's Essay on Superstition, and the Spectator. Bacon prefers Atheism to Superstition. Quære de hoc.

[1] The note from Mr. Brooks accompanying the shares is missing. CFA's words suggest that he was under the impression that the stock was a special gift to ABA, perhaps occasioned by the birth of their child. Actually Mr. Brooks made the same gift this day to each of his children; he valued the shares at $1,000 each (Waste Book). The Cocheco Manufacturing Co. of Dover, N.H., was a relatively new company formed from the failure and recapitalization of the Dover Manufacturing Co. (Caroline F. Ware, *The Early New England Cotton Manufacture*, Boston, 1931, p. 92, 135).

TUESDAY. 6TH.

Morning clear and pleasant. Took a ride with my Wife and lengthened it considerably as I found her better able to bear it. But it brought me to the Office very late and I had no morning. Mr. Rupp the Clerk of the Boylston Market called and I spoke of the proceedings of yesterday, and doubted the expediency of so large a Dividend, as they decided upon.[1] I afterwards said the same thing to Mr. Child whom I met.[2] Mr. Rupp gave me one or two desperate debts to collect for the Company which I promised to do with as well as I could.

The rest of the time was passed in running about town, and finally in going for a book to the Athenæum.

I have concluded to go back to Cicero and consequently began the Letters to Atticus this Afternoon. It is hard that so great a man should rarely be free from suspicion. Guthrie the translator even denies him credit in the famous Conspiracy of Catiline, and intimates that he made full as much of it as it would bear.[3] The idea has certainly crossed my mind when considering the apparent power enjoyed by the enemies of Cicero when accusing him upon this matter, yet on the whole I am led to think it unfounded. Summary punishment was and is a very unpopular, though occasionally a just measure—And we have the evidence of an Enemy, Sallust, besides. Read Bacon's Essay upon Travel, Fenelon, Boileau's Longinus and the Spectator, besides translating a page of Cicero, de optimo genere Oratorum.

[1] The newly declared semiannual dividend was at $4 a share where the preceding one had been at $2.50 (M/CFA/3).

[2] Doubtless Joshua Child, secretary of the Boylston Market; see above, vol. 3, entry for 24 April 1830.

[3] CFA's practice in the afternoon was to read from the Latin text. Apparently he was here reading a commentary on and perhaps some of the translation of the letters preliminary to studying the text itself. William Guthrie was the editor and translator of an edition of *Epistles to Atticus* published at London in 3 vols. in 1806.

WEDNESDAY. 7TH.

I have begun by way of a little variety to read the Oration of Demosthenes accusing Æschines on the matter of the Embassy to Philip. I did not think I should have begun upon him again, but the more I see, the more I am satisfied that the knowledge of the force of Eloquence is only to be got from a study of those specimens in which it is most displayed. I will get the mastery of the Greek Language if it can be done, by perseverance. Rode with my Wife as far as Brookline, making nearly six miles. She seemed to bear it pretty well.

At the Office, but Isaac Hull Adams soon came in to inform me that my Mother and Miss Roberdeau[1] were in town at the Athenæum Gallery. I went to see them and consumed a good proportion of the morning. My Mother informed me of the illness of the Judge my Uncle, and urged my going to see him. After leaving her I saw Mr. Foster and Edward Miller and their Account dissuaded me, for I can be of no use.[2]

Returned home and in the Afternoon read the Letters to Atticus which are pleasant but degrade the character of Cicero very much. It is impossible to deny it. He was a very weak great man and as for his patriotism it was not the patriotism of Cato. Read Bacon's Essay on

Empire in which he shows the same profoundness of mind which always distinguished [him], mixed with a little of the weak prejudice of the age. Translated Cicero and read the Spectator.

¹ Mary Roberdeau, of Philadelphia, had several times during JQA's Presidential term paid extended visits to the Adamses in Washington. She had arrived at Quincy on 31 Aug. for a visit of some weeks. Her presence occasioned a number of evening gatherings that, because she sang prettily, were frequently musical. JQA, Diary, 3 Sept.; above, vols. 1 and 2 *passim*; LCA to Mrs. JA2, 27 Sept. (Adams Papers).

² TBA had been in declining health for some months. Currently his illness was diagnosed as a nervous fever, characterized by involuntary convulsive motions of the limbs and delirium. Unexpectedly, his condition took a favorable turn on the 8th and he became for some time thereafter convalescent. JQA, Diary, 4 Sept.; JQA to JA2, 9 Sept. (Adams Papers).

THURSDAY. 8TH.

As the Judge is so sick, it is on the whole lucky that I invested the last remnant of T. B. Adams Jr's money yesterday,¹ for after his [TBA's] death I imagine there will be no further opportunities.

The day was cloudy with rain so that my Wife did not go out and I read Demosthenes very slowly and imperfectly gathering the Sense from a first perusal. Then to the Office.

I had three Clients today. One, Mr. Curtis to draw a Deed which occupied me all the Morning. One a tipsy Baker who had just been sued and came to me to know what it meant. The third Mr. J. Minot, a reformed Custom House Officer,² who came in consequence of my letter of Collection. He seemed to think he had suffered enough on my father's account not to be troubled by the Son. I felt sorry, but how can I mend the matter?

Returned home and read Cicero making no great progress. The Letters to Atticus are excessively difficult, from their concise style and the allusions to subjects now forgotten. If I remarked the same upon the familiar Letters how much more I have occasion to do so now.

Evening quiet at home. I finished a rough and literal translation of Cicero de Optimo genere Oratorum.³ How hard any translation is? Read Bacon on Counsel and the Spectator.

¹ CFA bought for Thomas B. Adams Jr. one share of State Bank stock (M/CFA/3).

² John Minot had been an inspector for the Custom House in Boston and Charlestown during the Presidency of JQA (*Mass. Register*, 1828), but he had apparently lost his post upon the change of administration. On the use of "re-

formed" in this sense, see above, entry for 29 May.

³ CFA used two editions of Cicero's *Opera*: the large-paper edition published at Oxford in 10 vols. in 1783 and the typographically undistinguished but more useful one edited by Ernest and published at Boston in 20 vols. in 1815 (see above, vol. 3:328, 364–365; below,

entries for 11 and 12 Jan. 1832). His practice seems to have been to translate from Ernest's edition, then compare the text with the Oxford edition, entering errors or variants in the margin there and even his translation itself (below,

entry for 13 Sept.). The "De optimo genere oratorum" is in vol. 3 of Ernest's edition; in vol. 1 of the Oxford edition, the copy of which at MQA contains CFA's translation in his hand (p. 540–544). See above, p. xvi–xvii.

FRIDAY. 9TH.

Morning clear and pleasant instead of having the Storm we anticipated. After reading Demosthenes as usual in the hour before going to the Office, and not riding with my Wife, as Mrs. Frothingham took my place, I passed much time in drawing up the Mortgage corresponding with the Deed made yesterday—The whole much more tedious than profitable. I did little else; Judge Hall called to ask about my Uncle and I had some conversation with Mr. Peabody; then returned home.

Afternoon passed in reading more of the Letters to Atticus, which display in pretty strong colours the condition of Rome and the motives of the principal Actors. I do not find any person exempt from reproach excepting Cato, and he is much the least popular of all. Cicero plainly considers him *foolish*. Read Bacon's Essay on delay which is excellent. Tried my hand over again at Cicero in translating. Read a Lecture of Blair for the purpose of encouragement and finished with the Spectator. Wife and Child well.

SATURDAY. 10TH.

Morning pleasant. I read my usual time in the Oration of Demosthenes upon the false Embassy. Then to the Office where two hours were taken up in talking with Mr. Curtis, Mrs. Boylston and Mr. J. Brooks who called as parties to a Deed but as I had not received it from my Father at that time, it could not be executed. I then went down and drew the several Dividends in the Massachusetts Fire and Marine Insurance Company, and examined all my Accounts for the purpose of making them correct previous to leaving town which I talk of doing.

As Mr. Brooks wished to rectify the Deed in case of any mistake, he appointed the afternoon at my Office for the purpose so that I went down and lost my labour.

The time being too much split up for regular study, I read my father's Eulogy of Mr. Monroe which is just out. It is a brilliant piece of writing, and displays his usual extent of mental capacity, but I think it written with less care and more strain than the generality of his compositions. Read an Essay of Blair. Translated more of Cicero, and the Spectator as usual.

SUNDAY. 11TH.

The day clear but exceedingly warm. It seemed as if the Season was coming back upon us instead of advancing to Winter. My Wife felt the effect of it a good deal and was more languid and low spirited than at any time. Recovery in cases of this kind is so slow and accompanied with such a variety of trifling yet vexatious drawbacks that it is not wonderful if courage sometimes fails.

I employed my morning in reading Demosthenes. Attended divine service as usual and heard Mr. George Whitney, in the morning from John. 16. 12. "I have yet many things to say unto you, but ye cannot bear them now." The discourse was intended to illustrate the progressive improvement of the world, a very favourite theory with the present generation. Under the "many things" of the text the preacher considered as now able to bear when it was not at that time, he included a disposition to check War, the detestation of slavery, the decrease of the power of mere public opinion &ca. Yet if we look round the world does he not hug a delusion. Peace has lasted but fifteen years since a long and desolating War, and at this moment the elements of Civil Society are in greater confusion almost throughout the Christian World than they have been for ages. Slavery is not only no where checked, but it positively increases and that immensely in many parts of the world. As to the third opinion, it is somewhat original with the author in itself. He considers the omnipotence of public opinion as an evil. Most persons regard it as a blessing. The difference lies in the definition of the words. The preacher considers it as prejudice for good or for evil, slow to be moved and as quick to go under bad influences as good ones. He therefore thinks the world has improved from a superior susceptibility to the action of leading individual minds. That it is more susceptible is probably true. But so far from this decreasing the force of public opinion, I should think it had increased it a thousand fold. Whether this has not produced a considerable degree of habitual subserviency in leading minds I will not undertake to say, but this I will say, that you see less originality than you did. So much for Mr. Whitneys morning Sermon. It remains only to say, that his manner pleased me and that he displayed more ability than I gave him credit for.

In the afternoon he preached from Hebrews 2. 15. "And deliver them who through fear of death were all their life-time subject to bondage."

In other words an exhortation to be prepared at all times for death. It was not particularly interesting.

On my return home I read as usual one of the Sermons of Massillon. Text. Matthew. 21. 5. "Behold, the king cometh unto thee, meek." Subject—the dangers awaiting the piety of the great, 1st through indolence in piety and disinclination to perform the duties of their station, 2d through timidity and irresolution, 3d through prejudiced piety. On the whole very good, but Massillon's style bears the stamp of too regular labour to last long agreeable. This Sermon is however very remarkable for the popular doctrine it addresses to the King upon his original right to the Crown.

Read Bacon's Essay on Wisdom for a Man's Self and Blair's Lecture on Taste. A plain but a clear style.

Evening, working upon Cicero, and the Spectator.

MONDAY. 12TH.

The temperature altered so much as to make the weather fine and clear and cool today. After reading Demosthenes again, I went to the Office and was busy for an hour in finishing the Deed and Mortgage &ca. but at last got the Parties to execute it and thus the transaction was made complete. The whole of this gives me a tolerable fee and supplies my deficiencies for some time past as a Lawyer.

T. B. Adams Jr. called in for half an hour with a Note from my father.[1] He talked a little about his funds and I concluded from his application to lend him a sum of Money on his Note, in preference to his drawing away the amount of his Dividends. Perhaps I am wrong. But I mean to check what I see to be a growing disposition to extravagance.[2] If not he must add one more to the long list of men who having good advice neglects it.

Returned home and in the afternoon read the third Book of the Letters to Atticus in which is the series of womanish complaint[s] at his exile and persecution. Cicero is not a great man in his personal character. Read Bacon's Essay on Innovations and a little of Blair. Tried more of my translation, closed with the Spectator. My Wife was much better today.

[1] JQA to CFA, 11 Sept. (Adams Papers); a warm iteration of LCA's invitation to ABA for the family to come to Quincy at once and to stay until mother and child had gained strength and were in good health: "I pack up my expectations in Patience till the end of this week."

[2] On other qualities of a related sort displayed by Thomas B. Adams Jr., see above, entry for 9 May, note.

TUESDAY. 13TH.

Morning cool and clear. Pursued the study of the Oration against Æschines which has a great deal of power. Indeed it is worth full the same study as a specimen of Attack, that is bestowed upon the famous Crown Oration as a Defence. I then went to the Office and occupied myself in writing my Journal. Tried to take my Grandfather's book upon the American Constitutions. But it is absolutely too dull and I give it up. I then went to the Athenæum where I lounged half an hour in the Gallery and another half hour in the reading room. Looked at one or two of the political Papers and regretted that the state of public affairs should look so gloomy. But a most astonishing combination of events is favouring the most unprincipled Rulers we as a Nation have ever had.

Returned home and after dinner read the Letters to Atticus, Book 4th. No man probably ever had his whole soul so fully laid open to the public as Cicero. This may be said in palliation of the faults of the man, but it condemns all men. Human nature is not perfect, every body knows. Nor is Cicero the best specimen of that nature. Read Bacon's Essay on Dispatch which is as sterling sense as any of the rest of his Works.

Evening, made a little further progress in my translation. I have copied it, into the margin of the Quarto Copy of Cicero which I have.[1] This is perhaps wrong. The translation is rather difficult from the concise style of the Text. He rather touches than opens his ideas. This is unusual with him but he had written a great deal upon Oratory and was probably tired of detail. The Spectator. My Wife and Child tolerably.

[1] See entry for 8 Sept., above.

WEDNESDAY. 14TH.

Morning clear and quite cool but it soon clouded over. I pursued my usual study of Demosthenes, until it was time to go to the Office. Began today a review of the Federalist which I propose now to examine more thoroughly than I have yet been able to do.[1] It is becoming every day of more importance to know what the framers of the Constitution did really and in truth mean. One man says one thing, another thinks the opposite to it is the proper sense, and none are willing now to bow to the decision of any common arbiter. If there is any thing more particularly dangerous than the rest, to our prospects of continuance as a Nation, it is this growing indisposition to compromise. A disposition which if cherished in the minutest concerns of life makes unhappiness, must be destructive when it is prevailing in the divisions of a People. If I should ever be called to deliver any address, I think this would be a useful subject. No body called today. I passed an hour in reading George's Papers, particularly his letters to Mary. How sorrowful they make me. And when I look back, what causes have I to be grateful to the protection of a divine Providence.[2]

Returned home and passed the afternoon in reading the Letters to Atticus. An Essay of Lord Bacon on Seeming Wise, and in the Evening Translated the rest of my task excepting the last Section, and the Spectator. My Wife was pretty well, the Child with a little cold.

[1] CFA's earlier reading in *The Federalist* was in 1826; on the Adamses' copies, see above, vol. 2:29.

[2] See above, vol. 3, entry for 8 Sept. 1829. No letters from GWA to Mary Catherine Hellen (Mrs. JA2) are known to survive.

Quincy

THURSDAY. 15TH.

The day was cloudy, and it rained in showers all along, until it set in more heavily towards night. After reading a part of the Oration of Demosthenes, I went to the Office and occupied myself in my usual avocations, attending particularly to my Journal and Accounts.

Mr. Kirke came in and notified me of his being ready to take us out, so that accordingly I made ready. This visit to Quincy is an unexpected one to me. I had resolved not to go again and had it not been for the strong recommendations of both Doctor and Nurse I should have wished to avoid it.[1] Returned to my house and found it in disorder and my Wife under the impression that leaving a place almost always creates.

We got through the ride very well, but the circumstances attending our arrival were not pleasant. Madame was sick, Miss Roberdeau unwell, the day gloomy—All together combined to dispirit. My Wife was strongly under the influence,[2] and I escaped it more only from occupying myself in making my arrangements to establish myself in the Office independently of any other person's room.[3] I have come here this time on a new footing. I remain here all the time instead of passing my mornings in Boston, and I abstract myself more in order to avoid being entangled in the results likely to occur from diversities of sentiment between my father and myself.[4] These results made my last stay here unpleasant, and unless I prevent it by decided conduct will this.

Read Bacon's Essay on Friendship, but rather negligently, and two numbers of the Spectator as usual.

136

¹ ABA had not regained her strength, had lost considerable weight, and was not able to resume her management of the household; LCA2 had had to have a tooth extracted before she was a month old. The conditions that impelled the removal to Quincy and the benefits effected by the visit are evident in LCA's letters to Mrs. JA2:

"[Y]ou would be shocked to see how she [ABA] has fallen away to a mere shadow. Her spirits were almost as much affected as her health but they are recovering and I hope much from her visit tho' I fear it will take a long time to restore her. The Boston system of nursing does not suit me at all from what I see of it. . . .

"The Baby grows finely and I think promises to be like our stock; she will have dark eyes like her Mothers I think but every body here calls them *Blue*. Her head is quite bald in front and so exactly like her Grandfathers that it is hardly possible to look at her without laughing. Poor little thing her tooth was obliged to be extracted by a dentist who was under the necessity of making an instrument for the purpose. It was in the under jaw with a perfect root the top of it indented and as white and sound as that of Infants at the regular age. This circumstance has set all the doctors to work at their books but hitherto it is said there has no case been found recorded. If it is to be productive of so much research it must at all events be called a wise tooth" (20 Sept., Adams Papers).

"Dr. Holbrook . . . says Abby's . . . child [has] . . . a very uncommon head the bones of which are more formed than that of a much older Child, and the shape of it is exactly like her Grandfathers which makes her look as wise as an Owl. She bids fair to be as lively as her Mother" (13 Oct., Adams Papers).

See also, LCA to Mrs. JA2, 27 Aug., 5, 10, and 27 Sept. (all in Adams Papers); and below, entries for 21 Sept. – 11 Oct. *passim*.

² That is, influenced by the surrounding gloom.

³ On "the Office" at Quincy, not to be confused with CFA's office in Boston, see below, entry for 17 Sept. and note.

⁴ The subjects which were the cause of friction were JQA's financial affairs and his antimasonic politics. See above, entries for 22 May, 18 and 19 July, 25 August.

FRIDAY. 16TH.

Morning cold with the Wind setting from the Eastward and every prospect of a long storm. This is rather a gloomy beginning. My night's rest was considerably disturbed by the child, the care of which now falls upon her Mother entirely. I arose early and began my way of life by spending my time morning and afternoon in the following order, this being what I propose to establish during my residence out here. First, my Diary, then, as I cannot find here the Oration upon the Embassy, the first Philippic in an Edition by one Richard Mounteney,¹ which has been interlined by my father, and which shows his labour though not his scholarship. At least he makes several errors. Then the Papers of the Federalist connected with the History of the Confederation and Constitution. This makes the morning.

Afternoon, the Letters to Atticus. This, with the usual small Tasks such as the Essay of Bacon and the Spectator, will make the amount of my labour.

Evening, I sat a little while with Madame and then walked with my Father to my Uncle's, the Judge's. Found him rather better I thought than when I went away. He talked more and with rather more spirit. I returned to him the trifles he put into my hands and was very glad to be relieved of the responsibility attending them.[2] We returned home and I after reading a little of Mrs. Royall's *last*,[3] retired rather early.

[1] Demosthenes, *Selectæ orationes*, Cambridge, England, 1731, in Greek and Latin. The present whereabouts of JQA's interlined copy is not known. However, there is a copy of a London, 1771, edition among JA's books in the Boston Public Library (*Catalogue of JA's Library*, p. 72).

[2] See above, entry for 1 July.

[3] The most recently published of Mrs. Anne Royall's travel books was *Mrs. Royall's Southern Tour, or Second Series of the Black Book*, Washington, 1831, "in three or more vols."; at MQA is vol. 2 only. On Mrs. Royall see also vols. 1:xxix, 2:150, above.

SATURDAY. 17TH.

The morning opened cheerless and dark, but we established a good counterpoise to the effect of the weather without, by making comfortable fires. I went to the Office however and remained there until driven in by the cold.[1] Performed my usual series of duties. Finished the first Philippic which I regard as a very powerful production. Short but clear and developing a policy according to the rules recommended by the Rhetoricians, in such a manner as to instruct, to please and to excite his Auditors. I am glad circumstances turned my Attention to it. Continued reading the Federalist and examined the Numbers relating to the dangers to the States. It is a little singular that the contingency likely to take place, was never foreseen by any of the Writers for the Federalist. They judged only from what they had seen, partial insurrections in particular States, but they did not extend their vision to what seems now as one of the most easily to be foreseen occurrences, the discontent of a State. The *spirit* of the reasoning however goes to show the total absurdity of the doctrine now advanced respecting the part that the States as separate Governments have in the original compact.

Afternoon, after an hour in the Garden, I continued the Letters to Atticus. The period of Cicero's Proconsulship is on the whole one of the most creditable portions of his career. He abstained from the Commission of any of the enormities so usual with the Roman Provincial Governors. Yet so little had he in his mind the principles of true morality, which directs human conduct in the path of virtue, by motives drawn from its innate value, that in all the letters to Atticus, it is plain he regards the fame, the reputation of this world as the great object to be gained. Perhaps even this is a great deal, apart from the knowledge given us through the religion of Christ.

Read Bacon's Essay on the true greatness of Kingdoms and Estates, and two numbers of the Spectator. Evening with the Ladies, read aloud from the Young Duke.[2]

[1] Until the building was torn down in 1869, a part of the second floor of the old farmhouse, located within the grounds and just to the north of the Old House, was known as "the Office." The second floor had been added in 1798 to serve JA as an office in Quincy and to house his library. His books remained there until after JQA's death.

When the building was remodeled to its new purposes an outside stairway was built to provide direct access to the office. At the same time a chimney opening and fireplace in the room were provided for. If the office, at the time

of CFA's use of it, was kept unheated, it was perhaps through fear of fire.

Cotton Tufts to AA, 31 March, 17 April, 12 May 1798; AA to Cotton Tufts, 16 April, 25 May 1798; Mrs. Richard Cranch to AA, 23 April 1799 [i.e. 1798] (all in Adams Papers). See also Charles E. Peterson, The Adams Mansion, Historic Structures Report, U.S. Department of the Interior, National Park Service, 1963 [typescript], p. 57–59.

[2] Benjamin Disraeli's most recently published novel, London and N.Y., 1831.

SUNDAY. 18TH.

Morning clear with a pleasant wind from the Westward and altogether an agreeable day. After my morning's occupation, I attended divine Service and heard a Mr. Edes, a young man not yet settled,[1] preach two very respectable Sermons upon 1st. the servitude of sin. Text John. 8. 34. "Whosoever committeth sin is the Servant of sin." He drew a contrast between the disgust commonly entertained at the slavery of the body, and the indifference with which the slavery of the mind is regarded. And filled his Sermon by citing examples of the influence of the passions upon man. His afternoon discourse was upon 1. Peter 1. 13. "Be sober" and was of rather a higher order. He inculcated the necessity of sobriety in all matters of life, whether in pleasure or in business, in happiness or in misery. The subjects of neither one new. But then what can be new that relates to the Christian faith? The latter subject is as old as the μηδὲν ἄγαν of the Greek wise man.

Read one of Massillon's Sermons in the afternoon, upon the Obstacles to the truth existing in the heart of the great. His text from Psalms 2. 2. "The kings of the Earth set themselves, and the Rulers take Counsel together, against the Lord and against his Anointed." He divided these obstacles into two: The Jealousy of all distinction which does and will always exist among men to depress true honour and virtue, and the self interest which pushes to the acquisition of fortune. He shows how these Passions operated to attempt the destruction of the Saviour and how he finally triumphed over these passions. This makes the substance of the Sermon, in which the parts are worked with very considerable power. But the eloquence of Massillon is not the eloquence of business, it is the stately movement of a studied uncontested style, not the fire and steel as Cicero calls it of the real battle of Wits. I read Bacon's Essay on Regimen of Health.

Evening passed with the family. I read a part of the Spectator and a little of the Review of Affairs in 1830 in the Cabinet Cyclopedia. Mr. and Miss Whitney[2] called upon Miss Roberdeau and Abby.

[1] Both Edward Henry Edes and Henry Francis Edes, Brown 1828, graduated in divinity at Harvard in 1831 (*Harvard Quinquennial Cat.*). JQA further identified the preacher as the son of Dr. Henry Edes (Harvard 1799)

of Providence, and as newly installed at Taunton (Diary, 18 Sept.).

[2] That is, Rev. Peter Whitney and his daughter Caroline (vol. 1:164; 2:153, note).

MONDAY. 19TH.

The day was a very fine one. I arose later than usual from having disturbed rest on account of the Baby. I have tried her three nights and have slept but about half as much as I commonly do. Isaac Hull went to Boston with his brother Thomas. I therefore[1] did not continue with Demosthenes. My father stopped me with a few moments Conversation. He entertains the intention of purchasing the Patriot Newspaper as a Speculation, in case of his not being nominated for any situation which should make it improper, and he suggested to me the idea of becoming it's editor, to be assisted by him as a Contributor.[2] This is a matter for consideration. Some circumstances might make the situation quite desirable to me while the care, responsibility and hazard would rather alter my present smooth way of living. I told him that I would consider of it. Read a little of the Federalist, but my attention was shaken by thinking upon this subject. I copied a letter for my Father which took up a good deal of time.[3]

Afternoon, walked with him to the Orchard at Mount Wollaston, and examined the condition of the Trees. Found them pretty well, but overgrown with suckers about the root, which I felt obliged to Clip. So that my afternoon's work was somewhat laborious. We got home by Sunset, and I read Bacon's Essay, of suspicion.

Evening, from my walk, and my sleeping so little of late, I was very drowsy. Read the Spectator and retired early.

[1] Because CFA had to assume for the morning Hull's duties as JQA's amanuensis.

[2] The possibility of acquiring the *Boston Patriot* arose, it would seem, from the ill health of John Brazer Davis, the

paper's publisher and editor. CFA continued for some time to weigh the question (see the next entry below, and that for 12 Nov., note). JQA rejected the idea finally as "too hazardous. I have no doubt you may employ yourself usefully to yourself and to your own interest in writing occasionally for the public Journals, but it would be a desperate case to connect yourself in pecuniary interest with any one of them" (JQA to CFA, 22 Nov., Adams Papers). However, CFA continued to advert to the possibility (below, entry for 31 Jan. 1832).

[3] The letter from JQA to A. H. Everett, 18 Sept., in JQA's letterbook is in CFA's hand; on the letter, see entry for 23 Sept., below.

TUESDAY. 20TH.

Morning clear, warm and very pleasant. Occupied myself this morning in my usual way. Read a large part of the first Olynthiac of Demosthenes, in which he tries to encourage the People of Athens in their struggle with Philip. He uses in this a figure which struck me before in the Oration for the Crown. Here it is amplified—The pains and aches which remain concealed in a healthy body, but break forth again upon the Attack of any new Disease. Is not this coming close to the border of the Rule as to unpleasant objects?[1] I also read attentively the Numbers of the Federalist written by Mr. Madison upon the powers and nature of the Government of the United States. They certainly qualify my Father's position in his late Oration and increase my doubts formerly entertained of the solidity of it.[2] I mean to say that though I think the argument he urges is eminently necessary for the safety of the Union, yet that it was not at the time of the formation of the System the intent of its makers to rest upon it.

Afternoon, read a part of the letters to Atticus, but I am so little provided with the necessary Notes and explanations here, that I do not take their force so fully. Bacon's Essay on Discourse, which contains a great deal of sense, as usual. This little book might be made a practical guide for human conduct though not always for good. The wheat must be winnowed.

Evening at home. Conversation with my Mother. I communicated to her my father's proposition and talked with her over it. I have reflected upon it considerably. Yet it is hardly of importance until we shall see what a month may bring forth. The objections I find rest in my political opinions, and in my father's decided temper which leads him to neglect tact, and make the prospects of the paper's support suffer. These may be avoided if I can obtain the management of [*i.e.* obtain management for?] the fiscal concerns and confine myself to the literary portion of the Paper in the editorial department. On the other hand the advantages are numerous. It will give me an employment, at once creditable and useful, perhaps profitable, and it may enable me to obtain reputation sooner than in the beaten road.

Read the Affairs of 1830 in the Cyclopedia, finishing the first Volume, and the Spectator.

[1] That is, "subjects"?   [2] See above, entry for 4 July.

WEDNESDAY. 21ST.

Morning cloudy and cold, threatening an unpleasant day, but it cleared away and was on the whole pleasant enough. My Wife is now suffering from a boil on her Nose. A thing calculated to try her patience considerably, though perhaps not otherwise serious.

I read in the morning the remainder of the first and part of the second Olynthiac, and was struck with the philosophical character of the remarks they contain. The want of this is an objection made by my father to the style of this Orator, but I cannot think there is any soundness in it. To be sure we never have the Dissertations which Cicero calls common places, but it is a question by no means settled whether they, however beautiful they may be, are not out of place. I also read with attention the numbers of the Federalist which treat of the powers conferred in the various Articles of the Constitution upon the National Government, all of which numbers strange to say, are the composition of Mr. Madison. It is perhaps a pity that Mr. Hamilton did not contribute one or two of these, as it is now highly desirable that the opinions of the framers should be known, and Hamilton was understood to differ somewhat in several doctrines from his coadjutor.

Spent half an hour in the Garden giving directions about the fruit for next year. Afternoon, reading the Letters to Atticus, and noticing the great trepidation in which the Writer was at the breaking out of the civil war, and his vacillation about the proper course for him to pursue. Had he possessed any military ability he might have settled the Republic himself. Every thing combined in his favour. A Consular Government, a Parthian invasion just alarming enough to authorize him to keep a large army on foot, and great personal popularity. But the vis was not in him. He was therefore floated about at the mercy of the winds which blew upon him from different quarters.

Evening, Mr. T. B. and Miss E. C. Adams came down, and we had music [1] and a pleasant time. I continued the Review of Events in 1830 and read the Spectator. Also Bacon's Essay on Plantations, which with some truth contains many errors.

[1] Piano and singing (JQA, Diary, 21 Sept.).

THURSDAY. 22D.

Morning cloudy, but on the whole tolerably warm. I passed my morning in reading Demosthenes in the latter part of the second Olynthiac. It is wonderful how clear his argument always is. He has no dimness in his conceptions. This is the very first requisite of a powerful Orator. He must know his subject so fully as to have not the least hesitation in unfolding it. And then he must take care not to entangle himself with irrelevant matter. I also read some numbers of the Federalist. Half an hour spent in the garden for exercise, in which I set a bed of Strawberries from the Keen's seedling roots purchased in the Summer. I found the original Plants in pretty poor condition, but there had grown several very healthy ones from the Runners. T. B. Adams Jr. dined with us.

Afternoon the letters to Atticus. But I feel heated after dinner, probably from eating too much, and I am not able to pursue the study so fully as I might. Besides, the want of Notes is a terrible thing. It takes away all the interest of a Book to understand it but partially. I read Bacon's Essay "Of Riches," which is very good. A large part of the Evening was passed with my Wife who seemed a good deal discouraged by her little trials. The rest with the Ladies, and reading the Affairs of 1830 as well as the Spectator.

FRIDAY. 23D.

Morning cloudy and dark but it did not rain until night. I went to Boston today. Called at my Office but could not get in. I left my Key at Mr. Elliot's,[1] and he went to Salem where he left his. So that both of us were in fine condition. Had Mr. Peabody come at the same moment his plight would not have been one bit better. It was lucky for me that I had other occupation. My father had requested me to call upon Mr. A. H. Everett and give him the MS about the Federalists.[2] After going to my House and making the arrangements which I proposed, I went to his. And though I had intended remaining for fifteen minutes Mr. Buckingham the Editor of the Courier came in, and I immediately retired. Perhaps it might be a curious question to know how this alliance has been forming.[3] But I meddle not with such secrets. I then went to see Mrs. Frothingham, then to the Athenæum, then to see Mr. Brooks, then on various Commissions, then to see Edmund Quincy and so the morning was consumed. I returned to Quincy to dine.

Afternoon, finished the ninth book of the letters to Atticus still describing his distress, his shame, his fear and his knowledge of the right with his indisposition to pursue it. Bacon's Essay on Prophecies.

Evening heavy showers. Sat with the Ladies. Music. Afterwards, Affairs of 1830 and the Spectator.

[1] William Elliot Jr., an attorney, occupied the office in the 23 Court Street building formerly rented by D. A. Simmons (M/CFA/3).

[2] On 16 Sept. A. H. Everett in a letter to JQA (Adams Papers) had reminded him of his promise to lend Everett "your last letter to the Boston Gentlemen on the Hartford Convention." JQA had replied (see above, entry for 19 Sept., note) saying that he would send the MS according to promise but that "it would not be fit for public inspection without severe revisal"; asking Everett to mark those passages "of which you would advise the omission" and to make comments to accompany the MS on its return (The letter is printed in *AHR*, 11:340–343 [1906]). In December, after a "little *fillip*" from JQA, Everett returned the MS to CFA (JQA to CFA, 13 Dec.; CFA to JQA, 31 Dec., LbC; both in Adams Papers). Because JQA and Harrison Gray Otis were moved by political developments toward a reconciliation in 1832, JQA then abandoned any thought of publication; see below, entry for 17 Dec. 1832, note. On the later history of the MS, see vol. 3:63.

[3] CFA's and JQA's subsequent mistrust of A. H. Everett's political stance may, in part, reflect this incident.

SATURDAY 24TH.

Lovely day after the Rain. Amused myself in writing my Diary, then in reading a part of the third Olynthiac. This I find is commonly put as the first of these three. It is much in the style of the rest. The same clearness, the same force. They are all worthy of attentive study, and while here I believe I shall confine myself to them. They comprise the whole book of Mounteney which I am now studying. Read some Numbers of the Federalist upon the Constitution of the House of Representatives. T. B. Adams Jr. called in and consulted me about the form requisite to make a Will. I gave him the best advice I could.

After dinner, read the tenth book of the Letters to Atticus to which I may apply much the same remarks I made yesterday. My way of life here is almost too quiet for my benefit if not for my taste. When I get into the common bustle of the City, it bewilders me. Yet if I had my way, I would not do any thing else. The din of arms or of Carts is not to my taste. Read Bacon's Essay on Ambition, which has much politic truth, but little moral truth.

Evening with the Ladies. Afterwards I finished the Affairs of 1830 and the usual numbers of the Spectator.

SUNDAY. 25TH.

The day was very fine. As usual I attended Divine Service all day. Mr. Lamson of Dedham preached.[1] Texts. Matthew 6. 34. "Take therefore no thought for the morrow: for the morrow shall take thought for the things of itself. Sufficient unto the day is the evil thereof." 1. Thessalonians 4. 11. "That you study to be quiet and to do your own business." The first Sermon was an examination of the doctrine of the Text, which does in fact require explaining—The Epicurean system being based upon very much the same words. Mr. Lamson thinks the intention was to deprecate over-anxiety to the obtaining of the things of this world. This takes off the attention of man from higher objects and worthier feelings, and so indeed it is. The passion for wealth is perhaps the most universal on the Globe. Its operation is to narrow the liberal feelings, to check nobility of soul. If there is any reproach to be made to people in this Quarter it is this. The Afternoon Sermon was upon the Meddler, the busy body and his unfavourable influence upon Society. Both discourses were sensible and adapted to the practical course of life. This is the use of a Clergyman. Mr. Lamson and Miss Smith dined with us.

I read in the Afternoon a Sermon of Massillon's, making the last of the Petit Carême. It was upon the triumph of Religion. Colossians. 2. 15. "And having spoiled principalities and powers, he made a shew of them openly, triumphing over them in it." He shews that the glory of the world has three great obstacles in it's way. The Envy of greatness, the influence of the Passions, and the decay of all things. Religion is the only basis upon which stability is marked. This addressed to a King was undoubtedly sound advice. But this and all the rest might as well have been pronounced to a Stone. Louis 15 was corrupt, and his Court profligate beyond most of his predecessors. And Massillon's Oratory remains to explain another moral lesson of the weakness of human nature.

Evening, the Misses Greenleaf[2] and Mr. and Mrs. J. Quincy Jr. Some Music. I read afterwards a part of Gillies Greece[3] and the Spectator.

[1] Alvan Lamson was the Congregational minister at Dedham (*Mass. Register*, 1831).
[2] The daughters of Thomas Greenleaf, Eliza and Mary Ann; see vol. 2:153.
[3] John Gillies, *The History of Ancient Greece, Its Colonies, and Conquests*, was first published in 2 vols. at London in 1786. A copy of this edition is among JA's books at the Boston Public Library (*Catalogue of JA's Library*, p. 102) and of another among JQA's at the Boston Athenæum (*Catalogue of JQA's Books*, p. 97).

MONDAY. 26TH.

The day was cloudy and dark with occasional heavy rain though not cold. I occupied myself as usual. Finished the third Olynthiac of

Demosthenes. I propose now to devote some time to a careful review of them—So that I may know them at any time at sight, without difficulty in construction. They are all specimens of a style but very little known in our day. The concise, persuasive, popular style. I wonder that somebody or other has not studied this manner for use in the present day. Our haranguing style is very indifferent. Read some numbers of the Federalist upon the arrangement of the Senate, and then examined an old volume of Debates in the Convention of Massachusetts that diverted me.[1]

Afternoon, read the eleventh Book of the letters to Atticus, which is another scene of trepidation after the defeat of the Pompeian party. Who would have been Cicero with all his glory and all his weaknesses? For my part I should prefer to remain what I am, a quiet, inoffensive mortal. Read Bacon's Essay on Masques and Shows.

Evening with the ladies, after which I continued Gillies, and read two of Addison's Essays upon the Imagination.

[1] This was presumably *Debates, Resolutions and Other Proceedings, of the Convention . . . of Massachusetts, Convened, on the 9th of January, 1788, . . . for the Purpose of . . . Ratifying the Constitution Recommended by the Grand Federal Convention*, Boston, 1788. A copy is among JA's books in the Boston Public Library (*Catalogue of JA's Library*, p. 161).

TUESDAY. 27TH.

The morning was dark and we had rain at intervals throughout the day. So that I could not execute my intention of going to Boston. Instead of it, I occupied myself in reviewing a large part of the first Philippic of Demosthenes. I find it quite easy, though as usual I perceive more beauty and more connexion, in this perusal. I then read several numbers of the Federalist upon the powers of the President which contain much strong reasoning that I never noticed before, upon the feature of the system restraining the election to four years of Office and admitting a continuance. I have been very much inclined to the other side, but these arguments are certainly worth considering.

Continued the Debates in the Massachusetts Convention, and was struck with the Speech of Mr. T. Dawes of Boston who was decidedly in the opinion that Manufactures were to be protected.[1] I think I can make use of this, some time or other.

Afternoon, the twelfth book of the Letters to Atticus in which I made considerable progress. Also Bacon's Essay upon Men's Nature. Thus passed a day as quiet as they generally go here.

Evening with the Ladies, after which Gillies and two of Addison's Papers.

[1] The speech of Thomas Dawes Jr., of Boston, was in support of the adoption of Article I, sect. 8, giving Congress the power to lay and collect taxes, duties, imposts, and excises. On Dawes, see further, *Commonwealth Hist. of Mass.*, 4:36, 41.

WEDNESDAY. 28TH.

The day was clear with occasional gusts of wind very high. I went to town at last. My time was taken up in a great variety of ways. My course was first to the House, then to the Office where I was occupied first in my Accounts, then in receiving Calls. Mr. A. H. Everett came with a letter from himself to my father.[1] He discussed political matters for a little while, and was interrupted by a Mr. Allen who came about an application of his to my father for money which I passed off as soon as I could. This man I recollected once before as coming about that business of Farmer's. He apologized for it today. Mr. Brooks came in to get Copies of my Father's addresses sent to Mr. Davis of New York.[2] I went over to see Sidney Brooks about it.

Mr. Josiah Bradlee had invited me to dine, but I was informed that he was sick and could not receive us. So I called at Mrs. Frothingham's and was asked to go there. The remainder of my morning was spent in other Commissions for the family. Met at Mr. Frothingham's Sidney and his Wife, Mr. Brooks and two Miss Phillips'es. Dinner pleasant enough, but somehow or other I do not fancy that set. The older I grow, the greater is my repugnance without knowing indeed the true and real cause of it. The true reason probably is that I feel as if I was always under criticism and observation. This *stiffens* me and makes me appear to disadvantage.

After one or two more Commissions I returned home to Quincy. My Mother had invited the Quincy people to spend the Evening.[3] And it was got through tolerably well. I read the Spectator afterwards.

[1] Everett's letter is missing; doubtless it was a reply to JQA's letter of 18 Sept., on which see above, entry for 23 Sept., note.

[2] Charles A. Davis, partner in the firm of Davis & Brooks, 28 South Street, New York City, with whom Sidney Brooks was associated (above, vol. 3:4; *American Almanac, N.Y. Register and City Directory*, 1827–1828).

[3] The guests, in addition to the TBA family, were "the Baxter's, Beale's, Greenleaf's (Thomas and Daniel), Marston, Miller's, Quincy's, and Whitney's, Mr. Gourgas and Mr. Hallett" (JQA, Diary, 28 Sept.).

THURSDAY. 29TH.

My time slipped away so fast this morning that I had only half an hour to continue Demosthenes. Walked into town with my Wife to make purchases. I think she is becoming gradually stronger, and hope that another fortnight will quite restore her. I read the numbers of the Federalist upon the Judiciary and was much pleased with them. As an instance of how much passes from the mind, it may as well be said that I have read the Federalist twice before, and yet it is now quite new to me. Continued the Debates in the Massachusetts Convention which amuse me more and more. The mind of man is generally but a weak affair, and no better proof of it can be produced than the incorrectness of the objections made to the Constitution, the features which have proved most faulty, were those least opposed or most approved.

After dinner I went down for amusement to fish, but I could not find that there were any smelts come up yet. I spent two hours in doing nothing and then returned. Read Bacon's Essay on Custom and Education.

Evening a Party of Quincy People at M. T. Greenleaf's, from which I was glad to get home and read the Spectator.

FRIDAY 30TH.

Morning cool but fine weather. I remained quietly at home and finished the review of the first Philippic and of the first Olynthiac, but I want Reiske's edition to make the study thorough. I do not think I ever saw a work more complete in itself than that edition of Reiske. As a model for editions to satisfy students it is deserving of imitation, though rather too heavy for very general use.[1] I finished to day the numbers of the Federalist and have been on the whole very much benefitted by this examination of it. I now propose to read the Debates in the Conventions of the several States. They are curious enough.

Afternoon, began the letters to Atticus, but I thought that for exercise I would try to fish again, with yesterday's success. Read Bacon's Essay upon Fortune and in the evening went with the ladies to Mrs. Josiah Quincy's. We found a few of the same set, and had a musical party. Miss Roberdeau and Mr. R. Apthorp[2] making the substance of it. Returned at ten, myself walking, and finished by reading two numbers of the Spectator.

[1] On John Jacob Reiske's edition of *Oratorum Græcorum*, in which vols. 9–11 contain the *Apparatus criticus ad Demosthenem*, see above, vol. 3:245.

[2] Robert Apthorp (LCA to CFA, 30 Oct., Adams Papers). He may be the person referred to at vol. 1:326 and there surmised to be George H. Apthorp.

SATURDAY. OCTOBER 1ST.

Morning cold but fine and clear, being a good specimen of our Autumn weather. I accomplished a little of my usual duties, previously to going to Boston with my father, mother and Miss Roberdeau. We reached there quite late, and I was very busy the whole of the time before dinner. This being Quarter day, I made up my Accounts for the Agency, completed the Copy of it for my Father, and settled all the other matters pertaining to the coming Quarter. Received Miss Oliver's Rent punctually on the day for the first time since I have been Agent. Called to see Mr. Curtis at the Merchant's Insurance Office and gave him my father's letter to Petty Vaughan.[1] Then arranged my balances at the Bank and returned home to dine with the ladies at my House. My father dined at A. H. Everett's.[2] We had a pleasant time, and I did on the whole much better than I anticipated.

After dinner, walked with Miss Roberdeau to shew her the town, and to see several Cabinet Makers, about a Commission of her's. Returned for my Mother, and after shopping a little for her, we went down and took tea at Mrs. Frothingham's. After which some sacred music. Returned to Quincy at seven, Mr. Kirke driving us with considerable rapidity. Talked a little with Abby, after which being fatigued read the Spectator and retired early.

[1] The letter is missing.

[2] The dinner, attended by JQA and some fifteen other gentlemen, "among whom were the two French Commissioners of the Government Tocqueville and de Beaumont who have been sent to this Country to visit and examine the Prisons" (JQA, Diary, 1 Oct.), has taken on a more than ephemeral interest from the fact that the substance of JQA's table conversation with Tocqueville, who was seated next to him, on such subjects as slavery and the South, the state of religion in the United States, political conventions, and the movement westward was entered in his notebooks by Tocqueville and has been printed. In Alexis de Tocqueville, *Journey to America*, edited by J. P. Mayer, New Haven, 1960, the conversation with JQA is at p. 60–63.

SUNDAY. 2D.

Morning clear and delightfully pleasant. My Wife was however in considerable suffering from her little troubles, which will not leave her. I attended divine Service all day and heard Mr. Whitney preach in the morning a Communion Sermon. Text 4. John. 34. "Jesus saith unto them, My meat is to do the will of him that sent me and to finish his work." I am not easily able to fix any thing in the Sermon way in my mind and certainly not Mr. Whitney's efforts in that line, but I gathered from this a degree of liberality about the Communion which would go far towards destroying it altogether. At least, I think so.

Afternoon Ecclesiastes. 7. 10. "Say not thou, What is the cause that the former days were better than these for thou dost not inquire wisely concerning this." An argument from this text to show the folly of lauding the past, and the perfectibility of man. I do not believe this doctrine when pressed by more powerful minds, and at this time I heard nothing new.

Mr. Degrand and Miss Smith dined with us. The former brought out the information that Mr. Wirt had been nominated by the Antimasonic Convention at Baltimore, for the Presidency.[1] I am very highly delighted with this and, both from my father's *not* being named and Mr. Wirt being the man, am almost a disciple.

Read a Sermon of Massillon's being the last in the Volume. Text Matthew. 4. 8, 9. "The Devil taketh Jesus up into an exceeding high mountain, and sheweth him all the kingdoms of the world, and the glory of them." "And saith unto him, All these things will I give thee if thou wilt fall down and worship me." The Sermon was upon the Vices and Virtues of the Great, and though divided into many heads, the substance of it was that their exalted station as it aggravated the faults and crimes they were guilty of, so it increased their merits and virtues—The influence of each being not confined to themselves.

Evening. Walked to my Uncle's and settled the Quarterly Account for him. There was a great deal of Quincy Company there. We sat a little while and then returned home. Read Bacon's Essay, of Usury, which betrays a very limited knowledge of Political Economy. This science has been created since his time and is even now in its infancy. Also the Spectator.

[1] The *Boston Patriot* of 3 Oct. (p. 2, col. 1) carried news of the nomination of William Wirt, former attorney general.

MONDAY. 3D.

Morning clear and fine. I rode to town accompanied by T. B. Adams Jr. My time was taken up in a great variety of occupations as usual. Arranging my Accounts and paying such of them as I found due, and brought to me. Then to the House, then to see Mrs. Frothingham and Mr. Brooks. And some time upon various Commissions intrusted to me.

Dined at Mr. Frothingham's and had a pleasant conversation with him. Attended the Meeting of the Directors of the Boylston Market Association, Messrs. Williams and Child the only ones present. I drew up the records and completed the business that was waiting my presence to form a Quorum. Conversed a little about the Antimasonic proceedings in relation to the Presidency and the Governorship. This party is under bad guidance here. Returned to my Office where I met Thomas, and we proceeded to Quincy again. Evening with the

Ladies. I was overfatigued. Read one of Bacon's Essays and the Spectator.

TUESDAY. 4TH.

The morning was clear but an East wind soon blew up the Clouds for a Storm. I thought I would try a little fishing this morning and so went down. The tide was high and my success was tolerably good. The fish now begin to run up.[1] Returned at noon and wrote my Diary. This is not the detail of a very satisfactory morning, but one thing may be considered, I do not spend many such.

Afternoon. Read the remainder of the twelfth book of Letters to Atticus. They are very short and relate rather to business, particularly to the purchase of Gardens wherein to build a monument to his daughter. It is remarkable to notice how earnestly he was engaged in this scheme. In our day, these things are little considered of. Read Bacon's Essay Of Beauty, and Attended a Party at Mr. Beale's given to Miss Roberdeau. The usual Quincy Company. Mr. B. came out very handsomely with a Supper Table.[2] Returned home, read my Spectators and went to bed.

[1] JQA recorded that the fishing party was "at the Creek" (Diary, 4 Oct.), that is, Black's Creek, a tidal inlet to the north and east of the Old House.

[2] In the course of Mary Roberdeau's stay in Quincy, George Beale became an attentive admirer. Within the fam-ily circle, some expectation of a proposal of marriage was entertained, but that point was not reached before the end of her visit. LCA to Mrs. JA2, 4, 18, and 26 Oct.; LCA to CFA, 30 Sept. [i.e. Oct.] (all in Adams Papers).

WEDNESDAY. 5TH.

Dark with drizzle and an Easterly Wind. Arose late. I spent my morning in a variety of ways. Completed my Journal in the first place. Then took a turn to the Wharf to fish but found the Tide had been too quick for me. Wet my feet in trying to get bait without effect. Got back and after changing my dress, read the letters of Pacificus and Helvidius upon the proclamation of neutrality. Also, more of the Debates in the Massachusetts Convention. All the talent in the State was arrayed in its favour, against the majority perhaps in numbers. Had the objections been better conducted the decision would perhaps have been less fortunate.

After dinner read part of the 13th book of Cicero's letters to Atticus, but the afternoons are growing so short that the progress in them is not so great. Read also Bacon's Essay, of Deformity. Conversation with my father upon Politics, and then we all went to Mrs. Baxter's party. Few or no Quincy People but some from Milton. It was quite handsome though dull. My father and I walked home and I read the Spectator.

THURSDAY. 6TH.

Morning clear and fine but a North Wester sprung up that made it pretty cool. After breakfast, I thought I would go down and fish. The sport was fine for about an hour and a half. I caught thirty and returned home quite satisfied.

Afternoon, finished the remainder of the thirteenth book of the Letters to Atticus. But it was so cold in the Office as to make staying there quite uncomfortable. Every thing now strongly reminds me that I ought to be at home. Yet I know my Wife will feel so badly at being left upon her own resources, that I do not like to press her going. Nothing of any consequence during the day. Read Bacon's Essay on building and in the Evening Mr. Beale and his daughter spent the evening. I resumed Gillies and read the Spectator.

FRIDAY. 7TH.

Morning clear and warm. I passed it in a pretty unsatisfactory way, unless I may consider myself as having provided my father's table with its best dish. I went to fish, and soon after my Mother and I. Hull joined us. We had excellent sport, catching more than seven dozen of Smelts among us. But it took us until dinner time.

On my return it was growing cooler. And the Office is so uncomfortable without a fire, I passed the time in weeding a bed of Strawberries in the Garden. My father in all practical matters wants the power of executing any thing like a connected system. The consequence is that his farm, his house, his garden are all exhibiting the progress of decay. His Property generally is in the hands of his Agents, a matter depending more upon their honour than his attention.

Miss E. C. Adams passed the Afternoon and Evening here. I tried to read a little of Cicero but the letters to Atticus require great attention. Finished all of Dr. Gillies' history that related to the period of Demosthenes and was surprised to find how meagre it is. Also the Spectator.

SATURDAY. 8TH.

Morning clear, but the wind came round East and the consequence was that it clouded and became cold. Miss Roberdeau accompanied me in a Chaise to town. We reached there at ten o'clock. And I immediately set about the business of collecting the Dividends due this month. This occupied me two hours as I was obliged to go to the Boylston Market. On my return, I found Mr. Conant from Weston, with whom I made a settlement of the sales of Wood at Weston last year and agreed upon a time for another sale. I hope that it will do better this Season, than it has yet done. I then went to the House to make a settlement with my Man Servant, and after this consumed the rest of the morning, in making up the Accounts. This Quarter has been unusually productive.

I went to dine at Mr. Frothingham's, with a party of several of our own family, i.e. my Mother, Wife and Miss Roberdeau. We started early and got into Quincy before Sunset. Evening, I could do little being fatigued from my exercise. So I read the Spectator and went to bed.

SUNDAY. 9TH.

Morning cloudy, and heavy rain from the South, throughout the day. I attended Divine Service throughout the day and heard Dr. Lowell of Boston preach. His morning Discourse was from 2. Timothy 1. 5. "When I call to remembrance the unfeigned faith that is in thee, which dwelt first in thy Grandmother and thy Mother; and I am persuaded that in thee also." It was written with great pathos. The subject the relative duties of Parents, especially Mothers, and Children. The ideas were few and simple, but the management of them was very well calculated for the principal end of preaching, effect upon the people. The Clergyman dined with us. Afternoon. His Sermon was from Colossians 3. 3. "For ye are dead and your life is hid with Christ in God." The nature of Piety, and its influence. I thought it much less interesting.

Read a Sermon of Massillon's upon the benediction of the Standards of the Regiment of Catinat. Text from Psalms. 73 by the Vulgate and 74 in the English Translation. V[erses] 4 and 5, but the text is so imperfectly translated that I shall not try to insert it. The purpose seemed to be an exhortation to piety, to the abandonment of the usual desires which engross the mind of a warrior. It must have been an affecting discourse, as it was bold.

Evening. Quiet at home. Read Lord Bacon on Gardening. In the evening from the North American Review and the Spectator.

MONDAY. 10TH.

Heavy rain all day with the Wind from the Eastward. I remained quietly at home reading the remainder of the Debates in the Convention of Massachusetts, and going over a part of the second Olynthiac of Demosthenes. There was very little variety and therefore very little to record. I read a part of Mr. Jefferson's famous Memoir of himself in the beginning of his Works,[1] and was much interested by it.

After dinner my father entered into Conversation and we talked more than an hour upon the course of the Messrs. Everett politically and personally, and he then gave me an Account of the ΦBK Affairs, at their late Meeting in August.[2] T. B. Adams Junr. came in afterwards and I passed the remainder of the afternoon, in transacting business with him, and in completing the loan which he had solicited from me.[3] I also conversed with him a little upon his views which are to redeem himself from these difficulties as soon as possible. This young man is now feeling the first mortification of an extravagant man.

In the evening, we all sat and discussed Poetry[4] and my father read to us Gray's Bard and Progress of Poesy. After which I read the North American Review and the Spectator.

[1] The "Memoir," written by Jefferson in 1821 of events in his life up to 1790, is in his *Memoir, Correspondence and Miscellanies,* 1:1–89, on which see above, vol. 3:74.

[2] See above, entry for 25 July, note.

[3] The loan of about $200 was still outstanding a year later (M/CFA/3).

[4] "This Evening we read a number of passages of Poetry by American Poets —Percival, Halleck, Dana, Bryant, Peabody, Willis and a review of their compositions gravely settling the pretensions to precedence among them and placing Dana at their head" (JQA, Diary, 10 Oct.). See also the entry for 22 Oct., below. The poets mentioned are all represented in the work there named.

TUESDAY. 11TH.

Very high wind with heavy rain during the day. I could not remain at the Office with any comfort. So I concluded to abandon my regular plan of study, and to go into the House, where I might take up Mr. Jefferson's Memoir. This I did and read a considerable portion of it relating to the period of our Revolution. But as it stopped raining I thought I would for exercise go down and try fishing, but the wind was so high I could catch nothing so that I soon returned home.

Afternoon. Read but slowly and superficially some of the fourteenth Book of Letters to Atticus. The Afternoons now grow so short as to prevent much study. I was also excessively drowsy and required exertion to keep me awake.

Today, I experienced for the first time a strong desire to be at home—As the weather makes the House here pretty cheerless. My

Wife has however recovered so much that I feel quite thankful for our visit here. Miss Roberdeau was quite dull today and could not enliven herself with music. I read one or two Articles in the North American Review, and was very much disgusted with them. Read an Essay of Bacon's "Of Negotiating" and the Spectator. We had an alarm from a Chair cover catching fire in my Wife's room.

WEDNESDAY. 12TH.

Morning cloudy with high wind from the Westward throughout the day. I was occupied the larger part of the morning in reading parts of one of Almon's Volumes of Prior Documents. They contain Papers relating to the early period of our commotions in this Country before the Revolution, which are highly valuable as historical memorials.[1] Indeed it is not easy to see the truth without their assistance. I had my mind very much enlightened in the course of the very short time which I could devote to them. Strange as it may be, I had at best but a very undefined idea of the Congress of 1765 which was the first Assemblage of Representatives from the different States.

Occupied myself an hour afterwards in pruning and arranging the Trees which I have been rearing for some years. Afternoon, reading Cicero's letters to Atticus and finished the fourteenth book. Evening, Miss Roberdeau, Abby and I went to my Uncle the Judge's. Found there the usual family. But I take very little pleasure in visiting now at that house, as the tone at present prevailing there, is not to my taste at all. Returned early. Read an Essay of Bacon's on Followers and Friends and two numbers of the Spectator.

[1] John Almon, a London bookseller and editor, published in 1777 *A Collection of Interesting, Authentic Papers, . . . 1764 to 1775*, often referred to as "Prior Documents"; see JA, *Diary and Autobiography*, 3:313.

THURSDAY. 13TH.

Morning very bright though cool. I went to town. My time was very much taken up first in paying a visit to Mrs. Frothingham's, then to my house, then to collect Dividends and afterwards at my Office making up and settling Accounts. Mr. Forbes called and settled his Account and I payed him an Amount pretty large for Six Months. The hours flew and I was barely in time to get home to dine. Mr. and Mrs. Frothingham were there as they had agreed to be and Mr. Alexr. Townsend was also there without any agreement. This was one of those cross accidents which will sometimes happen to mar intended sport. My father could not well avoid being civil to him much against his Will. We had plenty of music and some very good.[1] They went early and left us again quite alone at home. But there soon came a supply of Company. For all the Quincy People seemed to come together as if by invitation.[2] They spent the evening. I read Bacon's Essay on Suitors, and the Spectators as usual.

[1] "There was some music of the Piano, and singing by Mrs. Frothingham and Mary Roberdeau from which I had formed some expectations of amusement to myself which were disappointed. Mr. Alexander Townsend came out to visit me, and remained and dined with me. This gentleman is a lawyer in Boston of great eccentricity of character. I have a very slight acquaintance with him, but on two or three different occasions he has manifested a regard and friendship for me which is entitled to my gratitude. He came now to visit me in consequence of my civil answer to his enthusiastic Letter upon my declining the Antimasonic nomination [for Governor]. He told me that he himself had informed Governor [Levi] Lincoln, who was his Classmate at Cambridge, of my having declined [to run against Lincoln] .... Mr. Townsend's visit would have been more agreeable had it not accidentally crossed that of Mr. and Mrs. Frothingham" (JQA, Diary, 13 Oct.).

[2] The Quincy visitors were Col. and Mrs. Josiah Quincy Jr.; Eliza and Mary Ann Greenleaf; George W. Beale and his daughter Ann; and from the TBA household, ECA, Thomas B. Adams Jr., and Mary Harrod (same).

FRIDAY. 14TH.

Morning fine and warm for the Season. I was engaged during the whole time previous to dinner in working in the garden. My father has not many persons who are willing to attend precisely under his superintendence and so when he wishes a thing done, it is my particular province to do it. I accordingly devoted this time to the formation and transplantation of a set of raspberry vines for a new bed now to be formed. This involved the pruning of the old set which I retained exclusively to myself and which I accomplished.

The afternoon was taken up in a fishing bout with my Mother and I. Hull; we had good sport which induced us to stay until after Sunset. And when we returned it was that I began to feel the fatigue of standing and work all day. This disabled me from doing any thing of importance. Even Lord Bacon's Essay on Studies—One of the best in the whole collection, could hardly keep me awake and I got through with the Spectator.

Quincy-Boston

SATURDAY. 15TH.

Morning clear and beautiful. This was the day fixed for our final return to Boston. Accordingly about six o'clock, I arose, and made all the preparations to start. Mine were much sooner regulated than those of my Wife and Child. We finally got off at about ten o'clock. I must confess I never left with so much regret and never went to my own home with so little satisfaction.[1] This I do not consider a favourable symptom in myself. The strong stimulus of ambition which has pushed me on for two years to deny myself many of the pleasures of life, has given way before the prospect which circumstances now present to my view. My mind wants healthy occupation. It wants also something that may prove useful to myself as well as to others. Perhaps I have less confidence in my own resolutions, and more disposition to look to the pleasures of life. Here as everywhere my trust is in the Deity. Conscious that my present path is one of difficulty unusual to a man so young, I rely upon that aid which has never yet deserted me.

At the Office before and at home after dinner. My house was comfortless—Every thing being as yet out of order and going on roughly. The Jar of little things upon the Nerves is perhaps the hardest lesson of Patience in the world. Great misfortunes rarely come in numbers, and are met with greater courage, and most often are anticipated from afar. I read Bacon On Faction and the Spectator.

[1] "This day my Son Charles with his wife and child ... left us. . . . It left a painful void in the house. Their Society is extremely pleasing to me and in proportion as we grow old, the want of Society, and the aversion to Solitude increase" (JQA, Diary, 15 Oct.).

SUNDAY. 16TH.

Morning clear and fine weather. I arose feeling as awkward and lowspirited as if I had not ever left my Parents and had a home of my own. Occupied in my study bringing my books and things into my usual train. Attended divine Service all day as usual and heard Mr. Frothingham in the morning from Exodus 32. 1. "And when the People saw that Moses delayed to come down out of the mount, the people gathered themselves together unto Aaron, and said unto him, 'Up, make us Gods which shall go before us: for as for this Moses, the man that brought us out of the land of Egypt, we wot not what is become of him.'" The moral to be drawn from this is the ingratitude of man, and his forgetfulness of all favours shewn him, also the patience taught by the divinity in concealing his end beyond our understanding. Men are apt to repine but the purposes of the Lord are pure and righteous altogether. Afternoon Text. Job. 38. 4. "Where wast thou when I laid the foundations of the earth? declare, if thou hast understanding." A lesson strongly deserved by the presumtuous confidence of our day by which man is exalted. Now man is a weak

157

and ignorant and consequently fallible mortal, which makes it highly necessary that he should be modest.

On my return home I read a Sermon of Massillon's upon Fasting. Text. Matthew. 6. 16. "When ye fast, be not, as the hypocrites, of a sad countenance." The division was into the obligation and the extent of the Rule. It was a severe censure of the habits of the idle and luxurious who evaded this principal injunction of the Catholic faith. To me, it had of course no material interest. Fasting does not strike me as a part of the dispensation of Christ who teaches us to use the things of this life as not abusing them. Read an Essay of Lord Bacon's on Ceremonies and Respects. Quiet Evening with my Wife and the Spectator.

MONDAY. 17TH.

My nights are a little more disturbed since my return to town and we again have the Baby, in the room. I arose early and immediately after breakfast started to go to Weston according to my engagement. Called for my old acquaintance Richardson and completed my business in the course of an hour or two. This was as usual the marking out of Wood for the yearly sale. Returned home soon after my usual dinner hour. The weather being uncommonly warm today, made my precautions against the cold rather troublesome.

Afternoon at home. Took up the letters to Atticus and read one or two, but was stopped by a visit from T. B. Adams Jr. who stai'd to tea. He is going off tomorrow morning to Charleston after having passed four or five months here with his family. He appeared more like himself in the simplicity of his character today, than I had seen him for a long time. Nature is after all the great secret, of manners. He left us early and Edward Brooks came in for the remainder of the evening. I read Bacon's Essay of Praise and the Spectator.

TUESDAY. 18TH.

I begin to feel a little more settled now, and fall gradually into the routine of duty which I had formerly. The day was very fine and uncommonly warm for the Season. I went to the Office after spending an hour in reviewing the first Olynthiac of Demosthenes in the Edition of Reiske. This is the third in that of Mounteney. I find my reading of it has been more superficial even than I expected. Occupied at the Office in Accounts and in reading a part of the Debates in the Convention of the State of New York on the adoption of the Constitution.[1]

Went to the Athenæum and made several little calls which consumed a large part of the Morning. On the whole, I begin to feel again the content which my quiet way of life here gives me.

Afternoon at home. Continued the fifteenth book of the Letters to Atticus, but my progress was slow, and the text grows more obscure as I go on, it seems to me. Read Bacon's Essay, Of Vainglory and in the evening, tried to sketch off a little political Article for the Press. But I did not succeed in my effort. Finished by the Spectator as usual.

[1] The proceedings of the New York ratifying convention of 1788 were included in vol. 2 of Jonathan Elliot, ed., *The Debates, Resolutions, and Other Proceedings, in Convention, on the Adoption of the Federal Constitution . . .*, 4 vols., Washington, 1827–1830. CFA was reading in a copy borrowed from the Boston Athenæum.

WEDNESDAY. 19TH.

This is really delightful weather. An Indian Summer though why it is called so is unknown to me. I finished the first Olynthiac before going out of the house this morning. Then to the Office. Occupied myself there in scribling a political Article, of which I may never make any use. But it is exercise. I find it every day harder to write so as to please myself, and if I do not get over this, it will hardly be possible for me soon to put pen to Paper. Went into a Shop to buy a Hat, and while there purchased a Fur for my Wife which I intend as her Winter's present. Returned home after a short walk, and in the Afternoon read a portion of the Letters to Atticus. Mystery and corrupt text combine to impede progress as well as to injure the pleasure of reading. My hours also are not yet so perfectly divided as I wish them to be. It takes time to arrange one's self, especially as I feel now somewhat differently from what I have done. More languor, a disposition to do my duty with less anxiety as to any definite result. A more implicit reliance upon the support of the Deity. These seem to affect me now with much more force. I have been wrong in paining myself too much about the future, for what can I do to ward off the ills of fate? My own conduct is all I can regulate.

Evening quiet at home, read Bacon. Mr. and Mrs. Frothingham called and passed an hour. Wrote a little and retired early.

THURSDAY 20TH.

Morning fine. I read a large part of the second Olynthiac which I find was more thoroughly read at first, than the other was. Then to the Office where I was occupied in writing in continuation of my political squibs. This took all my time so that I did little of a more useful kind.

My father came in at about one o'clock and according to agreement we proceeded to Medford. My mother with Miss Roberdeau, Abby and the child had already gone. We arrived there rather late, but in time for dinner. Had a pleasant time enough. My father seemed to be in pretty good spirits and Mr. Brooks quite comfortable. It is a long time since I have been out there. And the autumn with its falling leaves and chilly wind reads a moral to the mind that remembers last the richness of Summer vegetation and the extreme of heat. I have no fancy for the Country after the sharp frosts, at least in this climate.

We returned home shortly after dinner calling on the way at Mr. Angier's where Miss Roberdeau was left to stay for a day or two. I felt upon going home almost as unsettled as at first. This is not pleasant. I wasted the Evening, reading only Bacon and the Spectator.

FRIDAY. 21ST.

Morning pleasant although rather cooler than it has been. Finished the second Olynthiac of Demosthenes before going to the Office. Find it easier than the last. When at the Office was engaged in writing but as usual my productions did not satisfy me. All my late efforts come to nothing. This is mortifying and discouraging. I went to the Athenæum and from thence home. Afternoon finished the fifteenth book of Letters to Atticus. It is lucky they are drawing to a close or my patience would hardly hold out the difficulty of extracting any sense from them.[1]

In the evening, Read to my Wife the beginning of the History of George 4th which will I hope do much to fill a void in my information and yet be entertaining enough to read aloud.[2] Afterwards I read some Chapters of Miss Edgeworth's book on Practical Education which deserve serious consideration.[3] On the whole, this day was passed more to my satisfaction than usual. Read Bacon's Essay upon Anger and two numbers of the Spectator.

[1] Sentence thus in MS. Doubtless "against" was intended after "hold out."

[2] Newly published in Lardner's Cabinet Library was William Wallace, *History of the Life and Reign of George IV*, 3 vols., London, 1831.

[3] CFA's bookplate is in the edition, earlier GWA's, at MQA of *The Works of Maria Edgeworth*, 13 vols., Boston, 1824–1826. *Practical Education*, separately published, 2 vols., Boston, 1815, is also at MQA, with JQA's bookplate.

SATURDAY. 22D.

Morning fair. I began reviewing the third Olynthiac this morning, and finished a considerable portion of it. Then to the Office but my time was wasted very much. The mason was at work in the next room upon the fireplace there and I felt obliged to oversee him so much that I left myself little else to do. This is the way my best plans come to an end. I ought to sit down and work hard and I cut up my time into such shreds as to do nothing. Took a short walk before dinner.

Afternoon spent pretty quietly at home continuing the Letters to Atticus of which I have got into the sixteenth and last book. My time now passes so quietly, I have little or nothing left to record. Read Bacon's Essay upon the Vicissitude of Things making the last of his finished ones. I have been about two Months reading these, for the third time. And the more I read them, the more I admire the profoundness of their Author.

Evening, read Miss Edgeworth. Miss Julia Gorham was here and I read aloud from the Specimens of American Poetry.[1] Finished by the Spectator.

[1] Samuel Kettell, *Specimens of American Poetry*, 3 vols., Boston, 1829. The set at MQA has JQA's signature. See also, above, the entry for 10 Oct., note.

SUNDAY. 23D.

The day was mild and beautiful. I passed my morning in reading Miss Edgeworth's Practical Education until the arrival of my father and Mother who came from Quincy for the day. We had fixed this as the time for the public baptism of our Child. Mr. Frothingham had appeared inclined to have me pursue this course and therefore I did. My own aversion to public exhibitions is so great that I should not myself have inclined much to it.

Mrs. Frothingham had hers christened at the same time. After much consideration, I concluded to have mine named from my Mother, Louisa Catherine.[1] This was not my first choice. But my Wife seemed so very little pleased with the idea of her own name, that I thought proper to give up. We got through the Ceremony well,[2] and I offered up my Prayers solemnly and humbly to the Almighty Power, that he would look with mercy and with favour upon this new Servant of his, that he would teach her the ways of wisdom and virtue, and that he would sustain her Parents in their endeavours to guide themselves and those who depend on them in a strait forward and upright course. I hope I feel the responsibility and the proper gratitude with humility for all kindness, which has been showered upon me. Mr. Frothingham's manner was impressive. His Sermon afterwards was from Titus. 2. 14. "He gave himself for us, that he might redeem us from all iniquity, and purify unto himself, a peculiar people, Zealous of good works." The subject was an examination of the Christian morality.

and of it's influence upon the World. He defined its nature, and the difference in its application from any morality before known containing the same general precepts. He then described the two excesses in which sects are apt to follow. The one ascribing too much effect to the operation of the Christian Dispensation and the other too little. And then proceeded to define wherein he thought the truth actually was. This was done with Judgment and discrimination. And on the whole I thought the Sermon more than usually striking.

My father, mother and Miss Roberdeau dined with us and the first went to Meeting again with me in the afternoon. Mr. Greenwood preached from Psalm 42d. 2. "When shall I come and appear before God." There was little in the Sermon beyond the old subject of a prepared state of mind. I never heard him when I thought him so sleepy. The Afternoon was passed with the family. I read after they returned [*to Quincy*], leaving Miss Roberdeau and Mrs. Nowlan with us, a Sermon of Massillon upon Conversion. Text from 2. Corinthians 6. 2. "Behold, now is the accepted time; behold, now is the day of salvation." The substance of it was that no time was to be lost in devoting one's self to the service of the true God. But I read it with less preciseness than any yet; owing to the derangement of my time.

Evening, Miss Roberdeau went out. Edward Blake came in and passed the larger part of the Evening with us. I was glad to see him and we had a pleasant talk. After he went I took a walk to Mrs. Frothingham's for Miss Roberdeau but did not find her. Read Miss Edgeworth and the Spectator.

[1] The baptisms of Louisa Catherine Adams [LCA2) and of Ann Brooks Frothingham are entered in the records of the First Church in Boston (Col. Soc. Mass., *Pubns.*, 40:452).

[2] "The two Sisters held their own Children. Mr. Frothingham took his child into his own arms and Charles held his. The Service began with these baptisms" (JQA, Diary, 23 Oct.).

MONDAY. 24TH.

Morning fair, but it afterwards clouded up and rained very heavily in the Afternoon. After reading nearly all the rest of the third Olynthiac, I went to the Office and occupied myself in writing but to little purpose. My Articles did not suit me and what is more I doubted the expediency of my writing any at all. But that must be judged of at the end. I must confess every day adds to my conviction that I can not write now with so much ease as I could have done a year ago.

Returned home early. Found my Mother who had come in again. I forgot to mention that I called upon Mr. Brooks and he entered into conversation upon his prospects for the Winter. I gave him an invitation to pass it with us, and he seemed pleased with the idea. He spoke with a good deal of feeling of his situation, and made me sympathize with him a great deal.[1]

After dinner I was compelled to attend a Meeting of the Board of Directors of the Boylston Market Association on the usual business of a month, though the day had been set forward to accommodate the Clerk of the Market.

Returned in the rain and got myself quite wet. My Mother concluded not to leave town tonight.

Evening, I went out to a party at Mrs. Wm. Smith's given to the bride of her Son.[2] The rain had disappointed her of much of her company but there were still many. It cleared when I went home. Read a little of Miss Edgeworth, and the Spectator.

[1] On the course taken by Peter C. Brooks in deciding upon a winter residence, see below, entry for 25 November.
[2] See above, entry for 4 May.

TUESDAY. 25TH.

Morning fair. My Wife was informed that one of her Domestics was taken ill in the night and this put us in considerable confusion. My Mother and the rest left town at ten, and I do not expect to see them again this year.[1] I regret their absence more and more. We have all spent the Summer in an unusually pleasant manner, and I have been myself relieved from a good deal of care and responsibility. It is a little singular that during this Summer we should have been so unlucky in Housekeeping, and perhaps it is the worse from the contrast it presents to living with others. I regret more on the account of others than myself.

Went to the Office, but my time passed without much profit. I am a trifler in life and all my good resolutions are vanishing into thin Air. So much for me. Took a short walk and returned home. Finished in the Afternoon the letters to Atticus. I am glad I have had the perseverance to accomplish them. Indeed they are on the whole interesting, and give the only true key to the character of the man. But they require great attention. The Greek bits of quotation are pleasant but sometimes obscure, the allusions are totally lost or but partially seen.

Evening very quiet. I read a part of Miss Edgeworth's Practical Education. I like this book much. There are many very sensible views in it of the nature of Children's minds. My own impression is that *clearness* is the great requisite and that this is lost nine times in ten because Children catch the *words* of their superiors without their ideas. Read the Spectator.

¹ The family's departure from Quincy on the 28th was timed to allow them to reach Washington well before the opening of Congress, with stops en route of some duration at New York and Philadelphia. (JQA, Diary, 28 Oct. – 5 Nov. *passim.*)

WEDNESDAY. 26TH.

Morning pleasant. I forgot to say that I was busy last Evening as well as this morning in correcting a proof Sheet of my father's contribution to Blunt's Register.¹ It came so late that I could not send it yesterday so that I thought I would save the lost time by sending him the corrected proof instead of the first copy. It is something of a labour to correct these as I found, and it requires a much more practised eye than mine to see the mistakes in letters at a glance. I looked it over three times and found new ones each time.

Went to the Office where I passed my time as usual. Read a good deal of the Debates in the New York Convention and went about upon several Commissions. But At noon I felt so unwell that I thought I would go and walk. Before I had reached School Street I was taken quite sick at my Stomach, which continued with great violence for a Couple of hours. It seems impossible to say what the cause was, but so it was that I was incapacitated from doing any thing today. Last year I had very much such a turn, though it was then accompanied with head ache. Today it came without any notice. I laid down feeling chills, but as the Night came on grew better so that after Tea I sat down and continued Miss Edgeworth. Interrupted soon by Mrs. Frothingham, Miss Lydia Phillips and Edward Brooks who came in and were quite agreeable the rest of the evening. Mr. Frothingham came also afterwards. I read Miss Edgeworth and the Spectator.

¹ A draft in JQA's hand of the chapter on "England 1829–1830," written for the *American Annual Register for the Years 1829–1830*, is in the Adams Papers, Microfilms, Reel No. 494. The proofs were received from the Boston printers Gray & Bowen (JQA, Diary, 27 Oct.).

THURSDAY. 27TH.

Morning at the Office without being able to do much before going there. Our family is so much disorganized at present as to make it difficult to study at all. It began to rain soon, and continued doing so all day. I wrote a little and read a little but on the whole did not do much. My father came in to accomplish a little of his final business. Nothing particular was necessary to be done excepting to supply himself with Cash and to get his Chronometer which had been broken.

He went about however and amused himself as usual until nearly two o'clock when he left town and I bid him Good bye. I could not help feeling dull at the departure, but went immediately to try and get over it at Mr. Frothingham's where Abby and I dined.

After dinner I returned home and began Cicero's letters to his brother Quintus, the first of which seems to me one of the most admirable of his works. Evening at home passed quietly. Read a Chapter or two of the History of George 4th. which was interesting, and some of Practical Education. After which began the seventh Volume of the Spectator.

FRIDAY. 28TH.

Morning cloudy but it did not rain. I was busy in Commissions during the larger portion of the morning. So that at the Office I had only time to read a mere trifle of the Debates in the New York Convention. Mr. Hamilton seems to have sustained the whole weight of the Constitution and in doing so he certainly deserves great praise. This Constitution, it is now the work of many to destroy, though as yet, it has brought us nothing but good. Went to the Athenæum where I took up Mackintosh's History of England,[1] and carried it home to read.

Afternoon, read the letters to Quintus 2 and 3 in the first book. I find little to except and a great deal to admire in these. Cicero in the tone of his morality was unquestionably far beyond the age he lived in. And in his recommendations to his brother he excels his usual style.

My wife was still in trouble about her household which does not get settled. I read part of Mackintosh's History in the Evening and part of Miss Edgeworth on Education. The first I found dry. The second entertaining and instructive as usual. Spectator as usual.

[1] The *History of England* by Sir James Mackintosh was published over many years in *The Cabinet Cyclopædia*, on which see entry for 9 Aug., above. Volume 1 had appeared in 1830, vol. 2 in 1831.

SATURDAY. 29TH.

Morning fine. This being the day of departure for my father and his family,[1] it is rather an agreeable circumstance that it should be fair. After reading a part of the first Philippic of Demosthenes, I went to the Office and spent my time in reading the New York Debates. Received a Note from my Father which gave me two or three Commissions to perform.[2] Mr. Peabody asked me also to accompany him to a sale of Dutch Flower roots, which I did and purchased several according to my Mother's request for her. They went pretty dear. My time was thus all consumed and partly in matters which really did not pay their way.

Returning home I passed my Afternoon in reading the Letters to Quintus, most of which are excellent. He moans too much about his exile however. Continued Mackintosh's History of England which seems to me to be bald, Cicero's Attic Style with a vengeance. The driest of dry things. Finished Practical Education, parts of which I propose to myself to read over for deeper reflection. The subject has been often written upon, and like that of Government has been in the hands of Theorists, most frequently. It appears to me that this book comes nearer the true principle by which to reach what we want, than any. It collects examples of the operation of things upon Children. In this science as in others induction will be used to advantage. And yet how little has been done in this way. Finished the Evening with the Spectator.

¹ An error; see above, entry for 25 Oct., note.
² JQA to CFA, 27–28 Oct. (Adams Papers).

SUNDAY. 30TH.

Morning clear but cool with a Northerly Wind which was not over agreeable to us, though it may have helped my father and family on their way. I tried to make a Fire in my study but the wind was in the smoky quarter and I desisted, not however until after I had been almost blinded.

Attended divine Service all day and heard in the morning Mr. Pierpont from Matthew 20. 27. "And whosoever will be chief among you, let him be your Servant." The whole Sermon was upon the difference between the essentials of Christian superiority and that of the world. The latter finding its substance in display, in luxury, in passion and vice, while the former was derived from self subjection for the benefit of others. This is common place enough but still good. Mr. Frothingham preached in the Afternoon from 65. Isaiah 5. "I am holier than thou," in other words the disposition of men to excuse to themselves their faults, by comparisons with others. This generates censoriousness, uncharitableness, and the various social sins. The Sermon was sensible.

I took two walks for exercise and on my return read Massillon's third Sermon in Careme. "Verily, I say unto you, I have not found so great faith, no, not in Israel." It was a defence of the Christian faith against Infidelity rested upon three grounds. 1. The reasonableness of it, 2. the glorious character of it, 3. its necessity. An Englishman would have relied mainly upon the first point. Massillon adheres to the Catholic doctrine of implicit faith and therefore makes that the least. Among the curious parts of the Sermon is that it deplores the condition of England and argues from it the necessity of the Catholic faith to make People happy. It does not seem to have entered his head, that to allow men to differ is sometimes the surest way of making them agree. To force them to unite ensures constant division.

My family is still in a very unsettled state. The sickness of this woman is a little discouraging. Evening. Continued Mackintosh's History, and began the Abbé Condillac's Art d'Ecrire,[1] which seems to be nothing more than showing the faults of other Writers in order to avoid them. Many of the remarks are good as general ones, and many being confined to points of French nicety in criticism, of no use to us. Read also the Spectator.

[1] In the edition at MQA of the *Œuvres* of Etienne Bonnot de Condillac (31 vols., Paris, 1803), *Art d'écrire* is in vol. 10.

MONDAY. 31ST.

The day was cloudy with occasional drizzle. I went to the Office as usual. Time wasted as it always is. My Office hours appear to bring little accession to my fortune or character. They pass in a kind of barrenness neither useful nor creditable. Occasional attention to accounts, with a visitor now and then for the payment of a bill or so and reading Newspapers take up nearly all my time. Shall this continue? I am afraid so, as I have never yet been able to remedy it.

Returned home and in the Afternoon, attempted another fire which today burnt beautifully, and put me quite in good humour with my new Coal. Read a large portion of the Letters to Quintus which please me a good deal. Also part of the life of Michael Angelo published by the Society to diffuse Useful Knowledge in England, which contains a sketch of the progress of Sculpture.[1]

Evening, reading loud to my Wife. After which the Abbé Condillac, and the Spectator. Our family goes on better.

[1] One of the *Lives of Eminent Persons* then being issued in parts in the *Library of Useful Knowledge* published by the Society for the Diffusion of Useful Knowledge. CFA had read a number of the lives as they began to appear in 1829; see vol. 2 *passim*, and above, vol. 3, entry for 3 Oct. 1829.

TUESDAY. NOVEMBER 1ST.

Morning cloudy but it did not rain. Having finished my Review of the first Philippic I began today for the second time the Oration upon the Embassy of Æschines. This is very long but I hope gradually yet slowly to work it off. At the Office where I have no better account to give of my time than usual. Much of it goes in conversation with Mr. Peabody which I ought to stop. It worries him and does not profit me. Took a short walk and then home.

Afternoon, finished the letters to Quintus, and read the larger part of those to Brutus and from him. In these I think Cicero appears badly by the side of the nobility of soul which prompted his Companion to do right in spite of all consequences. I admire this lofty character. It may not be well suited to success in life, but it is the most splendid eulogy after it.

Read to my Wife in the Evening part of the reign of George 4th. which is a curious mass of political prejudice and disgusting truth. Afterwards, I attended a Party given to the Bride Mrs. Smith by Mrs. S. A. Otis. A large Collection of persons many of fashion and it was altogether fine though I have been so long out of society as to make it flat to me. Returned early. Read a little of Condillac upon *point* in style, and the Spectator as usual.

WEDNESDAY. 2D.

Morning cloudy with occasional showers of rain, but the air was quite mild. After reading a little of the Oration on the Embassy, I went to the Office and busied myself today with a little more effect. I finished today the Debates in the New York Convention. They seem at last to have reached a considerable degree of personal bitterness and perhaps lay open the secret of the subsequent hatred of Hamilton entertained in New York as well as in the Union generally. It is the fortune of warm and, I may add, generous minds to make enemies from their superiority, but as an offset to this they have warmer friends than others.

Returned home and in the Afternoon finished the remaining letters of Cicero to Brutus. They confirm me in my previous impressions. I have now concluded two great divisions of Cicero's Works, the Rhetorical and the Epistolary. The Philosophical portion remains.

Evening at home. Mr. and Mrs. Frothingham and Miss Phillips came up and spent the Evening. And we had a little Supper and on the whole a pleasant time. I read the Spectator.

THURSDAY. 3D.

Arose early as this was the day fixed for the sale of Wood at Auction in Weston and as I have always made a practice to attend it. Immediately after my breakfast was despatched, I started. Called at Richardson's, and found he had mistaken the day so that I was sorry he had engaged himself but was obliged to proceed without him. Arrived in very good Season and went to the ground.

The Company in the morning was thin but increased at Noon. The first Wood sold went low, and for the sake of the experiment I bought a lot on my own Account to see how the wood would turn out, and judge pretty clearly of the profits of the purchasers in these cases. I had it struck off to me at 6.62 1/2 and after it is measured the price by the Cord will appear. After noon, the prices ranged very high and on the whole the wood may be considered as having sold well. I stopped in time to prevent a glut and after taking tea at the Conants returned home. It was dark and late however before I arrived. This is the third year I have conducted these sales and I hope they have been managed with success to my Employer. Each year, the wood has been said to sell high, but on this, the advanced price in the Market has done much more than usual.[1]

Short evening as I retired early. Spectator.

[1] See above, vol. 3:20. The 1831 sale netted $762.90 (M/CFA/3).

FRIDAY. 4TH.

Morning cloudy and threatened though it did not rain in fact. I wasted my time very much in preparing my defences for the Winter. Then to the Office where I received letters. One from my Mother[1] and one from Mr. James Brown of Cambridge making application about my father's book which has already been grasped at by several.[2] Several visitors, upon dunning and paying errands. Mr. Tenney as punctual as usual. Jos. Adams about J. Q. Adams' bills which I paid, having been long due.[3] Started to perform some Commissions which Mr. T. B. Johnson sent to my Mother to have done.[4] I went through with several of them and then took quite a long walk to get rid of an incipient headache.

Returning home, found my Wife in trouble about her Woman who is much worse and fears are entertained for her life. Read part of the Academic Questions,[5] though imperfectly today. My fire troubled me again today. I have not yet got the Art.

Evening at Mr. Frothingham's. Mrs. Parkman, Miss Hall, two Miss Phillipses and W. G. Brooks. Rather stupid. Returned at ten and my head was so bad I went to bed after the Spectator.

[1] New York, 30 Oct. (Adams Papers).
[2] The letter from James Brown, printer, is missing; however, CFA's reply to him, 8 Nov. (LbC, Adams Papers),

makes it clear that Brown, like others, had been led to believe by an item in a newspaper that JQA's biography of JA was approaching readiness for publication.

[3] Joseph Harrod Adams apparently had come as a messenger from John Angier to whom CFA had written a few days earlier that Angier had submitted no bill for J. Q. Adams Jr.'s schooling with him during the more than three months he had been there. On this day CFA paid out $48 on J. Q. Adams Jr.'s

account. CFA to Angier, 1 Nov. (LbC, Adams Papers); M/CFA/3, and M/CFA/4.

[4] LCA's brother, Thomas Baker Johnson (vol. 1:443 and Adams Genealogy), had requested LCA to purchase for him in Boston, shells, candles, spectacles, and socks (CFA to LCA, 5 Nov., Adams Papers).

[5] "Academicæ quæstiones" and "Academicarum quæstionum" are in vol. 14 of CFA's edition of Cicero published at Boston in 1815.

SATURDAY. 5TH.

Morning fine and cool. I read a little of Demosthenes and then went to the Office. Nothing of any consequence. I was busy in my usual way, spending half an hour however in writing to my Mother the exact state of our affairs. How sick our woman was and how much my Wife had been worried by various cares.[1] Called to see Mr. Brooks and went to find Mr. Curtis about the Boylston matters, but did not make out. I was not able to take much of a walk.

Returned home and passed the afternoon in reading the fragment of the 1st book of Academic Questions, which with the assistance of Enfield's Philosophy I made out to comprehend. Metaphysics in themselves exceedingly difficult of comprehension even in the language with which a man is most familiar, embarass much more in any other. The technicals must all be settled first, and after all a great deal of the Ancient philosophy resides in hard words.

I spent my evening quite actively and read Mackintosh comparing him with Goldsmith.[2] In this way I find his superiority in philosophical reflection though his style is singularly careless. Surely he ought to have set the present age a better example. Read a little of Condillac and the Spectator.

[1] CFA to LCA, 5 Nov. (Adams Papers). On this letter, see further the preceding entry and the entry for 25 Nov., below.

[2] Oliver Goldsmith, *History of Eng-* land. The edition at MQA, published at London in 3 vols. in 1794, has the signature of GWA, with annotations in his hand indicating that he had purchased and read the *History* in 1817.

SUNDAY. 6TH.

The Season has been an uncommonly fine one this year, and though growing cooler is yet very pleasant. Morning passed reading Sir James Mackintosh, then to Meeting as usual. Mr. Frothingham preached all day. Morning from 2. Esdras. 1. 27. "Ye have not as it were forsaken me, but your own selves, saith the Lord." It was upon the self-indulgence of men which subverted all ideas of duty. I did not follow it from my unlucky habit of abstraction. The Afternoon's discourse was from Micah 4. 5. "For all people will walk every one in the name of his God, and we will walk in the name of the Lord our God for ever and ever." The idea of the deity, the religion of man has been different in different ages. The worship of God has been construed often to mean the strangest series of actions. But the true worship is the cultivation of the virtues, to that let every one adhere. I will not say that I succeed in giving any notion of the Sermons, perhaps nothing more than my own reflections upon the Texts guided by what I hear.

Read a Sermon of Massillon upon the forgiveness of injuries. His division was in two parts. 1. The Motives to forgiveness derived from the insufficient reasons we have for hatred and revenge. 2. The rules of pardon, which he defines to require more than the false reconciliations among men. The character of Massillon's Oratory is singular. It depends upon the meanest view of human nature. He seems to have read Rochefoucauld to some purpose. Take for Example his definition of the friendship of men. He says three motives cause it. Similarity in taste, Interest or Vanity. This may be true but there may be a mixture at least of something better. All his eloquence is therefore fulminating.

Evening, read part of the Life of George 4th. Thoroughly Foxite. E. B. Hall called and paid a visit. I continued Mackintosh and read my usual Spectators. The Woman continues about the same.

MONDAY. 7TH.

The day was lovely. I did not read any of the Oration because I went out earlier than usual. The days have become short and my hour is therefore very much pressed upon. Indeed I am much inclined to think I must give up my Greek for the Winter. So it is. My energy is fast disappearing. The common current of life is too strong for my swimming against it. And I must soon be content to be swallowed up in its vortex. The last six months have produced a wonderful revolution in me. They have done more to extinguish the fire of my character than years. Perhaps the reflection that I have a child has been the secret of it,[1] that I am not a close in the course of the family. Be this as it may, here am I with much less spirit and more indolence.

Read a good deal of the Debates in the Virginia Convention[2] and wondered at the folly of Mr. Henry who seems to have worked himself into madness at the idea of the grand consolidated government.

Took a walk. Afternoon read part of Cicero's Lucullus. It contains an argument against the Philosophy which doubted of matter, but it requires with me a second perusal.

Evening finished the 1st Volume of the Life of George 4th and went to Mrs. Pickman's party to the Bride Mrs. Smith. All the fashion there. Returned early. Read the Spectator. The Woman still the same.

¹ Having observed CFA with his daughter, LCA wrote that "Charles perfectly doats on her" (to Mrs. JA2, 26 Oct., Adams Papers).
² In vol. 3 of Elliot, *Debates*, &c.

TUESDAY. 8TH.

Weather continues fine. I went to the Office a little earlier than usual. Engaged in a variety of occupations. Wrote to J. Brown about an application made for the printing of my father's biography.¹ Also to J. Minot and J. Y. Champney dunning letters.² Then to the Athenæum where I spent nearly two hours gleaning the Newspapers, and looking at new publications of which there is certainly an abundance. Then home.

In the Afternoon I continued the Lucullus of Cicero to which I give in the first place a very superficial reading. The argument is a singular one but the truth probably was not precisely on either side. As usual, it will be somewhere in the middle.

Evening, read to my Wife a little more of the Life of George 4th explaining a period of history of which I am shamefully ignorant. Particularly, the causes of the Addington Administration. Afterward as I could not get Mackintosh's second Volume, I began Fuseli's Lectures in order to gain some ideas of Painting,³ as on this subject my knowledge is very superficial. How many things there are of which we know absolutely nothing. We who claim the reputation of educated men. The Spectator as usual. The woman is slightly better. Her Mother in coming to her has met with an accident and dislocated her shoulder.

¹ See above, entry for 4 November.
² These letters are missing.
³ Henry Fuseli (1741–1825), Swiss-born painter and member of the Royal Academy, London, was a professor of painting there (DNB). His *Lectures on Painting* were published separately at London in 1801. However, they were included in John Knowles, *Life and Writings of H. Fuseli*, 3 vols., London, 1831; and it was in that work that CFA seems to have been reading some weeks after the present entry; see below, entries for 17–22 Jan. 1832.

WEDNESDAY. 9TH.

Morning pleasant, but the wind changed soon and it grew hazy with all the appearance of bad weather. After attending to the expediting of the Flower Roots for my Mother, I went to the Office and was occupied there as usual. Received a short letter from my Father at New York which I propose to answer as soon as I think he will get to Washington. He seems to me not to be taking judicious measures.[1] Read some of the Virginia Debates in which I was struck with the views of Mr. Madison. They seem to me to reach the truth. Took a walk.

Afternoon finished Lucullus. But I must read it well over again. The doctrine is necessarily obscure. It takes me a great while longer than it ought to attend to my fire. This must be mended.

I spent the evening reading Fuseli excepting a couple of hours at Mr. F. Parkman's where my Wife took Tea. There was a party of that family which is extensive and clans together very much. We returned at ten. I read a little of Condillac and the Spectator. I find a peculiarity in most of Steele's papers which betrays very much the character of his mind. The constant introduction of some allusion to sex, showing that he was one of a numerous class who indulge their imaginations until it becomes a habit.

[1] JQA to CFA, 6 Nov. (Adams Papers). JQA wrote that he had agreed to pay for the board of Isaac Hull Adams at TBA's, three dollars a week through the winter, in return for which Hull was to continue copying JA's journals under CFA's supervision.

THURSDAY. 10TH.

Morning pleasant but it became cloudy and wet before night. I went to the Office and passed my time in my usual wasting way. Mr. Eddy called with a Notice of meeting of the Middlesex Canal. I spent a little time with Mr. Peabody, and the balance in reflecting upon the subject of Antimasonry which the Debating Society have taken up as a part of their subjects and the one to be discussed on Saturday. I may be called out upon it. Mr. Minot asked me to step in and look at some odd volumes of Mr. Welsh's books which might have belonged to my Father. I did find a Volume of the Causes Celebres at which I was mightily pleased for this was one of my father's broken sets.[1]

Afternoon. Began reading over Cicero's Lucullus and from consulting Enfield and Middleton I found myself making much more rapid way than before. In Latin, a great deal depends upon having the subject well fixed in your mind.

In the evening I read to my Wife part of the Biography of George 4th, giving an account of the War on the Continent under Napoleon.

I must read Walter Scott's Biography of that wonderful man.[2] Finished Condillac's Art d'Ecrire from which I have got no new ideas. Indeed by this time I ought to know my A. B. C. and be out of leading strings. Read the Spectator.

[1] JQA's bookplate is in each volume of the 22-vol. set at MQA of F. Gayot de Pitaval, *Causes célèbres et intéressantes*, The Hague, 1745–1746. That the first volume was the one that had been borrowed and was now reclaimed is suggested by JQA's name in it, in CFA's hand, on the verso of the front end-paper.

[2] But see below, entry for 26 April 1832, note.

FRIDAY. 11TH.

Morning warm with a Southerly and very heavy rain, which did not last. I went to the Office after stopping to make inquiry about the woman of Dr. Stevenson. She is a little better today and if she goes on improving I have pretty much made up my mind to have her moved. My time at the Office was taken up in Accounts and my Diary. Attended a Meeting of the Directors of the Middlesex Canal called for the purpose of assenting to the sale of a piece of land in Charlestown. It is a mere formality as the regulation of all those affairs will lie with two or three, and the other Directors know but very little about it. Took a short walk.

Afternoon, made some progress in the review of Lucullus, every step in which I comprehend better as I go. The old Philosophers were always stumbling upon a mass of crude stuff their ingenuity formed which only embarrassed the perception of truth, and retarded the progress of knowledge.

Evening read Fuseli's Lectures upon Invention, Design and Chiaroscuro. They pleased me much. My Wife was so fatigued I did not read to her, so that I amused myself by writing something that may be of use to me hereafter. Read the Spectator.

SATURDAY. 12TH.

Fine day. Went to the Office after wasting a good deal of time at Market. The greater part of my leisure was taken up in writing a long letter to my father. It does not say what I wished to say, nor is it in the manner I wanted to use, but I cannot wait to do better. My opinions upon the subject of his course of life are plainly given, and my views of my own situation at present with a request of advice from him, accompany them. His course for the last fourteen months has not been calculated to raise him in the judgment of the public. The examples of Washington, Jefferson and Madison have produced so strong an effect that a departure from their line of policy is considered as a departure from true dignity. I think his only course is to set seriously about writing a biography of my Grandfather and a thorough examination of his papers.[1] My whole time was taken up until the time for my regular walk.

Afternoon finished the Lucullus, and began the Treatise de finibus[2] which opens with an elegant defence of the study of philosophy, as unpopular it would seem at Rome as it is now. Copied part of my father's letter.

Evening went to the Debating Society. Found nobody there and the Society defunct. Called at Mrs. Frothingham's for my Wife and returned home. Copied and read the Spectator.

[1] CFA to JQA, 12 Nov. (Adams Papers). The letter was partly an effort, in which there were elements of desperation, to win JQA again to literary pursuits and away from politics, and partly a plea for JQA's help in resolving his own dilemma brought to crisis by JQA's proposal to acquire the *Boston Patriot* for CFA to edit (above, entry for 19 Sept.).

As occasion for the renewal of his entreaty to JQA to give himself to the writing of JA's life, CFA seized upon the editorial note by Robert Walsh in the *National Gazette and Literary Register* (Phila., 29 Oct., p. 1, col. 1) accompanying the publication in the same issue of a lengthy extract from JQA's eulogy of James Monroe. After giving high praise both to the eulogy and to the 4th of July oration delivered at Quincy, Walsh wrote, "We trust that he will not be satisfied with these occasional contributions to our political literature. . . . Political elevation, official labors . . . merely, do not suffice to give durable and solid posthumous renown. . . . We shall not be content with Mr. Adams until he has finished a volume of history; under which denomination we would place such a Life of his venerable father as he is said to have undertaken."

Thus emboldened, CFA attacked before directing his fire upon himself:

"Three years have now elapsed and they have been witnesses to the most extraordinary irresolution I ever knew you seized by, which was continually laying upon the future what the present was the best time to execute. I have not been gratified by your election to Congress, I have felt little satisfaction in your occasional productions, for the reason that they employ the time in momentary objects, which should be devoted to a durable monument to your reputation. It seems idle to say that you can benefit the Country by doing in a subordinate situation what you have already had opportunities of doing in higher ones. The Nation wants a national Literature. It wants objects to attach itself to, apart from the English Idols set up to lead them astray—And these objects can come from none but men of high literary reputation. The Poet who devotes the time to trifles which might produce a sustained work is condemned immediately as an indolent Gentleman of genius. Why shall not the same rule be measured to others? I know that you can never be charged with any thing like Indolence in fact, but the moral effect is the same as if you could. I know that upon leaving here you expressed a decision as to the next Summer which would seem to supersede the necessity of my saying all this. But I have heard nearly the same words before and I have accustomed myself to believe that to rely upon what a man is to do some time hence is only one mode of building Castles in Spain. As Mr. Webster says, there are many incidents happen which cause 'a change of position to meet new circumstances.'

"I have said nothing of another view of the subject because I know that it never will have any effect on you. You have lived in an age when Literature in this Country was at its lowest ebb, and have not watched the progress which it has made to be a profitable occupation. The present state of it is, that literary *names* carry success, provided the subject is popular. Any work, if it was not too large, would be good in a pecuniary point of view if you thought proper to make it so. The eagerness of publishers for this proves it—And to me, no other method presents itself of repairing your broken fortunes, so likely to be certain; but your system has been through life to pay no regard to considerations of this kind in writing, and I confess that I have not much expectation you will do so now.

"Perhaps what I have said ought not to have been said. If so, I regret it. My way is to express opinions freely without meaning the least disrespect. My own very profitless way of life ought and does prevent me any confidence of language as it respects others. But I have to start from the beginning, to get the materials before I can use them, and the process of acquiring is slow and uncertain. You have long possessed them without question, and nothing remains but to use them.

"It is useless to speak much of myself, but to you I may at least indulge more than to others. Sensible that I have now reached a time of life when action ought at least to commence and desirous as I feel myself of not throwing away time which ought to be useful, I see nothing but difficulty in the way. My

position is perhaps a peculiar one. Entirely destitute of friends and relations here, either from accident or my peculiar character, yet enjoying a degree of respect and reputation from hereditary and other advantages, I am on one side without any artificial aid to raise me, and on the other, forced to act with greater caution that I may at least lose no portion of the ground already gained. My custom always has been to rely upon myself mainly in my course, and this, while it has freed me from all advice, has also tended to make me fearful of results. In this state of things, if there is any course which you think I can take, it would be agreeable to me if you would suggest it for my consideration.

"You will readily suppose that much of the preceding is occasioned by the proposition you made to me before you left here. On many accounts I would gladly have embraced it and I should now like exceedingly to connect myself with some publication though a literary would be more agreeable than a political one. But my vanity is not sufficient to drown my sense of the risk of a new undertaking and old ones are already overcrowded. It is not labour I would refuse if I could see any prospect of getting any thing by it. But I do wish to have some little certainty to go upon; to go backwards would be folly while I have so much to lose. It would be better for me to sleep twenty years."

[2] In the edition of Cicero CFA was reading, "De finibus bonorum et malorum" concludes the 14th volume.

SUNDAY. 13TH.

Morning cloudy but it afterwards cleared away. I finished copying the letter to my father which is always a tedious operation. Attended divine Service all day and heard my Classmate Hedge. His Sermons pleased the mass, but they were very dull to me. So much so that I know little beyond the Texts. That of the morning was from Matthew 23. 26. "Thou blind Pharisee! cleanse first that which is within the cup and platter, that the outside of them may be clean also," upon the value of internal Piety. The afternoon's was from James. 1. last verse. "Pure religion and undefiled before God and the father, is this, To visit the fatherless and widows in their affliction, and to keep himself unspotted from the world." The word religion he affirmed to be a wrong translation, the proper word being "service." The text is a beautiful one. It means more than any Commentary.

I afterwards read a Sermon of Massillon's from Matthew 4. 4. "Man shall not live by bread alone, but by every word that proceedeth from the mouth of God." The subject, attention to the word of God. Division twofold. 1. The Disposition proper to go to Church with. 2. The Disposition with which we listen to the word. Subdivision 1st. part. 1. In order to benefit yourself by a wish to improve. 2. In a spirit of humility and self debasement. 3. In a spirit of thankfulness. 2d. part. 1. With an earnest and sincere conviction of the divine authority of the word delivered. 2. In a spirit, not of critical niceness to judge of the Speaker, but with a sense of the value of religious instruction. The Sermon was a very good one. But the very regular and invariable mode of building a Discourse by the French becomes tedious through its uniformity.

Evening read a little of the Life of George 4th but not much, as my Wife was not quite well. Finished the Lectures of Fuseli with which I have been pleased. They have given me a good deal of knowledge of the Artists and of the different portions of the Art itself. Finished as usual with the Spectator.

MONDAY. 14TH.

Morning cloudy with rain. I went to the Office as usual. After writing my Diary which on this day of the week always takes much time, I went over to vote—This being the day in which by the new law, all the State Officers are chosen together. The distracted state of public feeling here leads to exceedingly divided votes. And this owing to the wretched mismanagement of the party called the National Republican. This party, not having any particular grounds to adhere with, splits into a thousand divisions upon the most trifling causes. As a party I have done with it, and instead will try to stick to an independent judgment even though by it I throw away my vote.[1] Took a short walk, stopping first at the Athenæum.

Afternoon. Read Cicero's first book De finibus, containing an examination of the Epicurean Doctrine. It is delightful from the flowing easy nature of the style and the clearness of the argument.

Evening. Read Mason's translation of Du Fresnoy on Painting with the Notes of Sir Joshua Reynolds,[2] and after it the latter's Journey in Holland and Flanders.[3] All these things give me new ideas. Read the Spectator.

[1] The contests for the offices of governor and lieutenant governor were without interest. Numerous tickets, often overlapping, were offered in the races for the state senate and house of representatives. Within the National Republican party there were special tickets offered by the grocers, by those favoring abolition of imprisonment for debt, &c. Outside the party there were the Jackson and the Antimasonic tickets (*Boston Patriot*, 15 Nov., p. 2, col. 1).

[2] Charles Alphonse Dufresnoy, *The Art of Painting*, translated by W. Mason into English verse with notes by Sir Joshua Reynolds, York, 1783.

[3] This was at least in part a rereading; see above, vol. 3, entries for 8 and 11 June 1830.

TUESDAY. 15TH.

The rain which fell heavily during the night ceased and gave us a very beautiful morning. I went to the Office as usual and was occupied after writing my Journal in reading the Journal of the Virginia Convention. Patrick Henry seems to have been as mad as a March hare upon the subject, and therefore totally unable to give distinct reasons for his course. Mr. Monroe was much more sensible. Mr. Marshall came out here in defence of the system. Took a walk as usual.

Afternoon, read a large part of Cicero's second book de finibus in which he endeavours to refute the Epicurean doctrine. The selfish nature of it is well exposed, but I think he hardly argues on the true basis when he does not admit the definitions of his Opponent. The Epicurean doctrine as explained by Torquatus in the first book is a harmless one if not the true one. It does in fact make virtuous conduct the happiness of life.

Evening. Read Sir Joshua Reynolds' five first discourses which are exceedingly sensible, then dressed myself to go to a Ball at Mrs. J. L. Gardner's with my Wife.[1] It was the most splendid affair I have seen since I have been in Boston, and I enjoyed myself pretty well. Returned by eleven and read the Spectator.

[1] On Mr. and Mrs. John Lowell Gardner, see vol. 2:165, 179. They lived on Beacon Street at the corner of Somerset (*Boston Directory*, 1831–1832).

WEDNESDAY. 16TH.

Morning clear and calm. I went to the Office as usual and passed my time in writing and reading a little more of the Debates in the Virginia Convention. This displays as clearly as any thing the character of the People. For they spent a great deal of time in talking about nothing; in going round the question, in general debate and furious declamation and little in a philosophical Analysis of questions of Government.

At twelve, I went with Mrs. Frothingham, Miss Dexter, Miss Glover and my Wife to see a new Picture by W. Alston. The subject taken from the "Italian."[1] I think it is in many respects a superior picture. The expression of the frightened figure is very powerfully done, as well as the effect of the lamp light upon the faces of the pair. But I have doubts upon the head of the Friar and the Unity of the Picture, by this I mean the difference in the direction of the eyes of the two figures. Would it have been better, had they had the same? On the whole, this specimen of the Artist's manner is creditable.

From thence I went to look at some Engravings advertised to be sold,[2] which turned out much better than I anticipated. Dined at Mr. Frothingham's. Nothing of very material interest.

Afternoon, finished the second and began the third book of the Moral Treatise de Finibus. Evening quiet at home. Read some of Sir Joshua Reynolds, and as usual, the Spectator.

[1] Apparently Allston's painting was being exhibited privately at this time. On its public exhibition and on its subject, see below, entry for 26 Jan. 1832.

[2] An auction of engravings, selected in London by E. Little of Philadelphia, was scheduled for 18 Nov. by J. L. Cunningham at his rooms, corner of Milk and Federal streets (*Boston Patriot*, 16 Nov., p. 3, col. 5).

THURSDAY. 17TH.

Morning clear and pleasant. Went to the Office as usual and occupied myself in continuing the Debates in the Virginia Convention. Read the Speeches of Messrs. Madison, Lee and Nicholas,[1] which all of them confirmed me in my former opinions. Some of my time was also taken up in money matters and in writing my regular Diary. Also a short time at the Athenæum, and a walk.

Afternoon. Read the rest of the third book de Finibus containing an explanation of the Stoic or Doctrine of Zeno. Much of it is obscure and unintelligible, justifying the supposition of Cicero that the School was made to be a distinct School rather than from variance in doctrine. The vanity of the former Philosophers did more mischief to the intellectual character than their ingenuity reflected credit.

Continued Sir Joshua Reynolds' Lectures and in the evening read the Life of George 4th to my Wife previous to our going to the Ball at Mrs. N. Appleton's.[2] It was an excessively crowded party, very much mixed from the necessity of the case, he being the Representative from this district in Congress. I did not enjoy myself much. Many of the People I did not know, others I did not have any opportunity of seeing as I wished. So that I was glad to get away. But they were both very brilliant affairs, these two balls, and I am glad I attended them though

I cannot say I wish to be going again. Glad to get home and close by reading the Spectator.

[1] Richard Henry Lee of Westmoreland, George and Wilson Nicholas, delegates to the 1788 ratifying convention.
[2] The residence of the Nathan Appletons was at 39 Beacon Street (*Boston Directory*, 1831–1832).

FRIDAY. 18TH.

Morning fine and clear. I went to the Office but did not remain long as I intended going to the sale of Engravings. Perhaps it would have been better for me if I had been prevented, but it consumed my whole morning and a considerable sum of money besides. But my purchases though luxuries are cheap, to any one who can afford them. The most valuable was a large Collection of landscapes of Rubens, Claude, Gaspar Poussin, Rembrandt, Salvator Rosa and one other which I gave 35 cents each for. How can I who am poor pay for all these things? A love of the fine Arts, though it is a real pleasure which others who have it not are therefore so much the less happy, is yet a dear thing.

Returned home. Afternoon taken up in reading part of the fourth book de Finibus or the refutation of the Stoic doctrine, part of which is as obscure as the doctrine itself. Evening quiet at home. My Wife wrote to my Mother[1] and I read Sir Joshua Reynolds. Then, the Spectator.

[1] This letter is missing.

SATURDAY. 19TH.

Morning fine after a rainy night. I went to the Office as usual: thence to obtain the Engravings purchased yesterday. I sent them home and paid for them. Then returned to the Office and was busy in writing my Journal. Deacon Spear called from Quincy and made a settlement about wood. He paid me a considerable sum and gave his Note for the rest. This with two others payable on the first of May will make seven hundred dollars and there will be about enough due from Weston to make up a thousand, so that Wood is not an unprofitable business. If my father had not embarrassed himself with this miserable flour ⟨business⟩ concern, this would have been a productive year to his private fortune.

Went to the Athenæum for a book or two upon the fine arts and took a short walk. Afternoon, occupied in reading the rest of the fourth book de Finibus which is a pretty satisfactory reply to the Stoics.

Evening quiet with my Wife. Read part of the Life of George 4th which as it comes down is more exclusively political than ever, and if possible still more prejudiced. Afterwards, read the Lectures of Sir Joshua in continuation and the Spectator.

SUNDAY. 20TH.

Temperature colder, and Clouds, which dispersed in the course of the day. I read part of the Dictionary of Painting this morning in order to gain information upon the subject of Engraving, as strange to say, this book of Bryan's answers much better to that.[1]

Attended Divine Service all day and heard Mr. Frothingham in the morning from Acts 17. 22. "Ye men of Athens, I perceive that in all things ye are too superstitious." This is the beginning of the famed and beautiful Address of Paul to the Athenians—One not excelled by any of the most distinguished Oratorical efforts of Antiquity. The subject chosen by the Preacher was not the general one but the mere question of superstition, and an argument for charity in the construction of what it is. He stated that the real translation of the Greek words is "over religious." Words much better adapted to the general purpose of the Speech than the ones used, though the original will bear both meanings. Superstition however is the excess of religious feeling commonly, though the reverse may not be true. It is therefore a more pardonable extreme than the total want of it, which is it's opposite.

The Afternoon Sermon was from 2. Timothy 3. 7. "Ever learning, and never able to come to the knowledge of the truth." He applied this Text to those among men who occupy their time not in the solid acquirements for a life of virtue and usefulness, but in the curious controversial topics of Sectarianism or the unimportant minutiæ of mental occupations. Upon some points I did not assent to the Doctrine. He slighted the certainty of Historical knowledge when it seems to be [*i.e.* me?] to bear considerably upon the moral character of man, that the lessons he reads from other experience should carry no doubt with them as to their truth.[2]

At home read a Sermon of Massillon upon the future State. He derives his argument from two heads. 1. The certainty of it as founded upon reason. 2. The necessity of it, as agreeable to the idea of a wise Deity, and to the private conviction of every man in the existence of such a being.

Evening reading to my Wife more of George 4th. Then the rest of the Lectures of Reynolds which are very sensible, and the Spectator.

[1] Michael Bryan, *A Biographical and Critical Dictionary of Painters and Engravers*, 2 vols., London, 1813–1816.

[2] The meaning of the passage, though poorly expressed, would seem to be about as follows: To slight the importance of the effort to arrive at certainty in matters of historical fact by terming it a study of unimportant minutiæ is something I cannot agree with. To the extent that man's principles are formed out of the sum of men's experiences, the effort to ascertain what is true in history is an occupation that bears considerably upon the moral character of man.

MONDAY. 21ST.

Morning clear and cold. I went to the Office as usual. After devoting some time to the performance of my Diary, I sat down to write to my Father. My letter was for the most part upon business matters. The question now comes upon him how he is to meet the Notes made by him in the Spring for this flour business.[1] He will probably do it by sacrificing productive property. I consider him as in a pretty poor way and am not perfectly clear as to how he will come out of it. Probably his perseverance in the business will accomplish his ruin. Took a walk.

Afternoon, reading Cicero de Finibus, Book fifth, in which he undertakes to explain his own ideas upon the Subject, and he does it in a clear and lucid manner. I did not quite finish it. One can immediately see the difference in the style when he writes with relish and a conviction of the truth of his position.

Evening finished the second Volume of the Life of George 4th which brings the history down to the occupation of Paris by the Allies the first time. I have on the whole gained something by it. Afterwards. Copied part of my father's letter and read the Spectator.

[1] CFA to JQA, 21 Nov. (LbC, Adams Papers). Francis J. Oliver, the president of the American Insurance Office, had notified CFA that JQA's note could be renewed only at a substantially higher interest rate because of the demand for money.

TUESDAY. 22D.

Upon opening our eyes this morning, we found a most tremendous flurry blowing hail and rain and snow together, and lasting only a few minutes after a Clap of thunder. The atmosphere afterwards became decidedly more chilly. I went to the Office but my time was wasted even more than usual. This is a melancholy state of things from which something must come soon to relieve me or I shall become a drone. Several persons called to see me upon various matters of business and I went to the Athenæum afterwards where I wasted the time when I should have walked. The neglect of exercise in my present condition is as bad as the neglect of study, for it makes the latter less likely to be performed when greater occasion may call for it.

Afternoon, finished the 5th book De Finibus, which is on the whole an interesting Dissertation though it settles nothing. I completed my Copy of the letter to my Father and sent it.

Evening. Read to my Wife a part of the Romance of the Italian which Mr. Alston's Picture has brought up again.[1] I am rather inclined to think the world has lost nothing by allowing these books to sleep on the shelves of Circulating Libraries in Peace. They consult[2] Passions and terrors which are hardly beneficial to man. I continued a sketch for future use which I think I mentioned as begun a few nights since and read the Spectator.

[1] CFA had read in *The Italian*, Mrs. Ann Radcliffe's novel, in 1824; see above, vol. 1:293.
[2] Thus clearly in MS; probably in the sense of "have an eye to" (*OED*).

WEDNESDAY. 23D.

Morning clear with a high wind from the South West. I went to the Office and passed my time after the usual matters, in reading Moore's Life of Sheridan which I have never examined before.[1] The thing amused me exceedingly. Sheridan's is a fascinating character. The brilliancy of his Wit is charming while the generous nature of his feeling makes one sympathize in all his fortunes. Nevertheless Sheridan had very little in his personal character which entitled the man to respect or esteem. He had no fixed principles of conduct, no sterling qualities. His life was a course upon a boundless and agitated Sea without chart or compass to guide him. Took a walk.

Afternoon, reading the first book of Tusculan Questions, upon Death. It is curious as the Argument of a Heathen Philosopher upon the Immortality of the Soul unaided by Revelation or any thing but the light of his own Reason.

Evening, the Italian to my Wife after which I continued my sketch, the materials for which grow upon me. I think better of it as I advance. Not what it is, but what it is capable of being made. Read the Spectator.

[1] Thomas Moore, *Memoirs of the Life of ... R. B. Sheridan*, London, 1825.

THURSDAY. 24TH.

Morning clear and cool. I went to the Office and was occupied in my usual way. First in my Diary and Accounts and then in the Life of Sheridan which afforded me a great degree of amusement. His attempts when compared with his subsequent performances are enough to encourage writers like myself who have no great confidence in themselves. He pruned and polished with a care which is not consistent with the general character of indolence sustained by him. Took a walk.

Afternoon finished the first Tusculan upon Death, which is one of the most pleasing to me of all Cicero's works. I like the spirit in which it is written, the philosophy which it inculcates and the acquaintance with nature it displays. Cicero is the first remarkable instance in Antiquity of Versatility of Powers. He was a Poet, a Philosopher, an Orator and a Statesman. In three of these he reached the first rank, and his claim in the other is not settled. Perhaps he may be considered as the only instance for Voltaire was no Orator, not much of a Statesman and though dealing in many things was superficial in all but his Poetry.

Evening, reading the Italian, to my Wife who is suffering from a Cold. After which I continued my sketch, the substance of which is much better than the way it is managed. Read the Spectator.

FRIDAY. 25TH.

Morning clear and cool. I went to the Office as usual and was occupied while there in reading and my usual duties. I continued the Life of Sheridan with unabated interest, and was fascinated by the account of his successes as a Speaker. Indeed little could be supposed more delightful to a man than the union of such brilliant wit as to put him at the head of one department of the Drama and the highest powers of eloquence. It is an example of the versatility of human powers which I was thinking of yesterday.

Col. Russel Freeman interrupted my meditations. He came to pay me a short visit and to complain of the course of the Courier. I told him pretty freely my sentiments upon the present state of parties. He is in quest of place and like all men of that kind feels twenty cords pulling in various directions.[1] He stated his case pretty plainly, but all I could do was to be sorry for him. Took a short walk.

Afternoon reading the second of the Tusculans upon the Question "Whether pain is an evil." A point which however ingeniously discussed requires only a little common sense to be resolved.

Evening reading the Italian, until Mr. Brooks came in. He has just moved from Medford and is now under all the discomfort of a change to a man at his time of life. I pity his case.[2] He gave us a direct invitation to go out there, next Summer. I did not know what to say. After this I went to a party at Mrs. J. Welles' which was pleasant enough.[3] But returned early being without my Wife. Read the Spectator.

[1] For an earlier estimate of Freeman, see above, vol. 3:165.

[2] Charlotte Brooks Everett's decision to accompany her husband to Washington for the approaching session of Congress presented Peter C. Brooks with the choice of a winter alone at Medford or living in Boston with one of his children. He had remained for some time undecided. ABA and CFA had invited him to come to them; presumably others had done the same. A solution was found when Mrs. Eliza H. Otis, the widow of Harrison Gray Otis Jr., decided to pass the winter in Washington and offered her Boston house at 8 Somerset Street "just as it stood . . . at a reasonable rate" to Gorham Brooks, who earlier had planned to remain through the winter at his home in Watertown. He

took it, "Mr. Brooks to occupy a part." The decision, while accepted by the family as a good one, raised some apprehensions about the future. It was at least LCA's view that the "gay widow" had set her cap for Mr. Brooks, and that in some way her course was directed toward that single end. Peter C. Brooks to ABA, 7 Oct.; CFA to LCA, 5 Nov.; LCA to CFA, 7 [i.e. 9] Nov.; LCA to JQA, 10 Nov. (all in the Adams Papers); CFA [to Peter C. Brooks], Dft, without date (Adams Papers, Microfilms, Reel No. 319); Brooks, Waste Book, 26 Nov.; *Boston Directory*, 1831–1832.

[3] The John Welles residence was at 59 Summer Street (*Boston Directory*, 1831–1832). Mr. Welles is identified at vol. 1:334.

SATURDAY. 26TH.

Morning clear and cool. I went to the Office as usual. Rather surprised not to find any letters from home.[1] This requires some explanation, and I can give none of an agreeable Character.[2] Spent my time pretty much as I did yesterday. Wrote my Diary, read my usual quantity in the Life of Sheridan. A work that has interested me exceedingly. His wife was a fascinating being. She seems to have entered into his feelings and partaken his labours whatever they were. Yet who can feel a regret for her death. I thought it on the whole a mercy, for her husband was already going down, though not yet with any sensible motion. Had she lived, she would probably have had nothing but bitterness in store for her. The bitterness of misfortune brought on by the follies and vices of the man she had married. As it was, she saved all that and saw only the situation which he had reached by his abilities. But the reading made me dull and it was aided by an indigestion. I was imprudent in eating at Mrs. Welles' last night which gave me a sick headache. The consequence was that I did not read Cicero in the Afternoon to much effect, nor do any thing in the evening, but take some Medicine and read the Spectator.

[1] From his parents at Washington—a curious reversion to a habit of thought and expression of some years earlier.

[2] The explanation that would have come immediately to mind was offense taken at CFA's letter to JQA of 12 November.

SUNDAY. 27TH.

Awoke this morning to see the first snow this Season. The day was rainy and unpleasant. I attended Divine Service in the morning and heard Mr. Frothingham preach from Luke 9 v. 16 Chapt. "Make to yourselves friends of the Mammon of unrighteousness." A singular text but a very good one as managed by him. For he illustrated it to mean the proper conduct of life in regard to Riches. First, prudence in the acquisition, second, liberality in the dispensation. The latter including all the Charities of which man should be capable to his fellow men, the former increasing the means, and preventing any resulting injury to its exercise. It was a Charity Sermon as a Collection was made for the Poor immediately afterward. The Attendance was thin from the bad weather.

I returned home immediately and passed my Afternoon very quietly as my Medicine and the Weather made it quite as advisable to remain at home. Read a Sermon of Massillon's Text Matthew. 21. 12. "And Jesus went into the Temple of God and cast out all them that sold and bought in the temple." Upon the true attendance upon the House of God, which should be: 1. in a spirit of Justice and benevolence, 2. in a spirit of humility. Passed an hour afterward in writing a sketch of a Dissertation upon Cicero which I had in my mind though to tell the truth I am not equal to it. Evening quietly at home. Read to my Wife a little and afterwards read a little upon Architecture, and the Spectator.

MONDAY. 28TH.

Morning cold with a little flight of snow in the Night. I went to the Office as usual where I was busy in writing and reading the Life of Sheridan in which I made great progress. The Account of his decline is hurried over and excused as much as possible but after all it is bad enough. Nothing material took place. I took a short walk and returned home.

Afternoon finished the third Tusculan of Cicero. In the Evening Mr. Brooks came in and sat a couple of hours very pleasantly. After which I began reading Pope's translation of Homers Iliad.[1] And the Spectator as usual.

[1] Two editions are at MQA, one, bearing JQA's bookplate, published at London in 1771 in 5 vols., the other, also a London edition, in 2 vols., 1818–1829.

TUESDAY. 29TH.

The weather is turning off quite cold, which coming after an uncommonly mild season makes it more severe to the feelings. I went to the Office and received a letter this morning from my father which has been so long expected. I was on the whole very well satisfied with it.[1] It answered my request for advice by recommending me to keep quiet for the present, which coincides with my own sentiments. Yet I wish some occasion would present itself for me to work upon. I read this letter over and over, and what with reflecting upon it, and attending to what little business I had, especially from the receipt of Money from Conant of Weston, I did not read at all, nor did I get a chance to take a walk.

Returned home and in the Afternoon Read the fourth Tusculan of Cicero. These two have a little too much of the leaven of the Schools. There is a jingle of words which mean nothing and lead to no practical end. The truth lies in a Nutshell.

Evening quiet at home. Read to my Wife a little but not with any interest and afterwards, continued Pope's Iliad which I have never opened before. Also as usual, the Spectator.

[1] JQA to CFA, 22 Nov. (Adams Papers). JQA found in the year's first winter storm the opportunity to quote, from *As You Like It*, Duke Senior's speech on flattery as more painful than any of nature's blasts. Thus reminded, he professed satisfaction in the knowledge derived from CFA's letter of 12 Nov. that there was no need to fear flattery from him:

"And God forbid that you should flatter me. I had rather hear truth from you, however unwelcome, than flattery. I wish to say as little as possible of myself, and therefore I shall not offer an apologetic exposition of the causes which have contributed to the waste of my last three years, so far as concerns the purposes to which I had devoted them in my intention. But I go into Congress, with the opinions of those who are nearest and dearest to me in the world, declared against the measure. I go there with expectations of any thing but pleasure, honour, or even profitable service to my country, to be derived from the necessary sacrifice of my Time within the Walls of the capitol. I go to experience slights, mortifications, insults, loss of reputation, and perhaps exposure of myself by infirmities of temper, unsuited to the trials which I am to encounter. Think you that I see a bed of roses before me? Or ask you *why* with all these consequences in my view I persist in the determination to take my seat in the Legislative Hall? Because I am acting under a sense of duty. For this I know I shall have no credit upon Earth. If the dearest of my friends refuse to receive it as my justification, I have no right to expect from any other human being a more candid interpretation. If I have no credit for it, with him who knows the heart, it is because my own heart deceives me, which I know is not impossible. My election to Congress was a *Call*, unsolicited, unexpected, spontaneous, from a portion of my Countrymen, into the public Service. Forty years before it might have been an object of laudable, ardent personal ambition. *Now*, it was an invitation to descend from the highest ranks of public dignity to a station of far less eminence and power. The call so far as opinions could be ascertained was nearly unanimous in the district; and it was from the dwellers on my native land. From the scenes of my childhood—Almost from the Sepulchres of my fathers—This Call, I could not find it in my heart to suppress or to reject, by a flat, ungracious refusal, for which I could have given no reason, but an overweening sense of my own personal comfort or personal dignity.

"I therefore accepted it, and with the blessing of God shall take my seat. There are rumours that it will be contested, upon the ground that I was not eligible in the district at the Time of the Election. If the House should so determine I may be relieved at an early day from all obligation of duty to the political service of my own generation, and shall be at Liberty to resume the labours which you consider as having been neglected only by my own unaccountable irresolution.

"I have so short a remnant of life before me, that it is comparatively speaking of little consequence what may befall myself. I have infinitely more concern for the prospects of my children and particularly for yours. You wish to take an independent, and respectable stand in Society, and yet to keep yourself disentangled from all the snarls of political strife as you have done hitherto. My advice to you then is, to confine your attention to such business as you have. To use all laudable exertions of Industry to defray the necessary expenses of your family and to avoid involving yourself in debt, and to devote all your leisure to study, practising rigorous economy, and seeking no political distinction, not even to find a place upon the list of sixty or seventy Representatives of the City in the general Court."

WEDNESDAY 30TH.

A considerable part of my Morning was consumed at Market. And for the season of Thanksgiving I do not think that the display I saw today was very great. For some years past I have thought it advisable to go down and see the sport, but have never before been much in the humour of buying. Today I got quite into the spirit of it.

Returned to my Office and was busy as I generally am. Finished the Life of Sheridan which is a miserable concern in its close. I don't mean Mr. Moore's book. It has affected me a good deal. Mr. John Angier called about J. Q. Adams Jr. and I had a conversation with him in which I spoke freely about the prospects of his Wife's family. This took so much time that I went home directly.

Afternoon spent partially in reading Cicero and partly in some little occupations to guard against the cold which is now coming upon us. Quiet evening at home. I read to my Wife a little of the Bible and to myself the Review of Mr. Moore's book in the Quarterly, which is bitter enough. But there is some ground for it.[1] I afterwards sat down and wrote half a letter to my Father in answer to his. And closed the day with the Spectator.

[1] The review of Thomas Moore's *Memoirs of . . . Sheridan* was that in the *Quarterly Review*, 33:561–593 (March 1826).

DECEMBER 1831.
THURSDAY. 1ST.

This was Thanksgiving day. Last year we spent it at Quincy and it was a bright cool day. This time we opened our eyes to see the snow falling fast and to realize the arrival of Winter, in all its dreariness. I spent my morning in finishing my Letter to my Father which is unusually long for me.[1] Then attended Divine Service at Mr. Frothingham's and heard him preach from Psalms 147. 13. "For he hath blessed thy children within thee." It was a good Sermon for the occasion, as he adopted the plan of discriminating the objects for the possession of which we should be grateful. These he stated to be Health, Peace, Liberty and Plenty. He presented the contrast between our condition and that of Europe quite forcibly.

Returned home and finished my work upon the Copy of the Letter excepting a half page which I did in the Evening. Went down to dine at Mr. Frothingham's. He expected several, but there was only Mr. Brooks, Gorham's wife, Abby and myself. The dinner was over bountiful. I felt as I always do after such a festival, a little too heavy, but I returned home and read a little of Cicero, before finishing the Evening at Mrs. F's. Walked home with Mr. Brooks. Read the Spectator. It was very cold and clear.

[1] CFA to JQA, 30 Nov. – 1 Dec. (Adams Papers):

"With respect to your going to Congress ..., it was not my intention to enter into the question of it's propriety.... Whatever opinion I may hold upon it is founded upon a construction of our system of government which like many other matters of that kind with me, is not entertained by you. I lay claim to no infallibility particularly where my conclusions are opposed to your's. And I may in this case add that I shall be glad to find myself wrong.

"But if the Call on the part of your Constituents was of such a Nature as to make this acceptance of it a *duty*; was it so imperious as to put in the back ground other Calls which perhaps are not less urgent, yet must be postponed? ... You say the call was 'from the scenes of your Childhood.' Is there not another associated with the same scenes which moreover can be answered by no one else? You say, it is '*Almost* from the sepulchres of your fathers.' There is another, from which '*Almost*' may be suppressed. There are services to a man's own generation, and it would be difficult to say you had not already done your share of them. But grant, the only question is, how these can be now multiplied. I say, not so well by your being in

Congress, if it should endanger your furnishing to the present and *future* generations what *you only* can furnish. This is the gist of the matter."

Continuing, CFA pressed upon JQA both the uniqueness of his equipment to edit JA's papers and the extraordinary importance of the task:

"Does my Grandfather's reputation stand so high that it will need no mending or restoring? Examine every Eulogy of him that was delivered and ask why it is that a veil is suddenly thrown upon his figure immediately upon his reaching the Presidency, when some intimate a fall from his great career, while even the most friendly drop the subject. Is this right? Shall it be, that his course as President of these United States belied all his former career, and proved him An Anti Republican unworthy of further confidence? Even at this moment, a deliberate attempt is made to rob him of all credit for knowledge of political affairs in a trying Crisis and moreover to prove him wrong where he has always been thought right. Is this nothing? Here is a gross perversion of history, in all its essential attributes, obtaining the authority of time and prescription, while the destruction of it is still left to chance.

"I am not nor ever was the unqualified admirer of my Grandfather, neither do I ever expect to be of any man living or dead. It is enough for me that human nature is concerned to distrust all notions of perfection. But from the clearest lights of my understanding I do feel impressed with a conviction that his story is not fairly told. . . . [H]is defects lying all on the surface impressed men, judging as men ordinarily do, unfavourably; while his rival was only rotten where nobody could see it, at the Core. . . . You know it all better than I do.

The only deduction I wish to make from the whole is this. If this is an important duty, which you and you only can perform, is it wonderful that I feel provoked that the performance of it should be hazarded by Orations, and Eulogies, Poems and Annual Registers, and last though not least by the doubtful (to say no more) advantages of the harassing, perplexing, all engrossing, all exhausting political warfare of a Seat in the House of Representatives?"

FRIDAY. 2D.

The winter sets in with great severity. The cold this morning for the season was very great. I went to the Office. Engaged there in drawing up my Accounts for last Month and balancing my Books. My father's affairs in pretty good condition. Did not experience so much inconvenience from yesterday as I expected. But I took a walk notwithstanding the cold in order to obviate any probable difficulty. Then home. Abby had a letter from my Mother giving but a poor Account of the health of John's child.[1] I am afraid that is a bad business.

Read in the Afternoon a considerable part of the fifth Tusculan upon the happiness of virtue. In which it appears to me the ancient Philosophers entangled themselves in their own webs. I did not quite finish it, because Gorham Brooks came wishing us to go to the Theatre. Mr. Hackett performed his usual Caricatures of American Character. Mr. Fletcher a series of Attitudes from Classical designs which are worth seeing and a man imitated the Actions of a Monkey.[2] Such is the Dramatic taste of the present day! Returned home and read the Spectator.

[1] LCA to ABA, 30 [i.e. 27] Nov. (Adams Papers). JA2's younger child, Georgeanna Frances ["Fanny"] was suffering from the "Canker," an extremely painful ailment, characterized, according to LCA, by ulcerations of the mouth and lungs.

[2] The Tremont Theatre offered James Henry Hackett as Col. Wildfire, a Kentuckian, in *The Lion of the West*, a comedy in four acts. The play was followed by "Mr. Fletcher, from the Theatre Royal Drury Lane" in "Venetian Statues"; a scene from *Down East*, a farce; and a drama in one act, *Savage of the Island, or the Ourang Outang*, in which M. Gouffe took the part of the orangutan (*Boston Patriot*, 1 Dec., p. 3, col. 4). On Hackett (1800–1871), see *DAB*; on Fletcher and Gouffe, see Odell, *Annals N.Y. Stage*, 3:569.

SATURDAY 3D.

Morning cloudy with slight snow. I went to the Office as usual. Nothing of material consequence took place. I was engaged in writing up my Journal and began to read the Speech of Burke upon the Nabob of Arcot's debts.[1] This Speech is very celebrated and Mr. Moore speaks so highly of it, I think I must look it over again. It takes more than one reading to judge of a Speech upon a subject of so little interest to us. Took a walk to the Athenæum and round High Street home. My purpose was to see the Address to the Public from Mr. Bailey which involves a charge against my father.[2] I could not how-ever find it. The Free Press is left at the Athenæum but is not in esti-mation enough to be preserved long. Returned home.

Afternoon, finished the reading of the Tusculans and began the Essay, "De natura Deorum." But I made no great progress. My After-noons pass like my Mornings without proper profit.

Evening, reading to my Wife—After which, the third Book of Pope's Homer, and the Spectator.

[1] The speech, delivered on 28 Feb. 1785 and published separately in the same year, is in vol. 2 of the edition of Edmund Burke's *Works* at MQA, pub-lished at London in 1792 in 3 volumes.

[2] The alleged attack on JQA by John Bailey of the Antimasonry party was later denounced by Bailey as fraudulent and an outright falsehood (JQA to CFA, 13 Dec., Adams Papers).

SUNDAY. 4TH.

I have not escaped a violent cold which has troubled me yesterday and today. The Snow had been falling all night and was so deep on the ground, besides the increase momentarily going on, that I thought it advisable not to attend Church today. I remained quietly installed in my Chair and instead read a Sermon of Isaac Barrow's and one of Massillon's. The first was from the well known text "And her ways are ways of pleasantness, and all her paths of peace." Upon the pleasant-ness of Religion. A sound though not to me a remarkable Sermon. That of Massillon was from Matthew 12. 45. "And the last state of that man is worse than the first." Upon the dangers of relapse. He con-sidered first its enormity, then its danger. The leading idea was the loss of that freshness of soul which is never to be recovered, that first spring of piety which once defiled can never regain its purity. On the whole a very good Sermon. Read an Essay or two of old Montagne who has had great reputation for thought.[1] I want to find it. My time was not all used to the best advantage.

Evening. Read to my Wife a portion of the Bible especially the beautiful Chapter in Corinthians upon Charity. Also a part of Byron's Deformed Transformed.[2] Afterwards, Pope and the Spectator.

[1] Of the three editions of Montaigne's *Les essais* at MQA, that published at

Rouen in 1619 has CFA's bookplate. [2] On the editions of Byron at MQA, see above, vol. 3:185. The order in which CFA read the poems during the next several days suggests that he was using the edition which had belonged to GWA, in which the poems appeared in the same order.

MONDAY. 5TH.

The Storm continued with wind very high all the morning, so that instead of going out, I sat down in my Study quietly and continued reading Cicero de Natura Deorum in which I made considerable progress. I find my faculties are much more quick in the morning which makes me feel what a pity it is that they are so much thrown away always. Yet if I was to alter my way of life, however much I might improve by it, my reputation for business would not, so that I must even submit to the present arrangement.

I went to the Office at one o'clock, for a minute, but returned immediately. Found the walking better than I expected, so I went down after dinner to the Boylston Market to attend the Meeting of the Directors. Found only Messrs. French and Child. We soon accomplished our business and I drew up the record for the last and this Meeting thus getting a matter off my hands which has troubled me. Returned at sunset and read a little more of Cicero.

Evening, read to my Wife the rest of the Deformed Transformed and Heaven and Earth. After which Pope's Homer and the Spectator.

TUESDAY 6TH.

Morning clear, but this snow storm has brought the Winter upon us a Month before its time. I found it cold going to the Office and when there did not accomplish any more than common. Made up my Accounts, received a Quarter's rent from a man about whom I had doubts and deposited on my own account. This done, took a walk. Returned home and felt unusually well with an appetite to correspond. How it is that I have suffered so much of late I cannot tell but for two or three days I have been as I was a year ago.

Afternoon, engaged in reading Cicero de Natura Deorum which contains the strangest Medley of most ridiculous notions entertained by the old Philosophers. It seems to have been made a Sport of the intellect to see how many ridiculous fancies could be started upon the subject of all the most serious. Cicero certainly shines among them very much. Most from comparison. My fire troubled me.

Evening quiet at home. My Wife was quite sick with a cold. Read to her a part of Byron's Island, which for him is poor though it has good strong verses. Afterwards, read Pope's Iliad and finished the seventh volume of the Spectator.

WEDNESDAY. 7TH.

Morning clear and cold. I went to the Office and from the sickness of my boy had the gratification to find my own fire to make. This done and after a time to get warm, I went through my usual duties, the performance of which left me only about an hour to continue the Speech upon the Nabob of Arcot's debts. I read however a fine parcel of the best of it especially the remarkable passage describing the irruption of Hyder Ali into the Carnatic. I. Hull Adams called with some sheets of Journal and requesting Stationary which I gave him. Then I went on my regular business of purchases and to the Athenæum which consumed my hour until dinner.

Afternoon. Read a considerable portion of the second book De Natura Deorum giving a defence of the Theory that the Earth is a Deity which has for its only merit a little sophistical but ingenious reasoning. My Wife was quite sick with the Influenza all day so that she retired early. I began Gibbon this evening,[1] and the 8th Volume of the Spectator.

[1] The only edition of *The History of the Decline and Fall of the Roman Empire* at MQA, CFA's, is that published in 6 vols. at London, 1846. However, there are two 18th-century editions, each imperfect, among JA's books in the Boston Public Library, one of them bearing JQA's bookplate as well as JA's autograph (*Catalogue of JA's Library,* p. 101–102).

THURSDAY. 8TH.

Morning very cold. The sudden rush of the severity of the Season upon us is somewhat unusual. I went to the Office and occupied myself in my common way. Read the rest of Burkes Speech upon the Nabob of Arcot's debts. A very able thing and worth attentive study by a man who is likely to be a Speaker. For myself it seems so doubtful whether I shall have any chance to shew myself in this way, that I must be content to speculate upon its effect and the means by which such a thing was composed. Nothing of any particular consequence took place. I went to the Athenæum and then took a short walk. My Wife still continues very unwell from her cold. This is a great annoyance and one of the Taxes of our Climate.

Afternoon. Continued reading the Work, "De natura Deorum" and was much pleased with it today. The reasoning from Nature's Works to the existence of a Deity is admirable and can be improved by nobody.

But the idea that the Earth is that Deity is realizing the step from the sublime to the ridiculous. On the whole the book is a valuable historical relic.

My Wife felt so much indisposed that I could not read to her, but went on with Gibbon. His opening Chapters are excellent. They make so good a starting point. I then read a Book of Homer's Iliad, but was almost overpowered with drowsiness. Finished the evening with two numbers of the Spectator.

FRIDAY. 9TH.

Morning cloudy but rather more mild than it has been. After going to Market and making some purchases for a few days, I went to the Office. Received a short letter upon business from my Father, in consequence of which I was engaged in making the necessary inquiries. Called at Mr. Oliver's Office, State Street, and settled with him, then saw Degrand for one or two moments, and returned to reply to my father which I did before one o'clock.[1] Then took a walk.

Found Abby so sick upon my getting home that I concluded to send for the Dr. A married man must expect this as one of his greatest cares—The health of his Wife and Children if he is blessed with any. Ever since my Marriage, my Wife has been delicate, and she has lost the superintending care of her Mother which was her principal reliance. I do not know what to do. And therefore send to Physicians to take the responsibility off from my mind. Read Cicero the whole Afternoon. Cotta's Confutation of the Stoic follies, though himself guilty of a few. Evening Gibbon and Homer's Iliad. After which, the Spectator.

[1] JQA to CFA, 4 Dec.; CFA to JQA, 9 Dec., LbC (both in Adams Papers). JQA's decision was to renew his note rather than sell securities, if it could be done at an interest rate of less than 6 per cent. CFA found, when he went to the American Insurance Office, that the President, Francis J. Oliver, was willing to renew for six months or a year at 5½ per cent.

SATURDAY. 10TH.

Morning severely cold. I went to the Office as usual and passed my morning besides my usual occupations in reading the Life of Caesar in Suetonius[1] which I did as a kind of assistance to my view of the Decline and Fall of the Roman Empire. Nothing of any particular consequence occurred and after taking a walk, returned home. Found my Wife laid up by her Cold. My Man sick in bed from the same thing and the House again all out of order. I had flattered myself that my troubles had ceased when my Woman went out of the House, but it seems that now I am to have some more. The family was in so much disorder that I concluded to pass my Afternoon at the Athenæum the result of which was that I did little or nothing.

Returned and as there was nobody to make my Fire, I sat in my Wife's room all the Evening. Continued Gibbon and made more progress than I expected. A man ought to have the power of fixing his attention upon a book in situations not the most convenient to him, or else he will lose a great deal of time that might have been made valuable to him. This has been so little felt by me that I have suffered by it. But I am likely to be so much tried as to make me learn better. Read my usual Numbers of the Spectator. Mr. Brooks spent a part of the Evening here.

¹ All of the numerous editions of the *XII Cæsares* of Suetonius in the several Adams libraries are in Latin.

SUNDAY. 11TH.

Morning clear but attended with the degree of cold we have been having which is so unusual. I arose after having had an uneasy night and attended Divine Service through the day. Mr. Frothingham preached in the morning. Text taken from Psalms 145. 8. "Snow and vapour; stormy wind fulfilling his word." It was upon the idea so frequently expressed that the severities of the Atmosphere were Judgments of God. Resisting this as an improper construction he proceeded to reconcile the rigour of the elements with the beneficent character of the Deity, and produced a conclusion that was agreeable to the words of the Text. I did not succeed in grasping the Sermon and am therefore reduced to this lame account of it. Mr. Parkman preached in the Afternoon a Sermon that happened to be peculiarly suited to my state of feeling. Romans. 11. 33. "How unsearchable are his Judgments and his ways past finding out." It was an examination of the apparently unequal operation of Providence upon the merits of Men. The exaltation of the vicious in health, fortune, friends and honor, and talent, with the corresponding depression of the Virtuous by severe trials in all these. He came to the conclusion from these that it is not for man to exercise his Judgment in questioning the correctness of such dispensations, but it is for him in faith and hope to trust that the Deity envelopes in darkness that which it would not befit us to know, but that which is in fact the certain course of his Justice. I said this was suited to my State of feeling, because it seemed as if I was myself somewhat tried. On subsequent reflection however, I felt ashamed of myself for considering any thing which I was experiencing as trial.

And though I had never remitted a moment my trust in the Deity, I thought I was sinful in repining at all when I had been so eminently favoured throughout my life.

Read a Sermon of Massillon's. Upon Prayer, from Matthew 15. 22. "Have mercy on me, O Lord, thou son of David." He considers the reasons urged against Prayer in two heads. 1. That Men do not know how to address the Deity. 2. That they are not in a fit state to do so. These he refutes. But I do not consider the Division or the refutation very striking. The fitness of individual Prayer can not be questioned. To the most miserable it is a relief.

Evening read one of Barrow's Sermons upon the Profitableness of Godliness which seemed to me more masculine. Then the Spectator.

MONDAY. 12TH.

My Wife is slowly but gradually getting better. My man still continues sick and the rest of my family are worked enough to wear them out. I went to the Office feeling under most anxiety for the Child who has taken her Mother's sickness.

Occupied in various ways, drawing Accounts and writing my Journal. Purchased today some more Suffolk Insurance Shares.[1] This is hardly a prudent step in my present situation as my expenditure cannot be foreseen at all as it could be a year since. And unless my Dover Stock[2] should bring me off safe, I shall have to retrace my path at the hazard of loss in a falling Market. I am fully sensible of this but my anxiety is so great to improve all reasonable opportunities of enlarging my means, that I feel under the necessity of straining a little. And on the whole the risks are now in my favour, and at worst I can only sell out Stock that is good.

Dined at Mr. Frothingham's to save trouble at my House. Afternoon reading Cicero and Evening, Gibbon. The Child gave us much uneasiness and kept us up to a late hour. Read the Spectator.

[1] On earlier acquisitions of Suffolk Insurance stock see above, vol. 3, entries for 6 Nov. 1830 and 5 Jan. 1831.
[2] That is, stock in Cocheco Manufacturing Co. of Dover, N.H.; see above, entry for 5 September.

TUESDAY. 13TH.

The Weather holds on unusually cold. My Wife grows slowly better but her patience is giving way under the constant pressure of her sickness. The Baby is rather better. My man has gone to other Quarters and so on the whole I feel myself much relieved. I went to the Office, although from these peculiar circumstances quite late. Time was spent in writing up my Journal and Accounts and drawing up my statement for T. B. Adams Jr. of his Affairs in my hands. Returned home and went from thence to Mrs. Frothingham's to dine. Then back but my Fire was in so poor a state that I consumed some time in getting it up, and therefore did little more than finish the third book De Natura Deorum which contains all that can be said in favour of Atheism. The Argument is undoubtedly a plausible one but after all it is weak. What is Man that he should set himself up as the creature of accident? What known state of things resulting from chance could ever authorize an argument in its favour as the cause of all the regularity of Nature? It is harder to believe in accident than in a Deity. Evening. Read Gibbon. Second Volume embracing the latter Roman Emperors of the Western Empire. His Style though satiating is still very good. Read two good Numbers of the Spectator.

WEDNESDAY. 14TH.

Weather excessively cold. I went to the Office. My Wife not quite so unwell as she has been though her spirits are exceedingly depressed. The family in utter confusion, and comfortless as possible. Engaged all the morning in writing and after all accomplished only a Letter to T. B. Adams Jr. covering my Account up to the 12th instant, and a short one to my Father.[1] This was no great matter but it was better than nothing. And the air is so sharp that it freezes the powers and nips one almost into nothing. The duty was performed and that always gives gratification.

Dined again at Mr. Frothingham's. His brother was there. Is the Cashier of a Bank here and a respectable though evidently not a bright man.[2] Returned home to chill again over a poor fire and accomplished nothing but copying my Letters. This is a miserable waste of life, and comfortless as miserable but what is to be done?

Evening. Carried my Letters to the Post Office and received one from my Mother with a Commission in the Navy for J. H. Adams.[3] We shall now see the result. Read Gibbon, the Iliad Book 9th and the Spectator.

[1] The letterbook copies of both are in Adams Papers.

[2] Ephraim Langdon Frothingham was cashier of the Traders' Bank, Boston (*Boston Directory*, 1831–1832).

[3] LCA to CFA, 10 Dec. (Adams Papers). For LCA's part in securing the commission for Joseph Harrod Adams, see above, entry for 26 June.

THURSDAY. 15TH.

Morning snow and very cold. The Thermometer for the last fifteen days has averaged little above 10°. of Fahrenheit. My Wife a little better and quite revived by the appearance of her Nurse from Medford.

Went to the Office and was occupied in writing Letters to Mrs. Adams and Joseph in relation to the Commission received last Night.[1] I then tried to sketch off an Article upon the Treasury Report lately published but did not finish it as I went home to oversee my fire. Took the precaution to make one up myself today, such as would probably last. Then went and dined at Mr. Frothingham's. Mr. Brooks was there. We had some conversation but I did not enjoy my dinner.

Returned home and read a part of Cicero's first book De divinatione discussing a peculiar part of the character of Man—His attachment to signs and wonders. Probably the greatest change that has taken place in this generation is the comparatively small operation of this feeling. But it is still powerful.

Evening. Attended a Caucus of Mr. Sullivan's friends. I went as one of them although I had no personal feeling for him, simply because I thought him the best man.[2] Returned and set to work upon my Article. Read the Spectator.

[1] The letters to Mrs. TBA and to Joseph Harrod Adams are missing.

[2] In the voting on 12 Dec. to elect a mayor of Boston, William Sullivan had placed third behind Charles Wells and Theodore Lyman Jr., but since no candidate had received a majority of the votes cast, a second election was called for 22 December. At the caucus of citizens supporting Sullivan's candidacy held at the New Court House on School Street on 15 Dec., a letter from Sullivan was read in which he withdrew from the race (*Columbian Centinel*, 14 Dec., p. 4, col. 7; 17 Dec., p. 2, cols. 6–7).

FRIDAY. 16TH.

I found the difference during the Night, in sleeping in a cold room without any fire. Arose and after warming myself as well as I could went to the Office. Was busy there in writing a part of my Paper upon the Treasury Report. But I could not finish it at all today. No material occurrence took place. Received an answer from Mrs. Adams just such as I expected to receive—Expressing no decided answer but wavering and talking.[1] These people do not deserve kindness. Took a short walk and returned to dine at home.

Afternoon passed in reading the first book De Divinatione which contains all the wonderful predictions that took place in Antiquity. Yet no one can suppose they were any thing but the effect of accident or good judgment in the Officer. In such cases Posterity has for a judgment only the prophecies which came true, while those that did not are left out of sight.

Evening, continued Gibbon and reached the famous Chapters, upon the Christian Religion. Read the tenth book of the Iliad, and two numbers of the Spectator. This Volume is certainly the most valuable.

[1] The letter from Mrs. TBA is missing.

SATURDAY. 17TH.

Morning Cloudy and cold. I went to the Office and worked hard at my first Article on the Treasury Report so as to finish and send it to the Patriot today.[1] This required pretty constant diligence for I was interrupted by Jos. H. Adams who came about his Commission. After a little conversation with him I thought it would be best to make him finish the business and sign the Papers. He accordingly took the Oath, and I despatched him to Quincy after dining with me, and the Papers to Washington.

Afternoon. Read the rest of the first book De Divinatione containing all that can be said in favour of the art of predicting from natural or unnatural signs. It is ingenious but not conclusive. The Stoic doctrine was a strange compound of superstition, firmness, virtue, sophistry and Nonsense. But such is the character of man wherever you find him. I read a part of the fifteenth Chapter of Gibbon but not much, as considerable time was consumed in reflecting upon the matter for my second number relative to the finances. These are labours of love, without any thanks. The night was excessively gusty at times, making me fearful for my windows. Closed the evening as usual with two numbers of the Spectator.

[1] A communication, "The Treasury Report—No. 1" signed "F.," appeared in the *Boston Patriot* on 24 Dec. (p. 2, cols. 5–6). The writer proposed to take up in a series of articles his disagreements with the report of the Secretary of the Treasury, Louis McLane. Initially concentrating on the section relating to the public debt, he offered a rationale for opposing the proposed acceleration in the rate of debt retirement by raising special revenue. For an earlier estimate of McLane, see vol. 1:69.

SUNDAY. 18TH.

The cold which has been very great since the month came in was today greater than ever. And I felt it sharp enough in attending divine service through the day. Heard Mr. Frothingham preach in the morning from Luke 16. 25. "But Abraham said, Son, remember that thou in thy life-time received thy good things and likewise Lazarus evil things: but now he is comforted and thou art tormented." The whole of the parable he considered to mean nothing more nor less than the justice of God which made compensation in the future for the sufferings of this life. The circumstances he thought were totally allegorical and meant to put the case more strongly before the minds of the People, who had previously been habituated to ideas of Heaven and Hell according to the Pagan Mythology. But this business of allegorizing the Scriptures is next to conjectural criticism upon the Text, the most easy handle for every change. Afternoon. Text Matthew 5. 16. "Let your light so shine before men, that they may see your good works, and glorify your Father which is in heaven." The object seemed to be to direct to action, to the performance of virtue to the extent of ability and situation. How sensible I am of the urgency of the call upon me. But perhaps the time with me has not yet gone by for *preparation*.

Read a Sermon of Massillon's upon Prayer, on the same Text as that last Sunday. A division more practical as I think, for it advised Prayer in the first place for what was proper, in the second, in a proper manner. This is the real difficulty of all Prayer. Even Massillon occasionally errs in his conjectures upon it. At one moment he talks of appeasing an angry God, at another of doing violence to him in order to obtain a desired object through importunity. How low such ideas place the attributes of a Deity.

The remainder of my time was taken up in writing out my second Number upon the Treasury Report and in the evening, reading Barrow's second Sermon upon the profitableness of Godliness, recommending Piety as the best policy, as well as the most worthy quality. After it the Spectator.

MONDAY. 19TH.

Morning at the Office, engaged writing my Journal &ca. But I. H. and J. H. Adams called in soon from Quincy and prevented my paying any farther attention to my Article as I contemplated. The latter had just received Orders from the Navy Department to join the Peacock and to report himself therefor to Com. Morris at Charlestown. In consequence of this Mrs. Adams wrote me in a letter about the want of funds necessary to equip the youth to sea, and more than half intimating an unwillingness that he should accept.[1] I saw that decision on my part would be the only thing to save him so I determined upon advancing him a small sum of money, just enough to take away the excuse, and upon taking at once all the measures which should engage him irrevocably almost to the Service. I accordingly declined the

Company of I. Hull, and went with Joseph myself to Charlestown. We did not find Com. Morris, so that we were obliged to return home with the object unaccomplished. I did not feel like giving Joseph a chance to see his Mother again, so I kept him at my House this night. My morning was thus pretty much consumed.

Afternoon, read Cicero de Divinatione Book 2d. containing a refutation of the Stoic Argument. Evening, Gibbon and the Spectator. My Wife came downstairs to dine.

¹ The letter is missing.

TUESDAY. 20TH.

Morning cool but clear. After going through my regular labours I started off again with Joseph and this morning we were successful. I had some conversation with him [*i.e.* Commodore Morris] about the outfit necessary and found it was by no means so great as I anticipated. That his [Joseph's] principal expense of uniform might be dispensed with and that he might wear whatever he had already, on board the ship. If Mrs. A. had any Judgment, this would be the easiest matter in the world but the misfortune seems to be every thing must be done in spite of her. My principal object however was accomplished and on our return Joseph went immediately to Quincy. I passed the rest of the morning at the Office. Deacon Spear called and consumed half an hour and some time passed in writing my Journal.

Afternoon, busy in reading Cicero. Forwarded an answer to my Father's letter received this morning which sent me an inaccurate Note. His Congressional Affairs now turn his head as much as others formerly did. He runs into every thing headlong.¹

Evening finished the sixteenth Chapter of Gibbon, which is indeed a curious specimen of insidious warfare. Read my two Spectators.

¹ CFA's letter to JQA (LbC, Adams Papers) was, in fact, an acknowledgment of the receipt of two letters from JQA, one of 13 Dec., the other of 15 Dec. (both in Adams Papers). The defectiveness of the new note arose from the omission of the phrase "with interest."

The letter of the 13th was a response to what JQA styled CFA's "objurgative letter" of 30 Nov. — 1 Dec., "charging me with a violation of the most sacred of my duties. . . . I *could* say much in reply, but *will* only say that there might be violations of duty, more discreditable." On other matters alluded to in JQA's letter, see the entries for 23 Sept. and 3 Dec., above; and for 21 March 1832, below.

In a letter to LCA from CFA, 21 Dec. (Adams Papers), the exchanges between him and JQA, which have been excerpted in the notes to the entries of 12 and 29 Nov., and 1 Dec., above, are characterized by CFA to good effect: "We keep up a kind of warfare that gives the letters a little spirit, and though apparently differing very much, agree well enough in the main. I tie my faith to no man's sleeve, and perhaps indulge opinions altogether too speculative and impracticable, but it hurts nobody and keeps me up at least with a sense of independence and justness of feeling, without which I should be as a broken reed."

For a different view of the spirit

manifested in the interchange, less sympathetic in its appraisal of the motivation for CFA's remonstrances, see Bemis, *JQA*, 2:220.

WEDNESDAY. 21ST.

This was a mild morning—The thermometer being only at about freezing point. It may be called the first of the kind we have had this winter. I went to the Office and was engaged there in various ways without touching any part of my Article. Wrote a letter to my Mother about Joseph &ca.[1] And Mr. Degrand called in for a few moments. So that I had no length of time at my disposal.

Returned home and in the afternoon, finished the second book De Divinatione. Which is on the whole pretty convincing, although parts of the refutation are not so entirely sound as the author seems to think them; for instance his taking to pieces the strong syllogism of the other party. He questions positions because they are not generally admitted, but at the same time does not deny that he thinks they are right. Now if they are sound as to him, the refutation from the opinions of others is not complete.

Evening, sat downstairs two hours with my Wife. Then read a little of Gibbon's third Volume, and the eleventh book of the Iliad and Spectator.

[1] See the note to the preceding entry.

THURSDAY. 22D.

The weather again severely cold. The Season is unprecedented. We have had more sharp weather during the month of December than during the whole of our ordinary winters. This comes at a time of scarcity in fuel and of extraordinary sickness, so that on the whole the suffering in the poorer classes must be severe.

I went to the Office and passed my time in drawing up my second Article upon which I sickened a little of the whole job. Davis does not publish and the thing is getting stale.[1] It takes me a good deal of thought to write a Paper of this kind and I get no pay in money or in reputation. So it is. My efforts all turn out poorly yet I *will not* be discouraged. Went to the Athenæum, and suffered more on my return home than I have before this Winter.

Afternoon, Read Cicero's De Fato, which is a species of supplement to the rest, as a refutation of the Stoic doctrine of Fate. Perhaps this is the most puzzling point human ingenuity has ever exercised itself upon. This has come down to us only with a different name. The question of predestination and free will amounting to about as much.

Evening, my Wife spent downstairs and I read to her part of Harriet Lee's Canterbury Tales.[2] Afterwards Homer's 12th Book of the Iliad, a little of Gibbon and the Spectator.

[1] The extensive space being devoted in each issue of the *Boston Patriot* to the race for the Boston mayoralty, preliminary to the election on the 22d, crowded out all communications on other subjects, including CFA's first number on the Treasury Report. It was published on the 24th; see the entry for 17 Dec., above.

[2] Harriet [and Sophia] Lee, *The Canterbury Tales*, 5 vols., London, 1797–1805. All were by Harriet Lee except "The Young Lady's Tale" and the "Clergyman's Tale."

FRIDAY. 23D.

Morning at the Office. Weather still holding on very cold. I passed my time for the most part in writing off my second Article upon Mr. McLane's Report. But it does not altogether please me. The strength of the argument does not seem to be fully laid down. And I have doubts about some part of it. I thought I would go to the Athenæum to look at the Debates of the period, but I so dawdled away my time as not to have any of consequence for my purpose when I got there. Returned home.

In the Afternoon, read Cicero's first book "de Legibus," which is but a repetition of what has already been said in the books de Finibus. But the treatise is a noble one. It conveys an idea of Law far above the grasp of petty Attorneys.

Evening, Mr. Brooks drank Tea here and spent an hour in conversation. He is a singular man. I respect his practical good sense and unassuming manners, but I do not feel at ease with him from a want of union in Taste. After he went, read to my Wife, part of the Canterbury Tales, and afterwards Gibbon, Homer and the Spectator.

SATURDAY. 24TH.

Morning at the Office. Weather changed this morning to a heavy rain and complete thaw, so that the Streets were in pretty wretched condition. I was busy part of the morning at my Office, but being desirous of some information in regard to the Arguments used in favour of the Charter of the Bank, I passed much the largest space of time at the Athenæum. The Debate was but poorly reported. I saw enough of it however to satisfy myself that Mr. McLane's view was not correct, and I went home determined to modify my Article already written a little, in order to introduce what I had found.

After dinner I read the larger part of Cicero's second book de Legibus which is a species of Commentary upon the Institutions of the Romans respecting Religion. And the work is curious as displaying the policy upon which the greatness of the Romans was founded. Upon this subject I must read Montesquieu again. In the evening I read to my Wife a part of the Canterbury Tales. They are written with a pleasing flow of style, and are easy, light and amusing. Afterwards, read the 13th book of the Iliad over, a little of Gibbon, and the usual numbers of the Spectator.

SUNDAY. 25TH.

This was Christmas day. A day the celebration of which spreads itself over a very large portion of the Globe. A day however which carries with it less festivity now than it did in former times, and less here than it does elsewhere. It was clear and mild. I attended Divine Service all day. Heard in the Morning, Mr. Frothingham, in the Afternoon, Mr. Emerson. They were both Sermons upon the day. The former drew his Text from Matthew 2. 11. "And when they had opened their treasures, they presented unto him gifts: gold and frankincense, and myrrh." His idea seemed to be that these words conveyed a beautiful idea of the species of worship acceptable in the sight of the Deity. They were each images, the gold of purity, the frankincense of prayer the myrrh of sorrow or tears. I confess I am somewhat of mortal mould, and take things more as I find them. Mr. Emerson was from Isaiah 9. 6, 7. "For unto us a child is born, unto us a son is given." "Of the increase of his government and peace there shall be no end." He compared the influence of the life of Christ with that of most of the mortal conquerors known to fame. That of these latter he affirmed to have been good though from no act of their own. I think the position questionable. That of the former was throughout perfect and so intended to be. A perfect example. He closed by predicting the spread of Christianity over the world. Mr. Emerson engages the attention, but I do not think him often conclusive. Read Massillon upon returning home. A fine Sermon upon the Catholic practice of Confession. Text from John. 5. 3. "In these lay a great multitude of impotent folk, of blind, halt, withered, waiting for the moving of the water." He said the defects in confession might be likened to the three species of defects above named. 1. The blind, or those who from want of self examination did not know their own sins. 2. The lame, or those who made a partial or insincere confession. 3. The withered, or those who made it without sorrow and without repentance. The whole examination manifests considerable knowledge of human nature. But it is the gloomy side of it. There is no difference between the rigid Catholics and the rigid of all other Sects.

In the Evening, after reading to my Wife a part of the Canterbury Tales, I sat down and wrote off the larger part of my Second Number upon Mr. McLane after which The Spectator.

MONDAY. 26TH.

Morning cold again. I went to the Office as usual. And was very busy all my time in finishing the second Number began yesterday. This was written several times over. I closed it by one o'clock and sent it away.[1] Then went down to the Athenæum where I killed an hour in which I ought properly to walk for my health. Indeed I felt a little uncomfortable today from a Cold and head ach which seemed to foretell the far-famed Influenza.

In the Afternoon I finished the Treatise of Cicero "De legibus" which is in many parts defective. The Commentary is interesting but in some respects I think his brother Quintus is more than half right. The Roman Republic is a study for a Legislator. Though many of it's best Institutions were borrowed from the Greeks. After all that we can say about it, this was a wonderful people and the world is more indebted to them than to any mere men it ever produced. They shone through the powers of the mind. While the Romans always shared this superiority more equally with that which came from the body.

Evening, the Canterbury Tales to my Wife, after which the Iliad, Gibbon and Spectator.

[1] The second number of CFA's series on the report of Secretary McLane appeared in the *Boston Patriot* on 29 Dec. (p. 2, cols. 1–2). In it, issue was taken principally with the means proposed by which the national debt could be redeemed at an accelerated rate. The argument was advanced that for the government to require the sale to the United States Bank of the shares in the Bank held by the Treasury would be unfairly disadvantageous to the Bank and to its private stockholders and unsound as a national policy.

TUESDAY. 27TH.

Day cloudy and moderate. I went to the Office as usual. My time taken up in writing my Journal and a variety of incidental occupations. Called at Mr. H. W. Kinsman's to ask him about the service of a Writ in Norfolk County. Having made my Writ, I went to the Athenæum and obtained from there the Volume of land laws in order to criticize Mr. McLane a little upon that subject. I confess I was surprised to find the extent of my own ground when I came to examine this book—Which by the way is an exceedingly useful compilation.

Returned home and passed the Afternoon in reading Cicero de Officiis—Perhaps the very best of all his philosophical works. I have read it before, I well recollect when. It was when I came to Boston under a new impulse of existence,[1] and sat down doggedly to study as the purpose of my life, instead of dissipation and folly. I was now therefore not so much interested in it.

Evening, continued reading the Canterbury Tales which are very certainly well told. After which, Mr. Brooks spent an hour conversing with us. I then studied the subject of the Land laws and finished with my usual numbers of the Spectator.

[1] That is, 4 Feb. — 10 April 1828; see vol. 2:210–228 *passim*.

WEDNESDAY. 28TH.

Morning at the Office as usual. The day mild and very thick with haze. I was occupied the larger part of my time in writing my third Article upon the Treasury Report upon so much of it as relates to the Public lands. I found it so easy that I made but one draught of the first half leaving the conclusion only not done. I had some trifling interruptions but on the whole worked well. Took a walk though hardly such a one as I was bound to take.

In the Afternoon I read the rest of the first and a part of the second book of Cicero de Officiis. His translator Guthrie writes with the most singular mixture of praise and prejudice that I have seen.[1] Yet the latter very far outweighs the former in his Judgments. He makes me as much in favour of Cicero by his harshness, as my father generally makes me against him by his partiality.

Evening with my Wife. I read part of the Canterbury Tales, a most interesting story. Afterwards, reviewed the 14 book of the Iliad. Read Gibbon and the Spectator.

[1] On the book, see above, vol. 3, entry for 13 January.

THURSDAY. 29TH.

We had a fall of snow during the night and it was dark and cloudy today. Went to the Office, finished my third Number upon the public lands with which I was well pleased and sent it.[1] The Vanity of an Author is perhaps the most deceptive thing in the world. I write and write. Nothing of mine has ever yet been at all taking, and yet I flatter myself along, that what has not yet been, may nevertheless be.

So is it with the young. My next task is fully equal to all the ability I can muster. Went to the Athenæum and tried to look up the subject.

Afternoon, continued and finished the second book de Officiis. But instead of going on with the Treatise I began to reflect upon Mr. McLane's discussion of the Tariff.

Evening, after reading to my Wife, part of the Canterbury Tales, I sat down to commit my ideas to Writing, but I found infinite difficulty in giving clearness to them. The subject of Political Economy is even now a most puzzling subject to the most thorough student of it, because its laws are not yet fully understood. To me who see but as through a glass darkly, though I know Mr. McLane's error I can not quite describe it. My attempts did not please me at all. I left off late to read the Spectator.

[1] In the third number of CFA's reflections on Secretary McLane's report, the first on the section relating to the public lands, CFA expressed the view that any scheme that would cede or sell public lands to any one of the states was a danger to the Union itself. On the publication of the third number, see below, entry for 31 Dec., note.

FRIDAY. 30TH.

Morning clear after a fall of snow sufficient perfectly to renovate the sleighing and make it even better than ever. I went to the Office and after having been occupied in drawing up my Agency Accounts for the close of the Quarter and the year, I devoted the remainder of my time to making up my fourth number upon the Treasury Report. I then went to the Athenæum to obtain another Book for my Wife's amusement and thence went home.

After dinner, I read the first half of the third book de Officiis which came very pleasantly as a well known acquaintance of times past. Interrupted by Mr. Nathl. Hall of Medford a Cousin of my Wife who came to take Tea. He did not however remain long. Afterwards, I fell into conversation with my Wife and I believe from the result we derived mutual benefit. In married life, every thing should be regulated by the spirit of concession, and with my unbending character, it is very necessary for me to keep rigid watch over my disposition. Prosperity has had considerable effect in making me forget my faults, until they have grown upon me. May I have resolution to set about checking them immediately.

Evening, Homer's Iliad Book 15th. Wrote a draught of my 4th Article and read the Spectator.

SATURDAY. 31ST.

Morning cloudy and very cold. Found upon opening my morning's Newspaper, a union announced between it and the Daily Advertiser. A union as unexpected as disagreeable to me. My Articles fall through of course.[1] Such has been the uniform result of all my efforts. And now I feel myself more perfectly shut out than ever from any prospect of succeeding as a Writer. Went to the Office and from thence to Market. Having spent an hour there I returned with a very short space of time to accomplish a great deal of work in. Received a letter from my Father with the Note of hand I expected and called immediately upon Mr. Oliver to finish that transaction.[2] I then went back to my Office and sat down to draw off my Quarterly Account for my Father. As the case was a simple one I accomplished it much more quickly than I have been accustomed to do. The Paper was drawn up besides my attending a sale of Stocks before one o'clock. The Stocks were low enough, a sign to me that Money is becoming daily more scarce. This has been expected by me. And now is the moment I ought properly to invest. But I have not as much as will keep me along. Took a walk before returning home.

In the Afternoon I wrote a letter to accompany my Quarterly Account[3] and read but did not finish the third book de Officiis.

Evening quietly at home. Read to my Wife a part of the Canterbury Tales. After which I read the fifteenth book of the Iliad and my Spectators. A few minutes were then spent in reflection. It was the close of the year. A year that to me had been an eventful one. It had added to my happiness too materially to be soon forgotten. It had dispelled doubts and fears which for many preceding years had slightly shaded my path, and had justified me to myself for my conduct in some important particulars.

Let me be grateful.

[1] The announcement that the *Patriot* and the *Advertiser* would be merged effective 1 Jan. 1832 and that the surviving paper would be called the *Boston Daily Advertiser & Patriot* was made by Nathan Hale for the *Advertiser* and Ballard & Co. for the *Patriot*. Identity of political viewpoint, support of the National Republican party, was the announced reason for the merger. Hale would become editor and proprietor of the new paper with the assistance of John Brazer Davis, the editor of the *Patriot*, "who has found his health again impaired" (31 Dec., p. 2, col. 4). CFA's fears for his articles proved groundless; his third number appeared in the newly combined paper on 5 Jan. (p. 1–2). See also, below, entries for 6–17 Jan. *passim*.

[2] JQA to CFA, 25 Dec. (Adams Papers). On JQA's note to the American Insurance Office, see the entries for 9 and 20 Dec., above.

[3] CFA to JQA (LbC, Adams Papers).

No. 7 Diary

1 January 1832

31 December 1833[1]

[1] Titlepage of D/CFA/9 (Adams Papers, Microfilms, Reel No. 61), which begins where D/CFA/8 ends and contains all the journal entries CFA made between the terminal dates indicated here. CFA repeats these terminal dates on a page (omitted) following the epigraph and preceding the entry for 1 January.

An explanation of the discrepancy between CFA's numbering of his Diary volumes and the Adams Papers serial numbering is given at vol. 1:xxxvii–xxxviii. For a description of this Diary MS and of the other MSS from which the printed text of vols. 3 and 4 derives, see the Introduction.

Cease from anger, and forsake Wrath.

Psalms. 37. 8.

JANUARY. 1832

Boston

SUNDAY. 1ST.

The opening of a new Year has usually been laid hold of by me as an opportunity for reflection as well upon the past as the future. This year a still further occasion is presented as at the same time I begin a new volume of my Diary. If there is any benefit to be traced most clearly from the practice of a daily record, it seems to me to be that arising from the habits of speculation it forms through the power of comparing the feelings of one period with those of another. In the course of a year, two or three occasions are presented upon particular days to look back and consider how you stand that moment as contrasted with the same moment in the years before. These if improved open a wide field for self examination and amendment in what is faulty, congratulation for what is good in you. I hope I may say that I have not allowed any day to pass without making some effort to derive advantage from cultivating the practice. The hopes and fears which give their colouring to one period of life change and are forgotten in those which succeed unless some faithful monitor remains to bring them up before the mind, as a lesson what shadows we are and what shadows we pursue.

I commence this Book and this year principally under a deep sense of Gratitude to the Divine Being for the manifold blessings which have been showered upon me as well in the past as in preceding years.

When I look back to what I was when my Diary first began, a Youth first entering College, and consider the course of events through the intermediate years, I am filled with wonder at my escape from the many snares which beset my path, and am often tempted to think there was a singular providence watching my steps, which caused many of the events deemed by myself at the moment to be evils, in order to withhold my too eager pursuit of the means for my own destruction. How closely in Man's life are approached the roads of happiness and of misery. How critical the turning points of his fate. Three times in my Existence already can I perceive the operation of influences upon my success in life. Of these three times, twice I was rescued from wretchedness and vice, once I was carried to the happiness I now enjoy. And in each time, the causes of the result might seem strangely inadequate if I did not invariably reflect with the Poet,

> There's a divinity that shapes our ends
> Rough hew them as we will.

In looking back upon the past I derive a satisfaction in the reflection that each year as it has passed has done something to add to my stock of virtue as well as to the sum of my happiness, and that the last have done more than the first. The one I am immediately considering has materially affected me in both respects. It has given me a Child. It has laid upon me new duties with my new relations, the importance of which I feel too much not to set about more earnestly than ever the work of self improvement, and the increased cultivation of all those virtues without which man cannot be what he ought. It has added to the already abundant share allotted to me of the goods of Fortune, the value of which I hope I shall learn not to rate too highly nor to despise too much. If this same Year has done so much for my happiness in these respects, perhaps it has not done less in checking the excess of my ambition which had set its aim far too high to avoid the mortification of occasional disappointment. I am now pretty much in the same situation as last year so far as it respects my station in Society. And so far from expecting now as I did then to make way for myself by a sudden leap to distinction, I am beginning to habituate myself to the idea that mine is already so respectable a situation that more is hazarded in the attempt than would be gained by success. Yet I would fain believe this is not the whisper of Indolence. Whatever I may find to do, that will I do with all my might, but as yet the only regret I experience if so I can call it, is that I shall not obtain sufficient chance to do enough to prevent me from yielding to indolence, unless some event happens which at present I cannot foresee. Of such an event it becomes not me to despair, but rather in devout gratitude to God for the number of favours he has already heaped upon my unworthy head, to trust that what will happen will prove for the best, and that in the meanwhile I will rest securely in the performance of my present duties. The hour may come when the Servant may be called to Action. May he in that hour not be caught asleep. So ends the rather longer series of personal reflections, than it has hitherto been my practice to indulge in.

The morning was clear and cold though so much less than yesterday that it seemed quite pleasant. I attended Divine Service all day. My Wife went in the morning, the first time since she had her Cold now nearly four weeks. Mr. Frothingham preached in the morning from John 11. 9. "Jesus answered, Are there not twelve hours in the day?" A Sermon upon the New Year and the necessity of employing time in order to give a good account of it. I did not like it so well as Mr. Young's in the Afternoon from John 12. 43. "For they loved the praise of men more than the praise of God." He tried to show the evils resulting from too great a desire of the applause of the world. These he considered principally in two classes. Evils of Vanity. Evils of Ambition. And closed with an exhortation to independent conduct and to the desire of the praise of God. I have at various times since my regular attendance at Church felt some benefit resulting from it to myself, in consequence of applications of the chance words of the Preacher to myself personally. They do occasionally go to my heart, either by warning me of faults which I try to conceal from myself or encouraging me to the performance of my duty when my zeal has begun to flag. Those of this afternoon were of the latter description.

On my return home I read a Sermon of Massillon's without much benefit. Matthew 17. 4. "Then answered Peter and said unto Jesus, Lord, it is good for us to be here." Upon the dangers of temporal prosperity. 1. Because the temptation to fall from religious faith and practice is almost irresistible. 2. Because repentance is scarcely possible. The subject is a noble and affecting one. But from some cause or other, which even I do not comprehend, this Writer touches me very little. Yet if he has any reputation it is more particularly for pathos.

In the evening I am in the practice of reading to my Wife besides the Canterbury Tales for amusement, a portion of two Chapters of the Bible nightly for instruction. It is a little remarkable however that I should myself be so little able to instruct in the meaning of the difficult parts of the Epistles from the Apostles. This is a future study I propose to myself. After Abby retired I was engaged in writing, and did nothing in any of my usual studies, always excepting the regular numbers of the Spectator.

MONDAY. 2D.

Morning clear and cold. I went to the office as usual and was busy all the time in the Accounts and calculations which happen at the opening of a new Year. My affairs are on the whole in a favourable situation though I do not as yet quite see clearly through them. Had a visit from Mr. Lyon a Man I sued a day or two since, who did not seem inclined to pay me and asked a delay. I granted him a delay considering that no harm could be done by it to any person. But my law business does not turn out so profitable as it might from this disposition of mine to indulge foolish desires. Took a short walk and seized a stray minute to go and see a picture of young Burke the Actor painted by a new Artist, Osgood who is gathering a little reputation from Portraits.[1] We saw several, and recognized one or two of them as acquaintances. But his painting is not good. I went with Mr. Peabody.

Returned home and was engaged in the Afternoon with attendance upon two Meetings. The first was the usual one of the Directors of the Boylston Market. The other the Proprietors of the Athenæum. The usual business was transacted at both places and I reached home to tea. Quiet evening. Mr. Brooks called and spent an hour. Afterwards I read a book of the Iliad and the Spectator.

[1] Probably Samuel Stillman Osgood (1808–1885), who began exhibiting at the Boston Athenæum in 1831 and was represented there annually for several years thereafter; see Groce and Wallace, *Dict. Amer. Artists*, p. 480; Mabel M. Swan, *The Athenæum Gallery*, Boston, 1940, p. 259.

TUESDAY. 3D.

Morning snowy and cold. I had some doubt about my executing my intention of going to Quincy but as it cleared up at noon decided in favour of it. Passed the morning however in constant labour with my pen, and transacting business. Called to receive my Dividends especially that upon the Dover Stock which makes me comfortable at once. I do not recollect for a long time so thoroughly employing my Morning. Mr. Brooks dined with us and kept me until after three, so that I started late in a Sleigh with my man for Quincy and did not get to my Uncle's before Sunset. Took tea and transacted all my business with the family, had as little conversation as I could about

Joseph's affairs dreading the moans and groans from all quarters, and got home to my own fireside by seven o'clock. My Uncle looks ill and is singularly affected in his Nerves as I never observed before. On the whole this was a day actively spent. I was fatigued in the evening and read only the rest of the sixteenth book of the Iliad as well as my Spectators.

WEDNESDAY. 4TH.

Morning excessively cold again. As this is the day fixed by the new System for the Political Year to begin and as business was not done by most People,[1] I thought I would remain at home. Accordingly I sat down and occupied my morning in reading Gibbon which has for some days past been suspended. His Chapters upon the Christian Religion are worth studying not so much for the matter as the skilful manner of Attack. Took a short walk to the Office and met Mr. Geitner who paid me his Rent. Returned home and spent the Afternoon quietly. Finished the Treatise de Officiis and a large half of Cato Major or the defence of Old Age. A beautiful trifle thrown off without any effort. Such is the power of Art seconding a happy Nature. In the evening I read to my Wife part of the Canterbury Tales. Afterwards, I read the seventeenth book of Homer's Iliad and finished the third volume of Gibbon, besides the usual Spectators. On the whole a pretty lazy day for an uninterrupted one.

[1] Whether "Election Day" would be observed according to the usage of former years upon the convening of the General Court despite the change in the political calendar was a matter of uncertainty. The closing of businesses was not uniform; however, the public procession to the Old South Church, the ceremonies on the Common, &c., were carried out much as before (*Boston Daily Advertiser & Patriot*, 4 Jan., p. 2, col. 1; 5 Jan., p. 2, col. 1).

THURSDAY. 5TH.

The day was cloudy but mild. I went to the Office as usual and was occupied almost all my time in business. After looking over the large amount of my bills for the Quarter, I began to pay them and in a very short space of time disposed of the considerable sum received the other day. I also disposed of several of my father's Accounts, and received his Dividends. These are again more than a fair average yet the bills seem to be almost inexhaustible. I think on the whole, I shall do well to make all things square in each case. The few days since the business of the year came in have been pretty thoroughly engrossed.

Dined with my Wife at Mr. Frothingham's. Mr. Brooks, and Miss Frothingham his Niece were the only persons present. The dinner was tolerably agreeable although I felt the usual constraint in offering my opinions. Returned home and finished the Treatise de Senectute but as it was late I did not go on with the next, but diverged to look into the subjects of the present number of the North American Review. Continued this in the evening after spending the usual quantity of my time with my Wife and reading to her a part of the Canterbury Tales. Read an article upon Croker's Boswell, upon Reform in England and upon the Tariff. The first I admired, the second terrified me and the third appeared to me most unusually weak for the Quarter from whence it comes.[1] Finished the evening with my usual Spectators.

[1] All were in the January issue of the *North Amer. Rev.* (vol. 34). The review of Croker's edition of Boswell's *Johnson* was by W. B. O. Peabody (p. 91–119); the article on "The Debate in the House of Commons on the Reform Bill" was by Edward Everett (p. 23–56); that on the tariff was by A. H. Everett (p. 178–198).

FRIDAY. 6TH.

My time was taken up this morning in the usual way. Making up balances after the payment of all dues, and being a little surprised at the great amount that has been called for. Received letters from my Parents both of whom wish me all manner of joy.[1] There came also a change of orders for Joseph H. Adams which I very much regretted.[2] But so it is. As Mr. Hale has published my third number on the Treasury Report and intimated he would continue them, I sat about the fourth today though without progressing a great way. The day was warm with rain, and rendered the Streets so bad that I could not walk.

In the afternoon, read almost the whole of the Treatise de Amicitia which is another pretty trifle. Read also a good Article in the American Quarterly upon the Diplomatic Correspondence,[3] and a flashy one from Mr. Everett upon Greece in the North American Review.[4]

Evening. Read to my Wife a large part of the rest of the third volume of Canterbury Tales. The only objection to them is that they are too much drawn out. Finished with the Spectator as usual.

[1] JQA to CFA, 31 Dec. 1831; LCA to CFA, 1 Jan. 1832 (both in Adams Papers).

[2] Along with his letter, JQA sent an order from the Navy Department to Midshipman Joseph Harrod Adams assigning him to the frigate *United States*, Commodore Patterson, scheduled to sail for the Mediterranean in April or May for extended service there.

[3] Jared Sparks' edition of *The Diplomatic Correspondence of the American Revolution* (12 vols., Boston, 1829–

1830) was reviewed in the *American Quarterly Review*, 10:417–443 (Dec. 1831). The review, without being anti-Franklin, is in large part a ringing defense of Jay's and Adams' position. In the course of an extended and cogent account of the negotiations in France, the reviewer writes of JA:

"Dr. Franklin ... describes Mr. Adams, 'as always a great man, often a wise man, and sometimes absolutely out of his senses.' With all the deference due to the sagacity of the veteran philosopher, we must say, that in relation to Mr. Adams's conduct towards the Court of France, with regard to which this remark was made, and on the evidence contained in these volumes, the unfavourable part of this character seems to us wholly inappropriate.... Mr. Adams was a stern and a bold man, but with all the severity and rigour that characterized him, there seems to have been no incapacity for the refinements and courtesies of diplomatic intercourse, no insensibility to benefits conferred, and no reluctance gratefully to acknowledge them. He belonged to a peculiar class of revolutionary men. His was the temper of his earlier associates, ... men who ... knew that all they gained was to be gained at the sword's point.... The most that can be said with regard to his feelings towards European allies, is, that he was not willing to sacrifice much to obtain what he knew his country could do without.... In relation to the importance of perfect fidelity to France, Mr. Adams's opinions do not seem ever to have varied.... It was neither by whim or caprice, nor by any imaginary affront, that his good will seems to have been alienated.... It was his theory that friendly and mutually beneficial relations should be established with every government of Europe, and that their friendship, if not offered, should be solicited. The object of the French alliance he believed to be principally to have assistance in severing the bonds of our own colonial subjection, and when any thing occurred to countenance the suspicion that the primary was sacrificed for a secondary object, his pride as an American, his stern sense of duty as the representative of an independent community, impelled him to indicate the source of danger. ... Every sentiment, erroneous or not, on the subject of the French connexion, expressed in this correspondence [with Vergennes], seems to have been the result of cautious deliberation, and patriotic impulses."

The reviewer concludes his justification of the policy of Adams and Jay by noting that that policy became the touchstone of American foreign policy, characterizing it in the words JQA had used in his eulogy of President Monroe: "We have now, neither in the hearts of personal rivals, nor upon the lips of political adversaries, the reproach of devotion to a French or a British faction.... We have no sympathies but with the joys and sorrows of patriotism; no attachments but to the cause of liberty and man." In doing so, the reviewer clearly intended to establish a lineage for American foreign policy extending from father to son, whom the reviewer characterized as "a living great man, himself the most distinguished of the diplomatists of our hemisphere."

⁴ Edward Everett's review of Rufus Anderson, *Observations upon the Peloponnesus and the Greek Islands* (Boston, 1830), appeared in the *North Amer. Rev.*, 34:1–23 (Jan. 1832).

SATURDAY 7TH.

The day was a disagreeable one. I went to the Office as usual. My time was engrossed first by the usual Accounts which are not quite closed, and afterwards by writing the fourth number of my series, the rough draught of which was at last accomplished. It has cost me a good deal of labour. Went to the Athenæum and took a very short walk.

In the Afternoon, finished the Treatise de Amicitia, and had two hours in which I completed the fair Copy of my Article. These lag on so much that if I do not make a desperate effort to finish them I shall not do it. There remains but one Number to embrace all I have to say. But this will cost me some trouble. I do not know that the profit is worth the trouble.

Evening. I went down at a Meeting of the Debating Society. This had gone on so heavily that it was considered advisable to discuss the expediency of stopping it altogether. For myself though I should have been pleased to continue a really effective Society, yet I had no manner of doubt as to what should be done with this. Eloquence is not in very great favour with us if we are to judge of the total indifference to it on the part of the young men. Returned home regretting a foolishly spent Evening. Corrected my Article and read a little of the North American Review after which the Spectator.

SUNDAY. 8TH.

The day was cold and raw. I arose quite late. Attended divine Service all day and heard Mr. Frothingham preach. His Text in the morning was from Luke. 2. 32. "A light to lighten the Gentiles." A Commemoration of the Epiphany, or manifestation of the Saviour. He considered it as giving distinction to three points of his history. The adoration, the baptism and the first Miracle of Cana. The afternoon was from John's 1st Epistle. 3. 2. "It doth not yet appear what we shall be." The subject the disposition of mortality to know futurity and the fortunate limit that is set to our knowledge. I cannot follow his Sermons in detail. They are hard to take in from the disconnection of the reflections.

After my return, I read a Sermon of Massillon's upon final impenitence. Text from John. 8. 21. "I go my way, and ye shall seek me, and shall die in your sins." His division was this—1. The impossibility of an effectual repentance at the last moment from the state of the Creature 2. from the will of the Creator.[1] The state of the creature might be owing to a sudden death, to a fear occasioned by remorse or to physical inability from disease. The will of the Creature to a total alienation from the abuse of every blessing and indulgence. The Text explains more clearly than the Preacher. For the latter in the second branch of his subject imputed to the Deity so many human and unworthy passions, that a pure mind must shrink with disgust from the idea of so singular a Divinity. Indeed this is the principal fault of Massillon. His zeal and his Oratorical exaggeration present to the imagination dreadful shapes. He sketches out an avenging being full of vengeance and destruction instead of the awful image of Justice and of Mercy. One other peculiarity I noticed in this Sermon. He says distinctly that each man bears stamped on his forehead at his birth the character he afterwards assumes, and that it is seen and formed by the Deity then. If so, how is man responsible for his faults and why should he be eternally condemned to torment for what no act of his could foresee or prevent? Such a faith does not suit me.

Evening. My Wife wrote to Washington[2] and I read Articles in the North American and Quarterly. With some of which I was pleased. Afterwards I read over the seventeenth book of Pope's Homer containing the battle for the body of Patroclus. The translation is wonderfully spirited. I wish it would not take too much time to read the original. Finished my Evening as usual with two numbers of the Spectator.

[1] The sentence's initial difficulty derives partly from the placement of the numerals, partly from the word "Creator." The two sentences following in the text provide the beginning of an explanation of the meaning. From them it seems clear that "the impossibility of an effectual repentance at the last moment" is owing 1. to the state of the Creature 2. to the will of the *Creature*. However, beyond the two explanatory sentences, the text reveals that the confusion in the writing reflected CFA's view that Massillon himself in the second section had confused "Creator" and "Creature," or made them all but identical. A sentence with a meaning congruent to the whole passage on the sermon might then read: "His division was this—The impossibility of an effectual repentance at the last moment 1. from the state of the Creature 2. from the will of the Creature and of the Creator."

[2] Letter missing.

MONDAY. 9TH.

Morning mild and the rain which had fallen heavily during the Night made the Streets very unpleasant to walk in. I went to the Office and despatched No. 4 of the Review.[1] I was then busy the remainder of the morning in various ways quite sufficient to take up my time and yet not sufficient to justify myself for its use. Went to the Athenæum to look up Papers for my next number but could not find them. So that I shall have to change my plan. Returned home again omitting to take a walk. How often this happens.

Afternoon. I read the Paradoxes of Cicero and began my fifth and last number. There is certainly one thing in writing. It consumes time very insensibly. My afternoons fly even faster than my Mornings.

Evening read to my Wife a part of the German's Tale in the fourth volume of the Canterbury Tales. This is made the foundation of Byron's Tragedy of Werner; in the preface of which that author very highly commends it.[2] Afterwards, I went on writing and did nothing else besides, excepting the usual Spectators.

[1] The fourth number in CFA's series on Secretary McLane's report was printed in the *Advertiser & Patriot* on 12 Jan. (p. 1-2). In this he took an outright protectionist position, opposing, as damaging to American manufactures, reduction in tariff duties despite the evidence adduced by the Secretary that the existing tariff was producing revenue in excess of government needs.

[2] In 1821 Byron dramatized "Kruitzner" or the "German's Tale" and pub-

lished it under the title of *Werner, a Tragedy.* The preface, in which Byron acknowledged his source, is at p. 384 of the edition CFA was reading (above, entry for 4 Dec. 1831, note).

TUESDAY. 10TH.

Morning mild and pleasant. I went to the Office as usual and after my regular duties, continued and finished the rough draught of my last Paper upon the Treasury Report. It is rather bitter upon the Secretary but not more so than he deserves for the very extraordinary course he has thought proper to pursue. The more I reflect upon it, the more I am satisfied there is some treachery at the bottom. It may seem rather presumptuous in me to deal so freely with the Secretary but I cannot conceal the impulses of my feelings in writing. Walked up as far as J. D. Williams' Store to try Wine but I could not make up my mind to choose.

Afternoon. Read the Treatise of Q. Cicero upon the mode of soliciting the Consulship. A dry thing when compared with the inimitable grace of his brother's style. Read also the famous dream of Scipio which is on the whole the most remarkable ancient Paper I ever read. It is impossible not to admire the genius which could have struck out so bold, so singular and yet so reasonable a path without any resources out of itself.

Evening, continued reading to my Wife a part of the German's Tale, Kruitzner, the interest of which is remarkably sustained. Afterwards, I read the eighteenth book of Homer's Iliad, an Article or two in the American Quarterly Review and the Spectators.

WEDNESDAY. 11TH.

Morning mild and pleasant to the feeling but a very bad day in respect to the walking. I went to the Office as usual and made use of all my time, first in making up my Diary and Accounts, and then in taking off the fair Copy of my last Number of the Treasury Report Review. I did not complete it. This is a much greater task than it seems to be. It has filled five Sheets of Foolscap Paper and that written pretty closely on all four sides. The exercise however has been a very good one. I have found the benefit of it as well in clearing my own ideas as in subjecting me to labour and finish the explanation of them.

I had a considerable number of Commissions to attend to so that I went out early and spent an hour and a half in performing them. Mr. Brooks dined with us quietly. After dinner, I sat down to read the

Treatise ascribed to Cicero, called Consolatio, written by him after the death of his daughter, but I do not for some reason think it is the genuine one. I therefore left off in the middle to begin Ernest's Critical Preface.[1] Evening, finished the German's Tale which is very ably done from first to last. Afterwards, read over the 18th book of the Iliad and the Spectator.

[1] To complete his survey of the works of Cicero, CFA, having finished the volume devoted to works not definitely in the canon, the last in his edition, now turned to the first volume, in which were the editorial prolegomena and the works on rhetoric. See the following entry.

THURSDAY. 12TH.

The Morning was cold again and felt worse than if we had never had mild weather. I went to the Office as usual and consumed my Morning in finishing the fair Copy of my fifth number upon the Treasury Report. This concludes the work much to my satisfaction.[1] It is rather remarkable but I think I wrote the three last numbers better and more easily than the two first. It is probably the facility which exercise upon some given subject produces. My mind having thought in the exact manner which can only produce clear writing. This it is I must cultivate. Clear and accurate thinking. From which speaking and writing both follow. Took a walk and returned home.

Afternoon read the rest of the Critical Preface of Ernesti, and part of his Dedication to Stigliz which I admire very much.[2] It conveys what I have often thought. Yet the remarks he makes of the spirit of the period when he wrote apply with increased force to the present day.

Evening. My Wife and I executed our long purposed visit to Edward Brooks and his Wife. I saw their Child which is a small, lively little creature, and their new House which is somewhat more in character with the situation he ought to hold in Society.[3] After our return, I read the reviews and the Spectator.

[1] The final number of CFA's series of articles on the Treasury report was printed on 17 Jan. in the *Advertiser & Patriot* (p. 1–2). It consists primarily of an attack on what seemed to CFA a drift in the report toward a weakening of the Federal Government by the Secretary's stand against any measures which would create a Treasury surplus. CFA's position was that it was imperative to create and maintain a surplus for such *national* uses as would almost certainly emerge.

[2] In the *Opera* of Cicero in John August Ernest's recension published at Boston in 1815 (see above, vol. 3:364–365; also above, entry for 8 Sept. 1831), both the preface and the dedication to Christian Ludovic Stigliz, to which Ernest's name is affixed, are of substantial length.

[3] The Edward Brookses had moved from Bulfinch Place to 31 Chesnut Street (*Boston Directory*, 1832–1833). Anne Gorham (1830–1848) was the youngest of their children (Brooks, *Medford*, p. 531).

FRIDAY. 13TH.

I cannot give a very good account of myself this morning. A considerable time was taken up in Marketing which I do generally once a week for the whole of the succeeding one. And my purchases seem to me to grow on a larger scale every day. At my Office, I pursued my usual exercises, and had one or two interruptions from bills. I also went down to see my friends Davis and Quincy to ask them to dine with me but found only the former. I then took a short walk though the day was fine and I ought to have taken a long one.

Afternoon at home quietly. Read the greater part of the Dedication to Stigliz and was much struck with it. It deserves study, not reading. Price Greenleaf from Quincy called to pay me a short visit and to offer his services which I think I shall avail myself of for the purpose of the horticulture of my Father's Estate.[1]

Evening. Continued reading the Canterbury Tales with the Scotsman's Tale, with which I was much pleased. Indeed I have admired them all though I think I see a good deal of difference in them. Read over afterwards the 19th book of the Iliad, the reviews and the Spectator.

[1] On Ezekiel Price Greenleaf, often consulted by JQA on budding fruit stocks and other horticultural matters, see vol. 2:156, 229; JQA, Diary, 5 Sept. 1831.

SATURDAY 14TH.

Morning fine. I went to the Office as usual. But I can give no very good account of the disposal of my time. Mr. Curtis called and paid me my Fees for a considerable portion of all the Law business I did last year. Little or nothing of any consequence besides. Next week I must turn over a new leaf. Took a walk before returning home.

Mr. Davis and E. Blake dined with me and we had a very pleasant time. It consumed so large a portion of my Afternoon however that I did nothing except finish the Dedication to Stigliz and the Preface to the Rhetorical Works. On the whole my day cannot be said to have been a very profitable one, but I have of late discovered that I have hardly seen company enough. And that in order to keep up the proper quantity of social feeling I ought to devote at least one day in the week to it.

Read a little to my Wife in the evening but not much as we finished the Scotsman's Tale and had nothing else to go on with. I afterwards began writing a letter to my father but had only time enough to finish one page. Somehow my facility of letter writing is decreasing from want of practice. Finished the Evening with the Spectators.

SUNDAY. 15TH.

The day was really lovely, much like the weather we frequently used to have at Washington as the first notice of Spring. I went to Meeting all day. Heard in the morning Dr. Lowell from Ecclesiastes 11. 9. "Rejoice, O young man in thy youth; and let thy heart cheer thee in the days of thy youth, but know then, that God will bring thee into Judgment." This is only one half of the verse and that so chosen as entirely to vary it's meaning from the original intention. I have many doubts how far this is allowable or proper. The principal object of preaching is to expound the Gospel. Now this is altering it. The verse as it stands, conveys a warning to the young to abstain from such indulgences as will subject them to the justice of the Deity. Dr. Lowell made it mean an encouragement to the joyful character of youth. A doubt of the expediency of forcing a premature gravity of thought and action. The Sermon was Common place but on the whole sound. My only objection would be that he might have found a more suitable Text. Mr. Frothingham drew his Afternoon's Discourse from Mark. 7. 37. "And they were beyond measure astonished, saying, he hath done all things well; he maketh both the deaf to hear and the dumb to speak" but I must candidly confess that further than the text, though I listened with some attention, I made nothing out of it whatever. This I consider as quite a misfortune. But I can devise no way to remedy it.

Returned home and read a Sermon of Massillon upon the Esteem of the world. Text from Matthew 23. 5. "But all their works they do for to be seen of men." His division was three fold. 1. The crime of neglecting duty for the sake of worldly regard. 2. The folly of it from its temporary nature. 3. The incorrectness of it as the world finally respects the man more who acts independently. Perhaps there is no kind of subject which deserves so fully to be treated as this. I regret my time was so short I did not give this Sermon its full weight. In life, every man meets with occasions in which there is a conflict between his duty and his interest. Most men overlook the former, but on the whole do not gain any thing by it. Yet it requires some character to bear even the temporary alienation of one's fellows.

In the evening I read to myself one of Barrow's Sermons upon the duty of honouring God and the reward of it. Afterwards, resumed my letter to my father, but became disgusted and left it.[1] Read Homer's Iliad and the two last numbers of the Spectator.

[1] The letter remained uncompleted. CFA to JQA, 21 Jan. (Adams Papers).

MONDAY. 16TH.

Morning delightful. This weather must be a monstrous relief to poor People whose supplies of wood have been so freely drawn upon by the unusual coldness of the preceding month. I said last evening that I had finished the Spectator by reading two numbers regularly since the month of March last. It is the first time I ever went regularly through them. And on the whole I think I have gained something. It has given me a more correct idea of the beauty of Addison's style, although I am yet far from impressed with that admiration of it which is common. I like a more flowing, forcible current.

Went to the Office and wasted my time. Read a long Debate in the Intelligencer[1] and took a long walk as my head was a little out of order. After dinner, I was obliged to attend a Meeting of Directors of the Boylston Market to consult upon a Plan for certain alterations to be made, and this kept me there the whole Afternoon. The last Director's Meeting this Year, and I decline the position next year.

Evening, went over and paid a visit to Mr. and Mrs. Gorham Brooks, found them at home, and Mr. Brooks came in soon after. On the whole a pleasant Evening. Returned early, read the 21st book of the Iliad and two numbers of the Guardian.

[1] In the House of Representatives on 5 Jan. on a motion to recommit to the Committee of Claims the bill for the adjustment and settlement of the claims of South Carolina against the United States, the debate was opened by JQA and joined by Messrs. McDuffie, Speight, Everett, Burges, Williams, Reed, Drayton, Davis, Barbour, and others. The remarks of each were printed at length in the *Daily National Intelligencer*, 9 Jan., p. 2–3.

TUESDAY. 17TH.

Another very agreeable morning. I went to the Office as usual but owing to the want of a book again wasted my time. My last number appeared in the Daily Advertiser this morning and adds one more to the list of my labours of love. I wrote my Journal and went over Accounts which with more than an hour consumed in other occupations out, as going to the Athenæum and Commissions for my Wife, on the whole made away with the time.

Mr. Brooks and Mr. Frothingham dined with me upon venison and we had a very pleasant time. The former incidentally asked me who was the Author of the numbers upon the Treasury Report in such a manner as to be highly flattering to me. On the whole this little trifle pays me for the labour I have taken. After dinner, I read the first book of the Rhetoric to Herennius and found it a meagre summary of the various Works of Cicero, having little or nothing original to recommend it.

Evening. Read to my Wife a part of a Canterbury Tale. After which I read over the 21st Book of the Iliad and began a short biography of Fuseli the Painter.[1] Nothing further excepting the usual numbers of the Guardian.

[1] That contained in John Knowles, *Life and Writings of H. Fuseli*, 3 vols., London, 1831, which work consisted largely of Fuseli's lectures. See above, entry for 8 Nov. 1831; below, that for 22 January.

WEDNESDAY. 18TH.

Morning rainy but warm. I went to the Office as usual. But as I did not recollect my materials for study, my time was again spent idly. Read the Newspapers and Mr. Clay's Speech.[1] And mused upon the course which political events are taking. It is now totally impossible to foresee to what they tend, but I hope to something safe. The elements of our Government are however a little too floating. Looked over my Accounts. Paid one or two bills and attended to my father's affairs. These with Commissions of various kinds consumed the morning.

Afternoon. Read the second book upon Rhetoric nearly through and had no occasion to change my opinion. Went with my Wife this evening to Mrs. P. C. Brooks Jrs. and found there, Miss Mary B. Hall, Mr. Brooks, Gorham and his Wife, Mr. and Mrs. Frothingham, and Edward Brooks. Quite a family affair. Inasmuch as I have become more accustomed to the members of it, and more at my ease, my time was passed more pleasantly. We returned home at ten, but I had no time to do more than read one or two pages of the Life of Fuseli, and the Guardian.

[1] Henry Clay's speech on the tariff in the Senate on 11 Jan. was reprinted from the *Daily National Intelligencer* in the *Boston Daily Advertiser & Patriot*, 18 Jan., p. 2, cols. 2–4.

THURSDAY. 19TH.

Morning very mild and pleasant. It would seem as if this month and the last had changed their places. I went to the Office and after my usual regular occupations, spent some time in reading the fourth volume of Gibbon's History which contains the Romance of Julian. I call it a Romance because the Author evidently writes with great relish. He sets before us the fair side of the Picture very strongly. But this is perverting history. Spent half an hour in conversation with Mr. Peabody and an hour in walking.

Returned home and passed the Afternoon in reading part of the books 2 and 3 to Herennius. They continue the abstract. As a book to consult for the purpose of filling up a skeleton of a subject I should think it might be useful. But it is dry as a work to read.

Evening. Read a part of the Canterbury Tales to my Wife but we were interrupted by a visit from Judge Hall who came and passed an hour in conversation. He looks old and haggard. He says he is taken up very much by the business of his Office. Perhaps this is a very fortunate thing for him. His situation is now so lonely. After he went, I continued the sketch of Fuseli's life and read some critical Articles inserted at length. But I do not think the Account makes a favourable impression. Read the twenty second book of the Iliad and the usual numbers of the Guardian.

FRIDAY. 19TH [*i.e.* 20TH].

Morning at the Office. Weather tolerably pleasant, though not quite so warm as it has been. My time passed quickly in settling Accounts and reading another Chapter of Gibbon upon the history of Julian. To show how much interest this author takes in his sketch it would only be necessary to look at the space it occupies in the general history. A mere period of sixteen months in which, though an attempt of some consequence was made, yet proved abortive and produced no permanent change, takes up half a volume. And the character of the man is brought forward rather as a slur upon the Christian faith, than as illustrating any portion of his period. Julian was undoubtedly remarkable in many points, but Constantine was more so. The latter brought about great things, the former very little.

Took a walk and in the Afternoon read part of the third and fourth books upon Rhetoric, the Commencement of the latter has some point to it. The Argument is a striking one, though the reasoning is scarcely conclusive.

Evening. My Wife and I went to Mr. Frothingham's to hear his Choir sing. I was not much affected. Somehow these things got up for an occasion are laboured. The performers all seem to want to do too much. Retired and had time only to read the Guardian.

SATURDAY. 20TH [*i.e.* 21ST].

Morning at the Office. At ten o'clock I attended a Meeting of the Board of Directors of the Middlesex Canal to examine the state of affairs for the year. We had an uncommonly favourable Account, and declared a Dividend of Twenty two dollars upon a share, being by far the largest ever made. This gives my father quite a large sum for his share. And I do not know what to do with it, but my present mind is to invest it if possible.[1] Took a short walk to the Athenæum and home.

My Afternoon was consumed partly in bottling Wine, partly in attending upon a Committee to examine the Agent's books and certify to the Proprietors of the Canal that they are correct. This is a tedious affair. It took up about two hours. The encouragement this will give to the holders of Canal Stock will probably raise the price of their Shares and bring on some speculation. Would it not be wise for some large Proprietors like my father to take advantage of it? I will consult him upon it. Returned home and passed the rest of the evening in reading to my Wife. Afterwards I read Fuseli's life which is a poor thing, and the usual numbers of the Guardian.

[1] CFA invested the proceeds of the Middlesex Canal Co.'s dividend by negotiating a loan of $1,200 to Henshaw & Co. for 6 months—$1,000 from JQA's funds, $200 from his own. CFA to JQA, 31 March (LbC, Adams Papers).

SUNDAY. 22D.

Morning more like Winter but still pleasant. I attended Divine Service all day and heard Mr. Frothingham preach in the morning from Mark. 10. 13, 14. "And they brought young children to him, that he should touch them: and his disciples rebuked those that brought them. But when Jesus saw it, he was much displeased, and said unto them, Suffer the little children to come unto me and forbid them not; for of such is the kingdom of God." The sermon was upon the necessity of purity, upon the consequent duty of education to bring the young to a state of excellence. One of the peculiarities of the doctrine of Christ was the attention enjoined by him to be paid to youth. Their improvement has however been rather a chance matter in most ages. It may well be doubted whether the proper cultivation of even a very ordinary natural intellect would not produce results far superior to those which we derive from the most highly favoured. Afternoon, Mr. Greenwood from Psalms 42. 1. "As the hart panteth after the Waterbrooks, so panteth my soul after thee, O God." A very good Sermon it was, no doubt, though not sufficiently stirring to excite my attention. I am afraid I am almost incorrigible on this head.

Upon my return home I sat down and copied a letter to my Father written yesterday,[1] after which I read a Sermon of Massillon's twice over. It was from 20. Matthew 20, 21. "Then came to him the mother of Zebedee's children with her sons, worshipping him and desiring a certain thing of him. And he said unto her, What wilt thou? She saith unto him, Grant that these my two sons may sit, the one on thy right hand, the other on the left, in thy kingdom." The subject was upon the vocation or calling of men. This he said was regulated by so many extraneous incidents that nothing was more common than mistakes. 2d. Nothing was more dangerous. There was a good deal of sense in his reasons, but many of them apply so particularly to the meridian of France as it was in his day, that the general force of the Sermon is weakened.

As my Wife was writing to Washington,[2] I did not read to her, but finished the remainder of the Life of Fuseli. His Lectures have a good deal of substance in them but the style is singularly inverted. Half the time it is necessary to trace out the connection by an effort. Afterwards I read the twenty second book of the Iliad over again containing the death of Hector, and the principal interest of the Poem. After it, a paper upon the Iron Manufacture in England and two Guardians. Thus mixed are my studies.

[1] CFA to JQA, 21 Jan. (Adams Papers). Despite the intent expressed in the preceding entry, the letter, largely on the tariff and related national affairs, made no mention of the desira-bility of JQA's taking advantage of the rising market that CFA foresaw in the immediate future for Middlesex Canal shares.

[2] ABA's letter is missing.

MONDAY. 23D.

Morning quite cold again but it was a beautiful day. I went to the Office as usual and spent my time in looking over my Accounts, and indeed wasted a part of it, I must admit. Such is the case too often. Reading the Newspapers and writing my Diary engrosses a considerable share of the short mornings we have. And I go out at one o'clock to obtain the exercise I ought regularly to take. Today for once I enjoyed my walk.

Afternoon, read a part of the fourth book to Herennius containing a brief account of the various modes of adorning and enlivening a discourse which are curious rather than useful. Nature ought to be the prompter in these cases. The man who should use Rhetorical phrases merely secundum artem would prove but a poor Orator after all.

Evening quiet at home with my Wife. Read to her a part of the last Canterbury Tale as well as her usual Chapters in the Bible. Afterwards I read the twenty third book of the Iliad, looked over the paper upon Iron, and perused the two Guardians. This is an inferior work.

TUESDAY. 24TH.

Morning quite mild and cloudy. The alternations of weather are worse than continued cold. I went to the Office as usual. After the regular duties, I saved an hour for the purpose of reading Gibbon, but a part of it was encroached upon by a call from Mr. Degrand whom I had consulted about investing some money, so that I in fact accomplished only a portion of a Chapter. Then took a walk. The day was not favourable but I thought it better to take exercise notwithstanding. My health is now excellent and I ought to keep it so. Indeed when I consider my present situation, it seems to be as near happiness as man can well get. So much so that the only danger is the chances of an unfavourable change are so much greater than either remaining as I am or doing better. In all things, however, good or evil I trust in a power far above this world.

Finished the fourth Book to Herennius this Afternoon which compels me to look round for some new subject to employ my mind upon. It is a chance whether I shall be so well satisfied. I leave the works of Cicero as one parts with an old acquaintance, quite unwillingly. Evening I had intended going to Mr. Everett's but Gorham Brooks and his Wife came in and kept me. Read the 23d book of the Iliad and the Guardian.

WEDNESDAY. 25TH.

Morning mild and foggy. I went to the Office and occupied myself much as usual. Tried to put a little more method into my private Accounts, a thing I have been in vain attempting ever since my Marriage. Read also a little of Gibbon embracing the account of the death of Julian and the accession of Jovian. He seems to slight the indiscretion of the former and to press upon the consequent misfortunes of the latter. Probably because he had taken his side upon the subject of Christianity and thus failed in the first duty of the historian. The weather was so bad I did not walk.

Afternoon. Concerned in bottling the rest of my new wine and in making some alterations in my Library with a view to a little more room and also to setting apart my Classical Department by itself. This consumed the whole of my time until it was the hour fixed to go to Mrs. Frothingham's. The weekly parties of the family are to be resumed. Found there in the course of the time Edward Brooks, Gorham and P. C. and Wives, Mr. Brooks, Mr. and Mrs. Parkman, Miss Hall and ourselves. Mrs. F. was quite unwell. The time was pretty agreeable.

Returned home in time to read the last book of the Iliad and the Guardians.

THURSDAY. 26TH.

Morning severely cold again. As an example of the variable character of our Climate, it may be stated that within twenty four hours the Thermometer had fallen more than fifty degrees. It was now below zero of Fahrenheit. I went to the Office as usual, but was engaged all day in making up Accounts, and was surprised to find that from some cause or other they did not come out right. What was worse I could not discover where the mistake was, and left it unfinished. Called in to see Alston's Picture again rather to pay my portion to the exhibition than from any wish to see it. It did not appear to me so favourably placed as it was there.[1] I think however that it is on the whole a very fair specimen of his powers.

Dined at Mr. Frothingham's upon venison with Mr. Brooks, and Gorham's Wife. The meat was not so tender as mine. But it was very good. Pleasant dinner enough. Returned home and found my fire gone out. The coldest day for a fortnight. Such is the luck. Read a little of the beginning of Quintilian's Institute, of Eloquence[2] but on the whole lost the Afternoon.

Evening. Finished the Canterbury Tales, and Fuseli's Lectures. Finished also the translation by Pope of the Iliad of Homer with which I have on the whole been even more pleased than I expected. Read the Guardians.

[1] Washington Allston's painting, "Spalatro's Vision of the Bloody Hand," based on the 20th chapter of Mrs. Radcliffe's *The Italian*, had been on public view at No. 2 Joy's Buildings during January "for the artist's benefit." Painted for a gentleman in South Carolina, the work "from the circumstance of its size—it being but a cabinet picture"— had not been thought earlier "an object of sufficient importance to form of itself an attractive exhibition" (*Boston Daily Advertiser & Patriot*, 3 Jan., p. 3, col. 4). Appreciations of the painting, together with the passage of which the painting is an illustration, appeared in the same newspaper, 21 Jan., p. 2, col.

6; 25 Jan., p. 2, col. 4. The whereabouts of the painting when CFA first went to see it is not clear; see above, entry for 16 Nov. 1831.

[2] Three editions in Latin of Quintilian's *Institutes*, each having CFA's bookplate, are at MQA: *Institutionum oratoriarum*, Venice, 1521; *Oratoris eloquentissimi de institutione oratoria libri xii*, Paris, 1549; and *De institutione oratoria*, 2 vols., London, 1822. Also at MQA are editions in Latin, French, and English bearing JQA's bookplate. However, CFA at this time was using the edition of P. Burman, published at Leyden in 1720, which he had borrowed from the Athenæum.

FRIDAY. 27TH.

Another severely cold morning. I went to the Office as usual and after looking thoroughly over my Accounts and discovering the cause of the error alluded to yesterday I sat down and made some progress in Gibbon. But the best employment of a morning does not give me more than about an hour of attention to reading. And this is not so thoroughly done as it would be at my study at home. I went afterwards to the Athenæum and obtained some books for our evening's occupation.

In the afternoon, I continued reading Quinctilian who is certainly exceedingly sensible. His argument on the merits of private and public education is a very pleasant one. It is so natural and clear. I do not accomplish much in an Afternoon. Indeed it is impossible to imagine a life of so much apparent occupation and so little real result as mine. I finish a few pages of easy Latin and that is all. Miss Julia Gorham dined with us.

Evening. Read to my Wife a part of Hazlitt's Conversations with Northcote the artist.[1] Some of the ideas are very good, others are merely striking. But Hazlitt presses his own into view full as much as he does his friend's. Began Pope's version of the Odyssey[2] and read the Guardian.

[1] William Hazlitt, *Conversations of James Northcote*, London, 1830.
[2] An edition published at London in 1771 in 4 vols. is at MQA.

SATURDAY. 28TH.

According to my observations the cold was greater this morning than it has been either day of the last three. But it gave way in the course of the day. I was occupied much as usual at the Office. Mr. Degrand came in and I accomplished the investment of the sum of money in my hands. This is an experiment. I have some doubts and fears owing to my want of experience in business. Read a little of Gibbon but on the whole did not do much. The weather was so bad, I did not walk. Read more of Gibbon who keeps up the interest of his history tolerably. This is a repetition showing the want of ideas in me, but I will not deface the page by erasing it.

Afternoon, continued reading Quintilian. A very dry piece of grammatical discussion which made me almost repent I had taken him up. It is undoubtedly true that nothing is to be done without a knowledge of grammar, but except as a matter of mere curiosity it is of no consequence to us how the Latin is to be arranged or spelled. Evening, read aloud to my Wife more of Northcote's Conversations. After which I read the version of the second book of the Odyssey and the Guardian.

SUNDAY. 29TH.

A snow storm. The temperature of the air much milder of course. Read a little of Fuseli. His Aphorisms are striking, but there are two defects. The one a straining for effect, a desperate exertion to force grandeur out of words and ideas which gives a very artificial appearance to the style. The other a consequence of this, the use of far fetched and pedantic words.

Attended divine Service all day. Heard Mr. Frothingham in the morning from 1. Peter 3. 8. "Be courteous." It was a very good Sermon. He expatiated upon the advantages of courtesy in the treatment of others distinguishing what he meant from the heartless external civility enjoined by the rules of the world, as it operated to produce internal softness of disposition while the other created only hypocrisy. He then regretted the change that had taken place in the manners of youth towards age, alluded to the decaying class of people called the old school, and inclined to think that this was not one of the improvements of the age. The Afternoon Discourse was from 4. Galatians 18. "It is good to be zealously affected always in a good thing." The purpose was an examination of the charge often made against the sect of Christians of which the Preacher was one, of coldness and want of zeal. He endeavoured to shew that this was an error. Unless they were disposed to adopt with the zeal of other sects their creed which impelled them to the work of proselytism as an article of duty. That a man should seek his own salvation by acting upon his Neighbours was one of the doctrines which he could not see the propriety of, but he had no objection to, or rather he was clearly in favour of his turning the direction of his efforts towards himself.

Read afterwards a Sermon of Massillon's. Text. Luke 16. 24. "I am tormented in this flame." Or in other words the Story of Lazarus. He endeavoured to show from it the character of the Rich man, not guilty of positive crime, but of negative character. In other words guilty of being rich, of luxury, of indolence, and of no virtue. This was what subjected him to the severe punishment described in the Text. A punishment the more acute as there was a compensation in it, that is to say the rich and the poor changed places. The former was to feel the contrast of pain the more strongly as he perceived the contrast of pleasure existing more strongly in the latter.

Read also in the evening the larger part of Fletcher's Play of the Faithful Shepherdess. Which I have nearly forgotten.[1] As usual, the regular book of the Odyssey and the Guardian.

[1] CFA had read the plays of Beaumont and Fletcher over a period of several

months in late 1825 and early 1826; see vol. 2:18–33. JQA's bookplate is in the edition at MQA published at London in 1811 in 3 volumes.

MONDAY. 30TH.

The Snow of yesterday changed to rain today and the Streets were in consequence in a shocking state. I went to the Office as usual and after the regular duties went on with Gibbon as far as the close of the reign of Valentinian. On the whole this history begins to enter the dreary barren waste in which man was probably at his extremest state of ignorance and depression. There is little to relieve the eye or the mind. Even Christianity sinks to a mere cover for sensual indulgence and sloth. The Monks degrade it by misunderstanding the spirit of it's doctrines.

Returned home and read Quinctilian, finishing the first and I hope the driest book. Some of the reasoning however upon early education is to me conclusive. The mind must not be left without exertion. Had mine been trained by care and experience, what might I not now have been. Memory is my deficiency. In the evening, read to my Wife from Northcote's Conversations. A great many substantial ideas. Afterwards, Fuseli's Account of Michael Angelo. The fourth book of the Odyssey and the Guardians.

TUESDAY. 31ST.

Morning pleasant. I went to the Office as usual and did not occupy myself much. My mind was running upon the possibility of obtaining a Newspaper or some employment in order to write and secure me an occupation which now I want.[1] For this purpose I went to Carter and Hendee's to see if I could not make a little acquaintance with them to this end.[2] But I lost an hour. Read a little of Gibbon and then took a walk. I thought I would go down and see the new buildings going on in the North part of the town, especially the new Hotel built by Mr. Williams which is to be sure a pretty great establishment.[3]

Afternoon, reading Quinctilian but my progress was slow. I was thinking of other things. And my period of study was shorter than usual, inasmuch as it was the day we were invited to go to Mrs. Gorham Brooks', a regular family party. Mr. and Mrs. Parkman, Miss Hall, and Miss Frothingham the only persons not immediately connected. I forget Mr. Shepherd. The time was not particularly agreeable but it did very well. Returned home at ten o'clock and had time to read the fifth book of the Odyssey over besides the usual numbers of the Guardian.

[1] On an earlier plan to the same end, see above, entry for 19 Sept. 1831.

[2] Carter & Hendee, at Washington and School streets, were publishers as well as booksellers and stationers (*Boston Directory*, 1832–1833).

[3] Perhaps the reference was to the Chelsea House, late the mansion house of Thomas Williams, located in Chelsea at the mouth of the Mystic River facing on Boston harbor, now greatly enlarged and improved, with spacious gardens, bowling alleys, and livery stables, ready for leasing beginning 1 April (*Boston Daily Advertiser & Patriot*, 26 Jan., p. 2, col. 6).

FEBRUARY 1832
WEDNESDAY. 1ST.

Morning cool but on the whole quite fine. I went to the Office and from thence to perform some Commissions as well as to attend the Meeting of the Directors of the Middlesex Canal, and the subsequent one of Proprietors. There were very few members present and the business was transacted before I got there. I did not even discover whether I was re-elected a member of the Board. Not that I care any thing about it if I was not. Did little or nothing in the way of reading but took a good walk.

On returning home the first thing I perceived when within sight of my house was that the Kitchen Chimney was on fire. This alarmed me as my flue had never been sound. No damage was done although I found my fears realized as to the cracks in the flue at my study. We got off with the alarm but I felt as if I was paid for neglecting to sweep it. The circumstance was the more provoking as I had asked Mr. Brooks and Mr. Frothingham to dinner. The former returned home, but we did very well on the whole. I read a little and but little of Quinctilian.

Evening spent by invitation at Edward Brooks. Mr. B. and Gorham the only persons there. We had not a very remarkably pleasant evening. Returned at 10. Read a Book of the Odyssey and the Guardian.

THURSDAY. 2D.

Cloudy and mild. I did little or nothing at the Office as I felt a little indisposition from head-ach. Engaged in writing and Accounts, after which I took a walk to get the air. My principal difficulty appears to me now to be want of some interesting occupation. I wish I had some inducement to the exercise of the powers I possess. But it is of no use to wish, and perhaps the best way is to let things take their course. My best plan is to keep on exercising myself to prepare for trial.

Returned home and read after dinner the latter part of the second book of Quinctilian. Whether Rhetoric is an Art. The question is tolerably absurd. It does not affect *things* the least in the world whichever way you settle it. While Eloquence is a means of power it will be sought, whether by acknowledged high road, or by cross paths is no kind of consequence. Of such a kind are half the arguments in the world. They turn upon words.

Evening quiet at home. I felt glad to get back again to my own fireside, the pleasure of which is more fully felt by now and then departing from it. Finished the Conversations of Northcote. His share of them I like. Hazlitt's I do not. And he closes with an opinion about Cicero which is shallow enough. Afterwards, the Odyssey. Fuseli and the Guardians.

FRIDAY. 3D.

Morning exceedingly mild. I went to the Office as usual and passed my day with the same degree of indolence which is usual with me. Received a letter from T. B. Adams expressing his satisfaction with my Accounts.[1] Read a part of one of the numbers of the Farmer's Series upon the Horse, with which I was pleased. I have purchased the set and consider it as more valuable than the general Series published by the same Society.[2] But I must turn over a new leaf in the employment of my time of a morning. Took a walk to the Athenæum thence home.

Afternoon continued Quinctilian Book 2 and 3. The division of Rhetoric, the Account of the Authors upon it and their particular theories, none of which is either interesting or peculiarly valuable. I came across an idea of perspective which seemed to me to settle the question whether the Ancients knew it or not.[3]

Quiet evening at home. Read to my Wife part of Leigh Hunt's book about Byron.[4] It is evidently a thing for sale, containing mean anecdotes and grovelling doctrines stuck on to distinguished names. The writer having had opportunities to see a little of some famous men in his day. Afterwards, finished Fuseli, read over the 7th book of the Odyssey and the usual Guardians.

[1] The letter is missing.

[2] *The Horse; with a Treatise on Draught*, London, 1831, was the first number to appear in the continuing Farmers' Series of the *Library of Useful Knowledge*, published by the Society for the Diffusion of Useful Knowledge.

[3] CFA entered the passage from bk. 2, ch. 17 of Quintilian in his literary commonplace book, p. 234 (Adams Papers, Microfilms, Reel No. 312).

[4] *Lord Byron and Some of his Contemporaries; with Recollections of the Author's Life*, Phila., 1828.

SATURDAY. 4TH.

Another mild day. I went to the Office as usual and passed my time in the same way. It was cut up today partly by attending a Meeting of the Directors of the Middlesex Canal for the purpose of organization for the next year. I had also one or two interruptions. Took a walk to the Athenæum. On the whole nothing to boast of in my morning. Read part of Quinctilian in the afternoon containing his distribution of the various species of Oratory and the subdivisions of which it is capable. In my opinion a great deal of time consumed in trifling matters. The subject of Rhetoric seems to me to have been very much mystified in former days. The division is simple enough, into deliberative, demonstrative and judicial. Though the second name hardly applies to the class it intends to cover.

Evening at home. Mr. Brooks took tea and spent two hours in conversation. So that I did not read. Afterwards I wrote a short letter to my father for the purpose of telling him what Deacon Spear requested as to the state of his farms at Quincy.[1] But my Correspondence with him this Winter has amounted to nothing at all. Afterwards, the Odyssey and Guardians.

[1] CFA to JQA, 5 Feb. (LbC, Adams Papers).

SUNDAY. 5TH.

The Snow was falling heavily and the day was on the whole so cheerless that I did not stir out of the House. My habit of going to Church is now so fixed as to make it appear very strange to me to stay away. I employed myself singularly as it turned out. For in looking over some of my old attempts I read the review of Williston's book with which I was so much pleased as to be tempted to cut out a part for publication. I accordingly copied about as much as I thought would do for Mr. Willard's new Review.[1] This and copying part of my father's letter which I did not finish yesterday took most of the day.

Read over twice a Sermon of Massillon's upon the Parable of the Prodigal Son. Luke 15. 13. "The younger son gathered all together, and took his Journey into a far country, and there wasted his substance with riotous living." I thought it one of the best of his which I had read. He first examines the nature of the vices charged upon the Son, their degrading character both to mind and body and then explains the Charity and benevolence of the Deity in a case of Repentance from so hardened a state of guilt. This constituted about all my doings today and I was not a moment idle. Read the Guardian as usual.

[1] Sidney Willard had begun the publication of the *American Monthly Review* at Cambridge in 1831. On Willard, see *DAB*. CFA's article seems not to have been published.

MONDAY. 6TH.

My Diary is a pretty monotonous record of the very even tenour of my life. I believe it is of use to a man to accustom himself to keep one, but the profit is derived not from any value attached to the record itself so much as the ease it gives to one's pen.

It was quite cold again this morning, and I went to the Office to do nothing. I. Hull Adams came into town from Quincy to ask my advice about the offer of a Commission at West Point.[1] I discussed the matter with him pretty closely and he promises very fair. Mrs. Adams has now all her Children disposed of and ought to have no more anxiety about the future, excepting what her husband gives her. Took a walk, after which I read a good deal of Quinctilian. His advice upon the Exordium of a Speech is good and to the point. Moreover he condemns as I have done the subtleties which he explained.

This was the regular evening for the Annual Meeting of Proprietors of Boylston Market. I went and the whole of the time was consumed in various matters. I "demitted" as Director and was chosen Clerk. This suits me much better. After performing the regular business I went home and had time to read a book of the Odyssey and the Guardians.

[1] On 25 Jan. JQA had requested of Secretary of War Lewis Cass an appointment to West Point for Isaac Hull Adams. Cass had replied to JQA on the following day with a warrant of admission, and JQA on the 27th notified Hull, instructing him to forward his acceptance to Secretary Cass (Cass's letter and LbC's of JQA's letters are in the Adams Papers).

TUESDAY. 7TH.

Morning at the Office. Nothing of any consequence. I tried to finish the fourth Volume of Gibbon but did not make out. Occupied in reading Newspapers which consumes much time and writing my Journal. I then started for a walk, but what with my hair [to be cut?] and two or three orders for purchases I did not get very far.

Afternoon. Finished the remainder of the fourth Book of Quinctilian in which he gives excellent advice upon the distribution of the essential parts of an Oration. The narration, proof and conclusion. This is illustrated principally from Cicero's practice, which proves that this author did not agree with the idea of Cornificius or whoever is the author of the four Books to Herennius.

As my Wife was out, I read also Gorboduc or Ferrex and Porrex by Lord Sackville which is the first attempt at the Drama in the English Language.[1] It is curious but on the whole hardly pays the perusal.

Afterwards, I went down to Mrs. Carter's where my Wife was spending the Evening with her daughter, and stupified[2] for a little while. I am not now fit for young ladies Society. Returned home at ten. Read a little of the 8th book of the Odyssey over again and the Guardian.

[1] Volume one of *Old English Poets,* 4 vols., London, 1820, is devoted to Thomas Sackville's works, including *Gorboduc.* The copy at MQA has CFA's bookplate.

[2] CFA's apparent meaning, to indulge in stupid conversation, is derived from the intransitive and already rare use of *stupefy*: to become stupid (*OED*).

WEDNESDAY. 8TH.

Morning at the Office. Weather dull and disagreeable. The Child had caught a severe cold and was dull all day and restless in the night. This is so unusual with her that it made us both restless. My morning was spent as usual. Conant from Weston came in and paid me a sum of Money which gave me a little business. I read Gibbon, finishing the short remainder of the fourth Volume, and took courage to despatch my writing to Mr. Willard with what success I know not. Property in this Country is so precarious that a man ought always to make himself of value if possible, in order that he may in time of need have the benefit of reputation. I try hard enough.

Mr. Brooks dined with us and I remained conversing with him until four o'clock. So that I had very little time for Quinctilian. The consequence was that I read only fourteen pages of the fifth book upon the examination of witnesses and treatment of evidence. One thing struck me. His giving advice as to the management of false testimony for a cause, and yet laying it down that no man can be an Orator if he is not virtuous.

Evening quiet at home which I enjoyed very much after being out a night or two. Read part of Hunt's book. Afterwards, the rest of the 8th and the 9th Odyssey *over*, and the Guardians.

THURSDAY. 9TH.

The Child still seemed heavy and restless so that I felt uneasy all day with a sensation of undue depression of spirits. I went to the Office as usual and employed myself but my time was broken in upon by various interruptions, more particularly that occasioned by taking in a new supply of Coal to last me as I hope for the remainder of the Winter. Mr. Peabody and I divide half a Chaldron. Read a little of Gibbon but without making much real progress. The Snow was falling all day so that I did not take my usual walk.

Afternoon. Continued reading Quinctilian upon Common places

and Arguments, all of which was very good. But my progress was not very great. My Wife received a letter from Washington in very good spirits.[1] They seem to be doing quite well there.

Evening quiet with my Wife. Continued Leigh Hunt's book, which is a compound of truth and malignity, of just reflection and a low spirit, of indignation and book making. Afterwards, I went on with the tenth Odyssey, and read a little of Graham's second Volume of American History,[2] with the usual Guardians. My night was again anxious and disturbed on account of my Wife and child.

[1] No letter of about this date to ABA from any member of the family in Washington is known to survive.

[2] See above, vol. 3:27, 213.

FRIDAY. 10TH.

The Child seemed so much more uneasy and in pain that I concluded to send for a Physician rather than be anxious about her so I called for Dr. Stevenson as I went to the Office. The day was a mild one. Passed my time here much more profitably than usual as I had time to do all my usual business and read a large extract from Gibbon beside. After spending two hours usefully in this way I always feel much better satisfied. Took a walk afterwards and returned home with an unusual feeling of elasticity. The Child had seen the Doctor and he had prescribed for her.

Afternoon, rather drowsy from the interruption of my night's rest, but on the whole I managed to accomplish a good deal of Quintilian. After all the subdivisions of Rhetoric are too minute. A great deal must be left to the feeling of the moment, which will prompt figures without a man's knowing that they are so. The only instruction to any purpose is the knowledge how to add to their effect.

Evening, continued Hunt's Book which becomes a little tedious after he quits his personalities against Byron. This is a sure sign that what is interesting in the book is scandal and detraction. The eleventh Book of the Odyssey took up an hour and a half of my time. After which I read two numbers of the Guardian. Steele carried on this latter publication almost entirely, alone. His Papers are some of them good but generally a little dry.

SATURDAY. 11TH.

Morning at the Office. A pleasant day after the Snow. I was engaged in Accounts and Journal until my Client Lyon came in who was very averse to settlement indeed but after reasoning and scolding, he paid the demand.[1] I settled forthwith with my Employer and then went up to the Boylston Market for the purpose of making a record of the Annual Meeting of Monday last. It was so long that it took me until nearly dinner time. Returned home. The Child seemed to be much better.

Afternoon. Read Quinctilian continuing his Account of the various kinds of reasoning, the acting upon the Passions and the Peroration. My time flies and I do not know that I make the best of it.

Evening quiet at home. Read to my Wife Hunt's singular character of Shelley and his love of generalities. I also read regularly a portion of the Bible which I do not mention because a repetition of so many duties seems too monotonous. I have some idea of making a Reform in my Diary. It began to rain and then poured violently through the night. Read the twelfth Book of the Odyssey and the Guardians.

[1] Lyon, who was being sued by CFA for another, was CFA's client only in the loosest, or possibly in an ironic, sense. See above, entry for 2 January.

SUNDAY. 12TH.

In conformity with my resolution of yesterday or I might rather say, my project, I intend not to mention any of my regular duties, considering them as having been performed without there is some notice given of the exception, or as they are incidentally noticed in commenting upon any of my reading.

Filled up my morning by looking over Spence's Anecdotes which may truly be called a lounging book,[1] holding some pretty good things and many trifling ones. Then went to hear Mr. Frothingham preach from John 9. 34. "Dost thou teach us," directed principally to the prevailing arrogance in the world of listening only to the suggestions of established reputation and slighting truth on account of it's source. There is much to be said on that subject and I am of opinion no where to more purpose than here. The attachment to prescription here is very inveterate. In many respects it leads to good, but in some it's operation is all evil. The Afternoon Sermon I liked the best however. It was from James 4. 7. "Resist the devil and he will flee from you." A mere examination of what the devil is, and an eloquent refutation of the idea that man has not the power to resist, with a touch at the orthodox doctrine of predestination. The fact he thinks that for *power* you may read Will. Mr. Frothingham did better than usual because he was more animated, and therefore felt strongly the words he was delivering. When this happens he gets out of the sing-song which he has formed for himself as the beauty of delivery.

Returned home and read a Sermon of Massillon from Luke 11. 26. "And the last state of that man is worse than the first." It was upon the character of the vacillating and inconstant in religion. He thinks their's is the most hopeless case of all. Because they derive no benefit from the knowledge of the truth, from any taste for religion which it forms nor from the administration of the Sacraments. The liability to return to the paths of vice deadens all their morality and renders them entirely unfit to be depended upon in any way. Their case is therefore more desperate than that of the hardened sinner.

Evening. Read Grahame's second volume but found I had got the substance of it pretty well in my first reading. I also found the idea I was in search of which I think will do for the foundation of an Essay. The Child was fretful today but did not appear much unwell.

[1] Joseph Spence, *Anecdotes, Observations and Characters of Books and Men,* London, 1820; primarily a record of Pope's conversations and those of members of his circle.

MONDAY. 13TH.

I spent more than an hour reading the Newspapers. I suppose if a man wishes to appear informed in this Country he must keep up with the debates in Congress at least. But even this takes much time. Things at Washington are getting into a most confused miserable state and it is really impossible to foresee what the result may be. The prospects of the Nation so far as they depend upon Rulers are poor enough. And what road there is to reach improvement is not so clear. But I am not particularly concerned so that I shall not trouble my head with croaking.

After dinner. Continued Quinctilian. A Dissertation upon Wit similar to that which is in the second book De Oratore of Cicero. It is pretty plain from both of these that this Article will not bear keeping. Much of it is totally lost, much so dim as to be no longer amusing, and much really very bad. Perhaps a man might moralize to some purpose in a case like this. The Jest of Yorick will hardly outlast his skull.

Evening. Reading to my Wife from Hunt's book. Recollections of several characters who have made a noise in the world, put in to aid the sale. They show the author however to more advantage as they are of an amiable cast. Indeed he is as partial to Keats and Shelley on one side as he is to Byron on the other. His Judgments are very far from being critically sound.

TUESDAY. 14TH.

At the Office as usual. Read a part of Gibbon's fifth volume and the detail of the miserable condition of the Countries of Europe under the Government of such Puppets as Arcadius and Honorius. I have often thought of a remark made either by Robertson or Roscoe which at the time I transferred to my Commonplace, that the period which may be considered that of the world's utmost degradation dated from the close of the reign of Theodosius till the Revival of letters.[1] Nothing material occurred.

Mr. Peabody and Mr. Quincy dined with me. The thing was rather dull. The latter gentleman has altered considerably and not for the better since his engagement. I had not time to pursue my studies today so that I took up Beaumont and Fletcher reading the four first Acts of the Maid's Tragedy, and wondering what it was gave to them their reputation.[2] Probably the loyalty which runs through it. A King is represented as bad as possible, and the persons he most injured will not touch him because he is a King. The Woman repents of her sin in the most sudden and unnatural manner merely because her brother rants a minute or two and threatens to kill her. Just so, this brother afterwards quarrels with Amintor and is reconciled again in neither case with any adequate motive. The transitions are violent and unnatural, and the Poetry is not particularly distinguished. Evening quiet, continued Hunt's puerile recollections of himself, the epithet will apply in more than one sense.

[1] William Roscoe's *The Life and Pontificate of Leo the Tenth* and *The Life of Lorenzo de Medici* are among the most frequently quoted works in CFA's literary commonplace book (Adams Papers, Microfilms, Reel No. 312), but no passage copied there from either bears on this point. However, there are two relevant passages (p. 30 and 186) from William Robertson, *The History of the Reign of the Emperor Charles V, with a View of the Progress of Society in Europe from the Subversion of the Roman Empire to the Beginning of the 16th Century,* one a general statement on the measurement of degeneration in a society, the second on the specific characteristics of society in the Middle Ages. Neither says quite what CFA remembers. Three editions of Robertson's *History* are at MQA. The two published at Philadelphia in 1770 in 3 vols. and at Basel in 1793 in 4 vols. have JQA's bookplate; the 2-vol., London, 1809, edition bears GWA's signature and his notation that he read it while at Harvard in 1818–1819.

[2] See above, entry for 29 Jan., note.

WEDNESDAY. 15TH.

I devoted nearly two hours to Gibbon and felt quite well pleased with myself in consequence. The rest of the time passed as it usually does. I accomplished a walk also in very wet streets, but it was not half as long as it should have been. Mr. Brooks dined with us, but did not appear to me to be very lively.

I was very superficial in Quinctilian. The truth is I have read enough about the Theory of Oratory. It has become so tedious and dry as to benefit me little. I have some notion of giving up the study of it, having accomplished six books being one half of the Work. But the truth is I am not clear what to do next. Perhaps I may take up Livy, perhaps Virgil or go back to a minuter analysis of the Orations of Cicero.

Quiet evening. Continued Leigh Hunt. His imprisonment for a libel, his opinion of himself &ca. On the whole, he seems a tolerably amiable man to have seen so much difficulty. His book was made up however to sell.

THURSDAY. 16TH.

The Cold seemed to be coming on again today. I was in hopes it was going away permanently. Occupied nearly all the morning in trifles so that I gave only a short time to Gibbon. I must plead guilty to half an hour of pure indolence. A thing by the way I feel to be growing upon me. I have not the energy to shake it off entirely. I took a long walk after it reflecting upon vanity and vexation of spirit.

In the afternoon I felt so disgusted with Quinctilian that I laid him aside and returned to the Oration in defence of Cluentius which is admirable. The Narration is a peculiarly brilliant part of this effort. It has all the merit of terseness, vigour and elegance which ought to belong to it. I find however that my previous reading was pretty thorough.

Evening, the family of the Brooks' came to pass the usual time with us. There is not much cultivation among them. I must say for this that I have not fallen exactly into a connection of like taste with my own in this regard. But they are on the whole educated and though not so agreeable as a man might form persons in his fancy, yet more so than you generally find them in life. They went at ten. I did not read any of the Odyssey. The rest as usual.

FRIDAY. 17TH.

A return of sharp cold upon us this morning. The Winter is long and trying to people who are not in good circumstances. I accomplished a good deal of Gibbon at the Office not having quite so many Newspapers to read. But the detail of the breaking up of the Western Empire is dull. Nothing but a series of rapine, and devastation with the greatest barbarity. The effeminacy of civilization contrasted with the energy of untaught nature. Took a walk and enjoyed the day cold as it was.

Afternoon, engaged still upon the Oration for Cluentius, the examination of the condemnation of those Judges concerned in the trial of Oppiancius. Argumentative and as it seems to me very satisfactory. I believe when I read it before, the Account of the crimes of Oppiancius and Sassia is the only thing very hard for me to swallow. It seems scarcely conceivable that such a man and such a woman could be kept in Society at all. Much less in Rome famous for it's Laws.

Evening quiet at home. Read the latter part of Hunt's book to my Wife, into which he throws every thing he can muster. His account of his trip to Italy is in some respects better than any of the rest. It has his faults but more beauties.

SATURDAY. 18TH.

My Record of today can have but little of interest in it. I pursued my reading of Gibbon without material interruption. Finished the fifth volume and the Roman Empire under Arcadius and Honorius. No letter from my father. His occupation in the House now employs him so much that he will not give me a syllable even upon the most necessary topics. My Mother writes occasionally.[1]

Afternoon quiet at home. Finished the Oration for Cluentius, which on this reading strikes me as about the summit of this kind of Oratory. The vigour and yet the flow of the language is admirable. I wonder if I could form to myself any thing like the same style. It would be worth all the gold in the world.

Evening quiet at home. Finished the Bible. We have been reading the Chapters of Revelation. Of which neither she nor I can make any thing. Part of it certainly betrays ignorance of the doctrines now received of the Constitution of the Universe and no apparent light to supply it's place from above. It makes the sun and moon and stars much more tributary to the earth than their relative size and importance in the Creation would seem to justify. I must confess it looks to me much more like the vision of a heated brain than the natural result of the mild and heavenly doctrine and practice of the Saviour. In him there was no rant, no extravagant visions, every thing is adapted to reason and to the conduct of life. Perhaps this single point is one of the greatest in which he can be contrasted with all mere men who have arrogated similar powers. They all more or less display the weak parts of the human mind. An imagination inflamed into wild enthusiasm, and showing itself in visions and ravings. He on the contrary works miracles and preaches Peace. Finished Hunt's book. And Began Rose's translation of Ariosto.[2]

[1] CFA had received on the day before, LCA's most recent letter (11 Feb., Adams Papers), in which she reported JQA well but "overwhelmed" with the business of the House.

[2] *Orlando Furioso. Translated into English verse. With notes by William Stewart Rose*, 8 vols., London, 1823–1831. The copy at MQA has CFA's bookplate.

SUNDAY. 19TH.

Nothing can be worse than our Weather has been for a considerable time past. The Alternations have been so rapid from cold to warm, and from dry to wet that the systems of People must be severely tried. I attended Divine Service all day. Heard in the morning a young man by name Chapman,[1] a brother of him who was my Class-mate at College. His Text from Matthew 18. 3. "Verily I say unto you, except ye be converted, and become as little children, ye shall not enter into the kingdom of Heaven." The subject, the purity necessary to a holy character. The Preacher did not lean to the doctrine of innate depravity for he spoke of Children as perfectly innocent and pure. Indeed it is difficult to make any thing out of the Text unless we suppose Children to be pure. Yet what becomes of the great orthodox doctrine if we do. Mr. Ripley preached in the Afternoon from Matthew 14. 23. "And when he had sent the multitudes away, he went up into a mountain apart to pray." He inculcated the propriety of private meditation and secret prayer, giving in the mean while something of a reproof to the prevailing fashion in these days of resorting to sympathy and public excitement for religious feeling. There was much sense in what he said, but he is dry in manner, as are nearly all of our Clergy.

I lounged over Spence's Anecdotes of Pope an hour or two and read Massillon's Sermon upon the small number of the elect. "And many lepers were in Israel in the time of Eliseus the Prophet, and none of them was cleansed saving Naaman the Syrian." He gives three reasons why there can be very few saved. 1. They must either be innocent, or having been sinners, truly repentant. Of the first there are scarcely any, and no great number of the other. 2. Most people are led away by the voice of the Majority, and pay implicit deference to the regulations of the world which are not compatible with their salvation. 3. The rules which are most commonly rejected, are the most necessary to that salvation. This must be the Sermon which is said to have produced so powerful an effect that all the Auditors rose at one passage. That bold one in which he imagines the presence of Christ. On the whole the Sermon is a very powerful though far from a convincing one. There is too much effect in it, too much harshness in sentiment to be agreeable to my notion of the Deity and Religion.

Quiet Evening. Began the Old Testament to my Wife which I propose to read to her two Chapters nightly. Read a good deal of Grahame's second volume.

[1] George Chapman, Harvard 1828, had completed his divinity studies there in 1831 (*Harvard Quinquennial Cat.*).

MONDAY. 20TH.

Snow, rain, and hail. Every disagreeable thing in the way of Weather. My morning was mostly taken up in reading the Memorial of Mr. Gallatin upon the Protecting duties, which my Father sent me this morning.[1] It is long and I did not get through it. It seems to me well adapted to the purpose intended of destroying the Restrictive System and contains many arguments so specious as to make them appear to most people who do not probe, perfectly sound. I wonder if I could answer them. This is setting my powers in a pretty high Scale. But "faint heart ne'er won fair lady." I will study it over at least. Went home directly as it was rather too wet to take a walk.

The Afternoon was passed in reading the first Oration against Antony which is a mere excuse of himself for going away and returning with some strictures upon the wonderful facility with which the Consul issued new parts of Caesar's last directions. Here was the great error of the Patriotic party. They confirmed all the Acts of the Tyrant when dead, whom they were so desirous to get rid of while living because he was a Tyrant. They established the Government and destroyed only the Man. No wonder then, that another was soon found to fill his place. Quiet evening at home. Read part of Ariosto to my Wife.

[1] On 30 Jan. the Speaker presented to the House a memorial drawn up by Albert Gallatin as chairman of a committee appointed by the supporters of free trade in convention at Philadelphia, Sept.–Oct. 1831. The memorial, a pamphlet of nearly ninety pages, immediately became the most authoritative of the statements of the antiprotectionist position. Henry Clay, in his tariff speech in the Senate, 2–6 Feb., in defence of the "American System" (see below, entry for 6 March), devoted much of his attention to a refutation of Gallatin's arguments, and he may have been drawn to speak at all at that time by the appearance of the memorial. JQA had received a copy even before its presentation in the House. (*Daily National Intelligencer*, 1 Feb., p. 3, col. 4; HA, *Gallatin*, p. 640–642; JQA, Diary, 27 Jan.)

TUESDAY. 21ST.

A little snow. Morning at the Office where I finished reading Mr. Gallatin's Memorial and also Mr. McDuffie's Report from the Committee of Ways and Means upon the same subject.[1] The latter is a ranting thing altogether unworthy of a public body such as our Congress. I reflected more upon the other, and concluded at least to make an experiment of commenting upon it. Went to the Athenæum to get a Book upon the subject of the Trade with Great Britain and from thence went home. In the Afternoon I wrote as much as I thought would make one Paper upon the general view of the subject but postponed going into a particular examination until I had thought and read more upon it. Quiet Evening at home. Read some of Lord Sheffield's famous Pamphlet which laid down the doctrine how we should be treated after we had succeeded in being independent.[2]

[1] George McDuffie of South Carolina, chairman of the Committee of Ways and Means in the House, had submitted the Committee's report, drawn up by him, on 8 Feb.; the report was flatly opposed to protectionism (*Daily National Intelligencer*, 9 Feb., p. 3, col. 4).

[2] *Observations on the Commerce of the American States*, London, 1783, a pamphlet by John Baker Holroyd, 1st Earl of Sheffield, in opposition to the bill introduced by Pitt proposing to relax the navigation laws in favor of the United States.

WEDNESDAY. 22D.

This day was set apart here for the celebration of the Centennial Anniversary of Washington's birthday. A considerable apparatus was got up to make the thing do,[1] but I could not make up my mind to take any part in it. The influence of Washington's character was undoubtedly highly favourable to the prosperity of this Country and indeed even to it's existence, and I doubt whether any body surpasses me in my admiration of his peculiar merits, but with me it needs no noise to increase the estimation of them, nor high wrought Eulogy to blunt my discrimination of his true qualities of greatness.

After taking a short walk, I sat down at home and occupied myself busily all the morning in reflecting and writing upon Mr. Gallatin's Memorial which is a very able Paper. Mr. Brooks and Miss Julia Gorham dined with us and we had a pretty good time. As I gave the Memorial to Mr. Brooks to read, I could not go on writing, so I passed my time in looking over Lord Sheffield's Pamphlet and the minutes of evidence taken before the Committee of Manufactures some years since upon the subject of the protecting duties.

Evening Mr. J. Gorham passed an hour here after which Miss Julia, my Wife and I paid a visit at Dr. Stevenson's and spent an hour pleasantly enough. So passed the day. I did not read a book of the Odyssey tonight.

[1] The Boston celebration of the Washington centennial was arranged by a committee of the legislature. The observance included a public procession to Old South Church from the State House, with the principal address delivered by Francis C. Gray. There was also a civic dinner arranged by the

Council in Faneuil Hall, a parade of the Boston Fire Department, and the ringing of bells at intervals throughout the day (*Boston Daily Advertiser & Patriot*, 22 Feb., p. 2, cols. 1–2).

THURSDAY. 23D.

Another shocking day. Snow, rain and wind. At the Office, but passed my time most unprofitably. I neither pursued the subject of Mr. Gallatin's Memorial nor read Gibbon nor did any thing but consume an hour with Mr. Peabody talking, and then look over Accounts. I do not know how I can justify it to myself to make a confession of this kind so often.

Afternoon, wrote the number I design for the first one over again and as I thought did something to improve it, but of this it is impossible to judge. I am grappling with the results of one of the clearest minds in the Country, and the very effort is one requiring no small share of confidence in myself. But the exercise is good, and I never refuse work. My progress is greatly impeded from the want of a Pamphlet.

Evening, at home with my Wife. Read some of the Minutes of evidence alluded to before and was surprised at the unanimity among the woollen Manufacturers. Yet they were not minded.

FRIDAY. 24TH.

The weather changed to sharp cold again. This has been on the whole a Winter of greater severity than any I have known since I have lived in New England, whether in regard to amount of cold or it's duration. At the Office. Occupied in correcting and writing over what I have to say upon Mr. Gallatin's Paper. There certainly is a good deal worth noticing in it, and the more closely I look at it the more I am satisfied with the fact. But I want very much a channel through which to communicate my opinions to the world. I am living in a town where the whole Press is inhospitable to me and my name. My time was not economized however. Notwithstanding the cold, I took a walk and felt better for it.

Afternoon. Looked over the Annual Registers for two or three years and found a good deal in them that suited my purpose. Of all the things in this world, information is the thing that sets a man on an eminence. Speculation can then be brought to bear with great force upon any given topic. I think this gives the advantage in our day.

We passed a quiet Evening at home and I read a little more of Ariosto. He is rather free as are all his Countrymen. There is genius and imagination in his Poem but not much of the high soaring of

Poetry. Looked over some numbers of the Albion Newspaper which
has good extracts from the prevailing literature in England.[1]

[1] The *Albion* was a weekly newspaper published in New York City.

SATURDAY. 25TH.

Morning cold with snow. At the Office where I was occupied in
reading a little more of Gibbon. But it is heavy work. The style of that
author is cumbrous. His regularly balanced periods become tiresome
after a certain time. And his sneers are too constant to vary materially
the monotony. Attended a Stock sale but made no purchase. Manufactures appear to be very much at a stand. Took a walk.

Afternoon. Took up Virgil and read his five first Eclogues.[1] I have
read them so often before that I am enabled to do a good deal at once.
They are fine specimens of the highest polish of which verse is susceptible. Vigorous yet smooth.

Evening. Continued Ariosto and finished Pope's version of the
Odyssey. On the whole I think the criticism of Longinus correct.
Homer does nod in this Work pretty often. The Iliad is a splendid
performance for its vigor, and its beauty. This has less of the former,
but yet in places more of the latter. It is as the female in comparison
with the male. Finished also the first Volume of the Guardian.

[1] Of the numerous editions of Virgil in Latin, French, and English at MQA, two London editions of the *Opera*, 1818 and 1824, have CFA's bookplate; and that of 1824 has marginalia in CFA's hand. CFA noted there that the source of most of his comments was the edition of Heyne published at Leipzig in 1798, "with which I have compared [this]." Above his signature he has entered, "January 21, 1834. I this day finished this volume."

SUNDAY. 26TH.

The weather at last looks a little more in conjunction with the
Season and the closing of Winter. Yet the whole surface of the Earth
was covered with Ice this morning, making the walking difficult. I
went to Meeting all day. Heard Mr. Frothingham from Ecclesiasticus
50. 6, 7, 8. "He was as the Morning star in the midst of a cloud: as the
rainbow giving light in the bright clouds: and as the flower of roses
in the spring of the year." It was upon the respect to be paid to great
men; occasioned more immediately by the celebration of Washington's
Anniversary. He considered the objections that had been made in
two lights. First, as being directed against the practice of paying extraordinary devotion to man, second, as underrating the merits of others
who were partners of the same struggle and producers of the same
success. These he combated as unreasonable fears, for in the first place

the man was dead, and could do no harm, in the second, nothing was claimed for him to the disparagement of others. He was in a degree the creature of circumstances which placed him at the head of our Revolution. He was a fitting Instrument chosen by Providence for a definite purpose. He then closed, by some severe strictures upon a Preacher who had vilified our Presidents at Albany. The whole in a strain of Eloquence of the first Order, and very far beyond the usual tone of the Preacher. A Mr. Green [1] preached in the Afternoon from Acts 8. 30. "Understandest thou what thou readest?" There was no eloquence in him, but I obtained some information. He explained the manner in which the Testament should be treated. He considered it as the record of revelation and not the revelation itself. As designed not to be a system of morals to apply universally, but as intended for the information of the era in which it was written. It followed from this that in construing the Passages of the Testament, we should have regard to the local character of the illustrations and set it apart as distinct from the general rule which it conveyed. The first were used merely to impress the latter more strongly upon the mind, but have no binding force upon us. The rule however remains forever. He instanced several texts. I confess this gave me new ideas, though I suppose they are not original with him.

Afternoon at home. Read a Sermon of Massillon's upon the mixture of virtuous and wicked in the world. Text Matthew. 18. 15. "If thy brother shall trespass against thee, go and tell him his fault between thee and him alone: if he shall hear thee, thou hast gained thy brother." He considers this mixture as beneficial in two ways. 1. Because the virtuous are either the safety or the condemnation of the wicked. By leaving them no palliation for misconduct 2. Because the bad teach lessons of instruction or conduce to the merit of the virtuous. I read it rather superficially.

Evening, did nothing. Conversation with my Wife. Read Dryden's Absalom and Achitophel which contains many very masterly lines.[2] Vigour is the great merit of them.

[1] Samuel Green was the minister at the Union Church in Essex Street, Boston; James D. Green was the minister at a Congregational church in Cambridge (*Mass. Register*, 1832).

[2] The poems of Dryden read on each of the next several evenings are in vols. 1–2 of the edition of his *Poetical Works* at MQA owned by CFA; see vol. 2:369.

MONDAY. 27TH.

Very disagreeable day with snow. At the Office as usual. Passed the larger part of my time reading Gibbon and his doleful account of the sack of Rome and the spreading of the Barbarians over the face of the earth. It is all barren desolation. Received a very short letter from my Father merely saying that his engagements would be such, he should be entirely unable to write to me any more during this session. At the same time appointing me to the superintendence of his Affairs in Quincy, to the same extent at which I have those in Boston. I do not feel particularly pleased with the Job though it may add a trifle to my Compensation. The Cost of going out there to superintend will more than balance what I receive.[1] Took a walk and then home. Afternoon I finished the Eclogues of Virgil besides writing an answer to my Fathers letter.[2] This consumed my whole time.

Evening: my Wife had made an engagement to go and visit the Mother and Sisters of Mr. Frothingham.[3] I accompanied her and Mr. & Mrs. F. There were several People there. I got through it pretty well. But my character is most exceedingly unfit for this kind of thing.

[1] JQA to CFA, 20 Feb. (Adams Papers). CFA had proposed in his letter of 5 Feb. to JQA (LbC, Adams Papers) that he assume the management of JQA's affairs in Quincy which had suffered somewhat when under the oversight of Deacon Spear. JQA's acceptance included his agreement to CFA's proposed charge for the service: 5 per cent "upon all Receipts from that Quarter."

[2] CFA to JQA (LbC, Adams Papers). For this letter, see below, entry for 7 March, note.

[3] Mrs. Joanna Langdon Frothingham, the widow of Ebenezer and the mother of Rev. Nathaniel Frothingham, lived at 28 South Street. Her two unmarried daughters were Priscilla Langdon and Abigail Langdon, later Mrs. Thomas B. Wales (*Boston Directory*, 1832–1833; Thomas B. Wyman Jr., *The Frothingham Genealogy*, Boston [1917], p. 42, 58, 96, 126).

TUESDAY. 28TH.

More disagreeable weather. At the Office. Read Gibbon and had but one interruption. Mr. I. Farrar from Quincy to pay a portion of his rent. He is about to quit the Farm not at all to my regret for he is a very wretched farmer. But whether he will have a successor at all better is a question still. Took a short walk and returned home.

Afternoon, the first Georgic of Virgil. I did not quite finish it. Copied also, the letter to my Father and sent it.

Evening at Mr. Frothingham's. A family party. P. C. B. Jr. the only one not there of those commonly present. It was pretty well. There seemed however to be some under-current. I congratulate myself that I have kept out of all difficulties arising from Jealousies, which assuredly I could not have done if I had shown the least disposition to accept the invitation to live at Medford. I regard the death of Mrs. Brooks as a great misfortune to this family. Returned home. Read

Dryden's Mac Flecnoe. Distinguished by his usual beauties and faults, but not so good as Absalom I think.

WEDNESDAY. 29TH.

A fine day. Morning passed at the Office very quietly reading Gibbon, and the close of the Western Empire. Nearly five Centuries from the commencement of the Christian Era and Twelve from the foundation of Rome. A very long period for the continuance of a Nation in power. The Romans were a fighting people and died from excess of conquest. They are the only persons who can be said with any truth to have governed the world. And they manifested most clearly that the thing could not be made to last. The Globe is too large; even one division of it is more than can be managed. Our Country has grown out of our means to control it. Interests are so various and so opposite that it is not easy to say what the result will be. Took a walk with Mr. Peabody.

Mr. Brooks dined with us and staid so late that I only got a chance to read a small part of Virgil's second Georgic. My energy for study seems certainly to be much damped. I do not clearly see what the result may be. But I am as far off as possible from any thing in which I can be of use to myself or to others. Evening quiet at home. Read Dryden's Religio Laici and Threnodia Augustalis. The first remarkable as the author soon after turned Catholic; the second as being a Panegyric upon one of the most execrable kings who ever sat upon the English throne.[1]

[1] Charles II.

THURSDAY. MARCH 1ST.

Day fine though cooler than yesterday. I went to the Office as usual and passed my time pretty diligently. Finished a Chapter of Gibbon upon the origin and progress of the Monastic habits and also of the Christian religion among the Barbarians. Though he is very much prejudiced and consequently never altogether fair in his Account, there are yet some things of value in his criticisms. That the Religion of Christ has been abused to a most extraordinary degree will admit of little doubt. The visions of Plato have done something but fanaticism resulting from excessive ignorance far more. Took a walk with Mr. Peabody at one.

Afternoon at home. Read portions of the second and third Georgic. The author has handled ticklish subjects with considerable delicacy.

But after all, there is not much to be said for the details of rural Economy. Like Mr. J. Randolph's stud advertisement which amused me this morning, there is too much of sex in it.[1]

Evening, resumed Ariosto to my Wife. He rises as he treats of the storm of Paris. Indeed this is the only place where I have seen a great deal of vigour. The personification of Silence and Discord, the latter particularly is very good. Read Dryden's Medal and the first part of the Hind and Panther.

[1] In the *Daily National Intelligencer*, 25 Feb., p. 3, cols. 5–6, there appeared a full two-column advertisement in the form of a letter signed by John Randolph of Roanoke. In announcing that his three stallions (Janus, Gascoigne, and Rinaldo) were at stud for the year, he provided in picturesque detail, of which a sample is given below, the information thought appropriate about each horse, with incidental comment on current taste and fashion:

"Janus has more of the blood of old Janus (his great great grandsire) than any other horse living, and his action surpasses that of any other animal of his species that the writer of this advertisement ever saw, his dam Frenzy only excepted. . . . He won several times—among others at Tree Hill, when Gen. Lafayette was there—but although a real racer, with great speed, he was a very unlucky one. . . . He beat the far-famed Henry . . . the two first heats out of five, of one mile each, the best three in five; and could he have been kept back, so as to throw away a heat, it is believed that he would have won the race—(Such was the opinion, among others, of that model of the Old Virginia Planter and Sportsman, the late Edmund Irby, Esquire.) But . . . his ungovernable temper caused his defeat. . . . Janus at sixty dollars and one dollar to the Groom; forty dollars the leap, to be paid at the stable door, *before the mare is led away.* . . . Any mare not proving in foal shall be covered next season gratis by Janus or Gascoigne. . . .

"[Rinaldo] is a horse of vast strength and great activity. He, too, was bred after the dam, most luckily, for easier trotters, or a more hardy and thrifty race of horses never existed; they will keep fat upon what will barely keep alive the leggy, long-backed *Garsons* that are now all the rage, and which are fit for nothing but a long race, or a collar and hames; whereas, the true serviceable horse is the quarter horse, being active, sure footed, speedy, and capable of breaking down the fashionable stock in a hard ride of fifty, or even five and twenty miles. . . . Rinaldo is of the best running blood, as will be seen. His neck was injured by too early smelling at mares. His body and limbs cannot be surpassed by any horse. His head is large and bony. . . . His feet are of the old horny and *cupped* description that distinguished the Virginia horse before Colonel Hoomes inundated our country with worthless Stallions, and introduced the flat, thin-soled, weak crusted foot that can hardly hold a shoe, and cannot travel five miles without one. Our old-fashioned horses never required shoeing except in hard frosts, or hard work on stony ground. The new stock must be shod when not at work, or they fall lame. . . .

"There cannot be a higher bred horse [than Gascoigne], and he is of immense power. . . . He is a most beautiful creature, not tall enough to suit the present depraved taste for leggy horses. . . . As a stallion he is untried, having only covered last year privately. He is eight years old next grass. . . . He will cover at one hundred dollars. . . . Any winner or breeder of a winner of respectability shall be covered gratis. . . . And one hundred dollars will be paid to the proprietor of Ariel for permission to cover her, and to the owner of Reality also, provided she be not past bearing. . . . Profit, it will be seen, forms no part of the object of Gascoigne's master."

CFA's allusion to the advertisement without naming the *Intelligencer* suggests that he had taken to reading the Washington paper regularly, perhaps since his father's term in the House began. This is confirmed by CFA's general awareness, evident in his letters, of JQA's actions and speeches in the House, even where no explicit reference is made in a journal entry. An example is JQA's speech of 8 Feb. against a proposed revision in the ratio of representation in Congress to population, his first major oratorical effort in the House, printed *in extenso* in the *Daily National Intelligencer*, 28 Feb., p. 2, cols. 1–4.

FRIDAY. 2D.

Morning fine, but it afterwards grew cloudy and disagreeable. I went to the Office and found there a letter from T. B. Adams Jr. requesting me to appropriate his funds to the education of Joseph until he should go to Sea.[1] This is generous on his part but hardly fair, for Joseph ought to pay his own expenses. Continued Gibbon and passed on the whole a fair morning. My time better occupied than heretofore. One or two interruptions of Tenants to pay Money. My father's Affairs are now pretty easy here and would go to relieve him very much if he had not contracted such a debt from his speculation of last Summer as throws back every thing for some years. Took a walk with Mr. Peabody as usual.

Afternoon. Read parts of the third and fourth Georgic. There is an amazing sweetness in these Poems. They present agreeable images. Country scenery, quiet, innocence and peace. Not that the thing is real, for human passions are the same every where but the eye loves to rest upon a green spot, even if it is only an illusion.

Evening at home. Continued Ariosto, but my Wife votes it monotonous and a bore, so that I shall be obliged to drop it. Read the rest of Dryden's Hind and Panther. A religious discussion in verse. I became drowsy over it.

[1] The letter is missing.

SATURDAY. 3D.

Fine day. I went to the Office as usual and was occupied in making up Accounts after which I finished the sixth volume of Gibbon which closes the History of the Decline and Fall of the Roman Empire in the West. A work in itself of immense labour and erudition. I admire it upon the whole. The disposition of the historian seems to have been warped by a sense of real injury done to virtue through the Agency of hypocrisy and fanaticism. He goes to one extreme from a dislike of the other. Attended a meeting of the Bar at one o'clock, and from thence went to the Athenæum, so that I did not walk today.

Afternoon. Finished the Georgics and the story of Aristæus which is considered as the greatest ornament. They are models for that species of composition, a sign of which is that all subsequent times have only imitated them.[1] Quiet Evening at home. Read part of Goëthe's Memoirs to my Wife.[2]

[1] At the conclusion of the section devoted to the Georgics in the London, 1824, edition of Virgil's *Opera* at MQA, CFA has written, "These books have never been equalled."

[2] An English translation was published at New York in 1824.

SUNDAY. 4TH.

This was another fine day though a little more cool. I attended divine service all day and heard Mr. Frothingham's Sermon in the morning from 2. Corinthians 5. 15. "That he died for all, that they which live should not henceforth live unto themselves, but unto him which died for them and rose again." It was upon that particular feature of the Christian doctrine which manifests an abandonment of self for the sake of others. One remark of his I was particularly struck with, that if we were to judge of the mass of men by the rigid justice of this Rule, we should find exceedingly few who lived up either to the letter or the spirit of it. Selfishness is the characteristic of the race. But I lost the trace of the discourse generally for which I am the more sorry as it was a good one. The text of the Afternoon has also escaped me though its subject was the character of the Deity as a Judge, the dispensation of rewards and punishments here and hereafter. He considered it probable that this was much more equally done even in this life than our limited faculties can form an idea of, but he did not deny that there were still inequalities which could only be explained consistently with our idea of the Deity, by a state of compensation in future.

On returning home I read Massillon though superficially so that I was obliged to read him at night again. Matthew 15. 8. "This people draweth nigh unto me with their mouth, and honoureth me with their lips, but their heart is far from me." He considered the nature of the true worship of God. Dividing the subject into two parts. First, the neglect of all formal worship and the reasons assigned for so doing. He considered these to be what in fact they most often are mere excuses for neglect of all religion. He thought some attention to external devotion beneficial on various accounts, the strongest of which is the effect upon other and weaker members. But second he took up the idea that attention to form was very injurious when it was made to take the place of real piety, when as in the text the lips speak but the heart is hard. A very good Sermon.

I felt depressed as the Child seemed unwell. Mr. Blake called and spent a couple of hours very pleasantly.

MONDAY. 5TH.

Heavy rain and apparently a disperser of our snow and ice. I went to the Office and read Gibbon. Beginning the sixth volume and the decline of the Roman Empire in the East. A thing that never had any solid foundation of it's own. A man may on the whole feel very grateful with us that he has been placed where he is. Perhaps the pleasantest period for life may be considered to have taken place during the last half of the last Century in England, and the first half in France. Though the thing may admit of some consideration. I am speaking of the pleasure of life to an educated man. In these days we are all educated.

Although it stormed hard, I attended the Meeting of the Directors of Boylston Market and they transacted the business expeditiously. They are pretty practical men all of them and understand the business of building. There is something to be got from almost every body in this world.

Returned home. The Baby was so unwell I sent for the Dr. She has been now in a poor condition for a month past. I know no anxiety equal to this. Read a part of Goethe's Memoirs to my Wife. Afterwards I finished Grahame's second Volume, and read some account of Dryden, but I cannot easily read over and over.

TUESDAY. 6TH.

A gloomy day. Besides the want of rest caused by the fretfulness of the Child, our anxiety about her was very considerable. She shows every symptom of illness and we feel it the more as we are so little accustomed to it. My time was passed at the Office in reading Mr. Clay's Speech upon the Tariff which strikes me as rather above the usual character of his writings, and only defective in prudence.[1] It took the whole of my time.

Afternoon. Read the first Book of the Æneid with great ease and much pleasure. The pictures are graphic, the versification smooth and the language elegant. In short about as good as one can imagine a thing of the kind.

Evening. My Wife retired so early that I devoted two hours and a half to the diligent study of Montesquieu upon the greatness and the decline of Rome.[2] A book containing a great fund of reflection. He studied History as it should be studied, for the sake of the general conclusions he could draw to instruct the human race. But though both in this work and in the spirit of the laws he seems to have much method, in fact his books are but bundles of thoughts irregularly spread.

¹ The speech delivered in the Senate by Henry Clay on 2, 3, and 6 Feb. "In Defence of the American System" was printed by the *Boston Daily Advertiser & Patriot* on 6 March as a 4-page extra section. Also published separately, CFA had a copy in his pamphlet collection (Adams Papers, Microfilms, Reel No. 326). See also, above, entry for 20 Feb., note.

² In the edition of the *Œuvres* of Montesquieu at MQA which CFA used (above, entry of 1 May 1831), "Considérations sur les causes de la grandeur des romains, et de leur décadence" is in vol. 6.

WEDNESDAY. 7TH.

Isaac Hull Adams came to town this day and established himself at our house for the purpose of preparing himself for West Point.¹ I was at the Office. Anxiety for the Child not materially diminished. Took a walk to a house in Cedar Street for the purpose of looking at some of the Furniture which I wanted. It did not at all answer my expectation. This and a regular walk at one o'clock fatigued me considerably as I had passed but a middling kind of a night. Read a considerable quantity of Gibbon however, upon Justinian and Theodora. Bad enough in all conscience.

Afternoon. Mr. Brooks having dined with us, I remained down stairs considerably longer than usual, so that I accomplished only about five hundred lines of the second Æneid, with the description of the taking of Troy. I think it is a very great mistake committed to make boys or men read Virgil first and Homer afterwards. One would think the true way to be exactly the reverse. For the former takes up the subject just where the other drops it. Perhaps it is one of the most curious of occurrences that perfection in this kind of style should have been reached so early.

Evening, we omitted our usual reading. Mr. Degrand came in, and passed an hour. I read more of Montesquieu, and progressed in my irregular study of the harmony of the Gospels.

¹ CFA had invited Isaac Hull Adams to stay with him and ABA until Hull's departure for West Point in June. "He will have the use of my study part of the time entirely to himself and always without interruption. Though no great hand at the Mathematics I also agreed to do what I could to help him, as a Teacher." CFA to JQA, 27 Feb. (LbC, Adams Papers).

THURSDAY. 8TH.

Fine morning. I went to the Office but did not improve my time to the utmost. In the first place I was busy about Commissions for an hour, then went to the Athenæum besides taking a walk at one. So that I only made up my Diary, in itself a tolerable Job, and read Mr. McDuffie's Paper upon the Bank of the U.S.[1] Our political affairs are becoming more and more black. For my part I see little prospect for us.

In the Afternoon I continued the Æneid, finishing the second and part of the third books. The Child seemed slightly better, although very fretful and apparently suffering. The total want of power to convey an idea of its sensations to others makes the sickness of an infant extremely distressing.

Quiet evening at home. I read part of Goethe's Memoirs which seem to me to be rather a record of trifles remembered by an old man. Mr. T. Davis came in and spent part of an Evening very agreeably. He has a great deal of conversation and that of a sensible kind. After he went, I continued Montesquieu, and my study of the Bible.

[1] The speech of George McDuffie in the House on 27 Feb. in support of the United States Bank was reported in the *Daily National Intelligencer* (28 Feb., p. 2–3; 29 Feb., p. 2–3). His "paper" on the subject is probably his report as chairman of the Committee of Ways and Means, which on 10 Feb. accompanied the introduction of a bill to recharter the Bank (*Daily National Intelligencer*, 11 Feb., p. 3, cols. 2, 4).

FRIDAY. 9TH.

This was one of the lovely days of which we have but a very few in the Spring season, though those few are perhaps the more valued on that account. I got out early this morning and went to the Office. My time was consumed without much profit to myself. Went to the Athenæum and passed so much time in lounging there that I lost my usual quantity of exercise. The consequence of which was rather less appetite than usual.

In the Afternoon I passed a quiet time reading the rest of the third and a part of the fourth books of the Æneid, the morality of all which is not the less doubtful because he makes it originate from Gods and Goddesses. The pious Aeneas is little better than a rascal for the desertion of Dido after seducing her. But Poets cannot make out their Story without such aids. And after all it is agreeable to nature. Evening at home. Nothing material. Finished Montesquieu, which is a very valuable Treatise.

SATURDAY. 10TH.

Another delicious day. My time was spent for the most part in the Street. I was engaged in Commissions for my Wife, of Furniture, but was unable to get any to suit me. The walking besides my regular exercise fatigued me considerably. And the day was weakening. Deacon Spear called to see me with reference to the auction to take place at Mr. Farrar's, and also upon Affairs in general. I gave him my general instructions as to what was to be done and agreed to go to Quincy next week on the same business. I was informed by him as well as from other sources that my uncle the Judge was now lying very low without probability of his going many weeks more. I do not know that this is to him a misfortune but it is bad that his death should happen while my father is absent.

Quiet Afternoon at home. Continued Virgil and read the fourth and part of the fifth books. The latter containing the Games in honour of Anchises. An imitation of the Games in Homer, at the funeral of Patroclus. The boat race is an improvement. Quiet evening at home. Began Scott's Life of Napoleon Bonaparte.[1] A book which will probably lead me fully into the history of a period about which my head is not now quite clear.

[1] CFA was reading the edition now at MQA, published at Philadelphia in 1827 in 3 vols.; see below, entry for 26 April, note.

SUNDAY. 11TH.

The Child seemed today decidedly better. And it is the first day upon which my pleasure has exceeded my anxiety for her, since her sickness. The Wind was cold and raw, the sky clouded. I attended Divine Service all day. Heard Mr. Putnam a young man settled in Roxbury. His Morning's Sermon was from 97. Psalms 1. "The Lord reigneth." But I did not find that he made much of the subject. At least my memory is a blank about it. I did rather better with the Afternoon. The text upon that occasion was from 1. Peter 12 "which things the angels desire to look into." The argument tending to show the intellectual character of the Christian religion, and based upon the authority of the greatest minds making it a study. This young man however does not direct his powers to any object of value. Milton, Hale,[1] Newton, Jones[2] and Locke though all of them undoubtedly men of first rate mind, yet did little or nothing to sustain the character of Christianity, for the simple reason, that the religion was at once adapted to the simplest and poorest comprehension, and set at nought all the distinctions of mental power. I of course mean the practical doctrine without reference to the mystery which equally defies the greatest and the smallest comprehension.

On my return home I read a Sermon of Massillon's upon lukewarmness in religion. Text from Luke 4. 38. "And Simon's wife's mother was taken with a great fever and they besought him for her." As it seems to me with very little propriety. He spoke of the dangerous effects of lukewarmness as it makes our rectitude of purpose uncertain 1. by retarding the endeavour to attain perfection, 2. by confusing in the mind the consciousness of crime or sin, 3. by making charity doubtful.

I had a very quiet evening. Read to my Wife a part of the Lives of British Painters, those of Opie and Morland.[3] They are interesting. Other studies as usual.

[1] Sir Matthew Hale (1609–1676), Lord Chief Justice of the Court of King's Bench and immensely learned in law and religion (*DNB*).

[2] The reference would seem to be to William Jones (1675–1749), mathematician and early expounder of the Newtonian philosophy, or to his son, Sir William Jones (1746–1794), orientalist and legal scholar, who enjoyed a reputation in England and America almost unrivaled for breadth of learning in literature and science; see the notices of each in *DNB*.

[3] Allan Cunningham's *The Lives of the Most Eminent British Painters and Sculptors* had recently been republished in *Harper's Family Library*, 3 vols., N.Y., 1831–1832. The lives which CFA chose for reading on this and the following evenings all appear in the second volume. On John Opie (1761–1807) and George Morland (1763–1804), see *DNB* notices of each.

MONDAY. 12TH.

Rain with occasional claps of thunder. I went to the Office as usual and was occupied in my Journal and a variety of small duties all day. Wrote a letter to my Mother which took more time than it ought to have done.[1] On my return home I found that Hull had received such information from Quincy as rendered it necessary for him to go there. I am fearful his father's end is approaching.

Passed the afternoon at home and began another attempt upon the Spanish language. I have made several, and my principal difficulty has always been that it seems too easy. It defies application and yet can not be read without the labour of a Dictionary. But I will now make a persevering attempt by reading some of it every day. I began again the Moorish letters and read the Preface.[2] Quiet evening at home. Read a part of the life of Barry the Painter.[3]

[1] The letter from CFA to LCA is missing unless the letter from and to the same, dated 9 March (Adams Papers) is the one referred to.

[2] CFA had studied Spanish as a junior at Harvard and in Washington during 1826 (vol. 1:100–133; 2:37–51 *passim*). The copy at MQA of José de Cadalso, *Cartas Marruecas*, Tolosa, 1820, has CFA's bookplate.

[3] James Barry (1741–1806), member of the Royal Academy (*DNB*). His life appears in Cunningham, *British Painters*, at 2:54–123.

TUESDAY. 13TH.

I received at breakfast this morning the intelligence that my Uncle the Judge expired yesterday at about one o'clock, before I. Hull reached there. In consequence of this intelligence and of a request of Mrs. Adams to see me I went out immediately. Upon arriving there I found Mrs. Adams and the children apparently in considerable distress but not unreasonably nor foolishly excited. After advising as much as I could, and going to the House of my Father for the necessary Papers &ca., I returned to town where I arrived before dinner.

The afternoon was taken up first in writing to my Father the intelligence with a request for orders thereupon.[1] The death puts us all in an embarrassing situation. His Estate is probably of no material consequence and the settlement of it is from the peculiar circumstances of my Grandfather's Will rather distressing.[2] The absence of my Father adds very much to the embarrassment of the whole thing. If I was disposed to moralize this event would easily afford matter for it. But it would be at the expense of a man now beyond the reach of reproach or benefit, of a man who paid a bitter penance for his follies and left his Children to share the same as his only legacy.

I read a little of the Moorish letters. Quiet evening at home until eight o'clock reading the Life of Napoleon. After that I went to P. C. Brooks Jrs. where there was a family party. Returned early and I soon retired.

[1] CFA to JQA, 15 [i.e. 13] March (LbC, Adams Papers). JQA received the letter bringing him intelligence of the death of his "dear and amiable brother" by messenger from JA2 while the House was in session on the 17th (JQA, Diary). His letters to Mrs. TBA and to CFA written immediately thereafter are in the Adams Papers.

[2] According to the terms of JA's will, the portion on which TBA was to receive the income during his lifetime devolved at death to his children, each of whom would receive an equal share ($520) of the principal when he or she came of age. Mrs. TBA would receive from the devise only the interest accrued to the date of TBA's death. Thereafter the interest due each minor child, along with the interest on the share left by JA to each of them directly and formerly paid to TBA, would be paid by JQA as JA's executor to a guardian. ECA, at her election, would have her portion added to her own devise from JA which she had allowed to remain at interest, taking a new note from JQA for the principal as increased. The portions of Thomas B. Adams Jr. and of Abigail (Adams) Angier would be payable to them on demand.

Beyond JQA's obligations arising under JA's will, JQA held mortgages on TBA's house and farm at Braintree and on the farm at Medford. He instructed CFA to take possession of these properties and to notify the tenants that rents would be payable to him. His further instruction was to inform Mrs. TBA that all rents received by him from the properties during the lifetime of Mrs. TBA would be paid over to her and that at her death the properties would be conveyed in equal parts to the six children.

JA, Will (Adams Papers, Microfilms, Reel No. 607); JQA to CFA, 5, 17, 21, 30 March (Adams Papers); CFA to JQA, 15 [i.e. 13], 16 March (LbC's, Adams Papers). See also vol. 2:398.

WEDNESDAY. 14TH.

After going to the Office for a few minutes, and calling upon Miss [*Louisa C.*] Smith to accompany me, I went to Quincy in a Carriage according to request. The day was so cold that I felt comfortless all the way out. I got out at the House of my Father for the sake of obtaining from among his Papers two or three which I found necessary. These I succeeded after considerable search in getting. I then went up to the House now occupied by the Widow. I sat very quietly alone for some time as I was early. But before three, persons began to come and the House was soon quite full.

Mr. Whitney made a very good Prayer, and the whole thing was conducted with the greatest propriety. We followed the body to it's long home. I went into the place as I came down and it gave me the least unpleasant idea of the grave that I ever had. The Coffins six in number were arranged on each side, and the place was clean and airy. There repose Mr. & Mrs. Cranch, Mrs. Smith the Mother of Louisa C. Smith and Mrs. Smith the sister of my Father, poor George and an infant child of the late deceased who today was added to the number.[1] My Grandfather and Grandmother have been removed to a spot beneath the Church. Such places are generally gloomy but this was less so than I expected. After every thing was over, we went back to the House and from thence to town. I was quite glad to get to my warm fire at home.

[1] JQA had instructed CFA that upon TBA's death CFA should pay the expenses of the funeral and interment from JQA's funds, and that TBA's remains should be placed in the Adams family vault in the First Church burying ground (in what is now Quincy Square) "by the side of my Sister and my Son and of his own [TBA's] infant child" (JQA to CFA, 5 March, Adams Papers; see also, above, vol. 3:85). The three others named by CFA as reposing in the vault were AA's sister, Mary (Smith) Cranch (1741–1811); her husband, Richard Cranch (1726–1811); and Catharine Louisa (Salmon) Smith (1749–1824), the wife of AA's brother, William Smith. On all these, see Adams Genealogy. It would appear from the present passage that the floor of the vault at that time was at or near ground level and that entrance to the vault was through a door or grille, though now (1967) only the topmost part of the vault, above the line of any door or aperture, is exposed.

THURSDAY. 15TH.

Fine morning but still cold. I went to the Office and was occupied most of my time in writing up my Diary which has been unusually interrupted, and also in drawing up lists of the Stockholders of the Boylston Market for the Treasurer. There was a transfer this day. It is a long while now since I have been able to open a book in the morning.

Returned home and passed the Afternoon in reading Spanish. I found it easy and quite pleasant. On the whole I believe I shall make it a regular pursuit and perhaps begin Italian thus dividing the Afternoon.

A quiet evening at home. I concluded the life of Barry to my Wife and began that of a man by name Bird of whom I have not heard. Which probably only argues my own ignorance.[1] Mr. Brooks came in for half an hour and interrupted us. We talked pleasantly. After he went I continued Scott's Life of Napoleon and began to obtain a much clearer idea of the horrors of the revolution than I had ever had. The triumvirate of Robespierre, Danton and Marat, and the blood in streams I had indistinct notions about, but fully supported by the reality.

[1] Edward Bird (1772–1819), member of the Royal Academy (*DNB*). His life appears in Cunningham, *British Painters*, 2:208–222.

FRIDAY. 16TH.

Fine morning though windy. I started early to perform my engagement to Deacon Spear and arrived there at Quincy at nine o'clock the time stated. Met him and Mr. Field with whom I settled the Terms of his Lease[1] and then gave directions to Mr. Veazie after which I met the present and future Tenant of the Farms and we decided upon what was to be done in regard to my father's interest. The whole took me about two hours.

I then went up to see Mrs. Adams for the purpose of requesting instructions with regard to the affairs of the Judge. I conversed with her about two hours, explained to her, her situation as well as I could, and begged of her to know what she wished to do. The whole thing was about as disagreeable as any I ever had to do with. I left her however without having settled any thing. She is a woman without any energy of character. Her life would have been a very pleasant one if she had married a wealthy, showy man. But she has met with nothing but asperities.

Returned to town to dine, and consumed the afternoon in writing the result to my father.[2] Evening at Mr. F. Parkman's. A family party and a very dull affair.

[1] Before his departure for Washington JQA had notified his tenant, Isaac Farrar, that his lease, which would expire on 1 April, would not be renewed; JQA also had made arrangements for new leases to Harvey Field and to John G. Carr (JQA, Diary, 23 Sept., 17 Oct. 1831; see also, above, entry for 28 Feb. 1832).

[2] CFA to JQA, 16 March (LbC, Adams Papers). For this letter see above, entry for 13 March.

SATURDAY. 17TH.

Morning dark with violent wind and rain. I went to the Office and was busy in writing up my Diary which the preceding days had thrown behind hand. This with more walking in rain for furniture consumed nearly all my time. I did buy something at Auction today however though I am not sure my bargain was a very good one.[1] I also went to see about more fuel as my Coal is exhausted. This has been a most consuming Winter. We have had nothing but cold Weather.

Returned home and passed the Afternoon in reading Spanish. I continue to find it easy. My study this afternoon accomplished ten pages which I thought quite fair for a beginner.

My Evening was passed quietly at home. I read a good deal of Scott's Life of Napoleon as my Wife was engaged. The French Revolution is as interesting as the best Novel. It presents human nature in a singular aspect. All things magnified and inflamed. A people committing the most atrocious crimes under cover of the fairest names. Worked up to madness by the most fascinating temptation of liberty. On the whole, few things in the world are of a kind deserving more intense reflection. I afterwards finished the life of Bird to my Wife which after all does not amount to much. His pictures are probably of no permanent character. Finished this evening my comparison of the Gospels.

[1] The sale was at the auction rooms of J. M. Allen & Co. on Milk Street (*Boston Daily Advertiser & Patriot*, 17 March, p. 3, col. 6).

SUNDAY. 18TH.

The sight of snow again this year was not very agreeable. And the day was cold and blustering. I attended divine service and heard Mr. Frothingham preach all day. Morning. Text from Matthew 3. 9. "For I say unto you, that God is able of these stones to raise up children unto Abraham." He then explained the passage. John the Baptist had been surprised to find the Pharisees come to him, and he warned them to put no dependence upon their advantages. These they deemed to be of two sorts. One that they being the Descendants of Moses were the chosen of God, and that through their agency alone could any be expected to gain salvation. He said that there were sects now in the Christian Religion who held to similar doctrines and he proceeded to castigate their reasons for them. Afternoon. Text from Matthew 18. 33. "Shouldest not thou also have had compassion on thy fellow servant, even as I had pity on thee." It was upon forgiveness of sins. A very good Sermon explaining the nature of the Parable, the character of the Christian Religion, its mildness, its inculcating forgiveness and the necessity of the practice of that virtue to a disciple of Christ.

On my return home I read a Sermon of Massillon's according to custom. It was upon the same subject as that of last Sunday. In extracting the Text then however I did not take quite the whole of the Verse as I ought. He endeavours more clearly to show the application which he made of it. He says that a mere fever was a very unusual thing for Jesus to be called to cure. His cures were generally those of persons dying, or even dead. He therefore infers this to mean a state of moral debility. But why it should be lukewarmness and represented by a fever passes my comprehension. His argument against the danger of indifference in Religion today was again threefold. 1. It prevents the special grace requisite for the full support of piety. 2. It inclines man to sin from confusing his nicer distinction of right and wrong. 3. It renders the usual means useless or dangerous, as prayer, the communion &ca. a relapse from which is fatal. The ideas are not much varied in either. Evening quietly at home. Continued the French Revolution.

MONDAY. 19TH.

Morning clear but cold. I went to the Office as usual. Nothing of particular consequence in the time. I could not read a line yet my time did not appear to be adequately occupied. Busy upon a lease for one of the Tenants at my new Agency in Quincy. I then took a walk with Mr. Peabody to the North end to observe all the improvements that are making in that quarter. And from thence returned home.

I. Hull Adams returned from Quincy this morning to remain at my House until he goes away. Afternoon I continued my Spanish book with tolerable success.

We took tea early for the purpose of going to the Play. Our party consisted of Mr. Brooks, Mrs. Frothingham, Mrs. G. Brooks and her husband, my Wife and myself. The piece was Cinderella, that part performed by Mrs. Austin.[1] It has been got up with much trouble and expense, and is performed on the whole with much better success than I could expect. The music took me back to New York and the period when I heard the Italian Company perform.[2] There is a fascination in the style of Rossini though I should hardly think it would bear time and repetition. We returned home at eleven, highly pleased.

[1] Rossini's opera *Cinderella* [*Cenerentola*] with Mrs. Austin in the title role was performed at the Tremont Theatre preceded by a comic opera in two acts, *Music and Prejudice*, in which Mrs. Austin sang the role of "Alfred (an

263

English Gentleman on his travels)" (*Boston Daily Advertiser & Patriot,* 19 March, p. 3, col. 5). On Mrs. Austin, beautiful and with a voice of great purity and range, see Odell, *Annals N.Y. Stage,* 3:309–312 and *passim.*

[2] That is, June–July 1826; see vol. 2:54–60.

TUESDAY. 20TH.

Morning at the Office. I this day managed to accomplish all my usual work and make a little progress in Gibbon besides. I lament the misuse of my time very much. But this has been so often done and so little amendment has followed that I think I may as well say but little more about it. Took a walk with Mr. Peabody over Craigie's Bridge to Charlestown and home.[1]

Afternoon, continued the reading of Spanish and dabbled a little with Italian. I think I have too many Irons in the fire, according to the old Proverb. But it is better to have too many than too few. It gives occupation and extends the means of enjoyment.

Quiet evening at home. I continued the lives of the Painters, read the Account of Blake who was little more than a Madman,[2] and commenced that of Fuseli.[3] Continued the Account of the French Revolution and began reading over Paley's Evidences.[4]

[1] Craigie's Bridge, when opened in 1809, connected Boston with Lechmere's Point in Cambridge. Some time after the bridge was built, a spur was constructed to Charlestown, taking off from the main bridge before it reached the Cambridge shore. The spur became known as Prison-point Bridge (C. H. Snow, *A Geography of Boston,* Boston, 1830, p. 125).

[2] The account of William Blake in Cunningham, *British Painters,* 2:124–155, while it reveals a sensitivity to his genius, gives such emphasis to his madness and to anecdotes illustrative of it as to explain CFA's observation.

[3] In Cunningham's *British Painters,* Fuseli's life is at 2:223–273. CFA had two months earlier read a different life of Fuseli, which had not satisfied him; see above, entries for 17–22 Jan. *passim.*

[4] William Paley, *A View of the Evidences of Christianity,* first published in 3 vols., London, 1794, went through 17 editions in the next 27 years. The reading of it was required in the junior year when CFA was an undergraduate at Harvard (above, vol. 1:12).

WEDNESDAY. 21ST.

I made my morning much more profitable today, accomplishing a Chapter of Gibbon upon the victories of Belisarius. The Author has thrown an Interest into his History which one could hardly have expected, considering the time and places he was writing about. I have found it very easy to go through now nearly seven volumes and if I had more time should still be willing to employ it in the same manner.

I was a good deal interested in a debate that took place in the House of Representatives upon a request of my Father to be excused from serving on the Committee of Manufactures. The excessive praise that was paid him from Quarters three years since the most violent against him, and the cautious course of those formerly of his party, now friends of Mr. Clay, are worthy of remark.[1] They show what I have long since expected that he stands now between two forces which may or may not crush him.

The weather was bad and I did not walk, but I was occupied in Commissions for about the same length of time. Mr. Brooks dined with us so that one hour was taken from my afternoon. I devoted one hour to Spanish, another to Italian, which I have determined to try to learn. Evening quiet at home. Read the Account of Fuseli and after it, the French Revolution and part of Paley.

[1] The debate in the House on 16 March occasioned by JQA's request to be excused from further service as chairman of the Committee on Manufactures was reported in the *Daily National Intelligencer* on 17 March (p. 2–3). The announced reason in justification of the request was his impending absence from the House for a considerable period required by his membership on the select committee to investigate the United States Bank. In the debate which followed the motion those who were opposed to granting the request were strongest in their praise of JQA as uniquely able to resolve the sectional conflict over the tariff, as almost alone enjoying the confidence of all parties. Those who spoke in this vein were C. C. Cambreleng of New York, William Drayton of South Carolina, James Bates of Maine, Jesse Speight of North Carolina. Of those who spoke in favor of granting the request for a variety of reasons, the most laudatory of JQA was John S. Barbour of Virginia. Edward Everett, who moved to postpone, and H. A. S. Dearborn, both old supporters, were more temperate in their words of praise. The debate ended when JQA withdrew his motion, reserving the privilege of renewing the request at a later date.

JQA's effort to have himself removed from his onerous chairmanship was of longer standing than was suggested in the debate. When he took his seat in the House in Dec. 1831, he had wished assignment to the Committee on Foreign Affairs, the chairmanship of which seemed to some naturally his by virtue of the offices he had held. But JQA had been kept from the Committee by the fact that he and President Jackson were not in that easy communication that seemed essential for the proper functioning of the Committee. Instead, the Speaker, Andrew Stevenson, had appointed JQA to the most sensitive and perhaps most thankless position the Speaker had to confer, that of guiding a tariff bill through a bitterly divided House. JQA had recorded that it was "a Station of high responsibility, and perhaps of labour more burdensome than any other in the House ... for which I feel myself not to be well qualified" (Diary, 12 Dec. 1831); and on the next day wrote to CFA (letter in Adams Papers) that he believed the Speaker "took me for a *Jack*, which any Mason or Anti-mason might have told him I am not. The Camel kneels to receive his burden, and so did Caesar's horse. I shall rather resemble the Horse of Sir Hudibras and kneel to cast my burden off." On the whole episode, see Bemis, *JQA*, 2:240–242.

THURSDAY. 22D.

I staid at my Office very quietly all the morning because one of my father's Tenants complained he could not find me to pay his Rent. He did not come and I a little suspect that it is a take-in.[1] I read a Chapter of Gibbon and had a visit from Mr. Gourgas which related to the two Farms belonging to the Estate of my Uncle. I could not give him any definite information but suppose some will soon come, so I promised to let him know. We had some conversation with regard to the condition of Mrs. Adams and her prospects. He takes out Administration himself but does not as yet know the extent of the demands upon the Estate. Received a short letter from my Mother postponing her intentions with regard to this Quarter.[2]

Dined at Mr. Frothingham's with Mr. Brooks and my Wife. A pleasant day enough. Afterwards I went home and read a little of Spanish and Italian as usual. Evening quiet at home. Read to my Wife from the Appendix to Croker's Boswell.[3]

[1] A swindle.

[2] LCA to CFA, 17 March (Adams Papers). Her hope to return to Quincy in early April had given way to a new date in early May.

[3] To the text of *The Life of Samuel Johnson* which John Wilson Croker had edited (5 vols., London, 1831), he had added in vol. 5 a General Appendix consisting of a miscellany of Johnsoniana including recollections of Dr. Johnson by Miss Reynolds, a selection of letters and prayers of Johnson, a collection of anecdotes, &c.

FRIDAY. 23D.

Pleasant day, not so cold as it has been. I read two hundred and odd lines of Virgil's sixth Book of the Æneid before going out and hoped it was a sign of improvement for the future. Finished Gibbon's seventh volume at the Office which was also quite a gain. I again remained at my Office all day for the purpose of seeing my Tenant and he did not come. I lost my walk thereby and did not feel so well for it.

Afternoon I progressed very successfully in Spanish, and pretty well in Italian. I think I shall succeed in acquiring both languages. My Afternoon's are thus pretty fully taken up, yet I cannot help recollecting my Grandfathers injunction to me, "studium sine calamo sommium."[1] I am doing nothing for my reputation.

We went in the Evening to a party at Mrs. A. Thorndike's.[2] Small but very pleasant. I have no great taste for such things now, but my neglect of them has had the effect of making me a stranger in my native town. This will not do. Returned before Midnight. Omitted Paley.

[1] Although it is not known precisely when JA enjoined CFA to record what he learned or suffer it to be lost altogether, JA did use the same quotation in a letter to CFA's brothers as they were about to leave Boston to join their parents in England (JA to GWA and JA2, 3 May 1815, Adams Papers. The sentence is quoted in its full context in L. H. Butterfield, "The Papers of the

Adams Family: Some Account of Their History" in MHS, *Procs.*, 71 [1953–1957]:334).

[2] The Augustus Thorndikes lived at 1 Otis Place (*Boston Directory*, 1832–1833).

SATURDAY. 24TH.

Beautiful morning. I went to the Office after reading a considerable portion of Virgil's beautiful sixth book of the Æneid. This on the whole is I think the masterpiece. The imagination, the description the versification combine wonderfully. My time at the Office was somewhat wasted from the want of another volume of Gibbon I had left at the House. I dawdled until I found nothing to do had brought me to my walking hour. Deacon Spear called to see me and let me know about the Farms. I find the people at Quincy have great respect of persons, but it is rather Reversing the common apprehension of things.[1] An agreeable walk.

Afternoon, reading the Moorish Letters in Spanish, and the Peruvian Letters in Italian, a translation of Mad. de Grafigny's work.[2] I think I make progress in both.

Quiet Evening. Read a few anecdotes of Johnson. After which my usual work upon the French Revolution. My mind is quite enlightened on this subject since I began. I do not realize my progress in knowledge.

[1] CFA's meaning would be clearer if following the comma he had written, "and this rather reverses what is commonly thought to be characteristic of small-town social attitudes."

[2] Françoise d'Issembourg de Happoncourt de Grafigny, *Lettere d'una Peru-viana, tradotte dal francese . . . , da G. L. Deodati*, Avignon, 1817. The copy at MQA bears the notation in CFA's hand: "Finished reading this book—the first Italian I ever attempted. April 25, 1832."

SUNDAY. 25TH.

Another fine day. Attended Divine Service and heard Mr. Bulfinch[1] preach Sermon taken from 2. Timothy 4. 6, 7, 8. "For I am now ready to be offered, and the time of my departure is at hand. I have fought a good fight, I have finished my course, I have kept the faith: Henceforth there is laid up for me a crown of righteousness." It was upon the truth of the Christian Religion, drawn from the character of Paul. The substance of the whole, a repetition of the old argument, that it was more difficult to disbelieve the evidence of his disinterestedness, than to assume it. A pretty ordinary production, I thought.

Mr. Frothingham's Sermon in the Afternoon was from 2. Timothy 3. 15. "That from a child thou hast known the Scriptures which are able to make thee wise unto salvation." This of course he said referred to the Old Testament. He proceeded to illustrate the value of the reading the Bible as a whole. He considered it beneficial in three points of view. 1. As it expresses more forcibly the divine Commandments 2. As it proposes bright examples for imitation 3. As it sets forth a clear promise of reward in a future state. A sensible Sermon.

I read Massillon in the Afternoon. The Text cited was from 4 John 5 "Then cometh he to a City of Samaria which is called Sychar," but the subject in fact extended to the whole story of the Samaritan Woman. From her replies to the various inquiries of Jesus, the Preacher draws several moral reflections. He considers the obstacles to the operation of divine grace to be fairly represented by them. They form excuses of these kinds. 1. Excuses of condition. That is that Persons are not in a state fit for grace, as the Samaritan Woman pleaded her being of a different Community. 2. Excuses of difficulty or want of means as she objected the depth of the well. 3. Excuses of confusion, in other words, that from the endless jarrings of sects and doctrines it was not of any use to attempt to follow the subject. This gives a singular view of that passage in the Bible, and as I said of that last Sunday, to me not a natural one. The Woman appears to have been ignorant and sinful, but there is no evidence that she intended to resist the effort of divine grace to save her. She meets an unknown person at a well. That person is of a Sect who refuse all connection with her own, and she naturally wonders at the unusual advance. It is not until the third question is put and he tells her of what was known only to herself, that she can form any idea of the character of the person addressing her. And she then declares it. All this is simple enough. It is just the natural working of a common mind. There seems no intentional resistance of grace about it. And the whole of the preacher's ingenious edifice falls to the ground. Apart from the Text and its application however, the moral of the Sermon is very well. Quiet evening at home.

¹ Perhaps Stephen Greenleaf Bulfinch, who had graduated in divinity in 1830 (*Harvard Quinquennial Cat.*).

MONDAY. 26TH.

I received this morning upon reaching the Office, definitive letters as to the settlement of my Uncle's landed property, and the other business relating to the Will of John Adams.¹ I called upon Judge Leland and conversed with him upon the subject. After obtaining his ideas about it, I returned and wrote the necessary Papers.² My principal anxiety is to release my father from the great burden of debt he has laid upon himself, as soon as possible. I talked with Mr. Brooks about the propriety of taking legal possession, but he seemed to think peaceable possession would do as well. I was engaged most of the Afternoon in writing and copying Letters to Mrs. Angier[3] and to J. M. Gourgas.[4] This with a little Spanish took my whole time.

Evening. Began reading aloud to my Wife Bulwer's last Novel of Eugene Aram.[5] A wild thing taken from the shocking story which cuts such a figure in the Newgate Calendar. I do not admire these kind of things. Afterwards, I finished Bell's Account of the French Revolution which is a mere compilation.[6]

[1] JQA to CFA, 21 March (Adams Papers). In this JQA essentially confirmed his earlier instructions given in his letters of 5 and 17 March, on which see entry for 13 March, above.

[2] CFA consulted the judge of probate in Norfolk co., Sherman Leland of Roxbury, primarily on the question of guardianship for the minor children. Judge Leland, though inclined not to favor the appointment of widows as guardians, agreed to appoint Mrs. Adams if she should wish it. It was also his opinion that the portions of the minor children, now vested in them, should be paid to their guardian at once or that notes should be executed in their favor with interest paid to the guardian. CFA to JQA, 27 March (LbC, Adams Papers); *Mass. Register*, 1832.

[3] In his note to his cousin, Abigail Angier, CFA wrote that her portion of TBA's devise from JA, with interest from the date of TBA's death, was ready to be paid upon demand. In the course of the next several days she and Thomas B. Adams Jr. were paid the sums due them. CFA to Abigail A. Angier, 26 March; CFA to JQA, 31 March (both

LbC's, Adams Papers); M/CFA/3.

[4] CFA notified Gourgas, who had qualified as administrator of TBA's estate, that it was JQA's intent to take possession of the real property under his mortgages "by regular legal process if necessary, or by a mere notice to the Tenants and pacific entry with your Consent as Administrator"; further that JQA proposed to pay all rents derived from the properties to Mrs. Adams during her lifetime, deducting only the expenses incurred. The letter also carried notice of the necessity for Mrs. Adams to become guardian for her minor children or to nominate someone to serve. CFA to J. M. Gourgas, 26 March (LbC, Adams Papers).

When Mrs. Adams' decision was reached it was that Phineas Foster, her brother-in-law, should become guardian for the children, provided JQA did not wish to serve. Foster's appointment was subsequently confirmed. CFA to JQA, 31 March (LbC, Adams Papers); M/CFA/3.

[5] Published in 3 vols., London, 1832.

[6] John Bell, *History of the First Revolution in France*, London, 1831.

TUESDAY. 27TH.

Fine morning but somewhat colder than it has been. I read a part of the seventh book of the Æneid before going to the Office, where I was occupied in writing a letter to my Father,[1] giving him the necessary information as to my progress in the affair of the Judge's Estates and the settlement of the whole matter. I then went to the Athenæum and from there took a walk, the wind blowing very violently made it not so agreeable.

In the Afternoon. After copying my letter, I devoted an hour each to the two languages. Received the unwelcome intelligence that

Graves had run off, without giving me any notice, leaving the House empty and his partners in a pretty rascally manner.[2] I never thought much of that fellow. My next business is to let the House again, and fortunately for me there seems to be some demand.

In the evening, there was a family meeting at Gorham's,[3] where we had a more than usually pleasant time. All parties appeared in a humour to be suited which is not invariably the case. We returned at ten. I read more of Napoleon.

[1] LbC, Adams Papers.
[2] In Sept. 1831 P. Graves had succeeded Joseph Libby as the tenant of tenement No. 3 at 101 Tremont Street (M/CFA/3).
[3] At 8 Somerset Street; see above, entry for 25 Nov. 1831.

WEDNESDAY. 28TH.

Morning cool but clear. I went to the Office after my progress in Virgil which has now become so regular that I shall omit noticing it every day. My time was taken up with affairs. Let my House again at an advanced rent[1] so that it is an ill wind that blows no good. A proverb embodying as much truth as any of them. I read a little of Gibbon but was interrupted by Mr. Gourgas from Quincy who came upon the subject of my letter. He talked and the result of it was that I was very little pleased with the tone of the family. If I was the manager of these concerns, they should have Justice and nothing more. I did not take any walk today.

Afternoon. Mr. Brooks having dined here and taking up a considerable time, I passed the rest in my pursuit of Spanish and Italian. This last is coming easier to me. I read two or three pages without difficulty. I shall have made no trifling acquisition if I can succeed in mastering these two languages. Indeed I consider myself already as knowing Spanish pretty well.

Evening, continued reading aloud Eugene Aram. Bulwer has a great deal of talent, but he is extravagant, and frequently takes for sublime what is only unnatural. I made some progress in the Life of Napoleon, and read a little of Paley's Evidences of Christianity. A little of this kind of study is always beneficial. And this is a simple exposition which puts to the rout, all Gibbon's insidious deductions and miserable sarcasms.

[1] E. A. Hovey was the new occupant of the tenement vacated by Graves the day before; the new rent was set at $140 a year, an advance of $8 (M/CFA/3).

THURSDAY. 29TH.

Cold chilly morning with occasional snow falling lightly to remind us that Winter was not yet distant from us. I read a quantity of Virgil pleasantly and at the Office was busy in making out my Quarterly Account for the close of the week. It is long and requires a little explanation. Took a walk, and in the course of it, went to examine the condition of the vacated House. Found it better than I had anticipated. On my return home I found Mrs. Angier from Medford. She talked a little with me and received a draught of a receipt for her to sign previous to her taking the legacy due to her. She also talked of other affairs from all which I gained important information.

My Afternoon passed in my usual studies. In the evening we went to a Ball given by Mrs. Charles Thorndike. It was to the Bride.[1] The company was small but I enjoyed myself at it, full as much as one can at any of these things. The course of life however warns me that I am not in the front rank. The day is past when I was welcome to the un-married ladies. Home early.

[1] The home of the Charles Thorndikes was at 5 Otis Place. The ball, like the recent party given by Mrs. Augustus Thorndike (see above, entry for 23 March), was doubtless in honor of the former Ann T. Dickey of New York, who in January became the second wife of the Thorndikes' brother, Israel T. Thorndike Jr. When her engagement to Mr. Thorndike was announced CFA had written that she is "about the age of his eldest daughter, Miss Sally Ann." CFA to LCA, 5 Nov. 1831 (Adams Papers); *NEHGR*, 13:94; *Boston Daily Advertiser & Patriot*, 28 Jan., p. 3, col. 2; *Boston Directory*, 1832–1833.

FRIDAY. 30TH.

Morning cool but pleasant. I went to the Office as usual. Employed in my Accounts which I finished drawing up. They are on the whole favourable not containing any loss excepting this last one of Graves' which is a bad business. I suppose it is not the fate of any one to steer totally clear of loss of some kind or other. The only thing [is][1] to make them as few as possible. I have done my best and suppose that I have only my share. I did not get a chance to read much. Took a walk with Mr. Peabody. Afternoon, read a little of Spanish and Italian. The latter is on the whole, I think the easiest, or else I have an easier work to begin with. The Peruvian letters are french love letters. No Indians ever had any idea of such things. Evening, reading Eugene Aram and the life of Napoleon.

[1] Word omitted in MS.

SATURDAY 31ST.

I was very busy after I reached the Office today. I went over the Account which was already drawn up and after proving it's correctness, drew up an explanatory letter to my father.[1] I recommended to him his future measures also, by which he might relieve himself of all further responsibility as it related to the legacy of the children. I do not know whether he will pursue my suggestions, but it seems to me that if he does, he may see light through his engagements, before long. If on the other hand, he should not he will only plunge himself deeper and deeper every moment. For he seems to have lost most of his interest in the management of Property. I waited at the Office until two o'clock for Mr. Angier to come and get his Money but he did not appear. The day was warm but blustering.

Afternoon. Copied my letter to my Father and settled with Mr. Angier by Checks which I drew for Monday. He remained half an hour in a matter that required only a few minutes. I felt the want of exercise so much that I consumed the rest of the Afternoon in a walk. Evening at home. Read Eugene Aram.

[1] LbC, Adams Papers. On this letter see further, entries for 13 and 26 March, above.

SUNDAY. APRIL 1ST.

An excessively gusty day with a few drops of rain in the afternoon, but on the whole clear. I attended Divine Service all day and heard Mr. Frothingham preach, though with not much benefit to myself I regret to say. The Texts were from 12. Jeremiah 5 "If thou hast run with the footmen, and they have wearied thee, then how canst thou contend with horses? and if in the land of peace, wherein thou trustedst, they wearied thee, then how wilt thou do in the swelling of Jordan," and from 9 Matth. 13. "Go ye and learn what that meaneth, I will have mercy and not sacrifice." I am ashamed to admit that I can do nothing in the way of analysis of the Sermons.

Afterwards I read one of Massillon's Sermons and as I thought a very good one upon Charity. Text 6. John 11. "And Jesus took the loaves: and when he had given thanks he distributed to the disciples and the disciples to them that were set down." He considers the Chapter from which this is drawn as embodying the common excuses made against Charity. 1. The deficiency of means, and the demands of necessity. 2. the poverty of the times. 3. the multiplicity of objects. After successively confuting these, he lays down the true rules for dispensing Charity. 1. That it should be secret. 2. That it should be general. 3 Done with mildness and delicacy. 4 With discrimination and vigilance. On the whole it seems to me that this Discourse contains a summary of the Doctrine and in fact exhausts the Topic. And it is the first of all those I have read by this Preacher that deserves that kind of praise.

I perfected the first volume of Scotts Napoleon and am on the whole satisfied with all the views of the Work excepting those in which Great Britain is concerned where he is altogether laudatory. This in human affairs is scarcely ever possible and the mere fact of it's happening throws suspicion upon the disposition of a Historian. I read a little of Eugene Aram to my Wife but not much. And I thought I would turn back and review the first seven Chapters of Paley.

MONDAY. 2D.

I went to the Office and passed my time rather lazily I suppose for I cannot account well for it. My Accounts however at the commencement of a Quarter always consume a great deal of time. I have so many branches and they extend into so many minute subdivisions that they run away with the hours. Perhaps it would be better for me if it was simplified but from some cause or other, I can not. It is as much as I can do if I keep a clear look out ahead, taking care above all things not to embarrass myself. This becomes every day more difficult. Demands for additional expense press upon me with unusual force. And I am only clear from the corresponding improvement of my Revenue. How long will this last? I hope, some time. Afternoon I went to a meeting of Directors of the Boylston Market but there was no Quorum so that I returned home and accomplished a little Spanish. Evening. Read a little of Eugene Aram to my Wife.

TUESDAY. 3D.

The days are generally clear but the air is extraordinarily cold still. We have as yet little that could be called pleasant weather. I went in a driving snow storm today to the South part of the town to collect Dividends for my Father and self, and I accomplished in the course of the morning, the collection of a considerable sum. But I was disappointed in the amount to be received. Insurance Stock is treacherous this year. My time at the Office was taken up very much in drawing up Accounts and balancing books. As to reading it seems to be totally laid aside. Nothing else of interest occurred. Afternoon quietly at home. I devoted my time to the Spanish and Italian as usual. Hours passed in so regular and unimportant a round of study can have little interest to any one. Evening at home as usual. Completed some Chapters of Eugene Aram.

WEDNESDAY 4TH.

Clear and cold. At the Office as usual and busy collecting more Money. The whole does not make up what I want. But we push along by all kinds of contrivances. I paid some Accounts and passed my whole Morning in such things. Am now in Treaty for a Horse and Chaise with Mr. Forbes, this involves a considerable outlay and a little risk. But my expense on this Account has been so great in past years that I think I shall in the end save money by it. My system has been heretofore of great caution, and I have done well by it. I hope that no change will take place in my character with the improvement of my fortune.

On returning home, found that I. H. Adams had gone to Quincy and I was quite surprised at the difference his absence seemed to make.[1] He says little, but there is something in the presence of a human being which you don't understand either when one is with you, or when you never have it, but which becomes perceptible when one to whom you have become accustomed leaves you. I read Spanish and Italian as usual. In the evening, to my Wife, Eugene Aram.

[1] See above, entry for 7 March.

THURSDAY. 5TH.

This was the day appointed according to custom for the keeping a general fast. A practice now somewhat nominal as the prosperity of the Country has been such that it is very unnecessary. The Clouds that seem now to be rapidly gathering over the political horizon may alter the case considerably.

I attended Divine Service in the morning and heard though I gathered little or nothing from a Sermon by Mr. Frothingham on repentance. Acts 3. 19. "Repent ye therefore and be converted." My attention is a capricious thing. It will not stick by a Speaker or a book unless constantly forced. I am training myself more and more but yet do not accomplish the whole.

I did intend to go again in the Afternoon but was caught by a Nap until over the hour. Read a considerable part of the North American Review for April which is unusually dull. Evening quietly at home.

FRIDAY. 6TH.

The days are clear but exceedingly cold for the Season. The quantity of ice made at the North chills us through whenever the wind is from that Quarter. I went to the Office and was occupied all my time in making Leases, drawing Accounts and a Writ against the Graves's. This to be effectual ought to have been done at first. Now I expect very little from it. Finished my bargain for my Horse and Chaise which I think on the whole a pretty fair one for the other party. Took a walk with Mr. Peabody.

Afternoon Rode to Quincy. Called at the House and arranged with Carr, the Tenant, then went to Mrs. Adams'. Transacted the little business I had up there. Conversed with her upon various matters relating to herself. And returned to town in time for rather a late Tea. Then went with my Wife and I. Hull, who came back today, to Mrs. Frothingham's to hear the Church Choir perform some of their Music. They did a great deal better today. And some two or three pieces I was charmed with. But the voices are not good. Returned home early, but being fatigued omitted all but the Spectator.

SATURDAY. 7TH.

Fine morning. Engaged at my Office in writing my Diary which has fallen behind hand and finishing the Draughts of Leases which I had made for Quincy. At Noon I attended a Stock Sale but purchased nothing. I afterwards made a Contract however with Mr. Brooks who had more than he wanted, for some Shares in the Union Bank for T. B. Adams. This purchase strips me of every thing I have in every capacity. But it is an object to get through with the business of discharging those children [1] at all events. I took a walk as usual.

In the afternoon I read my usual quantities of Spanish and Italian. But wasted the Evening excepting that I resumed the reading of the Bible to my Wife which had been some time interrupted. Received this morning a short but kind letter from my father.[2] Nothing else material.

[1] That is, the claims of TBA's children.
[2] 30 March (Adams Papers). For the letter see entry for 13 March, above.

SUNDAY 8TH.

The cold keeps on and renders us all very uncomfortable. I read this morning the numbers of the Society of Useful Knowledge on Planting.[1] They are valuable Treatises although they want an elementary fare to be extensively beneficial. I had some idea of writing upon the subject. Attended divine Service and heard Mr. Newell of Cambridge preach. His Text in the morning was *I think*, Deuteronomy 4. 9, but I am not sure, so will not quote it. The afternoon's was stated to be from 2 Chronicles 20. 11 but I could not find it there. His productions were both of them pretty ambitious ones upon self review. But I think I have stated before that he is not a favourite in my mind, and I find no reason now to alter my opinion. The duty of the Clergy is an arduous one and they should not be harshly criticized, but the duty of the listener is also arduous, sometimes, and he must sometimes be excused.

For the first time for a month my head was not in order from indigestion and it as usual discomposed me. I read twice over however a Sermon of Massillon's upon Slander. His text from John 2. 24. "But Jesus did not commit himself to them because he knew all men." He divided the Apologies for Slander into three heads. 1. That they are about trifles. 2. That the reports are general. 3. Drawn from the Zeal for the faith. This was another valuable Sermon because it is drawn from an insight into human nature and calculated for good practical benefit. Quiet Evening. Went to bed early on account of my head.

¹ *Useful and Ornamental Planting*, London, 1832, was a recent issue in the Farmers' Series of the *Library of Useful Knowledge* published by the Society for the Diffusion of Useful Knowledge, London.

MONDAY 9TH.

Morning clear as usual but cold. I made great progress in Virgil, concluding the tenth book. There is a charm about his Poetry which I never felt before, a pathos in the expressions and a polish in the thought which is passed over by boys always with no more feeling than if it was not there. It is a great mistake I think to submit such things to be hammered over in such a way until return to them at a future moment is disgusting from the Associations it brings up.

At the Office. Did very little. Paid for Stock. Drew the remainder of my Dividends, and before I went to dinner, having settled with Farrar, I found myself more totally denuded of money than I ever recollect being since I have had the care of any.

Returned home and passed the Afternoon in my usual studies which went on very easy. A person called with a request from Miss Longhurst which I propose answering tomorrow. Quiet evening at home. I omitted reading Paley.

TUESDAY. 10TH.

This is the first day upon which we have felt any thing like pleasant weather. I accomplished a good deal of the Æneid before going to the Office. But performed little more there than I usually do. Had a visit or two from Quincy people with whom I talked considerably. They let me into the state of feeling in the upper part of Quincy. These Country towns are shocking places for men reputed to possess property. If they do not allow themselves to be mangled and mauled to the satisfaction of every man who calls himself poor, the cry against him is that he is hard. My father in the mean time is sucked dry by a parcel of hangers on, who see how things go and wink at it all.

I went in the Afternoon to Quincy, saw the proceedings of the man who has gone there to work, examined the young trees in the Nursery, which I find very much injured by the field mice, and directed what was next to be done. Then went and gave the painter some directions about painting and to Mrs. Adams' where after remaining a few minutes we returned to town. By we, I mean I. Hull and I, for he accompanied me.

Evening quietly at home, where I read the account of Eugene Aram and his trial in the Newgate Calendar.[1] Afterwards Mr. Brooks came in and sat a little while. These expeditions to Quincy ought to be trifling and yet they are fatiguing. Read a little of Bonaparte and Paley.

[1] Bulwer-Lytton's novel was based upon the actual case of Eugene Aram, schoolmaster, who was tried and executed for murder in 1759.

WEDNESDAY. 11TH.

Morning mild but wet. I omitted reading Virgil being occupied in the studies of I. H. Adams, who is preparing to go to West Point. This attention will be beneficial to myself who neglected these pursuits when in College. I have improved in Geometry and Arithmetic since attending to him.

At the Office. Busy in accounts and the usual etceteras so that I did nothing else. Took a walk, but I am so anxious for the reception of some Money at present that I do not like to be long absent from the Office. I have drained myself so greatly that I want to get out of the risk of any demand which might embarrass me.

Afternoon, quietly at home. Continued my French and Spanish reading. And I find I understand the languages sufficiently to take some interest in the Stories. Evening quiet at home. I read to my Wife a little of the Newgate Calendar, but it is a disgusting book. The monotony of Crime is painful. Pursued Napoleon and read the Guardian, but omitted the Spectator.

THURSDAY. 12TH.

A beautiful day. After reading a considerable extract from Virgil

I went to the Office and was engaged as usual in reading Newspapers and writing Journal, with Accounts. This took up much time, which together with a walk to the Athenæum, a short lounge and temptation at the sale of Mr. Eliot's books,[1] and a walk with Mr. Peabody consumed the rest of my time.

Afternoon, I went to Quincy. Isaac Hull accompanying me. Found Mills the Painter at work busily and he informed me that he must have Vezey with him so I went up immediately for Vezey. Called in on the way to see Mr. Brigham and make some inquiry about the Canal. I found this year it paid for two years upon it's Notes, so that I was quite satisfied. On the whole the present prospect of things is tolerably favourable. I hope to be able this year to bring up a considerable arrear into which my father's affairs have fallen. But it is impossible to say how this will be, until I can see through the next Month. I gave orders about the grounds and the work to be done about the House — Returning home by seven.

We had the last family assemblage for the Season this year at our house. All present but P. C. Brooks Jr. and his Wife. It was on the whole pleasant, although I felt heated and tired. They all went at ten and I afterwards finished the Guardian, being the third in the series of Essayists.

[1] The books belonging to the late William H. Eliot were being sold at Cunningham's Auction Rooms in two sessions, 11 and 12 April (*Boston Daily Advertiser & Patriot,* 11 April, p. 3, col. 5).

FRIDAY. 13TH.

A very lovely day. I went to the Office after making some progress in the reading of Virgil though not so much as I wished. I did hope to finish Virgil this week. My day was somewhat wasted. The weather was so fine I could not make up my mind to remaining at the Office. Received an urgent letter from my father inviting my Wife and myself to spend the Summer with them. I suppose I must accede to it. If it was not for the inconvenience that it puts us to I should like it very much.[1] Spent an hour with Mr. Davis in which we had very pleasant literary Conversation. His mind is unusually cultivated. Took a walk, but the heat of the Sun was absolutely oppressive.

Afternoon. Read as usual but found my Spanish uncommonly hard. My only purchase yesterday was of a copy of Vasari's Works which I consider a great bargain.[2] But the consumption of money in these cases is quite prodigious.

Evening quiet at home. I read a little of the introduction to the first volume of Vasari. My Wife was out. Afterwards, I was interested in the account of the disastrous expedition to Russia in 1812. And the Rambler.

¹ "[Y]ou are necessaries of life to us, during the summer.... It is my ardent wish to devote the ensuing Summer to the memory of my father, and if I am permitted so to do, I shall want your assistance more than ever. I depend upon you for aid in my labours and for company in my Solitude.... [Y]our wife will be as necessary to the happiness of your mother, as you will be to mine" (JQA to CFA, 10 April, Adams Papers).

² The handsome set of Giorgio Vasari's *Vite de' più eccelenti pittori scultori e architetti,* 16 vols., Milan, 1807–1811, now at MQA, has CFA's bookplate pasted partially over the bookplate of William H. Eliot.

SATURDAY 14TH.

The weather cannot last fine a great while at this Season. The Wind was Easterly today and of course unpleasant. After reading Virgil, I went to the Office. My whole disposable time was taken up in writing a letter to my father.¹ This was hardly accomplished before two. The reason of this is that I had a long interruption in the shape of a woman who looked fond of the bottle and certainly talked to match her look. She was a kind of beggar. But I got along with her quite easy. My only loss was my time.² Deacon Spear also called and talked but I got no Money. I have never known a Season when this Article came in so sparingly.

Afternoon quietly at home. I read a little Spanish, but the largest portion of my time was devoted to transcribing my letter and accompanying it with the necessary papers. I was ashamed of it as a composition, yet was glad enough to get it finished at all. Evening short and quiet at home. I felt indolent. Mr. Nathl. Hall paid a short visit here. He is one of the perfectibilian tribe.

¹ LbC in Adams Papers.
² CFA recounted the visit at greater length in his letter to JQA, above: "Distinguished public characters reflect a little of their lustre upon persons nearly related to them in such a manner as those persons do not sometimes altogether relish. It is now an hour since I began writing to you, during which period my name is responsible for a shocking bore inflicted upon me in the shape of a tipsy woman by name Armstrong, who has been dilating upon all manner of things and sure all the time that if you was only here you would sustain all she says."

SUNDAY. 15TH.

Raw and cloudy with Wind still East. Passed the morning in finishing the Æneid with which I have been very much pleased. The thing seems to me to be an honour to the human intellect for imagination, for pathos, for perfect harmony, for beauty. And there is moral in it so far as the Ancients allowed themselves to have moral.

I attended Divine Service all day. Heard Mr. Frothingham preach. His Text, "Isaiah 21. 11–12. "He calleth to me out of Seir. Watchman, what of the night? Watchman, what of the night? The watchman saith, the morning cometh, and also the night: if ye will inquire, inquire ye: return, come." He explained in the first place the literal meaning of the Text. And then applied the words to the present state of things, to the future, and to the chance of death. The Sermon was admired but it did not strike me. His afternoon's discourse was much more simple, Nehemiah 9. 6. "Thou hast made heaven, the heaven of heavens with all their hosts, the earth and all things that are therein, the seas, and all that is therein, and thou preservest them all." It turned upon the attribute of God as a Creator, the doubt that had been early expressed by a particular sect of his having to do with so corrupt a thing as matter, and the belief drawn from phrases of the New Testament that the Saviour was the Creator of all things. He inclined to the construction of the *spiritual* creation of all things. It was useful but dry.

Read a Sermon of Massillon upon Scepticism, John 7. 27. "Howbeit we know this man whence he is: but when Christ cometh, no man knoweth, whence he is." Turning off from the discussion of the main question as to the truth of the religion, he considered only the motives for doubt of it in many cases. 1. Dissoluteness which resorts to disbelief as a protection. 2. Ignorance of a wilful kind. 3. Vanity of knowledge. He treats of them successively with great power. Evening quiet at home.

MONDAY 16TH.

Very cold disagreeable morning. Transferred for the present the Italian to be my morning study. Read a little of the Peruvian Letters which are very easy. Time at the Office variously spent. I was busy in collecting seeds for the Garden at Quincy, and other purchases which with the never failing business of accounts consumed the time. Found Joseph H. Adams had been at my House. He is ordered off and is preparing to start. I intended to have gone to Quincy but the setting in of the rain just as I was about to start prevented me.

Passed my Afternoon in reading the Moorish Letters. They contain a great deal of good sense. I know nothing of their Author however. The dearth of books relating to Spanish literature, speaking historically, is great with me, and I may also add with my father.

Quiet Evening at home. Did nothing—on the whole what a mass of my time is profitless. Read an excellent number of the Rambler on that point, this evening.

TUESDAY. 17TH.

Heavy rain with a high Wind from the Eastward. This will obviate the difficulty about vegetation but it is unpleasant enough in all conscience to the feelings. My mornings work has shortened since the dark weather. I read a little Italian and went to the Office. Had time to go over a little of Gibbon so that my account of my morning did not seem quite so blank. The weather did not admit of my going to walk.

Afternoon quiet at home. Occupied in attending to the Mathematics with Hull. I find I can learn something. My studies of this Science have always been exceedingly superficial. Read a good deal of the Moorish letters the end of which I am at last approaching.

Evening dull, doing nothing. I do not much admire this plan. Continued the wonderful Romance of Napoleon's history and was a little displeased with Scott's evident partiality. I also read Paley.

WEDNESDAY 18TH.

Heavy rain with more Wind. I read a little of the Peruvian Letters. Went to the Office, and from thence to the Athenæum where I lounged an hour without any profit. Returned and devoted a short time to Gibbon. Interrupted in this by a visit from my good friend Mrs. Armstrong whose face I never expected to see again. And indeed I can scarcely say I wanted to. My progress in Gibbon is slow but I hope to be able to persevere in finishing it.

Mr. Brooks dined with us. Not much to be obtained from dinners where the parties are dull. I felt but little disposed to make exertion and he seemed not very lively. Afternoon short, filled up with reading Spanish as I have transferred my Italian to the morning. I find the latter on the whole much the easiest language of the two. It is not filled with so many strongly idiomatic expressions and I think the Dictionary I have is better. But in this I think that there is great room for improvement.

Evening quiet at home. I read a few Chapters in the Bible to my Wife, an exercise designed to be regular, but from some reason or other often omitted. Finished the first division of Paley's work upon Christianity. It is remarkable for perspicuity and logic.

I have felt today a little depression of spirits. Now and then I am subject to them a little. They always show themselves in a kind of regret that I am not making the most of my time and abilities. Yet I have no opportunities. I know I ought to seek them. Have I not? When I reflect how much I am favoured in my situation I know I ought not to allow myself to repine, but I trust it is only from anxiety to support a mighty responsibility to my name, and therefore may be forgiven.

THURSDAY. 19TH.

Another cold and cloudy disagreeable day. Our bad weather all comes at once. I read a little Italian. Then to the Office. Time variously occupied. Read a little of Gibbon however. Had a long conversation with Mr. Peabody and afterwards a walk. One interruption from Mrs. Armstrong in the morning and three in the Afternoon. She is a very great nuisance. Finished reading the Moorish Letters of Cadalso. He is, I find, one of the Classical writers of Spain. I think his book a pretty trifle enough. I afterwards read the first Chapter of Mariana's History of Spain.[1] I doubt whether I shall have the vigour to go on with it. He begins with the Deluge. Read Mr. Everett's Memorial in favour of the restriction party. It seems to me very good. Though it is not entirely to my satisfaction. His strictures upon Mr. Gallatin are not agreeable to me. I am no friend of this gentleman, but I hate base measures.[2] Went to a party at Mrs. Frothingham's in the evening. Felt a little dull but on the whole got through it well. Read only the Rambler.

[1] There are two copies of *Histoire generale d'Espagne* by Jean de Mariana at MQA, one of the edition in 9 vols., Paris, 1723, the other of that in 5 vols., Paris, 1725. Both bear JQA's bookplate.

[2] On 26 March the Speaker conveyed to the House of Representatives and the Vice-President to the Senate "The memorial of a convention of Friends of domestic industry assembled at New York on 25 Oct. last," which was signed by A. H. Everett as chairman and dated Boston, 19 March 1832. Copies were ordered printed and became available on 4 April (Edward Everett to A. H. Everett, 23, 26 March; 4 April, Everett MSS, MHi).

The memorial was intended as a definitive statement of the protectionist or restrictionist position on the tariff and as a reply to the memorial of the Free Trade Convention in Philadelphia written by Albert Gallatin (see above, entry for 20 Feb., note). Like Clay's reply to Gallatin, but in a more veiled manner, the memorial attacked the "foreign origin" of the anti-protectionist ideas and alluded to the interests of "the Swiss manufacturer" being served by it (*Memorial ... of Friends of Domestic Industry* [Washington, 1832], p. 9; HA, *Gallatin*, p. 641).

FRIDAY. 20TH.

It is now one week that we have had very bad weather all the time. The rain of today was again mingled with snow and the whole appeared cheerless enough. I read some Italian and went to the Office, from thence to the Athenæum where I lounged an hour out of the reach of Mrs. Armstrong. But my time was a good deal wasted. I also managed to accomplish a little more of Gibbon. What a dreary waste, the history of the middle ages. Religion mystified,[1] morality forgotten, murder and robbery stalking over the earth, it seems as if all the elements of the social system had been separated and thrown aside. Nothing else material.

Afternoon, began reading Sismondi's History of the French.[2] I have some idea of writing something upon it. It takes up the same wretched period which I have just passed through in Gibbon.

Evening. Went to the Theatre and heard Mr. Sinclair and Miss Hughes in Cinderella.[3] They jointly make a pretty interesting entertainment. But the latter is not nearly equal in point of power to Mrs. Austin. She has a voice of a lower tone but does not seem to sing with so much ease to herself. He seems to have no middle key in his voice. He runs from a low one directly into a high one without being able to command any variety of tones. Yet his training is pleasant. I accompanied Mrs. Frothingham, her Children and my Wife. On the whole I was pleased. Returned rather late. Read only the Rambler.

[1] That is, made into a mystery.

[2] Jean Charles Léonard Simonde de Sismondi, *Histoire des Français*. The edition owned by CFA and now at MQA was that published at Paris, 1821–1844, in 31 volumes. The period up to the 15th century is treated in the first 12 volumes.

[3] The performance of *Cinderella* (*Cenerentola*) was the 28th of that opera in Boston and the final one of the engagement of Elizabeth Hughes and John Sinclair at the Tremont Theatre (*Boston Daily Advertiser & Patriot*, 20 April, p. 3, col. 4; on Miss Hughes and Mr. Sinclair, see Odell, *Annals N.Y. Stage*, 3:545–560 *passim*).

SATURDAY. 21ST.

The morning was cloudy but it cleared away in the course of the day. The wind being West for a short time but in general more to the Eastward. I occupied myself for a short time in Italian and then began upon a new undertaking, which is a regular Catalogue of my Library or rather the books under my care.[1] This is a thing I have been in considerable want of for some time past, and I think I can make it without very seriously interrupting any of my more valuable occupations.

At the Office. Read a little of Gibbon but far the greater part of my time was expended in a ramble with Mr. Peabody whereby I lost the presence of a Tenant at Quincy, Field, and as usual I had a fit of repentance.

Returned home and after dinner went to Quincy, accompanied by Isaac Hull. After arranging with Mr. Brigham and receiving from him the amount due upon the Canal Notes I went to the House and was busy there until the time to return. Reached home late and fatigued. Read only the Rambler with a little of Walter Scott.

¹ Doubtless the catalogue was another effort to preserve the identity of the books formerly owned by GWA which after his death became JQA's but remained in Boston for CFA's use. See vol. 3:325.

SUNDAY. 22D.

Clear but cold. After passing the morning hours in reading the Life of Napoleon, and doing something towards my library Catalogue I attended divine Service and heard Mr. Frothingham in the morning, Mr. Gannett in the Afternoon. Both upon the Resurrection of our Saviour—It being Easter Sunday. Mr. F's Text was from Luke 24. 5–6. "Why seek ye the living among the dead? He is not here, but is risen." It was upon the custom of reverting to the period of death without any practical purpose to the living but I must admit that as usual it quite escaped me. I cannot do any justice to it in an analysis. Mr. Gannett gave from Acts 2. 24. a short and well combined narrative of the facts attending the resurrection after which he drew an application to the immortality of the soul, not from the mere fact which he seemed to think insufficient but from encouragement it held out to faith. His manner is exceedingly unpleasant, and his style is a little too ambitious for his own power to display it. But I thought his Sermon in itself interesting.

Read one of Massillon's afterward, upon the Injustice of the world to the character of good men. Text, John 9. 24. "Then again called they the man that was blind, and said unto him, "Give God the praise: we know that this man is a sinner." His division was 1. That it was great rashness to ascribe bad motives where good ones could be inferred fairly. 2. That it was inhumanity, for even we ourselves might need the shelter of the virtuous. 3. It was impiety as discouraging from all hope or practice in religion. I thought this was the third good practical Sermon in succession in Massillon.

Evening quiet at home. I continued reading the Life of Napoleon which grows more English every day. This evening I resumed my reading of Paley with the second part.

MONDAY. 23D.

Morning at the Office. Hard frost last night by which all the vegetation must be somewhat retarded. I finished the Peruvian letters with which I have on the whole been pleased.¹ The idea is purely French. The Peruvian is somewhat civilized and exceedingly delicate.

But the observations are frequently just and the style has much of feminine sentiment. I was pleased.

My time at the Office was taken up by Accounts. Mr. Spear called to pay me from Quincy and I was thus relieved from a great deal of the pressure which I have been experiencing. Took a short walk. Joseph H. Adams came in from Quincy today for the purpose of starting for New York upon his final expedition for some time to come in this Country I hope.[2] He goes out in the *United States*. I gave him advice, and one or two letters,[3] with money enough to go to New York. This took so much of the Afternoon, that I devoted the little balance to my Catalogue.

Evening at home. My Wife having gone out to visit with her father, I read a large quantity of the Life of Napoleon and worked on my Catalogue.

[1] See above, entry for 24 March, note.
[2] See above, entry for 6 Jan., note.
[3] CFA to Sidney Brooks; same to Capt. Isaac Chauncey, commandant of the navy yard at Brooklyn (both LbC's in Adams Papers).

TUESDAY. 24TH.

Morning clear, but the weather holds on cold. Went to the Office. But passed my time without any very clear advantage. Joseph H. Adams went off this morning. May success go with him. I have felt anxious all along for him. But now I think he is in a fair way. I. Hull remains and of him I have considerable doubt. But he seems to have the will and I hope he will acquire the power. Time taken up in Accounts.

Afternoon, went to Quincy with him. Engaged the whole afternoon in superintending the transplanting and arranging trees. I think this year and the last have done a good deal in the way of improving the old mansion. It looks more like a Gentleman's place. It has been done at some expense but on the whole pretty economically. The distribution of the money has been fully made up by the added value to the place. It had been so suffered to fall into neglect that in a few years nothing would have answered but a complete repair, which would have been equivalent to a new house. Returned to tea.

Evening at home. Mr. & Mrs. Frothingham came in and spent an hour very pleasantly. Afterwards I felt so tired and sleepy I only read the Rambler.

WEDNESDAY. 25TH.

The day was exceedingly unpleasant although considerably warmer than it has been. I read a little of the Letters of Ortiz, an Italian book that I purchased at Mr. Eliot's sale.[1] Went to the Office. Passed an hour in writing and Accounts after which I was obliged to go out in quest of Fuel for my House. This involved a walk to the Southern extreme of the town. And I consumed the whole of my time in it before dinner.

The afternoon was all taken up at the Boylston Market there being a Meeting of the Directors to consider the expediency of making certain repairs &ca. There was a vast deal of discussion but no great conclusion. And I had little or nothing to do but to keep myself warm which was not perfectly easy. Got away quite tired at six o'clock. I have no great fancy for this situation. It is one of some labour and no great ease. I mean by this that the manual labour is all required.

Evening, went to a small party at Mrs. P. C. Brooks' given to Miss Fowle. It was not very agreeable yet not absolutely stupid. Returned home but read only the Rambler.

[1] Jacob Ortiz, *Ultime Lettere,* 2 vols. in 1, London, 1817. CFA has inscribed the information relating to his acquisition of the book in the copy now at MQA.

THURSDAY. 26TH.

At last we had a day that seemed to show some signal of the season of the year. It was very dusty however and windy, so that we did not enjoy it as much as we otherwise should have done. At the Office, very closely all the morning as Field had left word he should be here from Quincy today. He was not here at all. This is just the way I have been served more than once. I must pluck up more character and go to him. Finished the eighth volume of Gibbon with a Chapter upon the Sects of the Church. A little dry & dusty. My Wife received a letter from my Mother in which she makes no mention of her being likely to come on.[1] Indeed it seems now tolerably likely that Congress will not adjourn till July.

In the afternoon I read more of Mons. Sismondi but found him exceedingly dry. He discusses the origin of the French Monarchy which seems to be lost in a mass of doubt and fable. I shall make nothing of that.

Quiet evening at home. Mr. Brooks took tea here and passed the evening. Conversation principally upon the state of public affairs. He looks to singular authority for his politics. But though we do not often travel the same road, we generally come to the same conclusions. Afterwards I finished the Life of Napoleon by Walter Scott. A work of a Scotch Jacobite, who however amiable in his private relations and his literary spirit, is altogether unsafe as a political guide.[2] Omitted Paley.

[1] Letter missing.

[2] On 27 April CFA wrote on the fly-leaf of the first volume of the copy of the work now at MQA: "This is the work of a man whose whole life has been passed with feelings of hostility to the subject of this Memoir. He is a Scotch Tory, engaged in a work of apology and Justification of his own Country. All his statements, and reasoning upon them, must therefore be considered with distrust. Not that I admire the character of Napoleon. On the contrary, whether I regard his career or the influence of his name upon the age, infinite mischief seems to have resulted from it. But in order to bring this truth more fully to the eyes of the public, a little more appearance of impartiality would be desirable."

FRIDAY. 27TH.

A lovely day. I began reading Vasari's Works this morning which I have lately purchased. The Italian of this is tolerably easy. Went to the Office but wasted my time having forgotten to bring with me the next volume of Gibbon. My progress was therefore stopped. I amused myself in looking over the old Journals of my brother George which give a kind of melancholy picture of the past to me whenever I take them up. But so it is. Our days were deceitful ones then. The adversity which we have experienced has been a very fortunate thing for me who was young enough to be able to avail of the lesson. I have never yet known any thing that has happened to me which I thought at the time a misfortune not turn out in the end a very advantageous thing. Returned to my House.

Afternoon passed in reading Sismondi's Account of Clovis which is pretty good, but very dry. The history has nothing agreeable in it's details. Murder, Robbery and Violence form the monotony of the pages. Evening at home. I finished the publication upon France in the Useful Knowledge books[1] and read a little of Paley.

[1] A *History of France* by E. Smedley was being issued in parts in the *Library of Useful Knowledge* of the Society for the Diffusion of Useful Knowledge, London.

SATURDAY. 28TH.

The day was unpleasant with a cold Easterly wind and rain. I went to the Office after reading a little of Vasari. My time was not very well employed as I again forgot the Volume of Gibbon. I occupied it in reading the Account of several remarkable trials in a Collection I have at the Office. Among them those of Louis 16 and Marie Antoinette. They are interesting and since I have looked into it, I think better of the book than I did.[1] It seems much superior to the Newgate Calendar. Went down to purchase some Coal but failed.

Mr. Brooks dined with us today, after which in spite of the weather I went with Hull to Quincy. I thought if I delayed, it might be late in next week before I could go. The lateness of the season is surprising. Occupied myself in pruning and straitening Trees more particularly the Oaks which are taking shape surprisingly well. On the whole I was well satisfied with my progress and returned home to tea. Quiet evening at home.

¹ Perhaps the book was *Causes célèbres*; see above, entry for 10 Nov. 1831.

SUNDAY. 29TH.

Another cold and rainy day. Attended divine service after spending the morning partly in overlooking the Mathematics studied by Hull yesterday, partly in pursuing my Catalogue. Heard Mr. Frothingham preach a very good Sermon in the morning from John 12. 6. "Not that he cared for the poor, but because he was a thief." The subject was the tendency of substituting some plausible cause for the real one when a man commits any fault. There was much penetration into human nature in it. More especially when he touched upon the course of politicians and of zealots. Undoubtedly there is nothing in which we experience more of error in the substitution of sophistry for sound reasoning where self interest impels it. And there is a greater tendency that way as the powers of the intellect are improved. The path of life is an easy one where it runs through quiet spots, but upon entering the tempestuous scenes, Man manifests his feebleness prodigiously.

The Afternoon's Sermon was preached by Mr. Emerson. Proverbs 10. 9. "He that walketh uprightly walketh surely: but he that perverteth his ways shall be known." It was an attempt to show the folly of hypocrisy, because the character of a man cannot be concealed. He endeavoured to sustain this position by an argument showing that the general reputation of a man is the correct one. This like all other general propositions is partly true and partly false. A Man's whole character is rarely known, and in many cases the substitution in public opinion of certain leading traits occasions an entirely mistaken estimate. A man may be warmhearted in nature yet cold in his general manners. He is called haughty.¹ He may be ostentatious in his distribution of Money, and be reputed generous. The fact is that hypocrisy cannot be altogether attacked on that score alone. It is undoubtedly true that the world can sometimes, though it may not always, be deceived. The objections to it must rest upon somewhat higher grounds.

On my return home I read a Sermon of Massillon's upon Death. I think as I go on I relish these more. This is undoubtedly powerful. His Text from Luke 7. 12. "Now when he came nigh to the gate of the city, behold, there was a dead man carried out, the only son of his mother, and she was a widow." His division twofold. The uncertainty of the hour of death produces a foolish and illgrounded confidence. The certainty of its happening at some hour, leads to a dread of considering the subject at all. Upon these he descants, showing the necessity of constant readiness and therefore of immediate attention. There is some common place in this effort, but I have not the same horror of that which some entertain. There are but few new ideas in the world, and whether we know it or [not],[2] we do in fact only ring the changes upon old ones.

Passed my evening quietly at home and read some Chapters of the Bible to my Wife. I. Hull went to Medford this morning to see his Sister and did not return tonight. I am out of work now in the evening so that for a night or two I have taken up Sismondi, but he is very dry. Began tonight a famous Chapter upon the evidences of Christianity a part of which is noticed by my Father in his Letters.[3]

[1] An application to CFA's own case seems to have been intended.
[2] MS: it.
[3] That is, JQA's *Letters on the Bible,* concerning which see entry for 2 Aug. 1831, above.

[*Monday*] 30TH.

Heavy rain with cold Easterly Wind. I read a little of Vasari before going to the Office—His own Life which gives a sketch of his progress in the Art of Painting. I read today a political Article in the Daily Advertiser which not a little provoked me. I do not know why I should feel so disagreeably at such things, unless it is that I detest any thing like an attempt to mislead the public. I wrote a reply and sent it to be published in the Daily Advocate.[1] Perhaps I was not wise in letting my feelings out quite so much, but it was not very easy for me to help myself. My nature is to be frank and bold.

Afternoon, Engaged with the Directors of the Boylston Market in a tedious discussion of the projected improvement. This begins to be somewhat of a bore. And I am fearful that it is about to be often repeated which I confess was not anticipated when I accepted the situation. There is a love of talking as well as of dictating on the part of one member of the Board which is in the long run disgusting as well as tiresome.

Evening quietly at home. Had a little head ach from indigestion. Read the Bible &ca. as usual.

[1] The article entitled "Political Prospects" (*Boston Daily Advertiser & Patriot,* 30 April, p. 2, cols. 2–3) was the latest in a continuing controversy between the *Advertiser* and the *Boston Daily Advocate* over the desirability expressed by the *Advertiser* that the Antimasonic party subordinate itself to the National Republicans in the coming national election in order to elect Henry Clay. In the course of the article an attempt was made to distinguish between the situation in 1828 and in 1832: "Why did Mr. Adams lose his election? Because he could not command the support of the West. He had nothing to depend upon but his own section of the union. Is this the case with Mr. Clay? Is there any doubt of his getting the vote of New England, or a great part of it?" On CFA's reply see below, entry for 10 May.

TUESDAY. MAY 1ST.

Morning damp and cloudy again. I read a little of the Life of Vasari, and then went to the Office. My time was taken up as it often is in the close of one month and the beginning of another, by Accounts. My expenditure requires some attention as it has latterly somewhat exceeded its proper limits. And as I have received some intimation that my Stock in the Manufactures of the Country is not likely to yield any thing in future at least for a time, I suppose it will be expedient to draw in as much as possible. I accomplished a portion of Gibbon containing a Summary of the latter part of the History of the Western Empire.

Afternoon. Read Sismondi finishing the first volume with the account of Queen Brunehault, who seems to have had a tolerable share of the vices of her age. To a philosophical mind it seems not a little curious to look back over the past, and perceive the worthlessness of man in most of the situations where he is tried. Power is a much harder thing to struggle with than misery. For the latter prevents the execution of many vices which the former may indulge. But a truce to reflection.

I was engaged in going over my Library, one side of which I nearly finished. Nothing of any consequence occurred. Had a call from Mr. Rufus Davis which I got rid of as soon as possible. I have not seen his phiz for a long while. Quiet evening at home. I. Hull went to Quincy.

WEDNESDAY. 2D.

This is the month of May. It is necessary to know it or we might suppose it March. After reading a little of the Life of Vasari which I found tolerably dull I went to the Office. Occupied there in business a good deal. Deacon Spear from Quincy called and paid his Notes amounting to seven hundred dollars which is very agreeable. It may be fairly asserted that my Father's property, take it generally, is now at it's maximum of production. And certainly it need not be complained of. All the Real Estate is well rented, and the personal Estate makes a large average yield. This then is the time to devote the proceeds to redeeming the debts for which he stands charged. I have done all I could to promote this.

Afternoon, went to Quincy. The progress of the Painter is slow. I also superintended the arranging some trees in order as far as possible to shade the back part of the Estate. Returned home by seven o'clock and passed a quiet Evening at home.

THURSDAY. 3D.

Cloudy and unpleasant. I have been obliged to record this exceedingly often of late. I read a little more of the Life of Vasari, but it being nothing but a mere record of his work, I concluded to drop it, and begin the Life of Michael Angelo. It is necessary in learning a language to have interest enough in the book which you read to take off the tedium of looking for the meaning of words, and to aid a search for the construction.

Went to the Office. Read a little of Gibbon, but passed more of my time in reading Newspapers, a business as unprofitable as it is distracting. Took quite a long walk with Mr. Peabody and upon returning home found Miss Smith who dined and passed the day with my Wife. This latter received a letter from my Mother mentioning an intention of coming on in a few days.[1] I do not place any very great reliance upon what she intends, because I know how frequently they alter their plans. But I hope they will persevere in their designs this time.

Afternoon, read Sismondi, but my study was so chilly that I did not progress fast or pleasantly. Besides, the French History at least in the account of the first Dinasty is dull. Continued my Catalogue of Library. Evening walked home with Miss Smith to Mr. J. H. Foster's. Read a part of Sismondi's Novel of Julia Severa,[2] a kind of relaxation from his labours upon graver works. It wants vivacity. The tone is too much the staid and cold one of narrative which a historian adopts. The story is one of the era of Clovis. Read a part of Paley who merely condenses Lardner,[3] though in a very satisfactory manner.

[1] Letter missing.

[2] The edition in French at MQA of J. C. L. Simonde de Sismondi's *Julia Severa*, 3 vols., Paris, 1822, is without mark of ownership.

[3] Nathaniel Lardner, *The Credibility of the Gospel History*. The edition owned by JQA and now at MQA is in 14 vols., London, 1741-1762.

FRIDAY. 4TH.

Morning damp and rainy. After beginning Vasari's life of Michael Angelo, which I found pretty hard though a little more entertaining, I went to the Office and passed my morning pretty much as usual. Accounts took up a part of it and the rest was spent either in reading the Newspapers or in talking with Mr. Peabody. The present state of political matters interests every body and my father's singular[1] course at Washington as usual gives occasion to remark. He stands very much as I thought he would and he hazards his peace of mind for the sake of operating upon a parcel of very indifferent characters. The more I see of politics, the more I am satisfied of their nature. Took a short walk.

As it cleared up I went to Quincy and superintended the planting of more trees and the arrangement of the Garden. I think I shall materially benefit the place by what I do. Returned home. Mr. Brooks was sitting with my Wife, and he took tea with us. On the whole we passed an unusually pleasant evening. I afterward went on with Julia Severa, which grows more interesting, and my usual exercises.

[1] Probably to be understood in its original meaning of individual and independent. The immediate occasion of the observation is not clear. Since his return from the Philadelphia sittings of the Committee on the Bank of the United States, JQA had taken part frequently in the hearings on the charge of breach of privileges of the House against Sam Houston and in the debate on the Apportionment Bill, usually on procedural aspects (*Daily National Intelligencer*, 23–30 April *passim*). News of his objections to the presentation on 30 April of the report of the majority of the Committee on the Bank and of his dissent from that report would hardly have reached Boston by this date (same, 2 May, p. 2, col. 6; p. 3, col. 3).

SATURDAY. 5TH.

Cold and cloudy. A disagreeable variety of our miserable season. I read a little of Vasari and then went to the Office. My time not employed to any great profit. I read a little of Gibbon and was busy in Accounts &ca. as usual. As Mr. Field threatened to visit me I felt bound to remain until nearly two o'clock although I had no very serious idea that he would come. Upon my arrival at home I found that I. Hull had returned. He has lost a week of precious time and for the sake of indulging his mother in an unreasonable way. Read some of Sismondi and passed my Afternoon as well as I could without a fire. I do not however much approve of this plan of living so chilled. Evening quiet at home. Nothing to record.

SUNDAY. 6TH.

Clear for once. But the wind from the Eastward piercingly cold.

So that I was driven to repent of my clothing so thin in the morning. Attended divine service all day, and heard Mr. Frothingham preach. His first Sermon was from John 11. 25. "I am the resurrection and the life." The other from Matthew 7. 11. "If ye then, being evil, know how to give good gifts unto your children, how much more shall your Father which is in heaven give good things to them that ask him." I had a little of a headach this morning which disabled me from paying any attention to these Sermons, nor was I much more in a condition to gather the Sense of Massillon's Homily upon Lazarus. John 11. 34. "Come and see." The Text is not peculiarly appropriate. His division was something of this kind: The condition of Lazarus was emblematic of the corruption of a vicious character. This is the first. The second treated of the means, such as faith, by which life was recalled. The third of the motives which could produce the resurrection. I do not know that in this case I am exact, but if not it must be attributed to the head ach which went on increasing until it entirely disabled me from attention to any thing. And my system was driven to relieve itself. This has of late happened repeatedly and gives me sufficient warning that I am now in the second stage of life. I retired very early, reading nothing but the Rambler.

MONDAY. 7TH.

Clear and cold. I am informed that there was a sharp frost, and I do not wonder at it. Read more of Vasari which is now more interesting although the Text is not easy Italian. I am on this point somewhat struck with it's contrast to the Notes. Went to the Office where I read a little of Gibbon and spent an hour at the Athenæum. I see nothing encouraging in the state of public affairs. Nor do I think my father can aid them a jot. Indeed there is enough in the present prospect to discourage a great deal. Our Country has probably to see some bad days, and all that good men can do will be to fold up their arms and mourn.

Afternoon, went to Quincy. Called at Mr. Field's. Found he had moved from the House and yet circumstances seemed to authorize the supposition that it was only temporary. I followed him to where he lives but could not find him there either, so that I did not know what to do. He plagues me. Returned home earlier than usual. Evening quiet at home. Pursued all my usual studies.

TUESDAY. 8TH.

A warm day but a very windy one. I read Vasari as usual and went to the Office. Nothing material took place. As it was the period for returning books to the Athenæum, I went and amused myself an hour by reading an article in the Quarterly Review upon the state of America as contrasted with England. The subject of it is a book written lately by a certain Mrs. Trollop who has done much to justify her name.[1] There is notwithstanding all the abuse a foundation of Justice in her remarks. We are not a perfect nation very certainly, but this is not the question. It is whether on the whole Man is not in as advantageous a situation in the United States as any where on the globe. That is, whether the aggregate of human happiness is not greater and that of misery less. I did not do much of any thing else.

Afternoon. Passed an hour in reading Sismondi and then drove out in the Country with my Wife. We returned at six o'clock and at seven went down to Mrs. Frothingham's to spend the evening. She leaves town tomorrow for Medford to spend the summer. We had a pleasant time and returned home before ten. I felt sleepy however, so that I read only the Rambler and a little of Paley.

[1] The favorable review, unsigned, of Mrs. Trollope's *Domestic Manners of the Americans* in the *Quarterly Review,* 47:39–80 (March 1832), was by Lockhart; see the *DNB* notice of Frances Trollope.

WEDNESDAY. 8TH [*i.e.* 9TH].

A mild day with a South Wind. I read a little of Vasari and then to the Office. My time taken up very much by two persons. First, Mr. F. W. Field who came at last with a confession of Poverty which I have been expecting.[1] After conversation, I thought best to execute the leases upon his giving me his Note for the last half year—And promising to pay it previous to another Quarter's becoming due. I think it on the whole expedient not to take the place away from him. It would probably be unoccupied. I think he seems to have some sense of shame, so that while this is the case I shall feel as if I had a hold. Mr. Conant then came in from Weston, and I went over the affairs of the year with him. He settled his Rent up to the first of April. These are honest though not very enterprizing men. They get along by force of the assistance which I give them in one way or another, which is about equivalent to paying their rent. The Weston Farm yields little excepting in the Sales of the wood which have done very well. I had only a moment left to call and see Mr. Watkins who is here from Washington.[2] He was not at home. I went home, and after dinner, read Sismondi as usual. Evening quiet. Pursued all my usual occupations, dipping besides, a little into Dr. Franklin's Essays.[3]

[1] Harvey Field is spoken of elsewhere as a lessee of JQA's farm at Quincy; see above, entry for 16 March, note. [2] Probably Thomas L. C. Watkins,

sometime companion during CFA's years
in Washington (vols. 1 and 2, *passim*).
  [3] Benjamin Franklin, *Essays and Let-*

THURSDAY. 9TH [*i.e.* 10TH].

Morning clear. But the wind went round to the Eastward and kept the weather pretty chilly. I went to the Office and found my Article published in the Advocate. The Editor of this Paper has left town and this is probably the reason why they feel bold enough to give room for it on the *outside* of the Sheet.[1] I believe I have seen enough of the Advocate for the present. My success in publishing is mortifying. When my Articles are not rejected, they are laid up for a while, issued with apparent indifference, and immediately forgotten. Yet on reading them over, it seems to me there is more spirit in them than one commonly finds in Newspapers. But this is probably my vanity. No man can possibly judge of his own writing. I must therefore come to the conclusion that this is not my line.

Read Gibbon. His account of Mahomet is quite interesting and instructive. As to any parallel with Jesus Christ however, the thing is totally absurd. Took a walk, calling again without success upon Mr. Watkins. After dinner I continued Sismondi finishing the account of Charlemagne. Quiet evening. I read besides my usual business a part of La Harpe's Cours de Litterature.[2]

[1] CFA's communication to the *Boston Daily Advocate* replying to the article entitled "Political Prospects" in the *Advertiser* (see above, entry for 30 April) was signed "Q." In the issue of the *Advocate* for 10 May it was placed at the head of column one on page one, a page given over largely to advertisements. Although the letter was largely directed against the effort to gain support for the candidacy of Henry Clay, it professed concern that what was being asked of the Antimasonic party was "Total sacrifice of every principle for which they have been long contending." If the sentiments expressed represent more than an expedient antimasonry adopted for the occasion, they antedate by more than three months the firm position on the issue CFA arrived at after further study (see below, entry for 20 Aug.).

[2] See vol. 3:13.

FRIDAY. 10TH [*i.e.* 11TH].

Clear and tolerably pleasant day. After reading Vasari I went to the Office and was occupied as usual in reading Gibbon. This took up all my time excepting what I passed in walking and in Accounts. This latter is now a source of considerable embarrassment to me as my father's concerns are extensive and my own are in need of watchful vigilance. This is tautology. Returned home.

Afternoon, went to Quincy. I. Hull accompanied me. I went over the Garden and gave all the necessary directions remaining in regard to the House. I believe, it is now perfectly ready to see the family at any time. From the report of Mrs. Kirke I conclude that it will be as well for me to go out there on the 23d or 4th of the month, taking my chance of their arriving. Returned home by seven. No letters. Quiet evening. I was tired so that I omitted Paley.

SATURDAY. 11TH [*i.e.* 12TH].

A beautiful day. I went to the Office after reading a little of Vasari. Nothing of any moment occurred. I had two or three interruptions. Deacon Spear called from Quincy apparently only to talk. Some other persons for bills &ca. I was unable to read a word. Attended a sale of stocks at noon and found that manufactures were going downward. This is a severe blow to me as I had calculated upon a fair addition to my general income from my Cocheco Stock. But I cannot say that I have not had my eyes open to the probability of a fall in their value. The excessive importations make it probable that there will be but small profits for some time, and the Tariff is to be varied to finish the business. Walked with Mr. Peabody to E. Cambridge where I called for a Deed sent over last Summer and obtained, thus finishing a business which has been to be done a great while.

Afternoon. Rode to Medford with my Wife and saw Mrs. Frothingham there. Mr. Brooks dined in town. We remained a short time and returned. There is a loneliness about the House which would affect a great deal Mrs. Frothingham, I should think. She has been used to a large family and a bustling acquaintance. Evening quiet at home. The weather so warm, our windows were open, and it was very like Summer.

SUNDAY. 13TH.

Another lovely day. The air was soft and vegetation begins to give decided evidence of its influence. As it is probable I may soon go out of town, I occupied myself during all my spare time in continuing the Catalogue of my Books. An assistance which I absolutely need while it is necessary for me to keep them in double rows.

Attended Divine Service all day. Heard Mr. Frothingham and Mr. Barrett.[1] The former took his Text from Hebrews 12. 1. "Seeing we are compassed about with so great a cloud of witnesses." The subject was revealed religion, and it appeared to me very likely to have made a part of the Dudleian Lecture preached by him last week.[2] The Sermon of Mr. Barrett was from 55. Isaiah 10–11. "For as the rain cometh down from heaven and returneth not thither, but watereth the earth, and maketh it bring forth and bud, that it may give seed to the sower and bread to the eater; So shall my word be that goeth forth out of my mouth." He considered the Analogy, the necessity in the one case of planting the seed, before the promised benefits can be enjoyed. Of spreading the word before it will improve us. He then discussed how this might *best* be done and adverted severely upon the prevailing mode of worship in the stricter sects as narrow and bigoted. I think in this respect that there is great cause for complaint. Our religion is rather fanatical.

Afternoon. Read a Sermon of Massillon's upon the lighter kinds of transgression. John 11. 4. "This sickness is not unto death." He commences by adverting to the habit of disregarding such vices as are not mortal. He holds this to be injurious 1. as it affects the heart by hardening it, 2. as its consequences are fatal, first, as it acts directly, second as it has an indirect operation. Quiet evening at home. Omitted Paley.

[1] Probably Samuel Barrett, Harvard 1818, minister of the Twelfth Congregational Church, in Chambers Street, Boston; later an Overseer of Harvard College (*Mass. Register*, 1832; *Harvard Quinquennial Cat.*).

[2] To his sermon delivered in the University's chapel on 9 May as the year's Dudleian Lecture, Mr. Frothingham had given the title, "The Manifestation of Christ." The title was probably the ground for CFA's supposition that the sermon of the morning was but a repetition. However, the Dudleian Lecture was on the text of 1 Timothy, 3:16 (MS in MH-Ar:Dudleian Lectures).

MONDAY. 14TH.

A very warm day. Our Summer comes without any Spring. I continued and finished the rough draught of my Catalogue. This will require copying after which I do not think I shall give any further trouble to that matter. Went to the Office. Received a letter and documents. The former from T. B. Adams about his Property.[1] It will require an elaborate answer. Occupied in business and a walk. My time was not profitably employed however. Returned home.

Passed part of the afternoon in reading Sismondi, and rode out with my Wife the rest. Quiet evening at home. The Child was not very well today. This always affects my spirits. But independent of this I suffered considerably from depression all day.

The utter waste of my powers and my time which is taking place and the little prospect of any future improvement affect me. I have lost a great deal of the springy elasticity which distinguished me a year or two ago. My efforts fail, and my confidence in my own powers go with it. I hope this does not forebode what I have all along dreaded and what has been so often predicted of me, a life of ease, and of inglorious sloth. Advantageous as my situation is in a worldly point of view, I have nobler purposes to accomplish than the mere life of a fainéant. I belong to a race[2] who have refused no labour, and in comparison with whom my idleness would only present a pitiful picture of degeneracy. O, May this not be!

[1] Letter missing.
[2] CFA generally uses the word, as here, in the sense of "family."

TUESDAY. 15TH.

Morning pleasant but weather very warm. I went to the Office after sitting down to have some Conversation with I. Hull. He seems very much depressed and not altogether in so good a state of mind as I wished. I now and then repent of having offered him any convenience. But I suppose I ought not to.

Began my Catalogue which I propose to be pretty careful with. Read Gibbon. Had Several interruptions and walked with Mr. Peabody. The child is not very well which always troubles us. In addition to this, we get no information from Washington.

Afternoon, devoted to writing a long letter to my father—Upon the subject of Mr. McLane's report.[1] He will not thank me for boring him upon that subject. Read a little of Sismondi. Evening quiet. My wife went to Medford with Miss Fowle. It rained a little. I read some of Corneille's Cid. But am overcome with Drowsiness. Omitted Paley.

[1] Letter in Adams Papers. JQA had recently sent to CFA a copy of Secretary Louis McLane's plan for a "Judicious Tariff."

WEDNESDAY. 16TH.

Fine morning. I worked upon my Catalogue a good deal and then went to the Office. My whole available time was engrossed by my answer to T. B. Adams's letter. I draughted his Account for the last six months and explained my views of his interest.[1] This is a piece of business which I am pleased to finish. The whole is a voluntary labour without profit or satisfaction to me. I think I perceive one great difference in my own character as it is now and as it was two or three years since. Then I was anxious for occupation and responsibility. I assumed my father's agency with pleasure and T. B. Adams' with cheerfulness. To the former I am now indifferent, and the latter I should willingly be rid of. Experience of money affairs has made the hazards of it disagreeable. The only reason why I still adhere to my father's affairs, is that I give a little something in payment for my subsistence, and that I hope at least to prevent the shocking waste of his property which has heretofore taken place.

At one, I attended a Meeting of the Bar for the election of Officers, and nonsensical debates kept me there until two. Afternoon passed in copying Thomas' letter which I despatched. We had showers in the Evening. Read to my Wife Campbell's Gertrude of Wyoming. It is no great thing.[2] Read part of Corneille's Cid. And my usual tasks.

[1] CFA to Thomas B. Adams Jr. (LbC, Adams Papers).
[2] When first published in 1809, *Gertrude of Wyoming, a Pennsylvanian Tale,* established Thomas Campbell's reputation as a poet.

THURSDAY. 17TH.

The child has been suffering very much all day and gives us again a great deal of anxiety. I continued working upon my Catalogue. Then to the Office. I do not know how I passed my time. All I know is that it went very fast. Took a walk to Charlestown with Mr. Peabody. Mr. Beale called in about the affairs of Mrs. Adams children. His conversation seemed to me very conclusive upon the course which I think ought to be pursued. Certainly Mrs. Adams ought not herself to be the Guardian. Yet I shall say or do nothing about it.

Afternoon, rode to Quincy with my Wife. The Country has put on a very different face since I was last there. I looked through the Garden and found that we were likely to have a much neater place there than we had ever had heretofore. Indeed the place has I think been materially improved. We walked up and paid a short visit to Mrs. Adams who does not seem to gain courage. Returned home to tea. Quiet evening. Finished Corneille's Cid and the Comments upon it. A very restless night for the child.

FRIDAY. 18TH.

Morning cold. The change of wind has disposed of all our fine weather and given us in its place the easterly chill. Went to the Office. Passed my time in copying Catalogue and then to the Office where I read my father's Report upon the Bank. It has his usual vigour and his usual severity.[1] This is the reason why I think it disadvantageous to him to be placed in a public body. But in reading it as in reading all that is written by him one is carried away by the glow which he throws upon the subject. Washington has a heated Atmosphere unlike that of any other place in this Country. I do not think things are at all judged of in the same manner there that they are any where else.

Took a walk with Mr. Peabody. Then home. Mr. Frothingham dined with me, and we had some of my new wine which I think very good. Afternoon passed in reading a little of Sismondi as well as prosecuting my Catalogue. I did not work to effect however, feeling somewhat drowsy from my vigil last night. Quiet evening. My Wife went over to see Mrs. P. C. Brooks who is unwell. I went with her, though sitting solus, while she was upstairs. Continued my Catalogue.

[1] On 15 May the *Daily National Intelligencer* had devoted almost the whole issue (p. 1–3) to printing the text of JQA's separate Report on the Bank. Next day he sent a copy to CFA (JQA to CFA, 16 May, Adams Papers). A MS of the Report in several hands with notes and corrections in JQA's hand, dated 14 May and identified in CFA's hand as the "printers copy," is in the Adams Papers. On the wide distribution given to the issue of the *Intelligencer* containing the Report, see Bemis, *JQA*, 2:254.

JQA's Report was endorsed by John G. Watmough; these two in turn joined in signing the Counter-Report of the Minority prepared by George McDuffie which was presented on 11 May, was printed in the *Daily National Intelligencer* on 18 May (p. 2–3), and later appeared in pamphlet form along with the Report of the Majority.

SATURDAY. 19TH.

Morning cloudy and cold with rain. Isaac Hull left us this morning. On the whole I cannot say that I experienced any great regret. I asked him to stay with me from the best motives. I hope that he has received benefit from his time. I cannot help thinking however that he could have done more. Continued my Catalogue.

Then to the Office where I worked on my Diary and finished the ninth volume of Gibbon. This work from it's great length drags considerably. I finished the Account of the Conquests of the Saracens today. It is drawn up with great labour, evidently intended to counterbalance the influence of the argument drawn from the progress of the Christian Religion. But the cases are wholly dissimilar.

Returned home. The Child is still quite sick and gives us anxiety. I continued working upon my Catalogue all the afternoon and evening. The house seemed cheerless, and my spirits were much depressed.

SUNDAY. 20TH.

An exceedingly heavy rain all day and more particularly towards night. I laboured all my spare time upon the Catalogue, but attended Divine Service as usual. Mr. Frothingham preached in the morning from Matthew 11. 19. "Wisdom is justified of her children." I lost the thread so cannot retrace it. The afternoon was from 10 Job. 4–5 "Hast thou eyes of flesh? or seest thou as man seeth? Are thy days as the days of man." The subject was the justification of the dispensations of divine providence from the complaints of man by explaining the difference with which things are viewed. 1. Man is hasty. Providence is slow. 2. Man is confined to particulars. Providence sees the whole. 3. Man must form his opinions from superficial examination. Providence from things invisible. 4. Man's is limited in time, the Deity is eternal. It was a very good Sermon.

I read one of Massillon's Sermons afterwards. Upon the evidence of Christianity. John 8. 46. "If I say the truth, why do ye not believe me?" He takes up two objections to the practice of the Christian precepts, commonly urged. 1. That where conscience is at ease, there is no need of them. 2. Where these precepts are so differently construed and hard to be understood, they do not call for attention. He urges in opposition to this, the force of conscience and the simplicity of the spirit of Christianity. On this last point he is good.

The Baby is still sick and fractious which very much wearies us as well as affects our spirits. Finished reading Paley's book this evening with which I have been very much pleased.

MONDAY 21ST.

Morning clear but windy, cold and disagreeable. I continued my Catalogue and then went to the Office. Received a letter from my father informing me of the departure of my Mother from Washington and the probability of her being here some day this week. He also gives me news about the Tariff &ca. not of a very agreeable nature. He deserves credit for his very independent political course, but it is rather an injurious one in this Quarter, and likely to add to his unpopularity.[1]

After dinner, I went to Quincy. Found every thing in very good order. On the whole, more progress has been made in setting things right this year than during the three last. I am myself surprised at the result.[2] I gave all the directions that remained to give which were not in great number, and returned home.

The Dr. pronounces the child better, and I think she is, but I still doubt the expediency of carrying her away from him. He does not however, so that I ought to be satisfied. My Wife and I paid old Mrs. Dexter a visit this evening. She is a woman of sane mind with a rather broken body. Returned home and continued Catalogue.

[1] "I expect to report a [Tariff] *Bill* tomorrow; but what is to become of it and of myself for reporting it, is in the Council of higher Powers. My Bank Report extinguishes all the fire of my Southern friends. I suppose the Tariff Bill will demolish me in the North, and then —

"Why then for the Biography of the last and the Oaks of the next Century" (JQA to CFA, 16 May, Adams Papers;

printed in part in MHS, *Procs.*, 2d ser., 19 [1905]:519).

² LCA, on her arrival, expressed her pleasure in the changes she found at the Old House. To JQA she wrote, "I find every thing here in beautiful order and you would hardly know the Place" (26 May, Adams Papers); and to CFA, "I thank you very much for the improvements which you have made in the house which looks altogether different from what it was last year. And the Garden seems to be in fine order" (26 May, Adams Papers).

[*Medford*]

TUESDAY. 22D.

Cold and very windy with rain. I went to the Office and occupied myself in my usual way. Mr. Mills, the Painter from Quincy, called and I paid him more than I think he is entirely deserving of. But he is old and infirm and probably the surplus is beneficial to him so that I made no difficulties. On the contrary I corrected an error in his bill which gave him something more. Read a little of Gibbon and took a walk. Then home. Found there Horatio Brooks who dined with us. He has returned from his Voyage pretty much the same kind of a genius that he went away. About as wild.

After dinner I continued my Catalogue, until it was time to start off for Medford. This was the day that had been fixed upon by us to close up the House for the Summer and live among our friends. I hope we shall find the benefit of it.¹ The day was quite raw. Mr. Brooks sent in his Carriage for my Wife and the Baby, and I went out in my Gig. We arrived to tea and had a quiet evening among our friends. I did not read my Ramblers though I do not intend to discontinue them.

¹ "[W]hat astonishes me is that Charles has entirely broken up housekeeping shut up his Mansion and discarded all his help for the Summer" (LCA to JQA, 26 May, Adams Papers).

WEDNESDAY 23D.

Morning cold and cheerless. I went to town and to the House where I was quite occupied in various measures necessary previous to finally locking up all. I removed some of my Wine into my own Closet in order to see whether it would not keep better there than upstairs. Somehow or other I have made a very respectable collection of Wine. With my income this seems a little surprising and my saving as much as I have done. But with caution any thing is possible in this world. The only thing is to keep a proper attention to the adaptation of means to end *beforehand.*

I went afterwards to the Gallery and spent an hour very agreeably. Then to the Tremont House where I dined. Afterwards I went up to the House, superintended the departure of the last of my Servants, locked up the House, and proceeded to Medford. Quiet Evening. Read an Article in the Edinburgh Review upon the character of Hambden which I admired.[1] Read four Ramblers today.

[1] An essay-review of Lord Nugent's *Some Memorials of John Hampden, His Party, and His Times* in *Edinburgh Review*, 54:505–550 (Dec. 1831).

THURSDAY. 24TH.

Morning cloudy and disagreeable. It afterwards set in to rain quite hard. I went to town and passed my morning at the office excepting an hour's visit at the Gallery of Paintings with Mr. Peabody. Mr. Gulliver, the Tenant of one of my Father's houses in Tremont Street, after making so many difficulties that I gave him a notice to quit, sent me the Quarter's rent this morning. He is a most provoking man. I should not be sorry to get rid of him. Read nothing.

Returned to Medford in a heavy shower of rain from the Eastward. There were at dinner today, Mrs. Hall, Miss Hall, and Miss Henrietta Gray. These ladies spent the Afternoon. I felt fatigued and sleepy afterwards. Tried to read but accomplished exceeding little. So drowsy, I retired to bed early.

FRIDAY 25TH.

The morning opened with heavy rain and the wind from the Eastward. I concluded after reasoning about it, *not* to go into Boston. I thereby saved myself some discomfort from wetting and stood the risk of my Mother's arrival. My time was not over profitably spent, but I read Buffon's Article of the Horse and the Dog, several articles in the Edinburgh and some in the Quarterly Review. These are now full of the political discussions going on in England, and even all their incidental opinions upon other subjects derive a sharpness from their excited feelings upon Reform. The History of the Stuarts is condemned by the one while the excesses of popular violence are in all shapes alluded to by the other, with a warmth which it may be plainly perceived events so long bygone do not of themselves create.[1] Not a soul came near the House as it rained heavily. The Baby has I think been getting better ever since we left Boston. Today, she was very good.

[1] The allusion would seem to be to the article in the *Quarterly Review* for March (47:261–300) with the running-head title, "The Revolutions of 1640 and 1830."

SATURDAY. 26.

The morning was tolerably fair but cloudy, and it rained shortly afterwards. I received, upon arriving in town, a letter from my Mother at New York stating the reasons why the journey was delayed and mentioning the probable time of their arrival.[1] But judging from the weather I did not expect her so concluded to return to Medford. My time was somewhat cut up in fritters by Commissions of several kinds and Accounts.

Returned to Medford to dine and passed a very quiet peaceable time in the afternoon. Our stay here has been a singular one. For we have had scarcely any thing but rain since we came. I walked about the Garden and made some inquiries about the box, a poor attempt at resetting which I have made at Quincy. Read the discussion of the affairs of England for 1830 in the American Register, written by my Father.[2] It bears his mark. The more I think of it, the more I am astonished at the power of his mind. And its extent which has no equal in this or perhaps any Country.

Evening, we went by invitation to take Tea with Mr. and Mrs. Angier, and passed the time until nine o'clock. Mr. Stetson, and Mr. L. Angier were there. Returned in a heavy rain.

[1] LCA to CFA, 23 May (Adams Papers).
[2] See above, entry for 26 Oct. 1831.

SUNDAY. 27TH.

Heavy and continued rain all day. I remained at home as the Carriage was full going to Church in the morning. Most of my day was spent in reading the American Register which however does not equal in other parts that of my father's. I got hold of the Memoirs of Miss Hawkins the daughter of Sir John Hawkins.[1] They are trifling but not uninteresting.

It is an object of sincere regret that I cut up my time so much to waste. But I can do nothing. The avenues seem at present all stopped up. I have no friendly faces to encourage me to exertion, and not natural confidence enough to carry me on without them. I do not improve myself sufficiently. I do not give forth what I believe to be in me. The evening passed as the day did.

[1] The edition at MQA of Lætitia Matilda Hawkins' *Memoirs, Anecdotes, Facts, and Opinions,* 2 vols., London, 1824, has the signature of Horatio Brooks on the titlepage of the first volume. It would seem likely that CFA found the work among the books at Mystic Grove, had not finished reading it when he left Medford, and took it with him to Quincy.

Quincy

MONDAY. 28TH.

The morning was cloudy but much more like Spring. I went to town accompanied by Horatio Brooks. My time at the Office was taken up in reading my father's last Report upon the Domestic policy. I must confess that I have been dreading this considerably and find myself on the whole very much gratified and agreeably disappointed. It contains a clear and conclusive argument in favour of the system, while it concedes to the agitation of the South as much as it reasonably can, not because they are right in their demands, but for the sake of peace and harmony. On the whole, whatever the result may be, I must say, my father has exalted himself prodigiously in my opinion. There is a high souled independence in his course which suits my particular temper exactly.[1]

Not having received any Note or intimation of my Mother's arrival, I was in doubt as to what was proper to be done.[2] After consideration, I decided upon going at all events. The Road was shocking. But I arrived and found my Mother very quietly settled since Saturday night. Passed the rest of the day with her in conversation about one thing and another.[3] Rode up to Mrs. T. B. Adams' with her, to pay a visit, and spent the evening quietly. Remained at Quincy for the night.

[1] The report of the Committee on Manufactures submitted to the House on 23 May was printed in the *Daily National Intelligencer* on the 24th (p. 2–3). In its account of the session, the *Intelligencer* reported JQA's remarks which accompanied the presentation: "With respect to the report itself, which the Committee had indulged him (Mr. A.) with permission to present, it was to be considered an expression of his views alone. Different members, he added, approved different parts of the report, but there was, perhaps, no member of the Committee who approved the whole of it, except the reporter of it himself" (25 May, p. 2, col. 6). The *Report* later appeared as a pamphlet. A "First Draught," dated 23 May and chiefly in JQA's hand, is in the Adams Papers.

[2] Delivery of LCA's letter to CFA of 26 May (Adams Papers) announcing her arrival at Quincy was apparently delayed.

[3] Undoubtedly the conversation was in part on political questions. Next day LCA wrote to Mrs. JA2, "Mr. A–s is quite knocked up here it seems and will probably not be sent again. His Report is not admired and it is all over with him" (29 May, Adams Papers).

[*Medford*]
TUESDAY. 29.

Morning very lovely. It seemed to pay for all the bad weather we had had. I arose early and went to town after breakfast. Spent a considerable part of the morning in reading Gibbon and the rest in the Athenæum and at the Gallery of Paintings. Met at this last place my neighbour Mr. J. Fullerton. He is quite scientific in regard to pictures and discussed them with me very fully. I have never made any advances towards his acquaintance partly from indifference and partly from want of opportunity. He seems however to be a very gentlemanly man and of some though not extensive information.[1]

It was time to go, so I started again for Medford. Gorham Brooks and his Wife and Mr. Frothingham were there, and we had a pleasant dinner. Afternoon totally wasted, thrown away as if there had not been one. Evening, I accomplished the feat of reading my two Ramblers. Mr. S. Brooks and his sister called and staid an hour.

¹ J. J. Fullerton's residence was at 5 Hancock Avenue, next to that of CFA (*Boston Directory, 1832–1833*).

Quincy

WEDNESDAY. 30TH.

Against all expectation the day opened with the wind from the South and a very heavy rain. The question now was about starting, and after considering it well, I concluded that it would be best to do so. Accordingly I went off about nine o'clock accompanied by Mr. Frothingham, leaving my Wife to follow in Mr. Brooks' Carriage. Arrived pretty comfortably and occupied myself half an hour waiting for Kirke. As he did not come I went to the House, and occupied myself all the remainder of the morning in running about for my wife and family to get them off, which I finally did in a hackney Coach at Noon, starting myself an hour afterwards. I do not recollect ever having so unpleasant a ride. The rain was directly in my face and at times pelted considerably, so that upon my arrival I found myself wet quite through. My Wife and child had reached here in safety, so that on the whole I felt pretty well satisfied at our having at last attained permanent quarters.

My afternoon was spent in my father's Library making a disposition of some books which again threaten to overrun their limits. Quiet evening at home. I had some serious conversation with my Mother.

THURSDAY. 31ST.

I congratulated myself upon my decision of yesterday when I heard the Wind rise during the night, and much more so upon seeing the rain in the morning, so I concluded to remain quietly at home. Upon feeling the time heavy upon my hands I bethought myself what I should begin upon. At this moment I feel myself more out of reading than I have done for some years. In looking round over the Library I felt a great difficulty where to fix and in the process spent an hour or two reading a little fairy story of A. Hamilton.¹ And I then fell upon Gibbon's Memoirs of his own life,² a book that interested me so much that I continued upon it all the afternoon. I like his style in this work better than I do that of his history. It has not any of that excessive regularity which manifests any thing but the English language. His opinions are not always correct, on the contrary I should think most frequently they are the reverse. His politics were considerably inclined to ultra Toryism. Perhaps after all, they are right. I wrote a letter to my Father today.[3] Evening very quiet. I need hardly say that I persevere in my Ramblers.

[1] The *contes* or fantasies of C. Antoine Hamilton, mildly satiric of the taste for the marvelous in the mid-18th century, were included in his *Œuvres-mêlées en prose et en vers.* Two copies of the edition of 1749 are at MQA. A copy of the 4-vol., London, 1776, edition is also among JA's books at the Boston Public Library (*Catalogue of JA's Library*, p. 113).

[2] Edward Gibbon, *Miscellaneous Works with Memoirs of His Life and Writings ... by Himself.* A copy with JQA's bookplate of the 2-vol., London, 1796, edition is now at MQA. Another edition, 3 vols., Dublin, 1796, is also among JA's books at the Boston Public Library (*Catalogue of JA's Library*, p. 102).

[3] A lengthy and generally sympathetic analysis, though with reservations, on JQA's reports on the Bank and on the Tariff (letter in Adams Papers).

FRIDAY JUNE 1ST.

June in name but the day was more like September. My wetting made me determine not to risk another directly if I could avoid it, so I decided to remain at home. Morning was so cold I found it uncomfortable sitting without a fire in the Library. I continued reading Gibbon and finished his Memoirs with several of his letters to Lord Sheffield. I then took up Homer with a view to read the Iliad and finished fifty lines.[1] Upon consideration however, I concluded not to continue upon it. My line is History and Eloquence. So that I believe I shall settle down upon Thucydides.

My afternoon was passed in the Garden engaged in doing by little and little something in the way of improvement. So much seems to have resulted from my trifling efforts this year that I am much encouraged to go on. But I must check a tendency to expense. The adaptation of means to an end is a great secret of all economy. My work did me a great deal of good. Quiet evening at home.

[1] The Adamses had numerous copies of the *Iliad* in the original Greek. The edition in Greek and Latin published in 2 vols., London, 1754, is among JA's books at the Boston Public Library (*Catalogue of JA's Library*, p. 122); another copy is at MQA. JQA's bookplate is in editions published in 2 vols. at Leipzig, 1804; Oxford, 1811; and N.Y., 1826; all now at MQA. A presentation copy of the Grenville Homer (Oxford, 1800–1801) to JQA is now among his books at the Boston Athenæum (*Catalogue of JQA's Books*, p. 99–100).

SATURDAY. 2D.

Went to Boston this morning. Time engrossed in Commissions of various kinds and in copying the letter written the other day to my

Father. I was at the House where I executed all my final purposes. Perhaps this is one of the pleasures of being out of town, that when I come in, my time is so much taken up. It gives me occupation of an agreeable kind. But the mind runs to waste.

Returned to dinner. Passed the afternoon in the Library reading. Made some progress in Seneca whom I have taken up as a kind of relaxation.[1] His Essay upon Anger has some good ideas in it. The leading and best one is that anger is of no service. It denies the utility of it to the performance of great actions. It is undoubtedly true, but the occasional success which it gives blinds many to the fact. The real secret is that all such success is accidental and can never be counted upon. He who desires to make himself Master of Fortune must always be cool. Quiet Evening at home. I. Hull spent an hour with us.

[1] Seneca's philosophic works in the original Latin are well represented at MQA. Now there are editions published at Geneva, 1620, in 2 vols.; at Amsterdam, 1659, in 3 vols.; also an edition, *Philosophi . . . opera*, 4 vols., Biponti, 1782, with JQA's bookplate, a quotation from Dibdin on the flyleaf of vol. 1 in CFA's hand, and underlining characteristic of CFA in the essays "De iræ" and "De consolatione ad Helviam."

SUNDAY. 3D.

The Weather continues chilly and unseasonable. The Wind blowing pretty steadily from the Westward though without any rain. I attended Divine Service, and heard Mr. Whitney preach all day. But I have concluded not to give myself while in the Country the trouble of analyzing Sermons which often are not worth the trouble. Mr. Whitney is among the most commonplace of our Clergymen. He has grown old, and the Country is very fast outrunning him. I presume this will some time end in a separation. For my own comfort, I must say, I should admire it very much, but considering the Justice of the case I should be against it. The connexion is one where the single individual and the body are not fairly matched. The one grows old and helpless, the other remains the same. The one spends his best years in exertion, and his age deserves better treatment than to be turned off to want.

I read in the Afternoon, a part of Massillon's Sermon upon the death of Louis the 14th. It was only the first division relating to his careful management of power. The preacher says full enough in his praise, yet he does not conceal though he palliates the faults of his hero. Posterity can trace the Revolution of 1789 to them in part, but of course Massillon could do no such thing. In the evening, I went down to pay some visits, but stopped at Mr. Danl. Greenleaf's. She is an old lady full of her own consequence. He is a worthy man. I remained until nine.

MONDAY. 4TH.

Misty threatening rain. I was obliged to risk it, so I went to town. My time was entirely taken up in Commissions and in bringing up all accounts, which is my usual practice at the beginning of each month. I then had to go and see about some Trunks which are missing, that belong to the family. I could get no trace of them. The thing is somewhat extraordinary. It cost me something of a toil without any fruit.

Dined at the Tremont House and attended a Meeting of the Directors of the Boylston Market which consumed all the Afternoon. My prediction with regard to this, is about to be verified. The profits are to be stopped for some time. Returned to Quincy to tea, having escaped rain, and had a quiet evening.

TUESDAY. 5TH.

Weather tolerably fair, yet I concluded to remain quietly at home. I have no engagements of any pressing nature in Boston, and my time is usually wasted rather unprofitably. I read a portion of the first book of Thucydides [1] and I wrote a considerable part of my Diary which the distractions of the week had thrown in arrear.

In the afternoon I walked down to Mount Wollaston to see how the Orchard prospered and to do for it any thing I could in the way of pruning. I found the trees all alive, some of them however killed nearly to the ground and some looking quite sickly. And upon examination I dreaded the results of so unfavourable a Season. The succession of bad weather this Spring has been extraordinary and if it should continue much longer, there will be serious fears for the grain crops. The Corn looks ill and does not grow. And it is impossible to get any vegetables up. I spent the whole afternoon upon the Trees, returned home fatigued to Tea. Evening as usual.

[1] Among JA's books now at the Boston Public Library are two copies in Greek and Latin of Thucydides, *De bello Peloponnesiaco*: an edition published at Frankfort in 1594 which has JQA's autograph, and one published at Amsterdam in 1731 (*Catalogue of JA's Library,* p. 244–245). Now at MQA is the edition in 6 vols., Biponti, 1788–1789, with JQA's bookplate and, opposite the titlepage in the first volume, a quotation from Dibdin in CFA's hand.

WEDNESDAY 6TH.

It threatened to be pleasant but without success. I went to town. Found to my discomfiture that my Office boy was about to leave me.

This at this time is highly inconvenient. My time was consumed in going about on various commissions, in an attempt to find the missing Trunks, and in reading a little of Gibbon. One or two Tenants came to see me. One to pay rent, another to give me notice of his intention to quit one of the Tenements. I thought this would subject me to some trouble but before I left Boston, an application of a satisfactory nature was made for it. This is a very agreeable thing. Houses are no trouble when men are really in want of them.

I returned to Quincy to dinner. The whole Afternoon was taken up in superintending some improvements to the Garden which I really think is at last taking the appearance of a Gentleman's place. A little care and attention is all that is wanting. Paid a visit at Mr. T. Greenleaf's in the evening. All there but Mr. Price whose absence was not accounted for.

THURSDAY. 7TH.

Much the same cloudy, unpleasant weather which we have had all along. I remained at home today. Read a portion of Thucydides but my time was very considerably interrupted. I have now reached the causes of the famous War, and the author becomes more interesting. His style is peculiarly compressed. He leaves to the reader every thing but the leading word. It is like striking chords in music when you supply the rest of an octave. This to a man so superficial in Greek is not perfectly easy reading. Took a walk with my Wife at noon, and searched the Gardener's books afterward, but without much success. It is difficult to reduce theory to practice.

Afternoon, I finished Seneca's first book De Ira and passed an hour in the Garden. Seneca writes with an attempt to concentrate sense. It is as if you would feed a man always upon brandy. It is no doubt very fine but the human mind will put up with no such tax, and straightway forgets as much as is not most prominent. In the evening, read a little of the Memoirs of the Duc de St. Simon. A cynical historian of the age of Louis 14. But he probably tells much truth.[1]

[1]*Mémoires . . . sur le règne de Louis XIV.* JQA's bookplate is in the 3-vol., London, editions of 1788 and 1789, both now at MQA.

FRIDAY. 8TH.

The early part of the morning was so cloudy that I decided upon remaining at home. But it appearing a little finer at ten o'clock, I concluded to start with my Wife for Boston. She wished to go and see Mrs. Sidney Brooks who has come from New York to remain a day or two. I did not employ my own time to much advantage, it must be confessed. Read a Newspaper or two, performed a Commission or two, and talked a little with W. E. Payne who has just returned from Charleston,[1] about Nullification, at the Athenæum. This sentence is not properly constructed. This brought the hour for returning, and accordingly we reached home to dinner.

Afternoon, I passed partly in the Garden and partly reading Seneca, but I did not turn my time to so much advantage as I ought to have done. A quiet evening at home.

[1] William E. Payne, a counselor whose office was at 5 Court Street, lived at 20 Beacon Street (*Boston Directory*, 1832–1833).

SATURDAY 9TH.

The direction of the wind was changed this morning, but we nevertheless had a showery day. I concluded not to go to town. Occupied during the morning in reading Thucydides who becomes more interesting as he begins to describe the War between Corcyra and Corinth which gave rise to that of the Peloponesus.

The afternoon was passed reading Seneca with the exception of a little time passed in the garden. The Record of my days becomes more and more monotonous as I advance more into a quiet undisturbed way of life. Settled as we now are, it seems impossible to imagine any thing more secluded, yet to me it is very far from unpleasant.

In the evening my Mother concluded to make us a variety by going in to Boston and hearing the Messrs. Herrman. These are German Singers who have been making a tour of this Country with success.[1] We arrived in time and found a full and fashionable audience at the Masonic Temple. They are remarkable as singing in perfect taste and thorough harmony. But they want the relief of higher Notes and a better Room. For this did not appear to give the necessary sound. As Choristers I can hardly imagine any thing more perfect. We reached Quincy at about eleven, having performed our exploit without any difficulty and with some pleasure.

[1] For their second and final soirée musicale the Messrs. Herrmann, members of the Royal Conservatory of Munich, presented a program of music for male voices and for the cello by Weber, Cimarosa, Mozart, &c. (*Boston Daily Advertiser & Patriot*, 9 June, p. 3, col. 4); see also entry for 18 Sept., below.

SUNDAY. 10TH.

It is hardly necessary to make any allusion to the weather while we have constant clouds and rain. I have never known a season at all like this. The Crops will probably be very much cut off. Attended divine service all day, though I felt myself suffering from one of the head achs which have lately afflicted me occasionally. Mr. Mott preached and as I thought with considerable amendment since I last heard him. His morning Sermon was upon the cultivation of a pious character by the regulation of thought. That in the afternoon I felt unable to follow. Indeed my whole day was thrown away as it usually is in cases of such mental debility occasioned by bodily pain.

I looked over an old file of letters of my Grandfather without energy or method in re-arranging them. And I read the remainder of Massillon's Panegyric of Louis 14, with a part of that upon the Dutchess of Orleans, not having any ideas arise from it. It is prostrating to the vanity of the human intellect to think how totally a trifle may unnerve it. Evening, Mr. Price Greenleaf called and passed an hour pleasantly. I retired early.

MONDAY. 11TH.

I had designed going to town today, but the clouds threatened rain so much that I felt unwilling to trust myself. After balancing a longer time than was necessary, I sat down and made considerable progress in Thucydides. This writer is worth studying on account of his moderation and his sententiousness. I propose hereafter to translate some of the principal passages. The Sun came out with some force at Noon, and I felt a little the indisposition of yesterday so that I did not stay out long.

Afternoon, finished the second book of Seneca de Ira. I admire much of the wisdom contained in it. The forgiveness of injuries is perhaps the greatest pagan approximation to the doctrines of the Christian Religion. But he mixes with it advice which does not suit a Code of Ethics or a Moral Philosopher however well it may turn out practically in life. Submission to the caprices of the powerful is a maxim of policy for a tyrant's Court, not a principle of morals which lead to setting aside artificial distinctions. I passed an hour or more in a visit to our neighbour Beale who seems to feel alone in the world. He wants to be married again but hardly dares express it.[1] The night was clear.

[1] On the tentative approaches by the widower George Beale to Mary Roberdeau, see above, entry for 4 Oct. 1831. His shy probing continued and was duly reported to the lady: "Let me beg that you . . . come and take compassion upon your Swain who really seems to be in a deplorable state and complains bitterly of his loneliness" (LCA to Mary Roberdeau, 12[?] June); "Your Swain droops very much. . . . Mrs. Miller insists if you were here he would offer himself and

I have been sounded shyly more than once to know if I thought you would have him" (same to same, 28 Aug., both letters in Adams Papers).

TUESDAY. 12TH.

For once we had a very fine day. The whole force of the Season coming upon a very uncommon state of cold. I went to town and occupied myself in Accounts. The less I visit the City however, the more I find my time wasted when I do go. I do not know that I shall ever secure the quiet necessary for me to make great progress in learning, but at any rate I have more chance for it in the Country than I have in town. I went to the Athenæum and selected some books to hammer upon. It was so warm however that I was glad not to move about much. Returned to Quincy with pleasure.

The Afternoon was intended to be devoted to reading, but interruptions of one kind or another make me confess a very imperfect application. I commenced Vaughan's Memorials of the Stuart dynasty,[1] a work which if it suits my purpose I intend to review. I am not yet certain however that it will answer. The heat of the day drew together clouds in the evening with such rapidity as to produce a thunder gust with some rain.

My evening was passed at home reading the Newspapers which are full of matters from Washington. There seems little probability of any adjournment of Congress. My father's letters to me seem to express disgust but I doubt it.[2] Read the usual papers of the Rambler.

[1] Robert Vaughan, *Memorials of the Stuart Dynasty*, 2 vols., London, 1831. CFA was using a copy borrowed from the Boston Athenæum.

[2] JQA to CFA, 6 June (Adams Papers). Printed (in part) in MHS, *Procs.*, 2d ser., 19 (1905):521.

WEDNESDAY. 13TH.

The Wind Easterly and the day threatening rain. I went out to look at the weather, but concluded at any rate to stay at home. It cleared away however. I was occupied nearly all of my working day in reading Mr. Vaughan's book. It seems to be the Puritan side of the Account. I think very just, but it may not appear so much so to others whose feelings and prejudices take different directions.

My health has not been perfectly good during a few days past, but I hope it will not be materially touched. Without that, what is life to Man. It may be that he can bear it, but very certainly he cannot enjoy it.

Quiet evening. Miss Smith, Miss Adams, and Mr. Gourgas came in the evening and spent an hour very pleasantly.

THURSDAY. 14TH.

Morning cloudy, but it cleared and became a very warm day. I went to Boston, accompanied by my Wife's Nurse Mrs. Field who was sent in to perform Commissions.[1] At the Office where I was busy in Accounts but the generality of my time went as usual with but very little account of it.

Called at Mr. Brooks' room and at an Auction Room to see some Cut Glass. Found that the New England office again paid nothing, which cramps my father's means here again. But there is a kind of compensation always going on. When other things failed, that Office paid very largely, now this has failed, the Middlesex Canal and Wood take it's place. In the present condition of my father's estate, it is nevertheless to be regretted as this is the critical period. If he does not succeed in disentangling himself from his embarrassments in the course of these two or three years I think he will struggle on in them to the end of his life.

Returned from town after seeing the great military parade which was making in the case of some Philadelphia Militia who have come here.[2] All this is Vanity and Vexation of Spirit. Read Mr. Vaughan in the Afternoon. There is much in his book that I like. Quiet evening at home.

[1] Mrs. Field, the new nurse for LCA2, was "somewhat ponderous" (entry for 18 Aug., below) and at first seemed to LCA "a non descript character ... neither a Lady nor a Servant so I do not know how we shall make out" (to Mrs. JA2, 29 May); further observation of her, however, brought approval as "a very clever good temper'd creature ... who gives herself no airs and

we have a prospect of going on quietly and harmoniously (to same, 2 June; both letters in Adams Papers).
[2] The City Guards under command of Capt. Kinsman received the State Fencibles of Philadelphia on the Neck and together paraded through Washington, State, Court, and Tremont streets to the Common (*Boston Daily Advertiser & Patriot*, 14 June, p. 2, col. 1).

FRIDAY. 15TH.

Morning cloudy but afterwards exceedingly warm. The morning was passed in investigations for the benefit of my subject. The quantity of matter it leads me to read and look over would seem to be somewhat of a discouragement. But I hope it will have a tendency to fix in my mind the whole of a very important period when a contest was going on having a very great influence upon subsequent events.

At ten I went into Boston in the Carriage with my Mother and Wife. We stopped at Mrs. Frothingham's, and from thence I went with the former to the Gallery of the Athenæum, where after some time the latter joined us. I afterwards went to the Office where my time was taken up by a visit from Mr. T. Davis which I was obliged to cut short much sooner than I wished. Returned directly and we started from the Athenæum to Quincy. A hot ride.

I spent the afternoon in reading Vaughan without however making a great deal of progress. Warm evening.

SATURDAY. 16TH.

Cool in the morning but it became an exceedingly warm day. I remained at home, and on the whole applied myself pretty faithfully to reading Vaughan's book, the first perusal of which I finished, also reading Hume's Account of the Reign of James 1.[1] It certainly is pretty remarkable how he has varied from the truth in most important particulars. The influence of almost all of the English Historians has been thrown into the scale of high monarchy and the effect has certainly been considerable. But as it is the tendency of all misrepresentations to re-act when they are exposed, the final result may possibly be a tendency to the opposite popular extreme. From the aspect of affairs as they lately appear in England, there seems some ground to expect this pretty soon. The moderate popular party has been defeated. There seems only to be wanting a man of great character to hasten things to a crisis, involving the fate of King, Lords and Bishops. Evening, I drove my Wife out in my Gig. Mr. Beale afterwards spent an hour with us at home. It was so exceedingly warm I retired early.

[1] David Hume's *History of England ... to 1688* is among JA's books in the Boston Public Library in an edition in 8 vols., London, 1778 (*Catalogue of JA's Library*, p. 124). Now at MQA is an edition in 6 vols., Phila., 1795, with CFA's bookplate; also an abridged edition, 2 vols., London, 1795, with JQA's bookplate.

SUNDAY. 17TH.

Fine day but quite warm. I was occupied at home in beginning a draught of something upon Mr. Vaughan's book, and in reading further Hume and Brodie[1] in comparison. Perhaps this will only be another attempt added to a considerable list of things of that kind. But nil desperandum. It is better to give occupation to the mind and exercise to the pen.

I attended divine service all day and heard Mr. Kimball preach. He was formerly teacher of a school in Hingham which my brothers attended but has since moved elsewhere.[2] His morning discourse was upon the character of Martha in the Scriptures as understood from the correction applied to her by the Saviour—her over attention to the things of this world. The subject was odd enough, but the Sermon was what struck me as very commonplace. That in the afternoon was better so far as the nature of the subject and the manner of treating it. It was upon mental independence. Yet on the whole I could not help reflecting how low the standard of teaching must have been in this Country twenty years ago. I do not know how far it is better even now. But I hope something has been gained.

Evening. Took a ride alone to Mount Wollaston, returning not till after sunset.

[1] George Brodie, *History of the British Empire from the Accession of Charles I to the Restoration,* 4 vols., Edinburgh, 1822.

[2] Daniel Kimball, Harvard 1800 and tutor 1803–1805, preceptor of the Derby Academy in Hingham, 1808–1826, was ordained an evangelist in 1817. GWA and JA2 had lived at his house while they were students at the Academy. (*Harvard Quinquennial Cat.*; JQA, Diary, 25 Sept. 1818; [Thomas T. Bouvé and others], *History of the Town of Hingham,* 3 vols. in 4 [Cambridge], 1893, vol. 1, pt. 2, p. 139, 141, 202, 212.)

In addition to the two Adamses who were students at the Derby Academy other Adamses and their relatives were associated with the Academy from its founding in 1784. Richard Cranch, John Thaxter Sr., and Cotton Tufts were among the original trustees; and Cotton Tufts was president of the Board 1804–1815. TBA was a member of the Board 1804–1818. The Adams connection with the Academy was resumed when CFA became a trustee in 1850; he served as president of the Board 1856–1859; on resigning as trustee in 1861 he was succeeded by JQA2 (*History of ... Hingham,* vol. 1, pt. 2, p. 123, 135, 139, 140).

MONDAY. 18TH.

Pleasant morning and not too warm. I went to town and occupied myself at my Office as usual. The announcement of the arrival of the Asiatic Cholera on this side of the Atlantic at Quebec, seems to have excited great uneasiness and alarm.[1] For my part if it did any good to worry one's self at an irremediable evil, I certainly would do so, but as it does not, I hold the proper course to be to submit without any murmur to the dispensations of Providence. Called to see Mr. Brooks and performed some Commissions. A loose hour was devoted to reading Gibbon superficially. Returned to Quincy. Afternoon reading Hume whose history is nothing more than an Apology. Quiet evening. A thunder shower.

[1] Reports relating to the cholera occupied the major part of the news columns (p. 1–2) of the *Boston Daily Advertiser & Patriot* on 18 June.

TUESDAY. 19TH.

Morning cloudy with wind from the North and occasionally rain. I concluded to stay at home. Occupied all my morning in reading and beginning another and a more Review like Article. Whether I shall be able to persevere remains yet a mystery. But the subject is a good one, and I every day reflect that I ought to be doing something. There is a pleasure in definite occupation which pays one independently of profit. The action of the mind is nourished and that of the pen improved, while the passage of time is hardly felt.

In the afternoon I began to read over Mr. Vaughan in connection with the other writers. I believe I shall attempt to make a plan something like this. In the morning to put to paper the reflection of the preceding day. And thus go on until I have finished the volumes, after which I may cut down or enlarge and arrange as I may see fit. The evening was uncommonly cold. I was at home as usual.

WEDNESDAY. 20TH.

Morning clear but very cold for the season. In going to town, I felt the want of clothing even with my great coat. So upon arriving I went immediately to the house and put on my flannels. This I do with more willingness as I find it is recommended as a preventive against the Cholera, the approach of which seems to be much dreaded. The Boston people are in so much alarm that it will prepare the way finely for the disease. The Accounts from Canada are very indefinite. But it seems tolerably evident that the Country from the inundation of emigrants is suffering severely. I executed some Commissions, looked over Accounts and wasted my time a little, then returned to Quincy. The afternoon was passed reading Vaughan carefully. Evening as usual.

THURSDAY. 21ST.

Fine morning. Indeed I do not know that in the course of the year we enjoy much pleasanter weather than this day. I remained quietly at home. And was occupied all my time in reading over attentively the work of Mr. Vaughan. I find that it is much easier for me to write down as I go along, so that I have given up my former scheme as long as I am engaged upon the first draught. After that, as I find my mind is certainly clearer in the morning, I believe I shall take that exclusively for writing.

I now see how much I lose in Boston from my habits of life. The morning, by far to me the most effective portion of the day, is there totally wasted in trifles. Cut up by piecemeal in odd jobs and profitless reading even when I do read. As I live here, on the contrary, it seems to me to be productive at least of a little benefit to myself and consequently of self-satisfaction. I take exercise of an agreeable kind in the Garden, and am on the whole, at present free from any particular anxiety. For all this I am grateful. Quiet evening.

FRIDAY. 22D.

A beautiful day. I remained at home again all day, and in the morning began a fair draught of my remarks after going through with the material parts of Mr. Vaughan's book. I accomplished nearly five pages which I think I materially improved. And the passage of time was hardly perceptible to me.

My mother and Wife went into Boston in the Afternoon, but I concluded to remain. My Afternoon's work did not however satisfy me quite as well as the morning. I read the Preface to Fox's Historical Work,[1] with which I was on the whole quite pleased. I also went down to the Wharf below Mr. Greenleaf's and took a Salt-Water bath. The first this Season. The water was exceedingly pleasant. And I enjoyed myself much more than I had anticipated. The practice of moderate bathing, I believe to be one of the most wholesome possible.

Evening at home, all our evenings are peculiarly cold for the Season.

[1] CFA's bookplate is in two editions now at MQA of Charles James Fox's *History of the Early Part of the Reign of James II,* both published in 1808, one at London and one at Philadelphia.

SATURDAY. 23D.

Fine day. I went to town, and passed my time as usual in Commissions and lounging. Took up a volume of Gibbon but found that I had so lost the connection of his book as to make it difficult to pursue, and not interesting. I therefore passed an hour at the Athenæum, reading the Newspapers, and the Documents added to the Bank Report.[1] The Alarm about the Cholera seems to be subsiding.

Returned to Quincy and on the whole passed rather an idle Afternoon. I wrote a little upon my Essay, imagining it on the whole to be better to employ myself in some manner upon it, than to lose all my ideas upon the subject. After tea, I went down to the Water and took a bath. It was warm enough, but there being no wind the weeds came up and made the surface appear stagnant. Evening quiet at home.

[1] The allusion is probably to the supplementary report of the minority of the Bank Committee which contains extensive documentation; it was printed in the *Daily National Intelligencer,* 18 May, p. 2–3.

SUNDAY. 24TH.

Very cool with an Easterly wind. I was engaged in writing almost all day, excepting when going to Meeting. Mr. Ripley of Boston preached in the morning upon the immutability of religion. In the afternoon I was less attentive. Mr. Ripley is a good writer and a sensible man, but I am not much of an admirer of his Sermons. His manner makes them tedious. When he wishes to be solemn he becomes only slow, without adding a particle to the animation of his language. I often think, I could do better, but who can tell until he is tried.

Miss Smith dined with us, and Mr. Degrand called in the afternoon and took tea. He had little news of any kind to propose. Some farther notice of the Cholera which seems to be spreading along the St. Lawrence gradually. It is singular that it keeps water tracks, and would seem to sustain the doctrine of contagion. But whether contagion or not is of minor consequence so long as the mortality is great.

I walked up and passed an hour at Mrs. Adams' in the evening. She is dull and unhappy, and I could not console her. Called at Mr. Miller's but they were not at home.

MONDAY. 25TH.

Morning very fine. I remained at home today, and Completed the draught of the attempt I am now making. It has occupied me earnestly but continually for a week or fortnight, and it has led me to observe more closely the facts connected with the English History. I think I never before saw so clearly the demerits of Mr. Hume, nor so forcibly the real difficulties which followed the Revolution of 1640. These kind of researches are pleasant and profitable. They make learning appear less barren of good, and they fix the quantity of it. For the memory takes easier what has cost it a little unusual labour.

Not having any thing further to do, in the afternoon resumed Seneca and read part of the third book De Ira. As usual, a compound of wisdom and error. The checks to anger are wisely given. Yet by a species of syllogism he attempts to evade the maxim of Aristotle which is after all true in the main. Anger can give no strength. Anger is a kind of disease. Disease always weakens. Then anger weakens. Not remembering that the sick man can sometimes do an act which he never could have accomplished in health. Had he said continued strength, it might have been questioned, but with less reason. Evening, a long ride with my Wife. We lost our way and reached the Woods. Returned home safe and quiet.

TUESDAY 26TH.

Fine day. I concluded to remain very quietly at home as it was likely to be warm. I returned to the study of Thucydides which my late work had put a stop to. Continued the first book but I find I must not wear out my patience upon him as it only serves to retard my progress from understanding him less.

I attempted to do a little also towards methodizing rather more the Papers of my Grandfather. I came across many very curious and interesting letters in the process. It is much to be wished that these were put into a condition more likely to be durable. Yet my father's inclinations and occupations lead him in any direction rather than in this.

Took a bath. The water was cold. I find this to be occasioned by the comparative state of the atmosphere. Afternoon, occupied in reading Seneca's third book upon anger. A world of good advice upon the means of checking it. Took a ride with my Wife and quiet evening. My brother's child being quite sick creates some uneasiness.[1] Otherwise pretty comfortable.

[1] Since arriving at Quincy with her grandmother and during the whole of her stay there Mary Louisa suffered from a painful and stubborn rash and swelling that was particularly acute in the area of the eyes. LCA wrote twice or three times a week to JA2 or Mrs. JA2 throughout the summer providing details on the illness (letters in Adams Papers; see also entry for 4 July, below).

WEDNESDAY. 27TH.

Day cloudy and threatening rain. Nevertheless I went to Boston accompanied by my Wife who was anxious to see her sister, Mrs. Frothingham. At the Office, thence to the House upon search for some Papers that are necessary for the beginning of the Quarter. Upon my return, I thought I would prepare myself for this, by draughting as much of the general account as I could at this time. So that I should be able to finish all without any difficulty on Friday and Saturday. It is somewhat doubtful to me whether it is expedient to send it immediately as my father is so engrossed by the business before Congress that he will not probably look at it. This with a few Commissions and a slight examination of the great Pamphlet upon the Bank constituted nearly the whole of my occupation.

Returned home, though not quite escaping a Shower from the South. Afternoon, finished Seneca's third book de Ira. Quiet evening. I worked in the Garden somewhat.

THURSDAY. 28TH.

Fine day. I remained at home and resumed my writing. I gave in the first place a deliberate review to what I had done, and then I sat down with the intention of writing a correct copy. But as I went on, I found myself gradually altering the disposition of my materials until the new draught became a very different thing from the old one. I flatter myself it is better, this is one of the numerous self deceptions which writers always experience.

Afternoon. Read the larger part of Seneca's book of Consolation to his mother Helvia. Written to sooth her grief for his exile. The severity of this punishment is comparatively unknown to the moderns. Rome was the centre of every thing prized by its Citizens. It seemed to them to be the only place worth living for as it was the mistress of the world. Hence the complaint of Cicero and Ovid and the Consolation of Seneca.

Quiet evening at home. Mr. Beale called in for a short time.

FRIDAY. 29TH.

Fine weather. I went to town this morning. My ride was somewhat longer through the little green lane and over the Neck. I think this little place is one of the prettiest in the vicinity of Boston. It has the marks of extreme cultivation and the houses are both neat and ornamental. At the Office, but as John wished me to perform a Commission for him I thought I might as well do it today as any day. Accordingly I set off with Mr. Peabody, who has just returned to town, and we walked to Haggiston's Greenhouse at Charlestown, a small inclosure sheltered by a hill in which he raises various kinds of fruit and flowers. I gave my directions about the Strawberry Vines and took some of the fruit as a specimen. Returned to town just in time after having had a pleasant time.

I went back to Quincy directly. Afterward, I read Seneca finishing the book of Consolation to Helvia. I did not go on but wrote a little upon my work. It progresses slowly and is not much bettered by these breaks. Quiet evening at home.

SATURDAY. 30TH.

Fine morning. I went to Boston. Very busy all the time in finishing my Account. I accomplished it however and sent with it a short letter.[1] My father is so much engaged now that he will probably look at it a moment and then put it on file forever. I had one or two short interruptions of different kinds. Deacon Spear called to receive the Money for the new Church that is building.[2] On the whole I worked faithfully. Mr. Child came about the Boylston Market. A Meeting of

Directors this afternoon. I felt unable to attend so I asked him to make my excuses. Returned to Quincy.

Read in the Afternoon, the book of Consolation to Polybius. It shows Seneca under the torture of exile, abandoning his philosophy and his self-respect. Stooping to flatter without minding the terms. It has been thought that this is not a genuine work, but I think from the internal evidence that it is. Some passages of it are admirable if generally applied. Evening, I walked up to call upon Mr. Miller who was again not at home and then passed an hour at Mrs. Adams's.

[1] LbC in Adams Papers.
[2] On JQA's pledge of a contribution toward the construction of the new Episcopal church in Quincy, see entry for 8 Dec., below.

SUNDAY. JULY 1ST.

Clear morning but warmer than it has been. I was occupied in writing much of my time. Attended divine service in the morning and heard Mr. Whitney upon a future state. I was taken with so drowsy a fit that I could not pay any attention. In the afternoon I missed going from being asleep. This does not tell very much to my credit to be sure.

I read the very partial Account of Strafford's Trial,[1] and also the Chapter of Mr. Vaughan upon that subject. My opinion is on the whole pretty clearly made out. I drew off a little of it upon Paper, but did not please myself in this.

The Evening was far the warmest we have had. Mr. T. Greenleaf called in and passed an hour. He informed us of the passage of the Tariff bill through the House of Representatives.[2]

[1] Since CFA was reading simultaneously several historians of the struggle between king and parliament whom he regarded as partial to the monarchy, the account of the trial of Thomas Wentworth, 1st Earl of Strafford, here referred to cannot be positively identified (see above, entry for 16 June).
[2] Final action was taken by the House on 28 June and the bill approved by a vote of 132 to 65 (*Daily National Intelligencer*, 29 June, p. 3, cols. 5–6. The text of the bill as passed was carried in the issue of the 30th, p. 2, cols. 1–3).

MONDAY. 2D.

The weather is fine, but the continuance of the heat without rain is a trying thing for vegetation. I find many of the young trees which I have transplanted heretofore, begin to give evident signs of distress. One of my greatest vexations is the loss of so many fine young trees.

Went to town this morning and was occupied in drawing up Accounts for the beginning of the new Quarter. Struck my own balances and found my affairs just about as I expected. Had a little conversation with Mr. Peabody about this Tariff bill. He says it is a little more satisfactory to all parties than was expected. I hope it will not prove the bugbear that men's imaginations have made it. Returned to Quincy.

Read in the Afternoon part of the book of Consolation to Marcia, and as my father is now likely soon to come home I thought I would set down and write. But I did not satisfy myself at all. It is very disheartening to labour so much with so little profit. Quiet evening at home.

TUESDAY. 3D.

Another cloudy morning followed by a very bright day. I went to Boston again as it was about the commencement of the Quarter and persons might come in. There were but one or two however who did. My time was devoted as usual to a parcel of trifles. I walked down to the Old Theatre for the purpose of seeing some Pictures there for sale.[1] The owner seemed disposed to puff them as exceeding fine, but I saw nothing in them attractive to me. He did not appear to meet with much success. Returned to the Office and then called to see Mr. Brooks with whom I passed twenty minutes in pleasant conversation. Then went back to Quincy.

Afternoon, I took a bath in the Salt water, read a little of Seneca, continued my article and read a little of Ludlow's Memoirs.[2] Evening quiet at home.

[1] The sale of "elegant oil paintings" was advertised to take place "at the Saloon of the Federal street Theatre" (*Boston Daily Advertiser & Patriot*, 3 July, p. 3, col. 5).

[2] The *Memoirs* of Edmund Ludlow, one of the regicides, was composed during his long exile spent at Vevay. Its first appearance was in an edition published there in 3 vols., 1698–1699. This is the edition now at MQA with JQA's bookplate. Volume 3 of an Edinburgh, 1751, edition is among JA's books at the Boston Public Library (*Catalogue of JA's Library*, p. 152).

WEDNESDAY. 4TH.

Fine clear morning though much cooler than it has been for some days back. As this was the usual day of festival, I remained quietly at home. Last year, we had a day of great heat and noise, which for my own part I must confess I do not relish, as I did this today.

Occupied all the morning upon my Article which I at length finished. Took half an hour to go up and see my Tenants at Penn's hill to whom I presented my bills but got no money from them. At any rate this part of my duty is done. Returned and got the intelligence of the appearance of the Cholera in New York.[1] This will renew the

Alarm here, although that has already been so pressed that man's nature generally re-acts into confidence. My Mother has been for some days in a state of great and distressing anxiety on account of my brother's child, Mary Louisa, whose disorders seem to have settled in her eyes, and produce excessive suffering. Indeed the whole house experiences the consequence, particularly at night.

Afternoon, I read a good deal of Seneca's Consolation to Marcia. His pictures are too laboured. He dwells on what he thinks a striking thought until he has gone into every detail, and in fact wears it entirely out. Evening quiet. Elizabeth C. Adams was here at tea, and my wife and I accompanied her in her walk home.

[1] *Boston Daily Advertiser & Patriot,* 4 July, p. 2, col. 2.

THURSDAY. 5TH.

Fine morning. I went to Boston. Occupied when there in my own affairs and those of my father. Made some Collections and on the whole put the Accounts of the Quarter upon a tolerable footing. Called a few moments upon Mr. Brooks. My time was thus fully taken up. I returned to Quincy.

Afternoon, finished Seneca's book of Consolation to Marcia. I do not like it as well as the others. The topics of Consolation are few and simple. They require less art than almost any writing. Any thing formal becomes Parade. Passed an hour upon the Papers of my Grandfather. Elizabeth C. Adams dined and Mrs. Adams and Miss Smith took tea with us. I passed an hour at Mr. Beale's. The child seemed a little better today.

FRIDAY. 6TH.

I remained quietly at home all day. Weather warm and dry. I cannot say that I was properly occupied. After having read over my composition and feeling as usual exceedingly dissatisfied with it, I sat down to look over some old letters of my Grandfather's. I methodized the letters of the last few years of his life, and went over two Chests. There are now remaining only three Chests, but those are crowded. Looked over the last number of the North American Review. The Articles seem to me to carry no interest with them. Indeed this Review seems to me now to be mainly supported by Mr. Peabody the Clergyman.[1] Miss Elizabeth C. Adams took tea with us. The Child remains much in the same state. We sent in today for Dr. Reynolds.[2] But he did not come. Our baby, I thank Heaven, gives us, in the meantime, little trouble.

¹ That is, William Bourn Oliver Peabody, brother of O. W. B. Peabody and of Mrs. A. H. Everett (*DAB*).
² Edward Reynolds Jr., "the best oculist we have" (CFA to JA2, 7 July, Adams Papers; *Boston Directory,* 1832–1833).

SATURDAY. 7TH.

Fine morning. I went to Boston and was occupied much as usual. There was a good deal of news of different kinds. Bad so far as it denoted the spreading of this disease, good so far as it is political. I finished my composition and being tired of it concluded to send it at once to Mr. Everett, without hammering over it any more. I am sensible of it's imperfections. But to write a thing over three times is hard enough without wearing out the interest by perpetual correction.¹ I wrote also a short letter to John my brother, according to my Mother's request. It described to him merely the condition of his child and left it to him to decide what was fit to be done in the case.² I called to see Dr. Reynolds but was unable to find him.³ Thus the whole morning passed very rapidly. I returned to Quincy at the usual time.

The weather suddenly changed at noon and became cold and cloudy, with an Easterly wind. I read part of Seneca's book on Providence which attempts to justify the sufferings of good men. It will not do. Nothing but the belief of a future state will satisfy the mind in considering that question. I called in the evening at Mr. Miller's, saw him and sat an hour.

¹ On the subsequent history of CFA's essay-review of Robert Vaughan's *Memorials of the Stuart Dynasty* see below, entry for 25 Dec., note.
² CFA to JA2, 7 July (Adams Papers). The import of the letter was that Mary Louisa's condition was such that, despite JA2's own poor health, it would be well for him to come to Quincy if only to relieve LCA, "who is an altered woman from watching and anxiety."
³ Later in the day Dr. Reynolds did visit Quincy. After examining the patient he pronounced that Mary Louisa's sight would not be impaired; he saw no early end, however, to the severe disorder (CFA to JA2, 9 July, Adams Papers).

SUNDAY. 8TH.

Day cold and cloudy but without rain. I passed my time very quietly in reading at home, and in attending divine Worship. Heard Mr. Whitney. My life is if any thing still more quiet here than it used to be in town. I have no interruptions nor any of the anxiety which a family establishment of my own will necessarily give. The moment is exceedingly propitious for study, yet on the whole I have done little or nothing to answer for it. My time has been consumed by an article which appears to me tolerably indifferent. But now I feel at least as if something had been attempted, and I shall resume my regular studies with more satisfaction. I read today part of the report from Congress upon Steam Carriages, Roads, and Canals,[1] and I continued Ludlow's Memoirs that are amusing enough. The Child seemed somewhat better today.

[1] In February the House of Representatives had ordered printed "the report of the committee of the British House of Commons on the application of steam carriages to common roads" and so much of the earlier printed report of its own Committee on Internal Improvements "as relates to the actual and relative utility and cost of railroads and canals" (*Register of Debates in Congress,* 8:1842). This document was published with the title, *Report on Steam Carriages . . .* [with appended] *Documents in Relation to the Comparative Merits of Canals and Railroads . . .* (22d Cong., 1st sess., *House Exec. Docs.,* No. 101 ["Serial Set" No. 218]).

MONDAY. 9TH.

Cloudy and cold. But very little rain. I did not go to town. Time occupied between Thucydides and the examination of the old letters of my Grandmother, some of which I found quite interesting. Those of my father at an early age when he had his doubts of his success have much to produce reflection. They come to me with the more force as many of them were written at just my present age. It is true that our situations are very dissimilar and that in many respects my early life has been a very prosperous one. But this very circumstance assisted him in his subsequent course when it will be very likely to keep me down.

After dinner I finished Seneca's book de Providentia. The latter part is a justification of suicide. With the doctrine of the Pagans, there is no reason to object to it. But it would seem as if any person having sense enough to believe in a Deity, would see that the object of his creation was not to put his life in his own power. Elizabeth C. Adams was here all day. Evening at home. I read parts of the Bank Report.

TUESDAY. 10TH.

Morning cloudy and cold. I concluded however to go to town. At the Office a little while and from thence to the Athenæum—Where I returned my books without being able to find any new ones. My time passed rapidly enough notwithstanding. I had only a minute to pass and transact business at My Office with Mr. Geitner, and Gorham Brooks called.

Returned to Quincy. Passed the afternoon in severe exercise in remaking the Gravel walk which does not answer expectation. I worked hard myself and ought to be repaid in health. Indeed that has been very good this Summer. Quiet evening.

WEDNESDAY. 11TH.

The clouds and mist continued with occasional heavy rain during the day. I went to town contrary to my wishes, principally for the purpose of accommodating Gorham Brooks. This compelled me to go to my House, after which I went down to an auction of pictures at Mr. Cunningham's. There were a few good Paintings of landscape in the Dutch style, among a great many ordinary ones.[1] They were not sold for very high prices and yet they went beyond my mark. I am on the whole quite glad of it as I have no place to put more if I bought ever so many or few, and on the whole it is an idle taste. My whole morning was thus pretty much exhausted.

Returned to Quincy fortunately having the rain behind me. Miss Smith and Miss E. C. Adams dined here and celebrated my father's anniversary. He is sixty six.[2] Afternoon, read Seneca upon tranquility of mind, somewhat negligently to be sure. Evening quiet at home.

[1] "72 oil paintings just imported from Antwerp . . . several fine *landscapes* by Ruysdael, Teniers, Berghem and others" (*Boston Daily Advertiser & Patriot*, 11 July, p. 3, col. 5).

[2] CFA was in error. The birthday was JQA's sixty-fifth. The celebrants would have been cheered by the report of JQA's health and spirits contained in a letter written on 30 June to a friend in Boston by a "New England man and sojourner in . . . Washington" and printed two days before JQA's birthday: "I have never seen Mr. Adams look so well these ten years. He was much indisposed about the third year of his Presidency, which his friends thought was, in a great measure owing to his habit of cold bathing. . . . Every body, ladies and all, say he looks younger and sprightlier than when he stood at the head of the nation. . . . [T]his delicate and ungrateful business [the Bank investigation and the tariff] he conducted with a steady calmness and coolness that I hardly expected; but, at the same time with a promptness and decision characteristic of his patriotic predecessors of the same name, illustrious for their steady habits. He certainly, at this time, stands on an eminence deservedly high" (*Boston Daily Advertiser & Patriot*, 9 July, p. 2, col. 2).

THURSDAY. 12TH.

It rained occasionally throughout the day so that I concluded to remain quietly at home. Time taken up in reading Thucydides whose first book I finished and reviewed a considerable part of it. This makes rather an introduction to his History, than any part of the History itself. I think it valuable for its matter and manner, although a strict copy of it in these days would hardly be popular. The present age calls for more breadth as people take less time to think upon single subjects.

Afternoon read Seneca upon tranquility of mind. It is unfortunate for this author, that all his contempt of riches, and love for the most complete absence of cares arising from such a source, is set off against the fact in his life that he was himself immensely wealthy. Perhaps, abstractly considered there may be justice in his reflections. But I cannot help thinking the exercise of moderation in poverty, whether voluntary or involuntary, much easier, than in the possession of abundance. It is true that man's course is more sure and safe from avoiding temptation, but it is certainly more honourable to resist it. I believe Seneca has the greater merit. He was rich and yet frugal, not from a saving or accumulating spirit, but from a feeling of moderation. In the evening, I read Ludlow and the usual Ramblers.

FRIDAY 13TH.

Morning clear, but the day was cloudy with now and then a few drops of rain. I remained at home and passed my morning in reading Thucydides and the life of Pericles in Plutarch, which strikes me as rather unnatural this time. He ascribes motives of action to him worthy of the meanest Statesman and yet calls him the greatest. Even Thucydides who was opposed to him in the State, and who suffered from it, gives better and more probable reasons for his course of policy. Indeed Plutarch is a valuable writer for the temper which he usually treats things, but he is often incorrect and superficial in facts.

Afternoon, read the rest of Seneca upon tranquility. I am almost tired of him. He never varies from his strained, pointed and occasionally extravagant style. I stole an hour from him to read Sydney's life and Apology. He is one of the principal martyrs in the cause of liberty. He seems to have been a stern republican in his principles and pretty consistent in the support of them. His views of Government I believe I shall read.[1]

Evening, my Wife and I went over and paid a visit to Mr. Beale and his children. Nothing of consequence occurred.

[1] JA had among his books now at the Boston Public Library two editions of Algernon Sidney's writings which contained lives of Sidney: *Discourses concerning Government . . . to which is Added, a Short Account of the Author's Life*, 2 vols., Edinburgh, 1750; and *Works . . . a New Edition with Memoirs of His Life. Revised by J. Robertson*, London, 1772 (*Catalogue of JA's Library*, p. 230).

SATURDAY. 14TH.

Morning clear, but occasional showers, in the day. I went to town. Time passed in performing commissions and paying visits. I called to see Mr. Blunt of New York at Tremont House and from thence was obliged by a request of his to go to my House. I then went to see Mr. Brooks. The public seemed interested in the last news from Washington of the Veto which the President has put upon the Bank bill.[1] Such is the fate of our Country. All its creditable and useful institutions are to fall under the blows of ignorance and want of principle. Mr. Blunt again called upon me to obtain the Papers which I went to my House to obtain, and he delayed me rather longer than my usual time. I got home however in season for dinner.

Afternoon, read a little of Seneca, but most of my time was taken up in a long walk to Payne's [*i.e.* Penn's] hill for the purpose of collecting some of the rents due to my father. This carried me to several places, but I succeeded more than I expected. Quiet evening. Nothing of consequence.

[1] Report of the veto by the President on 10 July of the bill to renew the charter of the Bank of the United States was carried in the *Daily National Intelligencer* on 11 July (p. 2, cols. 5–6). *The Veto Message on Returning the Bank Bill with His Objections,* widely disseminated as a pamphlet, is in Richardson, ed., *Messages and Papers,* 2:576–591.

SUNDAY. 15TH.

Fine day though cool for the season. I attended Divine service and heard Mr. Newell of Cambridge preach. His Sermons were interesting, though disfigured by the peculiar manner which gives harshness rather than attraction to his style. I think he preached his morning discourse at Mr. Frothingham's although I do not find it.[1] The text was from Luke 12. 13 to 21 verses—The well known parable of the rich miser. The afternoon was upon righteousness. It is far better for a Congregation to have such a preacher as this, who will at least give them subjects for reflection, than the drowsy nothings of many of the old school. I asked him to come and dine with us, but he had been pre-engaged. Miss Smith came down.

Afternoon, nothing material. I read several articles in the Biographia Brittanica upon various persons of whose history I wished to know something.[2] Afterward a little of the life of Waller which I did not admire.[3] Quiet evening at home.

[1] That is, CFA thinks that he had earlier heard William Newell preach on the same text at the First Church, Chauncy Place, but this impression could not be confirmed by reference to the diary records of sermons heard.

[2] JQA's bookplate is in the edition of the *Biographia Britannica* published at London, 1747–1763, in 6 vols., now at MQA.

[3] Perhaps CFA was reading the life by Percival Stockdale prefixed to Edmund Waller's *Works* in the edition published at London in 1772, which, with JQA's bookplate, is now at MQA.

MONDAY. 16TH.

Pleasant day. I went to town principally for the purpose of obtaining from Mr. Blunt the Papers which I lent to him the other day. My time was taken up as usual in a variety of small ways. Read the Newspaper and found that my father had been getting himself into difficulty with the House which I do not admire. The affair terminated peaceably. But I am more and more satisfied that he is not suited to an assembly of this character. He cannot see a great many things that are wrong without strongly resenting it. Yet the attempt is often more dangerous to the person doing it than to the object attacked.[1]

Returned to Quincy and found the family quit for[2] a severe fright in the Carriage when riding this morning. I do not admire horses at all. The best of them are dangerous in the extreme.[3]

Afternoon, read Seneca and almost finished his book on the constancy or firmness of a wise man. I am tired of this writer and shall lay him up for the present I think. All the pointed, ambitious writers require some relaxation with a more flowing style. They will not do for constant companions. Quiet evening at home.

[1] The *Daily National Intelligencer* for 12 July revealed that JQA was actually embattled on two fronts. The difficulty to which CFA here alludes arose during consideration of a motion to censure William Stanbery of Ohio for an alleged indignity to the Speaker of the House. After objection to a vote until the charge had been investigated had failed to be sustained, and a roll call on the motion was ordered, "[Mr. Adams] asked to be excused from voting as he believed it unconstitutional to pass such a resolution until the facts of the case should have been ascertained." When the House refused to excuse him, he again refused to vote. The process was another time repeated, at which point the House turned to a consideration of how to deal with his recalcitrance (p. 3, col. 5). According to JQA's own account, written several days later, that consideration took the form of "a threatened resolution to expel me from this House or to commit me to the custody of the Sergeant at arms. . . . The Majority of the House were in a towering passion with me for declining to vote upon what I thought an Unconstitutional question. The next morning the House cooled down wonderfully" (JQA to LCA, 14 July, Adams Papers; printed [in part] in MHS, *Procs.*, 2d ser., 19 [1905]:526).

The second difficulty was the most recent of numerous clashes during the session between JQA and speaker An-drew Stevenson. The *Intelligencer* printed in full (p. 2, cols. 1–6) JQA's letter of 11 July to the Speaker protesting the conduct of the Speaker in having had printed in the *Richmond Examiner* while the Tariff Bill was under consideration, a private letter of James Madison "with the avowed purpose of affixing the brand of heresy upon a principle asserted by me prepared in discharge of a public duty." The full text is printed, along with other passages bearing upon the background of the controversy and the issues pertinent to it, in CFA2's paper, "J. Q. Adams in Twenty-Second Congress," MHS, *Procs.*, 2d ser., 19 (1905): 504–553.

[2] That is, "got off with" or "suffered nothing more than" (*OED: Quit*, adj., I, 1).

[3] "As we were ascending Pens Hill one of the Horses got his leg over the Pole and Kirk being alone could not dismount so as to assist him. . . . [F]ortunately a man came up and opened the door of the Carriage. When we got the Children out Mrs. Charles caught your Louise, and I just cleared the step when the Horses becoming entirely unmanageable upset the Carriage; and poor Kirk has broken one of his ribs and the Horse is much hurt. We are all well. It was in the morning and Kirk has behaved very well for a long time" (LCA to Mrs. JA2, 19 July, Adams Papers).

July 1832

TUESDAY. 17TH.

Fine morning. I concluded not to go to town today. My Mother received a letter this morning from my father mentioning the probability of his starting from Washington about this time, and my brother's family is to accompany him.[1]

I continued reading Thucydides—The Funeral Oration of Pericles, which partakes much of that style which foreigners are fond of charging upon us. I am also reading Sydney on Government, a work written to refute the singular system of Sir Robert Filmer.[2] It has many points, sarcasm, logic, ridicule, and vigor. But the only wonder is that a refutation should ever have been needed. The science of government has been prostituted to the designs of the few servile scoundrels who look to their own interest, cost what it may to the world.

Afternoon, finished the first volume of Seneca. Read also a part of the proceedings of the first Congress under our Constitution, relating to laying an impost.[3] How the Southern section of the Union can get over it, I do not see. Evening quiet. My Mother does not seem well at all, today.

[1] JQA to LCA, 11 July (Adams Papers). The plan for JA2 and his family to accompany JQA to Quincy was later abandoned because of the added hazard to travel imposed by the cholera. Instead, JA2 accompanied JQA as far as Philadelphia to consult a physician there about his own persistent eye trouble (JQA to LCA, 19 July, Adams Papers; entry for 19 July, below).

[2] Algernon Sidney's *Discourses concerning Government,* first printed in 1698, was written, probably as early as 1680, in answer to Sir Robert Filmer's *Patriarcha,* which was published in that year. See the *DNB* notices of each.

[3] Presumably in Thomas Lloyd, *Congressional Register; History of the Proceedings and Debates of the 1st House of Representatives of the United States,* 3 vols., N.Y., 1789–1790.

WEDNESDAY. 18TH.

Fine day. I remained quietly at home. My time was divided between Thucydides and Sydney in the morning. I read in the former the account of the plague of Athens, which has a peculiar interest at this time from the fact of their being such a thing now in the Country. There is no similarity at all in the symptoms of the two. The old plague seems to have been a fever arising from an overcrowded and ill settled population, this spreads in City and Country through three quarters of the habitable globe. In New York it continues with rather increased virulence, though on the whole it has as yet been tolerably confined in it's operations there.

Afternoon, I concluded for want of more attractive occupation to resume Seneca, so that I took up the second Volume and the Treatise upon Clemency in a Prince. It was addressed to *Nero.*

I took a drive with my Wife, and we went through Milton round the factories passing a house which certainly has a very imposing appearance. It is an old house lately repaired and much improved. Mr. Greenleaf very politely handed me a Newspaper which contained some late and important news from Europe. The French seem to be again in a state of commotion.[1] Mr. Beale and his daughter called in the evening.

[1] The *Boston Daily Advertiser & Patriot* for 17 July contained a dispatch from London of 7 June reporting a new insurrection in Paris (p. 2, col. 3).

THURSDAY. 19TH.

Morning fine. My wife accompanied me to Boston where she met her sister Mrs. Frothingham. I was engaged in various vocations, but very few of them of a useful nature. Received a letter from my brother stating his reasons for not coming this way.[1] There is much foundation for them. The alarm in relation to the progress of this disease is increasing, I think, and the consequent difficulty of transportation from New York here. Little or nothing else is talked of, and the public as usual in cases of panic does a great deal to accelerate it's fate.

Returned to Quincy just in time to save a violent thunder gust, though after all it passed principally to the south of us. The absence of thunder and lightning this season is I think one of the most remarkable signs of this remarkable year. I read some of Seneca upon Clemency and found much that was wise in it, although I could not subscribe to the slavish doctrines it professes. Quiet evening at home.

[1] See above, entry for 17 July; the letter from JA2 is missing.

FRIDAY. 20TH.

Fine day. I did not go to town. It is marvellous how little attraction there is for me in the heated streets. And the less I go, the less I feel inclined to. Occupied in reading the second book of Thucydides in which I have been very much interested. The very clear sketch of the sea fight kept me reading much beyond the time I commonly devote. I also progressed a little and but a little with Sydney.

The probable return of my father also makes it necessary for me to change my situation. It is now nearly two months that I have had the study entirely to myself, during which time I have not been entirely idle. Perhaps I ought to have done more, considering the advantages

I have in this collection of books. But on the other hand, though they make my progress seem small, it is well to resist the propensity to miscellaneous and desultory reading which would show it greater.

After dinner, I read but little of Seneca as in the first place I went to the bath and in the second my Wife wished to go to Weymouth, so I drove over there. Returned to tea but I felt unusually fatigued. After tea, my Mother, Wife, and I walked up to see Mr. T. Greenleaf and his family. No person was at home excepting Mrs. G. We remained a short time and returned before nine. I retired soon.

SATURDAY. 21ST.

A fine rain this morning, but it prevented my going to town as I had intended. Occupied in reading Thucydides, but I had a little touch of my headach, which prevented my pursuing studies very closely. Mrs. Frothingham with her brother Horatio came and spent an hour with us. They had nothing very new, but we were glad to see them execute their long talked of project. Afterwards I worked in the Garden.

Mrs. Adams sent home the old Journals which I. Hull had with him to copy, and I sat down and amused myself much in reading them.[1] He went through a great deal in his life of various sorts of fortune. He saw much of the world, and considering his situation, got through exceedingly well. But there is a spice of truth in what his enemies said of him, that he came home from Europe somewhat tinged with their notions. Perhaps it may be as he says, but Republicanism is the fashion of the day and that admits of no recognized distinctions. Evening, I called at Mrs. T. B. Adams'.

[1] JA's diaries; see above, entry for 9 Nov. 1831, note.

SUNDAY. 22D.

Fine day. I attended Divine Service all day and heard Mr. Flint of Cohasset preach. In the morning upon the fulfilment of vows made, in the Afternoon upon attendance on divine Worship. He is a very good Preacher so far as good sense may go but his excessively erroneous delivery is enough to cover every merit. The finest diamonds would never shine through so much mud.

At home, most of my day was taken up in reading the old Journals of my Grandfather relating to the very important period of the Treaty of 1783. A period which Mr. Sparks has been exerting himself to construe in his way against every circumstance of probability.

There is a Report of extensive circulation today that Mr. Clay has killed Mr. Benton in a duel at Washington. It wants confirmation very much.[1]

Evening, my Wife and I walked up to Mrs. T. B. Adams to pay a visit. Remained but a short time. Mrs. Angier and Mr. Joseph Angier came in from Medford just at this time. On our return we found Mr. and Mrs. Quincy.

[1] The rumor probably arose from accounts of the extremely bitter exchanges between Thomas Hart Benton and Henry Clay in the Senate during the debate on the President's veto of the bill to renew the charter of the Bank (*Daily National Intelligencer,* 16 July, p. 2; 19 July, p. 3).

MONDAY 23D.

Fine, clear day. I went to Boston and passed my time there with my usual waste. The accounts of the Cholera from New York are bad enough and the People seem to be able to talk of little or nothing else. Indeed to read the Newspapers much and to hear the talk are enough to give the disease almost. I went to the Athenæum, to my own house, to Mr. Brooks' room, &ca. and was glad when the time came to return.

Afternoon, read Seneca. Finished de clementia. It is very imperfect however. The treatise is full of fine sentiment. Occasionally the morality is of a very superior order, and it is only by considering the flattery of Nero and his subsequent character that we deduct from its merit. It is not possible to suppose him such an adept at dissimulation as to conceal his propensities. And Seneca must have known them if any body. He should therefore have spared his encomiums.

We have been slightly expecting my father today. The last news of him is of Thursday at Philadelphia.[1] We wish to hear of him *this* side of New York. Quiet evening.

[1] JQA to LCA, 19 July (Adams Papers).

TUESDAY. 24TH.

Fine morning. I went to town for the purpose of getting some information about my father. But I did not succeed. Time principally occupied in reading the Speech of Mr. Everett upon the Tariff. It is a dry, statistical performance, in some respects correct, in others questionable.[1] Had a visitor applying for the House in Tremont Street about to be vacated by Mr. Gulliver. We had a long conversation, and he finally asked me to come in to town tomorrow.

Returned to Quincy and passed the Afternoon in reading Seneca upon the shortness of life. Almost all of his subjects are Common places hackneyed by time. Yet they are well treated and contain a good deal of thought. Read also part of the debates of the first Congress. It is surprising to me that after these there ever should have been any question about the legality of protecting duties. Evening, walked with my Wife to Mrs. T. B. Adams's and passed half an hour.

[1] Edward Everett's *Speech on the Proposed Adjustment of the Tariff* (Washington, 1832), delivered in the House of Representatives on 25 June; a copy is listed in CFA's catalogue of his pamphlet collection (Adams Papers, Microfilms, Reel No. 326).

WEDNESDAY. 25TH.

Showery with more thunder and lightning through the rest of the day than we have had all the Season. I felt compelled to go to town where, after learning from casual report that my father had gone up to Hudson on the North River and reading some of Major Hordynski's book upon Poland,[1] my gentleman came and we proceeded to view the premises. After treating a good while, discussing this and that and the other thing, he concluded to take it at the advanced rent provided I made a great deal of repair. As on the whole it was not a bad bargain for me, I concluded upon it, although that House has already swallowed up far more than it's Rent.[2]

Returned to Quincy though somewhat later than usual. Afternoon, I read Seneca and finished the treatise upon shortness of life. His remarks upon the misemployment of time in trifling studies are valuable. Although as action is the universal wish, it may be doubted whether a division of labour which throws some of it into useless but innocent channels is not beneficial to man. It rained so much that we did not walk out. I read some of Mr. Canning's Political Life,[3] and finished the Rambler. Commenced the Adventurer.

[1] The edition at MQA of Joseph Hordynski's *History of the Late Polish Revolution, and the Events of the Campaign* is that published at Boston in 1832.

[2] From this date W. G. Ladd became the tenant at 103 Tremont Street (M/CFA/3, and see below, entry for 28 July).

[3] Augustus Granville Stapleton, *The Political Life of . . . George Canning*, 3 vols., London, 1831.

THURSDAY. 26TH.

Morning cold with a cloud of mist from the sea. I went to town notwithstanding for the purpose of giving directions in regard to the House, and also to see if I could discover any trace of my father. My time was taken up in running about after workmen, as I am without an Office boy, so that I had little at my own disposal. Found at Mr.

Brooks that Mr. Everett and family had arrived but that my father had gone up the river. Further I could not discover any thing.

Returned to Quincy and had just sat down to my usual lesson of Seneca upon happy life, when my father drove up in the Stage.[1] The rest of the day was passed in conversation. I think he looks very well but after the very flattering accounts not in such full health as I expected. Quiet evening at home.

[1] JQA wrote in a letter to JA2 a full account of his trip from Philadelphia to Quincy by way of Hoboken and up the Hudson to Poughkeepsie (stopping overnight with the de Windt's at Fishkill Landing), whence he proceeded by stage via Hartford (27 July, Adams Papers). His journal entries covering the period of the journey are printed in MHS, *Procs.*, 2d ser., 19 (1905):527–534.

FRIDAY. 27TH.

Fine morning. I did not go to town, from an anxiety to be out of the way as much as any thing. My new tenant will find plenty of things to think of I do not doubt, and I already do for him more than I feel justified in. Read Thucydides in the morning—The judgments upon the people of Mitylene and Platæa. The Athenians took the side of mercy with the former, the Lacedæmonians that of severity with the latter. Their habits in this respect were barbarous to a considerable degree. They killed the men and sold the women. So that there was always a prospect in Greece even among the most prosperous families of slavery or destruction. Read a little of Sydney but my progress in this is over slow.

In the Afternoon, I accompanied my Wife to Mrs. Quincy's. It was something of a walk for her. We found only the lady herself at home and sat there only time enough to take rest.

Evening, the life of Canning, and a conversation with my Father upon the character and influence of public men—Mr. Pitt, Fox, Burke, Sheridan. It kept me awake until after eleven o'clock. Read the Adventurers.

SATURDAY. 28TH.

Fine day. I went to town, and my time was entirely taken up all the morning. I had visits at my Office from T. K. Davis, Mr. S. Angier, and the new Tenant, Mr. W. G. Ladd. They consumed much time. After which I was engaged in some Commissions and in attending a meeting of the Suffolk bar. E. G. Prescott and R. S. Fay apply to be admitted as Counsellors. I might as well apply myself.[1] The facts were to be stated to the Court. Returned to Quincy quite late in consequence.

Afternoon, instead of my usual occupations, I was engaged in copying out a Will for a man in Quincy who came and asked it as a favour of my father.[2] It took me until late, when I walked with my Wife to see Mrs. T. B. Adams. Mrs. Angier there, still unwell.

[1] Richard Sullivan Fay and Edward Goldsborough Prescott were CFA's classmates at Harvard (vol. 1:120, 397–398). Fay was associated in the practice of law with another classmate, Jonathan Chapman Jr. (*Boston Directory,* 1832–1833).

[2] CFA drew up the will of Oliver Billings according to JQA's directions, and he and ABA witnessed Billings' execution of it (JQA, Diary, 28 July). As cases of cholera became more numerous the making of wills and the disposition of property began to absorb more and more persons. JQA began to work on his will on 4 Aug., completing it in October (Diary, *passim,* and Adams Papers, Microfilms, Reel No. 203). LCA also recorded her wishes as to the disposition of her personal belongings (LCA to JA2, 20 Aug., Adams Papers).

SUNDAY. 29TH.

Day pleasant and rather warm. Time occupied in copying a letter from my father,[1] and reading a little of Seneca whom, for the last Week, I have rather neglected. A discussion of the old subject of happiness which the Stoics would place in a perfect superiority to human feeling, and the idea of virtue. The thing is impossible and if it was attainable it would not make happiness—Such is human nature. Man is so much the creature of circumstances that he can never mark out for himself a time or way to be happy. The Stoics pursue the negative principle, but many a man feels at his heart without any need of reasoning long over the matter, that the absence of suffering from any cause does not satisfy his aspirations.

Mr. A. Bigelow of Medford preached a Sermon upon the doctrine of grace in the morning, and upon the perfect and upright man in the afternoon.[2] His matter was good, although I had such excessively drowsy fits that I was very much prevented from listening to him. This somnolent habit of mine, I fear, grows upon me.

Evening, called with my father, mother, and Wife at Mr. D. Greenleaf's. After our return I had an agreeable literary conversation with my father.

[1] The letter CFA copied in JQA's letterbook was that to JA2 of 27 July (see above, entry for 26 July, note).

[2] Rev. Andrew Bigelow also dined with the Adamses (JQA, Diary, 29 July).

MONDAY. 30TH.

Fine day, though it was cloudy in the morning. I went to town for the purpose of arranging my Accounts for a payment on the 1st instant, on my father's affairs. I shall do it with difficulty. Went to my House for a book or two and was engaged in several commissions. Thus the time passed. I did however succeed in reading several Chapters of the book of Major Hordynski. His book is principally military, but it conveys an idea of the bravery and success of the Polish troops greater than I had entertained.

Returned to Quincy and passed the afternoon in concluding Seneca, De vita beata. The latter portion of this is a defence of himself for possessing wealth and preaching poverty. His argument is undoubtedly sound, considered in itself. Though it might fairly be questioned how far he could be authorized to use it. It is idle to say that poverty is not an evil when so much care is taken to avoid it. The true rule is to consider wealth as not a primary object in life. And to divest it of all idea of value excepting insofar as it increases the virtuous enjoyments of life. Dr. Johnson somewhere remarks that Poverty is an evil, because it makes some virtues difficult to practise, others impossible.[1] This is not agreeable to the doctrine of Seneca. Quiet evening at home. A short walk with my Wife.

[1] Dr. Johnson many times expressed himself on poverty as an evil; probably the quotation CFA had in mind was contained in a letter to Boswell (7 Dec. 1782): "Poverty is a great enemy to human happiness; it certainly destroys liberty, and it makes some virtues impracticable, and others extremely difficult" (*Boswell's Life of Johnson*, ed. George Birkbeck Hill, 6 vols., Oxford, 1887, 4:157). CFA inscribed the quotation as a part of the epigraph on the front flyleaf of his personal account book, 1829–1844 (M/CFA/9).

TUESDAY. 31ST.

Clouds and showers with thunder and Lightning throughout the day. I remained at home and read Thucydides whose third book I finished. The picture it gives of the state of morals which the war introduced into Greece is shocking enough. Every City was divided into two parties, the aristocratic and democratic. The one favouring Sparta, the other Athens. It was a contest between two principles of government, neither of which are capable of well ordering mankind. It would seem however as if the world was on a larger scale destined to exhibit the same scenes. May they not close as before in a military despotism.

Read some of Sidney, who is rather dry. He is a staunch Republican. I also finished Seneca upon a question whether retirement is proper for a wise man. It is a pretty fragment enough. My other time was divided between the debate in the first Congress and the life of Mr. Canning. On the whole I now accomplish a good deal when at home.

Yet I ought to remember my Grandfather's constant advice, "Studium sine calamo somnium."

WEDNESDAY. AUGUST 1.

Morning cloudy, damp and cold. I went to town—My time there being almost entirely taken up in settling Accounts, and making up my books. Having received from Henshaw & Co. the amount of their Note and Interest,[1] I proceeded to Mr. Phineas Foster's and there paid over to him the sum due to the Minor Children of T. B. Adams Esq. from the Legacy to their Father, under the will of John Adams. This completes the amount of that legacy, and so far as it goes relieves my father's property from a charge of Interest of nearly two hundred dollars a year.[2] This business consumed all the morning.

In the afternoon, read a part of Seneca's first book upon benefits but on the whole did not effect so much as I ought to have done. How often does this remark escape me! but we are not masters of ourselves.

In the evening, Conversation with my father, principally political. He explained to me a great deal of the history of last winter—The plans of the various parties and his own difficult position between them. Perhaps considered historically this may be of some value to me. It certainly is worthy of deep remembrance.

[1] See above, entry for 21 Jan., note.
[2] See above, entries for 13 and 26 March, notes.

THURSDAY. 2D.

I went to town. Read a little of Major Hordynski's book and was engaged in a general examination of all my books of Accounts, which resulted in ascertaining their correctness. Little or nothing else material. The hours of the morning escape almost without any possibility of knowing how. Though in many respects the habit of coming to town is a very wasteful one, it has advantages in the exercise which it occasions.

Afternoon, I first went down to take a walk and a bath at Mr. Greenleaf's Wharf. The water was pleasant, but the eel grass was troublesome and I did not stay long. On my return, Mr. A. H. Everett and J. B. Davis called from Boston with Dr. Parkman soon after. They remained all the afternoon and most of the evening. Their object seemed to be to inquire of my father the political prospects in Pennsylvania and New York which if it was, they certainly did not get much satisfied in.

FRIDAY 3D.

Remained at Quincy all day. More of a Summer feeling in this than I have experienced for some time. Read a considerable portion of Thucydides, containing the history of the affair of Pylus and the Island of Sphacteria which brought the People of Sparta instantly to terms. The mistake was the grasping for more on the part of the Athenians. This is perhaps one of the unfavourable features of Republics. Read some also of Sidney who argues from the badness of one to the goodness of another, which is hardly right. The extremes of Government are equally pernicious.

Afternoon, finished Seneca's first book of Benefits containing all the common places relating to the manner of dispensing them. We had a brief shower after which I went and took a bath. I think I never felt the water more delightful nor saw it more clear. Engaged afterwards in copying. Quiet evening.

SATURDAY. 4TH.

My Wife accompanied me to Boston and thence to Charlestown to see Mr. and Mrs. Everett. We found them in tolerably good health and spirits. She was looking much better than I expected. I stayed only a minute and returned to town. I did very little however, after my arrival. A walk to the House after a book or two, with some two or three Commissions is all I could mention to account for my time. My Wife remained at Charlestown to come over with Mr. Everett. I called for her at one at Mrs. Carter's and we reached home to dinner.

Afternoon, I read a good deal of Seneca's Second book of benefits. As a moralist he certainly stands exceedingly high. I do not know any more pure and clear idea of Charity than that exhibited in this book, always excepting the divine commandment. Took an agreeable bath with my father at the Wharf and passed the evening quietly at home.

SUNDAY. 5TH.

Morning very warm with clouds, and in the afternoon some rain. I attended divine Service all day and heard Mr. Whitney. His morning Sermon upon the nature of the Saviour as a Communion Sermon. Some observations upon the inaccuracy of the Text. For my part, I think the substitute proposed is as expressive. I was not attentive however, my mind being somewhat in vacancy.

Read today, a part of the life of Canning. His biographer claims an undue share of credit to him for his influence in South American

Affairs. Mr. Canning recognized the independence of these States, not from any sympathy with them, nor from any regard to the question which had been existing for so long between the Colonies and the Mother Country. He did it because it suited the interest of Great Britain, because the commercial interest was to be consulted, and more markets were to be secured for the consumption of British Manufactures. Mr. Cannings principles were somewhat of a singular character. A stiff supporter of the aristocratic features of the Government of his own Country, he yet knew how to use the popular doctrines in his intercourse with foreign nations, when they availed his single purpose of benefitting England.

MONDAY. 6TH.

Cloudy with an Easterly Wind, which in the afternoon produced heavy rain. I went into town, accompanied by James Field, the son of Mrs. Field, the child's Nurse, who had come from Boston to see her. I had a quiet morning reading Major Hordynski and one or two of the Essays by Mr. Southey lately published in a separate volume. They are very amusing.[1] I also read Mr. Slade's Speech in the House of Representatives which is a severe invective upon the Administration of Gen. Jackson.[2]

Notwithstanding this account of my time I feel sensible that I am doing nothing for the benefit of myself or of others. But I do not clearly see any mode of amending my ways. The thing must be endured until some opening shall take place by which my labours can have a direction.

Dined at the Tremont House and went from there in a shower of rain to the Boylston Market, where a Meeting of the Directors was held according to custom. As usual a discussion arose which lasted until nearly six o'clock without any prospect of a termination. I was obliged to make a move, so that the business was transferred to a Committee.

Heavy rain during my return to Quincy. Quiet evening. There was an alarm respecting the Cholera in Boston in consequence of sickness at the State Prison.

[1] Robert Southey's earlier periodical contributions were collected and published as *Essays, Moral and Political*, 2 vols., London, 1832. Dr. George Parkman had lent the first volume to JQA a few days earlier. JQA's opinion of the essays differed from CFA's initial response to them: "They are like the withered flowers of a hortus siccus. Like stale Champaign wine. Like an almanack of a year long gone by. Like an old letter of my own writing. Like anything that once was fresh and lively and brisk and now is obsolete, flat and unprofitable. He

republishes them as if they were the vaticinations of Cassandra" (JQA, Diary, 7 Aug.).

[2] The *Speech on the Resolution Relative to the Collector of Wiscasset* (Washington, 1832) by William Slade of Vermont in the House of Representatives on 5 May, which proceeded from a consideration of the case of the Wiscasset, Maine, collector to a general attack on official corruption, was listed in CFA's catalogue of his pamphlet collection (Adams Papers, Microfilms, Reel No. 326).

TUESDAY. 7TH.

Clouds and occasional rain. I remained at home today. Began reading a Biography of Oliver Cromwell with the view of making something out of it.[1] I was led by it to look into the Parliamentary History and to make a kind of Analysis of the facts in the beginning of the Revolution.[2] I have thus cleared my ideas still more. Perhaps I should have written some passages of my last Essay differently at this time. But vox missa nescit reverti. I must stand the test of my own offering. My whole morning was taken up in this manner.

Afternoon, finished Seneca's second book of benefits. I certainly am agreeably disappointed in this work. He makes a great deal out of it. And what is more he hits upon a doctrine of extraordinary purity. He considers generosity as it's own reward, excepting so far as gratitude on the part of the benefitted heightens it. This gratitude acquits the debt. Though a kind of obligation yet remains, to be valid for the return of benefits, provided the thing is possible.

Evening, continued Mr. Canning. My life on the whole at Quincy is a studious one. I accomplish a good deal, though somewhat of a varied nature. It may fairly be questioned how far my plan is beneficial to me, but one thing is certain, that I know not how I can at present better myself. Perhaps if I was to write more and read less, it might be more useful, but I do not feel like taking so much trouble unless under the incitement of publication in prospect. This is a suggestion however worth thinking over again.

[1] Mark Noble, *Memoirs of the Protectorate-House of Cromwell.* CFA's bookplate is in the edition published at Birmingham, 1784, in 2 vols., now at MQA. However, only the day before, CFA had borrowed a copy of the work from the Boston Athenæum.

[2] An edition of *The Parliamentary or Constitutional History of England by Several Hands,* 24 vols., London, 1762, with JQA's bookplate is now at MQA.

WEDNESDAY. 8TH.

Weather continues showery. I remained at home and continued very earnestly reading the life of Cromwell. I finished the rapid Summary of events which the biographer places in the beginning. And I made a little abstract of them for my more clearly understanding the time. He will now proceed to develope the application of Cromwell's personal character to these events. I believe that a great deal can be said on this subject. My only interruption this morning was a bath.

Afternoon consumed without much profit—Pasting labels in my father's books, and a few pages of Seneca.

In the evening, continued Mr. Canning's biography—Account of the difficulties between Portugal and Brazil. He seems to have had full enough in his hands. In looking over the accounts of European diplomacy, it is curious to observe the intricate network which is laid over the whole division of Europe, and through Europe, of Asia and America. Is this necessary, or is it of the thousand and one puzzles of the human brain to enlarge itself.

THURSDAY. 9TH.

Heavy showers all day. This was the day appointed by Governor Lincoln as a day of fasting, humiliation and Prayer, on account of the disease which is spreading so generally through the Country.[1] For myself I felt disposed to observe the day according to the spirit of the declaration, abstaining from luxuries in eating and drinking as well as from any thoughts of an unworthy character. By an accident I was prevented from attending Church although I almost got there. Instead of it, I attempted as an exercise, an analysis of the three Chapters of Matthew which contain the Sermon on the Mount. I accomplished only the first.[2] Mr. Degrand came out from Boston and dined, and passed the Afternoon. He brought no news of particular consequence excepting as to the increase of the Cholera in Philadelphia. Quiet evening at home.

[1] Governor Lincoln by a proclamation of 27 July had named 9 Aug. as "a day of public fasting, humiliation and prayer." Businesses were closed and religious services were held generally (*Boston Daily Advertiser & Patriot*, 30 July, p. 1, col. 6; 11 Aug. p. 2, col. 4).

[2] See entry for 2 Sept., below.

FRIDAY. 10TH.

Heavy rain in the morning which prevented my going to town as I had intended. Occupied in pasting labels for my father so that I have not much to say in favour of my own progress. A bath at noon. The water was chilly and I had a cold so that I was not perfectly confident of the prudence of the measure.

I finished the first volume of the life of Cromwell, and was surprised to find how much could be said in his favour. Indeed there have been few men who have had so much injustice done them. All the fables about his early life seem to be conclusively disproved. And a great deal of stuff has been published about his private character, originating in the malignity of a subsequent, unprincipled age. I think I shall attempt to write something upon this subject.

Afternoon continued reading the third book of Seneca, upon benefits—Whether a Slave can confer a benefit upon his master. He settles it clearly. Evening quiet at home. The weather cleared but the musquitoes were troublesome. Finished the second volume of the Political life of Canning.

SATURDAY. 11TH.

Beautiful morning. I went to town. Time engrossed by the usual variety of little minutiæ which benefit nobody and vex me. It is making a considerable sacrifice to the few people who come to see me, to go and waste much of what might prove serviceable. Whether I am taking the right course or missing my way it is impossible to say. I do sometimes mistrust myself. But then I know that all that has been gained by me within three years has been the result not of acquirement at the Office but of reading and reflection in my Study at home.

Called at the Athenæum and from thence upon Mr. Audubon the Ornithologist with some letters which my father requested me to present to him.[1] He was not at home. Returned to the Office and read some of Major Hordynski. Mr. Jackson the Painter called about the House in Tremont Street. Returned to Quincy.

Afternoon, read Seneca, and finished the third book upon benefits. Can a child confer a benefit upon his father? Doubtless. Evening, Mr. Beale called in. Finished Adventurer, vol. 1.

[1] John James Audubon had had one of his sons, John Woodhouse or Victor Gifford, call on JQA at Quincy requesting letters of introduction for Audubon who was on his way to Maine "in pursuit of birds for the completion of his great work" (JQA, Diary, 10 Aug.). Copies of the letters which JQA wrote in Audubon's behalf to John Holmes, Benjamin Vaughan, and Peleg Sprague are in the Adams Papers (11 Aug., LbC's).

SUNDAY. 12TH.

Fine morning although we had a sea fog for half an hour. I attended the divine service all day and heard Mr. Capen of South Boston preach. I have gone back again in my habit of attention in Church since giving up the practice of examining the Text. I regret it but then what can be done? The generality of the Clergy who preach at Quincy certainly have exceeding little to attract any one—Manner very poor, and matter somewhat common place. This was not the case however with Mr. Capen.

I read a little of the second volume of Oliver Cromwell, and in the Afternoon continued my attempt to consider the Sermon on the Mount. This may prove a beneficial exercise to me. Miss Smith and Miss E. C. Adams dined here. Dr. Stevenson called to see the Baby and Mrs. Adams, on his road to Plymouth. Evening Mr. and Mrs. Miller, Miss Smith and Miss Adams paid a visit.

MONDAY. 13TH.

Fine morning and clear, warm day. I went to town and was engaged during the morning in my usual manner. Nothing of particular consequence took place. Finished the book of Major Hordynski upon Poland. I think I have gained a good deal of information as to the detail of military operations during the war, and a general notion of the causes and consequences of the struggle. This author does not seem at all to comprehend the real motives of action in any party. He limits himself to that which would probably interest his readers while it is more convenient to himself. I never thought that Poland could stand alone against Russia. My only real wonder is that France, who knew that a war with her was impending, did not assist her.

Dined at the Tremont House and from thence to the Boylston Market to meet a Committee upon Rents and Leases; which Committee took up the Afternoon. I returned to Quincy and passed a quiet evening. Mr. T. [*Greenleaf*] and Miss Greenleaf paid a visit.

TUESDAY. 14TH.

My Child has completed her first year. She has on the whole enjoyed a remarkable share of health and has given as little anxiety to her Parents as any infant so young could. May the blessing of Heaven rest on her progress.[1]

I went to town. The day was exceedingly warm. My morning was engrossed by a visit to my House and some trifling interruptions. I also had time to read several criminal trials among which that of the Queen of England. It is one of the historical monuments of that reign. I do not imagine that there can be much doubt of her guilt but the extenuation is to be found in the character of her husband. What morality can a King require in any body around or under him that he is not willing himself to practise?[2]

I dined at the Tremont house and from thence went to a Meeting of Directors of the Boylston Market according to adjournment. The afternoon was consumed by them in considering the new rate of rents, and they concluded upon an advance of about eleven hundred dollars. It now remains to be seen how the Tenants will like such a rise.

Returned to Quincy in the evening and after taking a solitary Tea, I went up into town to Mrs. T. B. Adams where the family had gone. Quiet evening. Mr. Gourgas was at home and was quite agreeable. Returned home at nine, and after a little conversation with my Father, and two Adventurers, retired.

¹ LCA's letters during the summer provide a picture of LCA2's health, appearance, and progress at the end of her first year: "She is a singular looking Child. . . . Her eyes are very dark her hair light and the form of her head exactly like your Fathers" (to JA2, 2 June); "the peculiar formation of her head seems to occasion some uneasiness to her father as the Dr. who attended her in Boston seems to think she will cut her teeth hard and that her head will be much affected in consequence" (to JQA, 6 June); "she has superb eyes but they indicate high temper and want sweetness" (to Mrs. JA2, 10 July); "your Father calls Abby's Baby a giant" (to JA2, 27 July); "we found she had cut three teeth last week without our knowing it. She is the picture of health but is so fat she has no idea of walking" (to Mrs. JA2, 13 Aug.; all the letters in Adams Papers).

² CFA's words and the fact that his historical reading at this time was in the 17th century make it clear that the reference is to Catherine of Braganza, wife of Charles II.

[*Medford*]   WEDNESDAY. 15TH.

Morning clear, and weather exceedingly warm. I went to town as usual preparatory to going to Medford for a week, as my Wife wished to see her Sister. At the Office where my time was taken up in reading the Criminal Trials of all ages and Countries.¹ A work got up with a good deal of judgment and success. It gives to be sure a very melancholy picture of the depravity of man, but perhaps it is not without a valuable practical moral in it. At noon, or a little after, I left town accompanied by Mr. Brooks.

Arrived at Medford and found my Wife and Child had reached there. Wasted the Afternoon excepting insofar as I read a part of the first division of Absalom and Achitophel by Dryden with Sir W. Scott's Notes.² These latter though decidedly party compositions yet do much to elucidate passages time has made difficult to understand.

Evening, I went down to Mrs. Angier's with Mr. and Mrs. Frothingham and my Wife. Some Company there. And singing, some of which was quite good. Returned a little after nine o'clock; a thunder shower took place which lasted some hours.

¹ The editors have not been able to determine which of the numerous collections of trials is meant.
² Scott's notes, "historical, critical, and explanatory," first appeared in the edition of Dryden's *Works* published at London in 1808.

[*Quincy*]   THURSDAY. 16TH.

Morning cloudy but it did not rain. After consideration Mr. Brooks concluded to go down to Nahant with his daughters, and as I was somewhat singularly left out of the party, nolens volens, I was reduced to the alternative of making my own day in some way or other. Mr. Frothingham accompanied me to town.

My inclination was to go to Quincy, and Mr. Degrand, coming in on a little application which required consulting with my father, confirmed it. We had official notice today of the breaking out of the Cholera in Boston. Not much alarm though the general topic of conversation. Kirke came in about the Carryal[1] which my father inclined to buy. He took me to see it and in that way consumed an hour. Reached Quincy to dinner.

Found my father and mother quite solitary and glad to see me so that I was paid for my decision. Mr. Brooks perhaps does not mean to hurt my feelings, yet he is always drawing lines between my Wife and myself which make my residence at Medford painful to me, and my recurrence to the kindness of my own Parents doubly delightful. Perhaps I have felt this instance a little too much, but it has been the strongest. I enjoyed myself far more than I should have done at Nahant. Quiet evening. Not having a copy of the Adventurer here I was compelled to omit my numbers.

[1] A light one-horse carriage with seats for four or more persons (*Dict. of Americanisms*: carryall).

Quincy—Medford   FRIDAY. 17TH.

Rain in the morning. I was in doubt as to what to do. Remained at Quincy until nearly ten o'clock when as it seemed to hold up I thought it best to start. My time was in this manner shortened in Boston very much. As there was no additional case of Cholera reported, the public seemed to be a little more quiet. Mr. Degrand called in and I purchased five shares of the Columbian Insurance Co. Stock, and the transfer was effected today. Two of these are on account of my father.[1]

Horatio Brooks accompanied me to Medford. I found the ladies had concluded not to go to Nahant yesterday, after I left there. So that I might have been saved my visit to Quincy. Mr. Brooks and Horatio went. There may have been other reasons for this change of resolution. I should regret it if I had prevented my wife from enjoying herself.

Quiet afternoon and evening. The weather cold. I read part of Mr.

Canning's life, Vol. 3d, in which he treats of the United States and the Colonial question. Also made up my numbers of the Adventurer.

[1] Purchased at $115.25 a share as a part of CFA's program to keep fully invested JQA's funds that might shortly have to be paid to JA's heirs (M/CFA/3).

SATURDAY. 18TH.

Morning cloudy. I went to town accompanied by my Child's Nurse who went in for the day. She being somewhat ponderous retarded my progress a little. Morning consumed very much as usual. I purchased and began to read the exposition of the Committee of the Rhode Island Legislature who investigated the business of Masonry and published a Report, the Copy Right of which was secured according to law.[1] A very extraordinary proceeding. I did not finish much of it. Returned to Medford to dinner.

Mr. and Mrs. Gorham Brooks dined here. Nothing of particular consequence occurred. I continued reading Stapleton's life of Canning, especially in the most interesting period of his life, the close. The account of the Portuguese War — "I called a new World into existence, to redress the balance of the Old." Somewhat of the bravado style. Nevertheless Canning deserves some consideration for his support of liberal opinions at a time when a formidable combination existed against them. He was ambitious, but that surely is not a Crime if directed to an honest purpose with honest means.

[1] Although there were a number of pamphlet publications purporting to be records of the legislative investigation in Rhode Island in 1831–1832, CFA seems to have been reading the *Report of the Committee Appointed by the General Assembly of Rhode Island to Investigate the Charges against Freemasonry & Ma-* sons ... *Together with All the Official Documents and Testimony Relating to the Subject*, Providence, 1832. This account, the fullest of those published, consisted of the committee report of 72 pages and an appendix of 148 pages containing documents and testimony.

SUNDAY. 19TH.

Is it possible that I should have finished my record of yesterday without recollecting that it is the completion of twenty five years of my life? What can I say of myself on this occasion — Have I done as much as I ought to have done? Am I what I should be? He must be eminently happy who can say yea conscientiously to these questions. I believe I can say that I am happy—That my share of prosperity has continued so far increasing rather than diminishing; at all times, I will humbly acknowledge, far beyond my deserts. But I must admit my exertions not to have equalled my duty, and my success to be trifling. Perhaps my position is not by any means as advantageous as it was, and the habits of retirement in which I am settling down, to be making it worse daily. If so it is, I regret it. But I never will do an act merely for the sake of popularity or public attention, nor will I court any man only to advance myself. My conscience must be clear or my position will be gone. Let me, as I trust I ever will, place my great reliance in the support of the Deity.

The day was excessively rainy. We attended divine service however and heard Mr. Stetson preach two respectable Sermons. The remainder of the day was passed quietly at home. I finished the life of Canning. He died at a critical moment for his fame. No one knows how affairs would have turned out. But he did not leave an equal behind him. How totally the face of Europe is changed since his death.

MONDAY. 20TH.

A beautiful morning. I went to town accompanied by Mr. Frothingham. Walked to the Athenæum to get a book, and from thence went to an auction room to see the library of my Uncle, the Judge, which is to be sold this week. It contains many valuable works.[1] Returned to my Office and read a little more of the Rhode Island Pamphlet. It is a very singular production. Arguing two ways at once—For the fraternity and against it. Warmly opposed to the Antimasons, and conceding the soundness of their principles. After a fair consideration of this question, I cannot avoid the conclusion that the Masonic Society as a principle is false and unsound even in the point of its charity and useful exertion. Its *exclusive* character, its secret character, its assumption of a sacred character, and inflicting of penalties, are all in my mind at variance with the foundation of society and government, of morality and religion.[2] Returned to Medford to dinner.

Horatio Brooks left this day on his voyage to Calcutta. He sails tomorrow. I walked to see the Rail Road—A great piece of work in crossing the Mystic River.[3] A good deal of company at the House. Mr. and Mrs. J. Hall,[4] then W. G. Brooks and his afiancée Miss Phillips,[5] then Nathl. Hall. Quiet evening. Read Frankland travels in Sweden and Russia.[6]

[1] The library of TBA was to be sold at Cunningham's Auction Rooms on the 22d and 23d by order of his executor. His general library of works in English, French, and German, and consisting of histories ancient and modern, biographies, and travel narratives; files of the *North American Review*, *Port Folio*, and *Analectic Magazine*; the works of Shakespeare, Byron, Scott, Moore, Burns, Sterne, Voltaire, Rousseau, Molière, &c., were to be sold on the first day. His law books and his books in Latin were to be sold on the second day of the sale (*Boston Daily Advertiser & Patriot*, 21 Aug., p. 1, col. 3).

[2] This marks CFA's first unequivocal statement of opposition to Freemasonry

and his first step toward identification with the antimasonic movement with which JQA had associated himself for a year. On the history of JQA's participation in Antimasonry in 1831 and 1832 see Bemis, *JQA*, 2:276–296; on CFA's early moves toward an active role in Antimasonry see Duberman, *CFA*, p. 45–48.

[3] The first railroad bridge across the Mystic River at Medford was a wooden structure built on pilings. When it was later damaged by fire, it was replaced by a granite arch with a fifty-foot span constructed by Asa G. Sheldon under the direction of Patrick Jackson.

Medford Historical Register, 12 (1909): 57, 65; 30 (1927):facing p. 48; the autobiographical *Life of Asa G. Sheldon: Wilmington Farmer*, Woburn, Mass., 1862, p. 169, 240.

[4] Perhaps Joseph Hall of Medford (b. 1759), whose mother was a member of the Brooks family (Brooks, *Medford*, p. 543).

[5] On William G. Brooks and Mary Ann Phillips, see vol. 3:132.

[6] Capt. Charles Colville Frankland, *Narrative of a Visit to the Courts of Russia and Sweden in 1830 and 1831*, 2 vols., London, 1832.

TUESDAY. 21.

Fine morning. I went to town accompanied by Mr. Frothingham. Morning passed quietly at the Office. Engaged in reading the Report on the Masonic Investigation. My own opinion is now pretty well made up. On principle I disapprove of every thing like Masonic Societies, not considering Morgan's murder as any thing other than one illustration of what such combinations can be made to do.[1] With regard to the persons who conduct the party,[2] and to the measures which they adopt to sustain it, I have always had much more doubt—At least so far as concerns this section of the Country.

Returned to Medford to dinner. Afternoon pretty much wasted. Took a walk with Mr. Brooks and heard him descant upon the beauty and merit of his land. It is rich certainly, and has been much improved by him. The scene is very lovely although not of the commanding kind which I confess I am more fond of.

On our return to the house P.C.B. Jr. came out with a stranger, and after his departure evening came on. I read a few pages of Frankland. Evening, Horatio Brooks came out—His vessel not ready.

[1] The abduction and murder of William Morgan in 1826 and the subsequent trials in New York State marked the beginning of political Antimasonry in the United States. JQA had earlier this month completed a thorough study of "The Murder of William Morgan" (MS,

5–17 Aug., Adams Papers). The subject became one of continuing interest to CFA, and in 1833 he published as Nos. 8 and 9 in his series of Antimasonic articles in the *Boston Daily Advocate*, the "History of the Morgan Abduction."

[2] That is, the Antimasonic party.

WEDNESDAY. 22.

Fine morning. For two or three days past I have taken a shower bath at the small house under the bank of the Canal, and I feel better for it. Went to town. Office, thence to the House, and thence to Mr.

Cunningham's Auction Room where the books belonging to my Uncle the Judge were selling. I purchased a few. But my father coming in I immediately quitted the field and betook myself to my usual occupations.[1] Finished the Masonic Pamphlet which on the whole has done much to convince me of the great impropriety of the Institution.

Returned to Medford. Afternoon wasted. Miss Gray passed the day with the ladies. The baby has for two or three days past been apparently labouring under an attack of the measles, but so slight that it is difficult to pronounce it to be so. Mr. Everett came up for fifteen minutes with one of his children. Mrs. Angier and Mr. Jos. Angier came to tea. Some music in the evening. A pretty do-nothing kind of life, but pleasant enough to those who have no admonitions from conscience of higher duties which they are neglecting.

[1] "I found Charles at Cunningham's Auction room where they were selling my brother's Books. I purchased a considerable number of them. They all sold very low. There were several of mine among them" (JQA, Diary, 22 Aug.).

THURSDAY. 23D.

Fine morning, quite unexpectedly to me for it was raining last evening. I went to town accompanied by Mr. Frothingham. Nothing of particular moment taking place there, I went to the sale of books at Auction and bid in one or two. On my return I found my father sitting quietly in my Chair. His object in coming in I do not understand, nor did I inquire.[1] He left me soon afterwards, and I saw but little of him. Occupied myself as well as I could with the Criminal Trials which is the only amusing work I have within my reach.

At noon I returned again accompanied by Mr. Frothingham. Afternoon wasted. Mr. Brooks had gone to Framingham. Mr. and Mrs. Everett called and paid a short visit. He seems either low spirited or indifferent to what others say or think whom it is not his immediate interest to conciliate. This is prostituting the best feelings of private life. Quiet evening.

[1] JQA came in to Boston to fulfill an engagement made with A. H. Everett, who was seeking to effect a compromise between the antimasonic forces and the National Republicans looking toward the selection of a mutually acceptable candidate for governor (JQA, Diary, 23 Aug.).

FRIDAY. 24TH.

Fine day. I went to town as usual. Morning passed as usual. I got a chance to go to the Athenæum and read a little, for my Office work is trifling. Even the business I usually transact has ceased. My father's

Tenants do not come near me. Read a little more of the trials. A work very judiciously compiled—The records of crime exhibiting the force of the passions. How one error invariably leads to another. How the best feelings of human nature once perverted can produce the worst of consequences. Adultery and murder, Robbery and murder, Gaming and robbery, Forgery and licentiousness, are constantly connected. These however do not surprise. How much more strange is it, when there is an absence of all motive.

Returned to Medford, being the only one of the gentlemen who did. I had a quiet afternoon in which I read a part of an apologetic life of Cromwell which I found in the library of Mr. Brooks. It is unsound. The reasoning is almost all of it false. He must be justified upon different grounds. Mr. Brooks and Mr. Frothingham came out in the evening and announced a new case of disease in Boston. Quiet evening.

Quincy
SATURDAY 25TH.

Fine day but the weather has turned off quite cold. I took my last shower bath this season and found it extremely pleasant. Left Medford after breakfast accompanied by Mr. Frothingham. My visit has on the whole been quite a pleasant one, yet I think I see alterations going on which will result in material changes before long. This is merely my own feeling. I hope and trust that we shall all be benefitted by them.

Time passed in town partly at the Office partly in going to the House to obtain some papers and Journals for my father who talks seriously of resuming his great undertaking,[1] a circumstance that I am very glad to see. This has been delayed too long already. Went also to the Athenæum for half an hour.

At my usual hour I rode to Quincy. My Wife had reached there before my arrival. Found the family much as usual, and spent the afternoon in reading the life of Cromwell. My absence has however broken the connection of my thoughts so much that I fear I shall have to give up my project or go over all the ground again. Miss Smith dined at the House but returned home in the Afternoon. I accompanied my Mother in a visit to Mrs. T. B. Adams and Mrs. Angier who is there. Returned and retired pretty early. A short conversation with my father upon political Affairs.

[1] That is, his life of JA. During the next several months JQA often, though not invariably, recorded in his journal that he had written a page of biography during the day (JQA, Diary, 28 Aug. – 2 Nov. *passim*).

SUNDAY. 26TH.

Fine Morning. I attended Divine Service all day and heard Mr. Green preach from the famous Address by Paul to the Athenians. This is the same man whom I heard on the 26 of February last, and have spoken of in this Journal. He sustained his reputation with me and perhaps increased it a little. His Sermons were somewhat Sectarian it is true, but his reasoning on the whole is good. His argument against the Trinity from the fact that Paul omits all notice of it in this explanation of Christianity to the Athenians, was curious and striking, though *not* conclusive.

Mr. Degrand came out and dined. In the afternoon, I continued my Analysis made of the Sermon on the Mount, without progressing very far. Evening, Mr. Beale came in. Conversation.

MONDAY. 27TH.

Inasmuch as my horse was quite tired by the amount of his work during the last fortnight and as my occupations did not prevent me from indulging, I remained at Quincy all day. Time occupied in reading the remainder of the life of Cromwell. I have lost my interest very much in my undertaking. Probably the whole thing will end in nothing. My time here is now not at my own disposal. I have not the quiet which aided me so materially in the commencement of the Season. Yet it is with regret that I give up undertakings of this kind, for I am advancing in life and they are the only means by which I can make any corresponding advance of character.

Afternoon, resumed Seneca. This break occasioned by my absence has done me much mischief. In Seneca I have lost the thread and it is almost useless for me to go on. A studious man never should allow interruptions in his occupations unless he has so arranged them that they divide nothing in halves. Evening quietly passed at home. Nothing took place of any consequence.

TUESDAY. 28TH.

Fine morning. I remained at home very quietly all day. My time was taken up partly in writing a slight and poor beginning upon Cromwell, partly in drawing off a sketch of some ideas for the Newspapers. I did not succeed very well in either of these attempt[s] from numerous interruptions which took place. Finished Mr. Noble's sketch of the Protector with that of some of his family. He ought to have some credit for rearing his children carefully. They do not seem to have possessed any portion of his energy of character, and considering the temper of the nation, perhaps it was as well for them.

After dinner read a little of Seneca. My father seems now to begin to take interest in the biography of my Grandfather and to feel a disposition to file and arrange his Papers. If this should come to any thing I shall feel obliged to turn my attention again to them after having given them up some time since in despair.

Evening, I accompanied my Mother and Wife in visits to Mr. Whitney and his family, and to Mr. Miller's. We got home by nine o'clock.

WEDNESDAY. 29TH.

Fine day. Remained at home again. Wrote off a fair copy of the draught which I mentioned yesterday and was engaged in reading again the first volume of Mr. Oliver Cromwell's book. But somehow or other I do not take to it now. The clearness of my ideas is all gone. Perhaps in a week or two it may come back again. In the mean time, my labour seems to be very much without an object. My spirits are not very good in this state of things.

After dinner, I sat about the old files and went over a considerable number of letters received during the period commencing with this Century.[1] There is a vast deal of trash with very valuable matter in this collection of Papers. I think it incumbent upon my father to take some course by which the latter shall be picked out and placed in a form to be made durable.

Evening at home. Read aloud in assisting my father the last Chapter of Sir Jas. Mackintosh's Dissertation upon the History of Ethical Philosophy.[2] Finished 2d vol. of the Adventurer.

[1] "I took up with Charles the project of assorting them, and after three hours occupation upon them found we had scarcely begun. I determined to begin by reducing all the Letters to Alphabetical files, and then subdivide them into collections from individuals, chronologically arranged. This labour will be exceedingly tedious and long" (JQA, Diary, 29 Aug.).

[2] The "Dissertation on the Progress of Ethical Philosophy" had been written for the *Encyclopædia Britannica* in 1830 and was also published separately in that year at Edinburgh.

THURSDAY. 30TH.

My father went this day to Cambridge to attend the exercises of the ΦBK Society. I rode to town and passed my morning in attending to matters of business. Called at the Athenæum and spent half an hour looking over the Newspapers, then saw Mr. Degrand. My time in this manner was pretty entirely consumed so that I did nothing in reading excepting to look over one or two old papers of Mr. Southey lately re-printed in form by him as if they were worth preserving from oblivion — A conclusion I have not been able to reach.[1]

Afternoon passed in assorting my Grandfather's Papers. One old trunk is left which contains great numbers. I worked hard upon them and made a material diminution in the amount. With the exception of Seneca for half an hour, I did little or nothing else. Evening, Captain Basil Hall's sketches to the Ladies.[2]

[1] See entry for 6 Aug., above; CFA returned to a reading of Southey by borrowing vol. 2 from the Athenæum.

[2] The 1st series of Capt. Basil Hall's *Fragments of Voyages and Travels* had appeared in 3 vols. at Edinburgh in 1831; a 2d series, also in 3 vols., in 1832.

FRIDAY. 31ST.

I did not go to town today. My father did, to dine with Mr. Coolidge.[1] I went on working upon the Papers of my Grandfather until I could say that so far as I knew how, all the letters were filed and assorted of which I had any knowledge. This is not however the worst part of the work. There is a re-examination of the whole which I cannot do, that will cost much trouble.

Afternoon accomplished something in Seneca nearly finishing the fourth book upon the question whether benefits should be conferred upon improper subjects or such about whom there is doubt. He comes across and modifies the Stoic doctrine as he proceeds. Worked for an hour in the garden by way of exercise clearing and pruning. Quiet evening. Continued Captain Hall.

[1] Other guests at Mr. Joseph Coolidge's included Governor Lincoln, Col. Josiah Quincy Jr., Peter C. Brooks, Edward Coles, Edward Tuckerman, and Rev. W. P. Greenwood (JQA, Diary, 31 Aug.).

SATURDAY. SEPTEMBER 1ST.

Cold morning but clear. I went to town. Time taken up partly in going to my House for Papers, partly in business transactions, and partly in a nameless kind of way which is fairly to be set down to waste. It is somewhat severe to be obliged to put down so large a quantity of precious time to no definite account. Some things however ought not to be done, some things it is more prudent not to do, and the rest as mere action is trifling. My only proper deportment is hard study and that I am sorry to say, I do not go through with. My spirits sink whenever I reflect upon what a useless life I lead. It is the only thing that annoys me in my present condition. I must go on trusting in my good conduct and in a higher Power who works my benefit even when I do not know it and imagine the reverse.

Returned to Quincy to dinner. Afternoon consumed in attending the public funeral of Dr. Phipps of this town. A worthy man who expired a day or two since without the least warning, and has left a large circle [of] mourners.[1] The Prayer by Mr. Whitney and the Sermon by his son were appropriate and impressive. I thought it a fine spectacle to see the voluntary homage paid by a Community to an Individual sustained by no recommendation beyond his own private character. It was not so affecting as Dr. Gorham's death, though that ceremony was marred by the want of genius in it's Orator.[2] Evening quietly at home.

[1] Dr. Thomas Phipps, who had succeeded his father Thomas Phipps in the practice of medicine at Quincy, died at forty-six of a heart ailment while on his rounds (George Whitney, *Some Account of the Early History and Present State of the Town of Quincy* [Boston, 1827], p. 58; *Boston Daily Advertiser & Patriot*, 1 Sept., p. 2, col. 6).

[2] On the funeral of Dr. John Gorham and the address on that occasion by Dr. James Jackson, see vol. 2:361.

SUNDAY. 2D.

Fine day although the Wind was Easterly. Attended Divine Service all day at the Meeting house and heard Mr. Whitney. We were quiet at home having only Miss Smith and John Q. Adams Jr. to dine.

I did not accomplish a great deal during the day. I finished however, the last Chapter of the Sermon on the Mount. I am sensible that this is very poorly done. But it may serve as an exercise and an improvement. It may teach me more complete familiarity with the sublime rules of Christian morality, and in this way may operate some good in my practice in life.[1] Evening, I walked with my father to Mr. Quincy's. Found there Mrs. Miller[2]—Mr. and Mrs. Quincy being absent, though they returned before we left—and Messrs. Miller and Beale. Conversation rather dull. Returned early walking, although the Ladies went in the Carriage. Roads unpleasantly dusty.

[1] Beginning on the Fast Day, 9 Aug., and continuing on the next four Sundays, CFA wrote an analysis and exegesis of the Sermon on the Mount (Matthew, 5–7), now in the Adams Papers (Microfilms, Reel No. 318), "rather as an exercise to help me to master the great truths which it teaches, than from any hope of further elucidating its sterling value."

[2] That is, Col. Josiah Quincy's mother-in-law, Mrs. Samuel R. Miller.

MONDAY. 3D.

Three years ago on this day, I was married. So far, I have never had occasion to repent it. Much has been said upon the danger of marrying early, but for a man constituted like me I believe it to be something of a safeguard.

Went to town with the expectation of remaining all day, but as the Boylston Market Directors did not meet I returned at the usual time. J. Q. Adams Jr. went in with me. I was engaged morning round in various errands, and doing little or nothing serious.

On my return, found my Mother had gone to town and was not yet returned. Afternoon, I read some of Seneca though not much from it's being shorter than usual from delay of dinner. Evening quiet at home.

TUESDAY. 4TH.

Heavy rain and cold. I remained at home all the morning, trying to revive my taste for the examination of Cromwell's life. I did not do much in that way as I could not find the authorities upon which the assertions against him are founded.

At noon, I accompanied my father to a Meeting of the Proprietors of Neponset Bridge. They generally have a Dinner at Squantum, Mr. Beale's place, upon that day. The weather was dreadful for so exposed a situation. Mr. T. Greenleaf, Mr. Miller, Mr. Gourgas, Mr. Beale, Price Greenleaf and I were the only persons there. Our dinner was Chowder, Wine and indifferent Fruit. It was so cold that I drank an unusual quantity of Wine.

We returned home, and I read to the Ladies part of the Book of Mr. Vidocq, a scoundrel of the French Revolution.[1] But my Wine being Claret and turning very acid upon my Stomach, I felt quite unwell before going to bed. I read the Adventurer as usual.

[1] Eugène François Vidocq, *Memoirs*, 4 vols., London, 1829.

WEDNESDAY. 5TH.

Fine morning. I arose feeling very unwell and my sickness did not abate for some hours. Indeed I do not know when my stomach has been so completely bouleversée as it was this morning. I am taught by this, first that I was very imprudent in my Diet, secondly, that I have been somewhat out of order, thirdly, that I drank more Wine than I ought and of an improper kind. It is rare that I find myself brought up to account on this score. And it is not a little astonishing to me that it should be at a time when prudence is essentially necessary to life. I was good for nothing all the morning and lost a pleasant dinner at which Dr. Waterhouse was present from Cambridge. Read a considerable portion of Stone's book upon Masonry — A treatise which goes very far to sustain the whole principle of Anti-masonry.[1] Evening. Conversation with my father upon it, until late. I retired to bed, taking Medicine and omitted the Adventurers.

[1] William L. Stone's *Letters on Masonry and Anti-Masonry Addressed to the Hon. John Quincy Adams*, N.Y., 1832, had been published in June (see Bemis, JQA, 2:294, and below, entry for 26 Nov.). The presentation copy from the author to JQA is at MQA.

THURSDAY. 6TH.

As I felt somewhat under the influence of medicine, I concluded to remain quietly at home during the day, though contrary to my original intention. Time occupied first in finishing W. L. Stone's book and then in reading irregularly with relation to Cromwell. My ideas are so totally out of method that I believe I must give the point up. Stone's book has given me for the first time a clear idea of the nature and extent of the Morgan excitement. I do not wonder at it. I wonder much more that the Institution should have baffled it[1] to so great a degree. I do not well make out how any fair minded man can read that book and not be astonished as well as shocked with the influence of Masonry.

Afternoon, I read a little of Seneca. Wrote a letter to I. Hull Adams in answer to one of last June[2] and worked a little in the Garden.

Evening, read a little of Vidocq to the ladies, but he is un peu fort. Made up the numbers of the Adventurer.

[1] That is, muffled or thwarted the excitement by confounding or concealing matters.
[2] Both letters missing.

FRIDAY. 7TH.

Fine morning. I felt better though not quite recovered from my sickness. Went to town in the Carriage with my Mother and Wife. Occupied in business at my Office—Looking over Accounts and making balances between my father and self. I also made a purchase of Mr. Degrand on my own Account, the whole of which transaction was completed today. Called at the Fire and Marine Ins. Office for the Dividends due which were on the whole rather better than for some time back,[1] and generally I did much more business today than usual.

At one, I was reminded to go and meet the ladies at Mr. J. H. Foster's where I found them, and we returned to Quincy. Afternoon, engaged in reading Seneca in whose fifth book De beneficiis I made much progress. Questions, how far a man can benefit himself and whether he can be grateful, whether there is such a thing as ingratitude by the definition of the Stoics, &ca. All which are mere turns of words and of exceeding small consequence in the moral system of the world. Had Seneca stopped this Treatise with the fourth book, I do not think much had been lost.

Miss E. C. Adams spent the afternoon and evening here. Mr. Beale, Mr. Gourgas and Mr. Beale coming in at eight o'clock.[2]

[1] Dividends of $1.50 a share were paid, or double the amount paid for the preceding six months (M/CFA/3).

[2] Thus in MS. CFA no doubt intended to write "Mr. Beale" and "Miss Beale" since Mr. Beale was accompanied by his daughter Anne (JQA, Diary, 7 Sept.).

SATURDAY 8TH.

Fine morning. I went to town. Time passed at the Athenæum and office. But I had no business to transact. The Tenants are as slow as ever. I amused an hour in reading a part of a late work of Chateaubriand upon French History.[1] He is a Royalist of the Bourbon species. A man now for the second time undergoing an eclipse. A good writer and a sensible man, though imbued with the prejudices peculiar to his caste. I have taken up his book from a curiosity to know how he will treat the history of France in its ancient stages. A remarkable thing is that he says nothing of Sismondi.

Returned to Quincy. Read and finished the fifth book of Seneca discussing whether a father or connection is bound by the act of conferring an obligation upon a son or relative. All this is refining. Worked a little in the Garden.

Evening, read to the ladies some of Dr. Granville's Journey to St. Petersburgh—A courtly physician.[2]

[1] In the edition of the *Œuvres* in 28 vols., Paris, 1826–1831, owned by the Boston Athenæum, Chateaubriand's "Etudes ou discours historiques" is begun in vol. 4, which CFA had borrowed.

[2] Augustus Bozzi Granville, *St. Petersburgh. A Journal of Travels to and from that Capital . . .* , 2 vols., London, 1828.

SUNDAY. 9TH.

Morning clear but day windy. I attended Divine Service and heard Mr. Lamson of Dedham — A good writer though not an attractive Preacher. He seems to have a good deal of sound sense conveyed in a simple manner. The first Sermon was upon progressive improvement, the other upon procrastination. But I cannot follow them. Somehow or other, I do not easily account for my time upon a Sunday although I am not sensible that I waste any.

Read in the Afternoon a Sermon of Mayhew upon Sobriety, being the first of a series addressed to young men.[1] I was a little disappointed in it's character though it is highly likely it was and is well adapted to the purpose which the Preacher had in view. Rode a little more than halfway into Boston to carry James Field, the son of my Child's Nurse on his way. Returned before Sunset. Weather quite cool. Evening, I read a little more of Dr. Granville.

[1] Jonathan Mayhew, *Sermons to Young Men.* JQA's copy now at MQA is of the 2-vol., London, 1767, edition. All the sermons in the collection relate to the virtues associated with sobriety or the evils that accompany its opposite.

MONDAY. 10TH.

Fine morning. I went to town having made an engagement with Mrs. Proctor to be ready to receive her rent.[1] This business completed, there was nothing else done. I sat at the Office some time and from thence attended a Meeting of Proprietors of the Fire and Marine Insurance Company. It was the Annual election of Officers and I thought I would take the opportunity to look a little into the state of the Stock. My examination was a very satisfactory one to myself. It proved to me pretty conclusively that the Company would do well to wind up inasmuch as it would probably pay back more than the par value of the Shares besides certain old claims that would perhaps turn out for something. But as a working establishment it is not likely to produce much for the future. Yet I see little prospect of it's being wound up. Most of the principal Stockholders have borrowed money upon their shares, which they would be obliged to repay, and the hardship of depriving the President, who is popular,[2] of his place deters others from attempting such a thing. I would advise selling, but nobody will buy.

Nothing particular happened and I returned to Quincy to dine. Afternoon, read some of Seneca. Quiet evening at home. Copied a long letter of my father's.[3]

[1] A. B. Proctor, dressmaker, occupied a tenement at 101 Tremont Street (M/CFA/3; *Boston Directory*, 1833).
[2] Aaron Baldwin; see vol. 3:303.
[3] JQA to William L. Stone, 10 Sept. (LbC, Adams Papers), on Antimasonry.

TUESDAY. 11TH.

Morning clear but windy. I accompanied my Mother to town in the Carriage this morning, and was busy during nearly all my time in commissions on her account. First, in buying provisions for her at Market and afterwards in obtaining fruit. I had therefore but little time to myself. We returned home pretty soon too.

Afternoon very much cut up. I was in the first place engaged in reading Seneca, then taken off in attending to Visitors, Gen. and Mrs. Sumner and her Son Mr. Perry,[1] and after them Mr. and Mrs. Tarbell. Then I had some Strawberries to plant in anticipation of a heavy shower in the evening.

A Country life is certainly pleasant enough in the Summer months, but it is very wasteful of time. I have become exceedingly careless on this subject, much more so than is proper, but what can I do? Without immediate object to give my studies a direction and without conveniences to make the most of the day, it is hard to do right. Quiet evening. I read Dr. Granville to the Ladies.

[1] On Brig. Gen. William H. Sumner of Dorchester see vol. 1:320 and below, entry for 27 September. His wife was the former Mary Ann (D'Wolf) Perry of Bristol, R.I. (*Columbian Centinel,* 7 Oct. 1826).

WEDNESDAY 12TH.

The rain and wind of the night ceased this morning to give way to a beautiful day. I arose and busied myself all the morning in reading M. Chateaubriand's Preface to his Etudes Historiques, alluded to the other day. His views are somewhat peculiar and curious. He considers society as founded upon three truths, as he calls them. Philosophical, Political, and Religious truth. The differences between these, or the influences which have represented them, and the preponderance of one over another unduly, have caused all the different stages of the progress of man, and the lessons of History. He has a further doctrine about the influence of the Catholic Religion, which being a Catholic is natural to him although in my humble opinion totally unsound.

We had to dine today, Mr. and Mrs. S. Brooks, and Mr. and Mrs. Everett. Pleasant enough and they went home about five. Quiet evening at home. The Cholera seems at last to be taking serious hold in the City. Read aloud a little of Dr. Granville.

THURSDAY. 13TH.

Fine morning. The weather is clear and cold. I am fearful the crop of Corn will not ripen. Passed my morning mostly in the Garden attending to my portion of it, the Raspberry and Strawberry vines. These will probably next year produce to us a full and fine quantity of fruit. I have done a good deal in my way and my exertions so far have been pretty well rewarded, somewhat unlike my father who has planted without definite plan, is encroaching on all sides upon his last resort, a garden, and in spite of perpetual losses finds himself embarrassed with trees which he knows not where to place with any prospect of ultimate existence. And yet he goes on and on adding to his difficulties, until the end of it will probably be a wild scheme engrossing a good deal of valuable farming land, only to terminate in complete failure of the whole. This is my present impression. My mind does not know the theoretical any farther than as it *clearly* guides to a practical end. No stumbling along in the dark.

I went with my Wife to Boston where she left me to spend an hour, and walk over to our common destination, Charlestown, which I did with Sidney Brooks. A family dinner party at Mr. Everett's, consisting of Mr. and Mrs. Frothingham, Mr. and Mrs. Sidney Brooks, Miss Davis[1] and ourselves. The dinner was a very pleasant one and ended in good time to have some singing from Miss Davis afterwards. We returned home to Quincy at five and reached it by sunset after having enjoyed ourselves very much. Mr. Everett has a very genteel manner of entertaining.

Quiet evening at home. Read a little of Dr. Granville and being slightly heated I retired pretty early.

[1] Maria, daughter of the Charles A. Davises of New York City (JQA, Diary, 29 Oct.).

FRIDAY. 14TH.

Fine morning. I remained at home very quiet and read a little of M. Chateaubriand, though far the largest portion of my time was devoted to putting the Garden in a state of somewhat better order than it has been of late. I pruned down the luxuriance of growth of the raspberry vines and Cherry trees. The greatest difficulty with us here is the excessive tendency to make wood.

In the afternoon, after having read a little of Seneca, I thought I would go down and visit the Orchard at Mount Wollaston. I found the Trees looking better than they did in the Spring, but still sickly and in a discouraging condition as to the future. I have interested myself in their success, believing the experiment to be a fair one. And I do not propose as yet to give it up, although things at present do not promise. I turned my eyes from the prospect to that of the scene around me, and thought I had never seen it look more beautiful. The day was one of the loveliest of the declining year. There was scarcely a breath of air and the setting sun threw a rich golden hue over every spot upon which it shone. I never was so much struck with the peculiar beauty of Mt. Wollaston. The Panorama is perfect and I felt for a moment as if I should be happy to possess a dwelling house on this situation.[1] It was however but for a moment. The enjoyment of the scenery can always be had at a cheaper rate. Returned home. Evening quiet. Read a little of Dr. Granville.

[1] On CFA's long-continued delight in Mount Wollaston, see vol. 3:268.

SATURDAY. 15TH.

Morning warmer. I went to town and was engaged my whole time in overseeing the putting of three tons of Coal into my Cellar at home. This is but a sorry account to give of time, but as I have no trusty person to place there and as the honesty of the Coal Carrier was not warranted, I felt obliged to be upon the spot. Found my House dry and the Cellar clean and in good condition.

I was detained until two o'clock and reached Quincy by three. Consequently, the Afternoon was very short. I read some of Seneca relating to the intent in conferring an obligation, but I have become satisfied the thing is altogether too much drawn out.

Quiet evening. Read a little more of Dr. Granville who, I think is amusing as well as instructive. The day was warm with a South Wind which terminated in a severe thunder gust at night. Finished the third volume of the Adventurer.

SUNDAY. 16TH.

The Storm produced a lovely Summer morning which I enjoyed exceedingly in a little walk with my Child in her little Carriage. Attended divine service all day and heard Mr. Gannet of Cambridge preach. I have a totally improper prejudice against the man. His afternoon Sermon contained however the argument which has always been convincing to me against the doctrine of natural depravity, and which I have stated in this book somewhere, drawn from the invitation of little children by the Saviour, "for of such is the kingdom of Heaven." I read a Sermon of Warburton upon Truth which I did not find remarkable,[1] and afterwards continued Chateaubriand. Mr. Degrand dined and spent the day. Quiet evening at home. Continued Dr. Granville and began Adventurer volume 4.

[1] Probably the sermon by William Warburton, Bishop of Gloucester, entitled "The Nature and Condition of Truth," which was the first sermon in the two volumes of his *Works* (12 vols., London, 1811–1841) devoted to sermons.

MONDAY. 17TH.

Fine morning. I went to town. Engaged in a few Commissions, and among the rest called at the Athenæum. Obtained there Mr. Vigne's, a young English lawyer's, six months tour in the United States,[1] and read it almost through in the morning. But one visitor, Henry Brooks, whom I have not seen before since his return from Europe. He is a good deal altered in appearance and manners, looks older and more settled if I may so call it. He staid but a few minutes.

Returned to dinner. Afternoon engaged in copying a Letter or two of the Arrears which have been occasioned by waiting for a new book.[2] This broke up so much of the time that I devoted the rest to pasting in Papers in his [JQA's] books. Short evening. Read Dr. Granville.

[1] Godfrey T. Vigne (of Lincoln's Inn), *Six Months in America*, 2 vols., London, 1832.

[2] That is, a new letterbook for JQA (now numbered Lb/JQA/27, containing copies of JQA's letters from 12 Sept. 1832 to 12 March 1834, Adams Papers, Microfilms, Reel No. 151). Following a long letter dated 12 Sept. in ABA's hand are four letters dated 14–17 Sept. in CFA's hand. For the remainder of their stay at the Old House ABA and CFA between them performed the duty of amanuensis for JQA.

TUESDAY. 18TH.

Lovely day. We seem at the termination of the Season and yet we have at no time had a pleasanter specimen than today. I remained at Quincy but did not do much in the way of study. My early morning was consumed in copying for my father, and the latter part of it in putting labels into the books. This business is endless. A whole morning's work seems like nothing when compared with what remains to do. Besides it is a shabby account to give of a man's time, if he claims any intellect at all, to say that he has been doing the work of a paper hanger.

Henry Brooks and Miss Julia Gorham came out here to dine, and we had quite a pleasant time. The afternoon passed.

Evening. My father, mother, Wife and I went into town to hear the Germans sing. After a tour through Canada since the 9th of June they were tempted by their good success to come again and get another harvest from Boston. The Room was full, music good, and we returned safe in good season.[1]

[1] See above, entry for 9 June. JQA pronounced the concert of the Herrmanns "pleasant and pretty, but the fashionable music has changed since I frequented Concerts and Operas — Rossini and Von Weber have taken the place of Paësiello and Cimarosa. They performed this Evening one Piece of Haydn and one of Mozart. The rest were all of new Composers. The House was well filled. Of my acquaintance very few. Another generation" (Diary, 18 Sept.).

WEDNESDAY. 19TH.

I remained absent from town again all day, though I can hardly say that I have a sufficiently good account to give of my time to compensate it. My morning was spent partly in the garden, partly in reading. Finished the first volume of Chateaubriand's Etudes Historiques. It is after all nothing but a skeleton. Mere annals so dry that I do not wonder at his saying in his Preface, nobody would read the book.

Afternoon, I continued the work of pasting in labels into the smaller volumes, occasionally dipping into them — Among others, the works of Crebillon the younger.[1] A French Writer who has done his utmost to deprave the imagination of his Countrymen. It is singular how much more of this style there is in French than in English Literature. The morality of France always has been very poor in its quality. But the reigns of Philip the Regent, and Louis the 15th completed the perversion of it. It is to be hoped that among the good effects of the Revolution this will prove one of the greatest. Private morals are the great foundation of a State.

Evening, at Mr. T. Greenleaf's. A few of the Quincy People. Conversation.

[1] Claude Prosper Jolyot de Crébillon *fils, Œuvres complètes.* The edition published at Maestricht in 1779 in 11 vols. and with JQA's bookplate affixed is now at MQA.

THURSDAY. 20TH.

Morning cloudy and looked very much like rain. The first thing that was announced to us was that the Baby had been sick during the night. She has so little sickness, that at this Season any thing like it alarms us. She was better during the day.

I remained quietly at home all the morning. Read the Preface of Bolingbroke to his Dissertation upon Parties, and some of this piece itself.[1] I find my views of the English History during the Stuarts generally born out by him. He has some power with his pen though he is frequently faulty. Spent an hour comparing and correcting MS Journals with my father,[2] and then rode in the Carriage with my Wife to Boston.

A dinner at Mr. Bradlee's.[3] Company consisted of Mr. Brooks, Sidney and his Wife and Henry, Mr. Frothingham and Wife, Mr. J. D. Bates,[4] a Mr. Teschemaker, and Mr. Mier, besides F. H. Bradlee and his Wife.[5] The dinner was quite a pleasant one. The two foreigners with the singular names did a great deal to enliven it. It is a little remarkable that the first of the two should have been an Englishman.

We left the table before six and returned directly to Quincy. I was fearful I had been imprudent in diet, though I know not why. I did not suffer.

[1] First published in *The Craftsman*, 1735, Henry Saint John, Viscount Bolingbroke's *Dissertation upon Parties* in its 10th edition, London, 1775, is among JQA's books now at the Boston Athenæum (*Catalogue of JQA's Books*, p. 122).

[2] "I began ... with Charles to compare my father's old Journals with the copies of them that I have had made"

(JQA, Diary, 20 Sept.).

[3] Josiah Bradlee's residence at 20 Pearl Street (JQA, Diary; *Boston Directory*, 1832–1833).

[4] John D. Bates, merchant, currently living at the Tremont House (*Boston Directory*, 1832–1833).

[5] Frederick H. Bradlee, associated in business with Josiah Bradlee, lived on Milton Place (same).

FRIDAY. 21ST.

As the Weather changed and the appearances were rather in favour of a Storm of some days, I thought I would go to town today instead of tomorrow. At the Office, most of my time occupied in various ways, doing as much as I could. Went to the House where I was glad to see the Mason had done his work pretty thoroughly. One or two applications for Houses and Offices and all told. Indeed the account which I can render of my [1] never corresponds to the quantity spent.

Returned to Quincy. After dinner, read Seneca de beneficiis, book 6. I have been a most incredibly long time about this business. Seneca is not one of those Writers in whom you find reason to hurry. His doctrine of the present book is upon the question how far particular gratitude is due for a general benefit. And how far it is due when the benefit is not voluntary. Minor questions these.

Notwithstanding the bad weather, my Wife and I concluded to go according to invitation to Mr. Whitney's. Nobody there but ourselves and the new Doctors who rushed into the town on the decease of Dr. Phipps—Gordon, Stetson, and Dorr. The two former are promising looking young men. The latter is an old acquaintance, having been a Classmate at College.[2]

[1] Word omitted in MS.

[2] Charles Gordon, a graduate of Brown, and James Aaron Stetson, of Trinity, had both taken their medical degrees at Harvard in 1832; Clifford Dorr had proceeded M.D. there in 1829 (*Harvard Quinquennial Cat.*).

SATURDAY 22D.

Morning cloudy and it rained occasionally throughout the day. I did not go to town and hardly stirred out of the House all day. My morning was consumed in another attempt to bring into order the Papers of my Grandfather. In this I undid a great deal of my last Summer's work and did it over in a new shape—Alphabetical instead of chronological. Passed an hour in comparing the Journals of my Grandfather written when he was twenty. They display a power of mind which is as striking as his conduct in any subsequent part of his life.

Read more of the Dissertation upon Parties. A charge that the Dissenters favoured James the 2d. Is it true? I think not. After dinner, continued the reading of Seneca. Question, whether a man is justified in wishing evil to his benefactor so that he may have an opportunity of acquitting himself of his obligation by rescuing him from it. Decided that he is not. For it is not in fact doing a kindness. It is wishing what would meet the views of a violent enemy instead of a friend. The case is simple enough, yet he explains its details with considerable success.

I took a short walk in the evening with my father, pasted in a few labels for my father, read a little of Dr. Granville to the ladies and retired early.

SUNDAY. 23D.

Fine clear morning with a much cooler air than heretofore. I was busy during the morning in pasting labels into my father's books. Not a very appropriate occupation but one which I feel never will be done unless I do it. How many things there are among those connected with Quincy, about which I have precisely the same feeling. Perhaps it is all vanity on my part.

Attended Divine Service and heard Dr. Lowell of Boston preach. His Sermons are always simple and impressive—Calculated to affect in a considerable degree a good many People. His morning discourse was upon the presence of God in all our actions. And he dined with us.[1] Afternoon I do not quite remember.

I passed my time after Service in working upon the new arrangement of the J.A. letters. Evening quiet at home. Mr. D. Greenleaf passed an hour.

[1] "Dr. Lowell dined with us, and his son James Russell, a boy eleven or twelve years old" (JQA, Diary, 23 Sept.).

MONDAY. 24TH.

Morning cold and clear. I went to town. The decay of the year again gives me a feeling of inclination to the haunts of men. There is a comfort in the accommodations of the City, not to be found any where else in Winter. And the true luxury of life is certainly to live one half the year in each way.

I was occupied in matters of business today. Brought up my

Quarterly Account which will terminate on Sunday next and collected nearly all the Rents remaining due from the Tenants. This has been a matter of anxiety to me, and I am glad to get through with it—Only however to begin again next week. Thus it is with the business of an Agency like mine. I let the empty Office below mine[1] and on the whole accomplished a very fair business day.

Returned home. Afternoon passed in reading Seneca, sorting Papers, and comparing copy. Evening. Conversation with my father and visit to Mrs. T. B. Adams. For the first time for some years, I suffered in my teeth.

[1] William Brigham was the new tenant; the office was that earlier rented to William Elliot Jr. (M/CFA/3; above, entry for 23 Sept. 1831).

TUESDAY. 25TH.

The day was cloudy with occasional heavy showers of rain but it finally cleared away. I remained at home but did not accomplish much. The pain in my teeth though coming on only occasionally was enough to keep me uneasy, and a considerable time devoted to a correction of Manuscripts of my Grandfather's Journals cut up the remainder of the morning. I pasted in labels of my father's books for the rest of the time before dinner.

This day was fixed for a dinner party. Mr. Brooks and Mr. Frothingham, Dr. Waterhouse and Mr. Henry Ware were to have dined here. The two first only came—The invitation having, by accident, been without limitation to them and excepting the weather in the other case. We had a pleasant dinner notwithstanding. The Afternoon however was consumed as almost all my other time is. Indeed I am running up a heavy account in this respect. In the evening, quiet at home.

WEDNESDAY. 26TH.

Fine day. I went to town and should have enjoyed my ride exceedingly if I had not felt a pain in my head, arising from indigestion and imprudence yesterday. This ought to operate upon me more in the way of warning than it does. My general health and my Constitution are on the whole so good that I ought to be ashamed to trifle with them merely in gratification of a momentary appetite. But so it is with man. In early life he wastes himself because he knows no better. In more advanced years, because he cannot resist temptation. Whether this is or is not so, I had a bad head ache and suffered accordingly.

My time in town was taken up in commissions and in attending a sale of Coal where I finally effected a purchase of my winter's Stock. Then returned directly to Quincy. Dr. Waterhouse and Mr. Ware came today. I regretted my indisposition the more as it entirely disabled me from enjoying their conversation. But as evening came on I recovered and passed a considerable part of it in reading Dr. Granville to the ladies.

THURSDAY. 27TH.

Having purchased my Coal, the next thing was to get it into my House and Office. For that purpose I rode to town, and was occupied about it nearly all the morning. Yet I did not succeed in more than one half the work, which will necessitate my going again tomorrow. I took advantage of the time on my hands to draw off my Quarterly Account, as far as I could previous to the termination of the month. Thus the time passed.

Returned to Quincy. Spent half an hour in correcting old Journals with my father, and we then rode over, My father, Mother, Wife and myself, to Dorchester to pay a visit to Gen. W. H. Sumner and his lady. He occupies a small but pretty rural place, but he was not at home and Mrs. S. was quite unwell so that we returned without entering the House. Our ride was on the whole a pleasant one. Evening quiet at home. I still feel uneasy about the teeth. Read more of Dr. Granville.

FRIDAY. 28TH.

I was obliged to go into town again today for the purpose of overseeing the putting my Coal into the Cellar. And it took up more than two hours of the morning. I am afraid I have been deceived as to the quality of this article which may tend to make our Winter uncomfortable. But it is too late to go back. I shall purchase some of the best quality to mix with it. Returned to my Office, I passed an hour in looking over Accounts &ca., and then went back to Quincy.

After dinner, went on with Seneca whose Treatise de Beneficiis, I have at last almost waded through. I am not satisfied that I have read it with advantage to myself. Seneca is a Writer who must be somewhat dwelt upon. His thoughts must be analyzed, must be weighed with care so as to measure what is good in them from what is bad. In this way his works may be of service. I have done nothing of this.

Had also a conversation with my father the nature of which is not for this Journal. I took the opportunity however to express my opinions upon a subject which appears to me of momentous concern to his future comfort. Having done so once from a sense of duty which I felt incumbent upon me, I have nothing more to say upon the subject and will leave it to take care of itself.[1] A quiet evening at home.

[1] Perhaps the conversation was related to some conclusions and expectations stated in JQA's next succeeding letter to JA2 (5 Oct., Adams Papers):

"I take it for granted that the business of the Mills has suffered greatly by the disability of Mr. Greenleaf following upon your own. These misfortunes crowding upon one another, have brought me to the conclusion that after the present Season that business must be given up. For the next year I shall if possible lease the Mills, and if that is impracticable, dismiss Speakman and the other workmen there and shut them up. For this I wish you to commence making preparation as early as possible. It is probable that the ensuing Winter is the last that I shall pass in Washington, and it will be my wish to dispose of all my property there as advantageously as I can." See also same to same, 19 Oct. (Adams Papers).

However, when the time came for the family's departure for Washington, CFA, who had earlier felt that JQA's political unpopularity in Massachusetts and in the Plymouth district would dictate his retirement from the House (LCA to JA2, 29 Aug., Adams Papers), had become convinced that "the President will probably remain in Congress as long as he has a mind, and I do not see but what General Jackson may have a lease equally long of the Presidency" (CFA to JA2, 8 Nov., Adams Papers).

SATURDAY. 29TH.

Morning cloudy and soon after eleven, hard rain for the rest of the day. This prevented our all fulfilling an engagement made to dine with Mr. Brooks at Medford, and my going to Boston as I had intended. I passed my time quietly at home, first in reading part of Lingard's History of England which I am going over,[1] and partly in comparing and correcting Text of Copy of Journals. William Greenleaf in making them was exceedingly careless. And the labour of altering is considerable. The Journals are to be sure in themselves very full of confusion, but they are worthy of rather more labour to arrange than was paid.

Afternoon, read Seneca. Minor questions, such as whether a man can be released from gratitude as an obligation, if he has made great efforts to repay it yet failed. Compared with a debt, the difference explained. These are small affairs inasmuch as they settle no principle. Passed half an hour at dusk in pasting in labels.

Evening, Dr. Granville to the Ladies, after which I continued Lingard for an hour. On the whole, the day is better accounted for than usual.

[1] There is at MQA, with JQA's bookplate, an edition of John Lingard's *History of England,* 12 vols., Phila., 1827–1830. However, perhaps to have a copy available both in Boston and Quincy, CFA continued to use the Athenæum's copy during the succeeding months in which he was engaged in the study of the work.

SUNDAY. 30TH.

Cloudy with sleet and occasional rain throughout the day. I passed my time in writing, dressing, and pasting labels before Service. Heard Mr. C. Brooks of Hingham preach. His two Sermons were upon a single subject, the primitive Christians, in whose character he recommended the features of unity, peace, love, and charity. The idea is a very good one and much more might be made of it. He dined with us and made himself quite agreeable. He seems a good hearted, kind, and withal tolerably well informed man.

Afternoon, engaged upon the old files of letters, a considerable portion of which I dispatched for the season, in their new form. It would seem as if there was a fate upon these Papers. The procrastination of my father upon this point is very extraordinary. Evening at home. P. Greenleaf came in and passed an hour.

MONDAY. OCTOBER IST.

Heavy rain all day so that I did not stir from the House. Occupied in various ways but in none concerning my own studies. Pasted labels. Compared Text of Journals and copied a long letter for my Father,[1] which must account for all my time until dinner and not much of it idled away either.

Afternoon, finished the seventh and last book of Seneca de Beneficiis. I am well pleased at this as in the course of this Journal, I have often expressed my weariness. Seneca is on the whole worth reading, but it would be better to take him by snatches than to attempt to read him through. One thought may be collected in this way which will be of value, whereas the subsequent ones in a long reading will jostle each other out of the memory. I then put a final hand for this Season to the old letter files, having set them under a new alphabetical instead of a Chronological arrangement. Whether this will answer or [*whether*] it will not be changed to some other next year remains to be seen. Quiet evening reading Dr. Granville—After which I made some progress in Lingard.

[1] Another in the series of JQA's letters to William L. Stone on Antimasonry (30 Sept., LbC, Adams Papers).

TUESDAY. 2D.

Fine day. I went to town early and was occupied the whole morning in attending to matters of business. It being Quarter day, I was obliged to give the finishing to the old Quarterly Account and to prepare my books for the new one. I then went to draw the Dividend of the Boylston Insurance Co. and was engaged in receiving and paying money the rest of the time. On the whole a pretty busy time.

Returned to Quincy to dinner. Found that the ladies had been also to town, and brought out with them Miss Julia Gorham to pass a few days. In the Afternoon I went down to the Creek to try after some smelts. But the Season is not yet sufficiently advanced. The fish will not bite until the frosts come pretty sharply. My Afternoon however was consumed.

Evening, I walked up to Mrs. T. B. Adams' to make my usual payments, and to pass an hour. Elizabeth was sick. Returned before nine o'clock. Evening, read a little of Lingard.

WEDNESDAY. 3D.

I did not go to town today. Morning taken up in writing for my father, correcting old MS and reading Lingard. I find this historian is somewhat influenced by his Catholic partialities. Yet now that the world is free from the dangers of Popish dominion, it may perhaps with truth be asserted, that historians have pushed to an extreme of prejudice their mention of Prelates and of Religion in early time. Dr. Lingard admits the principal charge against them, that of intermeddling constantly in affairs of State. After this it is surely somewhat immaterial whether the men were the vicious beings they are described. I mean immaterial in a historical point of view, because I think as a matter of Justice the mistake if any ought to be corrected.

After dinner, I read several Chapters of Quintus Curtius,[1] and passed half an hour in fishing, with better success than yesterday. Quiet evening. Read a part of Dr. Granville to the ladies and finished the Adventurer.

[1] At MQA are editions of Quintus Curtius' *Historiarum libri* published at Leyden in 1633 and at London in 1746 in 2 vols.; there are two copies of the latter edition, one of which has JQA's bookplate affixed.

THURSDAY. 4TH.

Fine morning. I rode to town feeling slightly unwell, though it did not disturb my comfort in the City. My time was engrossed as usual in a variety of occupations incident to the Accounts of my father and myself. Collected the Dividends due to T. B. Adams and myself upon the various kinds of Bank Stock we possess in small quantities. Arranged the charges on the different Stocks and collected some of the

Rents due to my Father. Had a conversation with Mr. Peabody upon political affairs, by which I gather that Mr. Wirts prospects here at least are not very bad. The result of the Election remains to be seen. I think the prospect is but a dismal one as yet, although it looks infinitely brighter than it has done.

Returned to Quincy and passed the Afternoon in setting out and clearing out the beds of Downton Strawberries. There are enough to make a pretty ample supply if the vines are good bearers which I somewhat doubt.

Evening at home until eight o'clock when I walked up to Mr. T. Greenleaf's whither my Wife and Miss Gorham had gone before me. Nobody there but Mr. and Mrs. Daniel Greenleaf, and the members of the family. Returned and read the Idler.

FRIDAY. 5TH.

Fine morning. I remained at home, and after spending an hour at the Wharf in a vain attempt to catch some Fish, I returned and spent the rest of my morning in reading Lingard and working hard in the Garden. This is about the proper time to make the arrangements necessary for the future. I transplanted all that were necessary of the Downton Strawberry which now make a pretty large bed. Next year will settle the question whether they are worth cultivating. I made considerable progress in the History and am on the whole pretty well pleased. He does not appear to me to do more than show a favourable side, without twisting documents unfairly as Hume does. My father being engaged at the usual time of dinner — It was put off so that the day was very unequally divided.

I passed the Afternoon in paying visits to the Tenants at Penn's hill and collecting their rents in which I was very successful. Mr. Degrand was here on my return. In the evening, the ladies and my father and I went to Mr. Daniel Greenleaf's, where we passed a good deal of time without being very dull. Home early.

SATURDAY. 6TH.

The morning thick and hazy. I went to town accompanied by my father. Of course got in somewhat later than usual. Time taken up in Accounts and collecting Money. This is now nearly accomplished. The first few days of a Quarter must always be devoted to Collections, and I congratulate myself somewhat that I have now got things in such a train that the money comes in with considerable punctuality.

At half past twelve o'clock, my father was very punctual, and we proceeded according to arrangement to Medford.

We reached Mr. Brooks' where we were to dine in time to go down and give my father the opportunity of taking possession of the farm under the Mortgage of Judge Adams to him. It is about a mile on the line of the Canal.[1] This done we returned and found as a Company, Mr. J. Parker, Jo. Tilden;[2] E. Everett, Gorham Brooks and his Wife, Mr. Shepherd, two Miss Phillips' and Mr. Brooks' family with our own. The dinner was not at all amusing to me, first, from my having a seat of the least interesting, second, from the tenor of the conversation which was all upon money. Mr. Parker is very wealthy, and cannot avoid discussing the only subject which engrosses his mind. I am not one of the men who consider riches in the character of a Philosopher, but I do not set them in quite so exalted a situation in life as to make them the subject of perpetual conversation.

My father returned with me and we reached Quincy early in the evening. The Ladies arrived soon after and we all retired early.

[1] See vol. 3:236.
[2] John Parker was a merchant, Joseph Tilden president of the Columbian Bank (JQA, Diary, 6 Oct.; *Boston Directory*, 1832–1833).

SUNDAY. 7TH.

Morning cloudy and mild. The Weather is on the whole fine for the Season. Morning passed in reading Lingard, previous to divine Service which I attended all day. It was Communion day, and Mr. Whitney preached two Sermons the purport of which did not make the least impression upon my mind. My habit of attention built up with so much care last Winter, has nearly vanished.

Miss Smith dined at our house. I can account for my Afternoon, by having read a little of Lingard and a Sermon of one John Balguy upon Censoriousness in a Collection called the English Preacher.[1] I tried to find some Account of the Author but did not succeed. We want a later biographical Work.[2] I thought the Discourse good, but not so superior as I had been led to expect from the character given to him in a number I once saw of the Edinburgh Review.

Quiet evening. Conversation. Finished the second Volume of Lingard, and read the Idler as usual.

[1] The collection of sermons published as *The English Preacher*, 9 vols., London, 1773, and now at MQA has JQA's bookplate in each of the volumes; however, the set was clearly that used over a long period of time by CFA. In 1838–1842, reading a sermon each Sunday and recording the reading in the volumes, he covered the whole collection. Archbishop Tillotson and Balguy are more exten-

sively represented than any other divines, Balguy having at least one sermon in each of the volumes and twelve in all.

² An account of the life of John Balguy (1686–1748), English divine and religious controversialist, appeared in a later edition of the *Biographia Britannica* than that in JQA's library and now at MQA; see above, entry for 15 July, note, and the notice of Balguy in *DNB*.

MONDAY. 8TH.

Morning cloudy but it did not rain. The weather remained doubtful until evening when it cleared away. I went to town. Engaged all the morning in Accounts, when after examination I settled my own and those of all parties. Received the various Dividends remaining due, and adjusted the balances all round. Walked to the Athenæum to read the News but found nothing of material consequence. My time was a good deal of it necessarily wasted from the fact that I have little or nothing at hand to do when a moment presents itself at my Office.

I remained in town until the Afternoon, for the purpose of meeting the Directors of the Boylston Market Association. It is now a long time since I have been present. Upon this occasion we were to look over the Accounts for the Work lately executed. And we found that my estimates so far from being exaggerated did not come up to one third of the cost incurred. The Dividends must therefore be cut off for a year. This is unpleasant to me so far as the Stock of T. B. Adams is concerned who invested here in consequence of our advice and who depends in some degree upon the Money. I cannot help thinking we have been a little extravagant. After going through the accounts, which took until near sunset, I returned to Quincy by a bright but cold moon.

Quiet evening at home. Nothing of particular consequence. Conversation and reading a little of Dr. Granville, after which Lingard and the Idler.

TUESDAY. 9TH.

Foggy morning but a very beautiful day. I remained at home all day and consumed a quantity of it in fishing in company with my Mother. We had very moderate success. Just enough to be tempted to try for more. On my return, passed an hour in comparing Text of the MS.

After dinner, my father wished me to accompany him to Braintree for the sake of taking possession of the Estate there belonging to the Judge.¹ I accordingly went with him in the Carriage and the business being accomplished returned home alone. The rest of the day was short and passed in reading Lingard.

Quiet evening at home. Mr. Beale and Mr. Price Greenleaf called in and passed an hour. I finished the reign of John in Lingard and Idlers as usual.

¹ JQA held a mortgage on the house and farm which TBA had owned and which was leased to Caleb Hollis (JQA, Diary, 9 Oct.).

WEDNESDAY. 10TH.

Morning cloudy, but I went to town notwithstanding, for the purpose of attending to the receipt of some Wood which I purchased the other day. I went to my House but left it in charge of the Office boy, for the purpose of performing Commissions of various kinds. The time has now come to make arrangements for our return to town, in order to which the household must be engaged which is now almost done. Returned to Quincy to dine.

Afternoon passed in reading Lingard in whose book I did not make much progress from the great shortness of the day. After tea, occupied putting labels into books until eight o'clock when I went up to Mrs. Adams'. The ladies took tea there. Mrs. Angier was there from Medford. I was very quiet hearing music until it was time to return home and read Lingard in whom I get along. I like his History so far, quite well.

THURSDAY. 11TH.

Clouds and occasional heavy rain. I remained quietly at home occupied in reading Lingard and comparing with Hume, and in correcting Text with my father. Few men have left closer pictures of their mind in youth, than my grandfather. And to all it is a study of some interest. We came today to the place where a transition of eleven momentous years to him occurred, and where you jump from his hopes and prospects, his wishes and his discouragements, to the hour of his success and establishment in the world. Is it not a lesson. He was six and twenty in the first instance.¹

Afternoon, lost my time in looking over an Account of the trial of two Mr. Sheares for Treason in Ireland in 1798.² Cruel enough. Evening with the family. Read Dr. Granville who is a little too minute to be interesting. Lingard and Idlers afterwards.

¹ In a small stitched booklet in which JA recorded his early reading and studies and in which he made some journal entries (D/JA/4 in the Adams Papers) there is a gap of eleven years between the entry for 20 Nov. 1761 and the next entry, that for 21 Nov. 1772. In the lat-

ter entry JA philosophized on the changes that had occurred during the interval (JA, *Diary and Autobiography*, 1:224; 2:67–68). CFA's words here should probably not be understood to mean that at this time he and JQA had not yet come upon some or all of JA's journal entries, somewhat irregularly made, during the intervening period in one or another of the booklets he used for his diary (same, 1:226, 235, 252, *et seq.*).

[2] *Report of the Trial for High Treason of Henry and John Sheares*, Dublin, 1798.

FRIDAY. 12TH.

Beautiful morning. I do not know that we have a pleasanter month than this when it is tolerably fair. I read a little, but passed most of my time in company with my Mother at the Wharf in an unsuccessful attempt to catch fish. This is rather a waste of time, but I do not do it very often, and it is at least a pleasanter way than that of which I am commonly guilty. Returned home and compared Text for an hour with my father. After which at dinner we had Company, Mrs. Angier and Miss Adams, Miss Anna Harrod[1] and Miss Smith. Nothing material passed.

Afternoon very short. Read but a very little of Dr. Lingard. His book interests me though I read it with distrust. His Account of Edward I and the conquest of Scotland is in some respects new and worth considering. I have long since lost my faith in most of the Romance of History. As the world was always much the same, [*as*] it is now, it is a mere illusion to suppose that perfect heroes are to be found any where. Yet virtue and vice have always been contending with each other, and the former is sometimes successful in a man as well as the latter. This makes our good public historical characters. Evening, Granville.

[1] Presumably one of the daughters of Charles Harrod, brother of Mrs. TBA (vol. 2:166).

SATURDAY. 13TH.

Mild and pleasant day. Miss Julia Gorham accompanied me to town today. She returns home much to the regret, I believe, of all the family.[1] The company of young ladies always contributes much to enliven a House, when they are not bent upon doing mischief. My principal occupation in town was to go to the House and see that every thing was in order there, to attend to several commissions and regulate Accounts. Henry Brooks called to see me a few minutes, and I conversed with Mr. Peabody upon political affairs. The proceedings of the Worcester Convention are to me very singular. The nomination of such a man as S. T. Armstrong for the place of Lieutenant Governor is a political catch like that of Wells last year, for the Mayor's situation.[2] The political news received this day from Pennsylvania is encouraging.[3]

Returned to Quincy, and read in the Afternoon the rest of the reign of Edward the first in Lingard which I afterwards compared with Hume. The material variations consist in the account of the course of the Clergy in resisting the exactions of the Crown, and in the accounts of the Scotch and Welsh conquests. I am inclined to think Lingard's, the nearest to the truth. Evening, read an Article in the North American Review upon Mackintosh which I thought good.[4]

[1] JQA found Julia Gorham "a very amiable and intelligent young woman" (Diary, 13 Oct.).

[2] On the 12th at the state National Republican convention in Worcester, Levi Lincoln was renominated as the candidate for governor and Samuel Turrell Armstrong of Boston was nominated for the lieutenant-governorship in place of Thomas L. Winthrop, who had declined to run again. Report of the nominations was not carried in the *Boston Daily Advertiser & Patriot* until the 15th (p. 2, col. 2). On Charles Wells, currently the mayor of Boston, and on his election in 1831 see above, entry for 15 Dec. 1831, and Winsor, *Memorial History of Boston*, 3:236. Armstrong was to become mayor in 1835 (same, 3:243).

[3] Returns in from Philadelphia city and county and Delaware county in the election for governor of Pennsylvania held on the 9th showed majorities for the anti-Jackson candidate (*Boston Daily Advertiser & Patriot*, 13 Oct., p. 2, col. 6).

[4] A review (unsigned) by A. H. Everett, of Sir James Mackintosh's *A General View of the Progress of Ethical Philosophy*, *North Amer. Rev.*, 35:433–472 (Oct. 1832).

SUNDAY. 14TH.

Morning cloudy but it cleared away towards night with a sharp North-Westerly Wind. I attended Divine Service all day and heard Mr. Whitney without the attention which I think is due to him. I shall set about a reform when I get back to town. Mr. Degrand came out and gave us the Newspapers containing very flattering Accounts of the Election from Pennsylvania. There is now a prospect that the Country may be redeemed.

Afternoon read a good Sermon of Mr. John Balguy upon the subject of Differences of Opinion leading to Discord. His discourses are short and plain, but well conceived and full of strong, downright sense. Evening, Josiah Quincy spent an hour. I afterwards read Lingard. But on the whole I have not an adequate account to give of my day.

MONDAY. 15TH.

Fine morning but very cold. I went into town and felt more chilled than I have done this autumn before. Time taken up at the Office writing. I am attempting another short article on politics. The present crisis is such that every little counts. The intelligence from Pennsylvania is very encouraging. It seems to show that the People have still a redeeming principle about them, that they are not at the feet of a man all the time without any exercise of judgment. Attended a sale of Coal and purchased at quite a reasonable rate a Chaldron of very excellent quality, and this winds up the Stock for the Year. Returned to Quincy.

Afternoon passed in reading Lingard and comparing him with Hume. There is no material variation in the Account of the Reign of Edward the second. Perhaps Dr. Lingard inveighs with more justice and warmth against the Murderers of this Monarch—The philosophical character of the other historian leading him to speak of vices and virtues with almost equal indifference.

Quiet evening. Mr. Beale came in for a few minutes with his daughter[1] who goes to school in Boston tomorrow. Afterwards, read Granville, and having finished Lingard's third volume without having the fourth, I passed an hour in looking over the Port folio—An Old periodical containing much of my father's contributing.[2] I could not help reflecting concerning it, how much of it was old and stale. Such is the fate of all writing for particular occasions and indeed of all review writing. If a mind cannot produce, if the power of invention is wanting, it is needless for him to expect any thing like durable reputation.

[1] Anne Beale (LCA to Mary Roberdeau, 28 Aug., Adams Papers).
[2] Among JQA's books now at MBAt are bound copies of each of the first five volumes of the *Port Folio* (Phila., 1801–1805) containing JQA's bookplate and TBA's autograph. One or the other of the two owners has indicated by initials those contributions which he knew to be by JA, JQA, or TBA, all of whom contributed to the magazine in its early years. JQA's contributions, much the most extensive, included his "Journal of a Tour through Silesia" (see above, vol. 3:233), translations in verse and prose, and articles on politics and literature. The connections of the various members of the family with the *Port Folio*, including a comprehensive list of the contributions of each, are given by Linda K. Kerber and Walter John Morris in "The Adams Family and the *Port Folio*," *WMQ*, 3d. ser., 23:450–476 (April 1966).

TUESDAY. 16TH.

Fine morning but cool. I rode to town to see about getting my Coal in, and was accompanied by my Child's Nurse, Mrs. Field. Morning very much taken up at my House. Yet I found time enough to finish and send what I wrote yesterday.[1] My father's advice to me is sound, not to engage myself in the mere easy, every day writing of political electioneering, but to discuss questions upon some clear and definite basis of a public nature requiring information and research.

Returned to Quincy, and wasted the Afternoon with my Mother in fruitless fishing. Evening at home reading Granville. Continued Lingard in the reign of Edward the third.

[1] Whether CFA's article on the current political situation was published is not known.

WEDNESDAY. 17TH.

Milder and clear. I remained at home all day. It was my intention to have employed my time very industriously but somehow I did not carry it into effect. My father gave me an account of the Executors to copy.[1] I then was busy in comparing the old Journals for correction, and this with pasting a few labels is all the rational Account I can give of the passage of time. It is manifestly inadequate.

The Accounts from Pennsylvania today are a little more discouraging. The result is very doubtful and we can only hope for the best.[2] I was hardly aware how much I was interested in the event of this election, until today.

My afternoon was consumed in fishing. A very vain attempt. But I had a pleasant walk along the bank of the Creek as far as Mount Wollaston. I shall put up my rod for some days. Quiet evening. Read a part of Mr. Webster's Speech aloud to the ladies.[3] It is the last effort of a man considerably excited both on public and private accounts against the President. He has wound himself up to inveigh against the Government with a bitterness which in political affairs is unusual with him. No wonder. What can be worse?

In the evening. Continued Lingard in Edward the third. It would be a curious labour to examine how many years in every Reign in England have been consumed in foreign wars upon groundless and frivolous pretences. How much of it's best blood has flowed upon every field of the Continent merely to gratify an idle desire for Conquest and fame. The Reign of Edward is a particularly striking instance of the mischief arising from such ambition. Probably France and England suffered as much during this as during any period of their history.

[1] The copy in CFA's hand of the 7th Report of the Executors of JA's Will is in the Adams Papers (Microfilms, Reel No. 181). JQA had finished the report on the preceding day; it was to be signed by the executors, JQA and Josiah Quincy, and presented to the Judge of Probate at Dedham on 6 Nov. (JQA, Diary, 16 Oct.).

[2] The earlier reported majorities for the anti-Jackson candidate for governor of Pennsylvania had been overturned as the votes were counted in the less populous counties (*Boston Daily Advertiser & Patriot,* 17 Oct., p. 2, col. 1).

[3] The first part of the speech delivered by Daniel Webster to the state National Republican convention at Worcester on the 12th appeared in the *Boston Daily Advertiser & Patriot* on the 17th (p. 2, cols. 2–4); the speech was continued in succeeding issues.

ANTIMASONIC CONVENTION IN VALDIMOR.

9. THE ANTIMASONIC CONVENTION IN BALTIMORE CARICATURED IN AN
ENGRAVING BY DAVID CLAYPOOLE JOHNSTON

See page x

11. THE REVEREND NATHANIEL LANGDON
FROTHINGHAM IN 1842. BY THOMAS BALL.

See pages xii–xiii

10. JARED SPARKS IN 1828,
BY GILBERT STUART

pe, peu ralliée, refusa de le suivre. On rapporte que, dans ce moment, un seigneur écossais, effrayé du danger personnel où s'exposait le monarque, ayant détourné la bride du cheval, ce mouvement, mal interprété, devint le signal d'une déroute qui entraîna tout.

L'armée parlementaire, qui n'avait éprouvé qu'une perte très-faible, fit cinq mille prisonniers, s'empara de l'artillerie et des bagages du roi, ainsi que de beaucoup de dames qui suivaient l'armée. On enleva même une cassette qui renfermait des papiers secrets, dont la publicité * devint un moyen de faire soupçonner la bonne foi du monarque dans les négociations, que naguères encore il entretenait avec les commissaires du parlement.

Cette victoire, si fatale au trône, fut le résultat de la réforme militaire, et sur-tout de la forte et pieuse discipline que l'influence de Cromwell répandait chaque jour dans la nouvelle armée. C'est la remarque de Clarendon : les troupes du roi **, lors même qu'elles avaient l'avantage, se railliaient avec peine. La première armée parlementaire, sous Essex et sous Valler, avait également montré plus de valeur que de constance et de

* Ludlow's memoirs, v. I, p. 167.
** Clarendon's history, p. 430.

Confound him. Why not speak plainer, or publish the letter to speak for themselves.

---

fera convaincu de la vérité de ce principe de notre auteur : que la bonne politique n'est point distinguée de l'excellente morale.

Fin du Tome septieme.

The unribbing remark is true but too will-serious of sentiment... must have any limited notion of the purposes of the Creator in forming Man, render a total want of common sense as to the practicability of any undulations in our day. A community of Interests is a fundamental error in any into, having for its end, the advantage of the human race. that is the desire of History new experience.

12–13. CHARLES FRANCIS ADAMS' MARGINAL COMMENTS ENTERED IN HIS COPIES OF VILLEMAIN'S "HISTOIRE DE CROMWELL" (AT LEFT) AND ABBÉ DE MABLY'S "DE LA LÉGISLATION, OU PRINCIPES DES LOIX" (ABOVE)

See page xv

We have discussed these matters rather more briefly than the subject will admit. More would be unnecessary however, to this our present undertaking - assuming then the position, that there is but one rank of excellence; let us consider what that is.

It is the same with that which flourished in Athens; from whence it happens, that the fame of the Attic orators has spread itself, while their real power is little understood. The greater number have confined their observation to a single point; the absence of any positive faults in them, so that it has rested but with a few to see the presence of a great many beauties. There are faults, whenever, either in the sentences there is any thing absurd, or foreign from the subject, or not to the point, or silly - or in the words there are low, or tame or not suitable; or harsh ones, or when they are used in a strained sense. almost all those called the attics as well as the persons who speak in the Attic style, have avoided these faults. So far as they have any merit, they may rest their claim upon being correct and plain. But like the scholars in a Gymnastic school, they may be never ceasing the course and yet never be fit to try for an Olympic crown - Let us place before ourselves as objects of imitation those who being equally free from faults, do not rest satisfied with this mere good health, and search for strength; for nerve; for blood; and also for the beauty of colour. If we cannot succeed in imitating these, it is better then to follow the persons who enjoy sound health (the peculiarity of the attics) than those of whom asia has produced so many, who are vicious from excess.

In order to succeed in this last pursuit (and success even in this is no trifle gained) let us, if we can, copy Lysias; none particularly in his simplicity; for he sometimes had flights. It was because he treated of many trifling causes about little things and these too for others to speak, that he seems rather dull; and from his intentionally paring down to adapt himself to handle lesser matters. He who does this so much as to lose the power when he had the will to rise, may indeed be called an orator, but he will stand in a very low rank. Yet it often happens that the greatest orator must have recourse to this plain style in the management of smaller cases. The difference is, that a Demosthenes can resort to it when he likes, but it is by no means equally certain that a Lysias can rise to the sublime when he likes. If there are any who fancy that, with an army stationed in the forum and the temples all round it, it would do to defend Milo in the same style one would use in a private cause before a single Judge, such persons estimate the price of eloquence from their own power at it; and by no means from the character of the science itself.

But the remarks of some persons have got abroad, a portion of whom claim to speak in the Attic style themselves, the rest affirm that none of us practise it. We shall pay no attention to the former set: a sufficient answer to them may be

eos: alterum pauci, laudabilia esse multa. Est enim vitiosum in sententia, si quid absurdum, aut alienum, aut non acutum, aut subinsulsum est. In verbis, si inquinatum, si abjectum, si non aptum, si durum, si longe petitum. Hæc vitaverunt fere omnes, qui aut Attici numerantur, aut dicunt Attice. Sed quatenus valuerunt, sani et sicci duntaxat habeantur, sed ita, ut palæstrice spatiari in xysto iis liceat, non ab Olympiis coronam petant. Qui cum careant omni vitio, non sunt contenti quasi bona valetudine, sed vires, lacertos, sanguinem quærunt, quandam etiam suavitatem coloris. Eos imitemur, si possumus; sin minus, illos potius, qui incorrupta sanitate sunt, (quod est proprium Atticorum) quam eos, quorum vitiosa abundantia est, quales Asia multos tulit.

IV. Quod cum faciemus, (si modo idipsum assequemur; est enim permagnum) imitemur, si poterimus, Lysiam, et ejus quidem tenuitatem potissimum. Est enim multis in locis grandior. Sed, quia et privatas ille plerasque, et eas ipsas aliis, et parvarum rerum causulas scripsit, videtur esse jejunior, quoniam se ipse consultò ad minutarum genera causarum limaverit. Quod qui ita faciet, ut, si cupiat uberior esse, non possit, habeatur sane orator, sed de minoribus: magno autem oratori etiam illo modo sæpe dicendum est in tali genere causarum. Ita fit, ut Demosthenes certe possit summisse dicere; elate Lysias fortasse non possit. Sed si eodem modo putant, exercitu in foro, et in omnibus templis, quæ circum forum sunt, collocato, dici pro Milone decuisse, ut si de re privata ad unum judicem diceremus; vim eloquentiæ sua facultate, non rei natura, metiuntur.

Quare quoniam nonnullorum sermo jam increbuit, partim seipsos Attice dicere, partim neminem nostrûm dicere; alteros negligamus. Satis enim his res ipsa respondet; cum aut non adhibeantur ad causas, aut adhibiti derideantur. Nam si arrideantur, esset idipsum Atticorum. Sed qui dici a nobis Attico more nolunt, ipsi autem se non oratores esse profitentur, si teretes aures habent, intelligensque judicium; tanquam ad picturam probandam, adhibentur etiam inscii faciendi cum aliqua

14. "EVENING, MADE A LITTLE FURTHER PROGRESS IN MY TRANSLATION.
I HAVE COPIED IT, INTO THE MARGIN OF THE
QUARTO COPY OF CICERO WHICH I HAVE."

See page xvi

THURSDAY. 18TH.

This morning upon getting up I found myself somewhat indisposed, and as there seemed to be no cause to which I could clearly trace it, I immediately concluded to take medicine. My father went into town to dine with Dr. Parkman. I remained quietly at home in some degree uncomfortable though not much so. My morning was consumed in pasting labels and in reading over with some attention Stone's book upon the Masons. As far as I went I took an abstract of the facts in the case of Morgan's murder as well to fix them more clearly as for future reference.

My afternoon was not passed so usefully. I continued pasting labels and only dipped a little into a volume or two of Bayle's Letters.[1] He teaches how to doubt, but that is useless unless he goes a step farther. Doubting is an easy business.

My father returned at about seven. I read to the Ladies a little of Granville and afterwards had some conversation with my father upon the subject of the Revolution. I find my own impressions were not incorrect in regard to the ancient history. If a man in reading coolly consults the right and the wrong he cannot very often be mistaken. There is a standard existing in his mind by which every thing can be tried. Yet my father suggested one idea to me this evening which I had not fully weighed.

[1] JQA's bookplate is in the edition of Pierre Bayle's *Lettres* published at Amsterdam in 1729 in 3 vols. and now at MQA.

FRIDAY. 19TH.

Cloudy day. I felt but poorly after the severe influence of my Medicine. I remained quietly at home engaged in looking over and abstracting Stone's book. The more I read upon that subject, the more I am struck with the extraordinary and disgusting nature of the whole transaction. The extent of the combinations, the calmness with which they were formed and the plans executed, and the disregard of means in executing them are truly wonderful. I was also occupied in comparing MS with my father, and copying two or three Letters for him.

After dinner, I read a few more of Bayle's Letters. They are amusing but pedantic, display a great variety of reading and a good deal of felicity in application, but are too much the efforts of a mere reader. The world has changed much since his time. It is less willing to hear the effusions of scholars which merely compile the sayings of their predecessors. Yet there is a charm to me in that kind of allusion that I never can get over. In many respects, I am not fit for the matter of fact world of this Century.

Evening. Read a little of Dr. Granville and afterwards Lingard, but not having rested well for the last two evenings, I felt drowsy and retired much earlier than usual.

SATURDAY. 20TH.

Morning cloudy but it cleared away afterwards and became warm. I went to town with the intention of executing much, but did in fact exceedingly little. Disappointed by the non appearance of my Office boy. It seems he has retired probably in disgust with my irregular attendance in town. I was consequently unable to notify the Directors as usual nor to do any thing I intended. Called to see T. K. Davis. Found him engaged with E. Blake but they finished in a minute. Got entangled in a discussion of Anti-Masonry. A thing I did not feel disposed to at all. That is a subject that stirs the blood. Returned to Quincy.

Passed the Afternoon reading Bayle, and pasting labels. The after dinner in the Country is so short, very little can be done in it.

Quiet evening at home. Read the Speech of Mr. Webster, part the 2d. Afterwards, Lingard. Finished the reign of Edward the third. He condemns the claims of the Pope and distinguishes his temporal and spiritual character.

SUNDAY. 21ST.

Morning clear but mild. I attended Divine Service all day and heard Dr. Gray preach.[1] I do not feel much interest in what he says. Indeed in the attention we pay to men, we are very much guided by the respect we pay to their character. Hence doubtless the origin of the Rule that an Orator must be a virtuous man. I have heard too much of the weaknesses of Dr. Gray to regard him in a proper light in the Pulpit. His afternoon Sermon was from the discourse on the mount, which is so often treated and so seldom fully considered.

Afternoon. Read two short Sermons in the English Preacher. One by Dr. Chandler on the Incurableness of Superstition which I did not think much of, and one by Dr. Hoadley upon the impossibility of serving God and Mammon, a good deal better.[2] Evening, Mr. and Mrs. D. Greenleaf and Mr. Beale came in. Afterwards, read Lingard.

[1] Dr. Thomas Gray of Jamaica Plain (JQA, Diary, 21 Oct.).
[2] These sermons of Samuel Chandler and of Benjamin Hoadly, Bishop of Winchester, are in the fourth volume of *The English Preacher.*

MONDAY. 22D.

Morning cold and cloudy. I went to town although feeling quite unwell. I have of late years enjoyed my health so well that any thing like sickness is tedious to me. No office boy and disappointed in getting one. I therefore had to do most of my Commissions myself. Several persons called to settle bills and arrange matters agreeably to my orders. I concluded to go and see Dr. Stevenson and request him to mend my condition at once. He puts me upon a diet, with gentle medicine. Remained in town, but as he restricted me so much I thought it useless to dine any where.

Read the Pamphlet on the Poor Laws of England, published by the Society for the diffusion of useful knowledge,[1] and spent an hour at the Athenæum reading the various Newspapers. Thence to the Boylston Market to meet the Directors of the association. The business was to provide ways and means for the payment of the balance due on Account of repairs. Voted to borrow not exceeding three thousand dollars of the Washington Bank. It will about consume another Dividend. I started a little before sunset, but before I reached Quincy, the Storm was pretty high from the North East. I felt very sick from a head ach and general discomfort, and retired to bed early. Omitted the Idler.

[1] *Hints for Practical Administration of the Poor Laws*, London, 1832, was a recently issued number of the Farmers' Series in the *Library of Useful Knowledge* published by the Society for the Diffusion of Useful Knowledge, London.

TUESDAY. 23D.

I felt much better this morning. My purpose is now to adhere strictly to the Diet prescribed for me. Remained in Quincy all day. Morning occupied in reading and examining Mr. Stone's book upon Masonry. The more I study the details of this affair, the more I am astonished at the daring and the deliberation with which it was conducted. Stone makes but a poor business of his defence of Governor Clinton. He exculpated him from all participation in the thing, but he cannot clear him from indifference in prosecuting the actors. He *might* have known the agency which Masonry had in the proceeding, but he did not care to inquire, and shielded his duty under a blind confidence in the general goodness of the Institution. Compared Text with my father.

Afternoon, amused myself with miscellaneous reading. Began an account of the teachers of Rhetoric by a certain Monsieur Gibert in a French Work called Jugemens des Savans. The work is by Baillet, but this is by way of Appendix.[1] It is so long however that I shall not be able to read it, nor should I, in all human probability, if I was. Quiet evening at home. Read Granville, and afterwards Lingard, besides making up the deficient numbers of the Idler.

[1] Adrien Baillet, *Jugemens des savans sur les principaux ouvrages des auteurs.* JQA's bookplate is in the 8-vol., Amsterdam, 1725, edition now at MQA. The titlepage of vol. 8 reads: *Jugemens des savans sur les auteurs qui ont traité de la Rhétorique . . . Par M. Gibert, ancien recteur de l'Université & professeur de rhétorique au Collège de Mazarin.*

WEDNESDAY. 24TH.

Morning cold and cloudy. I felt much better, and therefore went down to the Wharf fishing. My Wife seemed disposed to call it imprudent, but I did not experience any disadvantage from it. My sport for the last hour was very good. Passed an hour in comparing Text.

Afternoon. Reading one of the Causes Celebres of Pitaval. A man writes anonymous satires and lampoons against his friends. Those friends become indignant and trace the authorship nearly to him, for the purpose of avoiding the effect of which, he labours to fix it upon another person. A trial takes place and the evidence shows that four persons had been suborned to testify against him who was not the author by him who was.

I was interrupted in the midst of my meditations by a visit from Mr. Bussy and his grandaughter Miss Davis.[1] Nobody in the house but me — My Mother gone to take a ride, my Wife to Hingham with Mr. Beale and his children, my father in the woods, so I saw them. The object was to invite to dine on Monday. Evening quiet at home. Read Dr. Lingard.

[1] On Benjamin Bussey see vol. 2:417; his daughter Eliza had married Charles Davis of New York (vol. 2:157).

THURSDAY. 25.

Went to town accompanied by my father. His engagements were such as to require his presence in town at ½ past 9 o'clock which we just accomplished.[1] I went to the House and upon several Commissions. Had visitors to see my father, Mr. Marston, and Mr. Degrand. I wasted my time.

My father engaged me to dine at Mr. J. H. Foster's. This was somewhat against my will as I was not very fit to grace any other gentleman's table with my unqualified Diet. But when a man has adopted a system, it is not worth while to put it all out for a mere inconvenience. I stuck it out, but it was a very unpleasant affair. Mr. Frothingham was the only invited guest besides ourselves. My father was remarkably animated in conversation so that on the whole we did better.

We started at a little before five o'clock and reached Quincy shortly after Sunset. The night was cold. I read Lingard.

¹ JQA's principal mission was to have his newly drawn will (see above, entry for 28 July) witnessed by James H. Foster, Edward Cruft, and Col. Josiah Quincy (JQA, Diary, 25 Oct.).

FRIDAY. 26.

Morning was cold. I started shortly after breakfast, to go to Weston. My fingers ached and I otherwise began to experience in a good degree the approach of Winter. I went through Roxbury, Brookline and Brighton, and could not help noticing the great advances that are making in building and apparent prosperity throughout. This portion of the Country is now in an exceedingly flourishing condition. There is wealth and substantial independence to be seen in almost every direction. But it is by no means so stable, as it is great. The present aspect of public affairs portends changes which cannot fail to jeopardize all our success.

Reached Weston in about three hours and was disappointed in finding that Conant, the Tenant, had gone into town for the purpose of seeing me. Thus after four or five months of waiting, we each hit upon the same day to go in quest of each other. I remained but a short time and then made the best of my way home to Quincy where I arrived shortly after three. The distance is not less than forty miles.¹ I was chilled, and it took me all the afternoon to recover my natural state. Read Lingard.

¹ That is, to Weston and return.

SATURDAY. 27TH.

Clear morning and milder than it has been. I remained at Quincy in consequence of my father's having engaged a meeting of the Supervisors of the Temple and School fund here at twelve o'clock. How the time passed previous to that hour I can hardly say myself. I passed part of it in writing my Diary which had fallen backward some days and part in continuing the Causes Celebres, that part relating the story of the Sieur Rousseau. At twelve, all the Supervisors came, viz. Mr. Quincy, Mr. T. Greenleaf, Mr. Miller, Mr. Beale, and my father.

After transacting considerable business relating to the affairs of the Corporation,[1] we were joined by Messrs. D. and P. Greenleaf and Mr. Whitney which party dined here. After dinner, Mr. Beale spent an hour.

Evening quiet. Conversation until eleven o'clock with my father. One of the few which I catch in the course of a Summer, which are worth remembering. Consideration of the civil and the common law. Reasons of the superiority of the latter — A law of liberty and of purity. The civil Law looks entirely to the government of one man. It is a fair specimen of the sovereignty of a paternal king. The other is the Law of equals. The civil Law has no trial by Jury, no habeas Corpus, it is lenient in the construction of obligations, it is less observant of pure morality. Instances, the penalty of a bond, and the bastardy of children born before marriage. The one is a law of mercy, the other, of rigor. Some observations upon the character of modern study. The avoidance of labour seems to be the great end proposed. Nobody can arrive at greatness who makes that the object of life, hence the superficial character of modern acquirement. Fisher Ames said, Blackstone's book was the spinning jenny of the Law.[2] Blackstone was the most perfect specimen of method extant. Mr. Quincy the other day had depreciated Wood's Institutes, not so bad a book as he made it out to be.[3] Both had taken their arrangement from Justinian. The Roman Law had it's origin from the Greeks, and there is a striking coincidence between that of the latter and the Levitical law. All originated in Egypt. There is a difference however between Greece and Rome. The former especially at Athens was much more of a Government of law, and depended less upon individual authority. Gibbon calls the Roman Republic the proudest aristocracy that ever existed. A digression to the character of Cicero, his low birth, his immense difficulties in rising to an equality with Caesar, Pompey, Catiline &ca. should be taken into account in considering his compliances. On the whole, a very interesting and profitable conversation.

[1] Among the items of corporate business accomplished was the election and swearing in of CFA as clerk of the Adams Temple and School Fund. Because he was not a resident of the town of Quincy he was not eligible to become one of the supervisors (JQA, Diary, 27 Oct.).

[2] JQA's appreciation of Fisher Ames' metaphor on Blackstone's *Commentaries* is perhaps a confirmation of what JQA had long maintained was in fact his attitude toward Ames: admiration for the man and his talents as an orator and image-maker, strong dissent from his political views, especially his later ones from which much of New England Federalism derived. See JQA's *American Principles. A Review of Works of Fisher Ames*, Boston, 1809. See also the notice of Ames in *DAB*.

[3] Thomas Wood, *An Institute of the Laws of England*, 4 vols., London, 1720.

SUNDAY. 28TH.

Morning cold and cloudy. A few flakes of snow and some hail announced to us the rapid march of the Winter. I was engaged in the morning in making up my Diary and writing the unusually long Record of yesterday.

Attended divine Service and heard Mr. B. Whitney of Hingham. His morning discourse was upon the performance of duty — "She did what she could," that is ability to do the method of testing actual performance. The afternoon was upon the parable of the prodigal son. The preacher dined with us and so did Mr. Degrand who came out of Boston to spend the day. I read a Sermon of Mr. Balguy's upon the love of Enemies — The same general characteristic of strong sense unadorned and unpretending.

Mr. Degrand remained part of the evening and the rest was spent in conversation. I read Lingard — His account of the wars of the Roses.

MONDAY. 29TH.

Clear and cold. I went to town. Engaged all my time in commissions. My house is now to be opened and prepared for our reception. I was therefore engaged today in ordering grate &ca. for the Room to be devoted to the Nursery. I also was occupied in making a transfer and effecting a sale of some of my Bank Stock. It has been on the whole not very productive to me and as I can now part with it with a trifling gain to myself and turn it into a direction that may yield more, I have concluded to part with all I have excepting what is in the State Bank.[1] Should General Jackson succeed in his election and the Bank of the U.S. wind up, this Stock will appreciate. At any rate it will be a safe thing, where many of our Banks will be unsafe and I shall transfer my Deposits to it.

I was very much hurried and returned to Quincy later than I had engaged to. Dressed and proceeded with the ladies and my father directly to Mr. Bussy's.[2] Found there, Mr. and Mrs. Abbot Lawrence, General and Mrs. Wingate,[3] General and Miss Dearborn, Miss Wingate, Mr. and Mrs. Kuhn,[4] Mr. Pierpont and Dr. Gray, Mrs. and Miss Davis of course. The House, dinner &ca. was in a style of splendour quite above the ordinary character of gentlemen's establishments here. But the master and mistress are not at all in character. They are vulgar people. I sat next to Miss Dearborn and was on the whole as much amused as I could have been in any part of the table. Returned by moonlight. Read Lingard.

[1] CFA owned shares in the American Bank and in the Boston Bank (vol. 3:333).

[2] Benjamin Bussey's residence and farm in Jamaica Plain were left by his will to Harvard University as a part of his devise for the foundation of the Bussey Institution. The tract constitutes the largest portion of the lands which now form the Arnold Arboretum (information from Dr. Richard Alden Howard, Harvard Univ.).

[3] Joshua Wingate, Harvard 1795 (JQA, Diary, 29 Oct.), of a family identified with the New Hampshire militia for three generations (Joseph Dow, *History of the Town of Hampton, N.H.,* 2 vols., Salem, Mass., 1893, 1:268; 2:1045).

[4] George H. Kuhn, an associate of Benjamin Bussey in the Dedham Woolen Mills (Frank Smith, *A History of Dedham, Massachusetts,* Dedham, 1936, p. 255).

TUESDAY. 30TH.

Weather moderated, making one of the most delicious of our Autumn days. I rode into town for the purpose of making further arrangements in respect to my House. Found that it had not been opened yesterday. And I waited two hours without seeing a particle either of Chimney Sweep or Mason. The Woman came however, and I went down to effect the rest of the business relating to the Bank Shares &ca. My time is always so much taken up when I have no Office boy that I am always in a hurry.

Returned to Quincy. Miss Smith dined and spent the day. I had intended to employ the afternoon, but Mr. J. H. Foster and his daughter[1] came in and I was disappointed for my father left me to bear the brunt of it. They returned to town before tea.

Evening wasted in the Parlour. Read Lingard afterwards and finished the reign of Edward the 5th, the gloomiest period of the whole British history. Began the second Volume of the Idler.

[1] Mary Smith Foster (JQA, Diary, 30 Oct.).

WEDNESDAY. 31ST.

I staid at home this morning while my Mother and Wife went to town. Occupied very constantly though not much intellectually. My father wished me to go into the Garden and examine the Peach Trees which have been usually neglected and suffered to decay more rapidly than they grew after the second year. I did this after writing my Diary which has of late been kept rather irregularly. In our work, we were interrupted by Mr. H. Brooks and Miss Julia Gorham who came out to see the ladies. These disappointments are constantly occurring. They stayed only a few minutes. I passed another hour in pasting in labels. The ladies came home late.

After dinner, I went down to fish but had no sport. The water was too clear, and the winds have been so perpetually to the westward that the smelts remain in deep water. I do not know when we have had a more lovely day.

Returned to tea, and in the evening read Lingard. Richard and Henry the 7th. I think well of the history so far, and as to the wars of the Roses and all the subsequent events, prefer it to Hume.

THURSDAY. NOVEMBER 1ST.

Delicious day. The very perfection of our Indian Summer. I went to town accompanied by Mrs. Nowlan, leaving her at the Catholic Church. Time entirely taken up in Commissions connected with getting the House in order. Went up to the House twice. Went after the Mason and Chimney Sweep who both of them forgot my orders. Made the necessary purchases for the House and worked off as much business as I could. The drudgery attendant upon my not having an Office boy is very great.

I received an invitation to dine in town at my friend Blake's so that I disappointed my friend Mrs. Nowlan in coming out and had a little more time to take care of my own affairs. I went through my own Accounts and rectified my balances for the last month in as good a way as I could, though from the difficulties of small sums I find it pretty hard. Dined at ½ past two. Company consisted of Mr. and Mrs. S. Parkman Blake, Mr. and Miss Shaw, Mr. Payne, Mr. Shelton, Mr. Issarevlen, and the ladies of the family. Our dinner was pleasant and good.

I returned by Moonlight to Quincy. My road was also enlightened by the flames of a barn which was burning in Dorchester and the light of which shooting through a hazy atmosphere and illuminating half of the heavens gave a bright and picturesque appearance to the scene. Arrived at seven. E. P. Greenleaf spent the evening here.

FRIDAY. 2D.

My day was passed at home. I designed to have passed it very pleasantly in getting rid of some of the last occupations which must engage me before I leave Quincy. But Mr. Greenleaf and Mr. Beale came in and engaged me to look over the Library here with them, which occupation though a very troublesome one, I did not feel as if I could refuse. The books are very much out of order—Exposed to the injury of time, of damp, and mice, and utter neglect.[1] I feel an emotion of grief whenever I think of the misapplication of valuable funds in this instance. But what does it serve to lament circumstances beyond one's power to alter? There is enough happening in life in which man must himself be a responsible party, to worry and distress him. He need not seek for additional care beyond.

Evening at home very quietly. Read and finished the fifth volume of Lingard, which completes the first and least interesting part of English history. It is a little remarkable that out of a line of nineteen kings since William the Conqueror twelve held the Crown by force. Title to the Crown by descent is modern. In ancient times it is manifest that it came through the law of the strongest. Henry the 7th perpetuated his power in his own line, without the shadow of a title and from this false root comes the whole line which has since filled the throne of Great Britain.

¹ Thomas Greenleaf and George W. Beale had been deputed to examine the books in the library which JA gave in 1822 to the town of Quincy, and which still remained in the Office (JQA, Diary, 2 Nov.; and above, entry for 17 Sept. 1831, note).

SATURDAY 3D.

Fine morning though a little colder. I went to town accompanied by my wife. Left her at the house and soon afterwards went up there myself. Found all the workmen actively occupied in their various repairs and that my directions were at last in the way of being thoroughly executed. Left the house and did some business afterwards at the Office with Mr. Conant and others. Thus went the morning.

Returned to Quincy with my Wife at one. Engaged after dinner again with Mr. Greenleaf. Finished looking over the books and made up the missing list, which is considerable. A good many of them will however be found hereafter among the scattering works not numbered.¹

In the evening, Mr. Beale came in and passed two hours. Nothing new. Looked over Hume's Account of the Reign of Richard and Henry but found little that was new. Read also my father's Poem of Dermot MacMorrogh, which is just out. There is vigor in the lines, and occasionally a high order of poetry. But as a whole, the work wants invention and imagination. It is totally deficient in descriptive imagery and leans as almost all my father's poetry does, too much to the didactic style. This to the general is caviare. My opinion is, he would have done better *not* to have published it, but my opinion is worth very little in cases of this kind.²

¹ As a condition of the gift of his library JA required that a catalogue of his books be made and published. This was done: *Deeds and Other Documents Relating to the Several Pieces of Land and to the Library Presented to the Town*

of Quincy, by President Adams, Together with a Catalogue of the Books, Cambridge, 1823. Although the books are not numbered in the catalogue, it would appear that at the time of the preparation of the catalogue or earlier, numbers were affixed to most but not all of the books listed in the catalogue. The catalogue would have served as the basis for the inventory being made.

² On the bibliographic history of *Dermot MacMorrogh, or the Conquest of Ireland; an Historical Tale of the Twelfth Century*, see Bemis, *JQA*, 2:218. This narrative, "the subject of my own selection; the moral clear and palpable; the characters and incidents strictly historical; the story complete and entire," in 266 stanzas of Byronic *ottava rima*, was written principally in Washington from February to April 1831. JQA described the method: "I usually compose one, sometimes two, occasionally three [stanzas], before rising, between three and five o'clock, and usually from three to five in my walk round the Capitol Square. These stanzas I retain in memory, and write down after returning home,

sometimes before, sometimes after, breakfast. . . . I read every day to my wife what I have composed in the twenty-four hours" (JQA, *Memoirs*, 8:352, 355).

Nearly a year after publication, in Oct. 1833, when he was preparing copy for a second edition, JQA expressed his own judgment of the poem: "Scarcely any man in this country who has ever figured in public life has ever ventured into the field of general literature — none successfully. I have attempted it . . . in this poem of Dermot MacMorrogh, which is original, and at once a work of history, imagination, and poetry. . . . Like the rest of American poetry, it resembles the juice of American grapes — it has not, in ripening, the property of acquiring alcohol enough to keep it in preservation. I have pushed my experiment on the public temper far enough" (*Memoirs*, 9:24).

Copies of *Dermot MacMorrogh* in several stages of its composition, two in JQA's hand and one in CFA's, are in the Adams Papers (Microfilms, Reel Nos. 237, 242).

SUNDAY 4TH.

Morning windy but mild. I was occupied all day in finishing the various little occupations which have engaged me since my residence here and in returning to their places the various books, so as not to break up sets—A thing which in so large a library is exceedingly likely to happen.

Attended divine service and heard Mr. Whitney all day. My habit of inattention to him is very much fixed. Afternoon drew up the Records as Clerk of the Adams Temple and School Fund and put away the book for the Season.[1] Read a part of Brown's book on Antimasonry, the most extraordinary literary production of modern times. This is the book, that was sent to my father with these words in a fly leaf, "Read this and be cautious."[2]

Mr. Degrand and Mr. W. W. Clapp, Proprietor of the Evening Gazette,[3] came here and took tea and spent the evening. Much conversation upon Politics, the result of the Philadelphia Election, a movement of parties to bring Mr. Webster and my father into collision,[4] and some scientific discussion.[5] I read a few of the letters of Dr. Johnson and Mrs. Thrale.

[1] The Book of Records of the Supervisors of the Adams Temple and School Fund, beginning 3 Feb. 1827, is now held by the City of Quincy as a part of its municipal records at the City Hall, in the keeping of the City Historian, William Churchill Edwards. For a facsimile reproduction of CFA's first entry as clerk of the Supervisors see Descriptive List of Illustrations in the present volume p. ix–x.

[2] JQA's copy of the book is missing. The work referred to is probably that by Henry Brown, *A Narrative of the* *Anti-Masonick Excitement in the Western Part of the State of New York, 1826–1829*, Batavia, N.Y., 1829.

[3] "In Mr. Clapp's paper there are several extracts both from the preface [to *Dermot MacMorrogh*] and the poem with a commentary upon the whole favourable and criticism of no very high order" (JQA, Diary, 4 Nov.).

[4] "They . . . said something of a project talked of they knew not by whom, to place me in the Senate U.S. instead of Mr. Webster" (same).

[5] See below, entry for 18 Nov., note.

MONDAY. 5TH.

Morning cloudy but it cleared away pretty well so as to make it pretty agreeable notwithstanding an Easterly Wind. I went to town and was busy all my time in the preparation which is going on previous to our return. At my house twice. Found the Mason and Carpenter were out of it—And that they were in active preparation for us by clearing and cleaning. The anxiety of an establishment is great. So much responsibility devolves upon the master of a household, so much is to be examined with his own eye, that I do not wonder many people prefer to live single. Yet for myself I cannot say that I am of the number. There is comfort and independence, there is standing in Society and character in married and established life that fully compensates to me the inconveniences. And as to affection, that comes not into the question because it does not admit of comparison.

Remained in Boston, and dined at Mrs. Frothingham's very pleasantly. Attended a Meeting of the Directors of Boylston Market. Nothing of consequence done.

Reached Quincy at six. Ladies took tea at Mrs. Adams's. I walked up with my father at eight. Reported to him my conference with Mr. Webster this morning. I went by his [JQA's] request to see him and say to him that he (my father) had heard with great surprise that an attempt was making somewhere to put him in opposition to Mr. Webster at the election in the Winter. He knew nothing of the source of such a movement, nor did he intend to give it any countenance, for he should take an early opportunity, if he could find any fitting one, to declare his resolution not to allow his name to be used. Mr. Webster replied that he never had entertained the least uneasiness on the subject, that he had no reason to doubt the intentions of my father; the rumour probably originated in the suspicious temperament of Mr.

Buckingham who had wished to incite what friends he had to greater exertion. He had never attached any importance to it and of this he begged my father to be assured. Thus ended the conference.[1] At Mrs. Adams' was Mr. Beale, Mr. Gourgas, and the usual family. Rode home with the ladies. Moonlight and a fog. Read more of Brown's book on Masonry and the numbers of the Idler as usual.

[1] Webster wrote to JQA two days later expressing the same sentiments (7 Nov., Adams Papers).

TUESDAY. 6TH.

Cold and cloudy day with occasional rain. I went to town it being the last day allowed for preparation and arrangement. Time taken up at the house and in giving directions. Found all the furniture taking its old and accustomed places and began at once to feel pretty comfortable. Nothing is more disagreeable than making these changes in a domestic establishment. I mean in a small way. They create a want of a thousand things around one that have got out of the way by want of use. And they generally with us imply a new household which is among the most annoying of things.

Politics with Mr. Peabody. Prospects not very bright. Returned to Quincy to dine. Eliz. C. Adams spending the day. My mother was unwell in her own room for the first time today. I suppose anxiety as much as any thing — The prospect of going away. I expected Mr. Greenleaf, but he did not come. Amused myself by reading Marmontel's Nouveaux Contes Moraux.[1] Some of them are very good. What if I tried to translate?

[1] Jean-François Marmontel, *Nouveaux contes moraux.* JQA's bookplate is in the edition now at MQA, that published in 4 vols., Paris, 1801.

[*Boston*]
WEDNESDAY. 7TH.

The day has arrived when it is time to break up the Summer arrangement and begin the Winter one. It was cloudy and dull but not rainy as I had anticipated. It is now nearly six months since we have been at Quincy and I can say that I have enjoyed the time very much. The Society of my father and mother has been agreeable to us, and our's, we are assured, has not been unpleasant to them.[1] We have lived quietly, without the parade of public life and without its anxieties. Nothing has happened to annoy us with disagreeable or painful feelings, or harass us with care. Perhaps in the history of a life it may be difficult to say this for any period of six months time. It is my duty to be thankful and I hope I am so. Circumstances constantly occur to show me the advantages of my fortune. May they never lead me to calculate too securely upon them, nor to abuse them to useless and foolish purposes.

I came to town accompanied by my child's Nurse — My Wife in the Carriage with my Mother. Busy at my Office in various ways until one when I went home to put my study in order. Found myself in the afternoon as much at home as if I had been there a hundred years. Read several pamphlets, pro and con Masonry. I want to reach the bottom of this subject. It is not an easy one. As usual finished with the Idler.

[1] Of ABA, LCA wrote, "I have found her a lovely and charming companion throughout the Summer and it is a real trial to part with her" (to JA2, 12 Oct., Adams Papers).

THURSDAY. 8TH.

Morning cloudy but it cleared away quite cold. I went to the Office. Engaged a good deal in running about making purchases for the family of the things necessary to get them well going. I had therefore not much time to read though I did succeed in resuming Lingard. I am going to make another effort this Winter to improve my time more than I have done. My distracting occupations will I hope be fewer than they have been, and I shall be able to do more effectively what is in hand.

Called at the Athenæum to get a book or two. Thence home where I found my father. He announced to us that my Mother had left Quincy this morning considerably better in health. And that he had come in for the purpose of starting from our house to Providence in the morning. Of course I did very little else than attend to him. I took the opportunity however of answering a letter of John's inviting me to Washington,[1] and copied one or two others for my father. Read a little of Stone's book over again.

[1] On the letter to JA2 (Adams Papers) see above, entry for 28 Sept., note. JA2's invitation of 17 Oct. (letter missing), which CFA now declined, was elicited by the report contained in an earlier letter to JA2 from LCA (29 Aug., Adams Papers) that CFA proposed to spend a part of the next winter in Washington on the assumption that it would be JQA's last in Congress.

FRIDAY. 9TH.

My father left this morning early for Providence. He goes to Washington to assume new cares and incur more praise or odium according as chance may direct. The disastrous result of the Presidential Election throws a gloom over the political affairs of the Country which is deeper and darker than it ever has been before.[1] The fate of our currency is sealed, and the Judiciary is in imminent danger. Office ceases to be honorable and vicious principle is every where triumphant.

I went to the Office. Read Lingard apud Henry 8. Here begins the interest of *his*, alias a Catholic history. At noon, I returned home for the purpose of going out and paying visits with my Wife. The day was delightful. Called at Mrs. Webster's, Dr. and Mrs. Kirkland, Mrs. Crowninshields,[2] and Mrs. Sparks'—Two at home and two out. Mrs. Sparks is a bride and an interesting woman.[3] Dr. Kirkland has just returned from Europe and looks like an old Beau. His lean Pantaloon is "a world too wide for his shrunk shank," and he in the midst of his decay mental and corporeal indulges a foppery which never became or even would have been thought of in his early days. The spectacle is a melancholy one.[4]

Afternoon, reading over Stone's book. The luxury of my library is very great. Evening. Gardiner Gorham passed an hour,[5] after whom Edward Brooks came in. The rumor of the death of Dr. Spurzheim is not correct.[6]

[1] Although the election in Massachusetts was still three days away and the result in New York was not yet known, the voting in Pennsylvania, Maine, and New Hampshire had been so overwhelmingly in favor of electors committed to the reelection of President Jackson that the outcome in the nation already seemed clear.

[2] On Mrs. Benjamin Williams Crowninshield, see vol. 1:30; her residence was at 1 Somerset Place (*Boston Directory*, 1832–1833).

[3] In October Jared Sparks had married Frances Anne Allen of Hyde Park, N.Y. Although they were to occupy the Craigie House in Cambridge, it would appear that they were now living in Boston, perhaps at his former residence, 3 Somerset Court (*DAB*, under Sparks; *Boston Directory*, 1832–1833). Gilbert Stuart's portrait of Sparks is reproduced as an illustration in the present volume.

[4] Dr. John Thornton Kirkland had married Elizabeth Cabot only a few months before he resigned as president of Harvard. Following the resignation in 1828, they had traveled widely in the United States and abroad and had only recently taken up residence in Boston (vol. 1:12; vol. 2:226; and the notice of Kirkland in *DAB*).

[5] Gardner Gorham was a brother of Julia Gorham (CFA, Diary, 1 May 1833).

[6] See entry for 12 Nov., below.

SATURDAY. 10TH.

My health is declining in spite of myself. The distress I endure every morning is something more than the vision of a hypochondriac. Yet it is aggravated by want of occupation. I know not what to turn my attention to but this I know that something must be done or I shall be very good for nothing.

Went to the Office and read Lingard — The Catholic account of the Reformation. Prejudiced but not with any appearance of intentional unfairness. He has hit upon the great truth without appreciating it, and without seeing the effect it produces upon the whole of his history. The struggle of Luther was the struggle of the human mind, for *liberty*, moral, religious, political and ecclesiastical. Its consequences are not yet fully developed, both in good and in evil.

A walk at one. I propose to adhere strictly to exercise this winter. Afternoon, reading Antimasonry. I read and read but am not yet master enough of the subject to compose. Discouragement in all my preceding undertakings gives me little hope upon this. Evening. Read to my Wife two or three interesting lives of Painters — Copley and Mortimer.[1]

[1] A fourth volume of Allan Cunningham's *Lives of the Most Eminent British Painters and Sculptors* had recently been published in the *Harper's Family Library* edition (see above, entry for 11 March, note). John Singleton Copley, John Hamilton Mortimer, George Romney, William Owen, and Sir Henry Raeburn, whose lives CFA was reading during November, are all included in this volume, which CFA borrowed from the Athenæum.

SUNDAY. 11TH.

Beautiful weather. My father and mother are much favoured. Attended divine Service all day at the Church in Chauncy Place. Heard Mr. Frothingham, but my habit of inattention at Quincy has fixed upon me so much that I have all the old ground to go over again. My feelings were so bad also that I did nothing with zeal—A regular day of indigestion and suffering. Yet I took a long walk too.

Read a Sermon of Massillon's upon the immutability of the Law of God. Text from John 8. 46. "If I say the truth, why do ye not believe me." He considers three objections commonly made to the practice of Christianity. One drawn from the mutable nature of human affairs, one from the inequality of ranks in society, and one from peculiar contingencies and positions. To all he makes the same reply. Truth is eternal. The necessity of forming the invariable division of his Sermon drives him to repeat his idea in three distinct dresses. The first is the general position, the third is the particular position, and they both involve the second. I did little else.

In the evening read several of Marmontel's Nouveaux Contes Moraux. His style is charming. What could I do better than try to imitate it? I will attempt it, and take le trepied d'Helene for my first attempt. My labour was paralyzed by a head ach.

MONDAY. 12TH.

Another fine day. I felt better than usual. Went to the Office and found there a letter from my father at New York announcing his safe arrival in that place on Saturday.[1] And I saw in the Newspaper the account of the arrival of the Fornax here which is also good.[2]

This was the day of Election for State Officers and Electors with us. It was passed quietly enough. I voted the whole Antimasonic ticket with the exception of the Governor, one of the Senators and one of the Representatives.[3] My mind is now made up to vote uniformly against the influence of that Institution. It's effects in New York and Pennsylvania are strikingly perceptible in the late election.

Read Lingard and felt interested in his partial account of the Reformation. I am much afraid that here I must leave him in opinion. Afternoon at home—Digesting my notions of Antimasonry. Evening at Mrs. Frothingham's. Conversation respecting natural magic. The death of Dr. Spurzheim is now confirmed.[4]

[1] JQA to CFA, 10 Nov. (Adams Papers).

[2] In August JQA and LCA wrote asking that JA2 send the cases of books "which have been more than three years packed up at Washington" and their prints, pictures, &c. The cargo was later sent by the steamer *Fornax* (JQA, Diary, 11 Aug.; JQA to JA2, 11 Aug.; LCA to Mrs. JA2, 21 Aug., both letters in Adams Papers).

[3] The Antimasonic candidates were last in each contest. The whole National Republican ticket received majorities over the Jackson and Antimasonic tickets (*Boston Daily Advertiser & Patriot*, 14 Nov., p. 2, col. 1).

[4] Dr. Johann Gaspar Spurzheim, German physician, anatomist, and craniologist, a principal expounder of the new science of phrenology, died of typhus fever on 10 Nov. in Boston. From August to November he had delivered there and in Cambridge to large, distinguished, and enthusiastic audiences a series of seventeen lectures on phrenology. At the same time he delivered another series of lectures to the Boston Medical Society on the anatomy of the brain. His funeral at the Old South Church was the occasion of a great outpouring of persons. His impact upon the community had been profound. JQA recorded (Diary, 2 Nov.) that "Dr. Spurzheim is turning all our meditative brains by his Lectures. Since the days of Whitfield there has not been such a frenzy." (*Boston Daily Advertiser & Patriot*, 30 Oct., p. 2, col. 2; 12 Nov., p. 2, col. 3; 19 Nov., p. 2, col. 1; John D. Davies, *Phrenology, Fad and Science, a 19th-Century American Crusade*, New Haven, 1955, p. 16–20.)

TUESDAY. 13TH.

A fine day. I felt pretty well although a little uneasy. Went to the Office. Pretty industrious in reading Dr. Lingard. He affirms pretty positively that Anne Boleyne was the King's Mistress. I hardly believe it, first, because if she had been the King would not have cared about marrying her, second, because she had no children until after her true marriage. The fact that the child was premature is however somewhat in favor of his position. I do not know what to think but shall read Burnet.

Mr. Conant from Weston came in and we proceeded to make a

settlement of last year's Accounts, upon the sales of Wood. I somewhat regret that I have not better accountants to deal with as I cannot push these men to the exactness which all business requires, but if I believe them honest in substance I suppose that is as much as I ought to require. At least it is what I might not get.

Afternoon, continued writing upon the Anti Masonic subject but I do not at all satisfy myself. The intricacy of the detail is what discourages the attention of the many.

Quiet evening at home. Read to my Wife part of the life of Romney the Painter. It is interesting although the name and style of the painting is not familiar to me. Afterwards, I continued working upon the Antimasonry. Political results are curious enough. The whole nation seems to have gone by acclamation for General Jackson. Yet Can we believe him to be a good or a great man.

WEDNESDAY. 14TH.

Weather changed today and it became chilly and with a feeling of snow. I went to the Office. Time passed with tolerable industry. I make more progress in Lingard than I have been accustomed to in reading at my Office. The only interruption was William C. Greenleaf who has at last arrived and informed me of the place where the vessel is. I immediately went down, saw the Captain and made my arrangements with him for getting the boxes removed tomorrow. William C. Greenleaf has been here since Friday and might have stayed a month longer in all probability if I had not sent for the information that was necessary in the case.

Dined early at Mr. Frothingham's with him, our two ladies being gone to Medford, and started at two for Quincy. The Country looks desolate enough, and to go to a House deserted, which you have been accustomed to find full of persons of your own family is the climax of cheerlessness. I drove first to the Canal Wharf and found a sloop just starting for Boston with whose skipper I made a bargain, then to the House to give the necessary directions there. Mrs. Kirk seemed to be fixed quiet and solitary enough. I returned at sunset and had a comfortable evening at home. Continued working upon Antimasonry.

THURSDAY 15TH.

Cold but clear. On account of my ailing, I thought I would change my diet in the morning to Rice and Milk, but it gave me a head ach this morning so that I shall not try it again. Read Lingard all the time that I was not engaged in superintending the disembarkation of all my father's prints and things. To attend to these I left my house at eight in the morning and was busy about them in all two or three hours. I got the prints safely to my house and in the afternoon opened them. They are on the whole in as good a condition as I expected. Three or four of the glasses are broken and one or two otherwise injured, but the mass are pretty well preserved considering where they have been for eight years.[1]

Took a long walk. Time so much broken up in the afternoon that I had only a moment or two to look into Burnet for the purpose of examining the other side of the question of the Reformation.[2] My Wife took tea out so that I had the evening. Began translating "le trepied d'Helene," and was much entertained by my attempt. The style is peculiar. My first effort will be a lame one. It seems to come easy however.

[1] CFA dispatched twenty-four heavy cases of books to Quincy by lighter. "The remainder I caused to be landed on learning that some of them contained broken things. They contain your prints and pictures — Your little busts and Madame's china cups and saucers. Such as appeared in good condition have been sent to Quincy by Mr. Baxter. . . . The Glasses in three of the frames of prints were broken. . . . And many of the Engravings are otherwise injured from the cause that affected those last year. Such as required it most, and were worth it, have been sent to be cleaned and repaired. Some remain at my house to go to Quincy in the course of the Winter" (CFA to JQA, 18 Nov., LbC, Adams Papers).

To this report that his artifacts had been received and were being properly cared for, JQA responded: "Of all my Prints, that which you have of Cicero at his Villa, has the deepest and strongest hold upon my affections, and next to that, my six little bronze Busts, the two Philosophers, the two Orators, and the two Poets, come closest to my heart. I would not speak it profanely, but to me they are as household Gods. I have missed them from my mantle piece for the last four years, but hope to have them replaced there at Quincy next Spring, and that in due time they will pass from mine to your's" (JQA to CFA, 25 Nov., Adams Papers). In the will which he had lately drawn JQA identified the busts more precisely as those of Socrates and Plato, Demosthenes and Cicero, Homer and Virgil, "which I have been used to keep on the mantle piece of my writing chamber" (Adams Papers, Microfilms, Reel No. 203).

The busts in their place as here described are illustrated in the present volume; see the Descriptive List of Illustrations, p. vii.

[2] The edition of Gilbert Burnet's *History of the Reformation of the Church of England* published at Oxford in 1816 in 6 vols., which CFA owned, is now at MQA.

FRIDAY. 16TH.

Clear and cold. I went to the Office and was tolerably industrious the whole morning reading Lingard. He does not please me quite so much in his history of the Reformation. The reign of Edward 6. is one in which he has full scope. The difficulty I now find in him is that he attributes too much weight to the influence of the Crown. He makes

Henry and after him the Protector Somerset do pretty much what they have a mind to from motives the most equivocal, and insists upon it eleven twelfths of the People were against all change. This cannot be true. If it had been, the insurrections that took place could not have been quelled by the Protector so easily. The fact is that the reforming doctrines had taken deep root in the Country, and there was a general indifference to the Catholic Religion which paralized every exertion to counteract them. Even the Rioters claimed the ancient rites rather as matter of discontent with the Government, just as they did Agrarian laws, than from any fanatical enthusiasm. Had this existed in truth, Henry would have found himself at his wits end.

A walk, felt better today. Miss Carter and Miss Gorham, Abby's friends dined and spent the day here. I worked upon Antimasonry and upon Marmontel. My time has not for a long while been so faithfully spent.

SATURDAY. 17TH.

Cloudy and dull. At the Office, read a little of Lingard, but far the greater part of my morning was taken up in business. Deacon Spear called and made settlement for the wood sold at Quincy, and he is a slow moving body. I then was engaged in drawing up an Account for Thomas B. Adams as I received this morning his last Dividend for the year. I did not finish it before Mr. Ladd, a Tenant, came in and kept me settling with him until after my hour for dinner, not merely that for my walk. The consequence was that I encroached upon the afternoon to accomplish my work and take exercise, without which I cannot now get along.

The funeral ceremonies for Dr. Spurzheim took place this afternoon, but owing to my engagements I did not attend them. Quiet afternoon working upon German Catalogue. I find my ignorance of the language a very serious obstacle. After next month, one of my first labours must be to settle a system of study to acquire this language.

Evening at home. Read to my Wife the rest of Romney's life and the whole of Owen's—A coat and waistcoat painter. It is strange how little I know of the English school of Artists. Worked upon le Trepied d'Helene.

SUNDAY. 18TH.

The day was wet but warm. I was occupied in reading a little but principally in writing letters upon the matters I could not finish with yesterday. One to my father upon business in general,[1] one to T. B. Adams forwarding his semiannual Account.[2]

Attended divine service all day and heard Mr. Frothingham preach, in the morning from Numbers 20. 10. "Hear now, ye rebels, must we fetch you water out of this rock?" He briefly ran over the condition and prospects of the Hebrews in the desert and alluded to their distrust and the error of Moses. He applied the moral to present times, but as usual, the manner in which it was done has escaped me. The afternoon's discourse was from Genesis 1. 16 "he made the stars also." Upon the character of the account of the creation, the absence of all the superstition of ignorance without the knowledge which subsequent times have unfolded. Incidentally he alluded to the prevailing notion during the last year that a Comet would strike the world, but he did not follow out the idea, nor was there any of that forcible eloquence which came immediately to my mind in connection with the same subject as explained by my father a few weeks since before Mr. Degrand and Mr. Clapp.[3]

Read a Sermon of Massillon upon the employment of time. Text John 7. 33 "Yet a little while am I with you, and then I go unto him that sent me." His division was two fold. First upon the abuse or waste of time which is criminal, because it is the price of eternity, because it is short, and because it is irrecoverable; next upon the use of time, not in worldly occupations which engross the mind, nor even exclusively in duties which are useful or honourable to the world, but in the cultivation of the virtues which Christianity inculcates as preparation for a holier state. This is exactly in accordance with my own sentiments and therefore appears to me the soundest of all his Sermons. The illusion that men make to themselves on this subject is worthy of deep reflection.

Evening, quiet at home, reading with my Wife as a lesson of French to her, Marmontel's Tales. I afterwards continued working upon le Trepied d'Helene.

[1] (LbC, Adams Papers.) For this letter see above, entry for 15 Nov., note.

[2] To Thomas B. Adams Jr. (LbC, Adams Papers).

[3] Before the conversation with Messrs. Clapp and Degrand on 4 Nov., JQA had been "poring in the Astronomics of Manilius" and had been led by the current interest in phrenology to speculate that the "parallel between judicial astrology and phrenology might if well treated be presented in a very striking light" (JQA, Diary, 1 and 2 Nov.).

MONDAY. 19TH.

Cloudy with heavy fog. I went to the Office and my whole time passed very busily in copying Letters and Accounts written yesterday, so that in fact I did not waste a moment. Indeed, since my return to town I have felt considerable satisfaction in the confidence that as little of my time is unemployed as reasonably can be. Perhaps I do not occupy myself in the most useful manner, but as to that who is to judge. If I do as well as I can in my best way of forming an opinion what more can be expected from me.

Took a walk, part of the way with Edmund Quincy. His talk is of small things. He has narrowed his intellect from giving it a mistaken and frivolous direction.[1] Afternoon, writing upon Anti Masonry. Draughted No. 1 with important alterations. Evening with my wife, reading Marmontel and lives of Painters, and then the Tripod of Helen.

[1] What diversion had proved temporarily absorbing to Edmund Quincy is not known.

TUESDAY. 20TH.

Fine morning. Clear and windy as the day advanced which very rapidly increased the cold. Morning at the Office for an hour, arranging Papers, and draughting Accounts. I then went down to the Athenæum and to see two Pictures of the State of Man in Paradise and his expulsion; by a man named Dubufe said to have been painted for Charles 10.[1] They are good, the figures of the man and woman seem to me to express every thing that can be imagined of beauty in the human form. But I do not like the appearance of the Snake, the idea is that Satan is whispering into her ear, but there is no corresponding expression in her face. Purity and love, implicit faith in her husband are expressed but nothing like a conception of sin. The other and less pleasing picture is disfigured by a similar introduction of Satan. This may claim the greater technical merit as a powerful specimen of fore-shortening. It seems to me however to be liable to greater objections. The scene is an unpleasant one. It represents a storm, but there is no clearness in the background. No one can tell whether it is the sea or a river or any thing but water, and clouds and smoke. The effect of the light is however very well done. I passed an hour there and was gratified. These pictures however commonly meet with an objection here, that I do not urge because I do not think it sound, their indelicacy. We have vastly too much of the "seeming pure."

After a walk and dining, I rode to Quincy, examined the state of the things, gave orders respecting them, and returned home to Tea. Cheerless enough is the Country in winter. Mr. Brooks came in for a few moments. He goes to morrow to Washington. Finished, le Trepied d'Helene.[2]

[1] Probably Claude Marie Dubufe (1790–1864), whose work was included in later exhibitions (Mabel M. Swan, *The Athenæum Gallery*, Boston, 1940, p. 221).

[2] CFA's translation, "The Tripod of Helen," from Marmontel, first contemplated on 11 Nov. and begun on the 15th, is in the Adams Papers (Microfilms, Reel No. 318). The project may

have initially suggested itself to CFA during his recent reading of some of his father's contributions to the *Port Folio* (entry for 15 Oct., above). In the issues for 8, 15, 22, and 29 Oct. 1803 is a translation, "The Tripod of Helen," which in JQA's copy of the *Port Folio* now at MBAt is initialed as having been made by JQA. CFA began to read Marmontel on 6 November.

WEDNESDAY. 21ST.

Morning quite sharp. Upon going down to the Office I found the whole street in commotion, in consequence of a fire which had taken place in the City Hall and the opposite side of the Street. It seems that this morning a fire was discovered in the building in State Street occupied by Mr. Derby and other Lawyers—That it got in under the Slates and spread over the whole Roof. The loss is considerable to the City, as much from damage in extinguishing it as from fire—For in such cases the violence of two elements is about equally to be dreaded.[1]

Read Lingard very industriously today and compared him with Hume. He certainly makes a specious case. Walk before dinner. Afternoon, writing upon Antimasonry. Evening reading to my Wife. After which I dawdled over German grammar and four Stanzas of the first Canto of Ariosto.[2]

[1] The fire had been discovered at 4 A.M. in the building numbered 14 and 16 State Street, owned by the heirs of William Dehon and occupied by E. Haskett Derby, Cornelius Coolidge, and other lawyers and brokers. By 6 o'clock the fire had spread to the roof of the City Hall and was not extinguished for three more hours (*Boston Daily Adver-*

tiser & Patriot, 22 Nov., p. 2, col. 1).

[2] CFA's earlier reading of Ariosto's *Orlando Furioso* had been in an English translation (above, entry for 18 Feb.). The poem in the original Italian is in the first and second volumes of the edition of the *Opere* published at Bassano, 1771, in 4 vols., now at MQA. JQA's bookplate is affixed.

THURSDAY. 22ND.

Cloudy and dark with rain. I went to the Office as usual, but a considerable part of my morning was engrossed at Cunningham's Auction Room whither I went to buy a German Dictionary. I do not think that I made much by my bargain. In my opinion bargains are not very often made at auction. I did not succeed in getting any thing else I wanted. Walk notwithstanding the rain.

Afternoon, finished No. 2 on Antimasonry. *I* think it good. At any rate the occupation makes my time light enough upon my hands.

Evening quiet at home. Read with my wife part of the little Tale of Undine in French taken from the German.[1] And afterwards hung over the German Grammar, with a stanza or two of Ariosto. The acquisition of language is tiresome. I detest the mud of the Grammars. Received letters from both my parents who are safe arrived at Washington.[2]

[1] La Motte Fouqué's *Undine* had been translated into French by I. Montolieu and published at Paris in 1822 as *Ondine.*

[2] JQA to CFA, 15 Nov. (Adams Papers). The letter from LCA is missing.

FRIDAY. 23RD.

Morning clear and pleasant. Our weather is on the whole uncommonly mild. I hope it is not to be followed again by so severe a winter. At the Office where I accomplished much of Lingard. I think every body ought to read him who wishes to form a clear notion of English History, but not without closely comparing him with other writers. He admits something in regard to Mary. Others will explain the rest. He claims for her a merit she probably deserves, which in others she has not had attributed to her. He certainly is skilful in shading his pictures.

Took a walk and stopped to look at House 105 Tremont Street which has been lately vacated by Mr. Brackett. It must be repaired. Afternoon, worked hard upon Antimasonry and continued it in the evening. I have finished three numbers and shall now offer them for publication previous to going on with more.

Quiet evening reading Undine with my Wife. I this night finished the Idler, making the twenty fourth and last Volume of my edition of British Essayists. I have been two years, one month and thirteen days, in going through them at the regular rate of two Numbers nightly.[1]

[1] See above, vol. 3:337–338, 407.

SATURDAY. 24TH.

I sent this morning three numbers to the Editor of the Advocate, for publication.[1] The success of my writing has been so indifferent that I always regard it as rather a favour that the pieces see the light. If ever I had any pride of authorship, it has been pretty effectually humbled. Yet I feel as if my style was not without power and that it ought to take better. Perseverance may effect what my amount of skill cannot.

At the Office working upon Lingard with assiduity. The day was half and half. Took my walk notwithstanding. Afternoon, working upon No. 4. I have got into a train and must not break out of it.

Evening quiet at home, reading with my Wife. Undine is a pretty little thing. Afterwards, began upon Follen's German Grammar which seems to be composed of more simple elements.[2] But after all a man learns more by translating five sentences of a book than by reading twenty Grammars. Began reading the World. A periodical Essay though not belonging to my set of the Classics.[3] I pursue in this, the same method that has carried me so quietly and easily through all the others.

[1] Publication of CFA's series of anti-masonic articles in the *Boston Daily Advocate*, the organ of the antimasonic movement, began on 5 December. See below, entries for 6, 8, and 11 Dec.; Duberman, *CFA*, p. 47.

[2] In the years since Charles Theodore Christian Follen began to teach the German language and literature at Har-

vard in 1825 (see above, vol. 3:22) he had brought out several textbooks in the language.

[3] *The World*, an essay-periodical by Edward Moore, was published at London during the years 1753–1756. It was included in some editions of the *British Classics* and of Chalmers' *British Essayists*.

SUNDAY. 25TH.

Cold but clear this morning. I consumed my leisure time in reading Vasari's life of Corregio in Italian. I find it easier than Ariosto. This language is too easy to get thoroughly. I can never read a page without feeling enervated. The labour of examining thoroughly becomes so annoying when it is required seldom.

Attended divine Service all day. Mr. Greenwood preached in the morning from Revelation, 11. 12. "And they heard a great voice from heaven, saying, Come up hither." Mr. Greenwood has a flowing style, considerable power of language and some imagination. But he has not a particle of vigour of thought and he consumes himself quicker than any of our Clergy. A few pretty words upon the nature of creation, upon the beauty of holiness derived from the view of God's works, all of which may be found condensed in a few lines of Milton, and all is told. Yet Mr. Greenwood is a popular preacher, and is ranked before Mr. Frothingham. The sermon of the latter person in the afternoon was better than any thing of Greenwood's I ever heard. It was taken from 2. Thess. 3. 13. "But ye, brethren, be not weary in well doing." It was upon the duty of benevolence, and considering the two favourite objections which are commonly made against it. First, the great multiplicity of its objects which make selection difficult, second, the abuses which frequently take place in the employment of funds derived from benevolent people. There was no particular novelty in the ideas nor art in the management of them, but there was penetration into the every day feelings of men and consequent practical excellence. In this world of our's where there is such a vast deal of humbug, such an immense portion of stuff brought forward merely because each man thinks himself able to give the world a shove, it is refreshing to alight occasionally upon a little plain, natural good sense.

Read a Sermon of Massillon's. Text. John 7. 6. "My time is not yet come, but your time is alway ready." This was upon future happiness. Division two fold. 1. He considered the indifference manifested in securing it, as contrasted with the eager pursuit of temporal affairs, 2. the apathy as to the selection of the true and only way to attain it, the mistakes which are constantly occurring in the choice of a path, being occasioned by the easy satisfaction with which people remain as they happen to be placed.

Quiet evening. Read Undine with my Wife. We also again pursue the regular Chapters of the Bible as heretofore when at home. Read also a good deal of Vasari's life of Corregio with the supplement.

MONDAY. 26TH.

Morning mild but cloudy with high wind. At the Office as usual where I read and finished the seventh Volume of Dr. Lingard. He is very hard upon Elizabeth as he was upon her Mother before her. And I have done feeling an inclination to justify him. The mind of man is not equal to the comprehension of truth. Some human passion will always interfere to pervert objects to the sight of even the most conscientious. I am sensible of this influence myself, and see it strongly in others. Took a walk.

A silly paragraph is running the round of the Newspapers about my father and Mr. Van Buren. I feel a regret always rising that my father should have placed himself in any situation where the public must be constantly discussing his merits. It is true the general practice of bringing him in connection with every public trust shows the confidence which all the Community place in him, but this is not enough to make up for the having his name bandied about at every corner.[1]

Afternoon, finished No. 4, which is, I think, the best I have written. The Editor proposes to publish them. I must therefore proceed pretty steadily in the composition. Evening quiet at home. Read a good deal of the Life of Henry Raeburn, a Scotch Painter to my Wife, but did not finish it. Evening finished by reading the beginning of Follen's German Class Book.

[1] An item originally appearing in the *National Intelligencer* and reprinted in the *Boston Daily Advertiser & Patriot* (26 Nov., p. 2, col. 2) gave currency to the rumor that JQA would soon be appointed secretary of state in place of Mr. Livingston. It was alleged further that Mr. Van Buren not only favored this step but "had already suggested the propriety of naming Mr. Adams for the next Presidency, as under his broad National Banner all parties might unite, and that he himself would consider it 'glory enough' to serve one term as *Vice* under such a Chief as we now have, and another under such a Statesman as the Cincinnatus of Massachusetts!"

JQA's name had only a few days be-fore been given renewed prominence in the press with the publication of his let-ters to William L. Stone on Antimasonry. Written in August and September to Stone, who was one of the editors of the *New York Commercial Advertiser* and whose earlier letters to JQA on Freema-sonry had been published as a book in June (see above, entry for 5 Sept.), JQA's letters at his request had been withheld from publication until after the national election. Immediately following their publication in the *Commercial Ad-vertiser*, they were reprinted widely in newspapers over the country and in pamphlet form. (*Boston Daily Adver-tiser & Patriot*, 20 Nov., p. 1–2; Bemis, *JQA*, 2:294–295.)

TUESDAY. 27TH.

Fine morning. Mild as September. I thought I could not do better than to pay my last visit to Quincy, so after stopping half an hour at the Office, I went on. My ride was quite agreeable. And I found the Country did not look today quite so desolate. I looked over the books and regretted to find them in a very poor condition.[1] Many of them are consumed by mould and those that have fresh sheepskin bindings are full of worms. The four years that they have been packed up, have been productive of more injury to them than the twenty in which all the rest were kept in the Athenæum and in Mr. Lyman's Warehouse.[2] Returned home to dinner.

After dinner, began No. 5 upon Antimasonry. Labour in vain I fear, yet still it is labour and that is better than idleness. It makes me accustom myself to examine the minutiæ of transactions and try to show them to the best account.

Evening. Read one of Marmontel's Tales, "Il le falloit" rendering it in English aloud to my Wife. Afterwards. Slow progress in a German fable of Lessing's.[3]

[1] That is, the books recently received from Washington; see entry for 15 Nov., above.

[2] See vol. 3:32. JQA, in replying to CFA's letter informing him of the arrival of the books, wrote of his hopes upon the reassembly of his library: "[A]l-though I have been compelled to abandon the hope that I had cherished through a long life, of being able before its close to erect a building spacious enough to contain them all, and to give me the full enjoyment of them in my last days, I still indulge the anticipation that cooped and cabined as they are and must be, like the Soul within the Body, they will yet afford me pleasure and contribute to some useful purpose" (25 Nov., Adams Papers).

[3] JQA's bookplate is in the edition now at MQA of Gotthold Ephraim Les-sing, *Sämmtliche schriften*, 21 vols., Ber-lin, 1771–1774. The "Fabeln" are in the 18th volume.

WEDNESDAY. 28TH.

Cloudy with fog. At the Office, occupied in making up Accounts and writing Diary. And went to Market as usual before Thanksgiving day. The display was not very great. Mr. Conant from Weston came in and kept me an hour and more in drawing out the Accounts of the last year. After investigating the whole business and considering the difficulty in the way of settlement, I wound up by making them take the good debts in part payment of services and the balance due to me on account in full satisfaction. I assumed the bad debts where the wood remained standing, and this settled the thing. A walk as usual.

Afternoon, finished No. 5. I do not know that I succeed in being perspicuous enough. It is one of the difficulties of composition to know when one has done enough. Though the idea may be clear enough to oneself, it may want to another the accessaries which explain it, and yet the labour of making plain is often equally tedious to writer and reader.

Quiet evening at home. Company disturbs us less than ever. My Wife began a Story by Madame Cottin, Malvina.[1] I know nothing of it's merits. Continued the Fables of Lessing, but they continue to puzzle me.

[1] *Malvina* was contained in the first two volumes of the *Œuvres* of Mme. Sophie Ristaud Cottin (8 vols., Paris, 1817).

THURSDAY. 29TH.

This was the day appointed according to custom, for returning thanks to the divine being for so many favours and so much bounty as he has been pleased to bestow upon us. For my own part, I hope I am sufficiently impressed with a sense of my share of them. I hope I am properly aware of the duty of neither exulting nor repining at the situation in which I have been placed. How much during the last year as during every year, I have had cause to be thankful for. How unmixed my prosperity has been. My only prayer is to deserve by my conduct no discontinuance of these blessings—To do my duty in this world as I ought, in whatever relation I may be placed.

Read in the morning a good deal of Vasari's Life of Corregio and the supplement to it. Attended divine Worship and heard Mr. Frothingham from Job. 22. 17—18. "Who said unto God, What can the Almighty do for them. Yet he filled their houses with good things." An allusion to the practice of annual thanksgiving whether in good or evil fortune —A return for mercies bestowed even when the contrary seem to predominate. The practice of thankfulness forms a habit of grateful reliance upon the justice and mercy of the Deity. It is so, and must be so. Suffering in this world is natural. Prosperity is not so, if long continued. Therefore man must not complain if he experiences what he was born to experience, and he must be thankful for the good gifts which he has no right to claim.

Took a long walk. The day was lovely. I have not known such before in this climate, so late in the Season. Dined at Mr. Frothingham's. Nobody but my Wife and Henry Brooks. Drank Champagne and tea. Returned to my Study for two hours. Looked over Macbeth, and one of the Nouveaux Contes of Marmontel. Wondered at Shakespeare's perfect acquaintance with Dialogue. Returned again to Mr. Frothingham's for my Wife who spent the Evening there.

FRIDAY. 30TH.

Clouds and rain. At the Office. Received letters from both my Parents.[1] They are in a tone of uncommon despondency. My father seems to foresee nothing but storms in the approaching Session of Congress. I suppose he will have a due share of them. And his inflexible character will perpetually expose him to suffer by them when others would escape. Be it so. His mind is a deeply conscientious one. His course is always the consequence of a self impressed conviction of duty, which though it may occasionally be wrong, can never fail in the end to be appreciated. I ought not to feel any dread of consequences which may fall upon me. I am but a worm in comparison with the interests of the Country.

Passed a considerable part of the morning at the Athenæum. It was little better than wasted. Tried to walk but the weather was too bad. Afternoon, began No. 6. of Antimasonry. I find I can accomplish about the same quantity every day. Quiet evening. My Wife continued Malvina, and I read Nollekens.[2] Afterwards, I read a German fable with a little more ease.

[1] The letters from LCA written on the 24th and from JQA on the 25th are in the Adams Papers. For JQA's letter see the notes to the entries for 27 Nov., above, and for 8 Dec., below.

[2] That is, the life of the sculptor Joseph Nollekens (1737–1823) which is included in the 3d volume of Cunningham's *Lives of the Most Eminent British Painters and Sculptors.*

SATURDAY. DECEMBER I.

The first day of Winter brought with it the livery which the season commonly wears. Short days and long evenings with snow and cold are the attendants of the three succeeding months. They give fine opportunities for the cultivation of the mind and the production of ideas. But they are not the hours for physical enjoyment. I always see the first snow with a slight feeling of melancholy. Yet I know not why. For in our climate, it rather adds to our light in the darkest period of the year.

At the Office. Engaged some time in Accounts but I also accomplished somewhat of Lingard. The weather did not admit of a walk.

Afternoon, pursued my regular course. Mr. Hallett sent me a letter today, suggesting some alterations in the articles I sent to him.[1] They relate generally to positions of mine not quite Antimasonic enough for his taste. After reflecting upon them, as I found I could not quite assent to them, I replied by expressing my willingness to soften the terms without altering the expression of my own opinion.[2] Continued working upon No. 6, but I find it will not answer. I must read over all the information and new model it.

Evening quiet at home. Malvina. Finished Nollekens. A fable of Lessing.

[1] The letter from Benjamin Franklin Hallett, editor of the *Boston Daily Advocate*, is missing. On Hallett, see entry for 13 Dec., below.
[2] Letter missing.

SUNDAY. 2.

Bright morning and pleasant. But the snow gave a chill to the air that tells us of winter in no equivocating terms. I passed the greater part of my time in reading over the Story of Morgan all the facts relating to which I am anxious to master.

Attended divine Service and heard Mr. Frothingham from 1. Peter. 2. 21. "Christ also suffered for us, leaving us an example." It was upon the passion of the Saviour and calculated for the occasion of Communion day. Very well in it's way but not remarkable for any thing that I could perceive. Afternoon. Mr. Barrett from 10. Mark 21. "But one thing thou lackest." He discoursed upon the absence of a single virtue in a character destroying the value of all the rest. For instance a man wants prudence and he will find no benefit in benevolence, justice, honesty &ca. If he wants piety, his morality will serve him little. I was struck with one defect in the argument. All his examples were brought forward with an eye to temporal success. It was always, how he had failed to be esteemed, or to be distinguished, to have influence or wealth. As an illustration it might possibly do, if it did not tend to mislead ordinary minds as to the *end* of existence. Self should not be the standard either of morality or religion. The practice of all the virtues might easily be supposed and yet be unattended with worldly prosperity. Look for example at the character of Christ. Another objection occurred to me. Man is naturally imperfect. His virtues are many of them the result of his conscientious state of mind. To say then that because he fails in one, it is to ruin the value of all the rest, is in fact to discourage from the performance of any. I do not read the Text or the story thus. All merit is comparative. The Young man asked of the Saviour a question. What shall I do to inherit eternal life? The answer was to obey the commandments. Of course a grade of merit or it would not have been required. Upon his replying that he had done this from his youth upwards, Christ then suggested the performance of a still higher Act of virtue and this was too much for his questioner. That one thing he wanted. Yet I should not say that therefore he was no better than one who had never obeyed a Commandment but on the contrary had violated them all. It has always appeared to me that the whole of this Story is one of the most trying portions of the Testament. It requires a sacrifice from Man which but very few would make any sooner than the Young man. Human ingenuity has done much to modify the phrases that follow, but there is an expressiveness in them, notwithstanding, that is fearful.

Read Massillon. John 10. 31. "Then the Jews took up stones again, to stone him." Upon the discouragements to Piety. 1. They are many. 2. They are not so unpleasant as one imagines. 3. Not so unpleasant as those the World creates. 4. They are compensated by gratifications never found in the World. A good Sermon.

Quiet in the evening. My wife wrote letters and I read Marmontel. Afterwards. Read over the details in Stone's book.

MONDAY. 3D.

Cloudy, rainy and warm morning — The snow and ice disappearing nearly as fast as it came. I went to the office and was occupied nearly all my time in Accounts and writing up the long Diary minute of yesterday. My time disappears with rapidity and I find I improve it little more than I used to. My general occupation however is of such a kind that I ought not to reprove or trouble myself particularly about it. Took a walk with Mr. Peabody notwithstanding the Rain and returned home early. We found a letter from my Mother in much improved spirits.[1]

Afternoon, busy reading over the whole of the materials I am working upon and I found them of great use. But it will be necessary to write over No. 5 and 6 — A labour I might easily spare and which I do not know why I assume.

Evening quiet at home — Reading Malvina and the life of Mrs. Damer, Sculptress.[2] Afterwards I stopped my German, for the sake of examining the Antimasonry.

[1] Letter missing.

[2] CFA here, or a few days earlier (above, entry for 30 Nov., note), began to supplement his reading of biographies of painters (entries for 10 and 25 Nov., above) with the lives of British sculptors which were contained in the 3d volume of Cunningham's *Lives of . . . Painters and Sculptors*: Mrs. Anne Damer, John Bacon, Louis Francis Roubiliac, Thomas Banks, and John Flaxman.

TUESDAY. 4TH.

Cloudy morning and mild. I went to the Office. Occupied some time in making up my Accounts and writing Diary. I then went to the Athenæum for the purpose of examining the Anti Masonic Review in regard to the character of Morgan but although I had seen the book there some time ago, I could not now find it either on the shelves or in the Catalogue.[1] I seized the opportunity however to read the article in Mr. Walsh's Review upon the subject.[2] Found it to be miserably barren.

Took a walk and returned home. After dinner I began to rewrite my No. 5. Amplified and new moulded the reasoning so as to appear in a better form. The exercise of writing sharpens the reasoning faculties, while that of reading much, dulls them. I think I improve in my style. At any rate I make my afternoons fly. And I do not know that I could do more good in any other manner.

Evening, I read to my wife two Chapters in the Bible and we accomplished some pages in Malvina. Mr. and Mrs. Frothingham then came in and passed two hours. I conversed with the former upon the explanations of the Bible, and felt desirous of ascertaining whether I could obtain any brief Commentary that would answer the purpose. It does not seem that there is such a thing. We had a pleasant little Supper and broke up at a little before ten. I omitted my German again and continued writing.

[1] The *Anti-Masonic Review*, published at New York from Jan. 1828 to Dec. 1830, had become in 1831 the *New York Register and Antimasonic Review*.

[2] An essay-review of Stone's *Letters on Masonry and Anti-Masonry* in the *American Quarterly Review*, 12:57–87 (Sept. 1832).

WEDNESDAY. 5TH.

Morning cool and cloudy. I went to the Office. Time occupied much as usual. I wrote, calculated my accounts and went on with Mr.

Lingard. But I am pretty tired of his perpetual labour to justify that which cannot be justified. His candour is just sufficient however to keep me not absolutely provoked with him. I took a walk with Mr. Cazenove. The political news is of somewhat an alarming character. South Carolina has assumed a warlike attitude. She is about to fence with the Union, and God knows what the end of it will be.

Afternoon. Worked upon No. 5 which I finished and extended. It is altogether the best of the series in my estimation. But what is the benefit of all my labour. Nothing but vanity and vexation of spirit. The amount of power necessary to produce an impression upon the Public is four times what it used to be. Talent has come forward so rapidly under the impulse given by our system of government.

Quiet evening at home. Read Malvina with my Wife, and the Life of John Bacon the Sculptor to her. Afterwards, instead of German, hammered away upon No. 6.

THURSDAY. 6TH.

Cloudy and cool. At the Office. Received a letter from my Father, mentioning the sickness of my Mother, and apparently in a state of considerable depression. I do not know what the matter can be, but this I imagine, that all is not right in the family.[1] Whether the subject relates to my father's embarrassed affairs or to other concerns I can not pretend to divine. In consequence of his writing that I had not noticed his two last, I immediately sat down, and penned an answer,[2] which with the copying took my whole morning, with the exception of the time regularly devoted to walking.

After dinner. Worked in continuation of No. 6, which I finished, and without waiting to scratch them any more, I despatched the three numbers to Mr. Hallett. I ought to have mentioned that the first of the series appeared yesterday,[3] with a favourable notice from the Editor.[4]

My Wife and I went to the Tremont House and took Tea with Mrs. Gorham Brooks prior to going to the Theatre. The piece was a new Play of one Knowles called the Hunchback. The plot is very defective, the events ill combined and the developement meagre, but several single scenes have pathos, force and affect strongly. C. Kean and Hamblin. The former is a mediocre resemblance of his father. We remained only during this Play.[5] I could not study. Amused myself with Marmontel.

[1] JQA to CFA, 1 Dec. (Adams Papers). LCA's condition seems to have been at- tributable partly to her own discomfort from a return of erysipelas along with an

attack of "inflammable rhumatic fever," and partly to her concern at JA2's "almost total loss of sight" and at the continued ill health of his children (JQA, Diary, 15, 29 Nov., 1 Dec.; LCA to Mary Roberdeau, 21 Nov., Adams Papers).

[2] LbC in Adams Papers.

[3] "The Principles and Grounds of Anti-Masonry," signed "F," *Boston Daily Advocate*, 5 Dec., p. 2, cols. 3–4.

[4] "We ask particular attention to the series of numbers from an able pen, which we commence publishing today. . . . [W]e commend the candid and temperate manner in which our correspondent discusses the subject" (same, col. 1).

[5] The performance at the Tremont Theatre was the seventh and final one of *The Hunchback*, a play in five acts by James Sheridan Knowles. The play had had its première in London in the spring and in New York in June. Beginning in the fall of 1832 it became for a long time one of the more popular vehicles for Charles Kemble in the role of Sir Thomas Clifford and Fanny Kemble as Julia. Neither Thomas S. Hamblin as Sir Thomas, Charles Kean as Master Walter, nor Naomi Vincent as Julia achieved any reputation in their roles. On the same evening another company was presenting *The Hunchback* at the Warren Theatre. (*Boston Daily Advertiser & Patriot*, 6 Dec., p. 3, cols. 4–5; Odell, *Annals N.Y. Stage*, 3:558, 607, 617; *DNB* notice of Knowles.)

FRIDAY. 7TH.

The President's Message arrived today, or I should rather say was published in the Newspapers.[1] It gives no comfort to us in this Quarter. I regard the intimation as tolerably distinct that New England Interests are in the end to be sacrificed for the purpose of conciliating the jealous States of the South. I have expected this all along. Thank fortune, there is a constantly vivifying principle in the character of our inhabitants which will sustain them through difficulty. It is not so with the slave-holding South.

Time taken up in reading. Diary and Lingard. The mornings are very short and I do daudle considerably. Walk, the day was fine. Afternoon, not very diligent. I have got along so many papers in advance that I can afford to rest myself. Nevertheless I commenced No. 7. The thing becomes more intricate as I proceed.

Quiet evening at home. Malvina, and the Life of Roubiliac. I afterwards resumed my German and read two Fables of Lessing, one of which is the first that I understand in the point of it.

[1] Jackson's Fourth Annual Message was delivered to the two Houses of Congress on 4 December. The *Boston Daily Advertiser & Patriot* printed it complete on the 7th (p. 2, cols. 2–6). The text is in Richardson, ed., *Messages and Papers*, 2:591–606.

SATURDAY. 8TH.

Morning rainy and dark. I went to the Office as usual. The second of my numbers appeared in the Advocate.[1] I do not think it equal to the first. The editor has also made a few corrections, some of which are no improvements.[2] I see in one or two a distrust of my information, which I do not wonder at, but yet cannot admire. These are some of the difficulties against which young men always have to struggle, and I trust that they will not succeed in discouraging me.

Time taken up writing Diary and reading Lingard. A call from Deacon Danl. Spear of Quincy about the Pew of the Episcopal Church, the balance for which I paid.[3] Took my usual walk notwithstanding the rain.

Afternoon, working upon Antimasonry. Finished No. 7. but am much dissatisfied with it. Shall have to write it over. I have not got that power yet, which enables a person at the first dash to give thoughts their most effective form. How labour saving such a power is.

Evening quiet at home. My way of life here in Boston, is the most pacific, secluded kind of thing imaginable. I see few, know few and trouble myself with few. Read to my Wife, the lives of Roubiliac and Banks, Sculptors, and with her more of Malvina. Afterwards I hammered away upon German, and found my progress not so much impeded. Understand the point of two or three Fables. I have a notion that these are not the easiest things possible to begin with.

[1] Page 2, cols. 3–4.

[2] "You must make great allowance for errors of the Press. My sense is most shockingly mangled and my friend Hallett now and then amends a sentence in such a way as by no means to improve it" (CFA to JQA, 31 Dec., LbC, Adams Papers).

[3] JQA had subscribed $100 toward the building of Christ Church in Quincy and had authorized the purchase of a pew at a price not to exceed $25 (JQA to CFA, 25 Nov., Adams Papers).

SUNDAY. 9TH.

Mist in the morning and hard rain at night. I attended divine service throughout the day notwithstanding. Mr. Frothingham preached. Morning from 1. Peter 2. 16. "As free, and not using your liberty for a cloke of maliciousness, but as the servants of God." A discussion of true liberty with a general view of the effect of the Reformation in giving it a true signification. I am sorry I did not follow a sensible sermon more closely. Afternoon from Colossians 3. 15. "Be ye thankful" upon Gratitude as a social, a domestic and a Religious duty. One thing I have to reproach myself with, the allowing of unsuitable thoughts in the house of God. Why it is, I do not know, but it seems to me as if I no sooner was seated, than my mind begins to run upon some view of the subject of Masonry, or my temporal affairs, or any thing in short but what is before me. This must be corrected.

Read a Sermon upon the Story of the penitent female, from Luke 7. 37 and following verses, by Massillon. The text is too long, as it includes in fact much of the Chapter, for me to quote it. Subject. Repentance. Division, 1st the common idea that repentance is barren — not true, for it must be followed by reparation, 2d that it is bitter — not true, for it brings with it, its own peculiar consolation. Many of the Sermons of Massillon are not only repetitious in their parts, but also of each other. This however must necessarily be the case, where a man writes and preaches much.

Evening quietly at home. Read more of Malvina but as my Wife was writing Letters, I began Ruffhead's Life of Pope.[1] Afterwards, more of Lessing's Fables which I understand much better.

We heard today of the extraordinary result of a marriage intended to have taken place at Andover. My old acquaintance and my Wife's Relation, Elizabeth Phillips, was jilted on her wedding evening, when she was dressed for the Ceremony. "There's many a slip" &ca.[2]

[1] The edition at MQA of Owen Ruffhead, *The Life of Alexander Pope*, London, 1769, has JQA's bookplate affixed.

[2] "The hour appointed for the ceremony was eight in the evening — at *six* Mr. Spaulding made his appearance elegantly dressed, and found most of the family assembled in the sitting-room. Not seeing Elizabeth among them he expressed a wish to see her alone and passed through to the other parlor where she was sitting. She remarked to him as he entered, that he looked unusually pale and low-spirited and told him (in a joking way) that his appearance was to *her* not very flattering. He then said to her, 'I am perfectly miserable, I cannot be married this evening. You must consent that the wedding be deferred for a month.' Elizabeth with great spirit answered, 'We are married this evening or never.' After some little conversation with him she summoned her Mother who endeavored to draw from him an explanation of his extraordinary conduct, but he had none to give.... After remonstrating with him for a while Aunt Phillips desired him to leave her house *forever*, and with great deliberation he rose, put on his india-rubbers, tied a handkerchief about his neck and left the house.... The next morning he sent to Elizabeth the keys of his house and left Andover.... Previous to the evening of the Wedding he had been a most devoted lover, and had shown greater anxiety than any one else to have his new establishment in order for his bride" (Charlotte Everett to Edward Everett, 9 Dec.).

"The whole transaction, from beginning to end, has been published (without calling names) in the Haverhill paper ... much to the annoyance of Aunt Phillips and her family" (same to same, 12 Dec.; both letters in Everett MSS, MHi).

MONDAY. 10TH.

A beautiful morning. Instead of any appearance of this month, I should suppose it was hardly more than October. At the office, I read a little of Lingard but was out most of my time. Went to the Athenæum where I looked over the Newspapers and an article in the Edinburgh Review which I found pretty tedious. On the whole, my time was wasted. Mr. Tenney, my Tenant called in to pay his rent. He looks emaciated, says he believes he has had the Cholera. Came to talk about the renewal of a Lease of his House. Postponed it until May next.

I took my usual walk, and my spirits felt bright and lively — The action of the fine day being altogether invigorating. I felt as if it was to be a lucky day to me without my knowing or being able to assign any cause therefor. It passed off without my being sensible of it's having proved so. The feeling however was a buoyant one. And as I do not feel particularly anxious about my luck or rather what I would call in my graver moments by a more serious name, I was thankful for the momentary elasticity which it occasioned, without looking any farther.

Afternoon. Began upon Anti Masonry No. 8, but was stopped by want of information. The whole of the time was taken up in digesting materials. Evening, quiet as usual. Malvina and the Life of Flaxman. Afterwards, finished the Fables of Lessing in the German Reader.

TUESDAY. 11TH.

Another very beautiful day. What a contrast between this and last year. We then were suffering under the severest of the Winter. I look back upon that time with a lively remembrance of the anxiety and discomfort that attended it. Yet it was on the whole a prosperous Winter to me. This year, I have been much more free from care and trouble yet it may not turn out so successfully to me. Let me not worry my mind. I trust in a higher Power.

At the office—Engaged in Diary and Accounts. Went into State Street, and drew a Dividend upon my Columbian Ins. Shares. None upon my father's in the New England. My Affairs have done exceedingly well this year, while I regret to say those of my father have gone backward. One or two calls. A Mr. Flagg about some Boylston Market Shares he wanted transferred, and William C. Greenleaf respecting his return to Washington. I took the opportunity to make of him some inquiries about the state of things there, John's health, and the success of the Mill—The answers to which were not in any one point encouraging. The horizon looks black in that quarter. Took my usual walk—Mr. Peabody with me. He and I though now good friends, have not exactly the same agreement of opinions that we formerly had.

Afternoon quiet at home. At work upon No. 8. But I was not at all satisfied with the result. My No. 3 was published this morning. It does not meet my expectation, in print.[1] Quiet evening. Read Malvina and continued the life of Flaxman. Afterwards, I began an extract from Wieland but did not get through the first sentence which reached down the page.[2]

[1] "A Brief History of the Masonic Outrages in New York," *Boston Daily Advocate*, 11 Dec., p. 2, cols. 3–4.
[2] Christoph Martin Wieland's *Geschichte der Abderiten* had been published at least as early as 1781. From CFA's words, however, it seems likely that what he was reading was a selection from the work in a German reader, Follen's or another's.

WEDNESDAY. 12TH.

Warm, but heavy clouds and rain. At the Office much as usual. Read Lingard very attentively and finished the History of the Reign of Elizabeth. He treats her character very harshly, by heightening her follies and shading her good sense. She was nevertheless a very remarkable woman. Her successful career brought England up to the first rank among Nations. And her Ministers made themselves a lasting reputation for wisdom by their judicious management of a difficult game. From this last reading, however I am more and more satisfied that nothing positive can be deduced from the history of the modern world unless you put Religious feeling at the foundation. It is this to which we owe our civil liberty. But Dr. Lingard is not the man to make this discovery.

I killed half an hour looking over some books about to be sold, at Auction, and walked, though not far, owing to the weather. Afternoon, finished No. 8 which I shall be forced to write over again. And I then studied the division of the rest of my subject, which will require much reflection.

Evening at home, finished 1st volume of Malvina and the life of Flaxman. I afterwards finished two Paragraphs of Wieland's History of the Abderites.

THURSDAY. 13TH.

Colder. I went to the Office and after getting through with my usual duties went out to call upon Mr. Hallett, Editor of the Advocate, in return for a visit paid by him to me. I had never seen him before. He is older than I expected and not at all the kind of man, but his conversation is full of information and his appearance intelligent.[1] After a considerable stay, I went to the Athenæum where I obtained a book or two and from thence to a Sale at Mr. Cunningham's at which I purchased several works which I did not want. What a difference in satisfaction there is upon such occasions. When I buy a really useful book to me at Auction cheap, I am always glad of it. But when my purchase is merely for cheapness I regret it.

Afternoon, continued upon Masonry. Read several papers given me by Mr. Hallett, and began writing over No 7. I found it exceedingly hard work. My mind was not quiet. O, the difficulties of writing, and the uselessness of it. Yet day after day multiplies a thousand fold what man writes.

Evening quietly at home. Read Malvina, and began Lockhart's Life of Burns.[2] Apparently a tolerably agreeable book. Afterwards, travelled through two more paragraphs of Wielands. A paragraph is a sentence.

[1] Benjamin Franklin Hallett (1797–1862) was a graduate of Brown University, had practiced law, and had been a newspaper editor in Rhode Island before moving to Boston to become editor of the *Advocate* in 1831. He soon assumed leadership in antimasonic politics in Massachusetts. A fairly extensive correspondence between JQA and Hallett, largely on antimasonic affairs, began just at this time, on 10 Dec., and continued through almost the whole of JQA's interest in Antimasonry to 25 June 1836. An exchange of letters between CFA and Hallett covering a much briefer span, Nov. 1836 — July 1837, reflects the shift in CFA's interests also, but more significantly the change in Hallett's political stance and the end of CFA's use of the *Advocate* for the expression of his opinions. Hallett's later course, a refutation of his early principles, took him far from the Adamses' position on public issues. (*DAB*; Bemis, *JQA*, 2:279–351 *passim*; Duberman, *CFA*, p. 46–57 *passim*. Hallett's letters to and from JQA and CFA are in the Adams Papers.)

[2] John Gibson Lockhart, *Life of Robert Burns*, Edinburgh, 1828.

FRIDAY. 14TH.

Morning dark and gloomy. I felt a little out of spirits, yet for my life I do not know why. Went to the Office. Read there a Proclamation from the President upon the subject of the Carolina Ordinance. It is an ably written Paper—In several of it's passages reminding me of my father's style and turn of thought.[1] I do not know who could have been the Author. Read a good deal of Lingard, and felt very much interested in his Account of James 1. and the famous Gunpowder plot. An affair that did wonders in confirming the People's horror of Popery. Took my usual walk.

In the Afternoon, continued and finished the copy of No. 7. But one of these papers has been published this week. I shall have abundance of time. And if I had any vanity, there seems no great probability of my gaining material gratification from it. I believe after this I will wind up, write no more, and consent to go down the Stream exactly as Providence may direct.

Evening, Mr. Degrand called. Some conversation about the proclamation. It is attributed to my father. Because it is good and contains his principles.[2] Went with my Wife to a party at Mrs. Blake's.[3] We had a tolerably pleasant time. Returned at eleven. Miss Anne Carter was with us.

[1] JQA sent a copy of Jackson's Proclamation against the nullifying Ordinance of South Carolina to CFA on the 10th, the same day he had received it, and

followed it the next day with his comments:

"If the whole State of South-Carolina were on fire this Proclamation is of a size to cover it like a wet blanket, for an extinguisher.... I thought it contained much sound Constitutional doctrine, more indeed than properly belonged to the source whence it originated. It would make a very tolerable Lecture for a Lyceum. The Constitutional Law is however mingled up with equal portions of pathetic paternity, of comminatory expostulation, and of vindictive personality against Calhoun thinly covered with a veil of gauze."

On balance JQA found the strength of the national voice sounded in the Proclamation diminished by the policies weakening to the Union advocated in the President's Message to Congress. "Between the Message and the Proclamation, Nullification is triumphant, but the nullifiers are in a dilemma. There is no danger from them. The danger is all here" (JQA to CFA, 11 Dec., Adams Papers). The text of the Proclamation is in Richardson, ed., *Messages and Papers*, 2:640–656.

² "[The Proclamation] has produced an electrical effect here.... The first general impression here which found its way into the Newspapers, was that *you* wrote the Paper. The singular coincidence in it's opinions with those expressed in your 4th of July address certainly gave colour to such a suspicion. And although my own mind could sanction no such idea, yet I cannot help believing the writer of that Paper to have carefully studied that address, even if he has not conversed with you. I do not perceive that you assign any source for the composition. It is hardly possible that a Paper so unusually and in that quarter peculiarly good, should have come from any of the ordinary writers of the Party....

"[T]he old Federal and the Masonic parties are perfectly triumphant here.... You are the subject of the bitterest attack. And yet, after all, when General Jackson is found to have once in his life done a good thing, the whole Community involuntarily almost, looks for it against all probability, beyond him to you" (CFA to JQA, 17 Dec.).

The effect produced by the Proclamation in Boston is again described in CFA's letter to LCA of 23 December. JQA in his reply to CFA's letter to him reflects further on the political consequences of the Proclamation elsewhere, particularly in Kentucky (25 Dec.; all letters quoted and referred to are in the Adams Papers).

The Proclamation's authorship, which so interested CFA, is now generally attributed, at least that part which expounds the historical justification for the rejection of the nullification doctrine, to Secretary of State Edward Livingston. The view held by CFA that the doctrine asserted in the Proclamation was remarkable for its closeness to JQA's own thinking was corroborated amusingly. On the same day that the Proclamation was issued, JQA sent to a publisher in New York a preface (to appear unsigned) for a source book that as then planned would contain the Declaration of Independence, the Constitution, and Washington's Farewell Address. The publisher was so struck by the similarity of constitutional theory animating both Jackson's Proclamation and JQA's Preface that forthwith and apparently without notification to JQA he enlarged his plan so as to include both documents in the source book, which he issued as *The Declaration of Independence; the Constitution of the United States; the Farewell Address ... the Proclamation of Andrew Jackson ... to which are prefixed prefatory remarks by one of the most distinguished statesmen of the United States*, N.Y., 1833. (Bemis, JQA, 2:262–264.)

³ Probably Mrs. Sarah Blake, the widow of Edward Blake, whose home at 7 Bowdoin Square was also the home of CFA's friend Edward Blake (*Boston Directory*, 1832–1833).

SATURDAY. 15TH.

Morning mild, cloudy and wet. At the Office. Great talk about the proclamation, people seem to expect a new era. A letter from my father this morning seems to me to give very much the most sound view of this question. The Paper is good so far as it goes. But every thing else the Government is doing is calculated to depress the best interests of the Nation. Let us see the end of it.[1] I have little hope. A storm is coming and the only way for every man to do is to gather in his sail and lie quietly to. It may bring us fair weather and new breezes. Walk, after reading a good deal of our friend Dr. Lingard.

Afternoon, quietly at home reading and writing. Continued No. 8. But the publication of my numbers has ceased, in consequence of the more exciting topics of Carolina and Government politics. I am always unfortunate in my times, and never shall succeed as a political writer. Let me turn then as soon as possible to Literature. Even there, is a blank.

Evening quiet at home. Read part of Malvina. Lockhart's Life of Burns, a pleasing book, though I could never form such an estimate of the Poet as he and others have done. German as usual.

[1] JQA to CFA, 11 Dec. (Adams Papers). For the letter see above, entry for 14 Dec., note, and below, that for 17 Dec., note.

SUNDAY. 16TH.

Colder but still cloudy and dull. I went to Meeting all day. In the morning heard my Classmate Cunningham from Psalms. 107. 43. "Whoso is wise, and will observe those things, even they shall understand the loving kindness of the Lord." He discoursed upon the benefits as superior to the pains experienced in life. He considered the various supports of human nature in times of suffering as well as its enjoyments—Meaning to draw a favourable picture of human life. His discourse was terribly common-place. Cunningham has not yet fulfilled his early promise. He graduated first in my Class. I never stood near him in Scholarship. Yet now I think I could have written a rather better Sermon. Perhaps this is mere vanity for I am not likely to be tried. Afternoon. Mr. Parkman. 1. Corinthians 10. 12. "Let him that thinketh he standeth, take heed lest he fall." The vicissitudes of life, wealth and poverty, happiness, misery, reputation and disgrace. A good practical Sermon.

Read Massillon afterwards, upon the Communion. Matthew 21. 5. "Tell ye the daughter of Sion, Behold, thy King cometh unto thee." The question involved in this Discourse is one of deep interest to every Christian. I have endeavoured seriously to reflect upon it, and my conclusion has been that a man ought to be thoroughly confirmed in the habits of virtue, and of an age to authorize confidence in their continuance before he partakes of it. This Sermon goes even farther. It requires 1. Conversion. 2. Expiatory penitence. 3. Active Christian virtue. Here is almost too much, for that person shall have a marvellous self conceit who could bring to the Altar such claims of fitness in himself.

The days are so short I can do little else of a Sunday. Evening, my Wife was writing, so that I read Ruffhead's biography of Pope. Some striking lines from the Essay on Criticism. Afterwards Malvina, and German.

MONDAY. 17TH.

Morning warm with heavy rain. I went to the Office and from thence to Faneuil Hall. A meeting of the Citizens had been called for the purpose of expressing an opinion in answer to the President's Proclamation.[1] As one of the Community, I doubted the expediency of the call,[2] but I went to hear what could be said about it. The hall was quite full. Mr. F. Dexter began. He said not much and was quickly done. And one third of what he did say might in my humble opinion have been left entirely unsaid. Mr. Webster made some remarks, merely pledging himself here and elsewhere to support the proclamation. The most remarkable point was a poor excuse for absence from his public duty under the plea of private affairs. Mr. H. G. Otis then took up the Cudgel and laid about him handsomely. His striking point was a justification of the Hartford Convention. The old sore place. Seventeen years have not yet healed it. I pitied him and his Apology.[3] The Stone *will* roll backwards. Mr. J. T. Austin concluded.

I returned before he finished, and wrote a letter to my Father.[4] Part of the Afternoon was taken up in copying it. The rest in reading the beginning of Villemain's Life of Cromwell.[5] A miserably superficial production. I have been cheated in the book.

In the evening. Progressed in Malvina, in the Life of Burns and in my German. This last however goes on very slowly indeed. I find myself a tremendous time upon a single sentence. Not that it is the construction, but the singular difficulty of fixing the meaning of the words.

[1] The call, signed by the leading political figures of Boston, including surviving Federalists, was addressed to "friends of the Union of the States and of the Constitution of the United States" and had as its stated purpose "to take into consideration the late proceedings of the Legislature, and the Convention of the State of South Carolina, and to express their opinion thereon, and to respond to the sentiments expressed in the late Proclamation of the President" (*Boston Daily Advertiser & Patriot*, 17 Dec., p. 2, col. 3).

[2] In this view CFA agreed with his father, who had written, "I think there

422

is no occasion, and there would be little wisdom in a public Meeting at Boston at this time. Wait at least until the whole policy of the Administration shall be disclosed. It is rotten ice" (JQA to CFA, 11 Dec., Adams Papers).

[3] JQA, when he received CFA's letter (17 Dec., Adams Papers) reporting Harrison Gray Otis' speech, was led to revert to the old question of publication of his "Reply to the Appeal of the Massachusetts Federalists" (see vol. 3:63 and entry for 23 Sept. 1831, above): "I am now much nearer the disposition to have it committed to the flames. I rejoice that I did not publish it; and so totally is my resentment disarmed by his advances to a reconciliation, and by the modesty of his present position, that I am determined henceforth to bury it in oblivion" (JQA to CFA, 25 Dec.,

Adams Papers). By Otis' "advances to a reconciliation" JQA doubtless refers to the recent visit Otis and Col. Thomas Handasyd Perkins had paid him at Quincy (JQA, Diary, 14 Aug.).

[4] See the preceding note. For more on the letter see above, entry for 14 Dec., note. In his reply to CFA's detailed report of the meeting, JQA commented on the positions taken by the various speakers and suggested additional implications.

[5] In the edition of Abel François Villemain's *Histoire de Cromwell* at MQA (2 vols., Brussels, 1829) are CFA's bookplate, a quotation on the flyleaf from Montaigne, and copious marginalia throughout in CFA's hand. For more on these annotations see entry for 26 Dec., below.

TUESDAY. 18TH.

Morning cloudy with very high winds. I went to the Office as usual. Very busy in writing Diary which my engagement yesterday put me behind hand in. I afterwards made a good deal of progress in Lingard. He is now upon the track which I have pretty well beaten. His account is generally tolerable. But he is too severe upon most of the British men of genius. Every thing that is not Catholic, is open to his darts. He speaks with little severity of the Jesuit pamphlets or the Jesuit doctrines, he conceals the efforts of the Catholics against the Government, and he deprecates censure of Catholic noblemen. But Coke, Bacon, Raleigh, Burleigh, Walsingham and Hatton all are not to be spared. This is not fair. England has no names to be more proud of than some of these. Took my usual walk although it was very windy.

Afternoon, finished No. 8 of my Papers. Their publication is at a dead stand still. Why should I plague myself to continue them? Nothing but the want of something else to do more useful induces me. Read more of Villemain's miserable book. A Frenchman can form no distinct ideas of Constitutional liberty. Evening as usual. Malvina, Lockhart's Burns and Wieland, a discourse before the Abderites upon the Shadow of an Ass.

WEDNESDAY. 19TH.

Fine morning although somewhat colder than it has been. I went to the Office. Nothing particular. My spirits somewhat depressed. It is my wish to do something in the world, not to be a creature entirely useless. I have laboured a good deal and what has been the success? Little indeed in comparison. Yet is it not for me to be discouraged? I will bear up as well as I can under a species of ostracism which exiles me by negatives. My services are not wanted. The world can get along exactly as well if I do nothing. Perhaps better as there would be one less to crowd it. But this tone is incorrect. So long as I am placed in it, I must not reject my duty, because others do so. It is essential to me that my conscience should be clear.

I read Lingard, finishing the reign of James which does on the whole, reconcile me to continuing the book. Walk as usual. Afternoon, began No. 9 of my work, wrote a page and then read Villemain. Not worth a sixpence. I continued in the evening however, as my Wife had gone out to tea. I went for her at nine to Mrs. Gorham's. Miss Julia and Miss Carter, besides Mrs. Gorham and the young men. On my return, read German. I work slowly.

THURSDAY. 20TH.

Beautiful morning. I staid at home quite late on account of one of the Conants from Weston who came in with some Wood and some money, both of which were very acceptable. My father's affairs in this quarter look somewhat gloomy. The interest he pays on his debts is consuming,[1] and his management does not make what property he has most productive. I felt again depressed, but rather relieved by writing my Diary. Read Lingard and took a walk.

Dined at Mrs. Frothingham's. Company, Mr. Brooks, Mr. Gorham Brooks and his Wife, Mr. Stetson my Wife and self. Returned in the evening after a short interval at home.

Gorham Brooks is the most singular of the world. He advances startling doctrines upon all subjects. I always endeavour to keep my tongue quiet but there are moments when the impetuosity of my natural character will burst forth and then it rushes with tenfold violence. I was impelled to day as I ought not to have been. I may as well now as at any other time, take myself to task for the warmth of my temper. I ought daily to set before myself some monitory sentence to guard me from the natural and powerful tendency of my own passions. In other climates, it would matter little, but here where the natural character and manners are cold, mine appear unpleasantly. I must learn to press down, to restrain the intense force of my feelings. I must teach myself to dissent only in mind, to give no vent to thoughts let them rush up ever so thick, to assume nothing, to arrogate nothing. O! God, thou who lookest down upon all our efforts whether they tend to good or ill, who knoweth the inmost heart of man, guide me in the path when my steps are feeble, show me the true road when I am going upon a wrong one. Let me not fall when I may be weak. My will is to do well, but my power sometimes deserts me in my utmost need. I do not enough study the spirit of the Christian Religion. Read German after my return.

[1] LCA, two months earlier, had written that the debts on which JQA was paying interest amounted to $40,000 (to JA2, 20 Oct., Adams Papers). This figure seems excessive, however. In scheduling his debts in the course of preparing his will, JQA had listed $13,000 of bank loans and $14,404 due the heirs of JA (Adams Papers, Microfilms, Reel No. 203).

FRIDAY. 21ST.

Morning clear and fine. I went to the Office as usual. Then to the Athenæum for the purpose of getting some more of the volumes of Lingard. This took some time. I then went down to take up a Note of my father's and renew it paying the Interest. These various operations kept me so long that I had very little time to devote to my regular reading. Our days have now reached their shortest. And I hope my industry will increase as they will, in future. Under a depression of spirits which I can not understand and which is unworthy of me, I am likely to suffer time to pass without due improvement. The hope of being useful has stimulated me heretofore and under it the six weeks elapsed since my return home have been much improved. But I have been considerably disappointed in my success. I probably expected too much. Took a walk.

Afternoon, did not write a word. Continued Villemain. I find no reason to change my opinion. A superficial translation of Hume, varied occasionally by extracts from the party Memoirs of the period without any discrimination in regard to the weight of the evidence he uses. I am surprised at M. Villemain.

Evening, my Wife had company. Her brothers Henry and Gorham, with his Wife, Miss Carter and Miss Gorham with her brother. It was a little stiff, no very animated conversation. I read no German.

SATURDAY. 22D.

A severely cold morning. Went to the Office as usual. My No. 4 appeared in this morning's Newspaper and put an end to my doubts concerning its reaching its destination safely.[1] What the motive could have been so long to delay it, I cannot very readily conceive. I felt ashamed of my late depression of spirits on so very miserable an account.

Wrote at the Office and read some of Dr. Lingard. One or two interruptions. Mr. Eben. Adams from Quincy with a bill which I declined paying — My father's funds being rather scantily off. He is so sharp a man too that I care not much to have him look to me as the source for money. Mr. Geitner also, my Tenant. He came for a subscription to a Concert which I gave him. I consider it as a matter of interest. Though I have no objection to hearing good music. Walk with Mr. Peabody. The cold was biting.

Afternoon very quiet at home. My Wife met with an accident to her teeth which produced excessive pain, and as there seemed to be no alleviation, I sent for the Dentist. She went to bed, however in very great pain. I tried to continue my numbers but the fit was not upon me. I made no head way at all. Read some of Villemain, and German. Progress tonight encouraging.

[1] *Boston Daily Advocate*, p. 2, cols. 4–5.

SUNDAY. 23D.

The remedies taken by my Wife for the tooth ach, were so powerful as to produce intense suffering in the head all day. She did not rise and as I began to apprehend nervous fever towards evening I sent for Dr. Stevenson who administered a sedative that composed her. Most of her complaints affect her nervous system. I believe this is customary with all women. To me, it is exquisitely distressing.

I read some of Villemain, and attended Divine Service all day. The weather still exceedingly cold. Mr. Frothingham preached. Morning, a continuation of the subject of the other day. Text, the same as on the 9th, 1 Peter 2. 16. The effect of the light and liberty of the age upon the religious condition. He follows up by a consideration also of the moral and social state of the world. His arguments today directed against the idea of neglecting the outward duties of religion. I wonder if I should not do well to take a blank card and make an abstract on the spot. This was too good a Sermon to lose. Afternoon, Matthew 12. 42. An application of the character of Solomon by the Saviour. Took a walk.

Afternoon, read a fragment of a Sermon by Massillon upon the Communion, apparently intended in the first instance for an Introduction to that I read last Sunday. It considers the crime of partaking it unworthily as greater than that of the Jews in rejecting the Saviour. Of course, this implies the doctrine of transubstantiation. My attention was not complete. Henry Brooks was here and took Tea. He goes to New York tomorrow. Evening I wrote a wild kind of letter to my Mother,[1] and read German.

[1] Letter in Adams Papers. Written, because of ABA's indisposition, to acknowledge LCA's most recent letter to her (18 Dec., Adams Papers) and to provide a substitute for ABA's weekly "Gazette of our proceedings." More discursive than was his habit, CFA included observations on matters of family interest:

"The most remarkable incident of the last week is the arrival of Mr. Brooks at home [after a visit to Washington]. . . . He has seen abundance of new things and new people and his is a mind that interests itself so much in details that I wonder he has not travelled a great deal more. A traveller is a person who notices all things, who returns home with new ideas of the shape and size and position of every article under the sun. There are not many such. I am not such a one. My Journeyings have been for the most part of that character which Sterne describes as often occurring between Dan and Beersheba — I have found all barren. I know little of New York, less of Philadelphia, less still of Baltimore. My Journies to the tops of hills for 'voos' have rarely occurred when possible to avoid them, and I remember but one cascade. A shabby result from all my wanderings. Now Mr. Brooks has settled these matters far more effectually."

After other comments on health, the weather, politics, &c. he concluded, "baby walks and talks after a fashion."

MONDAY. 24TH.

Morning cloudy, but it cleared up and gave us one of the purest skies of our Winter Season—Objects at a distance being perfectly defined and the smoke rising to a great distance without mixing with the air. I was at the Office. My Wife much better, though weak in her nerves, from the effect of her remedies. Occupied in writing and reading Lingard. His Account of the Revolution still pleases me. Took a long walk. Met two Messrs. Dixwell and accompanied them.[1]

Afternoon at home. Could not write so I read Villemain. I am afraid the interruption has dished the remainder of my series. It is so much more easy to read, and comparatively so very indolent a business that I fall into it very naturally when I make no effort to the contrary.

Quiet evening at home. My Wife sat with me downstairs. Read Malvina and Lockhart's Burns. Afterwards German. Finished the first extract from the Works of Wieland. I think it comes easier. Going on regularly with the World.

[1] Epes Sargent Dixwell, Harvard 1827, and John J. Dixwell resided at 5 Somerset Place (*Boston Directory*, 1832–1833).

TUESDAY. 25TH.

Christmas and a beautiful day. I went to the Office. Occupied in writing, and read a portion of Lingard. In the account of the troubles, he writes with ease and fluency. And on the whole he does not attack the liberty of the subject. Yet where so much of public affairs was influenced by religious feeling, such an author is rather a dangerous guide. Took a walk with Mr. Peabody, and finding that I had some surplus time I went to the Athenæum but found nothing.

Afternoon, made considerable progress in the book of M. Villemain. The summary of Cromwell's character is most incorrectly drawn. He has just enough of the true qualities to puzzle himself and to be astonished by his far strained explanations. I do not know a historical character who has been less correctly drawn. It would be very well worth while to make an estimate of it. I will think of it perhaps if I ever feel encouraged to write again. But my hopes are low. I find my article written for the North American Review so long ago is put off for another three months and perhaps more.[1] No success. Well, I will give up and take my ease.

Evening quiet. My Wife still in torture with her teeth. Read German.

[1] CFA's renewed defense of the Puritans in the form of an essay-review of Robert Vaughan's *Memorials of the Stuart Dynasty* had been sent to the *North American Review* on 7 July. On 4 Jan. 1833 he asked for its return; on the 8th he began rewriting it, on the 15th completed it, and on the 26th dispatched it again. After further threatened postponements it was published in the issue for July 1833 (*North Amer. Rev.,* 37:164–189).

WEDNESDAY. 26TH.

Cloudy and dull day. I went to the Office and passed my time there in the usual way. First and most regularly writing up Diary. Second, making up Accounts for the close of the year. Third, reading Dr. Lingard. The days are so short, and I take my regular walk at one o'clock, that I have not three hours for all these occupations. The political news as to the state of the Country is gloomy. There seems to be hardly any prospect of saving the Union since the appearance of the Resolutions from Virginia.[1]

Afternoon, finished Villemain's Life of Cromwell. I have seen no occasion to alter the opinion already expressed. The Author was not equal to his task. It required a knowledge of Constitutional Law of England, a study of the springs of human action, and a familiarity with preceding events, that he did not possess. His reliance is upon Hume et id genus omne.[2] I afterwards read his Eulogy of Montaigne. Here he is on his legs. This is French literature, and many a Frenchman perfectly understands that for one who knows what the Institutions of England are.[3] I was induced to look into Montaigne. He has been much admired for his originality and profoundness of thought. I confess in the two Chapters I read tonight I found nothing of them. Neither have I ever before.

Quiet evening. My Wife's tooth ach was better. We were asked to pass the evening at Mrs. Gray's but declined. Miss Julia Gorham dined here.

[1] The first reactions expressed in the Virginia legislature to the President's Proclamation were that "Virginia would not see South Carolina crushed" and that a convention of the states should be called (*Boston Daily Advertiser & Patriot*, 20 Dec., p. 2, col. 4). More moderate sentiments, though still opposed to the assertion in the Proclamation of the federal power, seemed, according to the latest reports, to be on the ascendant (same, 26 Dec., p. 2, col. 4). On the actions taken in the several states in the wake of Jackson's Proclamation, see William W. Freehling, *Prelude to Civil War*, N.Y., 1966, p. 267–297 *passim*.

[2] CFA expressed his disagreements with Villemain's interpretation of Cromwell and of his times much more vigorously in the marginal comments and notes he wrote in his copy of the book (see above, entry for 17 Dec., note). These comments ranged from simple expletives: "humbug," "you goose," "flat Popery," "lie," "nonsense," "what a man," "stuff," "all slander," "brazen dog," and "French humbug"; to a kind of dialogue with the author: "You are talking about men whose principles of action, wrong or right, *you* could never understand"; and then to generalizing animadversions: "No Frenchman knows much about English Constitutional History"; "A Frenchman cannot understand morality. He considers it all as policy."

Another characteristic example appears in the facsimile of a page from CFA's copy of Villemain reproduced as an illustration in the present volume; see above, p. xv.

[3] In the edition of Villemain's *Mélanges philosophiques, historiques et littéraires* at MQA (3 vols., Brussels, 1829), "Eloge de Montaigne" is in the first volume. CFA's bookplate is affixed and his characteristic underlinings and markings appear throughout.

THURSDAY. 27TH.

Morning cloudy with occasional rain. Went to the Office. Nothing particularly new. Engaged in my regular occupations, the monotony of which destroys all the interest of a Diary. Pursued the study of Lingard and owing to the weather, did not take my walk.

Afternoon, rather idle. Read an Essay upon Criticism by Villemain with which I was very much pleased. I do not now wonder at his reputation as a Writer. To begin with him where I did is doing an injustice to his character.[1] I finished the Afternoon by looking over Voltaire's Account of the English Revolution.[2] It is written with vivacity but with the same French mind. He sees things only by halves. He cannot understand the true character of the English Puritan. He sees nothing but fanaticism. Yet there was conscientiousness, morality, faith in God, and immense firmness of purpose. All good qualities in their way and strongly in contrast with the unprincipled looseness of their opponents, in whom Loyalty was the principal merit and a sense of honour according to the worldly notion apart from morality or religion. Voltaire is however more fair to Cromwell's character, Dr. Lingard yet more so.

Quiet evening. Malvina, and Conversation. Afterwards, German.

[1] "Discours sur les avantages et les inconvénients de la critique" is also in the first volume of Villemain's *Mélanges philosophiques, historiques et littéraires.*
[2] Probably the section relating to England in his *Siècle de Louis XIV.*

FRIDAY. 28TH.

Fine day. I went to the Office and was engaged in my usual way. Read Lingard and had two or three interruptions on Account of bills. This is the season for the making up of all the yearly Accounts. And a shower of Papers falls upon one, who has only to deem himself lucky that he has wherewith to meet them. Took a walk as usual.

Afternoon, for the sake of refreshing my Memory, I took down a volume of Cicero, and read the Oration for Milo. It is admirable. I find I relish his style more and more. The flowing measure of his periods, the power of his phrases, the adroit management of the strong points of the case. All wonderful. It has been always a question whether Milo was really the attacked party in the scuffle, but who can doubt it when he reads Cicero's defence? As my Wife was out, I accomplished the whole of it at a sitting and afterwards read the rest of Voltaire's Summary of events during the time of the troubles. A singular mixture of penetration and absurdity.

At eight I went down to Mrs. Frothingham's. She had a few friends belonging to the family. Mrs. Hall of Medford, Mr. and Mrs. F. Parkman, Mr. and Mrs. Story and Miss Gray, W. G. Brooks, Gorham Brooks and his Wife, P. C. B. Jr. and ditto. Returned at ten. Heard of the loss of the frigate Constellation in the Mediterranean.[1] Bad enough. Hammered over some German.

[1] An unconfirmed report of the sinking of the *Constellation* off Rhodes was carried in the newspapers on the 29th, but information received within the two days following seemed to justify the denial of the whole story (*Boston Daily Advertiser & Patriot*, 29 Dec., p. 2, cols. 4–5; 31 Dec., p. 2, col. 2).

SATURDAY. 29TH.

Fine day notwithstanding a little flurry of snow that fell early in the morning. I went to the Office as usual. Time taken up in drawing off my Accounts for the beginning of the year. My father's funds never were so much in the Minority.[1] My fifth number appeared in the Advocate with a recommendation of special attention from the Editor.[2] I think I have already expressed an opinion that it was the best of the series. Whether they succeed or not in attracting attention, my duty is done. And in all future time, I shall endeavour to follow in that line which my conscience points out to me to be right, without any consideration of the mere results to myself. It may be that my interests may not be served by any such Quixotic course. But I feel as if there were other considerations than these to sway a man even on this earth. Difficult as it is to look constantly to the point of duty, yet I know no reason why I should not even consider it my interest to attempt it. Read some of Lingard and took a walk.

Afternoon, began the History of the Ligue by Anquetil.[3] A portion of the French Annals of great interest as displaying the manner by which the Reformation affected that people in contradistinction to the English.

As my Wife was out in the evening, I also read a part of the second Philippic of Cicero. Powerful it is indeed. The Attention coming to it fresh again relishes it much more. Mr. E. Price Greenleaf took tea with us. He has much pleasant conversation. Principally upon South Carolina which State is going perfectly mad. God only knows the consequences. Called for my Wife at Mrs. Gorham's at nine o'clock. Read German afterwards.

[1] The meaning would seem to be that never before was the income for the quarter so much less than the expenditures.

[2] The editor's note inviting "special attention to the 5th No. of our valuable correspondent 'F'" is at p. 2, col. 2, the article itself at cols. 3–5. Copy for No. 5 in CFA's hand, differing substantially from the printed text, is in the Adams Papers along with copy for Nos. 6–9 and notes for additional numbers (Microfilms, Reel No. 319). Publica-tion of the series stopped for a time with No. 5 but was afterward resumed (CFA, Diary, 21–22 May 1833).

[3] Editions of Louis Pierre Anquetil, *L'esprit de la Ligue ... les 16 et 17 siècles*, published in 3 vols. at Paris in 1771 and in 1783 are at MQA. The edition of 1771 has JQA's bookplate and an inscription on the half-title of each volume: "George Washington Adams from his Grandfather 1825." Also at MQA is CFA's set of *Histoire de France* by the same author, 15 vols., Paris, 1817.

SUNDAY. 30TH.

Fine day although rather cold. I passed an hour of my morning in reading Montaigne's Essays and this time I did succeed in finding a good deal that was original and striking. His ideas upon the subject of place and occupation and the agitation of human affairs are worth considering. A man most certainly may make himself very unnecessarily uncomfortable by meddling in matters where he has no occasion so to do. But then a man must not hide his talent in a Napkin. He ought not to go to sleep over his work.

Attended divine Service. Mr. Frothingham preached for the third time upon the danger of abusing the privileges of the age we live in. Text the same as last Sunday. He considered the three positions. Every man has a right to all the liberty he can acquire. Every man has a right to all the property and 3. to all the power and influence he can acquire. He defined and limited them. It was an excellent Sermon. A great deal of sense and spirit in the mode of treating the doctrines of the levellers of the present day. In the afternoon, we had Mr. Huntoon from Bangor, Maine—A man who was formerly settled at Canton and whom I have heard at Quincy.[1] Text from Ephesians, 4. 1. "I therefore beseech you that ye walk worthy of the vocation wherewith ye are called." Subject, the religious character. He urged the strictness of the injunctions of the New Testament, and condemned the Luke-warmness of nominal Christians. When a man talks after this fashion, it is just as well to call him to a strict, definite explanation of what he *means*. Does he mean to make a *Monk* of a Man at once, to spend all his time in devotion, or does he refer to the performance of all the moral, religious, social and political duties for which Man seems to be fitted by the Creator. If so, let him define how they can be best fulfilled. That is a practical end, and free from confusing generalities. Mr. Huntoon is nevertheless a strong thinker. Some of his views were clear and able.

Afterwards, I read a Sermon of Massillon's upon the Passion of our Saviour. Text, John, 19. 30. "It is finished." But it was a general view of the whole Chapter. Three points. The Passion of Christ was a consummation of Justice to the Deity, of Malice in Men, of love in the Saviour. The whole doctrine of the Saviour's atonement was involved in the first point. The Sermon was consequently less taking to my-self. I do not pretend to be quite equal to the comprehension of so re-markable a doctrine. Evening quiet at home. I read some of Ruffhead, and some of Montaigne.

[1] When CFA more than six years earlier had heard Rev. Benjamin Huntoon preach, he had been impressed (vol. 1:321).

MONDAY. 31ST.

Morning damp and warm. I went to the Office. Received a pleasant Letter from my Father upon passing events. He does not seem much disturbed by the indications that are manifested in Carolina, but he dislikes very much those at Washington.[1] Heaven only knows what the result may be. I was occupied in drawing up my Accounts. Finished my Quarterly Statement and forwarded it together with a short letter,[2] which occupied me all the Afternoon to finish and copy. As punctuality is a thing I always feel much disposed to rest upon, it gives me pleasure when the whole of it is well over. Took my usual walk.

My Wife went, and I accompanied her, to take tea and spend the evening at her sister, Mrs. Gorham Brooks'. They live for the Winter at the Tremont House. Gorham Brooks is a humorist, but when he chooses, he can be quite agreeable, and on this evening, he could talk and make the evening pass almost imperceptibly. I never feel as if I could discuss subjects with much freedom, nor even touch upon others. But there are enough in common to be able to make an Evening. His Wife is a charming Woman. Her great simplicity of manner united with a good deal of vivacity make her very fascinating to people in general. Returned home, and Dipped without much satisfaction into Shakespear's Comedy of Errors.

A strange thing to fall upon at the close of a Year.

I hope my life during the past twelve months has born no relation to Error. The Review of it is not an unpleasant thing to me. I have prospered in worldly affairs. I and mine have been most mercifully saved when others have suffered. A disease has passed over the land in the course of it and we have not fallen. My days have been pleasant and peaceful. And if I have not occupied them quite so fully as I ought, yet I have not been wholly idle. May the Lord who has showered blessings so bountifully upon me and those whom I love, continue his favours and at the same time make us worthy to receive them.

[1] JQA to CFA, 25 Dec. (Adams Papers). For other matters adverted to in the letter, see above, notes to the entries for 14 and 17 December.
[2] To JQA; LbC in Adams Papers.

Appendix

NOTE ON THE APPENDIX

The Appendix is an author list of the books which CFA borrowed from the Boston Athenæum from the first exercise of his privileges as a shareholder on 18 January 1830 to the date at which these volumes conclude, 31 December 1832. Because many if not most of the books he read were from his own or his father's or his grandfather's library, the Athenæum list of borrowings is of course a supplement to rather than a complete record of CFA's reading during this period. For those books he borrowed, the list does provide exact information as to the dates he had each in his possession and the editions he was reading. What is more important, perhaps, the body of books he is known to have read is increased substantially by those he is here recorded as borrowing but which he did not mention in the diary text. Each title to which CFA did refer in the diary and for which the editors subjoined a footnote bears as the concluding element of its entry in this Appendix a reference to the date in the diary at which the title is mentioned and annotated.

Multivolume sets listed in the Appendix were borrowed in entirety unless the entry specifies which volume or volumes were borrowed.

The Appendix has been constructed from the manuscript volume in the Boston Athenæum's archives labeled "Entry of Books Borrowed: I, 1827–1834"; the printed *Catalogue of Books in the Boston Athenæum,* Boston, 1827; and the *Catalogue of Books Added to the Boston Athenæum since . . . January 1827,* Boston, [1830]. The opening section of the pages relating to CFA in the "Entry of Books Borrowed" is illustrated in volume 3. See further the Descriptive List of Illustrations, vol. 3, p. xx.

Appendix

BOOKS BORROWED BY CHARLES FRANCIS ADAMS FROM THE BOSTON ATHENÆUM, 1830–1832

ARISTOPHANES. *Comedies*, transl. Thomas Mitchell. 2 vols., London, 1820.
Vol. 1 borrowed 18 Jan. – 3 Feb. 1830; annotated at 25 January.

ARMSTRONG, T. B. *Journal of Travels in the Seat of War, during the Last Two Campaigns of Russia and Turkey.* London, 1831.
Borrowed 12 March – 18 April 1832.

AUSTEN, JANE. *Emma.* 3 vols., London, 1816.
Borrowed 29 Jan. – 9 Feb. 1831.

—— *Northanger Abbey.* 4 vols., London, 1818.
Borrowed 2–12 Feb. 1831.

—— *Sense and Sensibility.* 3 vols., London, 1813.
Borrowed 14 Jan. – 28 Feb., 6–22 June 1831.

BARBIER, ANTOINE ALEXANDRE. *Dictionnaire des ouvrages anonymes et pseudonymes.* 2 vols., Paris, 1806.
Borrowed 14 July – 14 Aug. 1830.

—— Another edn. 4 vols., Paris, 1806.
Borrowed 14 Aug. – 7 Sept. 1830.

BARRINGTON, JONAH. *Personal Sketches of His Own Times.* 2 vols., Phila., 1827.
Borrowed 2–19 June 1830.

BARROW, JOHN. *A Family Tour through South Holland; up the Rhine; and across the Netherlands.* London, 1831.
Borrowed 22 Nov. – 7 Dec. 1831.

BEATTIE, WILLIAM. *Journal of a Residence in Germany.* 2 vols., London, 1831.
Vol. 1 borrowed 8–17 Dec. 1831.

BELL, JOHN. *History of the First Revolution in France.* London, 1831.
Borrowed 8–27 March 1832; annotated at 26 March.

BOILEAU–DESPRÉAUX, NICOLAS. *Œuvres.* 5 vols., Paris, 1772.
Vol. 4 borrowed 30 Aug. – 16 Sept. 1831; annotated at 31 August.

BOSWELL, JAMES. *Journal of a Tour to the Hebrides.* N.Y., 1810.
Borrowed 21–30 March 1831; annotated at 27 March.

—— *Life of Samuel Johnson,* ed. J. W. Croker. 5 vols., London, 1831.
Vol. 5 borrowed 12 March – 27 April 1832; annotated at 22 March.

BRODIE, GEORGE. *History of the British Empire from the Accession of Charles I to the Restoration.* 4 vols., Edinburgh, 1822.
Vols. 1, 2 borrowed 15 June – 10 July 1832; annotated at 17 June.

BROOKE, HENRY. *The Fool of Quality.* 2 vols., N.Y., 1818.
Borrowed 19 Feb. – 21 March 1831.

BRYAN, MICHAEL. *A Biographical and Critical Dictionary of Painters and Engravers.* 2 vols., London, 1813–1816.
Borrowed 19 Nov. 1831 – 17 Jan. 1832; annotated at 20 November.

BURNEY, FRANCES, later D'ARBLAY. *Camilla.* 3 vols., Boston, 1797.
Vol. 3 borrowed 17–29 Jan. 1831; annotated at 10 January.

—— *Cecilia, or Memoirs of an Heiress.* 3 vols., Boston, 1803.
Vol. 1 borrowed 18–20 Jan. 1830; vols. 2, 3 borrowed 12–19 Feb. 1831.

CHALMERS, GEORGE. *Political Annals of the Present United Colonies . . . to the Peace of 1763.* London, 1780.
Borrowed 15 April – 7 May 1830; annotated at 8 April.

CHATEAUBRIAND, FRANÇOIS AUGUSTE RENÉ. *Œuvres complètes.* 28 vols., Paris, 1826–1831 (*Etudes ou discours historiques, vol. 4*).
Vol. 4 borrowed 8–26 Sept. 1832; annotated at 8 September.

CICERO, MARCUS TULLIUS. *Epistles to Atticus,* transl. William Guthrie. 3 vols., London, 1806.
Vols. 1–3 borrowed 21 July – 27 Aug. 1831; vol. 1 borrowed 7–16 Sept.; annotated at 6 September.

—— *Epistolæ ad Atticum.* 2 vols., Amsterdam, 1684.
Borrowed 7 Sept. – 28 Oct. 1831.

—— *Morals,* transl. William Guthrie. London, 1744.
Borrowed 17 Nov. – 8 Dec. 1831.

—— *Orationes.* 6 vols., Amsterdam, 1696.
Vols. 5, 6 borrowed 2 May – 27 June 1831.

—— *Orationes cum interpretatione et notis P. C. de Merouville.* 3 vols., Venice, 1725.
Vol. 1 borrowed 29 Jan. – 3 March 1831.

—— *Orations*, transl. William Guthrie. 2 vols., London, 1806.
Borrowed 21 Jan. – 2 Feb. 1831.

—— *Three Dialogues on the Character of an Orator*, transl. William Guthrie. London, 1755.
Borrowed 26 Nov. – 17 Dec. 1830; annotated at 29 November.

COTTIN, SOPHIE RISTAUD. *Œuvres.* 8 vols., Paris, 1817.
Vols. 1, 2 borrowed 28 Nov. 1832 – 9 Jan. 1833; annotated at 28 November.

CUNNINGHAM, ALLAN. *Lives of the Most Eminent British Painters and Sculptors* (Harper's Family Library). 5 vols., N.Y., 1831–1832.
Vol. 2 borrowed 9–27 March 1832; annotated at 11 March; vols. 3, 4 borrowed 8 Nov. – 21 Dec. 1832; annotated at 10, 30 Nov., 3 December.

D'ISRAELI, ISAAC. *Commentaries on the Life and Reign of Charles I.* 5 vols., London, 1831.
Vol. 1 borrowed 20–26 April 1831.

ELLIOT, JONATHAN. *The Debates, Resolutions, and Other Proceedings, in Convention, on the Adoption of the Federal Constitution.* 4 vols., Washington, 1827–1830.
Vol. 2 borrowed 18 Oct. – 19 Nov. 1831; annotated at 18 October.

EUSTACE, JOHN CHETWODE. *A Classical Tour Through Italy, . . . 1802.* 4 vols., London, 1815.
Borrowed 2 April – 12 June 1830; annotated at 7 April.

FÉNELON, FRANÇOIS DE SALIGNAC DE LA MOTTE. *Œuvres.* 9 vols., Paris, 1787–1792 (*Dialogues des morts*, vol. 4).
Vol. 4 borrowed 27 Aug. – 16 Sept. 1831; annotated at 29 August.

"Few Days in Belgium" [not further identified by the editors].
Borrowed 2–9 April 1831.

FIELD, WILLIAM. *Memoirs of the Life, Writings, and Opinions of the Rev. Samuel Parr.* 2 vols., London, 1828.
Borrowed 5 June – 6 July 1830; annotated at 5 June.

FOURNIER, FRANÇOIS IGNACE. *Dictionnaire portatif de bibliographie.* Paris, 1809.
Borrowed 16 Sept. – 26 Nov. 1830.

FRANKLAND, CHARLES COLVILLE. *Narrative of a Visit to the Courts of Russia and Sweden.* 2 vols., London, 1832.
Borrowed 20–30 Aug. 1832; annotated at 20 August.

FRANKLIN, JOHN. *Narrative of a Journey to the Shores of the Polar Sea, . . . 1819–1822.* London, 1823.
Borrowed 9–13 April 1831; annotated at 9 April.

—— *Narrative of a Second Expedition, . . . 1825–1827.* London, 1828.
Borrowed 25 April – 30 May 1831; annotated at 25, 29 April.

GOETHE, JOHANN WOLFGANG VON. *Memoirs.* N.Y., 1824.
Borrowed 3–12 March 1832; annotated at 3 March.

—— *Sorrows of Werter.* Chiswick, 1822.
Borrowed 20 Jan. – 2 Feb. 1830.

GRAHAME, JAMES. *History of the . . . United States.* 2 vols., London, 1827.
Vols. 1, 2 borrowed 2 April – 7 May 1830; annotated at 25 Sept. 1829, 13 April 1830; vol. 1 borrowed 18–24 Aug. 1831; vol. 2 borrowed 4 Feb. – 8 March 1832.

GRANVILLE, AUGUSTUS BOZZI. *St. Petersburgh. A Journal of Travels to and from that Capital.* 2 vols., London, 1828.
Borrowed 8 Sept. – 7 Nov. 1832; annotated at 8 September.

GRIMM, FRIEDRICH MELCHIOR DE. *Correspondance littéraire, philosophique, et critique, 1753–1790.* 16 vols., Paris, 1829–1831.
Vols. 1–6 borrowed 2 May – 27 July 1831; annotated at 2 May.

HALL, BASIL. *Fragments of Voyages and Travels.* 3 vols., Edinburgh, 1831.
Vols. 1, 2 borrowed 30 Aug. – 17 Sept. 1832; annotated at 30 August.

HAZLITT, WILLIAM. *Conversations of James Northcote.* London, 1830.
Borrowed 27 Jan. – 3 Feb. 1832; annotated at 27 January.

HEAD, GEORGE. *Forest Scenes and Incidents in the Wilds of North America.* London, 1829.
Borrowed 27 May – 1 June 1830.

HEARNE, SAMUEL. *A Journey from Prince of Wales's Fort . . . to the Northern Ocean, . . . 1769–1772.* London, 1795.
Borrowed 2–9 April 1831; annotated at 3 April.

HUNT, JAMES HENRY LEIGH. *Lord Byron and Some of His Contemporaries.* Phila., 1828.
Borrowed 3–21 Feb. 1832; annotated at 3 February.

JUSTINIAN, *Institutions*, transl. George Harris. London, 1761.
Borrowed 2 Feb. – 7 March 1831; annotated at 17 February.

KNOWLES, JOHN. *Life and Writings of Henry Fuseli.* 3 vols., London, 1831.
Borrowed 8 Nov. 1831 – 4 Feb. 1832; annotated at 8 Nov., 17 January.

KOTZEBUE, OTTO VON. *A Voyage of Discovery into the South Sea.* 3 vols., London, 1821.
Borrowed 21 March – 9 April 1831; annotated at 23 March.

LA MOTTE FOUQUÉ, FRIEDRICH HEINRICH CARL DE. *Ondine*, French transl. I. Montolieu. Paris, 1822.
Borrowed 20–28 Nov. 1832; annotated at 22 November.

LEE, HARRIET. *Canterbury Tales*. 5 vols., London, 1797–1805.
Borrowed 7 Dec. 1831 – 27 Jan. 1832; annotated at 22 December.

LELAND, THOMAS. *History of Ireland*. 3 vols., London, 1773.
Vol. 1 borrowed 17 Sept. – 7 Nov. 1832.

LIND, JONATHAN. *Remarks on the Principal Acts of the Thirteenth Parliament of Great Britain. . . . Vol. 1, Containing Remarks on the Acts Relating to the Colonies with a Plan of Reconciliation*. London, 1775.
Borrowed 17–22 Dec. 1830; annotated at 21 December.

LINGARD, JOHN. *History of England*. 14 vols., London, 1825–1831.
Vols. 2–11 borrowed 26 Sept. 1832 – 12 Jan. 1833; annotated at 29 September.

LOCKHART, JOHN GIBSON. *Life of Robert Burns*. Edinburgh, 1828.
Borrowed 13 Dec. 1832 – 19 Jan. 1833; annotated at 13 December.

LOUDON, JOHN CLAUDIUS. *Encyclopædia of Gardening*. London, 1827.
Borrowed 26 May – 21 July 1831.

MACKENZIE, ALEXANDER. *Voyages from Montreal . . . to the Frozen and Pacific Oceans*. London, 1801.
Borrowed 16 April – 2 May 1831; annotated at 16 April.

MACKINTOSH, JAMES. *History of England* (Lardner's Cabinet Cyclopædia). 2 vols., London, 1830–1831.
Borrowed 28 Oct. – 8 Nov. 1831; annotated at 28 October.

—— *Dissertation on the Progress of Ethical Philosophy*. Edinburgh, 1830.
Borrowed 6–30 Aug. 1832; annotated at 29 August.

Manuel du Libraire, du bibliothécaire et de l'homme de lettres. Paris, 1829.
Borrowed 16 Sept. 1830 – 14 Jan. 1831.

MIDDLETON, CONYERS. *Life of M. T. Cicero*. 3 vols., London, 1750.
Borrowed 22 Dec. 1830 – 14 Jan. 1831; annotated at 26 Dec., 13 January.

MINUTOLI, WOLFARDINE A. L. MENU VON. *Recollections of Egypt*. London, 1827.
Borrowed 11–22 Dec. 1830; annotated at 14 December.

MORGAN, LADY SYDNEY. *Book of the Boudoir*. 2 vols., London, 1829.
Vol. 1 borrowed 26 Nov. – 11 Dec. 1830; annotated at 26 November.

NOBLE, MARK. *Memoirs of the Protectorate-House of Cromwell*. 2 vols., Birmingham, 1784.
Borrowed 6 Aug. – 8 Sept. 1832; annotated at 7 August.

OTIS, JAMES. *Rights of the British Colonies Asserted and Proved.* Boston, 1764.
Borrowed 14–24 June 1831; annotated at 14 June.

PARR, SAMUEL. *Bibliotheca Parriana. A Catalogue of the Library of.* London, 1827.
Borrowed 20 March – 8 May 1832.

—— *Works . . . with Memoirs of his Life and Writings . . . by John Johnstone.* 8 vols., London, 1828.
Vol. 1 borrowed 4–11 Aug. 1830; annotated at 4 August.

PARRY, WILLIAM EDWARD. *Journal of a Voyage for the Discovery of a North-West Passage, . . . 1819–1820.* London, 1821.
Borrowed 10–21 March 1831; annotated at 10 March.

—— *Journal of a Second Voyage, . . . 1821–1823.* London, 1824.
Borrowed 21 March – 9 April 1831; annotated at 21 March.

—— *Journal of a Third Voyage, . . . 1824–1825.* London, 1826.
Borrowed 9–13 April 1831; annotated at 9 April.

—— *Narrative of an Attempt to Reach the North Pole, . . . 1827.* London, 1828.
Borrowed 14–18 April 1831; annotated at 14 April.

PRIOR, JAMES. *Memoir of the Life and Character of . . . Edmund Burke.* 2 vols., London, 1826.
Borrowed 27 May – 5 June 1830; annotated at 27 May.

PYE, HENRY JAMES. *Commentary Illustrating the Poetic of Aristotle, with a Translation.* London, 1792.
Borrowed 21 July – 9 Aug. 1831; annotated at 23 July.

Quarterly Review, Edinburgh.
Vols. 18, 21 borrowed 15–18 April 1831; annotated at 15, 17 April.

QUINCTILIANUS, MARCUS FABIUS. *De institutione oratoria*, ed. P. Burmanno. 2 vols., Leyden, 1720.
Borrowed 27 Jan. – 21 Feb. 1832; annotated at 26 January.

REISKE, JOHN JACOB. *Oratorum Græcorum, quorum princeps est Demosthenes.* 12 vols., Leipzig, 1770–1775 (*Apparatus criticus ad Demosthenem*, vols. 9–11).
Vols. 9–12 borrowed 3 Feb. – 2 April 1830; annotated at 30 Sept. 1831.

ROSS, JOHN. *A Voyage of Discovery . . . for the Purpose of Exploring Baffin's Bay.* 2 vols., London, 1819.
Borrowed 12–16 April 1831; annotated at 12 April.

SCHILLER, JOHANN CHRISTOPH FRIEDRICH VON. *Don Carlos*. London, 1798.
Borrowed 16–21 July 1831.

SHEFFIELD, JOHN BAKER HOLROYD, EARL OF. *Observations on the Commerce of the American States*. London, 1783.
Borrowed 21 Feb. – 9 March 1832; annotated at 21 February.

SMITH, JOHN THOMAS. *Nollekens and His Times*. 2 vols., London, 1828.
Borrowed 22 Dec. 1830 – 28 Jan. 1831; annotated at 22 December.

SOUTHEY, ROBERT. *Essays Moral and Political*. 2 vols., London, 1832.
Vol. 2 borrowed 30 Aug. – 17 Sept. 1832; annotated at 30 August.

SPENCE, JOSEPH. *Anecdotes, Observations, and Characters of Books and Men*. London, 1820.
Borrowed 27 Jan. – 12 March 1832; annotated at 12 February.

STAPLETON, AUGUSTUS GRANVILLE. *The Political Life of . . . George Canning*. 3 vols., London, 1831.
Borrowed 15 July – 20 Aug. 1832; annotated at 25 July.

UNITED STATES. *Laws*. 20 vols., Phila. and Washington, 1796–1823.
Vol. 14 borrowed 17–29 Dec. 1831.

VAUGHAN, ROBERT. *Memorials of the Stuart Dynasty*. 2 vols., London, 1831.
Borrowed 12 June – 10 July 1832; annotated at 12 June.

VIDOCQ, EUGÈNE FRANÇOIS. *Memoirs*. 4 vols., London, 1829.
Vol. 1 borrowed 3–11 Sept. 1832; annotated at 4 September.

VIGNE, GODFREY T. *Six Months in America*. 2 vols., London, 1832.
Vol. 1 borrowed 17–26 Sept. 1832; annotated at 17 September.

VOSSIUS, GERARDUS JOANNIS. *Rhetorices contractæ, sive partitionum oratoriarum lib. V*. Leyden, 1627.
Borrowed 17–29 Jan. 1831; annotated at 17 January.

WALLACE, WILLIAM. *History of the Life and Reign of George IV* (Lardner's Cabinet Library). 3 vols., London, 1831.
Borrowed 21 Oct. – 22 Nov. 1831; annotated at 21 October.

WALPOLE, HORACE. *Memoires of the Last Ten Years of the Reign of George II*. 2 vols., London, 1822.
Borrowed 19 June – 4 Aug. 1830; annotated at 23 June.

WALSH, ROBERT. *Narrative of a Journey from Constantinople to England*. London, 1828.
Borrowed 18 April – 30 May 1831; annotated at 18 April.

WEDDELL, JAMES. *A Voyage towards the South Pole,* ... 1822–1824.
London, 1825.
Borrowed 2–9 April 1831; annotated at 2 April.

WIRT, WILLIAM. *The Letters of the British Spy in Virginia.* Baltimore,
1813.
Borrowed 18 July – 3 Aug. 1831.

Chronology

Chronology

CHARLES FRANCIS ADAMS, 1829–1832

1829

Sept. 4: "Established as a married man in Boston," residing at 3 Hancock Avenue and occupying a law office at 23 Court Street.

13: Begins to worship regularly at the First Church, Chauncy Place.

Oct. 25: Attends the dedication of the memorial to John and Abigail Adams that John Quincy Adams had caused to be erected within the Adams Temple in Quincy.

Nov. 24: Assists JQA in effecting the reburial of GWA's remains in the Adams family vault in the First Church burying ground, Quincy.

25: Receives from JQA by transfer his proprietor's share in the Boston Athenæum.

Dec. 13: Begins to read in JA's MS diaries and papers.

1830

Jan. 2: Speaks on the question of Indian removal at the Private Debating Society, Boston.

Feb. 1: Elected a director of the Middlesex Canal Company.

20: His essay on Eloquence is published in the *Massachusetts Journal*.

21: His mother-in-law, Mrs. Peter Chardon Brooks, dies after a long illness; his tribute to her is published anonymously in the *Columbian Centinel* three days later.

May 26: His article "The Next Presidency" is adapted and used as an editorial in the *Boston Patriot*.

June–July: Three articles by him signed "A Calm Observer" opposing a grant of municipal funds for the construction of railroads are published in the *Boston Patriot*.

Sept. 10: A second daughter is born to JA2 and christened Georgeanna Frances, adapted from the names of her uncles.

16: Reads and disagrees strongly with the proposal published in the *Boston Courier* that JQA be elected to Congress as representative of the Plymouth District.

Oct. 12: Completes the catalogue of JQA's library which he had undertaken along with JQA on 16 June.

21: His article supporting the National Republican candidate for representative in Congress from Boston is published in the *Boston Courier*, signed "A."

Nov. 1: JQA is elected to the 22d Congress.

1831

Jan.: His essay-review of James Grahame's *History of the United States*, written in April 1830, is published in the *North American Review*, in payment for which he receives $21.

March: Is admitted as an attorney at the Supreme Judicial Court of Massachusetts.

May: Three communications by him signed "Cimon" analyzing the background of "The Resignation of the Cabinet" appear in the *Boston Patriot*. Goes with ABA to live at the Old House in Quincy with his parents for two months, and begins the task of sorting and arranging JA's papers.

August: Despite his efforts of more than a year to prevent the appearance of a pamphlet making public the facts of GWA's relations with Eliza Dolph, *Report of a Trial* is published.

13: His first child, a daughter, is born at Boston and in October is christened Louisa Catherine (LCA2).

Sept. 2: Defends JQA against the attacks of Joseph T. Buckingham in a letter signed "A Looker On" in the *Boston Patriot*.

15: To relieve ABA of household responsibilities during her recuperation, takes family to Quincy for a month.

19: Takes under advisement JQA's offer of the editorship of the *Boston Patriot* if JQA should decide to buy the paper.

Dec. 5: JQA takes his seat in the House of Representatives.

24, 29: Two installments signed "F" of his critique of Treasury Secretary McLane's Report appear in the *Boston Patriot*.

1832

Jan.: The three final installments on "The Treasury Report" are published in the *Boston Daily Advertiser & Patriot* following the merger of the two papers.

Feb.: Adds the management of JQA's Quincy property to his responsibilities as manager of JQA's affairs in Boston.

March 13: His uncle TBA dies and is buried the next day in the Adams family vault in the First Church burying ground in Quincy.

May 10: His communication signed "Q" defending JQA's political antimasonry is published in the *Boston Daily Advocate.*

26: Upon completion of extensive repairs to the house and garden undertaken by CFA, LCA arrives from Washington to occupy the Old House and is soon joined by CFA, his wife, and daughter, who remain until November.

July: At the conclusion of the 1st session of the 22d Congress JQA returns to Quincy and is soon engaged in continuing his life of JA and with CFA in bringing JA's papers into some order.

Oct.: Succeeds TBA as clerk of the Adams Temple and School Fund.

Nov.: Serves with a committee of the Supervisors of the Fund in inventorying JA's library, which remained in the "Office" at the Old House.

7: Returns to his Boston residence with his family in anticipation of the imminent departure of JQA and LCA for Washington.

Dec.: Begins an active role in antimasonry with the publication in the *Boston Daily Advocate* of the first five of his series of articles signed "F" on "The Principles and Ground of Anti-Masonry" and "A Brief History of the Masonic Outrages in New York."

Index

NOTE ON THE INDEX

This Index covers volumes 3 and 4 of the *Diary of Charles Francis Adams* in accordance with Adams Papers practice of providing an index at the end of each published unit.

Every index is designed in some measure to supplement the annotation. With the aid of the editors the compiler has tried to furnish the correct spellings of proper names, to supply forenames for persons who appear in the text only with surnames, to indicate places of residence and occupations of persons whose forenames are either unknown or not known with certainty, and finally to distinguish by dates persons with identical or nearly identical names. Markedly variant spellings of proper names have been cross-referenced to what are believed to be their most nearly standard forms, and the variant forms found in the MSS are parenthetically recorded following the standard spellings. Undoubtedly the index contains mistakes and incomplete identifications; the editors would warmly welcome corrections of mistakes of this kind, and indeed of every kind, from users who can put them straight.

Wives' names, with a few exceptions for special reasons, follow their husbands' names. *See*-references under maiden names are used for members of the Adams and collateral families and for women mentioned in the text who married subsequently but before 31 December 1832.

Under major place names (e.g. Boston, Washington) there are appended separate gatherings of "Buildings, landmarks, streets, &c.," the items in which are arranged alphabetically rather than in order of their appearance (as other subentries are throughout the Index).

References in the form "*See* (or *See also*) Adams Genealogy" are to a compilation described in the Guide to Editorial Apparatus at vol. 3:xlvi.

The index to the first two volumes of the *Diary of Charles Francis Adams* was prepared by Mrs. Carl A. Pitha, who has also contributed heavily to the present index.

"A." *See* CFA

AA. *See* Adams, Mrs. John (Abigail Smith, 1744–1818)

AA2. *See* Smith, Mrs. William Stephens (Abigail Adams, 1765–1813)

ABA. *See* Adams, Mrs. Charles Francis (Abigail Brown Brooks, 1808–1889)

Abbot, Rev. John S. C., 3:346

Adams, Abigail. *See* Smith, Mrs. William Stephens (1765–1813)

Adams, Abigail Smith. *See* Angier, Mrs. John (1806–1845)

ADAMS, CHARLES FRANCIS (1807–1886, son of JQA, designated as CFA in *The Adams Papers; see* Adams Genealogy). *Note:* habitual activities such as daily walks, weekly church attendance, the identification of Bible texts used in sermons, &c. are not indexed

AGENT, PERSONAL ASSISTANT, AND DEPUTY FOR JQA

Personal and domestic matters: performs commissions and errands, 3:9–10, 44, 71, 93–97, 112, 224, 254, 331, 344, 353, 377, 387–88; 4:64, 72, 97, 156, 165, 399; supervises Sparks' use of JA's letterbooks, 3:88, 92, 143–44, 149, 160–63, 173, 205; 4:xiii; affixes bookplates, 3:176, 182, 257; 4:12, 50, 343, 364–88 *passim;* has books bound, 3:257; 4:50; catalogues library at Old House and books in Boston, 3:262–401 *passim;* amanuensis, 3:260, 331, 374, 407; 4:103–18, 140–41, 337, 360, 364, 371–72, 380–81, 391, 394; arranges books in library, 4:306, 391; caretaker of Old House, 4:402. *See also* Old House

Deputy in administering estate of JA and in payment of legacies: 3:31, 86, 101, 104, 145, 196, 199–200, 202–203, 374, 377, 394; 4:1, 6, 23, 46, 259, 268–69, 339, 348, 425; collects accounts, 3:196, 202–203, 215, 225, 408–409, 415; 4:180, 290

Manages investments: 3:3, 37, 41, 49–50, 106, 131, 135–36, 144, 150–52, 207, 234, 251, 260, 285, 381, 396, 404, 415; 4:23, 132, 225, 273, 372, 417, 425

Manages Boston real estate: 3:xxv, 3–4, 11–80 *passim,* 91–165 *passim,* 174–236 *passim,* 250–81 *passim,* 294–404 *passim,* 414–27 *passim;* 4:4–56 *passim,* 70–91 *passim,* 104, 113–14, 124, 132, 144–55 *passim,* 172, 183, 190, 196, 207–29 *passim,* 246, 252, 265–96 *passim,* 303, 309–24 *passim,* 334–75 *passim,* 389, 400–17 *passim,* 426–33 *passim*

Quincy rental properties: 3:xxv, 185–86, 195, 202–204, 251, 415; 4:10, 180, 234, 249, 257, 261, 263, 267, 275–77, 279, 285, 292–94, 323, 329, 373, 400; assumes management, 4:249

Administers Weston farm and woodland: 3:16–17, 19–20, 34, 64, 74–75, 93, 112, 127, 164, 204, 221, 254, 274, 317, 334–35, 354, 366, 381, 422; 4:30, 42, 60, 80, 153, 158, 168–69, 180, 187, 236, 294, 385, 397–98, 408, 424

BOOKS

arranges collection, 3:12, 19, 44, 226, 312, 319; 4:89, 227; makes catalogue, 3:51–60 *passim,* 65, 72, 256–58; 4:283–302 *passim;* delights in his study, 3:52, 71, 215, 319, 324, 361; brings duplicates and needed volumes from Old House, 3:91, 319; 4:89; on his collection, 3:234, 246; purchases, 3:344–45, 400–401; 4:9, 351, 418; prepares catalogue of pamphlets, 4:107–108, 113. *See also* JQA – Books; CFA – Agent &c. for JQA

FAMILY AND DOMESTIC LIFE

Boston residence, 3:x, 2; deaths, funerals, &c., 3:xxv, xxxi, 83–85, 169–72, 175, 184, 186, 337, 345, 405, 418–19; 4:87–88, 259–60, 356; births and baptisms, 3:xxv, 229, 317, 325, 326; 4:110–11, 161–62; gifts to, 3:8, 86, 394; 4:129; earlier lodgings, 3:8, 59, 183; on himself and Brooks family, 3:9, 21–23, 60, 70, 87, 98, 105, 112, 138, 169, 174, 193, 199, 274, 287–88;

ADAMS, CHARLES FRANCIS (*cont.*)
4:147, 223, 241, 249, 347; health and
minor illnesses, 3:11-12, 19-20, 27-31,
39, 126, 128, 138-39, 141-44, 158,
169-71, 173, 180, 186-87, 201, 215,
288, 291, 294, 341, 352, 358-59, 361-
62, 377-78, 380, 431; 4:1, 6, 60, 63-
64, 93, 120, 164, 169, 185, 191, 192,
227, 232, 276, 289, 293, 313, 333,
357-58, 368-69, 372, 381-82, 395-98;
domestic problems, 3:12, 84, 161, 276,
282, 325, 410; 4:2, 98-99, 112, 118,
153, 163-74 *passim*, 194-97, 232; baptism, 3:14; domestic purchases, errands,
tasks, 3:23, 47, 61-62, 75-76, 79, 85,
96, 120, 129, 161, 183, 185, 261, 312,
315, 328, 384, 405, 429; 4:52, 58-59,
60, 97, 104, 112, 114, 124, 174, 188,
208, 220, 222, 225, 227, 236, 256-57,
280, 286, 309-10, 321, 363, 369, 376;
on TBA family, 3:28, 260; 4:76, 82,
134, 155, 158, 200-201, 259, 261;
payment for wedding, 3:84; 4:18;
Thanksgivings, 3:87, 374; 4:188-89,
408-409; on his family, 3:112, 114-15,
260, 274, 277, 363; 4:50-51, 60, 92-
93, 125, 136, 156-57, 393-94 (*see
also names of individual members*);
makes a "noise" at Post Office, 3:118-
19; causes flurry by changing summer
plans, 3:242-44, 250, 252-53; arranges for horse and chaise, 3:242;
4:274-75; closing and reopening of Boston house, 3:282, 324, 327-28; 4:157,
302-303, 376, 387-90, 392; buys painting, engravings, 3:294, 325; 4:180;
household improvements, 3:324; 4:84,
87, 89-90; rising time, 3:329; 4:8-9;
wish to name daughter Abigail, 4:161;
concern over cholera, 4:316-19, 323-
25, 331-32, 334, 341, 343, 347, 352,
361, 433; physician prescribes diet,
4:383-84. *See also* Brooks family meetings; Medford; Old House; Quincy
Civic activities: votes, 3:104, 298,
353, 381; 4:22, 45, 177, 397; attends
town meetings, 3:190-91, 279-80,
292-93, 409; attends political caucuses,
3:344-45, 351; 4:198; attends public
meeting, 4:422

INTELLECTUAL INTERESTS
Boston Athenæum as resource, 3:xx,
120, 173-74, 246; 4:436-42; commit-
ment to studies, 3:xxxv-xxxvi, 56, 313,
319; 4:393; course of studies projected,
3:45, 97, 100-101, 113, 316, 327-28,

345, 356; 4:20, 89, 307, 342; editing
newspaper considered, 4:140-42, 175,
231. *See also* CFA – Agent &c. for JQA,
Books, Reading, Writings &c
Eloquence: observes pulpit style of
clergy, 3:42, 49, 90, 102-103, 110,
129, 149, 204-205, 220, 264, 287,
297, 314, 352, 371, 389, 394, 398; 4:
xvii, 238, 248, 319, 329, 333, 401;
speaks at debating society to acquire,
3:48, 109-10, 116, 123, 156, 162,
192, 198, 289, 341, 375, 380, 383-84,
412, 429, 430; 4:xvii; analyzes Webster's power, 3:85, 89; drawn to study,
3:85, 97, 100, 147, 350; 4:xvi-xvii;
compares oratorical style of JQA and
Edward Everett, 4:82. *See also* CFA—
Reading, oratory and rhetoric

LEGAL AND MONETARY AFFAIRS
Law practice and career: clients,
3:xxv, 58-65 *passim*, 72-73, 77-81,
105, 111-13, 118, 124, 138, 150, 185,
204, 221-22, 232-35 *passim*, 239, 242,
246, 263, 276-78, 281-83, 298-306
passim, 310-11, 314, 317, 319, 323,
328-40 *passim*, 347, 391-93, 395, 396,
399; 4:10, 18, 22, 26, 44, 65, 67-72
passim, 77, 79, 101, 109, 131-32, 212,
220, 237-38, 328-29, 337; office, 3:2,
140, 154-55, 159, 171-72, 342; direc-
torships, &c., 3:130, 150-51, 153, 185,
395, 409, 415, 424; 4:5, 225, 233-34,
341, 345, 375, 383, 385-86, 389-92;
bar, 3:422; 4:1-2, 37, 252, 299, 336.
See also GWA – CFA settles estate; CFA –
Agent &c. for JQA.
Financial: quarterly payments from
JQA and Peter C. Brooks Sr., 3:xxvii,
86-87, 94-95, 122, 253, 313, 376;
4:30-31; investments and investment
income, 3:3, 35-36, 49-51, 103, 104,
111, 113, 132-33, 136, 151-52, 154,
201-207 *passim*, 215-22 *passim*, 267-78
passim, 295-303 *passim*, 313, 317,
332-33, 344, 356, 388, 396, 414; 4:3,
16, 67, 70, 83, 86, 88, 129, 132, 153,
196, 208, 212, 229, 273, 276, 296,
347, 358, 363, 372, 387, 417; personal finances, 3:7-8, 32, 86, 91, 95,
120, 130, 138, 178, 396-97; 4:79,
227

OPINIONS AND COMMENTS
General: parties, 3:5, 99, 281-82;
4:266, 271; the Quincys, 3:11; 4:91;
probate law, 3:12; 4:44; mathematical

Index

ADAMS, CHARLES FRANCIS (*cont.*)
aptitude, 3:34; landowning, 3:38; 4:4; autumn, 3:51–52, 57; 4:160; wine, 3:61–62; social calls, 3:77; fulfillment of promise shown at college, 3:110, 149, 231–32; 4:421; foreigners' views of America, 3:115–16; conversation, 3:118; basis of respectability, 3:118; the French, 3:134; 4:xv, 365, 423, 428–29; unusual weather, 3:148–49, 282–83, 402; 4:228, 246, 311–12, 332; marketing, 3:161, 384; grief in the young, 3:182; opinionated men, 3:186; "words are things," 3:193, 198, 314; where merit lies, 3:205; danger to public men, 3:207; fasting, 3:208; 4:23, 158, 274; Great Britain, 3:211; folly in a widow, 3:230–31; misfortune in marriages, 3:235; diary-keeping, 3:238–39; 4:209; changes in Boston, 3:305; 4:11–12, 385; his college class, 3:311; crowds, 3:321; "Roué tribe," 3:327; death of a promising youth, 3:343; management of money, 3:356–57; English-speaking Germans, 3:417; public charities, 4:73; "a case fit for a moralizing romance," 4:77; political economy, 4:78, 207; public opinion and originality, 4:133; teaching children, 4:163–64; collecting paintings, 4:180; Christmas, 4:204; altering Biblical texts, 4:221; duty vs. interest, 4:221; the Boston press and the Adamses, 4:246; stud advertisement, 4:251; the commonplace, 4:289; military parades, 4:314; city and country living, 4:367; young ladies in a household, 4:377; doubt, 4:381; a splendid dinner, 4:387; compensations of married life, 4:392; painting and the "seeming pure," 4:402; acquisition of languages, 4:404; bargains in books, 4:418; a traveler, 4:427

Historical: Mitford's interpretation of ancient history, 3:58, 115, 117–18, 256–57; Franklin, 3:61–62; LaHarpe's interpretation of ancient history, 3:65, 72; Puritan contribution to American history, 3:207, 226, 284, 289, 355; Cromwell and British Puritans, 4:xv–xvi, 116, 343–44, 428, 429; Napoleon, 4:173–74, 286–87; Greece and Rome, 4:205; the middle ages, 4:240; Rome, 4:250; the 18th century, 4:254; Canning, 4:348; romance of history, 4:377

Literary: his own writing, 3:xxv–xxvi, xxxv–xxxvi, 6, 93, 99, 102, 103, 111, 203, 336, 394, 408, 416; 4:38, 42, 55, 93, 103, 235, 242, 404, 412, 421; *Edinburgh Review,* 3:96, 147; Jeremy Taylor, 3:103, 110, 162; reading, 3:114, 155, 256; 4:89; Demosthenes and Cicero, 3:165; French literature, 3:199; 4:167, 177, 365, 429; writing, 3:215; toryism in 19th-century British literature, 3:256; compensation of books, 3:288; Boswell and biography, 4:19; a writer's frustrations, 4:38, 413, 419, 424; disquisitions of commentators, 4:99; the great poet, 4:114; Steele's absorptions, 4:173; Virgil, 4:247, 250–51, 254, 256, 267, 276; Gibbon, 4:252; JQA's poetry, 4:390

Political: price of free government, 3:166; toryism among New Englanders, 3:271, 272; revolution and skepticism, 4:29; Jackson administration, 4:34, 394–95, 398; wildness of the age, 4:89; paradox of freedom and force, 4:167; the nation and expansion, 4:250; Southern states and New England, 4:414; Nullification Proclamation and JQA, 4:419–20; New England Federalists, 4:422

Religious: basis of stability in society, 4:29; Reformation in England, 4:400; basis of historical developments, 4:418, 428

Social: money and wealth, 3:xxx, 412–13; 4:30, 145, 338, 374; penology, 3:295–96; effect of system upon domestics, 4:98–99; "progressive improvement of the world," 4:133; learning, 4:254, 316; republicanism, 4:333

See also CFA – Personal; CFA – Writings &c.; JQA – Opinions &c.

PERSONAL

portrait by Charles Bird King, 3:xvi–xvii; discussion of, 3:xxv–xxxviii; response to natural scenes, 3:xxix–xxx, 37–40, 132, 268, 299, 309–10, 332; 4:362–63; desire for child, 3:xxx–xxxi, 33, 58, 70, 100–101, 237, 317, 332, 336–37, 393–94; 4:110; feeling for Adams heritage, 3:xxxi, xxxvi, 17, 55–56, 100, 116, 156, 317; 4:79, 115, 171, 282, 298; reliance upon divine beneficence, 3:xxxii–xxxiii, 1–2, 11, 13, 40, 100, 229, 237, 313, 393; 4:79, 101, 110–11, 115, 128, 136, 157, 159, 161, 195–96, 209–11, 227, 316, 349, 356, 408, 417, 425, 433; self-appraisals, 3:1, 6–7, 11, 13–15, 33, 39–41, 96, 100, 105, 111–16, 121, 138, 196, 213, 225, 250,

ADAMS, CHARLES FRANCIS (*cont.*)
303, 393; 4:55, 82, 101, 115, 157,
159, 161, 171, 207, 210, 289, 349,
356–57, 382, 417, 424, 427, 432–33;
comments on conditions of his life, 3:3–
4, 7–8, 40, 237, 292, 298, 303, 307,
312–13, 336–37, 393; 4:79, 110, 114,
126–28, 159, 167, 171, 209–11, 227,
232, 281–82, 287, 297–98, 304, 316–
18, 348–49, 355, 361, 392–94, 415,
423–25, 431–33; grounds for early marriage, 3:113–14, 128, 167; 4:110, 208,
356–57; fastidiousness in friends,
3:142; JQA's comments on character,
3:226; 4:9; resumes a friendship,
3:380; compared to JQA, 4:55, 326,
409; effect of neglecting parties, 4:266,
271

READING

Drama: ancient, 3:79–94 *passim*,
110–45 *passim*; English, 3:176–84 *passim*, 379, 419–29 *passim*; 4:230–31,
235, 240, 409, 433; French, 4:49–50,
89–90, 104–109, 186, 298–99
Education: 4:160–66 *passim*
Exploration and Travel: 3:xxix, 15–
16, 123, 133, 208–39 *passim*, 246–58
passim, 266, 268, 382–85 *passim*, 400–
409, 413; 4:6–39, 349–78 *passim*, 384
Fiction: 3:6–33 *passim*, 41, 43, 52,
63–84 *passim*, 92–104 *passim*, 111–32
passim, 142–44, 156–70 *passim*, 197–
206 *passim*, 370–78 *passim*, 386–99
passim; 4:203–228 *passim*, 269–74 *passim*, 291–92
Fine Arts: 3:256–58; 4:113–14, 167,
172–86 *passim*, 223–33 *passim*, 258–96
passim, 396–418 *passim*
History and Government: American,
3:xxvi, 26–27, 59–62 *passim*, 97–221
passim, 227–29, 235, 268–73 *passim*,
277, 284–307 *passim*, 319–34 *passim*,
340, 357, 381–88 *passim*, 419–20; 4:6,
17, 24, 71–84 *passim*, 99–106 *passim*,
108, 115–19, 135–79 *passim*, 237, 239,
244–45, 254, 294–95, 307, 328–40
passim; British, 3:246–54 *passim*, 266,
275, 280–92 *passim*, 386; 4:xv–xvi,
160–82 *passim*, 313–431 *passim*; French,
3:186–87, 192–93, 199; 4:257–310
passim, 359–65 *passim*, 431; Greek,
3:58–59, 85, 115–18, 250–57 *passim*;
4:145–52 *passim*, 307–12 *passim*, 320,
326–40 *passim*; Polish, 4:335–45 *passim*
Horticulture: 3:315–16; 4:275

Law: 3:20–34 *passim*, 44, 47, 53–
66 *passim*, 234, 424; 4:2–4, 61, 63, 68,
100, 386
Literature: British, 3:41–47, 56, 185–
96 *passim*, 200–201, 233–42 *passim*,
254–57 *passim*, 291–99 *passim*, 328–78
passim, 385, 402–407 *passim*; 4:7–8,
33–161 *passim*, 183–93 *passim*, 229–43
passim, 248–54 *passim*, 266–67, 316,
331–35, 341, 346, 355, 391, 416–32
passim (see also *Adventurer; Guardian;
Idler; Rambler; Spectator; Tatler;
World*); French, 3:41, 87, 315–23 *passim*, 328–96 *passim*; 4:39–50, 57, 60,
71–95 *passim*, 306–307, 365, 396–427
passim; German, 4:253–56, 407–31
passim; Greek, 4:93–109 *passim*, 186–
238 *passim*, 247, 307 (see also Æschines; Demosthenes); Italian language and
literature, 4:244–52, 261–86 *passim*,
403–404; Latin, 4:45–48, 72, 80, 85–
91, 109–10, 124, 127–30, 228–57
passim, 266–79 *passim*, 308–12, 319–
44 *passim*, 353–71 *passim* (see also
Cicero); Spanish language and literature,
4:258–81 *passim*. See also LaHarpe
*Natural History, Mathematics, Sci-
ence*: 3:34, 40, 51, 54, 60–61, 220,
300, 415–22 *passim*; 4:8–14 *passim*,
41, 233, 303
Oratory and Rhetoric: 3:54–66 *passim*, 85, 97–217 *passim*, 264–65, 286–
90 *passim*, 315–27 *passim*, 344–50,
356, 359, 386, 403–11 *passim*; 4:xvi–
xvii, 89–95 *passim*, 123, 129–30, 167–
74 *passim*, 183–93 *passim*, 383–84. See
also Æschines; Cicero; Demosthenes;
CFA—Intellectual Interests
Philosophy and Religion: 3:44–85
passim, 97, 103–10 *passim*, 135, 162,
243–56 *passim*, 328–29, 376, 380, 385,
388, 397–431 *passim*; 4:103–18 *passim*,
191, 196, 200, 211–12, 221, 226, 238,
242, 244, 255–56, 264, 270–301 *passim*,
354, 363, 374–82 *passim*. See also
Bible; Massillon
Trials: 3:303–304; 4:86, 269, 277,
287–88, 346, 352, 376, 384–85

SOCIAL LIFE AND RECREATION

outings, 3:xxv, 276, 281–82, 285,
305–306, 308; 4:149; wedding visits
and parties, 3:1, 4–13; friends, 3:1–2,
9, 23, 46, 79, 96, 117, 127, 141, 142,
223–25, 380; 4:10, 88, 115, 240, 402,
417 (see also *names of individuals*);
attends sales and auctions, 3:36, 230–

Index

ADAMS, CHARLES FRANCIS (*cont.*) 32, 241, 322, 330, 375; 4:6, 7, 18, 262, 314; book auctions, 3:73, 213, 234, 343, 400–401; 4:349, 351, 418; attends dinners, social functions, &c., 3:73–74, 90, 99, 106–108, 113, 121, 140, 276, 325, 336, 373; 4:41, 58, 65, 82–83, 125, 127, 151–52, 163, 168, 172, 178–80, 185, 266, 271, 365–66, 384, 387, 419; attends lectures, 3:81, 88, 96, 101, 108–109, 127, 133, 155; the theater, 3:153, 420, 423, 425; 4:viii–ix, 190, 263–64, 283, 413–14; art exhibitions and auctions, 3:234, 240, 255, 294, 410–11; 4:21, 46, 115, 118–19, 179–80, 212, 228, 303, 305, 314, 323, 327, 402; observes astronomical phenomena, 3:257, 421; 4:83; shower baths, 3:269–70, 273–74, 295, 318–19, 322; 4:350; music, 3:279; 4:156, 224, 275, 311, 364; salt-water bathing, 3:282–83; 4:59, 66, 70–72, 81–84, 89, 318, 320, 323, 339, 340, 343; measures girth of elms, 3:323–24; views new construction, 4:46–47, 231, 263, 385; fishes for smelt, 4:151, 156, 372–73, 375, 377, 379–80, 384, 388–89

WRITINGS, EDITORIAL AND ARCHIVAL WORK

Published: newspaper articles, 3:xxxvi (pseudonyms: "A," "A Calm Observer," "A Looker On," "Cimon," "F," "Orator," "Q"); *Life and Works of John Adams* (1850–56), 3:103; essay on eloquence in *Massachusetts Journal*, 3:145, 151–53, 158, 168; tribute to Mrs. Peter C. Brooks in *Columbian Centinel*, 3:170–71; essay-review of Grahame's *History of the United States* in *North Amer. Rev.*, 3:205, 209–21, 223, 225–27, 234, 262, 326, 330, 335–36, 342, 350–51, 353–57, 394, objected to, 3:428, 4:2, noticed, 4:39–40; "The Next Presidency" adapted in *Boston Patriot*, 3:240, 242, 244–46; three communications against railroad subsidy in *Boston Patriot*, 3:267, 271, 273–74, 278–79, 291–92; article supporting National Republican candidate for Congress in *Boston Courier*, 3:340–42; article against railroad subsidy in *Boston Daily Advertiser*, 3:406, 408, 409; three articles on "The Resignation of the Cabinet" in *Boston Patriot*, 4:37–39, 42, 44–45, 47–48; *Letters of Mrs.*

Adams (1840), 4:70, 103; defends JQA in communication to *Boston Patriot*, 4:125–26; five articles on "The Treasury Report" in *Boston Patriot* and *Boston Daily Advertiser & Patriot*, 4:198–200, 202–203, 205–207, 214–19; defends JQA's antimasonic stand in *Boston Daily Advocate*, 4:289–90, 295; essay-review of Vaughan's *Stuart Dynasty* in *North Amer. Rev.*, 4:315–23, 325, 428; nine articles, "Principles and Grounds of Anti-Masonry" and "Brief History of the Masonic Outrages in New York" in *Boston Daily Advocate*, 4:350, 397–431 *passim*

Unpublished: translation of Æschines and Demosthenes, "On the Crown" (incomplete), 3:58, 229; 4:xvii; essay on Williston's *Eloquence of the U.S.*, 3:97–99; 4:xvii, 234, 236; essay on eloquence, 3:143–44; 4:xvii; second article on the same, 3:154–55, 158–59, 170–71; 4:xvii; paper on Middlesex Canal (1829), 3:153; "Elements of Knowledge," commentary on apothegms of "seven wise men of Greece," 3:388–90, 392; 4:15, 28; translation of Cicero's "De optimo genere oratorum," 4:xvi–xvii, 131–35, illustration facing 380; two articles in answer to W. F. Otis, 4:90–91, 93–95; essay on tariff, 4:245–46; exegesis of Matthew 5–7, 4:343, 345, 353, 356; translation of Marmontel's "Le trépied d'Hélène," 4:396, 399–403

Projected: 3:45, 49, 52, 54, 105, 111, 114–15, 122, 125–26, 128–29, 131–32, 134, 239–42, 403; 4:xvii, 108, 117–23, 128, 159, 174, 183–84, 186, 239, 353–54, 357–58, 378–80

Personal Papers &c.: diary, MSS described, 3:xxxviii–xl, 1–2; minutes of Adams Temple and School Fund, 4:x, illustration facing 125, 391–92; marginalia, 4:xv–xvi, 9, illustration facing 380, 429

Archival and Editorial Activities: studies and methodizes JA's papers, 3:xxxvi–xxxvii, 103; 4:51–89 *passim*, 312, 320, 324, 354–55, 366–71 *passim*; collates JA's diary with copies made, 3:103; 4:365–84 *passim*; collates JA's letterbooks with copies made by Sparks, 3:141, 156–58, 173, 227, 242–43; stimulated to editorial work by Sparks, 4:xii–xiii; corrects proof for article by JQA, 4:164

457

Adams, Mrs. Charles Francis (Abigail Brown Brooks, 1808–1889, CFA's wife, designated as ABA in *The Adams Papers; see* Adams Genealogy): at bathing house, 3:xv, 277, 291, 304, 307; and CFA, their marriage, 3:xxviii–xxix, 3–5, 7, 12, 15–16, 18, 21–25, 29–30, 35, 41, 46–47, 52, 55, 77, 97, 121, 167, 222, 233, 237, 242, 326, 393; 4:127–28, 194, 207; friends, 3:2–4, 7, 25; schooling, 3:4; attends social functions, 3:5–6, 8, 11, 12, 90, 99, 106–108, 113, 121, 140; 4:41, 58, 148, 178–79, 271, 365–66, 419; indispositions and illnesses, 3:6, 14, 35–36, 42, 66–67, 122, 129, 182, 193, 197, 219–20, 233, 243, 246, 264, 266, 282–83, 286, 299–302, 312, 318, 321, 326–27, 339, 344, 353, 361–62, 380, 395–96, 406, 410; 4:24, 38, 67, 72, 83, 89, 93, 100, 177, 184, 192–98, 426–29; jewelry stolen, 3:7, 10–12, 15; gifts from parents, 3:8, 11, 93–94, 254; loneliness, 3:14, 35, 58, 78, 237; literarily inexperienced, 3:47, 52, 56, 176, 189; 4:252; rebuffs Degrand, 3:91; and JQA, 3:98–99, 155; 4:157; response to mother's illness and death, 3:138–40, 157, 162, 165, 167–72, 237; disturbed by cross occurrence, 3:153; amanuensis for CFA and JQA, 3:163, 422; 4:364; comments on CFA's essay, 3:221; makes wedding gift, 3:228; CFA improves her French, 3:287, 294, 297, 323, 328–406 *passim;* 4:401–30 *passim;* prefers to live among family, 3:297; 4:152; invites LCA to visit, 3:355; becomes pregnant, 3:393–94; gifts from CFA, 3:427; 4:159; birth of daughter, 4:110–11; confinement, 4:111–28; slow recovery, 4:133, 136–37, 142–43, 147, 155; at christening, 4:161–62; calls CFA imprudent, 4:384; and LCA, 4:394. *See also* CFA; Brooks family meetings; Medford

CFA reads to, evenings: Devereux, 3:6–20; *Man of Feeling,* 3:25–33; Scott's *Lives of the Novelists,* 3:41–52; *Clarissa Harlowe,* 3:63–144, 165–70, 197–206; *Sir Charles Grandison,* 3:149–63; Shakespeare, 3:176–82, 379; Sheridan's plays, 3:183–84, 422–23, 429; Byron, 3:185–87, 240, 361; 4:191–92; *Lalla Rookh,* 3:189–96; Eustace's *Italy,* 3:208–29, 246–56; JQA's *Silesia,* 3:233–39; Moore's *Byron,* 3:240–41; 4:33–39, 54; *Arabian Nights,* 3:245; Mason's *Gray,* 3:330–50; Wordsworth, 3:364; Lady Morgan's *Book of the Boudoir,* 3:370–78; Baroness Minutoli's *Egypt,* 3:382–85; *Pride and Prejudice,* 3:386; *Evelina* and *Camilla,* 3:390–99; Mackenzie's *Spain,* 3:400–13; *Douglas,* 3:419–22; *Jealous Wife,* 3:424–29; Parry's voyages, 4:6–30; *Journey from Constantinople,* 4:31–33; Bible, 4:39, 188–412 *passim;* Boswell, 4:47–48, 266–67; *George IV,* 4:160–82; American poets, 4:161; Mrs. Radcliffe, 4:183–84; Lee's *The Canterbury Tales,* 4:203–28; Hazlitt's *Northcote,* 4:229–33; Hunt's *Byron,* 4:233–42; Ariosto, 4:242–52; Goethe's *Memoirs,* 4:253–54; *Lives of the British Painters,* 4:258–65, 396–418; *Eugene Aram,* 4:269–74; *Newgate Calendar,* 4:277; *Gertrude of Wyoming,* 4:299

Adams, Charles Francis, 2d (1835–1915, son of CFA, designated as CFA2 in *The Adams Papers; see* Adams Genealogy): on CFA, 3:xxvii; on JQA in his "writing chamber," 4:vii; "J. Q. Adams in Twenty-second Congress," 4:330

Adams, Daniel (pump- and blockmaker), 3:315

Adams, Ebenezer (1704–1769; *see* Adams Genealogy), 3:39

Adams, Mrs. Ebenezer (Anne Boylston, 1706–1770; *see* Adams Genealogy), 3:39

Adams, Deacon Ebenezer (1762–1841; *see* Adams Genealogy), 3:39; 4:426

Adams, Elihu (1741–1775, brother of JA; *see* Adams Genealogy), 3:180

Adams, Elizabeth Coombs (1808–1903, daughter of TBA, designated as ECA in *The Adams Papers; see* Adams Genealogy): payments to, under JA's will, 3:31, 125, 202, 277–79; 4:84, 85, 259; engagement to John M. Gourgas, 3:90, 243; 4:60, 73, 313, 393; mentioned, 4:79, 86, 87, 91, 99, 142, 152, 156, 324, 326, 327, 345, 359, 372, 377

Adams, George Washington (1801–1829, CFA's oldest brother, designated as GWA in *The Adams Papers;*

see Adams Genealogy): at Adams Temple dedication, 3:xi; portrait by King, 3:xv–xviii, illustration facing 314; literary bent of, 3:xvii, xxvi, 6–7, 47, 85, 388–89, 406–407; 4:101; CFA reflects on himself and, 3:xxxi–xxxii, 6–8, 18–19, 41, 47, 73, 84–85, 191, 213, 216, 347, 388–89; 4:101, 287; CFA uses his ledgers and writing books, 3:xxxii, 73, 144, 373, 388; and Mary Catherine Hellen, 3:6–7; 4:136; CFA destroys part of papers, 3:7, 213, 217, 219, 347, 364; 4:101–103; remains transferred and reburied, 3:17, 36–37, 81, 83–85, 324; as JQA's agent in Boston, 3:17, 33, 47, 102, 119, 145, 165, 212, 217, 222; sale of books and personal effects, 3:18, 23, 30, 31, 41, 47, 91, 181, 194, 254, 276–77; CFA settles estate, 3:25, 34, 35, 43, 44, 46–47, 103–104, 132–33, 141, 151–52, 154–55, 157, 159–60, 167, 169–70, 172–73, 189, 191–92, 210, 263, 265, 267, 325, 359–60; 4:29, 284; affair with Eliza Dolph agitated, 3:23, 44–45, 50, 189–90, 192, 193, 222, 422–24; 4:32–33, 104–105; attends Derby Academy, Hingham, 4:315–16; mentioned, 3:2, 14, 46, 63, 110, 115, 147, 180, 185, 201, 206–208, 243, 256, 259, 365, 380; 4:39, 48, 170, 192, 240, 260, 431

Adams, Georgeanna Frances (1830–1839, daughter of JA2; *see* Adams Genealogy): birth, 3:317; christened, 3:326; named for uncles, 3:330; ill health, 4:190

Adams, Henry (1838–1918, son of CFA, designated as HA in *The Adams Papers; see* Adams Genealogy): on CFA, 3:xxvii, xxx; mentioned, 3:x, 2, 63; 4:vii, 111

Adams, Isaac Hull (1813–1900, son of TBA; *see* Adams Genealogy): amanuensis for JQA, 4:46, 140, 173, 333; refuses commission in Navy, 4:76; receives West Point appointment, 4:235; prepares for examinations at CFA's home, 4:255, 263, 274, 275, 277, 281, 285, 288, 289, 292, 298, 300; and death of TBA, 4:258, 259; mentioned, 3:28, 29, 179, 367, 431; 4:64, 66, 68, 70, 72, 81, 82, 84, 89–90, 103, 124, 130, 152, 156, 200 201, 278, 283, 290, 295, 308, 358

Adams, Deacon John (1692–1761, CFA's great-grandfather; *see* Adams Genealogy), 3:38, 39

Adams, Mrs. John (Susanna Boylston, 1709–1797, wife of Deacon John; *see* Adams Genealogy), 3:39

Adams, John (1735–1826, CFA's grandfather, designated as JA in *The Adams Papers; see* Adams Genealogy): creates Adams Temple and School Fund, 3:xi–xii, 24–25, 90; 4:ix–x; burial place, 3:xii, 56; 4:260; memorial tablet, 3:xii, 24, 27, 55–56, 247; likenesses, 3:xvi, 56, 146, 246, 247; 4:46; estate, 3:xix, 86–87, 101, 145, 151, 159, 180, 236, 364–65, 374, 377; 4:5, 380; projected biography of, 3:xxxiii, xxxvii, 257, 267; 4:84, 126–27, 175, 189–90, 352, 354; papers of, studied and methodized, 3:xxxvi–xxxvii; 4:51–89 *passim*, 175, 312, 320, 324, 354, 355, 366–71 *passim*; reputation attacked, 3:xxxvii; 4:xii–xiii, 189–90, 214–15; Boston law office, 3:2; legacies, 3:31, 202, 243, 293, 381–82, 394, 396; 4:1, 6, 46, 259, 268–69, 339, 348, 425; birthplace, 3:38; and Franklin, 3:62; 4:56, 214–15; books and library, 3:67, 316, 334; 4:x, 139, 145, 193, 307, 309, 315, 323, 389–91; Sparks' use of letterbooks of, 3:88, 92, 141, 143–44, 149, 156–63 *passim*, 172–73, 227, 242–43; 4:xiii, 333; diary of, read, copied, collated, 3:103; 4:173, 333, 365–84 *passim*; first law case (Field v. Lambert), 3:103; eulogies of, 3:193, 195; 4:82–83, 189; John Pierce visits and attends funeral, 3:269; compared to Jefferson, 4:69; Pickering's pamphlet attack on, 4:78–81 *passim*; injunction to grandsons, 4:266–67, 339; mentioned, 3:249, 268; 4:62, 85, 101, 125. *See also* Adams Temple and School Fund; Old House

Published writings: correspondence with William Cunningham, Jay, Jefferson, Arthur Lee, William Tudor, 3:60, 61, 241, 334, 387, 388; 4:64, 78–84 *passim; Novanglus,* 3:383, 387; *Defence of the Constitutions of Government,* 4:xvi, 97–103 *passim,* 121, 135

Adams, Mrs. John (Abigail Smith, 1744–1818, CFA's grandmother, designated as AA in *The Adams Papers*; *see* Adams Genealogy): burial place, 3: xii, 56; 4:260; memorial tablet, 3:24, 55–56; CFA on her correspondence, 4:69–70, 326; mentioned, 3:38; 4: 69, 268

Adams, John, 2d (1803–1834, CFA's older brother, designated as JA2 in *The Adams Papers*; *see* Adams Genealogy): portrait, 3:xv–xviii, illustration facing 314; CFA's attitude toward, 3:xxxi, 277, 280; 4:80, 95, 129; marriage, 3:7; correspondence with CFA, 3:23, 45, 242, 243, 318, 330, 349; 4:7, 8, 32, 72, 95, 96, 111, 325, 332, 394; letters removed from family papers, 3:45, 217; and flour business in Washington, 3:104, 243, 315; 4:46, 80, 91, 92, 93, 95, 417; robbery, 3:274; arrives at Quincy, 3:277; birth of second daughter, 3: 317, 318; joins CFA in urging LCA not to remain at Quincy, 3:348–49, 363; attends Derby Academy, Hingham, 4:316; ill health, 4:325, 331, 414, 417; mentioned, 3:14, 62, 190, 221, 275, 281, 282, 285, 289, 297, 300, 304, 428; 4:102, 126, 259, 320, 321, 332, 336, 370, 397, 425

Adams, Mrs. John, 2d (Mary Catherine Hellen, 1806?–1870; *see* Adams Genealogy): and GWA, 3:6, 7; 4:136; ABA and, 3:30; Quincy visit and CFA, 3:242, 243, 252, 253, 257, 260, 277; birth and christening of second daughter, 3:317, 326; returns to Washington, 3:348; mentioned, 3:xvii, 16, 30, 366; 4:320

Adams, J. Q. (printer) 3:260, 265

ADAMS, JOHN QUINCY (1767–1848, CFA's father, designated as JQA in *The Adams Papers*; *see* Adams Genealogy)

BOOKS
removed from storage to Old House, 3:32–33, 40; CFA on collection, 3:40, 56, 234, 313; size of collection, 3:55; at Old House, 3:55, 56; 4:vii, 407; at Athenæum as payment for share, 3:173; catalogue made with CFA, 3:262–302 *passim*; GWA's books, 3:324–25; 4: 283–84; a broken set restored, 4:173–74; gaps in collection, 4:280, 374; purchases at sale of TBA's collection, 4:351; sent from Washington to Old

House, 4:397–99; desire for building to house, 4:407. *See also* CFA–Agent &c. for JQA

CHARACTER, APPEARANCE, HABITS, DOMESTIC LIFE

Addiction to disputation and controversy: with CFA, 3:xxxiv, 332; 4:137, 201–202; political Antimasonry, 3:xxxv; 4:xi, xii, 53, 59, 65, 75, 86, 108, 120, 125–26, 191, 350–51, 358, 360–61, 381, 383, 395–97, 407, 419; with Massachusetts Federalists, 3:63, 332, 419–20; 4:144, 423; with Proprietors of Boston Athenæum, 3:73–74, 173–74; with Jared Sparks, 3:73, 92, 160–61, 202–203; 4:xiii; over Latin-American policy, 3:167; with John Randolph, 3:249; with Jonathan Russell, 3:365; in Calhoun-Jackson dispute, 3:406–407, 428, 430; over Nullification, 4:82–83, 420; CFA on, 4:82, 141, 330; over reform of Phi Beta Kappa, 4:97–98, 107, 109, 124, 154, 354; in Congress, 4:265, 292, 299, 330

Family: memorial tablet to JA and AA, 3:xii, 24–25, 27, 55–56, 247; wedding gifts to CFA and ABA, 3:8, 11–12; and LCA, 3:17, 348–49, 355, 374; and GWA, 3:17, 85, 216–17; assists TBA family, 3:28, 130–31, 159, 241; 4:76, 173, 235, 259–60, 269; and JA2, 3:45, 92, 348–49, 370; pride, 3:56; gives Athenæum share to CFA, 3:86–87; and ABA, 3:98–99, 155; on CFA, 3:226; 4:9; burdened by household cares, 3:253–54; devises heraldic seal, 3:410–11; LCA2 resembles, 4: 137, 346; offers CFA editorship of *Boston Patriot*, 4:140–42; pleasure in company of ABA and CFA, 4:157, 278–79, 393; on TBA, 4:259; family's ill health depresses, 4:413–14. *See also* CFA – Family and Domestic Life

Friends and Amenities: attends dinners and social functions, 3:5–6, 27, 73–74, 276, 285, 315, 336, 355, 373; 4:58, 83, 124–25, 127, 148–49, 151, 160, 355, 357, 364, 374, 381, 384–85, 387; entertains at Old House, 3:16, 89–90, 313; 4:65, 87, 145, 147, 155–56, 361, 367–69, 385–86; visits at P. C. Brooks house, Medford, 3:28, 86–87; receives visitors at Old House, 3:28–29, 90–91, 258, 262–63, 275, 278, 301–302, 310, 314, 329; 4:51, 57, 73, 75, 90, 131, 156, 339, 343, 353, 361, 378,

Index

ADAMS, JOHN QUINCY (*cont.*)
384, 387; Degrand, 3:33, 90–91; *Life of Arthur Lee* dedicated to, 3:60; J. B. Davis, 3:63; allows Sparks to use JA's Letterbooks, 3:88, 160–61; 4:xiii; and Dr. Thomas Welsh, 3:419; pays social calls, 4:62, 91–92, 356, 369, 373; attends ordination, 4:68; Thomas Welsh Jr., 4:88; contributes to building Episcopal Church, Quincy, 4:321–22, 415

Personal: disinterest in management of money and property, 3:1, 54; 4:79–80, 93, 152; ties to First Church, Boston, 3:14; cold and reserved manner, 3:110; likenesses, 3:145–47, 161, 166, 196, 246–47, 287, 411–12; 4:46; health, 3:164, 196, 239, 277, 333, 421, 425; 4:40, 50–51, 81, 336; depressed, languid, irritable, &c., 3:257, 260, 263–67, 270, 275, 277, 283–85, 332; 4:60, 81, 89, 92–93; indulgent to servants, 3:274; goes bathing, 3:310; 4:66, 70–71, 82, 84, 340; tendency to financial speculation, 3:425; vigorous, 4:87; makes will, 4:337, 385; CFA on inflexible morality, 4:409; on gardening and arboriculture, *see* Old House; JQA — Lands &c., Mount Wollaston

Residences: Washington, 3:xvi, 348; uncertainty in plans, (1829) 3:17–18, (1830) 349; birthplace, 3:38. *See also* Old House

LANDS, INVESTMENTS, AND ACCOUNTS
Boston rental property: Court Street (law office), 3:2, 48, 66, 155, 159–60, 184, 194, 307, 342, 351; Hancock Street, 3:13, 127, High Street, 3:210; Tremont Street, 3:17, 21, 25, 30, 54, 187–88, 191, 194, 294, 351; taxes on, 3:32, 367; annual reports on, 3:121, 393; 4:207, 432

Quincy property: ancestral farms and woodland (Penn's Hill), 3:37–40, 180, 185–86, 307; 4:180, 277, 400; Mount Wollaston orchard and farms, 3:186, 299, 306, 309–10, 316, 324–25, 332, 368–69, 374; 4:40, 52, 57, 85, 140, 309, 362. *See also* Quincy, Mass.; Old House

Weston farm and woodland: 3:17, 34, 298, 355; 4:180, 294

Farms acquired by mortgages: at Medford, 3:xviii, 236; 4:259, 374–75; at Randolph, 3:180; at Braintree, 4:259, 375–76

Fiscal situation: 3:86, 151–52, 207; 4:273, 290–91, 314

Columbian Mills (D.C.): 3:xxxi, 104, 107; 4:16–17, 46, 72, 80, 91–93, 95, 180, 182, 370, 417

Securities owned: 3:3, 37, 41, 50, 106–107, 125, 130–33, 137, 141, 150–51, 153, 208, 240, 242–43, 289, 293, 297, 381–82, 415; 4:16, 88, 225, 347–48

Accounts and notes payable: 3:86–87, 104, 145, 158–59; 4:17, 72, 79, 80, 92, 180, 182, 194, 201, 208, 425

Accounts and notes receivable: 3:215, 224, 225, 236, 242, 251, 408–409, 415; 4:5–6, 180, 225, 290, 339

Legatee and trustee under will of JA: 3:86–87, 151, 243, 293, 364–65, 377, 381–82, 396; 4:1, 5–6, 23, 46, 259, 268–69, 380

See also CFA — Agent &c. for JQA; JA — estate, legacies; Boylston, Thomas; Boylston, Ward N.

OPINIONS AND INTELLECTUAL INTERESTS
CFA's estimate: 3:xxxiv, 29, 56, 266, 316, 328–29, 331, 367, 410; 4:189–90, 201, 305, 362, 409, 419

Exchanges of views with CFA: JQA's re-entrance into politics, 3:xxxiii–xxxiv, 331–33, 391, 409; 4:9, 174–75, 187–90, 201–202, 339, 352; general issues, 3:xxxiv, 29, 94, 98–99, 123, 366–67; business matters, 3:56, 94, 391; American history, 3:73, 161, 226; 4:113, 381; CFA's program of studies, writings, and career, 3:100, 113, 135, 238, 316, 353, 391; 4:175–76, 188, 379; ancient and modern oratory, 3:129, 226; Indian removal, 3:139; Demosthenes and Cicero, 3:166, 413; 4:206; governmental authority and rights of the people, 3:226; French drama, versification, and Molière, 3:264; British politics of late 18th century, 3:265, 300; Bentham, 3:266; Antimasonry, 4:53, 59, 358; Milton's poetry, 4:76; response to political attacks, 4:126; A. H. and Edward Everett, 4:154; poetry and literature, 4:154, 337; the tariff, 4:305, 307; Bank of the United States, 4:307; civil law and common law, 4:386; Greeks and Romans, 4:386; Nullification Proclamation, 4:419–20

Historical, Literary, &c.: Shakespeare, 3:20; book-collecting, 3:43, 55; Jay

461

Index

ADAMS, JOHN QUINCY (*cont.*)
and Arthur Lee, 3:60, 161; Cicero, 3:239, 284, 410, 425; 4:vii, 399; fine arts, 4:vii, 399; Harvard oratorical style, 4:71; Southey's essays, 4:341–42; his own poetry, 4:391; astronomics, 4:391–92, 401; phrenology, 4:397, 401

Public men and issues: Panama Inter-American Congress, 3:167; politics absorbs, 3:264; 4:242; Fanny Wright, 4:76; James Monroe, 4:85, 120–21; expressed to Tocqueville, 4:149; touchstone of American foreign policy, 4:215; ratio of Congressional representation, 4:252; right to withhold participation in procedure deemed unconstitutional, 4:330; Fisher Ames, 4:386

PUBLIC LIFE

3:xxv, xxxiii, xxxvii, 57, 206, 304, 321, 329, 331–33, 342, 348–49, 353, 406–407; 4:x–xii, 52–53, 55, 78–79, 82–83, 85, 98, 107–108, 120–21, 124, 150, 222, 252, 264–65, 292–93, 330, 370, 385–86, 391–94, 406–407, 420. *See also* JQA – Character, Appearance, Habits, &c.; JQA – Opinions &c.; JQA – Writings &c.

WRITINGS, EDITORIAL AND
ARCHIVAL WORK

Published (before 1848): contributions to the *Port Folio* (including "Journal of a tour through Silesia," "The Tripod of Helen," &c.), 3:xxxv, 233; 4:379, 403; *Lectures on Rhetoric and Oratory*, 3:206, 208–209, 213–15, 217, 401–402; 4:xvii; *Letters on Silesia, Written during a Tour Through that Country*, 3:233–35, 239; chapters on Russia, Turkey, and Greece, in *Amer. Annual Register*, 3:257–58, 266–68; *Oration ... on the Fourth of July 1831*, 4:98; *An Eulogy on ... James Monroe ... 25th of August, 1831*, 4:120–21, 132; "England 1829–1830" in *Amer. Annual Register*, 4:164; *Remarks in the House of Representatives ... on the ratio of representation*, 4:252; [*Minority*] *report of the Committee ... to examine ... the books of the bank of the United States*, 4:292, 299–300, 307; *Report of the House Committee on Manufactures* (1832), 4:305; *Letters on Masonry, addressed to William L. Stone*, 4:360, 371, 407; *American Principles. A Review of Works of Fisher Ames,*

4:386; *Dermot MacMorrogh*, 4:390–92; "Preface" to *The Declaration of Independence; the Constitution ...*; &c. (1833), 4:420

Unpublished (before 1848): "Reply to the Appeal of the Massachusetts Federalists" in HA, *New-England Federalism*, 3:63, 418–20, 430; 4:43, 143–44, 423; "Satire upon the powers of the Nation," 3:228–29; "Memorial of the Life of John Adams" in CFA, *Life and Works of John Adams* (1850–56), 3:257; 4:84, 126–27, 169–70, 172, 175, 352; "Wisdom," a poem addressed to CFA, 4:13–14; "Letters on the Bible," in CFA, *Letters of Mrs. Adams*, 4th ed., 4:103–18, 289; "Murder of William Morgan," 4:350

Personal papers: inscription for tablet to JA and AA, 3:55–56; early letters, 4:55, 326; will, 4:385

Archival work: methodizes letters of JA, 3:xxxvii; 4:52–54, 59, 61, 83, 189, 320, 354, 366–71 *passim*; has amanuenses copy sections of JA's diary, 3:55, 103; 4:173, 333, 366, 370; collates JA's diary with copies made, 4:365–84 *passim*

Adams, Mrs. John Quincy (Louisa Catherine Johnson, 1775–1852, CFA's mother, designated as LCA in *The Adams Papers*; *see* Adams Genealogy): King's portrait of, 3:xvi; at Washington, 3:1–251, 384–431; 4:1–36, 170–301, 404–33; ill health and depression of spirits, 3:3, 16, 23, 27, 28, 135, 185, 257, 260–64, 267, 274, 277, 278, 280, 300, 310, 311, 349, 356, 357, 361, 363, 366, 367, 373; 4:38, 40, 50, 92, 120, 136, 331, 393, 413–14; and Brooks family, 3:28; 4:105, 160; and CFA, 3:165, 375; 4:393; journeys between Washington and Quincy, 3:251–53, 384–84 *passim*; 4:36–38, 163–70, 301–305, 394–404 *passim*; at Quincy, 3:253–374; 4:38–163, 305–394; CFA performs commissions for, 3:263, 267, 313, 315; 4:64, 166, 173, 360–61; purchases bathing tub, 3:268, 271; attends church, 3:274, 314; conversations with CFA, 3:315, 316, 328; 4:102, 103, 112, 141, 305, 306; opposition to JQA's aspirations to Congress, 3:329, 333, 348–49; visits CFA and ABA, 3:331, 336,

339–42, 361; 4:42, 93, 98, 101–107, 111–18, 120, 149, 162–63; comments on Lt. Thomas B. Adams, 4:44; entertains at Old House, 4:65, 147; obtains naval commission for J. H. Adams, 4:76, 197; on CFA as head of household, father, and uncle, 4: 98–99, 118; fall from hack, 4:121–22; fishes for smelt, 4:152, 156, 375, 377, 379–80; on CFA's improvements at Old House, 4:302; attends concert in Boston, 4:311, 364; on Mrs. Field, 4:314; nurses Mary Louisa Adams, 4:320, 324–25; carriage accident, 4:330; records wishes about personal belongings, 4:337; comments on LCA2, 4:346; on ABA, 4:394; mentioned, 3:45, 158, 223, 235, 244, 258, 264, 268, 312, 425; 4:58, 59, 60, 61, 70, 81, 104, 108, 116, 130, 134, 153, 185, 314, 333, 347, 352, 354, 357, 358, 369, 388, 397, 425

Adams, John Quincy (1815–1854, son of TBA, called "JQA Jr."; *see* Adams Genealogy): JQA provides for schooling, 3:130–31, 159, 241, 316, 425; 4:74, 169–70; mentioned, 4:71, 188, 356, 357

Adams, John Quincy, 2d (1833–1894, son of CFA, designated as JQA2 in *The Adams Papers*; *see* Adams Genealogy), 3:201, 268; 4:316

Adams, Joseph Harrod (1817–1853, son of TBA; *see* Adams Genealogy): in Navy, 4:76, 197–202, 214, 280, 285; mentioned, 3:317; 4:81, 169, 170, 213, 252

Adams, Joseph T. (editor, *Columbian Centinel*), 4:94, 95

Adams, Deacon Josiah (1763–1844; *see* Adams Genealogy), on farm survey, 3:38–39

Adams, Louisa Catherine (1831–1870, daughter of CFA, later Mrs. Charles Kuhn, designated as LCA2 in *The Adams Papers*; *see* Adams Genealogy): birth, 3:xxv, xxx; 4:110; CFA's comments on, 4:110–11, 128, 427; health, 4:118–19, 132, 135–36, 140, 236–39, 254–57, 297–303, 351, 365; appearance, 4:137, 346; baptism, 4:161–62; first birthday, 4:345; mentioned, 4:156, 158, 160, 302, 306, 314, 324, 345, 363

Adams, Mary (1845–1928, daughter of CFA, later Mrs. Henry Parker Quincy, designated as MA in *The Adams*

Papers; *see* Adams Genealogy), 4:49

Adams, Mary Louisa (1828–1859, daughter of JA2, later Mrs. William Clarkson Johnson; *see* Adams Genealogy): in Quincy, 3:252–53, 257; illnesses, 3:253, 328; 4:320, 324–26; and CFA, 4:98, 118; mentioned, 3:xvi, xvii, 329; 4:36

Adams, Thomas Boylston (1772–1832, CFA's uncle, designated as TBA in *The Adams Papers*; *see* Adams Genealogy): Medford farm, 3:xix, 236; 4:374; CFA's comments on, 3:28, 260; 4:155, 259; residence and household, 3:29; collects payments due under JA's will, 3:31, 124, 202, 203, 274, 330, 332, 395; 4:150, 212; collects payments for son's education, 3:159, 241, 316, 425; 4:74; CFA visits, 3:243, 260, 374; 4:17, 34, 70, 89, 138, 155; accident, 3: 367, 391; Clerk of Adams Temple and School Fund, 4:x; gives CFA custody of seal and medal, 4:80–81, 138; illness, 4:85, 130–32, 138, 213, 257–58; death and funeral, 4:259–60; settlement of estate, 4: 259, 261, 266, 268–69, 275, 339, 349, 351; trustee, Derby Academy, Hingham, 4:316; Braintree farm, 4:375–76; articles in *Port Folio*, 4: 379; mentioned, 3:65, 68, 73, 90, 131, 183, 206, 252–53, 266, 276, 277, 281, 293, 310, 313, 314, 386, 426; 4:14, 51, 53, 64, 65, 87

Adams, Mrs. Thomas Boylston (Ann Harrod, 1774?–1845; *see* Adams Genealogy): on Joseph Adams' joining Navy, 4:198–201; and death of TBA, 4:259; mentioned, 3:29, 279, 312, 313, 332, 408; 4:17, 63, 65, 79, 81, 87, 235, 259, 261, 266, 269, 275, 277, 299, 305, 319, 322, 324, 333–35, 337, 346, 352, 368, 372, 376, 377, 392–93

Adams, Thomas Boylston, Jr. (1809–1837, son of TBA; *see* Adams Genealogy): amanuensis for JQA, 3:2, 55, 103; lieutenant, U.S. Army, 3:2, 47, 50; 4:158; legacy under JA's will, 3:243, 293, 297, 382; 4:46, 259, 269; CFA acts as agent, 3:312, 337–38, 340, 342, 396; 4:7, 14–17, 24, 26, 67, 88, 131, 134, 144, 154, 197, 233, 275, 297–99, 372, 375, 400; appearance, manner, and character, 4:44, 134, 154, 158, 252; visits Mrs.

de Windt, 4:103; mentioned, 3:1, 9, 28, 29, 37–38, 424; 4:52–55, 57, 63, 80, 108, 115, 121, 140, 142–43, 150, 156

Adams National Historic Site. *See* Old House

Adams Temple. *See under* Quincy, Mass.

Adams Temple and School Fund: JA creates, 3:xi–xii, 24–25, 90; 4:ix–x; CFA as clerk, 4:x, 385–86, 391; Book of Records, 4:x, illustration facing 4:125

Addison, Joseph: critique of *Paradise Lost*, 3:376–77; papers and essays, 4:15, 146; style, 4:222

Adventurer, The, 3:238, 338; 4:335, 336, 344, 346, 348, 354, 357, 358, 363

Æschines: Auger's translation, 3:58, 60; CFA studies and translates, 3:58–60, 65–69 *passim*, 72–73, 77–85 *passim*, 88, 92–104 *passim*, 112–17 *passim*, 120–29 *passim*, 229–34, 239, 244–45, 251, 257–58; 4:xvi–xvii, 20–34 *passim*, 120, 124; and Demosthenes, 3:157–58, 177, 198, 235; 4:37, 47–48; Reiske's edition, 3:245. *See also* Demosthenes

Æschylus: preface to Potter's translation, 3:79; *Prometheus Chained*, 3:80; *The Supplicants*, 3:81, 86; *Seven against Thebes*, 3:88, 93; *Agamemnon*, 3:93–94; *Choephoræ*, 3:95–96; *Furies*, 3:110

Albion, The, 4:247

Alger, Rev. Horatio, 4:71

Allen, J. M., & Co. (auctioneers), 4:262

Allen, Mr., 4:147

Allison (artist), 4:ix

Allston, Washington: portrait by Stuart, 4:xii; paintings by, 4:119; "Spalatro's Vision of the Bloody Hand," 4:179, 183, 228

Almon, John, *A Collection of Interesting, Authentic Papers* ("Prior Documents"), 4:155

Amateurs and Actors (farce), 3:153

American Annual Register: chapters on Greece, Russia, and Turkey by JQA, 3:257, 258, 262, 266–68; "England 1829–1830" by JQA, 4:164, 304; mentioned, 4:126, 246

American Bank, 3:150, 206, 207, 268, 272, 333; 4:387, 388

American Colonization Society, 3:270

American commissioners, 3:59, 60, 195; 4:56

American Insurance Co., 4:72, 182, 194, 208

American Law Journal and Miscellaneous Repertory, 3:182

American Magazine of Useful and Entertaining Knowledge, 3:ix, xii

American Monthly Review, 4:234

American Quarterly Review, 3:205, 327; 4:36, 214, 217, 218, 412

American Revolution: CFA reads about, 3:62, 381–88 *passim*; discussed with Jared Sparks, 3:92; JA's letters and papers about, 3:387, 388; 4:54, 68, 69; discussed with JQA, 4:381; mentioned, 3:195; 4:xii

Ames, Fisher (U.S. Repr., Mass.): identified, 3:115; speeches of, 3:114, 122, 188; JQA's attitude toward, 4:386

Ammin & Smith (engravers), 3:xi

Anatomy, legalization of study, 3:128, 148, 409, 410

Ancient and Honorable Artillery Co., Boston, 3:255

Anderson, Rufus, *Observations upon the Peloponnesus and the Greek Islands*, reviewed, 4:214, 215

Andover, Mass., 3:145; 4:416

Andover Theological Seminary, 3:291

Andrews, A. (painter), 4:ix

Angier, John (1803–1863, son-in-law of TBA): identified, 3:271 (*see also* Adams Genealogy); visits Abigail S. Adams at CFA's house, 3:425, 426, 428, 430; 4:3, 6; and J. Q. Adams "Jr.," 4:170, 188; mentioned, 4:1, 63, 82, 160, 272, 304

Angier, Mrs. John (Abigail Smith Adams, 1806–1845, daughter of TBA): identified, 3:17 (*see also* Adams Genealogy); visits at Old House, 3:16, 267, 313; 4:82, 377; CFA visits, 3:26, 124, 203, 276, 400; 4:34, 48, 50, 81, 95, 105, 304, 334, 337, 346, 352; legacy from JA, 3:31; 4:1, 6, 17, 23, 24, 41, 42, 46, 259, 269; engagement to John Angier, 3:424; visits CFA, 3:179, 261, 340, 424–431; 4:1–6, 271, 351, 377; wedding, 4:58; party for, 4:65; mentioned, 3:271; 4:63, 289, 377

Angier, Joseph, 4:334, 351

Angier, Luther, 3:271, 304

Angier, S., 4:336

Anquetil, Louis Pierre, *L'esprit de la Ligue* and *Histoire de France*, 4:431

Anti-Masonic Review. See *New York Register and Antimasonic Review*

Antimasonry: JQA and, 3:xxxiv, xxxv; 4:xi, 53, 65, 87, 108, 120, 125, 350, 351; Baltimore convention, 4:x–xii, 150, illustration facing 380; CFA and, 4:x–xi, 295, 349–50, 391–431 *passim*; 1831 state tickets, 4:45, 178; state convention in Faneuil Hall, 4: 53, 65; JQA's correspondence with Stone on, 4:358, 360, 371, 381, 383, 395, 407; 1832 party ticket, 4:397; mentioned, 4:75, 173, 191, 290, 382, 419

Appleton, Nathan (U.S. Repr., Mass.), 3:340, 342, 344–45, 351, 353, 365; 4:180

Appleton, Mrs. Nathan, 4:179–80

Appleton, William, 3:395, 396

Apportionment Bill, 4:292

Appropriations Bill, 3:427

Apthorp, George H., 4:148

Apthorp, Robert, 4:148

Arabian Nights, 3:180, 245

Archibald, George, 3:8

Arey, Mrs. Elizabeth (tenant), 3:381, 383

Ariosto, Lodovico: Rose's translation of *Orlando Furioso*, 4:242–52 *passim*, 403; *Orlando Furioso* in *Opere*, 4: 403, 404

Aristophanes: LaHarpe on, 3:42; Mitchell's translation of *The Comedies*, 3:42; 4:437; *The Acharnians*, 3:136–37; *The Knights*, *The Clouds*, *The Wasps*, 3:140–44; mentioned, 3:145, 256

Aristotle: abstract of *Politics*, 4:9–10; *Poetics*, 4:93–106 *passim*, 109; mentioned, 3:20, 23, 401; 4:110, 319

Armstrong, Samuel Turrell, 4:377, 378

Armstrong, Mrs. (tipsy woman), 4:279, 281, 282

Armstrong, T. B., *Journal of Travels in ... Russia and Turkey*, 4:437

Arnold Arboretum, 4:388

Arts et Métiers, 3:73

Astronomics, 4:401

Athenæum, The, CFA's article noted in, 4:39, 40

Atlas Insurance Co., 3:81, 190, 198–206 *passim*, 267–78 *passim*, 285, 295; 4:80, 83, 121

Audubon, John James, 4:21, 344

Audubon, John Woodhouse and Victor Gifford, 4:344

Auger, l'abbé. *See* Æschines; Demosthenes

Augusta, Me., 3:259

Aurora borealis, 3:257; 4:83

Austen, Jane: *Pride and Prejudice*, 3: 386; *Emma*, *Northanger Abbey*, *Sense and Sensibility*, 4:437

Austin, Charles, 3:288

Austin, Mrs. Elizabeth (opera singer), 4:ix, illustration following 124, 263–64, 283

Austin, James T. (attorney), 3:344, 371; 4:422

Ayer, C. C. (tenant): identified, 3:174; CFA's difficulties with over rent, 3: 221–29 *passim*; mentioned, 3:204

Ayers (Ayer), Thomas (housewright): payments to, 3:95, 254, 397; mentioned, 3:96, 222, 352, 398; 4:6, 74–75, 87

Aylwin, Thomas Cushing, 3:302

Bacon, Francis: quoted, 3:101, 359; *Essays*, 3:200, 201, 390; 4:114–16, 119–61 *passim*; *Novum Organon*, 4:7–8; mentioned, 4:423

Bacon, John (sculptor), 4:412, 413

Bailey, John (U.S. Repr., Mass.), 3:329; 4:75, 191

Bailey, Mrs., 3:263, 264

Baillet, Adrien, *Jugemens des savans sur les principaux ouvrages des auteurs*, 4:383–84

Baker, Capt., 3:84

Baker, T. M., & E. Alexander, Jr. (auction rooms), 3:222

Baldwin, Aaron, 3:302–303; 4:360

Baldwin, George R. (surveyor), 3:xviii

Baldwin, James F., 3:248, 249

Baldwin, Loammi (1780–1838), 3: xviii, 296

Baldwin, William, and Andrew Knapp, *The Newgate Calendar*, 4:86, 269, 277, 287

Balguy, John, sermons, 4:374–75, 378, 387

Ball, Thomas, portrait of N. L. Frothingham, 4:xiii, xiv, illustration following 380

Ballard & Co., 4:208

Ballister, Mr. (of McLellan, Ballister & Co.), 4:91–93, 98

Baltimore, Md.: Antimasonic convention at, 4:x, xi–xii, 150; mentioned, 3: 232, 251; 4:36, 120

Bancroft, George, "Bank of the United States," 3:402

Bangor, Me., 4:432

Bank of the United States: JQA's account at Boston Branch Bank, 3:43; CFA's interest in, 3:100, 104–105, 108–10, 116; robbery at Boston branch, 3:271, 272; Bancroft's article on, 3:402; McDuffie's speech on, 4:256; JQA's investigation and report on, 4:265, 299–300, 307, 318, 326; bill to renew vetoed, 4:328–29, 334; mentioned, 3:145, 199, 229; 4:205, 387

Banks, Thomas (sculptor), 4:412, 415

Barbeyrac, Isaac. *See* Pufendorf

Barbier, Antoine Alexandre, *Dictionnaire des ... pseudonymes*, 4:437

Barbour, James (U.S. Sen., Va.), speeches, 3:177

Barbour, John S. (U.S. Repr., Va.), 4:222, 265

Baring Brothers & Co., 3:157, 158, 260, 261

Barnard, Capt. Moses, 4:41

Barney Brallagan (farce), 3:425

Barrett, Rev. Samuel, 4:296–97, 410–11

Barrington, Jonah, *Personal Sketches of His Own Times*, 4:437

Barrow, Isaac, CFA reads sermons of, 3:243–44; 4:191, 196, 200, 221

Barrow, John, *A Family Tour ... across the Netherlands*, 4:437

Barry, James (painter), 4:258, 261

Barry, William T. (Postmaster General), and CFA's violated letter, 3:118, 119, 130, 131

Barrymore, W. (theatrical director), 4:viii

Bartlett, Catherine. *See* Walker, Mrs. James

Bartlett, Dr. George, 3:113

Bartlett, Mrs. George (Mary Gorham), 3:113

Batchelder, Mr., and son, 3:336

Bates, James (U.S. Repr., Me.), 4:265

Bates, John D., 4:365–66

Bates, Joshua, 3:260, 261

Batteux, Abbé Charles: *Principes de la littérature*, 3:135, 286–90 *passim*; *Les quatres poëtiques*, 4:45, 48, 94, 109. *See also* Cicero

Baury, Rev. A. L., 4:28

Bausset, Louis François Joseph de, *Memoires anecdotiques sur l'intérieur du palais et sur quelques évènemens de l'Empire*, 3:186–87, 192–93, 199

Baxter (chain bearer), 3:38

Baxter, Mr. and Mrs. (of Quincy), 4:147, 151–52

Baxter, Mr., 4:399

Bayard, James A. (U.S. Sen., Del.), speeches, 3:120, 125, 145, 148

Bayle, Pierre, *Lettres*, 4:381–82

Beale, Anne, 4:147, 152, 156, 332, 359, 379

Beale, George W.: identified, 3:56–57; supervisor Adams Temple and School Fund, 3:90; 4:389–90; and Quincy Canal Co., 3:125; and Old House, 3:391, 392; 4:16; and JQA's 4th of July oration, 4:60; courtship of Mary Roberdeau, 4:151, 312–13; mentioned, 3:130, 275, 276, 282, 285, 307, 312; 4:147, 156, 299, 315, 321, 324, 328, 332, 344, 353–59 *passim*, 375–93 *passim*

Beals, Henry (tenant), 3:311, 323

Beattie, William, *Journal of a Residence in Germany*, 4:437

Beaumont, Francis, and John Fletcher: *Faithful Shepherdess*, 4:230–31; *Maid's Tragedy*, 4:240

Beaumont, Gustave de, 4:149

Belgium, 3:357, 392

Bell, John, *History of the First Revolution in France*, 4:269, 437

Belloy, P. L. B. de, *Le siège de Calais*, 4:82

Benjamin (servant). *See* Salter, Benjamin

Benjamin, Asher (architect), 3:xi

Bentham, Jeremy, 3:93, 266

Benton, Thomas Hart (U.S. Sen., Mo.), 3:199; 4:334

Berrien, John Macpherson (U.S. Sen., Ga.): speeches, 3:166, 167; on Cabinet resignations, 4:99, 100; mentioned, 4:125

Beverley, Robert, *The History and Present State of Virginia*, 3:206, 207

Bible: CFA reads, 3:44–64 *passim*; 4:39, 188, 191, 211–12, 226, 238, 242, 244, 255, 256, 275, 281, 289, 406, 412; quoted, 4:209; CFA's exegesis of Sermon on Mount, 4:343, 345, 353, 356

Bibliothèque de l'homme public, 4:xvi, 9–32 *passim*, 50, 51, 61, 72–73, 88

Bicknell, Capt., 3:32

Biddle, Nicholas, 3:43

Bigelow, Rev. Andrew, 4:337

Bigelow, Mr. (of Medford), 4:127

Bigelow & Bangs (merchants), 3:32

Billings, Oliver, 4:337

Biographia Britannica, 4:329, 375

Biot, J. B., life of Newton, 3:34

Bird, Edward (painter), 4:261, 262

Bittner, Mrs. Elizabeth, suit against, 3:52, 113, 215, 227

Blackstone, Sir William, 4:386

Blair, Francis P., 4:100

Blair, Hugh, *Lectures on Rhetoric and Belles Lettres,* 3:116, 117; 4:xvii, 132

Blake, Admiral Robert, Johnson's life of, 3:77, 78

Blake, Edward (deceased), 4:420

Blake, Mrs. Edward (Sarah), 4:419-20

Blake, Edward: identified, 3:2; and CFA, 3:1, 3, 6, 11, 35, 142, 394; 4:34, 162, 220, 254, 389, 420; and Private Debating Society, 3:34, 104, 106, 141, 147, 148, 154, 155, 378; mentioned, 4:382

Blake, George, 3:353, 354

Blake, Mr. and Mrs. S. Parkman, 4:389

Blake, William, 4:264

Blaney, Joseph, 3:286

Bloch, Marc Eliéser, *Ichtyologie,* 3:40-41

Blunt, Joseph, proposed life of JA, 4:126-27, 328, 329

Bodin, Jean, "Republic," 4:xvi, 10, 11

Boileau-Despréaux, Nicolas: "L'art poëtique," 4:48, 109, 115, 116; *Œuvres,* 4:124, 438; translation and critique of Longinus, 4:124-30 *passim*

Boleyn, Anne, 4:397

Bolingbroke, Henry St. John, Viscount, *Dissertation upon Parties,* 4:365-67

Bolívar, Simón, 3:208

Bonaparte, Napoleon. *See* Napoleon I

Bond, Charles (watchmaker), 3:254

Book of Common Prayer, 3:265

Booth, Junius Brutus (actor), 3:153; 4:viii

Boott, Elizabeth. *See* Brooks, Mrs. Edward

Boston, Mass.: map of (and adjacent towns), 3:ix, 275, 276, 307, 309, illustration facing 218; craft of engraving in, 3:ix; CFA's residence, 3:x, 2; anniversary of settlement, 3:x, 321, 322, 339; Greek Revival architecture in, 3:xii-xiv; theater in, 3:xiii; 4:viii-ix; bathing establishments, 3:xv, 305; White murder and ensuing trials, 3:xix, 207, 208, 303-304, 371; CFA's law offices, 3:2, 155, 172; CFA's earlier lodgings, 3:8, 59, 183; Grand Muster Day,

3:31, 334; fires, 3:62, 91, 92, 159, 160; 4:403; mayoralty, 3:63, 198, 203; 4:378; various scandals and subjects of gossip, 3:89-90, 230-31, 371-72; depressed real estate, 3:121; canals and railroads, 3:153, 173, 267, 271, 273, 280, 291-92, 298; establishment of Post Office, 3:159; Massacre, 3:183; town meetings, 3: 190, 191, 279-80, 292-93, 409; Election Week, 3:245, 255; 4:55, 213; bank theft, 3:272; Universalism in, 3:279; shark exhibited, 3:285-86; Unitarian-Congregationalist controversy in, 3:291; Salmon's paintings of harbor, 3:294; paintings exhibited, 3:294-95; 4:21, 179, 228, 323; topographical changes, 3:305-306, 308; 4:11-12; great elm on Common, 3:323, 324; political meetings and caucuses, 3:344, 351; 4:53, 65, 198, 422; marketing customs, 3:384; solar eclipse, 3:421; news of Cabinet resignations, 4:34-35; invites JQA to give memorial address on Monroe, 4:85; Independence Day celebrated, 4:90; Washington Centennial, 4: 245-46; parade of militia, 4:314; cholera alarm, 4:317, 341, 347, 352, 361; Jackson's Proclamation, 4:420, 422

Buildings, landmarks, streets, &c. (alphabetically arranged): Atkinson Street, 3:26; Avon Place, 3:59, 183; Back Bay, 3:ix, 308; Beacon Hill, 3:x, 2, 306; Beacon Street, 3:x, xiii, xiv, 308; Boston Common, 3:x; Braman's Baths, 3:xv, 305, illustration facing 219; Cambridge Street, 3:8, 311, 334, 339, 358; Charles Street, 3:308; Chauncy Place, 3:xi; Chelsea House, 4:231, 232; City Hall, 4:403; Common Street, *see* Tremont Street; Concert Hall, 4:2; Cornhill Square, 3:xi; Court Street, 3:2, 15, 159, 160, 172, 342; Craigie's Bridge, 4:264; Dock Square, 3:305; Faneuil Hall, 3:306, 344, 351; 4:53, 246, 422; Federal Street Theatre, 3:xiii; Fenno's coffee house, 3:394; First Church, 3:xi, 13, 14, 92, illustration following 218; 4:xiii, xiv; Hancock Avenue, 3:x, 2, illustration following 218; 4:xiii; Hancock Street, 3:63; Kenmore Square, 3:308; Long Wharf, 3:83, 304, 305; Lynde Street, 3:311, 334; Marine Railway,

4:46–47; Masonic Temple, 4:xi, 311; Merchants' Hall, 3:201, 286; Mill Dam, 3:ix, 308; Mill Pond, 3:ix, 305, 306; Neck, 4:321; Old South Church, 4:113, 120, 122; Old State House Reading Room, 3:320, 321; Park Street, 3:x, xiii; Pearl Street, 3:xiv–xv; Pond Street, 3:xiv–xv; Prison-point Bridge, 4:264; Quincy Market, 3:xii, 267, 306; St. Paul's Church, 3:xii; Sewell's Point, 3:308; South Boston, 3:283; 4:11–12, 344; State House, 3:x, 2, 139, 304, 305, illustration following 218; State Street, 4:403; Stone Chapel, 3:56; Town Dock, 3:305; Tremont House, 3:xiii–xiv, illustration following 218; 4:119–24 *passim*, 413, 433; Tremont Street (earlier Common), 3:xii, xiii–xiv, 17, 21, illustration following 218; Tremont Theatre, 3:xiii–xiv, 153, 419, illustration following 218; 4:viii; Union Wharf, 3:32; Warren Bridge, 3:ix, 130, 306; Western Avenue, 3:ix, 306. *See also* JQA — Lands &c.; Brighton; Charlestown; Dorchester; Jamaica Plain; Roxbury

Boston (ship), 3:251–52

Boston and Lowell railroad, 4:41, 42

Boston Athenæum: Pearl Street buildings, 3:xiv–xv, 124–25, illustration facing 219; picture gallery, 3:xv, 234, 235, 240, 255, 281, 295; 4:xiv, 115, 118, 119, 130, 212, 302, 303, 305, 314–15; catalogues and list of CFA's borrowings, 3:xx, xxix, 120, 133, 134, illustration facing 315; 4:436–44; proprietors' meetings, 3: xxx, 124; 4:212; JQA's proprietor's share and its transferral to CFA, 3:74, 86–87, 89, 173–74; Boston Society for Diffusion of Useful Knowledge lectures at, 3:78, 101, 155; CFA visits and uses, 3:106–108, 115, 148, 155, 191, 214, 224, 243, 245, 263, 293, 299, 301, 320, 338–39, 357, 368, 370, 381–83, 386, 390, 401, 403, 405, 412, 414, 421, 425; 4:2, 4, 13–19 *passim*, 28–45 *passim*, 56, 63, 67, 91, 94, 95, 99, 104–10 *passim*, 121, 124–25, 130, 135, 143, 159, 160, 165, 172, 177, 179–81, 191, 193, 195, 202, 203, 205, 207, 215, 217, 222, 225, 229, 233, 234, 245, 252, 256, 269, 278, 281, 282, 293, 294, 305, 311, 313, 318, 326, 334, 344, 349, 351, 352, 354, 359,

364, 370, 375, 383, 394, 396, 402, 409, 416, 425; CFA on, 3:246; and Harding's portrait of Marshall, 3: 411–12; mentioned, 3:32, 241, 400; 4:5, 307, 407

Boston Bank, 3:206, 207, 333; 4:387, 388

"Boston Bewick Company," 3:ix

Boston Commercial Gazette, article against JQA in, 3:365

Boston Courier: Edward Brooks' articles in, 3:22; nomination of JQA for Congress, 3:320, 321; CFA sends article to, 3:341, 342; comment on JQA's antimasonry stand, quoted, 4:125; mentioned, 4:45, 184

Boston Daily Advertiser: CFA's advertisements in, 3:11, 65, 66; CFA's communication on railroads, 3:409; report on amendment to Judiciary Act, 3:416; Ingham-Eaton correspondence, 4:78; on JQA's eulogy for Monroe, 4:121; merger with *Patriot*, 4:208; mentioned, 3:13

Boston Daily Advertiser & Patriot: new paper formed by merger, 4:208; continues CFA's articles on McLane's Report, 4:217, 219, 222; reprints Clay's speech, 4:223; controversy with *Daily Advocate*, 4:289, 290; dispatches on Paris insurrections, 4:332; reports National Republican state nominations, 4:378; prints rumor JQA to be secretary of state, 4:407

Boston Daily Advocate, CFA's articles in, 4:289, 290, 295, 404–31 *passim*

Boston Debating Society, 3:34

Boston Housewright Association, 3:136, 137

Boston Manufacturing Co., 3:59

Boston Masonic Mirror, 4:xi

Boston Medical Society, 4:397

Boston Patriot: CFA's advertisements in, 3:65, 66; CFA's articles in, 3:244–46, 268–74 *passim*, 290–92; 4:39–40, 45, 48, 125–26, 199, 205; Ingham-Eaton correspondence, 4:78; JQA considers buying, 4:140–42, 175; and Boston election, 1831, 4:203; merges with *Advertiser*, 4:208; mentioned, 3:xiii, 63, 277, 338; 4:150

Boston Society for the Diffusion of Useful Knowledge, 3:78, 81, 88, 101, 127, 155

Boswell, James: *Journal of a Tour to the*

Hebrides, 4:17-19, 438; *Life of Samuel Johnson*, 4:19, 338; Croker's edition, 4:214, 266, 267, 438; mentioned, 4:47, 48

Bourne, E. A., 3:254

Bowditch, Nathaniel: identified, 3:247; mentioned, 3:246, 409, 410; 4:xii, 41, 42, 46

Bowen, Abel (lithographer and engraver), 3:ix-xv, 24-25

Bowen, Daniel, 3:ix

Boyd, Mr. (law client), 3:395

Boylston, Anne. *See* Adams, Mrs. Ebenezer (1706-1770)

Boylston, John Lane, 4:127

Boylston, Susanna. *See* Adams, Mrs. John (1709-1797)

Boylston, Thomas (1721-1798): identified, 3:13 (*see also* Adams Genealogy); settlement of estate, 3:12-71 *passim*, 131-43 *passim*, 260. *See also* Curtis, Nathaniel

Boylston, Ward Nicholas (1747-1828, second cousin of JA): identified, 3:5 (*see also* Adams Genealogy); estate settlement, 3:4-5, 13, 77-147 *passim*, 196, 260-78 *passim*, 367, 370, 396, 409, 410; 4:121, 127; Weston property bequeathed to JQA, 3:17; and portrait of JQA, 3:146

Boylston, Mrs. Ward Nicholas, 3:5, 102, 107, 261; 4:93, 132

Boylston, Ward Nicholas, 2d, admission to Harvard, 4:127

Boylston Fire and Marine Insurance Co., 3:295-303 *passim*, 337, 342, 343; 4:372

Boylston Market: JQA's shares, 3:16, 36, 37, 209; dividends, 3:37; 4:129, 130; meetings of stockholders and directors, 3:144, 150-51, 417; 4:4, 18, 63, 78, 101, 103, 150, 153, 163, 192, 212, 222, 235, 254, 273, 286, 289, 309, 321-22, 341, 345-46, 375, 383, 392; CFA's shares, 3:154, 215, 219-20, 222; shares for TBA Jr., 3:312, 313, 337; CFA a director and Clerk, 3:417, 418, 424; 4:5, 16, 65, 67, 235, 238, 260, 417; mentioned, 3:157

Brackett, Rufus (tenant), 3:188, 190, 194; 4:404

Bradford, Alden, *History of Massachusetts*, 4:2

Bradford, Claudius, 3:7

Bradlee, Mr. and Mrs. Frederick H., 4:365-66

Bradlee, Josiah, 4:147, 365-66

Bradlee (Bradley), Mrs. Josiah (Joanna Frothingham), 3:108; 4:365

Braganza, Catherine of, 4:345, 346

Braintree, Mass., 4:259, 375, 376

Branch, John (secretary of navy), 4:35, 125

Brazer, John, 3:362

Breed, Ebenezer, estate of, 3:295, 296

Bridge, Samuel J., 3:320

Briggs, Rev. Charles, 3:211

Briggs, Cyrus, 3:259

Brigham, Josiah, 3:196, 202, 240, 408; 4:278, 283

Brigham, William (tenant), 4:368

Brighton, Mass., 3:308; 4:385

Brimmer, George Watson, 3:73-74, 145, 146

British Classics, The, 3:337-38, 407; 4:405

Brodie, George, *History of the British Empire from the Accession of Charles I to the Restoration*, 4:315, 316, 438

Brook Farm experiment, 3:149

Brooke, Henry, *The Fool of Quality*, 4:438

Brookline, Mass., 3:ix, 308; 4:385

Brooks, Abigail Brown. *See* Adams, Mrs. Charles Francis (1808-1889)

Brooks, Alfred (son of Jonathan), 3:317

Brooks, Ann Gorham. *See* Frothingham, Mrs. Nathaniel Langdon

Brooks, Anne Gorham (1830-1848, daughter of Edward): birth of, 3:407; mentioned, 4:219

Brooks, Rev. Charles (1795-1872, son of Jonathan), 3:318

Brooks, Charles (son of Cotton), 3:324, 346

Brooks, Mrs. Charles, 3:324

Brooks, Charlotte Gray. *See* Everett, Mrs. Edward

Brooks, Cotton Brown (1765-1834, brother of Peter Chardon), 3:132, 324, 346

Brooks, Edward (1733-1781, father of Peter Chardon; *see* Adams Genealogy), 3:325

Brooks, Edward (1793-1878, brother of ABA; *see* Adams Genealogy): CFA's comments on, 3:22, 73, 92-93, 112, 123, 201, 388; articles signed "Brougham," 3:22; birth of daughter, 3:407; move to Chesnut Street, 4:219; mentioned, 3:3, 14, 57, 65, 87, 107, 118, 143, 162, 168, 172, 194, 236, 241, 259, 266, 291,

293, 320, 350–51, 356, 363, 370, 381, 387, 419; 4:5, 11, 50, 104, 127, 158, 164, 223, 232, 395. *See also* Brooks family meetings

Brooks, Mrs. Edward (Elizabeth Boott, 1799–1865, sister-in-law of ABA; *see* Adams Genealogy): CFA's comments on, 3:73, 87, 112; mentioned, 3:3, 22, 51, 65, 92, 123, 143, 152, 236, 259, 291, 293, 320; 4:50, 104, 219. *See also* Brooks family meetings

Brooks, Edward (1822–1865, son of Edward [1793–1878]), 3:325

Brooks, Elizabeth (b. 1797, daughter of Jonathan), 3:70, 325; 4:306

Brooks, Gorham (1795–1855, brother of ABA; *see* Adams Genealogy): CFA's comments on, 3:259, 268, 293, 322; 4:424, 433; death of child, 3:337; moves to Boston, 4:185; mentioned, 3:22, 319, 345, 397; 4:190, 222, 223, 227, 232, 263, 305, 326, 327, 348, 374, 425, 430. *See also* Brooks family meetings

Brooks, Mrs. Gorham (1809–1884, Ellen Shepherd, sister-in-law of ABA; *see* Adams Genealogy): CFA's comments on, 3:259, 268, 293; 4:433; loss of child, 3:345; mentioned, 3:22, 322, 397; 4:11, 49, 189, 222, 223, 227, 228, 231, 263, 306, 348, 374, 413, 424, 425, 430

Brooks, Henry (1807–1833, brother of ABA; *see* Adams Genealogy), 4:364, 365, 377, 409, 425, 427

Brooks, Horatio (1809–1843, brother of ABA; *see* Adams Genealogy): accident, 3:354, 356, 357; mentioned, 3:340, 342, 343, 348, 350, 423, 425, 431; 4:2, 6, 20, 40, 41, 44, 63, 302, 304, 333, 347, 349, 350, 388

Brooks, John (Mass. governor), 3:53

Brooks, Jonathan (1765–1847; *see* Adams Genealogy): identified, 3:70; CFA's comments on 3:227, 232, 297, 323; mentioned, 3:273, 317, 318, 325, 371; 4:132

Brooks, Mrs. Jonathan (Elizabeth Albree, d. 1826), 3:70, 325

Brooks, Lucy Ann (b. 1810, daughter of Jonathan), 3:70

Brooks, Mercy. *See* Tufts, Mrs. Cotton, Jr.

Brooks, Peter Chardon (1767–1849, father of ABA): identified, 3:10 (*see also* Adams Genealogy); Mystic Grove, home of, 3:xviii, 10, 326; 4:41–42, 350; and CFA's Hancock Avenue home, 3:2, 32; wedding gifts to ABA, 3:8, 254; ties with First Church, Boston, 3:14; and loss of ABA's jewelry, 3:15; CFA's comments on, 3:22, 27, 138, 187, 205, 287; 4:203, 286, 347; winter residence in Medford and Boston, 3:26, 322; 4:162–63, 184–85; JQA and, 3:28; and Mrs. Sidney Brooks, 3:36; and Gorham family, 3:55; at Winthrop dinner, 3:73; invites JQA, CFA, and ABA for Thanksgiving, 3:86, 87–88; subscriber to *Edinburgh Review*, 3:89; on Degrand, 3:91; gifts to ABA, 3:93, 94; 4:129; financial provisions to children, 3:95; and Mrs. Brooks' illness, 3:140, 142–44, 147, 151–68 *passim*; at funeral of Mrs. Brooks, 3:171–72; after death of Mrs. Brooks, 3:174, 175, 231, 237; case of Farnam *v.*, 3:199, 200; CFA discusses plans and problems, 3:244, 265, 266, 299; 4:268–69; shower bath, 3:269, 270; health, 4:7; trip to Nahant, 4:347; trip to Washington, 4:402–403, 427; mentioned, 3:xxx, 4, 21, 27, 50–53, 68, 70, 76, 101, 107, 108, 113, 122, 128, 131, 132, 158, 160, 170–95 *passim*, 204, 209–11, 220, 221, 225, 229, 234, 236, 240, 247–62 *passim*, 269, 270, 276, 278, 280, 288, 290, 291, 294, 295, 307–25 *passim*, 345, 346, 350, 365, 367, 370, 372, 381, 386, 392, 403, 405, 410, 419, 423; 4:3, 14, 18, 88, 95–107 *passim*, 114, 121, 143, 147, 150, 160, 170, 186, 189, 195, 198, 206, 212, 213, 218–55 *passim*, 263–75 *passim*, 281–302 *passim*, 314–36 *passim*, 346–55 *passim*, 365, 368, 374, 424

Brooks, Mrs. Peter Chardon (Ann Gorham, 1771–1830, mother of ABA; *see* Adams Genealogy): death, 3:xxv, 169, 186; illness, 3:10, 18, 22, 26, 87, 98, 99, 117, 137–38, 140, 142–44, 152–69 *passim*; and ABA, 3:18, 114–15; 4:194; visit to Quincy, 3:28; on Mrs. Sidney Brooks, 3:36; CFA's affection for, 3:167–71 *passim*; CFA obtains plate for coffin, 3:170; funeral, 3:171–72; Sunday prayers for after death, 3:175; effect of death, 3:174, 193, 199, 237; 4:249; mentioned, 3:21, 51, 53, 55, 70, 106, 113, 181

Brooks, Peter Chardon, Jr. ("Chardon," 1798–1880, brother of ABA): identified, 3:4 (*see also* Adams Genealogy); CFA's comments on, 3:9, 24, 112, 125, 194, 196, 233, 347; host to CFA, 3:48, 101, 108–109, 138–39, 200, 335, 383–84, 396, 398; mentioned, 3:6, 10, 53, 59, 69, 98, 106, 113, 133, 152, 168–70, 174, 183, 191, 204, 215, 248, 285, 287, 298, 337, 339, 345, 351, 357, 376, 387, 397, 423, 429; 4:3, 33, 95, 105, 127, 350, 430. *See also* Brooks family meetings

Brooks, Mrs. Peter Chardon, Jr. (Susan Oliver Heard, 1806–1884, sister-in-law of ABA; *see* Adams Genealogy): and ABA, 3:1, 3, 6, 8; CFA's comments on, 3:9, 112, 233; accident, 3:335, 339; mentioned, 3:2, 10, 48, 53, 59, 98, 125, 133, 137, 168, 191, 196, 298, 337, 356; 4:95, 105, 223, 227, 278, 286, 300, 430

Brooks, Phillips, 3:132

Brooks, Samuel Reeves (1793–1870, son of Jonathan), 3:317, 323, 371; 4:306

Brooks, Sidney (1799–1878, brother of ABA): identified, 3:4 (*see also* Adams Genealogy); visits CFA, 3:33, 311, 324; 4:94, 361; transferral of GWA's remains, 3:36–37, 81, 324; mentioned, 3:12, 21, 164; 4:117, 127, 147, 285, 362, 365

Brooks, Mrs. Sidney (Frances Dehon, 1805–1861, sister-in-law of ABA): identified, 3:4 (*see also* Adams Genealogy); CFA's comments on, 3:35; parents, 3:36; social calls between CFA, ABA, and, 3:310, 311, 324–26; 4:84, 94, 361; mentioned, 3:12, 13, 21, 61, 333; 4:127, 147, 362, 365

Brooks, Thomas (1732–1799, great-uncle of ABA), 3:70

Brooks, Mrs. Thomas (Mercy Tufts, 1742–1813), 3:70

Brooks, Ward Chipman (1804–1828, brother of ABA; *see* Adams Genealogy): death of, 3:5, 10; mentioned, 3:55

Brooks, William Gray (1765–1834): identified, 3:132; visits, 3:131, 237, 346; mentioned, 3:324; 4:169, 349, 350, 430

Brooks family meetings, 3:73, 81, 86, 93, 99, 105, 112, 119, 125, 130, 137, 152, 158, 164, 182, 188, 194, 201, 207, 217, 222, 408; 4:227, 231, 241, 249, 259, 261, 270, 278, 362

Brooks & Co. (hardware), 3:324

"Brougham." *See* Brooks, Edward

Brougham, Henry, Lord: article on military education, 3:148; speech on law reform, 3:223, 224; *Account of Lord Bacon's Novum Organon Scientiarum*, 4:7–8

Brown, Henry, *A Narrative of the Anti-Masonick Excitement in ... New York*, 4:391–93

Brown, James (of Cambridge, printer), 4:169–70, 172

Brown, M. E. D. (artist), 3:x

Brown, S., 3:159

Brown, Stephen (stock auctioneer), 3:198, 285–87, 291, 312, 378, 379, 396; 4:88

Brown, Mr., on GWA's affairs, 3:50

Brumoy, Pierre, analyses in *Le Théâtre des Grecs*, 3:93, 96, 116, 118–19, 131, 137, 139, 142, 144

Bryan, Michael, *A Biographical and Critical Dictionary of Painters and Engravers*, 4:181–82, 438

Bryant, Gridley, 3:307

Bryant, William Cullen, 4:154

Buchanan, Andrew, 3:275

Buchanan, Mrs. Andrew. *See* Frye, Mrs. Nathaniel, Jr.

Buchanan, Robert Christie (1811–1878, first cousin of CFA): identified, 3:275 (*see also* Adams Genealogy); Quincy visit and CFA, 3:277, 280, 281, 297, 300, 304–10 *passim*

Buckingham, Joseph T. (editor, *Boston Courier*): and JQA, 3:32 , 342; 4:125–26; *Address Delivered before the Mass. Charitable Association*, 3:371; and A. H. Everett, 4:143; mentioned, 4:45, 48, 393

Buckminster, Rev. Joseph S., 3:49

Buffon, George Louis Leclerc, Comte de: *Histoire naturelle*, 3:319–20, 415–17, 422; 4:1, 4, 8–14 *passim*, 41, 303; CFA's comments on, 4:14

Bulfinch, Rev. (Stephen Greenleaf?), 4:267, 268

Bullard, John, 3:85

Bulwer, Edward George Earle Lytton (afterward Bulwer-Lytton): *Devereux*, 3:6–7, 14–20 *passim*; *Eugene Aram*, 4:269–77 *passim*

Bunker, Capt. (of *President*), 3:253; 4:38

Burges, Tristram (U.S. Repr., R.I.), 4:222

Burke, Edmund: Prior's *Memoir*, 3:246–52 *passim*; two articles on, 3:252; speeches, 3:253, 254; 4:191, 193; mentioned, 3:265, 382; 4:xvii, 336

Burke, Master Joseph (actor): characters played in Boston, 3:419, 423; 4:viii, ix, illustration following 124; CFA on, 3:420, 425; portrait, 4:212

Burleigh, William Cecil, Lord, 4:423

Burnap, Rev. George Washington, 3:53

Burnet, Gilbert, *History of the Reformation of the Church of England*, 4:397, 399

Burney, Frances (Fanny, later Mme. D'Arblay): *Evelina*, 3:390–99 *passim*; *Camilla*, 3:399; 4:438; *Cecilia*, 4:438

Burns, Robert, biography, 4:419–27 *passim*, 441

Bussey, Benjamin, 3:xxx; 4:384, 387, 388

Byrd, Mr., indebted to Robert New, 3:422

Byron, George Gordon Noel: CFA's response to, 3:xxix, 41; "Beppo" and "Parisina," 3:185; shorter poems, 3:187, 361; 4:191–93; biographies of, 3:240–41; 4:33–39 *passim*, 54, 233, 236–37, 239; *Don Juan*, 3:240; CFA paraphrases *The Giaour*, 4:127; *Werner, a Tragedy*, 4:217–18

Cabinet Cyclopædia. See Lardner, Dionysius

Cadalso, José de, *Cartas Marruecas* ("The Moorish Letters"), 4:258–59, 267, 280–82

Caldwell, Elizabeth (nurserymaid), 3:328

Calhoun, John Caldwell (vice-president): CFA's comments on, 3:246; controversy with Jackson, 3:406–407; *Correspondence between Gen. Andrew Jackson and*, 3:427, 428, 430–31; 4:8; *Sentiments upon the Subject of State Rights and the Tariff*, 4:116

"Calm Observer, A." See CFA

Cambreleng, Churchill Caldom (U.S. Repr., N.Y.): *Report on the Commercial Intercourse with Foreign Nations* and answer, 3:232; CFA's comments on, 3:232, 403; speech on Appropriations Bill, 3:427; mentioned, 4:265

Cambridge, Mass.: West Cambridge, 3:xviii, 181, 231, 248, 269, 322; First Church, 3:309; Fresh Pond, 3:354, 357; Lechmere's Point, 4:264; East Cambridge, 4:296; Craigie House, 4:395; mentioned, 3:xxv, 11, 117, 308; 4:104, 354

Campbell, George, *The Philosophy of Rhetoric*, 3:135, 188–90, 195–204 *passim*

Campbell, Thomas, *Gertrude of Wyoming*, 4:299

Canada, 3:28; 4:317, 364

Canning, George (Prime Minister of Great Britain), biography, 4:335–49 *passim*

Canton, Mass., 4:432

Capen, Rev. Lemuel, 3:283; 4:344

Capen, Gen. Aaron, 3:334

Carey, Alpheus, cuts inscriptions for tablet to JA and AA, 3:24, 25, 56

Carpenter, Thomas, *The American Senator*, 3:196, 201; 4:xvii

Carr, John G. (tenant, Quincy), 4:261, 275

Carter, Anne: identified, 3:2–3; CFA's comments on, 3:25; mentioned, 3:1, 8, 9, 26, 67, 113, 118, 170, 243; 4:236, 400, 419, 424, 425

Carter, Hannah. See Smith, Mrs. William

Carter, Mrs. James, 3:118; 4:236, 340

Carter & Hendee (publishers), 4:231–32

Cass, Lewis (secretary of war): article on Indians, 3:129–30; appointment to Isaac Hull Adams, 4:235

Cassius, Dion, *Roman History*, 4:71, 72

Causes célèbres. See Pitaval

Cazenove, Charles J., 4:413

Cazenove, Charles J., & Co., 4:46, 92

CFA. See Adams, Charles Francis (1807–1886)

Chadwick, Ebenezer, 3:247, 248, 341; 4:106

Chalmers, Alexander, *British Essayists*, 4:405

Chalmers, George, *Political Annals of the Present United Colonies*, 3:209, 213–15, 220, 227–29; 4:106, 438

Champney, John Y. (tenant): identified, 3:30; as CFA's client, 3:276, 301, 392; 4:22, 172; mentioned, 3:29, 72, 135, 179, 218, 233, 275, 311, 317, 399

Champollion, Jean François, 3:402
Chandler, Samuel, 4:382
Channing, Edward Tyrrel, CFA on, 3:382–83
Channing, Dr. Walter: identified, 3:81–82; lectures, 3:78, 81, 88, 96
Channing, William Ellery: *Sermon* for Election Day, 3:245, 262, 291; mentioned, 3:422
Chantrey, Francis Legatt, statue of Washington, 3:305
Chapman, Rev. George, 4:243, 244
Chapman, Jonathan, Jr.: identified, 3:127; and Private Debating Society, 3:126, 128, 198, 378; CFA's comments on, 3:380; later career, 3:381; mentioned, 3:147, 387, 393, 405; 4:337
Charles II, King of England, 4:xv, 250, 346
Charles X, King of France, 4:402
Charles River, 3:153, 296, 308
Charles River Bridge: Proprietors of, *v.* Proprietors of Warren Bridge *et al.*, 3:130–31; mentioned, 3:296
Charleston, S.C., 3:47, 50; 4:158, 311
Charlestown, Mass.: Bunker Hill Monument, 3:xiv, 307; Winter Hill, 3:13; Middlesex Canal terminus, 3:247–49; Mill Street, 3:249; Charlestown Neck, 3:249; bicentennial celebration, 3:270, 284; walk to Boston from, 3:295–96; 4:264; Breed's Hill, 3:295, 296; Navy Yard and dry dock, 3:295, 296; State Prison, 3:295–96; 4:341; Bunker Hill, 3:296; Rydal Mount, 3:296; Warren Bridge to, 3:296, 306; Prison-point Bridge to, 4:264; mentioned, 3:ix, 320; 4:200, 201, 299, 321
Chase, Justice Samuel, 3:178, 179
Chateaubriand, François Auguste René, "Etudes ou discours historiques," 4:359–65 *passim*, 438
Chatham, Earl of. *See* Pitt, William
Chauncey, Capt. Isaac, 4:285
Chauncy, Rev. Charles, 3:xi
"Chesterfield," defence of W. F. Otis, 4:95
Child, David Lee (editor, *Massachusetts Journal*): and GWA's uniform, 3:30, 31, 41, 181, 194; and CFA's essay on eloquence, 3:152, 158; mentioned, 3:292, 293
Child, Mrs. David Lee (Lydia Maria): *Juvenile Miscellany*, 3:223, 224; mentioned, 3:194

Child, (?)Joshua (secretary, Boylston Market), 3:219–20, 418; 4:129, 130, 150, 192, 321
Child, Stephen, Jr., 3:23, 328, 329
Cholera, Asiatic: in Canada, 4:316–19; in New York, 4:323–24, 331–32, 334; in Boston, 4:341, 347, 352, 361; and wills, 4:337; Fast Day in Mass. for, 4:343; mentioned, 4:433
Christian Examiner and General Review, 3:371, 381
Christian Watchman, CFA's review of Grahame criticized in, 3:428
Cicero, Marcus Tullius: LaHarpe on, 3:54, 62, 63, 65, 71; JQA reads, 3:166, 239, 284; Batteux's translation, 3:290–91; editions read by CFA, 3:327–29, 365; 4:131–32, 170, 176, 219, 438–39; Guthrie's translation, 3:372, 401, 412; 4:130, 206; JQA's bust of, 4:vii, 399, illustration facing 124; CFA translates "De optimo genere oratorum," 4:xvi–xvii, 131–35 *passim*, illustration facing 381; CFA drafts dissertation on, 4:xvii, 186; Voltaire on, 4:41; "Dream of Scipio," 4:218; Hazlitt on, 4:233; Quintilian compared, 4:235, 239; Gibbon on, 4:386; mentioned, 3:xxxiv; 4:140, 321
CFA *studies*: rhetorical works, 3:327–51 *passim*, 358–405 *passim*; 4:131, 223–27 *passim*; orations, 3:405–31 *passim*; 4:2–78 *passim*, 241–42, 244, 430–31; philosophical works, 4:1, 169–220 *passim*; epistles, 4:93–119 *passim*, 130–68 *passim*. *See also* Middleton; Plutarch
Cicero, Quintus Tullius: "Treatise," 4:218; mentioned, 4:205
"Cimon." *See* CFA
Cinderella. See Rossini
City Bank, 3:160
City Guards. *See* Massachusetts Militia
Clapp, Mr. and Mrs. Elisha, 3:338
Clapp, James (mason), 3:57, 60
Clapp, W. W. (proprietor, *Evening Gazette*), 4:391, 392, 401
Claude (Lorrain), 4:180
Clay, Henry: speeches on Bank, 3:109, 110; 4:334; speech on army bill, 3:158–59; as candidate for President, 3:342; 4:65, 126, 290, 295; speeches on tariff, 4:223, 244, 254, 255, 282; mentioned, 3:114, 167, 177; 4:265

Clayton, John Middleton (U.S. Sen., Del.), 3:214

Clinton, DeWitt: address, 3:197; mentioned, 4:383

Clough, Ebenezer, 3:159–60; 4:83

Cocheco Manufacturing Co. (Dover, N.H.), 4:129, 196, 296

Cohasset, Mass.: fishing at rocks, 3:281–82; mentioned, 3:xxv

Coit, Mr., 3:398

Coke, Edward, 4:423

Colburn, Joshua, 4:108

Cole, Thomas (painter), 4:119

Coles, Edward, 4:355

Coles, Mr. (of N.Y.), 3:248

Collins, William (poet), 3:xxix, 41

Colman, George, *The Jealous Wife*, 3:424, 428–29

Colombia, 3:208

Columbian Bank, 4:374

Columbian Centinel: CFA's tribute to Mrs. P. C. Brooks in, 3:171; mentioned, 4:95

Columbian Insurance Co., 4:347, 348, 417

Columbian Mills (D.C.). *See* JA2; JQA – Lands, Investments, &c.

Conant, Amory and Silas (lessees of JQA's Weston property), 3:16, 17, 34, 48, 75, 204, 221, 224, 254, 274, 317, 366, 381, 422; 4:30, 42, 80, 153, 169, 187, 236, 294, 385, 390, 397–98, 408, 424

Concord and Boston Boating Company, 3:395

Condillac, Etienne Bonnot de, *Art d'écrire*, 4:167–74 *passim*

Condorcet, Marie Jean Caritot, Marquis de, 4:xvi, 9, 29, 51. See also *Bibliothèque de l'homme public*

Congregationalism, factionalism in, 3:291; 4:34

Constellation (frigate), 4:430

Continental Congress, 3:60; 4:155

Cook, Capt. James, 4:21

Coolidge, Cornelius, 3:2; 4:403

Coolidge, Joseph: identified, 3:74; mentioned, 3:248, 249, 373; 4:73, 355

Coolidge, T. B., 3:373

Cooper, James Fenimore, *Notions of the Americans*, reviewed, 3:89

Copley, John Singleton: portrait of JA, 3:146; mentioned, 4:396

Corneille, Pierre: *Œdipe*, 3:132–34; *Le Cid*, 4:298–99

Cottin, Mme. Sophie Ristaud, *Malvina*, 4:408–27 *passim*, 439

Cotton, Rev. John, 3:14

"Country without a Government, The," essay in *Edinburgh Review*, 3:346

Cox, William (music critic, N.Y.), 4:ix

Crabbe, Rev. George, *Works*, 3:363

Crafts, Rev. Eliphalet P., 3:264

Cranch, Richard (1726–1811, brother-in-law of AA; *see* Adams Genealogy), 4:260, 316

Cranch, Mrs. Richard (Mary Smith, 1741–1811, sister of AA; *see* Adams Genealogy), 4:260

Crawford, William Harris, and JQA, 3:406–10 *passim*

Crébillon, Claude Prosper Jolyot de, *fils, Œuvres complètes*, 4:365

Croker, John Wilson. *See* Boswell, James

Cromwell, Oliver, CFA's interest in, 3:268; 4:xv–xvi, 342–58 *passim*, 422–28, 430. See also Villemain

Crowninshield, Mrs. Benjamin Williams, 4:395

Crowninshield, Richard, Jr., 3:249

Cruft, Edward (Boston merchant; *see* Adams Genealogy), 3:31, 126, 190; 4:51, 385

Cruft, Mrs. Edward (Elizabeth Storer Smith, 1789–1859): identified, 3:31 (*see also* Adams Genealogy); mentioned, 3:278; 4:41, 51

Cumberland, Richard: biography of, 3:47; on Æschylus, 3:80; translation of Aristophanes, 3:144; on Greek comedy, 3:145–47

Cunningham, Allan, *The Lives of the Most Eminent British Painters and Sculptors*, 4:258–65 *passim*, 396–418 *passim*, 439

Cunningham, Francis (CFA's classmate), 3:27, 28, 394, 395; 4:421

Cunningham, Joseph L. (auctioneer), 3:18, 19, 23, 344, 401; 4:179, 180, 278, 327, 349, 351, 403

Cunningham, William, *Correspondence between the Hon. John Adams . . . and the Late William Cunningham, Esq.*, 4:78–82, 84

Curtis, Charles Pelham: identified, 3:73; and Boylston estate, 3:72–79 *passim*; and Henderson's case, 3:80, 83, 84; mentioned, 3:424

Curtis, Rev. Jared, 3:296

Curtis, Nathaniel: identified, 3:5; and

settlement of Boylston estates, 3:4–31 *passim*; 60–137 *passim*, 196, 259–93 *passim*, 367–73 *passim*, 396, 410; 4:121, 132, 149, 170, 220
Curtis, Noah, 4:5
Curtis, Mr. (lessee of Quincy farm), 3:186
Curtius, Rufus Quintus, *Historiarum Libri*, 4:372

Daily National Intelligencer. See *National Intelligencer* (Washington)
Damer, Mrs. Anne, 4:412
Dana, Richard Henry (American poet), 4:154
Danton, Georges Jacques, 4:261
D'Arusmont, Mrs. Phiquepal. *See* Wright, Frances
Davenport, Rufus, 3:281
Davis, Charles A., 4:147, 362, 384
Davis, Mrs. Charles A. (Eliza Bussey), 4:384, 387
Davis, Dr. Edward G., 3:123, 240, 298
Davis, Isaac P.: and JQA portrait, 3:145, 146, 159–66 *passim*, 196; mentioned, 3:223, 331; 4:39
Davis, Mrs. Isaac P. (Susan Jackson), 3:224
Davis, Col. John Brazer (editor, *Boston Patriot*): identified, 3:63; accepts CFA's communications, 3:244, 246, 267; 4:37, 202; illness, 4:140–41, 208; mentioned, 3:31, 61, 119, 321, 329, 344, 377, 409, 410; 4:339
Davis, Maria, 4:362, 384, 387
Davis, Rufus (veteran), 3:96, 97, 127, 130; 4:290
Davis, Thomas Kemper: identified, 3:79, 223–24; and CFA, 3:44, 105, 126, 317, 381; 4:34, 88, 126, 127, 220, 256, 278, 315, 336, 382; Harvard commencement oration, 3:308–309
Davis, Warren Ransom (U.S. Repr., S.C.), 3:416; 4:222
Davis & Brooks (N.Y.; importers), 3:4; 4:147
Dawes, George, 4:91, 92
Dawes, Horace, 4:91, 92
Dawes, Thomas, Jr., in Mass. Convention on Ratification, 4:146, 147
Deane, Silas: *An Address to the United States of North America*, 3:194, 195; mentioned, 3:60, 92
Dearborn, Gen. Henry Alexander Scammell, 3:16, 17, 73–74; 4:62, 265, 387
Dearborn, Julia, 3:16, 17; 4:62, 387

Debating Society. *See* Private Debating Society
Debrett, John, *Peerage* ..., 3:280
Debt, imprisonment for, 3:180
Declaration of Independence, 3:411; 4:82, 420
Degrand, Peter Paul Francis: identified, 3:33; CFA's comments on, 3:33, 90–91, 359; stockbroker, 3:66, 67, 81, 107, 111, 113, 122, 132, 141, 200–202, 234, 242–43, 253, 267–68, 272, 278, 287–93 *passim*, 342, 356, 414; 4:64, 67, 72, 121, 227, 229, 347, 358; mentioned, 3:1, 37, 58, 127, 247, 314, 332, 363, 428; 4:40, 57, 106, 109, 150, 194, 202, 255, 319, 343, 353, 354, 363, 373, 378, 384, 387, 391, 401, 419
Dehon, Frances. *See* Brooks, Mrs. Sidney
Dehon, Mary M. (later Mrs. Edward Blake), 3:12–13
Dehon, William, 3:36; 4:403
Dehon, Mrs. William, 3:36, 140, 311, 333; 4:84
deJouy, Victor Joseph Etienne: *L'hermite de Londres*, 3:390–91, 395; mentioned, 3:388, 389
Demosthenes: LaHarpe on, 3:54, 59, 179; Auger's translation, 3:57, 58, 147, 179, 199–200; editions read, 3:58; 4:137–38, 148, 158; Æschines on, 3:80–82, 117; CFA on, 3:166, 382; JQA's bust of, 4:vii, 399, illustration facing 124; CFA drafts articles on, 4:117–22 *passim*; mentioned, 3:xxxiv. *See also* Æschines; Plutarch
    CFA studies and translates: "On the Crown," 3:58, 72, 150–99 *passim*, 229–30, 234–45 *passim*; 4:xvii, 35–48 *passim*, 129; "On the Embassy," 4:130–36 *passim*, 167–68; Philippics, 4:137–38, 146–48, 165, 167; Olynthiacs, 4:141–48 *passim*, 154, 158–60, 162
Derby, Edward, 4:60, 80
Derby, E. Haskett, 4:403
Derby, Richard C., 3:6, 305, 306
Derby, Mrs. Richard C., 3:6
Derby Academy (Hingham), Adams family and, 4:315, 316
de Roos, Lt. Fred. Fitzgerald, *Personal Narrative of Travel*, reviewed, 3:225
de Windt, John Peter (1786?–1870, son-in-law of AA2; *see* Adams Genealogy), 3:382; 4:336
de Windt, Mrs. John Peter (Caroline Amelia Smith, 1795–1852, daughter

of AA2; *see* Adams Genealogy), 4:103
Dexter, Franklin, 4:119, 422
Dexter, Samuel (JA's secretary of war), 3:81, 178, 179; 4:16
Dexter, Mrs. Samuel (Catherine Gordon), 3:80–81, 110, 111; 4:16, 107, 301
Dexter, Miss, 4:178
Dibdin, Thomas Frognall, 4:308, 309
Dictionnaire d'histoire naturelle, 3:195
Dictionnaire historique et bibliographique portatif, 3:315–16; 4:50, 62, 87
Diderot, Denis, 4:43, 45, 66, 86–87
Disraeli, Benjamin, *Young Duke*, 4:139
D'Israeli, Isaac: *Curiosities of Literature*, 4:33–34; *Commentaries on ... Charles I*, 4:439
District of Columbia, Rock Creek, 3:104
Dixwell, Epes Sargent and John J., 4:427
Dodge, Joshua, 4:57–58
Dodsley, Robert, 3:369
Doggett, John, & Co., 3:8, 107, 108, 146, 287
Dolph, Eliza, 3:23, 45, 423–24; 4:33
Dorchester, Mass.: Dorchester Heights, 4:11–12; mentioned, 4:369, 389
Dorr, Clifford, 4:366
Dorr, Alfred, & Allen, J. M. (auctioneers), 3:91–92
Douglass, Mr. (of Quincy), 3:90
Dover Manufacturing Co. (N.H.), 4:129
Down East (farce), 4:190
Drake, Nathan: *Essays ... Illustrative of the Tatler, Spectator, &c.*, 3:362, 364–65, 378, 385, 402–403, 407, 426; 4:4; sketch of Addison, 3:375, 376
Drayton, William (U.S. Repr., S.C.), 4:222, 265
Dryden, John, CFA reads poems of, 4:248–54 *passim*, 346
Dubos, Jean Baptiste, *Réflexions critiques, sur la poësie et sur la peinture*, 4:113–14
Dubufe, Claude Marie (painter), 4:402–403
Duff, Mrs. (actress), 3:153
Dufresnoy, Charles Alphonse, *The Art of Painting*, 4:177, 178
Dummer, Jeremiah, *Defence of the New England Charters*, 4:71, 72
Dunlap, Mr. (tenant), 4:90
Dwight, Timothy, *Travels in New England and New York*, reviewed, 3:228

Eaton, John H. (secretary of war), 3:130; 4:35, 77, 78, 100
Eaton, Mrs. John (Peggy O'Neale), 4:78
ECA. *See* Adams, Elizabeth Coombs
Eddy, Caleb, 3:153, 185, 248; 4:173
Edes, Rev. Edward Henry, 4:139–40
Edes, Dr. Henry, 4:140
Edes, Rev. Henry Francis, 4:139–40
Edgeworth, Maria, *Practical Education*, 4:160–66 *passim*
Edinburgh Review, 3:88, 89, 93–96, 144–45, 147–48, 200, 252, 290–92, 346, 361; 4:119, 303, 374, 416
Elba, 3:187
Elections. *See individual states by name*; United States – presidential election
Eliot, William H., 4:18, 19, 278, 279, 286
Elizabeth I, Queen of England, 4:406, 418
Elliot, Jonathan, *The Debates ... on the Adoption of the Federal Constitution*, 4:158–59, 164–73 *passim*, 178–79, 439
Elliot, William, Jr. (attorney; tenant), 4:143–44, 368
Ellis, David, 3:51
Elmes, James, *A General and a Bibliographical Dictionary of the Fine Arts*, 3:258
Embargo, speeches on, 3:144, 145, 148
Emerson, Charles Chauncy, 3:320
Emerson, Edward Bliss (brother of Ralph Waldo Emerson), 3:4
Emerson, Ralph Waldo: sermons, 3:xxviii, 102–103, 156; 4:17, 96, 204, 288; mentioned, 3:4
Emerson, Rev. William (father of Ralph Waldo Emerson), 3:4, 320; 4:17, 96, 204, 288
Emerson, William (brother of Ralph Waldo Emerson), 3:4
Emmet, Thomas Addis, speech, 3:178, 179
Encyclopædia Britannica, 4:354
Encyclopedia Americana, 3:101
Encyclopédie, L', 4:87
Enfield, William: *The History of Philosophy*, 3:376, 380, 385, 397–425 *passim*, 431; 4:1; 170, 173; apothegms of the "seven wise men" from, 3:388, 390, 392, 417; 4:15, 28; CFA on, 3:399–400
English Preacher, The, 4:374, 382
Epicureanism, 3:404; 4:145, 177, 178
Epicurus, 3:404

Ernest, John August, edition of Cicero, 4:131-32, 219

Europe, unrest in, 3:297, 356, 357, 392; 4:80, 85-86

Eustace, John Chetwode: *A Classical Tour through Italy*, 3:208-29 *passim*, 246-56 *passim*, 439; CFA's comments on, 3:223, 252

Evans, David, 3:207

Evarts, Jeremiah, speech of, 3:344

Evening Gazette, 3:58; 4:391

Everett, Alexander Hill (editor, *North Amer. Rev.*): and JQA, 3:57-58; 4:141-49 *passim*, 351; CFA on, 3:57, 129, 133; 4:25; writings, 3:133, 273, 299, 403; 4:214, 282, 378; and CFA's articles, 3:221-27 *passim*, 262, 326, 330, 335, 336, 342, 351, 353; office, 3:272, 336, 372; mentioned, 3:71, 73, 78, 86, 99, 186, 187, 266, 298, 321, 325, 333, 344, 367, 372, 379; 4:127, 154, 339

Everett, Mrs. Alexander Hill (Lucretia Orne Peabody), 3:57, 86, 99, 333, 336, 353; 4:65, 325

Everett, Ann and Charlotte, 3:245, 246

Everett, Edward (1794-1865, brother-in-law of ABA): identified, 3:6 (*see also* Adams Genealogy); CFA's comments on, 3:9, 10, 65, 255, 294, 295, 325, 410; 4:82, 127, 351, 362; dinner for ABA, 3:12; political career, 3:28, 109; as clergyman, 3:49; returns to Washington, 3:83, 371; quarterly payments from P. C. Brooks Sr., 3:95; articles and reviews, 3:115-16, 337, 402; 4:85-86, 214-15; speeches, lectures, and addresses, 3:194, 270, 284, 371; 4:6-7, 334-35; LCA's comment on, 3:197; dinner party, 3:336; mentioned, 3:8, 9, 13, 43, 53, 57, 65, 67, 69-70, 71, 73, 78, 262, 266, 273, 287, 296, 297, 319, 324, 333; 4:41, 60, 99, 113, 154, 222, 265, 336, 340, 361, 374

Everett, Mrs. Edward (Charlotte Gray Brooks, 1800-1859, sister of ABA): identified, 3:6 (*see also* Adams Genealogy); at Mystic Grove, 3:26, 370, 371; attitude on having children, 3:69-70; visits ABA and CFA, 3:99-100, 106-108, 245; and CFA on husband's career, 3:109; and death of Mrs. Brooks, 3:167, 169; birth of son, 3:229, 231, 237, 249;

CFA's comments on, 3:249-50, 255; goes to Washington, 4:185; mentioned, 3:5, 8, 9, 10, 43, 65, 67, 87, 95, 98, 123, 138, 166, 181, 187, 205, 245, 294, 297, 319, 324, 397; 4:41, 60, 65, 99, 340, 351, 361

Everett, Edward Brooks, 3:325

Exeter, Mass., 4:32

"F." *See* CFA

Faneuil Hall. *See under* Boston

Farmer, Miles: attempts blackmail, 3:23, 137, 164, 222; libel suit of, 3:183, 189-90, 193, 197, 422-24; 4:2; difficulties in publishing report of trial, 4:32-33, 104, 105, 107-108; mentioned, 4:95, 147. *See also* Storer, Dr. David Humphreys

Farnam, Henry, *v.* P. C. Brooks, 3:199, 200

Farrar, Isaac: gardens at Old House, 3:211-12; legal client for CFA, 4:26, 83; as tenant, 4:249, 257, 261, 276

Farrar, Professor and Mrs. John, 4:73

Fast Days, 3:208-209; 4:23, 274, 343

Fay, Richard Sullivan, 4:336, 337

Fayetteville, N.C., fire in, 4:73

Federalist, The, 4:135-48 *passim*

Federalists, Mass.: and JQA, 3:63, 332; 4:144, 422-23; mentioned, 3:248

Felt, Rev. Joseph Barlow, 3:236

Fénelon, François de Salignac de la Motte, dialogue on eloquence, 4:xvii, 123, 129-30, 439

Fergus, Henry, *History of the United States*, 4:108

"Few Days in Belgium," 4:439

Field, Barron, *Analysis of Blackstone's Commentaries ... in a series of questions*, GWA writes on, 3:73

Field, Harvey (Quincy tenant), 3:186; 4:261, 283, 286, 292, 293, 294

Field, James, 4:341, 360

Field, William, *Memoirs of the Life, Writings, and Opinions of the Rev. Samuel Parr*, 3:254-57 *passim*, 294, 299; 4:439

Field, Mrs. (LCA2's nurse), 4:314, 341, 348, 360, 379, 394

Field *v.* Lambert, JA's first case, 3:103

Fielding, Henry, Scott's life of, 3:43

Filmer, Sir Robert, *Patriarcha*, 4:331

Fire and Marine Insurance Co. *See* Boylston Fire and Marine Insurance Co.; Massachusetts Fire and Marine Insurance Co.

First Church, Boston. *See under* Boston

First Church, Quincy. *See under* Quincy

Fisher, Dr. John D., 3:118–19

Fishkill Landing, N.Y., 4:336

Fiske, Augustus Henry, 4:60, 80

Flagg, Mr., 4:417

Flash (sloop), 3:32

Flaxman, John, 4:412, 417–18

Fletcher, John, and Francis Beaumont: *Faithful Shepherdess*, 4:230–31; *Maid's Tragedy*, 4:240

Fletcher, Richard, 3:183, 190, 424

"Fletcher, Mr." (actor), 4:190

Flint. *See* Flynt

Florida, 3:406

Flynt (Flint), Rev. Jacob, 4:57, 58, 333

Follen, Dr. Charles Theodore Christian: identified, 3:22; CFA's comments on, 3:21–22; mentioned, 3:417; 4:405, 406

Fontenelle, Bernard Le Bovier de: *Pluralité des Mondes*, 3:300; *La République des philosophes* ..., 4:88

Forbes, William (stabler), 3:7, 8, 95, 212, 224, 227, 242, 254, 259, 400; 4:45, 155, 274

Fornax (steamer), JQA's books sent to Boston in, 4:397, 398

Forrest, Edwin (actor), as Falconbridge, 3:153; 4:viii, ix, illustration following 124

Fort Pickens, S.C., 3:47

Foster, Elizabeth Anne (1802–1875), 3:37

Foster, James Hiller (1773–1862, husband of AA's niece): identified, 3:13 (*see also* Adams Genealogy); bills to JQA agency, 3:12, 13, 215, 224–25; store burned, 3:91, 92; financial sagacity, 3:91, 92, 136, 137, 297; mentioned, 3:8, 37, 90, 133, 147, 150, 154, 187, 276, 285, 295, 367; 4:87, 130, 291, 358, 384–85, 388

Foster, Mrs. James H. (Elizabeth Smith, 1771–1854, niece of AA; *see* Adams Genealogy), 3:13, 17, 37, 90

Foster, Mary Smith (b. 1807), 3:90, 284; 4:388

Foster, Phineas: identified, 3:27; as guardian of TBA's minor children, 4:269, 339; mentioned, 3:26

Foster, Mrs. Phineas (Frances Harrod), 3:27, 124, 125

Foster, W., letters on railroads (signed "Honest Industry"), 3:267, 271, 273, 277

Foster, William, 3:110–11

Foster, William E. (son of James H. Foster), 3:276

Foster (Mr. Brooks' servant), 3:169

Fournier, François Ignace, *Dictionnaire ... de bibliographie*, 4:439

Fowle, Miss, 4:286, 298

Fox, Charles James: *History of the Early Part of the Reign of James II*, 4:318; mentioned, 3:265; 4:336

Fox, John (merchant), 3:8

Framingham, Mass., 4:351

France: Boylston claim against, 3:13, 131; shifts in government, 3:313, 314, 318, 357, 392; 4:332; relations with U.S. during JA's presidency, 4:55; mentioned, 3:120, 121, 187; 4:22, 79, 345, 380

Francis, Rev. Philip, *A Poetical Translation of the Works of Horace*, 4:91

Francklin (Franklin), Thomas, *The Tragedies of Sophocles, from the Greek*, 3:119, 121, 127

Frankland, Charles Colville, *Narrative of a Visit to ... Russia and Sweden*, 4:349–50, 439

Franklin, Benjamin: Arthur Lee and, 3:60, 92; CFA on, 3:61, 62; and JA, 3:161; 4:56, 214–15; Jared Sparks' opinion, 3:202; 4:xii; *Essays and Letters*, 4:294–95

Franklin, Sir John: *Narrative of a Journey to the Shores of the Polar Sea*, 4:25–26, 439; *Narrative of a Second Expedition* ..., 4:35–38, 440

Freeman, Col. Russell, 3:164, 165; 4:184, 185

Freemasonry: R.I. *Report* on, 4:348–51; mentioned, 3:xxxv; 4:x–xii, 59, 65, 83, 125, 394, 415. *See also* Antimasonry

Free Press, 4:125, 191

Free Trade party, 3:341; 4:244, 282

French, Mr., 4:192

French Revolution: in LaHarpe, 3:65, 72; debated, 3:375; CFA on, 4:xv, xvi, 262, 365; mentioned, 3:256; 4:43, 51, 267, 269, 308

Frothingham, Abigail Langdon (later Mrs. Thomas B. Wales), 4:249

Frothingham, Ann Brooks, baptism of, 4:161, 162

Frothingham, Ebenezer, 4:249

Frothingham, Mrs. Ebenezer (Joanna Langdon), 4:249

Frothingham, Edward Brooks, 3:325
Frothingham, Ephraim Langdon, 4:197
Frothingham, Rev. Nathaniel Langdon (1793–1870, brother-in-law of ABA; *see* Adams Genealogy): and First Church, Boston, 3:13–14; 4:xiii–xiv; sermons, 3:35, 42, 63–64, 83, 97, 102, 110, 135, 141, 208, 243, 259–60, 336, 341, 376, 380, 384, 389, 394, 407, 417, 421, 426, 430; 4:4, 12, 17, 21, 23–24, 30, 34, 96–97, 102, 106, 117–18, 128, 157–58, 166, 170–71, 181, 186, 189, 195, 199–200, 204, 211, 216, 221, 225, 230, 238, 247–48, 253, 262–63, 267–68, 272, 274, 280, 284, 288, 293, 296, 300–301, 396, 401, 405–406, 408–409, 410, 415, 426, 431–32; CFA's comments on, 3:71, 87, 262, 268, 272, 289, 325; 4:xiii–xiv; quarterly payments from P. C. Brooks Sr., 3:95; host to CFA, 3:50, 57, 61, 95, 107, 115, 118, 133, 191, 215, 224, 234, 242, 387, 419; 4:xiii, 78, 150, 189, 196–97, 213–14, 228, 266, 398, 409, 424; in Washington and New York, 3:149, 170–71; on CFA's tribute to Mrs. Brooks, 3:171; portrait by Ball, 4:xiii, xiv, illustration following 380; career, 4:xiv; baptism of daughter, 4:161–62; Dudleian lecturer, 4:296, 297; mentioned, 3:3, 29, 32, 33, 36, 43, 48, 59, 65, 73, 108, 109, 113, 197, 241, 258, 269, 332, 354, 385, 392, 428; 4:11, 28, 32, 38, 45, 63, 100, 147, 153, 159, 164, 165, 168, 169, 179, 198, 222–24, 232, 249, 285, 365, 368, 385, 412. *See also* Brooks family meetings
Frothingham, Mrs. Nathaniel Langdon (Ann Gorham Brooks, 1797–1863, sister of ABA; *see* Adams Genealogy): and husband at Medford, 3:9, 21–22, 26, 106, 137, 242, 255, 262, 272, 286–99 *passim*, 317–25 *passim*, 338, 397, 410; 4:41, 294, 296, 306, 346–52 *passim*, 398; illnesses, 3:88–89, 163–64, 170; child's illness, 3:98–99; CFA's comments on, 3:255; and ABA, 4:xiii; daughter's birth and baptism, 4:108, 111, 161–62, mentioned, 3:3, 14, 32–33, 34, 36, 41, 43, 59, 65, 68, 74, 95, 107, 109, 113, 115, 126, 141, 142, 148, 155, 162, 177, 191, 241, 243, 245, 258, 262, 300, 354, 367, 387, 392, 394, 405, 419, 429; 4:17, 21, 32, 36, 38,

52, 88, 93, 100, 112, 117, 132, 143, 147, 149, 150, 155–56, 159, 164, 168, 175, 178, 189, 197, 223, 249, 263, 275, 282, 283, 285, 320, 332, 333, 365, 392, 397, 412, 424, 430. *See also* Brooks family meetings
Frothingham, Priscilla Langdon, 4:249
Frothingham, Miss, 3:300; 4:213, 231
Frye, Nathaniel, Jr. (d. 1855, brother-in-law of LCA; *see* Adams Genealogy), 4:53, 72
Frye, Mrs. Nathaniel, Jr. (Carolina Virginia Marylanda Johnson, 1776?–1862, sister of LCA; Mrs. Andrew Buchanan by her 1st marriage; *see* Adams Genealogy), 3:xvi, 275
Fuller, Abraham W., 3:162, 186
Fuller, Henry H., 3:292–93
Fuller, John, 3:272
Fuller, Timothy, 4:65, 87
Fullerton, J., 4:305–306
Furness, Mr., 3:232
Fuseli, Henry: *Lectures on Painting*, 4:172–74, 177, 228, 231, 233; biographies, 4:223–26, 264–65

Gallatin, Albert: speech on British treaty, 3:114; articles on banks, 4:36; CFA on tariff memorial, 4:244–46, 282; mentioned, 4:75
Gannett, Rev. Ezra Stiles, 3:421–22; 4:284
Gannett, Rev. Thomas B. (of Cambridge), 3:249–50; 4:363
Gardner, Mr. and Mrs. John Lowell, 4:178
Gay, George (attorney), 3:2, 33, 86, 176, 201, 202, 276
Geitner, C. (tenant), 4:52, 91, 213, 326, 426
George IV, King of England: death, 3:297; Wallace's *Life*, 4:160–82 *passim*
Georgetown, Md. (now part of Washington, D.C.), 3:330
Georgia, and Indian removal, 3:115, 116, 123, 139
German language, CFA studies, 3:357–77 *passim*; 4:20, 403–31 *passim*
Gerry, Elbridge, 4:55
Gibbon, Edward: *The History of the Decline and Fall of the Roman Empire*, 4:193–206 *passim*, 213, 223–55 *passim*, 264, 266, 270, 281–318 *passim*; *Memoirs*, 4:306–307; mentioned, 4:386

Gibert, M., on teachers of rhetoric, 4:383–84
Gibraltar, 3:340
Gilbert, Mr. (possible tenant), 3:140, 142
Giles, William Branch (U.S. Repr. and Sen., Va.), speeches, 3:114, 125, 145
Gillies, John, *The History of Ancient Greece* ..., 4:145–46, 152
Gilman, Mr., 3:105, 138, 139
Gilson (Asa or Joshua), 3:124
Giusta, Antoine (White House valet), 3:62
Gleason, Mr., 3:144
Glover, Miss, 3:300; 4:178
Goethe, Johann Wolfgang von: *Memoirs*, 4:253–54, 256, 440; *Sorrows of Werter*, 4:440
Gold Hunter (ship), 3:65, 77
Goldsmith, Oliver: biography of, 3:52; *History of England*, 4:170
Gordon, Dr. Charles, 4:366
Gorham, Ann. *See* Brooks, Mrs. Peter Chardon (1771–1830)
Gorham, Benjamin (U.S. Repr., Mass.), 3:73, 74, 164, 262, 336, 341, 344; 4:127
Gorham, Elizabeth (1769–1845, sister of Mrs. P. C. Brooks Sr.), 3:9, 10, 113, 118
Gorham, Gardner, 4:395
Gorham, Dr. John (deceased), 3:3, 55; 4:356
Gorham, Mrs. John, 3:15, 32, 82, 100; 4:424, 431
Gorham, John Warren: identified, 3:55; dines with CFA, 3:54–55, 210, 215, 390; mentioned, 3:288, 289, 354; 4:29, 245, 425
Gorham, Julia: visit to Quincy, 4:372–78; mentioned, 3:1–3, 4, 6, 8, 15, 20, 32, 44, 54, 55, 59, 97, 134, 136, 141, 154, 157, 168, 170, 172, 215, 241, 258, 261, 286, 316, 358, 383, 390, 397, 421; 4:14, 17, 161, 229, 245, 364, 388, 395, 400, 424, 425, 429
Gottsched, J. C., *Le maître allemand ou nouvelle grammaire* ..., 3:358–60
Gouffe, M. (actor), 4:viii, ix, 190, illustration following 124
Gourgas, John M., Jr.: affianced to ECA, 3:90, 281; 4:60, 73, 313, 346; administers TBA's estate, 4:266, 269, 270; mentioned, 3:276; 4:147, 357, 359, 393

Grafigny, Françoise d'Issembourg de Happoncourt de, *Lettere d'una Peruviana, tradotte dal francese ... da G. L. Deodati* ("Peruvian Letters"), 4:267–85 *passim*
Grahame, James: *The History of the ... United States*, 3:26, 27, 204–20 *passim*; 4:115–19 *passim*, 237, 239, 244, 254, 440; CFA reviews, 3:209–27 *passim*, 350, 351, 353, 394, 428
Granite Railway. *See under* Quincy, Mass.
Granville, Augustus Bozzi, *St. Petersburgh. A Journal of Travels to and from that Capital* ..., 4:359–84 *passim*, 440
Graves, P. (tenant), 4:270, 271, 275
Gray, Francis A., 3:237
Gray, Francis Calley, 3:6; 4:51, 245
Gray, Henrietta, 3:7, 8, 11, 109, 237; 4:41, 303, 351, 430
Gray, Samuel (deceased), 3:107, 184, 278, 288
Gray, Mrs. Samuel (Mary Brooks): identified, 3:107; mentioned, 3:106, 109, 164, 184, 186, 236; 4:41
Gray, Thomas: Mason's memoir, 3:330–50 *passim*; poems, 4:154; mentioned, 3:xxix, 41
Gray, Dr. Thomas (of Jamaica Plain), 4:382, 387
Gray, Winthrop, death and funeral, 3:184, 186
Gray, Capt. (of *Gold Hunter*), 3:77
Gray & Bowen (printers), 4:164
Great Britain: JQA and CFA on Parliament's power, 3:xxxiv, 226; speeches on Treaty of 1794, 3:114, 122; articles on state of, 3:211; CFA on, 3:256, 303; 4:273, 380, 390; Reform of 1832, 4:63, 214; mentioned, 3:164–65, 232, 392; 4:245
Greece: theater, 3:118, 144; speeches on Greek Question, 3:163; JQA's articles on, 3:257, 258, 268; Lycurgus' Sparta, 4:xvi, 61, 100; law, 4:386
Greek language, 3:78, 426–31; 4:1–4, 20, 96, 97
Green, Rev. James D. or Samuel, 4:248, 353
Greene, Nathaniel (postmaster), 3:119; 4:108
Greene, Simon E., 3:150, 295, 296, 298
Greenleaf, Daniel: identified, 3:57; CFA's comments on, 4:308–309;

mentioned, 3:56, 90, 310, 311, 313, 367, 370; 4:59, 60, 147, 318, 337, 339, 367, 373, 382, 386

Greenleaf, Mrs. Daniel (Elizabeth): CFA's comment on, 3:313; 4:308–309; mentioned, 3:310, 311; 4:373, 382

Greenleaf, Eliza and Mary Ann, 4:145, 156, 345

Greenleaf, Ezekiel Price, 4:220, 310, 312, 357, 371, 375, 386, 389, 431

Greenleaf, Thomas: supervisor, Adams Temple and School Fund, 3:90; 4:389–90; mentioned, 3:276, 329, 374; 4:60, 61, 92, 145, 147, 148, 310, 322, 332, 345, 357, 365, 373, 385, 393

Greenleaf, Mrs. Thomas, 4:333

Greenleaf, William Cranch (1801–1868, grandnephew of AA; *see* Adams Genealogy): amanuensis for JQA, 3:55, 103; 4:370; JA2 employs, 3:243; 4:370, 417; mentioned, 3:85, 90; 4:398

Greenough, Horatio, busts of JA and JQA, 3:56, 246, 247; 4:46

Greenwood, Rev. Francis W. P., 3:49, 341, 426; 4:162, 225, 355, 405

Grenville, George Nugent Temple, *Some Memorials of John Hampden*, reviewed, 4:303

Grimm, Friedrich Melchior de, *Correspondance littéraire, philosophique, et critique*, 4:39–67 *passim*, 75–95 *passim*, 440

Griswold, Lt., 3:287

Grosvenor, Mr., buys New's property, 3:339, 378, 379

Guardian, The, 3:338; 4:222–38 *passim*, 247, 277–78

Guicciardini, Francesco, 4:xvi, 15

Guild, Benjamin, 3:248, 249

Gulliver, John (tenant), 3:420, 422; 4:4, 6, 303, 334

Guthrie, William. *See* Cicero

GWA. *See* Adams, George Washington

Hackett, James Henry (actor), 4:viii, ix, 190, illustration following 124

Haggiston's Greenhouse, Charlestown, 4:321

Hague, The, Netherlands, 3:57; 4:55

Haillan, Bernard de Girard, seigneur du, writings, 4:15–16, 18

Hale, Sir Matthew, 4:257, 258

Hale, Nathan (newspaper publisher), 3:12, 13, 57, 99, 333, 336; 4:208, 214

Hale, Mrs. Nathan (Sarah Preston Everett), 3:12, 13, 99, 255, 325, 333

Hall, Capt. Basil: *Travels in No. America*, 3:89, 115–16, 133; *Fragments of Voyages and Travels*, 4:355, 440

Hall, Rev. Edward Brooks (son of Nathaniel Hall): identified, 3:70; CFA's comments on, 3:69, 106, 297; mentioned, 3:67, 128, 286; 4:171

Hall, James E., ed., *American Law Journal and Miscellaneous Repertory*, 3:182

Hall, Judge Joseph, 3:253, 254; 4:93, 98, 100, 107, 108, 132, 224

Hall, Mr. and Mrs. Joseph (of Medford), 4:349–50

Hall, Mary Brooks (daughter of Nathaniel Hall): CFA's comments on, 3:123; stays with P. C. Brooks Sr., 3:181, 193; mentioned, 3:47, 51, 227, 299; 4:169, 223, 227, 231, 303

Hall, Nathaniel, 3:51, 70, 76, 77, 175, 273, 291

Hall, Mrs. Nathaniel (Joanna Cotton Brooks), 3:51, 70, 76, 77, 106, 123, 174, 236, 273, 323; 4:303, 430

Hall, Rev. Nathaniel (son of Nathaniel Hall, b. 1805): identified, 3:127–28; mentioned, 3:299; 4:29, 30, 207, 279, 349

Hall, Peter Chardon (son of Nathaniel Hall, b. 1809), 3:273

Halleck, Fitz-Greene (poet), 4:154

Hallet, George, 3:248, 249; 4:147

Hallett, Benjamin Franklin (editor, *Boston Daily Advocate*): identified, 4:419; and CFA, 4:410, 413–15, 418

Hallett, Mr. (of Quincy), 4:147

Hamblin, Thomas S. (actor), 4:413–14

Hamilton, Alexander: "Report" and "Opinion" on bank, 3:105–108; defense of Croswell, 3:177; on ratifying Constitution, 4:165, 168; mentioned, 3:193; 4:142

Hamilton, C. Antoine, fairy tales, 4:306–307

Hampden, John, 4:303

Hancock, John: speeches, 3:183; mentioned, 3:x, 2

Harding, Chester (portraitist), 3:410–12

Hardwick, Mr. (Quincy tenant), 3:186

Harper, Robert Goodloe (U.S. Repr., S.C.), speeches, 3:121–23

Harper's Family Library, 4:126, 258, 396

Harris, George, translator of Justinian, 3:424; 4:440

Harris, Rev. T. M., 4:111–12

Harrison, William Henry, 3:207, 208

Harrod, Ann. *See* Adams, Mrs. Thomas Boylston (1774?–1845)

Harrod, Anna, 4:377

Harrod, Charles (brother of Mrs. TBA), 4:377

Harrod, Mary, 4:156

Harrod, Susan D., 4:86, 87

Hartford, Conn., 3:378, 379, 380

Hartford Convention, 3:248; 4:144, 422

Harvard College and University: GWA and JA2 at, 3:xvii; Wadsworth House, 3:12, 309; W. N. Boylston's bequest of JA and JQA portraits, 3:146; JQA as Boylston professor, 3:206; transactions with Boylston executors, 3:263, 264, 266, 409, 410; overseers' meetings, 3:304; 4:60, 85, 124; commencements, 3:308–309, 311; 4:124; University Hall, 3:309; Jared Sparks and, 4:xiii; Theological School, 4:34; admissions procedure, 4:127; Dudleian Lecture, 4:296, 297; Bussey legacy, 4:388; mentioned, 3:22, 82, 113, 193, 287, 302, 383; 4:xiv, 51, 90

Haskell, J. (housewright), 3:193

Haskell, Levi(?), 3:165–66

Haskins, Misses (tenants), 3:191–92, 204, 418

Hastings, Joseph S. (merchant), 3:8

Hastings, Warren, 3:277; 4:5

Hatton, Sir Christopher, 4:423

Haverhill, Mass., 3:332

Hawkins, Sir John, 4:304

Hawkins, Lætitia Matilda, *Memoirs, Anecdotes, Facts, and Opinions,* 4:304

Hayden, D. (tenant), 3:346, 347, 368–69

Hayford, William (mason), 4:52

Hayne, Robert Y. (U.S. Sen., S.C.): speeches, 3:163, 164; on public-lands policy, 3:167, 168, 174

Hazard, Ebenezer, *Historical Collections ...,* 4:106, 107

Hazlitt, William: comp., *Select British Poets,* 3:358; *Conversations of James Northcote,* 4:229, 231, 233, 440

Head, George, *Forest Scenes ... in the Wilds of North America,* 4:440

Head, Joseph, and sons George and Joseph, 3:276

Head, Mr., 3:15

Heard, John, Jr., 3:48

Heard, Mary, 3:48

Heard, Susan Oliver. *See* Brooks, Mrs. Peter Chardon, Jr.

Hearne, Samuel, *A Journey ... to the Northern Ocean,* 4:21–23, 25, 440

Hedge, Rev. Frederic Henry, 3:123–24, 181, 310–11; 4:xiv, 176–77

Hedge, Levi, *Elements of Logick,* 3:258, 329

Hellen, Mary Catherine. *See* Adams, Mrs. John, 2d

Hellen, Thomas Johnson (1809–1833, nephew of LCA; *see* Adams Genealogy), 3:157–58, 311

"Henderson's case," 3:77–84 *passim,* 118

Henry VII, King of England, 4:390

Henry VIII, King of England, 4:397, 400

Henry, Patrick, 3:101; 4:172, 178

Henshaw, David (collector of customs), 3:50–51; 4:108

Henshaw, John, 3:51

Henshaw & Co., 3:51; 4:225, 339

Herrmann, Messrs. (of Royal Conservatory, Munich), 4:311, 364

Hewit, Mr., and Farmer-Storer matter, 4:32–33

Hill & Blodget, 3:340

Hilliard, Gray & Co. (booksellers), 3:34, 43, 143, 223, 229, 257

Hingham, Mass., 4:315, 316, 384

Hingham Gazette, 3:329

Hints for Practical Administration of the Poor Laws, 4:383

History of the Western World, 4:106

Hoadly, Benjamin, Bishop of Winchester, 4:382

Hobbes, Thomas, 4:68

Hobby, William, 4:52–53

Hoboken, N.J., 4:336

Holbach, Paul Thiry, Baron d', *La Politique Naturelle,* 4:xvi, 31–36 *passim*

Holbrook, Dr. Amos, 3:286–87; 4:137

Hollis, Caleb, 4:376

Hollis, Daniel: carpenter for JQA agency, 3:15–17, 24, 44, 61, 126, 135, 137, 165, 178, 179, 184, 218, 227, 233, 258, 266; services terminated, 3:294, 298, 299, 305, 311; mentioned, 3:52, 138, 140, 215, 323, 351

Holmes, John (U.S. Sen., Me.), 3:199, 200; 4:344
Holt, Mr. (paperhanger), 3:278
Home, Rev. John, *Douglas,* 3:419, 422; 4:viii
Homer: JQA's bust of, 4:vii, 399, illustration facing 124; Pope's translation of *Iliad,* 4:186-228 *passim;* Pope's translation of *Odyssey,* 4:229-38 *passim,* 247; *Iliad* in Greek, 4:307; mentioned, 4:94, 114, 255
"Honest Industry." *See* Foster, W.
Hood, Thomas, *The Comic Annual,* 3:366
Hopkinson, Dr. John P., 4:126, 127
Hopkinson, Judge Joseph: speech, 3:178, 179; mentioned, 4:126
Horace: *Art of Poetry,* 4:45-48 *passim,* 74, 80, 85, 86, 91, 109-10; mentioned, 3:45, 424; 4:93, 115
Hordynski, Joseph, *History of the Late Polish Revolution,* 4:335-45 *passim*
Horse, The; with a Treatise on Draught, 4:233
Houston, Sam, 4:292
Hovey, E. A. (tenant), 4:270
Howe, William (tinsmith), 3:91-92
Howes, Capt. Willis, 3:24
Hubbard, John, 3:30, 58-59
Hubbard, Mary Greene. *See* Sturgis, Mrs. Russell
Hubbard, Mr. (sexton at Quincy), 3:84, 85
Hubbart, Tuthill, 3:200
Hudson, N.Y., 4:335
Hudson River (North River), 4:335, 336
Hughes, Elizabeth (singer), 4:283
Hull, Commodore Isaac, 4:76
Hume, David: "Essay upon Eloquence," 3:264; 4:xvii; abstract of political essays, 4:13-14; *History of England . . . to 1688,* 4:315-16, 390; CFA compares with Lingard, 4:373, 378, 379, 389, 403; mentioned, 4:39, 319, 425
Humphreys, David (deceased), 3:231
Humphreys, Mrs. David (Ann F.). *See* Walewsky, Madame de
Humphreys, Lemuel (surveyor), 3:37, 38
Hunt, James Henry Leigh, *Lord Byron and Some of his Contemporaries,* 4:233-42 *passim,* 440
Huntoon, Rev. Benjamin, 4:432
Hurd, Bishop Richard, commentary on

Horace's *Art of Poetry,* 4:74, 85-86, 91
Hurlbert, Jesse P. (tenant), 3:183-84, 194, 203, 338; 4:6
Huskisson, William, death, 3:352
Hutchinson, Thomas, *The History of the Colony of Massachusetts Bay,* 3:212-13, 277, 284, 292-307 *passim,* 319-30 *passim,* 385
Huygens, Chevalier C. P. E. J. Bangeman, 3:5-6

Idler, The, 3:338; 4:373-404 *passim*
Inches, Elizabeth and Susan, 3:106-107
Independence Day: 1830, 3:274, 275; 1831, 4:82-83; 1832, 4:323
Indian removal, 3:xxxiv, 115, 116, 123, 129-30, 139; 4:6-7
Ingham, Samuel D. (secretary of treasury): resignation, 4:35, 36; controversy with J. H. Eaton, 4:77, 78; letter on President Jackson, 4:106, 107; mentioned, 4:100, 125
Ingham, Mrs. Samuel D., 4:78
Ingrey & Maddeley (engravers), 4:ix
Insect Architecture, 3:220
Inter-American Congress (Panama), 3:167
Irish Tutor, The (farce), 3:423
Issarevlen, Mr., 4:389
Italian language, CFA studies, 4:261-83 *passim*
Italy, 3:357, 392; 4:111
Ixion, 3:389

JA. *See* Adams, John (1735-1826)
JA2. *See* Adams, John (1803-1834)
Jackson, President Andrew: bank policies, 3:100, 105; Indian policies, 3:115, 116, 139; CFA's opinion of, 3:246, 247, 249; 4:3, 135; message to Congress, 1830, 3:379, 380, 383; controversy with Calhoun, 3:406-407, 428; Cabinet resignations, 4:34-35, 99; CFA's articles on Cabinet resignations, 4:39-40, 45, 48; vetoes Bank renewal, 4:328-29, 334; reelected, 4:394-95, 398; message to Congress, 1832, 4:414; Proclamation against nullifying ordinance, 4:419-29 *passim;* mentioned, 3:45, 232, 321; 4:265, 341, 370, 387
Jackson, Ebenezer (painter), 3:107-108, 178-81, 383; 4:56, 70, 344
Jackson, James, 4:356
Jackson, Patrick, 4:350
Jackson party ticket, 4:45, 178, 397

Jamaica Plain, Mass., 4:388

Jay, John, 3:161, 241; 4:xii, xiii, 55, 214–15

Jefferson, Thomas: *Memoir, Correspondence and Miscellanies*, 3:73, 74, 211, 235, 345; 4:154; on Bank, 3:105; CFA on correspondence with JA and AA, 4:64, 66, 69, 70; death, 4:85; mentioned, 3:xxxvii, 178, 193, 195; 4:174

Jennings, Robert, *The Landscape Annual*, 3:427

Jesus Christ, 3:45; 4:242, 411. *See also* Taylor, Jeremy

Johnson, Alexander Bryan (1786–1867; *see* Adams Genealogy), 3:382, 401

Johnson, Louisa Catherine. *See* Adams, Mrs. John Quincy (1775–1852)

Johnson, Col. R. M., 4:100

Johnson, Samuel: biographies, 3:52, 426; correspondence with Mrs. Thrale, 3:56; 4:391; life of Admiral Blake, 3:77–78; on Milton and *Paradise Lost*, 3:347–48, 377; life of Pope, 4:116; Johnsoniana, 4:266–67; on poverty, 4:338. *See also* Boswell, James

Johnson, Thomas Baker (1779–1843, brother of LCA; *see* Adams Genealogy), 4:169–70

Johnson, William Clarkson (1823–1893, husband of Mary Louisa Adams; *see* Adams Genealogy), 3:xvi–xvii

Johnston, David Claypoole, political cartoonist, 4:x–xii, illustration facing 380

Johnston (Johnson), Josiah Stoddard (U.S. Sen., La.), 3:336

Johnston, Thomas Jones, 3:336

Johnston, Mrs. Waldo C. M., 3:xvi

Johnstone, John, *The Works of Samuel Parr . . .*, 3:293–99 *passim*

Jones, J. B. (merchant), 3:8

Jones, Col. John (of Weston), 3:19–20, 64, 93, 112, 127, 164, 334–35, 420

Jones, John Coffin, 3:413

Jones, William (postmaster at Washington), 3:119

Jones, William (1675–1749), or Sir William (1746–1794), 4:257, 258

Jones, Mr., charge against JQA, 3:102

Jonson, Ben, 3:359

Journal des Sçavans, 3:67

Joy, Benjamin (architect), 3:xi

Joy, Joseph B., 3:248, 249

JQA. *See* Adams, John Quincy (1767–1848)

Julien Auction Room, 3:213, 295, 322; 4:21

Junius, letters, 3:265, 300; 4:90

Justinian, *Institutionum juris civilis expositio*, 3:424; 4:2–4, 386, 440

Juvenal, 3:45

Kames (Kaimes), Henry Home, Lord, *Elements of Criticism*, 3:134, 147–79 *passim*; 4:xvii

Kean, Charles (actor), 4:413, 414

Keats, John, 4:239

Kelley, Hall Jackson, and Oregon settlement, 4:96

Kemble, Charles (actor), 4:414

Kemble, Fanny (actress), 4:414

Kent, Abigail. *See* Welsh, Mrs. Thomas

Kettell, Samuel, *Specimens of American Poetry*, 4:161

Kidder, James (artist), 3:xii, 24

Kimball, Rev. Daniel, 4:315–16

King, Charles Bird (portraitist), 3:xvi–xvii, illustration facing 314

Kingman, Mr., 3:164

Kinsman, Henry W.: and GWA's loan to City Guards, 3:44, 79, 210; and Whitney case, 3:150, 160, 176, 210, 217, 218, 221; and Ayer case, 3:221–29 *passim*; and New's estate, 3:246; mentioned, 3:78; 4:205, 314

Kirk (Kirke), John (JQA's servant), 3:254, 258–59, 274, 318, 353, 361, 366, 369; 4:36, 56, 94, 103, 136, 149, 306, 330, 347

Kirk, Mrs. John (Elizabeth), 3:253, 387; 4:296, 398

Kirkland, Dr. John Thornton, 4:395

Kirkland, Mrs. John Thornton (Elizabeth Cabot), 4:395

Knapp, Andrew, and W. Baldwin, *The Newgate Calendar*, 4:86, 269, 277, 287

Knapp, Frank (John Francis), and murder of Capt. White, 3:xx, 248–49, 303–304, 371

Knapp, John (lawyer), 3:36–37, 135–36, 150, 215, 219

Knapp, Capt. Joseph J., Jr., 3:248–49, 303

Knowles, James Sheridan, *The Hunchback*, 4:413–14

Knowles, John, *Life and Writings of H. Fuseli*, 4:172–74, 177, 223–33 *passim*, 440

Knox, Vicesimus, essays, 3:260

Kotzebue, Otto von, *A Voyage of Discovery, into the South Sea and Beering's Straits,* 4:15–20 *passim,* 440
Krehmer, George, 3:322, 327, 328
Kronstadt, Russia, 3:77
Kuhn, Charles (1821–1899, husband of LCA2; *see* Adams Genealogy), 4:111
Kuhn, George H., 4:387–88
Kuhn, Mrs. George H., 4:387

Ladd, W. G. (tenant), 4:335, 336, 400
LaHarpe, Jean François de: *Lycée ou cours de littérature ancienne et moderne,* 3:12–13, 20–26 *passim,* 34, 35, 42–95 *passim,* 131, 142, 179; 4:49, 50, 109, 295; CFA's comments on, 3:34, 35, 42, 65, 72, 73, 76
LaMotte Fouqué, Friedrich Heinrich Carl de, *Undine,* 4:404–406, 441
Lamson, Rev. Alvan, 3:28; 4:144–45, 359
Languet, Hubert, "De la puissance légitime," 4:xvi, 61
Lardner, Rev. Dionysius: *Cabinet Cyclopædia,* 4:108, 140, 142–44, 165; *Cabinet Library,* 4:160, 443
Lardner, Nathaniel, *The Credibility of the Gospel History,* 4:291
Latin language, 3:329, 413–24
Laurens, Henry, 4:xii
Lawrence, Mr. and Mrs. Abbot, 4:387
LCA. *See* Adams, Mrs. John Quincy (Louisa Catherine Johnson)
Lee, Arthur: *Life of,* 3:59, 60, 62, 92; Sparks' view of, 3:92, 161, 202; 4:xii, xiii
Lee, Emily, 3:133
Lee, Harriet [and Sophia], *The Canterbury Tales,* 4:203–28 *passim,* 441
Lee, Henry, Free Trade Party nominee, 3:341, 351
Lee, Henry (1756–1818), eulogy of Washington, 3:188
Lee, Richard Henry (of Westmoreland, Va.), 4:179–80
Lee, Richard Henry, *Life of Arthur Lee,* 3:59–62, 73, 92
Lee, William, 3:355, 375; 4:112
Lee, Mrs. William (Ann Amory McLean), 3:355, 375
Leighton, Charles (housewright and tenant), 3:136–38, 140
Leland, Judge Sherman, 4:269
Leland, Thomas, *History of Ireland,* 4:441
Leonard, Daniel, "Massachusettensis" papers, 3:383

LeRoy, Caroline. *See* Webster, Mrs. Daniel
Lessing, Gotthold Ephraim, "Fabeln," 4:407–17 *passim*
Lewis, Mrs. Harriet (tenant), 3:53, 54, 71, 140, 180, 181
Lewis, Dr. Winslow (tenant), 3:53, 54, 66, 71, 119, 121–22, 181, 188
Libby, Joseph (tenant), 4:44, 45, 124, 270
Liberia, 3:270
Library of Entertaining Knowledge, The, and *Library of Useful Knowledge. See* Society for the Diffusion of Useful Knowledge
Lieber, Francis, lectures, 3:78, 101, 108–109
Lilly, Mr. (at Pension Office), 3:127
Lincoln, Gov. Levi, 3:29; 4:156, 343, 355, 378
Lind, Jonathan, *Remarks on the Principal Acts of the Thirteenth Parliament ... Vol. I ... Relating to the Colonies,* 3:386; 4:441
Lingard, John: *History of England,* 4:370–431 *passim;* compared with Hume, 3:373, 378, 379, 389, 403
Litchfield, Allen (mason), 3:31
Litchfield, Ward, 3:30
Little, E. (of Philadelphia), 4:179
Livingston, Edward (secretary of state): speeches, 3:177; author of Proclamation against nullification, 4:420; mentioned, 4:407
Lloyd, Thomas, *Congressional Register ...,* 4:331
Locke, John: analysis of essay on government, 4:14–15; mentioned, 4:257
Lockhart, John Gibson: review of Mrs. Trollope, 4:294; *Life of Robert Burns,* 4:419–27 *passim,* 441
Loker, Mr. (of Weston), 4:20
Longhurst, (Miss or Mrs.) Mary B. (milliner; tenant), 3:4, 11, 12, 15, 16, 25, 44, 99, 132, 133, 164, 175–93 *passim,* 209, 311, 346; 4:276
Longinus: LaHarpe on, 3:23, 24; *On The Sublime,* 4:124–30 *passim;* on Homer, 4:247
"Looker On, A." *See* CFA
Loring, John G., & Co. (coppersmiths), 3:82
Loudon, John Claudius, *Encyclopædia of Gardening,* 4:441
Louis XV, King of France, 4:97, 145
Louis-Philippe, King of France, 3:392
Louisiana, 3:147

"Lovelace," 3:371-72

Lovell, James, letters to JA and AA, 4:68, 69

Lowell, Rev. Charles, sermons, 3:134-35, 352; 4:25-26, 153, 221, 367

Lowell, Charles Russell, 3:305, 306

Lowell, Edward Jackson: library auctioned, 3:343-44; 4:xvi, 9; mentioned, 3:12

Lowell, James Russell, 3:xxviii; 4:367

Lowell, John: identified, 3:6; and Boylston estate, 3:142, 143, 261; mentioned, 3:161

Lowell, Mass.: proposed railroad to, 3:173, 248; mentioned, 3:28

Ludlow, Edmund, *Memoirs*, 3:323, 326, 328

Lufkin, Capt., 3:65

Lunt, George, 3:405

Lunt, Rev. William Parsons, 4:48-49, 122

Luther, Martin, 4:396

Lycurgus, 4:xvi, 61

Lyman, J. [Joseph?], 3:320

Lyman, Mr. and Mrs. Levi, 3:53

Lyman, Theodore (merchant), 3:32; 4:407

Lyman, Gen. Theodore, Jr.: identified, 3:144-45; CFA's comments on, 3:321; mentioned, 4:198

Lyon, Mr. (client), 4:212, 237-38

Mably, Abbé Gabriel Bonnot de: "De la législation," 4:61, 63, 68; CFA's marginalia on, 4:xv, xvi, 100, illustration following 380

McDonough, Bridget (cook), 3:328

McDuffie, George (U.S. Repr., S.C.): speeches, 3:168, 177; reports on Bank, 3:402; 4:256, 300; report on tariff, 4:244-45; mentioned, 4:222

Machiavelli, Niccolò, 4:11-12

Mackay, Capt. (of *Boston*), 3:252

Mackenzie, Sir Alexander, *Voyages from Montreal ...*, 4:29-33, 441

Mackenzie, Alexander Slidell, *A Year in Spain*, 3:123, 400-413 *passim*

Mackenzie, Henry: "Louisa Venoni," 3:25-26; *The Man of Feeling*, 3:26-27, 31, 33

Mackintosh, Sir James: *History of England*, 4:165, 170-71, 441; *Dissertation on the Progress of Ethical Philosophy*, 4:354, 378, 441

McLane, Louis (secretary of treasury): speeches, 3:163, 164; CFA's articles on report, 4:198-207 *passim*, 215-23 *passim*; CFA on a "Judicious Tariff," 4:298

McLean, Mrs. John (Ann Amory). *See* Lee, Mrs. William

McLellan, Ballister & Co., 4:92

Madison, James: on ratification of Constitution, 3:101; 4:173, 179; *Federalist* papers, 4:141, 142; mentioned, 3:xxxvii, 114; 4:174, 330

Maine, 3:77, 78, 259, 346; 4:344

Malcolm, Rev. Howard, 3:398-99

Manners, George (British consul), 3:323

Manuel du Libraire, 4:441

Marat, Jean Paul, 4:261

Mariana, Jean de, *Histoire generale d'Espagne*, 4:282

Marmontel, Jean-François: CFA translates "Le trépied d'Hélène," 3:xxxv; 4:396-403 *passim*; *Nouveaux contes moraux*, 4:393, 401-13 *passim*

Marshall, John: on ratification of Constitution, 3:101; 4:178; *Life of Washington*, 3:203-13 *passim*, 227-29; Harding's portrait, 3:411-12

Marshall, Samuel, *Treatise on the Law of Insurance*, 3:20-34 *passim*, 44-66 *passim*

Marston, John, 3:90; 4:81, 147, 384

Mary, Queen of England, 4:404

Maryland, 3:213

Mason, Rev. John M., speech, 3:188

Mason, Stevens T. (U.S. Sen., Va.), speech, 3:125

Mason, William: memoir of Thomas Gray, 3:330-35 *passim*, 337, 339, 343, 348, 350; translator, Dufresnoy's *The Art of Painting*, 4:177-78

Masonry. *See* Freemasonry

"Massachusettensis." *See* Leonard, Daniel

Massachusetts: CFA's feeling for, 3:xxxi; Federalists, 3:63; Secretary of Commonwealth, 3:65; Supreme Judicial Court, cases in, 3:85, 89, 130-31, 199, 200, 423-24; Fast Days, 3:208-209; 4:23, 274, 343; Governor and Artillery Election Day, 3:255; CFA on heritage, 3:284; Commission of Insolvency, 3:314, 319, 383; Court of Common Pleas, 3:423; 4:2; debates ratification of Constitution, 4:146-54 *passim*

Elections: Congressional, 1830, 3:340, 341, 352-53; state offices, 1831, 4:22, 45, 48; state offices, on new date, 1831, 4:177, 178; state offices,

1832, 4:377–78; Presidential, 1832, 4:395, 397

General Court: bill on railroads, 3:173, 409; act to amend mayoralty election procedure, 3:190, 191; convenes on "Election Day," 3:245; 4:55, 213; bill on autopsies, 3:409, 410

National Republican party: JQA nominee for Congress, 3:329, 333; Appleton nominee, 3:340; caucus, 3:344; in state elections, 4:45, 48, 177, 178, 397; merger of Boston papers and, 4:208; Antimasonic party and, 4:290, 351; state convention, 4:377–78, 380

Massachusetts Fire and Marine Insurance Co.: stock owned, 3:3, 104, 107, 182, 272, 291, 425; 4:5–6, 14, 16, 17, 132, 358–59; CFA on, 4:360

Massachusetts Historical Society, 3:241, 269, 411

Massachusetts Horticultural Society, 4:86

Massachusetts Hospital Life Insurance Co., 3:136, 137, 246, 247; 4:17, 46

Massachusetts Militia: GWA and "City Guards," 3:30, 31, 34, 41, 44, 79, 145, 154–55, 160, 181, 194, 210, 267, 276, 359, 360; parade, 3:334; 4:314

Massachusetts Journal: CFA's article in, 3:152, 153, 168; Child edits, 3:194, 293

Massachusetts Mutual Fire Insurance Co., 3:187, 190

Massachusetts Society for Agriculture, 3:321

Massillon, Jean Baptiste: *Sermons*, 4: xvii; CFA summarizes a sermon each Sunday, 24 July 1831 – 10 June 1832, and 11 Nov. – 30 Dec. 1832, 4:97–312 *passim*, 396–432 *passim*

Mathematics, 4:277, 281, 288

Mather, Cotton, *Magnalia Christi Americana*, 3:220–21

May, Henry K., 3:32

Medford, Mass.: Sparrell's plan of, 3: xviii–xix, illustration following 314; Mystic Grove (Brooks family home), 3:xviii, 10, 26, 250; 4:184, 350; Adams farm, 3:xix, 236; 4:259, 374; CFA and ABA visit, 3:xxv, 9, 21–22, 53, 69–70, 76–77, 87–88, 98–99, 106, 116–17, 123–24, 137–38, 166–69, 174–75, 181, 186–87, 192–93, 198–99, 204–205, 211, 216, 220–21, 227, 231–32, 236–39, 248–50, 254–55, 259–60, 262–63, 268–74, 286–300, 316–27, 328, 338, 345–46, 370–72, 397; 4:7, 41, 94–95, 105, 127, 160, 296, 302–306, 345–52; ABA visits, 3:23, 36–37, 157, 164–65, 242, 376, 418; 4:398; Brooks family's seasonal moves, 3:26; mentioned, 3:3; 4:63, 271, 289, 294

Buildings, landmarks, streets, &c. (alphabetically arranged): Brooks Stone Bridge, 3:236; Medford lock and aqueduct, 3:xviii, xix, 236, 248, 249, illustration following 314; Mystic Pond, 3:xviii, 249, 300; "The Partings," 3:xviii, 300; railroad bridge, 4:349, 350; Weir Bridge, 3:xviii. *See also* Middlesex Canal

Medford River. *See* Mystic River

"Medium," communication to *Boston Daily Advertiser*, 3:341

Meidinger, J. V., *Nouvelle grammaire allemande-pratique*, 3:358–60

Meisel, H., *Cours de style diplomatique*, 3:344–50, 356

Melmoth, William, Cicero's *Letters to His Friends: with Remarks by*, 4:99–100

Menageries, The, 3:51, 54, 60–61

Mercantile Marine Insurance Co., 4:88

Merchant's Insurance Co., 4:149

Meredith, George Augustus, 3:305–306, 308

Meriam & Brigham (wine merchants), 4:70, 71

Merrill, James C., 3:267

Merrimac River, 3:153

Michelangelo, biographies of, 4:167, 231, 291, 292

Middlesex Canal: route of, 3:ix, xviii, 153, 236, 247–49; mentioned, 3:260, 292. *See also* Medford

Middlesex Canal Co.: CFA as director attends meetings, 3:xxx, 150, 153, 173, 185, 395, 413, 415; 4:41, 173, 174, 224–25, 232, 234; corporate history and outlook, 3:150–54, 413, 417; Adams family holdings, 3:151, 152, 414; 4:225, 226

Middleton, Conyers, *Life of M. T. Cicero*, 3:389, 394, 400, 402, 407, 413; 4:49, 173, 441

Mier, Mr., 4:365

Militia, debating subject, 3:147, 148, 156, 161, 168. *See also* Massachusetts Militia

Mill, John Stuart, *Essays on Government*, reviewed, 3:94
Miller, Edward (of Quincy): supervisor, Adams Temple and School Fund, 3:90; mentioned, 3:276, 282, 285, 302, 314; 4:60, 61, 121, 130, 147, 319, 322, 325, 345, 354, 356, 357, 385
Miller, Mrs. Edward, 3:302; 4:147, 312, 345
Miller, Mrs. Samuel, 4:356
Mills, Mr. (Quincy painter), 4:278, 302
Milton, John: biographies, 3:339–48 *passim*; *Paradise Lost*, 3:350–52, 358–77 *passim*; *Paradise Regained*, 4:110, 113; mentioned, 3:250; 4:76, 114, 257
Milton, Mass., 3:27, 55, 247, 275, 286; 4:62, 152, 332
Minot, George Richards, *Continuation of the History of ... Massachusetts Bay*, 3:334, 340, 343
Minot, John (former customs inspector), 4:131, 172, 173
Minot, William(?), 3:338
Minutoli, Baroness Wolfardine A. L. M. von, *Recollections of Egypt*, 3:382, 384–85; 4:441
Mirabeau, Honoré Gabriel Riquetti, Comte de: "L'ami des hommes," 4:72–79 *passim*; mentioned, 3:198; 4:xvi
Mitchell, Thomas: translator, *The Comedies of Aristophanes*, 3:42, 136–37, 140–45, 256; on America, 3:142, 143
Mitford, William: CFA on, 3:58, 85, 115, 117–18, 136, 250–51, 256–57; *The History of Greece*, 3:59, 253–54; 4:119
Molière (Jean Baptiste Poquelin), 3:89, 264
Monk, James Henry, *Life of Richard Bentley*, reviewed, 3:346
Monroe, James: Harding's portrait, 3:411; death, 4:84–85; JQA's eulogy, 4:85, 113, 120–21, 132–33, 175, 215; mentioned, 3:406, 428; 4:45, 178
Montaigne, Michel Eyquem de: *Les essais*, 3:371; 4:191, 428–29, 431, 432; Villemain's "Eloge," 4:428, 429; mentioned, 4:423
Montesquieu, Charles Louis de Secondat, Baron de la Brède et de: *Œuvres*, 4:39, 254–55, 256; "De l'autorité

de," 4:xvi, 50; *De l'esprit des lois*, 4:22, 27–28
Montolieu, I., translator, *Undine*, 4:404, 441
Moore, Col. Abram, 3:89, 90, 323
Moore, Mrs. Abram (Miss Woodham; actress), 3:90
Moore, Edward. See *World, The*
Moore, Jared Sparks, 4:xii
Moore, Mary F. See Park, Mrs. John C.
Moore, Thomas: *Lalla Rookh*, 3:189–90, 195–96; *Letters and Journals of Lord Byron*, 3:240–41, 328–29; 4:33–39 *passim*, 54; *Memoirs of the Life of . . . R. B. Sheridan*, 4:183–88 *passim*; mentioned, 4:191
"Moorish Letters, The." See Cadalso, José de
More, Sir Thomas, *Utopia*, 4:20
Morgan, Lady Sydney, *Book of the Boudoir*, 3:370–78 *passim*; 4:441
Morgan, William, murder, 4:350, 358, 381, 410, 412
Morland, George (artist), 4:258
Morris, Commodore Charles, 3:295, 301, 336; 4:127, 200, 201
Morris, Mrs. Charles, 3:301
Morris, Gouverneur, speech, 3:125
Morse, Mr., 3:234
Mortimer, John Hamilton (British artist), 4:396
Morton, Eliza Susan. See Quincy, Mrs. Josiah (1773–1850)
Motley, Thomas, portrait by Stuart, 4:xii
Motte (Mott), Rev. Mellish Irving: identified, 3:111; sermons, 3:110, 376; 4:312
Mount Desert (Desart), Me., 3:78
Mounteney, Richard, editor, Demosthenes, *Selectæ orationes*, 4:137–38, 144, 158
Mount Wollaston. See Quincy, Mass.
MQA. See Stone Library
Music and Prejudice (comic opera), 4:263–64
Mystic Grove. See Medford, Mass.
Mystic River: in Medford, 3:xviii, xix, 236, 248; railroad bridge, 4:350

Nahant, Mass.: described, 3:x–xi, illustration following 218; outing at, 3:305–306; mentioned, 3:xxv, 281; 4:94, 347
Naples, death of King of, 3:392
Napoleon I: biographies of, 3:187, 192–93, 199; 4:257–87 *passim*; CFA's

comments on, 4:173–74, 287; mentioned, 3:231, 327; 4:xv, 173

National Intelligencer (Washington): Holmes' speech, 3:199, 200; Calhoun-Jackson correspondence, 3:427, 428; Cabinet resignations, 4:100; South Carolina debate, 4:222; Clay's speech on tariffs, 4:223; John Randolph's advertisement, 4:251; CFA reads, 4:251–52; debate on JQA's desire to leave chairmanship of Committee on Manufacturing, 4:265; JQA's Report on Bank, 4:300; Report of Committee on Manufacturing, 4:305; Bank Committee minority report, 4:318; reports JQA's political battles, 4:330; JQA as secretary of state rumored, 4:407

National Republican party. *See* Massachusetts – National Republican party

Neal, John, memoir of Bentham, 3:266

Negris, Alexander, editor, *The Orations on the Crown*, 3:58, 229–30, 235

Neponset Bridge Co.: stock, 3:41, 125–26, 207, 208, 370; annual meetings, 3:276, 315; 4:357

Neponset River, 3:xiv, 307

Neponset Woollen Co. (Canton, Mass.), 3:58–59

Netherlands, The, 3:357, 392; 4:55

New, Robert: estate, 3:221–22, 232–46 *passim*, 263, 276–83 *passim*, 298–408 *passim*, 422; 4:10, 18, 44–45, 65–79 *passim*, 101; life, 3:235; 4:77

New Bedford, Mass., 3:372

New Britain Museum of American Art, Conn., 4:xii

Newburyport, Mass., 3:164

Newell, Rev. William, sermons, 3:231–32; 4:26, 275, 329

New England: CFA on character, 3:xxxvi, 213, 214; 4:xv; and constitutional interpretation, 3:168, 199; in Grahame, 3:207, 208, 210, 218; in Chalmers, 3:228; Thanksgiving observance, 3:374

New England Marine Insurance Co., 3:106, 107, 251–52, 260, 317, 381; 4:67, 72, 314, 417

New England Soap Stone Co., 3:20, 30–31

New England Society, 4:6, 7

Newgate Calendar, The. See Knapp, Andrew

New Hampshire, 3:418; 4:395

New Harmony, Ind., 4:76

New Monthly Magazine and Literary Journal, 3:24, 219

Newton, Sir Isaac, 3:34; 4:257

New York (state): CFA on prisons, 3:295; debates ratification of Constitution, 4:158–59, 164, 165, 168; cholera, 4:323, 331, 332, 334; election of 1832, 4:395, 397; mentioned, 3:213; 4:339

New York City: JQA and LCA in, 3:380, 383; 4:36, 38, 164, 173, 304, 384, 396–97; CFA in, 1826, 4:263–64; mentioned, 3:4, 37, 83, 171; 4:viii, ix, 40, 75, 247, 310

New York Commercial Advertiser, 3:xiii; 4:407

New York Register and Antimasonic Review (formerly *Anti-Masonic Review*), 4:412

Niagara Falls, N.Y., 3:28

Nicholas, George and Wilson, 4:179–80

Nicolas, Nicholas Harris, *A Synopsis of the Peerage of England*, reviewed, 3:280

Niebuhr, B. G., *History of Rome*, reviewed, 3:346

Niles, Hezekiah, 3:232

Noble, Mark, *Memoirs of the Protectorate-House of Cromwell*, 4:342–45, 353–54, 441

Nollekens, Joseph, biography, 4:409–10

Norfolk co., Mass., 3:321, 329; 4:205, 269

North American Review: Sparks edits and writes in, 3:27, 161, 202, 203; 4:xii; A. H. Everett edits, 3:57, 222; and CFA's articles, 3:213, 234, 326, 330, 335, 336, 394, 414, 428; 4:39–40, 106, 428; office, 3:372; mentioned, 3:116, 123, 126, 129–30, 132, 211, 273, 274, 278, 299, 327, 328, 329, 337, 379, 381, 401–402, 403; 4:25, 27, 85–86, 87, 91, 153, 154, 155, 214–15, 216, 217, 274, 324, 378

Northampton, Mass., 3:53, 67, 106

North Carolina, 3:213

Northcote, James. *See* Hazlitt

Nott, Eliphalet, 3:193

Novanglus. See JA

Nowlan (Nowland), Mrs. (nurse), 3:252; 4:36, 101, 118, 162, 389

Nugent, Lord. *See* Grenville

Nugent, T. *See* Port Royal, Messrs. de

Nullification. *See* South Carolina

Old Colony Memorial, 3:329

Old English Poets, 4:236

Old House (Adams National Historic Site, Quincy): portraits at, 3:xvii; repaired, 3:9, 18, 23, 52, 57, 60, 80, 82, 203, 404; 4:16–17, 24–25, 277, 301, 302; planting and gardening, 3:211–12, 316, 366; 4: 156, 277, 288, 311, 318, 320, 322, 355, 358, 359, 361–62, 373, 388; CFA on condition of, 3:17–18, 202, 243, 244, 247, 282–83, 288; JQA reassembles belongings at, 3:32–33, 51, 90, 348; 4:vii, 397–99, 407; occupants, 1830, 3:254, 366; "Portico," 3:261; CFA improves grounds, 3:315–16; 4:27, 34, 285, 291, 292, 295–96, 299, 301, 302, 307, 310, 326, 362; gate posts, 3:391, 392, 396, 418–19; 4:14, 16, 25; JQA's "writing chamber," 4:vii, illustration facing 124; JA's "Office" and library, 4:x, 138, 139, 389–91; mentioned, 3:xxv, 56, 275, 408; 4:20. *See also* CFA – Agent, &c. for JQA; JQA – Books

Oliver, Miss A. B. (or A. R.; tenant), 3:42, 124, 125, 126, 127, 206, 207, 221, 230, 233, 276, 401, 404; 4:90, 114, 149

Oliver, Francis J., 4:182, 194

Oliver, N. K. G. (tenant), 3:127, 206

Oliver, Mr., 3:398

Olivet, P. J. Thoulier, abbé d', and J. A. Ernest, editors, Cicero's *Opera,* 3:368, 372

Opie, John (British artist), 4:258

"Orator." *See* CFA

Orcutt, David (cabinetmaker; tenant), 3:20, 21, 25, 32, 44, 48, 53, 54, 57, 59, 92, 102, 107, 108

Orcutt, Mrs. David, 3:44

Oregon settlement, 4:95, 96

Orne, Henry, 3:85

Ortiz, Jacob, *Ultime Lettere,* 4:286

Osgood, Rev. David (of Medford), 3:76–77, 124

Osgood, Elizabeth and Lucy, 3:76–77, 124, 273, 299

Osgood, Samuel Stillman (artist), 4:212

Otis, G. A., 3:159

Otis, Harrison Gray: and JQA, 3:63; 4:144, 423; speeches, 3:193; 4:422; mentioned, 3:58, 191, 292, 381

Otis, Harrison Gray, Jr., 4:185

Otis, Mrs. Harrison Gray, Jr. (Eliza H.), 4:185

Otis, James, *Rights of the British Colonies . . . ,* 4:67, 68, 72, 73, 442

Otis, Mr. and Mrs. James (of N.Y.), 3:8

Otis, Mary Ann (daughter of Mrs. Samuel Otis), 3:278

Otis, Mrs. Samuel Allyne (Mary [Smith] Gray, 1757–1839, cousin of AA; *see* Adams Genealogy), 3:278; 4:168

Otis, William Foster: *An Oration before the Young Men of Boston,* 4:89–95; *The Reviewer Reviewed,* 4:95

Ousatonic (steamer), 3:306

Ovid, 4:321

Owen, William (British painter), 4:396, 400

Oxford Elements of Logic, 3:250–58 *passim,* 329

Paine, Charles Cushing, 3:145, 147

Paley, William: *Works,* reviewed, 3:225; *A View of the Evidences of Christianity,* 4:264–301 *passim*

Palfrey, Rev. Cazneau, 4:128

Palfrey, Rev. John Gorham: sermon, 3:380; mentioned, 3:171, 172, 336, 373

Panama Question, 3:166, 167

Paris: American Commissioners at, 3:59, 60, 195; Treaty of (1783), 4:333

Park, Dr. John, 3:78, 155

Park, John Cochran: marriage, 3:89, 90; and Farmer-Storer trial, 3:423, 424; mentioned, 3:34–35, 82

Park, Mrs. John C. (Mary F. Moore), marriage, 3:89, 90

Parker, Chief Justice Isaac: career and death, 3:288; mentioned, 3:130, 131, 199

Parker, John (merchant), 4:374

Parker, Samuel D., 3:424

Parkman, D., 3:373

Parkman, Rev. Francis: identified, 3:51; CFA's comments on sermons, 3:204–205; 4:66, 195, 421; mentioned, 3:75, 373; 4:173, 227, 231, 261, 430

Parkman, Mrs. Francis (Caroline Hall): identified, 3:51; mentioned, 3:75; 4:169, 227, 231, 430

Parkman, Francis (son), 3:51

Parkman, Dr. George, 3:94, 373; 4:124, 339, 341, 381

Parks, Elizabeth or Rebecca, 3:69–70, 152, 153

Parks, Mrs. Warham (aunt of ABA), 3:70

Parliamentary or Constitutional History of England by Several Hands, The, 4:342

Parr, Samuel: Field's *Memoirs,* 3:254–57, 294, 299; *Works,* 3:293–99 *passim;* 4:442; *Bibliotheca Parriana,* 4:442

Parris, Alexander, 3:xii

Parry, Sir William Edward, voyages, 4:6–28, 30, 442

Paulding, James K., *The Lion of the West,* J. H. Hackett in, 4:viii, ix, 190, illustration following 124

Payne, William E., 4:311, 389

Payne, Miss (sister of Mrs. Clapp), 3:338

Payson (Henry) & Gutterson (Jacob), 3:48

Peabody, Oliver (of Exeter, N.H.), 4:115–16

Peabody, Oliver William Bourn: identified, 3:336; and CFA, 3:353, 378, 382, 386, 401, 402, 410, 420, 425, 428, 431; 4:6, 7, 10, 32–39 *passim,* 46, 119–32 *passim,* 143, 165, 168, 173, 212, 224, 236, 240, 246, 250, 252, 263, 264, 271, 275, 278, 282, 283, 291–303 *passim,* 321, 323, 373, 377, 393, 411, 417; death of father, 4:115; mentioned, 4:325

Peabody, William Bourn Oliver, 3:328; 4:154, 214, 324–25

Peacock (ship), 4:200

Pendleton, John, 3:ix

Penniman, J. R., 3:xi

Pennsylvania: election of 1832, 4:377–80, 391, 395, 397; mentioned, 3:213; 4:107, 339

Percival, James Gates (poet), 4:154

Perkins, James, and Boston Athenæum, 3:xiv, 124–25

Perkins, Thomas ("short Tom"), 3:62–63

Perkins, Col. Thomas Handasyd: and Boston Athenæum, 3:124–25; acquires Granite Railway and quarry, 3:307; mentioned, 3:63, 351; 4:423

Perry, Mr. (son of Mrs. Sumner), 4:361

"Peruvian Letters." See Grafigny

Peters, Pond & Co. *v.* Commonwealth Insurance Co., 3:85, 89

Phelps, Dr. Abner, 4:120

Phi Beta Kappa: addresses, 3:194, 197; JQA and efforts to revise charter and laws, 4:97, 98, 107, 109, 124, 154; mentioned, 4:354

Philadelphia, Penna.: JQA and LCA in, 3:98, 104, 251–52, 384; 4:36, 164, 331, 334; Stuart-Sully portrait of JQA at, 3:145, 146; Free Trade convention at, 4:244, 282; State Fencibles (militia) in Boston, 4:314; cholera in, 4:343; election of 1832, 4:378, 391; mentioned, 3:x; 4:77

Phillips, Elizabeth (ABA's cousin, later Mrs. William Stevens): identified, 3:146; visits ABA and CFA, 3:145–52, 156–57, 162, 165; at Medford, 3:192–93, 198, 397; 4:41, 95, 105, 374; jilted by Mr. Spaulding, 4:416; mentioned, 4:147, 169

Phillips, John, 3:132, 146, 286

Phillips, Mrs. John (Lydia Gorham), 3:132, 146, 286

Phillips, John (servant), 3:274

Phillips, Lydia (ABA's cousin), 3:22–23; 4:147, 164, 168, 169, 374

Phillips, Mary Ann (later Mrs. William Gray Brooks), 3:132, 360; 4:349, 350

Phillips, Thomas W., 3:107, 108

Phillips, Turner, 3:187, 190

Phillips, Willard, 3:123

Phillips Exeter Academy, 3:130, 131

Phipps, Dr. Thomas, 4:356

Phipps, Dr. Thomas (son of preceding), 4:356, 366

Phrenology, 4:397, 401

Pickering, Edward, 3:126–27

Pickering, John, 3:78, 423–24, 425

Pickering, Timothy, *A Review of the Correspondence between the Hon. John Adams and the Late William Cunningham,* 4:78–81

Pickman, Mrs. Benjamin, Jr. (Hannah Smith, 1794–1863, daughter of AA's cousin, William Smith; *see* Adams Genealogy), 3:278; 4:172

Pierce, Rev. John, 3:269

Pierpont, Rev. John: sermons, 3:129; 4:166; mentioned, 4:387

Pinkney, William, speeches, 3:163, 179, 180

Piozzi, Hester Lynch (Thrale), *Letters to and from Samuel Johnson . . . ,* 3:56, 57; 4:391

Pitaval, F. Gayot de, *Causes célèbres et intéressantes,* 4:173, 174, 288, 384, 385

Pitkin, Timothy, *A Political and Civil*

Index

History of the United States, reviewed, 3:161

Pitt, William, 1st Earl of Chatham: "Speech on the Seizure of Falkland's Islands," 4:6, 7; mentioned, 3:265, 382; 4:245

Pitt, William (the younger): and "The Rolliad," 3:300–301; mentioned, 3:265; 4:xvii, 336

Pitts, Mrs. Mary Ann (servant), 3:253; 4:36

Pittsburgh, Penna., 4:120

Plato: JQA's bust of, 4:vii, 399, illustration facing 124; analysis of *Republic*, 4:xvi, 19–20; *Laws*, 4:28; mentioned, 4:250

Plautus, 3:43

Pliny, elder and younger, 3:66

Plumer, William, Jr., 3:332, 418

Plutarch, *Lives*: Demosthenes, 3:96, 126, 165; Cicero, 3:126, 165; Pericles, 4:328; mentioned, 3:69, 245

Plymouth Congressional District, Mass., JQA elected to Congress from, 3:xxxiii, 328, 353

Poindexter, George, speeches, 3:147, 159, 160

Poland, 4:345

Pope, Alexander: *Works*, 4:116; translation of *Iliad* and *Odyssey*, 4:186–238 *passim*, 247; in Spence's *Anecdotes*, 4:239, 243; biography, 4:416, 422, 432

Porter, Jonathan, 3:278

Porter, Mrs. Jonathan (Catherine Gray), 3:278

Port Folio, the Adams family's contributions to, 3:xxxv, 233; 4:379, 403

Portland, Me., 3:324

Port Royal, Messrs. de: *A New Method of Learning with Facility the Latin Tongue*, trans. T. Nugent, 3:329, 413–24; *A New Method of Learning with Facility the Greek Tongue*, trans. T. Nugent, 3:426–31; 4:1–4

Portugal, 3:357

Portuguese War, 4:348

Potter, Rev. Alonso, 3:78

Potter, R.: translator of Æschylus, 3:79–81, 86, 88; translator of Sophocles, 3:121, 127

Potter, Rev. William T., 4:82, 83

Poughkeepsie, N.Y., 4:336

Poussin, Gaspar, 4:180

Pratt, Caleb, 3:307, 311–12

Pratt, Mr. and Mrs. G. W., 4:95

Prescott, Edward Goldsborough, 3:90; 4:336, 337

Prescott, Judge James, 3:182

Prescott, William, 3:85

President (steamboat), 3:253; 4:38

"Prior Documents." *See* Almon, John

Prior, James, *Memoir of the Life and Character of . . . Edmund Burke*, 3:246–52; 4:442

Prisons, CFA on, 3:295–96

Private Debating Society: CFA's preparation for and attendance at meetings, 3:34, 48, 76, 82, 96–97, 104, 109–110, 116, 122–23, 128, 141, 148, 155–56, 161–62, 168, 180, 186, 192, 198, 341, 357, 360–62, 375, 379, 380, 383, 384, 394, 398, 412, 416, 421, 426, 427, 429, 430; 4:xvii, 173, 175, 216; committee meetings, 3:104, 126, 128, 141, 148, 378; mentioned, 3:102, 154, 204

Proctor, Mrs. A. B. (tenant), 4:32, 360

Prout, S. (artist), 3:427

Providence, R.I., 3:252, 253; 4:38, 394

Public-land policies: Congressional debate on, 3:167–68, 177; CFA writes on, 4:205–207

Pufendorf, Samuel: *Les devoirs de l'homme et du citoyen, trad. du Latin par Jean Barbeyrac*, 3:68–85 *passim*; "Le droit de la nature . . .," 4:88–89, 95

Puritans, CFA's interest in, 3:xxxvi, 207, 208, 213, 226, 271, 284, 289, 355; 4:xv, 116, 429

Putnam, Rev. George, sermons, 3:412–13; 4:257

Putnam, Justice Samuel, 3:130, 131

Pye, Henry James, *A Commentary Illustrating the Poetic of Aristotle*, 4:95–104 *passim*, 442

"Q." *See* CFA

Quarterly Review, 3:144–45, 211, 223, 225, 228, 252, 256, 280, 283–84, 332; 4:29, 30, 188, 294, 303, 442

Quebec, Canada, 4:316

Quincy, Anna Cabot Lowell (1812–1899, later Mrs. Robert C. Waterston; *see* Adams Genealogy), 3:274–75

Quincy, Edmund (1808–1877, son of Josiah Quincy "the President"; *see* Adams Genealogy): and Private Debating Society, 3:34, 97, 416; CFA's comments on, 3:96, 141–42,

404; 4:240, 402; visits CFA and ABA, 3:3, 6, 7, 85, 120, 149, 163, 196, 210, 218, 228, 244, 245, 274, 276, 282, 318, 329, 335, 357, 372, 376, 382, 397, 411, 427; 4:6, 12, 31, 37, 49; mentioned, 3:224, 305; 4:2, 3, 18, 143, 220

Quincy, Eliza Susan (1798–1884, daughter of Josiah Quincy "the President"; *see* Adams Genealogy), 3:12, 38

Quincy, Josiah II (1744–1775, "the Patriot"; *see* Adams Genealogy), memoirs, 4:17

Quincy, Josiah III (1772–1864, "the President"; *see* Adams Genealogy): as President of Harvard, 3:12, 29, 308; co-executor of JA's estate, 3:86, 364, 365, 379; 4:380; resigns presidency of Athenæum, 3:124; speeches 3:147, 158, 159, 227, 322, 339; *Memoir of . . . Josiah Quincy, Jun.*, 4:17; supervisor, Adams Temple and School Fund, 4:385–86; mentioned, 3:263, 274; 4:83, 91, 124, 334, 356

Quincy, Mrs. Josiah (Eliza Susan Morton, 1773–1850; *see* Adams Genealogy): CFA's comments on, 3:11, 12; mentioned, 4:127, 334, 336, 356

Quincy, Col. Josiah IV (1802–1882, son of Josiah Quincy "the President"): identified, 3:29 (*see also* Adams Genealogy); secretary of Boston Athenæum, 3:73, 74, 89; birth of son, 3:89, 90; acts for father on JA's estate, 3:101, 145, 151, 158, 159; mentioned, 3:130, 142, 151, 224, 263, 274, 276, 301, 340, 410, 422; 4:145, 156, 355, 356, 378

Quincy, Mrs. Josiah IV (Mary Jane Miller; *see* Adams Genealogy), 3:263, 274, 306; 4:145, 148, 156, 356

Quincy, Josiah Phillips (1829–1910; *see* Adams Genealogy), 3:89, 90, 263

Quincy, Margaret Morton (Mrs. Benjamin Daniel Greene, 1806–1882; *see* Adams Genealogy), quoted, 3:x

Quincy, Maria Sophia (b. 1805, daughter of Josiah Quincy "the President"; *see* Adams Genealogy), 3:309

Quincy, Norton (1716–1801, uncle of AA; *see* Adams Genealogy), 3:268

Quincy family: CFA's comments on, 3:11, 12; seal, 3:411; mentioned, 4:147

Quincy, Mass.: CFA at, 3:16–18, 27–29, 37–41, 55–57, 89–91, 130, 202, 243, 252–53, 257, 260–68, 274–85, 300–16, 328–29, 331–32, 357, 366–67, 373–74, 387–88, 408; 4:16–17, 27, 34, 38, 40, 50–92, 136–56, 212–13, 259–61, 277–78, 283–85, 288, 291–93, 295–96, 299, 301, 305–47, 352–94, 398, 402, 407; Independence Day celebrated, 3:275; 4:60, 82–83, 101; Universalism in, 3:279; 4:76; CFA on townspeople, 4:60, 91, 267, 276–77; *Deeds . . . Relating to the . . . Land and to the Library Presented . . . by President Adams*, 4:390–91. *See also* CFA – Agent, &c. for JQA; JA; JQA – Lands, &c.; Adams Temple and School Fund; Old House

Buildings, landmarks, streets, &c. (*alphabetically arranged*): Black's Creek, 4:151; Canal Wharf, 4:398; Christ Church (Episcopal), 4:83, 322, 415; Classical School (Adams Academy), 3:25, 90; 4:ix, x; First Church (Adams Temple, Stone Temple), 3:xi–xii, 24–25, 56, 247, illustration following 218; 4:ix, 49, 82–83, 260; First Church burying ground (Adams vault), 3:56, 84–85; 4:260; Granite Railway, 3:ix, xiv, 275, 307, illustration facing 219; Greenleaf Wharf, 3:310; the Ledges, 3:307; Mt. Wollaston, 3:xxx, 56–57, 268; 4:316, 362–63, 380; old Plymouth Road, 3:37, 39; Penn's (Payne's) Hill, 3:ix, 37, 38, 180, 186; 4:323, 329, 330, 373; Railway Hotel, 3:275; Railway (later Bunker-Hill) Quarry, 3:xiv, 307; Ruggles House, 3:29

Quincy Bay, 3:268, 276, 310

Quincy Canal Co., 3:94, 125, 130–131, 196, 202, 203, 240, 408, 409; 4:278, 283

Quincy Historical Society, 3:38

Quintilian (Marcus Fabius Quinctilianus): *Institutes*, 4:228–41 *passim*, 442; mentioned, 3:48, 403; 4:xvii

Racine, Jean Baptiste: *Esther*, 4:49; *Athalie*, 4:49–50, 109; biography, 4:50; *Phèdre*, 4:89, 90, 109; *Iphigénie*, 4:104, 105, 109

Radcliffe, Mrs. Ann, *The Italian*, 4:179, 183–84, 228

Raeburn, Sir Henry, 4:396, 406

Railroads: Granite Railway, 3:xiv, 307;

Index

Middlesex Canal and, 3:150, 153, 173, 185, 248; CFA opposes public subsidy, 3:267, 271, 273, 278, 289, 291–92, 406, 408, 409; Boston debates and votes on subsidy, 3:279–80, 292–93, 298, 341; Congressional Report on, 4:326

Raleigh, Sir Walter, 4:423

Rambler, The, 3:338; 4:279, 281–86, 293–94, 306–307, 313, 328, 335

Randolph, Edmund, 3:101, 105

Randolph, John: nominated as minister to Russia, 3:247, 249; Harding's portrait of, 3:411; stud advertisement, 4:251

Randolph, Thomas Jefferson, editor, Jefferson's *Memoir ...*, 3:74, 211, 345; 4:64

Randolph, Mass., 3:180

Raynal, Abbé G. T. F., *Philosophical and Political History of the Settlements ... in the E. and W. Indies,* 3:210

Rayner, John, 3:159–60

Redwood Library and Athenaeum, Newport, R.I., 3:xvi, xvii, 412

Reed, Edward (U.S. Repr., N.Y.), 4:222

Reiske, John Jacob, *Oratorum Græcorum,* 3:245; 4:148, 158, 442

Rembrandt van Rijn, 4:180

Report of the Trial for High Treason of Henry and John Sheares, 4:376, 377

Republican Institution, GWA's share in, 3:159, 160; 4:29, 36, 39, 41

Review, or the Wags of Windsor, The (farce), 3:420

Reynolds, Dr. Edward, Jr., 4:324, 325

Reynolds, Sir Joshua: *Complete Works,* 3:256–58; 4:178–82; notes to Dufresnoy's *Art of Painting,* 4:177–78

Rhode Island: projected book on, 4:90; *Report of the Committee ... to Investigate the Charges against Freemasonry & Masons,* 4:348–51

Rice & Thaxter, 4:92

Richardson, Mr. and Mrs. Abel, 3:323

Richardson, John Hancock: visits CFA, 3:8–9, 23, 46, 59, 60, 66, 111, 117, 143, 155, 157, 178, 225, 243, 252, 259, 286, 317–18, 338; 4:115; CFA's comments on, 3:9, 23, 225; accompanies CFA to Weston, 3:19–20, 74–75, 334–35, 354; 4:158, 169; engagement and marriage, 4:115, 116

Richardson, Mrs. John Hancock (Lydia Anne Thaxter), 4:115, 116

Richardson, J., appendix to Franklin's *Narrative,* 4:35, 38

Richardson, Joseph (U.S. Repr., Mass.), 3:321, 329

Richardson, Samuel: Scott's life of, 3:41, 42; CFA reads and comments on *Clarissa Harlowe,* 3:63–144 *passim,* 165–67, 170, 197–206 *passim; The History of Sir Charles Grandison,* 3:149, 156–63 *passim,* 166

Richmond, Rev. Edward, 3:314

Ripley, Rev. George, CFA on sermons, 3:149, 336; 4:13, 122, 243, 318–19

Rip Van Winkle, 4:viii

Ritchie, Andrew, 3:211

Ritchie, Mr. and Mrs. William(?), 3:8

Robbins, Dr. Chandler, 3:78

Robbins, Dr. E. H., 3:36

Roberdeau, Mary: at Quincy, 4:130–31, 136, 140, 148–62 *passim;* George Beale as suitor, 4:151, 312–13

Robertson, J., editor, A. Sidney's *Works,* 4:328

Robertson, William: *The History of America,* 3:208–15 *passim; The History of the Reign of the Emperor Charles V,* 4:240

Robespierre, Maximilian François Marie Isidore, 3:65; 4:261

Rogers, Isaiah (architect), 3:xiv

Rogers, Capt., and Henderson's case, 3:80–81

Rolle, John, M. P., 3:301

"Rolliad, The," 3:300–301

Rollin, Charles, *De manière d'enseigner et d'étudier les belles lettres,* 3:315–27 *passim*

Rome: St. Peter's, 3:214; paintings of, 3:427; character in antiquity, 4:71, 205, 250, 321, 386

Romney, George, biography, 4:396, 398, 400

Rosa, Salvator, 4:180

Roscoe, William, *The Life and Pontificate of Leo the Tenth* and *The Life of Lorenzo de Medici,* 4:240

Rose, William Stewart, translator, Ariosto's *Orlando Furioso,* 4:242–47, 251–52, 403

Ross, Sir John, *A Voyage of Discovery ...*, 4:27–29, 442

Rossini, Gioacchino, *Cinderella (Cenerentola;* English adaptation by Rophino Lacy), 4:ix, 263, 283

Roubiliac, Louis Francis, biography, 4:412, 414–15

Rousseau, Jean Jacques: *Emile et Sophie*, 4:62–71 passim; CFA's comments on, 4:74

Roxbury, Mass., 4:4, 5, 62, 68, 257, 385

Royall, Anne (Newport), *Mrs. Royall's Southern Tour, or Second Series of the Black Book*, 4:138

Rubens, Peter Paul, 4:180

Ruffhead, Owen, *The Life of Alexander Pope*, 4:416, 422, 432

Rupp, Mr. (clerk, Boylston Market), 4:129

Rush, Richard, 4:125

Rush Light (steamer), 3:306

Russell, Jonathan, 3:365

Russell, Mr. and Mrs. Joseph, 3:301, 302

Russell and Randall (pumpmakers), 3:218

Russia: JQA's article on, 3:258; mentioned, 3:32, 247, 392; 4:279, 345

Sackville, Thomas, *Gorboduc*, 4:235–36

St. Helena, 3:187

St. Lawrence River, 3:153; 4:319

St. Petersburg, Russia, 3:322, 358; 4:103. See also Granville

St. Simon, Louis de Rouvroy, duc de, *Mémoires ... sur le règne de Louis XIV*, 4:310

Salem, Mass., 3:xix, 207, 247, 248, 288, 303, 304, 362; 4:143

Sallust, orations attributed to, 4:78

Salmon, Catharine Louisa. See Smith, Mrs. William (1749–1824)

Salmon, Robert, CFA purchases painting by, 3:294–95, 325

Salter (or Sawtell), Benjamin (servant), 3:84, 161, 202, 276, 282, 325, 387–88, 408; 4:16, 27, 34, 98–99, 101, 112

Salter, Mrs. Benjamin (Elizabeth; servant), 4:99

Sargent, Mrs. Ignatius (Charlotte Gray), 3:405

Sargent & Brooks (merchants), 3:4

Savage, James (1784–1873): identified, 3:241; seeks JA letter, 3:241, 242; CFA on his editing of Winthrop, *The History of New England . . .* , 3:269, 271, 273, 290

Savage of the Island, or the Ourang Outang (play), 4:190

Savérien, Alexandre, *Histoire des philo-sophes anciens jusqu'à la renaissance des lettres*, 3:245–46

Sawtell, Benjamin. See Salter, Benjamin

Schiller, Johann Christoph Friedrich von, *Don Carlos*, 4:443

Schlegel, Frederick, *Lectures on the History of Literature, Ancient and Modern*, 3:145–46

Schroeder, Mr. (of Baltimore), 3:336

Scott, Sir Walter: *Biographical and Critical Notices of Eminent Novelists*, 3:41–45, 47, 52; *Dramatic Pieces*, 3:346; *Letters on Demonology and Witchcraft*, 4:56; *Life of Napoleon Bonaparte*, 4:174, 257–87 passim; notes to Dryden's "Absalom and Achitophel," 4:346; mentioned, 3:256

Sega, Mr., 3:400

Selfridge, Thomas O., 3:178, 179, 288

Seminole War, 3:159, 406, 428

Seneca: LaHarpe on, 3:72, 73, 76; *Philosophi ... opera*, 4:308–12, 319–44 passim, 353–71 passim; mentioned, 3:405

Sergeant, John (U.S. Repr., Penna.), 3:163, 164

Sevigné, Marie de Rabutin-Chantal, Marquise de, *Sevigniana, ou recueil de pensées ingénieuses ...*, 3:315

Sewall, Rev. Charles C. (of Danvers) or Samuel (of Burlington), 3:149, 156, 162, 168

Sewall, Jonathan, 3:276

Sewall, Mr. (of Halifax, grandson of preceding), 3:276

Shadel, James, 4:107

Shakespeare, William: *Othello*, 3:20; *Macbeth*, 3:20; 4:409; *King John*, 3:153, 157; 4:viii; *Romeo and Juliet*, 3:176, 177, 425; *King Lear*, 3:177, 179, 182; *Hamlet*, 3:379; 4:9, quoted, 4:210; *Merchant of Venice*, 3:420, 425; *Richard III*, 3:423; *As You Like It*, 4:187; *Comedy of Errors*, 4:433; mentioned, 4:110, illustration following 124

Sharp, James (cabinetmaker), 3:8, 113, 138

Shattuck, Dr. George Cheyne, 3:419–20

Shaw, Chief Justice Lemuel, 3:85, 373

Shaw, Robert G., 3:373, 424; 4:389

Shaw, Miss, 4:389

Sheffield, John Baker Holroyd, 1st Earl of: *Observations on the Commerce of the American States*, 4:245, 443; mentioned, 4:307

Sheldon, Asa G., 4:350

Shelley, Percy Bysshe, 4:238, 239
Shelton, Mr., 4:389
Shepherd, Ellen. *See* Brooks, Mrs. Gorham
Shepherd, Resin D., 3:22, 158, 259; 4:84, 231, 374
[Shepherd, W.], *History of the American Revolution*, 3:381–83, 385
Sheridan, Richard Brinsley: *School for Scandal*, 3:183–84; *The Rivals*, 3:422–23; *The Critic*, 3:429; speeches, 4:xvii, 5; Moore's life of, 4:183–86, 188; mentioned, 3:265; 4:336
Sheridan, Mrs. Richard Brinsley, 4:185
Sheridan, Thomas, *Lectures on the Art of Reading*, 3:265
Shirley, Gov. William, 3:56
"Sidney, Algernon" (pseud.), pamphlet on Presidential succession, 3:229
Sidney, Algernon: *Discourses concerning Government . . . to which is Added, a Short Account of the Author's Life*, 4:328–40 *passim; Works . . . with Memoirs of His Life, Revised by J. Robertson*, 4:328
Silsbee, Georgiana, 3:293
Simmons, D. A. (attorney; tenant), 3:2; 4:144
Simple, Jonathan, 3:409–10
Sinclair, John (singer), 4:283
Sismondi, Jean Charles Léonard Simonde de: *Histoire des Français*, 4:283–300 *passim; Julia Severa*, 4:291–92; mentioned, 4:359
Slade, William (U.S. Repr., Vt.), *Speech on the Resolution Relative to the Collector of Wiscasset*, 4:341, 342
Smedley, E., *A History of France*, 4:287
Smith, Abigail. *See* Adams, Mrs. John (1744–1818)
Smith, Adam, 4:78
Smith, Elizabeth (niece of AA). *See* Foster, Mrs. James H.
Smith, Elizabeth Storer. *See* Cruft, Mrs. Edward
Smith, Hannah. *See* Pickman, Mrs. Benjamin, Jr.
Smith, John Thomas, *Nollekens and His Times*, 3:386–87; 4:443
Smith, Joseph E.(?), 4:70, 71
Smith, Louisa Catherine (1773–1857, niece of AA; *see* Adams Genealogy): legacy from JA, 3:379, 382, 394; mentioned, 3:16, 17, 31, 37, 55, 90, 267, 283, 304, 313; 4:62, 81,

87, 145, 150, 260, 291, 313, 319, 324, 327, 329, 345, 352, 356, 374, 377, 388
Smith, Mary (sister of AA). *See* Cranch, Mrs. Richard
Smith, Thomas Carter (1796–1880, grandson of Isaac Smith Sr.; *see* Adams Genealogy): engagement and marriage, 4:41; mentioned, 3:31; 4:163
Smith, Mrs. Thomas Carter (Frances Barnard), 4:41, 163, 168, 172
Smith, William (1746–1787, brother of AA; *see* Adams Genealogy), 4:260
Smith, Mrs. William (Catharine Louisa Salmon, 1749–1824, sister-in-law of AA; *see* Adams Genealogy), 4:260
Smith, William (1755–1816, first cousin of AA; *see* Adams Genealogy), 3:31
Smith, Mrs. William (Hannah Carter, b. 1764; *see* Adams Genealogy), 3:31, 278; 4:163
Smith, William (b. 1774, nephew of AA; *see* Adams Genealogy), 3:90
Smith, Col. William Stephens (1755–1816, husband of AA2, designated as WSS in *The Adams Papers; see* Adams Genealogy), 3:178, 179
Smith, Mrs. William Stephens (Abigail Adams, 1765–1813, sister of JQA, designated as AA2 in *The Adams Papers; see* Adams Genealogy), grave, 3:85
Smith family seal, 3:411
Smollett, Tobias: Scott's life of, 3:45; *The History of England from the Revolution to the Death of George the Second*, 3:266, 275
Snow, Caleb H., 3:ix, xi, xiii
Society for the Diffusion of Useful Knowledge, London: *Library of Useful Knowledge*, 3:34; 4:7, 167, 233, 275–76, 287, 382, 383; *Library of Entertaining Knowledge*, 3:51, 54, 60–61, 220
Socrates, JQA's bust of, 4:vii, 399, illustration facing 124
Solon, quoted, 4:122, 123
Somerset, the Protector (Edward Seymour), 4:400
Sophocles: *Œdipus*, 3:127, 131; mentioned, 3:35, 121, 124, 126
South Braintree, Mass. (later Randolph), 3:180
South Carolina: debate on public-lands policy, 3:168, 177; and tariffs, 3:337,

426; and nullification, 4:83, 419–22, 429, 431–32; debate on claims against U.S., 4:222, 413; mentioned, 3:213, 266

Southey, Robert: *Vision of Judgment* and *Sir Thomas More*, 3:291; *Thalaba*, 4:117; *Essays Moral and Political*, 4:341, 355, 443

Spain, 3:57, 357

Spanish language, CFA studies, 4:258–81 *passim*

Sparks, Jared: editor, *North Amer. Rev.*, 3:27, 222; 4:xii; *Diplomatic Correspondence of The American Revolution*, 3:73, 74; 4:xii, 214–15; uses JA letter books, 3:87, 88, 92, 141, 143–44, 149, 156–63, 172, 173, 179, 205, 227, 242, 243; 4:xii–xiii, 24, 333; reviews biography of Arthur Lee, 3:202; *American Almanac*, comp., 3:385–86; Stuart's portrait, 4:xii, illustration following 380; marriage, 4:395; mentioned, 3:26, 202

Sparks, Mrs. Jared (Frances Anne Allen), 4:395

Sparrell, John, plan of Medford, 3:xviii–xix, illustration following 314

Sparta. *See* Greece

Spaulding, Mr. *See* Phillips, Elizabeth

Speakman (employee, Columbian Mills), 4:370

Spear, A. (tenant), 3:415

Spear, Deacon Daniel: JQA's Quincy agent, 3:180, 185–86, 195, 202–204, 215, 224, 225; 4:10, 180, 249, 257, 261, 285, 290, 400; mentioned, 3:329; 4:25, 279, 296, 321, 415

Spear, John I. (tenant), 3:187–90, 192, 265–67, 269, 276, 401, 414, 418, 420

Spear, William (chainbearer), 3:38

Spectator, The, 3:338; 4:3–222 *passim*

Speight, Jesse (U.S. Repr., N.C.), 4:222, 265

Spence, Joseph, *Anecdotes of Books and Men*, 4:238–39, 243, 443

Sprague, Peleg, 3:177; 4:344

Spurzheim, Dr. Johann Gaspar, 4:395, 397

Spy Pond (West Cambridge, Mass.), 3:321, 322

Squantum, Mass. (now Quincy), 3:276, 285, 307, 315; 4:357

Staël-Holstein, Anne Louise Germaine, Baronne de, *Corinne*, 3:328–88 *passim*

Stafford Springs, Conn., 3:375

Stanbery, William (U.S. Repr., Ohio), motion to censure, 4:330

Stapleton, Augustus Granville, *The Political Life of … George Canning*, 4:335–49 *passim*, 443

State Bank, Boston: elections at, 3:49–51, 332; Adams stock, 3:50, 62, 66, 103–104, 107, 113, 132–33, 141, 196, 205, 234, 242–43, 253, 287, 293, 297; mentioned, 3:16, 254, 289, 296

Steele, Richard: CFA's comments on, 4:173, 237; mentioned, 3:403

Stetson, Rev. Caleb: CFA's comments on, 3:76, 326; sermons, 3:117, 123, 175, 181, 186, 198, 216, 227, 236–37, 292, 297, 322, 327, 371; 4:43, 349; payment for CFA's wedding, 3:84; 4:18; and funeral of Mrs. Brooks, 3:172; mentioned, 3:70, 259, 270, 286, 325; 4:58, 304, 424

Stetson, Mrs. Caleb, 3:70, 76

Stetson, Dr. James Aaron, 4:366

Stevens, William, 3:146

Stevenson, Andrew (Speaker of House), 4:265, 330

Stevenson, Dr. J. Greely: identified, 3:143; attends Mrs. Brooks, 3:157, 165, 166; attends ABA, 3:233, 353; 4:38, 72, 426; attends ABA's servant, 4:174; attends LCA2, 4:237; attends CFA, 4:383; mentioned, 3:171, 243, 300; 4:97, 245, 345

Stevenson, Mrs. J. Greely, 3:300; 4:97

Stewart, Dugald, *The Philosophy of the Active and Moral Powers of Man*, reviewed, 3:299

Stigliz, Christian Ludovic, edition of Cicero dedicated to, 4:219, 220

Stockdale, Percival, life of Waller, 4:329

Stoicism, 4:110, 179, 180, 194, 199, 201–203, 337, 359

Stone, Ebenezer W., 3:154–55, 276, 359

Stone, William J. (engraver), 3:411

Stone, William L.: *Letters on Masonry … to the Hon. John Quincy Adams*, 4:358, 381, 383, 394, 395, 407, 411; JQA's letters to, 4:360, 371, 407

Stone, Mr. (P. C. Brooks' tenant), 4:18

Stone Library (Adams National Historic

Site, Quincy; designated in these volumes as MQA), 4:vii, xvii

Stone Temple. *See under* Quincy, Mass.

Storer, Dr. David Humphreys: claims against GWA's estate, 3:44–50 *passim*; Farmer's suit against, 3:183, 189–90, 192, 197, 422–24; 4:2, 32–33

Storrow, Mr. (of Paris), 3:118–19

Storrs, Henry R., 3:177

Story, Franklin, 3:237; 4:430

Story, Mrs. Franklin (Elizabeth Gray): identified, 3:106–107; mentioned, 3:109, 237; 4:430

Strafford, Thomas Wentworth, 1st Earl of, 4:322

Stuart, Gilbert: portraits of Adamses, 3:xvi, 8, 146; portrait of Sparks, 4:xii, illustration following 380; mentioned, 4:90

Stuart, Moses, *A Letter to William E. Channing*, 3:291

Sturbridge, Mass., 3:376, 377

Sturgis, Russell, 3:30

Sturgis, Mrs. Russell (Mary Greene Hubbard), 3:30, 35

Suetonius, *Life of Caesar*, 4:194–95

Suffolk co., Mass.: Probate Court, 3:13, 65, 169, 250, 302, 399, 408; 4:18, 26, 45; bar, 3:422; 4:1–2, 37–38, 252, 299, 336

Suffolk Insurance Co., 3:356, 357, 396; 4:196

Sullivan, James, 3:153

Sullivan, William: and Middlesex Canal, 3:153, 154, 248, 413; mayoralty candidate, 4:198; mentioned, 3:78, 344

Sully, Thomas, and Stuart's portrait of JQA, 3:145, 146, 387

Sumner, Brig. Gen. William H., 4:361, 369

Sumner, Mrs. William H. (Mary Ann [D'Wolf] Perry), 4:361, 369

Susan and Phoebe (ship), 3:83, 84

Swan, Dr. Daniel, 3:163, 166, 175, 216, 297

Swan, Mr. (of N.Y.), 3:250

Swett, Samuel, 3:294–95

Swett, Miss, 3:294

Symmes (Aberjona) River, 3:249

Symmons, Charles, "Life of Milton," 3:339–45 *passim*

Tarbell, Thomas: identified, 3:59 (*see also* Adams Genealogy); sends legal work to CFA, 3:58, 61, 80, 81, 105, 112–13, 129, 138, 139, 150; mentioned, 3:183, 354, 407; 4:41, 361

Tarbell, Mrs. Thomas (Lucy Tufts; *see* Adams Genealogy): identified, 3:59; mentioned, 3:354; 4:361

Tariff: articles on, 3:132, 133, 232, 337; 4:214; Webster on, 3:351–52; Congressional debate, 1824, 3:163–65; CFA's viewpoint, 4:217; issue of, 1830, 4:223, 244–45, 254, 255, 265, 282, 301, 307, 322, 323, 330, 334, 335; mentioned, 3:342, 426; 4:207, 296

Tatler, The: CFA's daily comments on, 3:373; GWA's comments, 3:406, 407; mentioned, 3:338–431 *passim*; 4:1–4

Taylor, Jeremy: *The Life and Death of ... Jesus Christ*, 3:46, 49, 64, 83, 97, 103, 110, 135; sermon, 3:162; mentioned, 3:68

Taylor, William (JQA's servant), 3:251, 274

Taylor, Mr., on TBA's accident, 3:391

TBA. *See* Adams, Thomas Boylston (1772–1832)

Tenney, William (tenant), 3:128, 143, 148, 225, 353, 414, 415; 4:39, 104, 169, 416–17

Terence, 3:43

Teschemaker, Mr., 4:365

Textile manufactures, 1829 depression in, 3:59

Thanksgiving Day, 3:87, 374; 4:188–89, 408–409

Thatcher (Thacher), Peter O., 3:248, 249, 373

Thaxter, John, Sr. (1721–1802, uncle of AA; *see* Adams Genealogy), 4:316

Thaxter, Levi, 4:116

Thaxter, Lydia Anne. *See* Richardson, Mrs. John Hancock

Thayer, Rev. Christopher Toppan, 3:287

Thayer, John Holbrook, 3:287

Thayer, Dr. and Mrs. Nathaniel (of Lancaster), 3:237

Theatrical exhibitions, debating subject, 3:192, 198

Thomas, John (JQA's servant), 3:37, 63

Thompson, Moses (plasterer), 3:164

Thorndike, Mrs. Augustus, 4:266–67, 271

Thorndike, Mrs. Charles, 4:271

Thorndike, Israel T., Jr., 4:271

Thorndike, Mrs. Israel T., Jr. (Ann T. Dickey), 4:271

Thorndike, Sally Ann, 4:271

Thrale, Hester Lynch. *See* Piozzi, Hester Lynch

Thucydides, *De bello Peloponnesiaco*, 4:307–12 *passim*, 320, 326–40 *passim*

Ticknor, George, 4:62

Tilden, Joseph, 4:374

Tillotson, John, Archbishop of Canterbury, 4:374

Titcomb, Mr., claim against, 3:61, 62, 64, 77, 108, 112

Tocqueville, Alexis de, conversation with JQA, 4:149

Todd, Henry John, "Life ... of John Milton," 3:345, 347

Tooke, John Horne: *The Diversions of Purley*, 3:331–32, 334–35; mentioned, 3:265

Tories, English literary, 3:256

Torrey, S., 3:248

Towne, Gen. Salem, 3:78, 86, 107

Townsend, Alexander, 4:155–56

Trask, S. and W. (roofing), 3:25

Trial of Warren Hastings, The, 4:5

Trollope, Mrs. Anthony (Frances), *Domestic Manners of the Americans*, 4:294

Trueman, Robert, 3:135–36, 144

Tuckerman, Edward, 4:355

Tuckerman, Rev. Joseph, and Eliza Dolph, 3:423–24, 425

Tudor, William: JA's letters to, 3:334, 387; mentioned, 3:379

Tufts, Cotton, Jr. (1757–1833, cousin of AA; *see* Adams Genealogy), 3:59; 4:316

Tufts, Mrs. Cotton, Jr. (Mercy Brooks, 1763–1849; *see* Adams Genealogy), 3:59, 70, 304, 305

Tufts, Lucy. *See* Tarbell, Mrs. Thomas

Tufts, Mercy (1742–1813). *See* Brooks, Mrs. Thomas

Tufts, Mercy (daughter of Cotton Tufts), 3:304, 305

Tufts, Nathan, CFA on gardens of, 3:295, 296

Turkey, JQA's chapter on, 3:258, 266

Tyler, Col. J. S., 3:263–65

Union Bank of Georgetown, 4:72

United States: Presidential election, 1832, 4:394–95, 397–98; *Laws*, 4:443

United States (frigate), 4:214, 285

United States Branch Bank, Boston. *See* Bank of the United States

United States Congress: Jackson's messages to, 3:100, 105, 115, 116, 139, 379, 380, 383; 4:414; speeches in Williston, *Eloquence*, 3:114, 120–25 *passim*, 144–45, 147–48, 158–68 *passim*, 176–77; public-land debate, Senate, 3:168, 199, 200; early debates, 3:196, 207; 4:335, 338; tariff reports and debates, 3:232; 4:223, 244–45, 254, 255, 265, 282, 301, 307, 322, 323, 330, 334–35; *Report of Committee of House ... on Post-Offices ...*, 3:327; 1830 election, 3:340–41, 344–45, 351–53; beginning of term and session, 1831, 3:366; bank debates and reports, 3:402; 4:256, 265, 299–300, 307, 318, 326, 328–29, 334; House debate on repeal of section of Judiciary Act, 3:415, 416; amendment to Appropriations bill, 3:427; *Report on Steam Carriages ... Canals and Railroads*, 4:326; speech on Wiscasset collector, 4:341, 342; 1832 election, 4:397

United States Constitution: ratification debates, 3:101; 4:146–79 *passim*; speeches on amendment governing Presidential elections, 3:168, 177; *Federalist* papers on, 4:135, 137, 138, 142

United States Military Academy, West Point, N.Y.: I. H. Adams prepares for, 4:235, 255, 277; mentioned, 3:275

United States Navy, commission for J. H. Adams, 4:76, 197–98, 200, 214

United States Telegraph, Eaton-Ingham correspondence in, 4:78

Universalism: history, 3:279; and Fanny Wright, 4:76

Useful and Ornamental Planting, 4:275, 276

Utilitarians, 3:93, 94

Valpy, Richard, *The Elements of Greek Grammar*, 4:4–7

Van Buren, Martin, 3:246; 4:35, 407

Van Rensselaer, Henry Bell, 3:333

Van Rensselaer, Stephen, 3:333, 336

Vasari, Giorgio, *Vite de' più eccelenti pittori scultori e architetti*, 4:278–79, 287–96 *passim*, 405, 406, 408

Vaughan, Benjamin, 4:344

Vaughan, Petty, and Boylston claim,

3:13, 62, 63, 65, 131–32, 137, 142, 147, 157, 260; 4:149

Vaughan, Robert: *Memorials of the Stuart Dynasty*, 4:313–22 *passim*, 443; CFA's essay-review, 4:316–17, 323, 325, 428

Vaughan, William, 3:131–32, 143, 260

Veazie (Vezey), George (carpenter): posts for Old House, 3:391, 418–19; 4:16, 17, 24–25; mentioned, 4:261, 278

Vernet, Claude Joseph (artist), 4:119

Victory (steamboat), 3:380

Vida, Girolamo, "Art of Poetry," 4:109–10, 112–15

Vidocq, Eugène François, *Memoirs*, 4:357–58, 443

Viger, François, *Greek Idioms . . . translated by Rev. J. Seager*, 4:96, 97

Vigne, Godfrey T., *Six Months in America*, 4:364, 443

Villemain, Abel François: *Histoire de Cromwell*, CFA's marginalia in, 4:xv–xvi, 423, 429, illustration following 380; study and comment on, 4:422–28; *Mélanges philosophiques . . .*, 4:429–30

Vincent, Naomi (actress), 4:414

Virgil: JQA's bust of, 4:vii, 399, illustration facing 124; CFA on, 4:114; *Eclogues*, 4:247, 249; *Georgics*, 4:249–53; *Æneid*, 4:254–79 *passim*

Virginia: debates ratification of U.S. Constitution, 3:101; 4:171–73, 178–79; history of, 3:205, 206, 215, 217; and Jackson's Proclamation, 4:428–29

Voltaire, François Marie Arouet de: *Mélanges litteraires*, 3:87–89; *Rome sauvée, ou Catilina*, 4:41; *L'orphelin de la Chine*, 4:47, 50; *Siècle de Louis XIV*, 4:429–30; mentioned, 3:46, 134; 4:39, 49, 62, 90, 184

Vossius, Gerard J., *Rhetorices contractæ . . .*, 3:403–11; 4:xvii, 443

Wait, R. G., 3:276

Wales, Samuel, Jr., 3:189, 191–92

Wales, T. B., 3:276

Walewsky, Col. de, 3:231

Walewsky, Madame de (formerly Mrs. David [Ann F.] Humphreys), 3:230–32, 234

Walker, Rev. James: identified, 3:113; CFA on sermons, 3:102–103, 220; 4:8; visits ABA and CFA, 3:160; mentioned, 3:224, 325

Walker, Mrs. James (Catherine Bartlett), 3:113, 160, 228

Walker, John, *A Rhetorical Grammar . . .*, 3:171, 182–85

Wallace, William, *History of the Life and Reign of George IV*, 4:160, 165–82 *passim*, 443

Waller, Edmund, *Works*, 4:329

Walpole, Horace, 4th Earl of Orford: *Castle of Otranto*, 3:64; *Memoirs of the Last Ten Years of the Reign of King George II*, 3:266, 275, 280–92 *passim*; 4:443

Walsh, Robert (ed., *American Quarterly Review*): on JQA, 4:175; on JA, 4:214–15; mentioned, 3:205; 4:412

Walsh, Robert, *Narrative of a Journey from Constantinople to England*, 4:31, 33, 38–39, 443

Walsingham, Sir Francis, 4:423

Warburton, William, Bishop of Gloucester, "The Nature and Condition of Truth," 4:363

Ward, Judge Artemas, 4:16

Ward, Mary Gray, 3:273

Ward, Thomas W., 3:273, 288

Ward, Mrs. Thomas W. (Lydia Gray), 3:273, 288

Ward, William, identified, 3:288

Ware, Rev. Henry, 3:6, 192–93; 4:368, 369

Ware, Mrs. Henry, 3:6

Warren, Dr. John C., 3:166, 307

Warren, Joseph, oration, 3:183

Warren, Mr., trees sold to CFA, 3:324, 370–71

Warren Bridge, case against proprietors of, 3:130–31

Washington, George: Farewell Address, 3:185; eulogies of, 3:188; Sparks' view, 4:xii; centennial, 4:245–46; mentioned, 3:xxxiv, xxxvii, 105, 196, 329; 4:69, 174. See also Marshall, John

Washington, D.C.: GWA in, 3:xvii; JA2 in, 3:xvii, xxxi, 23; CFA and, 3:xxxi; 4:221, 299, 394; JQA's houses in, 3:xvi, 348; Post Office, 3:118–19; N. Frothingham's trip to, 3:149, 170, 171, 197; Russian legation, 3:322; corporation stock of City of, 3:414; P. C. Brooks' trip to, 4:402–403, 427. See also JQA; LCA

Washington Bank (Boston), 3:209, 210, 220, 303; 4:383

Washington Globe, The, 3:426

Waterhouse, Dr. Benjamin, 3:265; 4: 90, 124, 357, 368, 369

Waterloo, 3:187

Watertown, Mass., 3:22, 259, 292, 375, 376

Watkins, Dr. Tobias, case of, 3:45

Watkins, Thomas L. C., 4:294–95

Watmough, John G., 4:300

Watson, Mr. (stockbroker), 3:291

Webster, Daniel: law students in office of, 3:7, 74, 79; president, Boston Society for Diffusion of Useful Knowledge, 3:78; engagement and second marriage, 3:79; CFA on court appearance, 3:85, 89; Congressional speeches, 3:163–68 *passim*, 174, 182; *Discourse Delivered at Plymouth ... 1820*, 3:194, 210; eulogy of JA and Jefferson, 3:195; as P. C. Brooks' attorney, 3:200; at Boston political meetings, 3:344; 4:422; on tariff, 3:351–52; Harding's portrait of, 3: 410–12; speech at Worcester, 4:380, 382; possibility of JQA's opposing, 4:391–93; mentioned, 3:6, 109, 262; 4:175

Webster, Mrs. Daniel (Caroline LeRoy), 3:79, 262; 4:395

Weddell, James, *A Voyage towards the South Pole ...*, 4:21, 444

Welles, Arnold, 3:305, 306

Welles, Mr. and Mrs. John, 4:185

Wellington, Arthur Wellesley, Duke of, 3:352, 392

Wells, Charles (mayor of Boston), 4: 198, 378

Wells, Frances Boott, 3:152

Wells (Welles), Mrs. M. (tenant), 3:53, 54, 179, 201, 269, 278, 299, 301

Wells, William, Jr., 3:152

Wells, Mrs. William, Jr. (Frances Boott), 3:152

Wells, Miss (daughter of tenant), 3: 201, 224

Wells, Mr. (son of tenant), 3:92

Wells & Lilly (Boston publishers), 3: 364, 365

Welsh, Harriet (d. 1857, stepdaughter of AA's cousin Abigail [Kent] Welsh; *see* Adams Genealogy): GWA's indebtedness for rent, 3:189, 191, 192; mentioned, 3:63

Welsh, J. A., 3:367

Welsh, Dr. Thomas (1752–1831, husband of AA's cousin Abigail [Kent] Welsh; *see* Adams Genealogy): death

of, 3:418; ties with Adamses, 3:63, 418–19; mentioned, 3:66, 69, 192

Welsh, Mrs. Thomas (Abigail Kent, 1750–1825, cousin of AA; *see* Adams Genealogy), 3:63

Welsh, Thomas, Jr. (1779–1831, son of AA's cousin Abigail [Kent] Welsh): identified, 3:63 (*see also* Adams Genealogy); prospective sale of house, 3:62, 66; CFA's comment on, 3:148; brings New's estate to CFA, 3:185, 221, 246, 277, 340; rental debt, 3:192, 202, 210, 368; death of, 4:87–88; mentioned, 3:2, 73, 182, 197, 307; 4:6, 24, 26, 32, 90, 173

Wendell, Dr. (tenant), 3:179–81, 197

West Boston Bridge, 3:41, 207, 208, 278

West Cambridge. *See* Cambridge, Mass.

West Cambridge Pond. *See* Spy Pond

Westminster Review, 3:94

Weston, Mass., CFA's trips to, 3:19–20, 74–75, 334–35, 354–55; 4:158, 168–69, 385. *See also* JQA — Lands &c.

Weymouth, Mass., 3:37; 4:333

White, Capt. Joseph (of Salem): murder of, 3:xix–xx, 207, 208, 247, 248–49, 288, 303–304; *The Trial in the Case of the Commonwealth, versus John Francis Knapp, for the Murder of*, 3:xx, 304, illustration facing 315

White, Col. Joseph M., 4:123–24

Whitney, Caroline (daughter of Peter Whitney), 4:88, 140

Whitney, Rev. George (son of Peter Whitney): ordination, 4:68; mentioned, 4:133, 356

Whitney, Rev. Nicholas Bowes (of Hingham): identified, 3:91; sermons, 3:90, 301; 4:91, 387

Whitney, Rev. Peter (of Quincy): sermons, 3:55, 274, 279, 306, 331–32, 366, 374; 4:53, 62, 81, 86, 149, 308, 322, 325, 340, 374, 378, 391; officiates at marriages and funerals of Adamses, 3:85; 4:58, 260; view of Fanny Wright, 4:76; mentioned, 3:56, 90; 4:68, 140, 147, 354, 356, 366, 386

Whitney, Mrs. Peter, 4:88, 147

Whitney, Prentiss (tenant), 3:2, 128, 136, 137, 150, 151, 160, 174–80 *passim*, 188, 193, 195, 200, 203, 206, 210, 212, 217, 218, 221, 222, 236, 247, 250, 251

Whitwell, Mr., 3:248

Wieland, Christoph Martin, *Geschichte*

der Abderiten, 4:417–19, 423, 427

Willard, Sidney (publisher, *American Monthly Review*), CFA submits article to, 4:234, 236

Willard, Solomon (architect), 3:xii, xiv, xv

William (CFA's servant), 3:15, 84

Williams, Henry, 3:292, 293

Williams, John D. W., 3:150–51; 4:150

Williams, John D. & Moses (wine merchants), 3:52, 61, 302–303, 429; 4:124, 218

Williams, Lewis (U.S. Repr., N.C.), 4:222

Williams, Roger, 3:428

Williams, Thomas, 4:231, 232

Willis, Nathaniel Parker, 4:154

Williston, E. B., comp., *Eloquence of the United States,* 3:97–200 *passim,* 372; 4:xvii, 234

Winchester, Mass., 3:249

Wingate, Gen. and Mrs. Joshua, 4:387–88

Wingate, Miss, 4:387

Winthrop, George E., 3:44

Winthrop, John, "Journals," published as *The History of New England from 1630 to 1649,* 3:268–69, 271–73, 286, 288, 290, 357

Winthrop, Brig. Gen. John Temple, 3:34, 145, 267

Winthrop, Robert Charles, 3:74

Winthrop, Lt.-Gov. Thomas Lindall, 3:6, 73–74, 322; 4:125, 378

Wirt, William: eulogy of JA and Jefferson, 3:193; Antimasonic candidate for President, 4:xi, xii, 150, 373; *Letters of The British Spy in Virginia,* 4:444; mentioned, 3:200

Woburn, Mass., 3:xxv, 248–49, 323

Wood, Thomas, *An Institute of the Laws of England,* 4:386

Woods, Mrs., and New's estate, 3:263, 264

Woods, Mr. (son), 3:265

Wool, Gen. John Ellis, 3:326

Worcester, Mass., 3:376; 4:377, 378, 380

Wordsworth, William, *Poetical Works,* 3:364–65

Working-Men's Party, 3:371, 383–84; 4:45, 76

World, The, 3:338; 4:405, 427

Wright, Frances (later Mme. Phiquepal D'Arusmont), 4:76

Wyttenbach, Daniel Albert, 3:364

Yazoo River, 3:116

Young, Rev. Alexander, Jr., CFA on sermons, 3:49; 4:211

Zeno, 4:179

Zeuner, Charles (composer), 3:x; 4:xi

❡ The *Diary of Charles Francis Adams* was composed on the Linotype and printed directly from type by the Harvard University Printing Office. Rudolph Ruzicka's *Fairfield Medium*, with several variant characters designed expressly for *The Adams Papers*, is used throughout. The text is set in the eleven-point size and the lines are spaced one and one-half points. The photolithographic illustrations are the work of The Meriden Gravure Company. The cover fabric is a product of the Holliston Mills, Inc., and the books were bound by the Stanhope Bindery. The paper, made by the S. D. Warren Company, is a new grade named *University Text*. It was developed by Harvard University Press, for first use in *The Adams Papers*, and bears its mark. The books were designed by P. J. Conkwright and Burton L. Stratton.